DEADPOOL

We Don't Need A[illegible] Hero

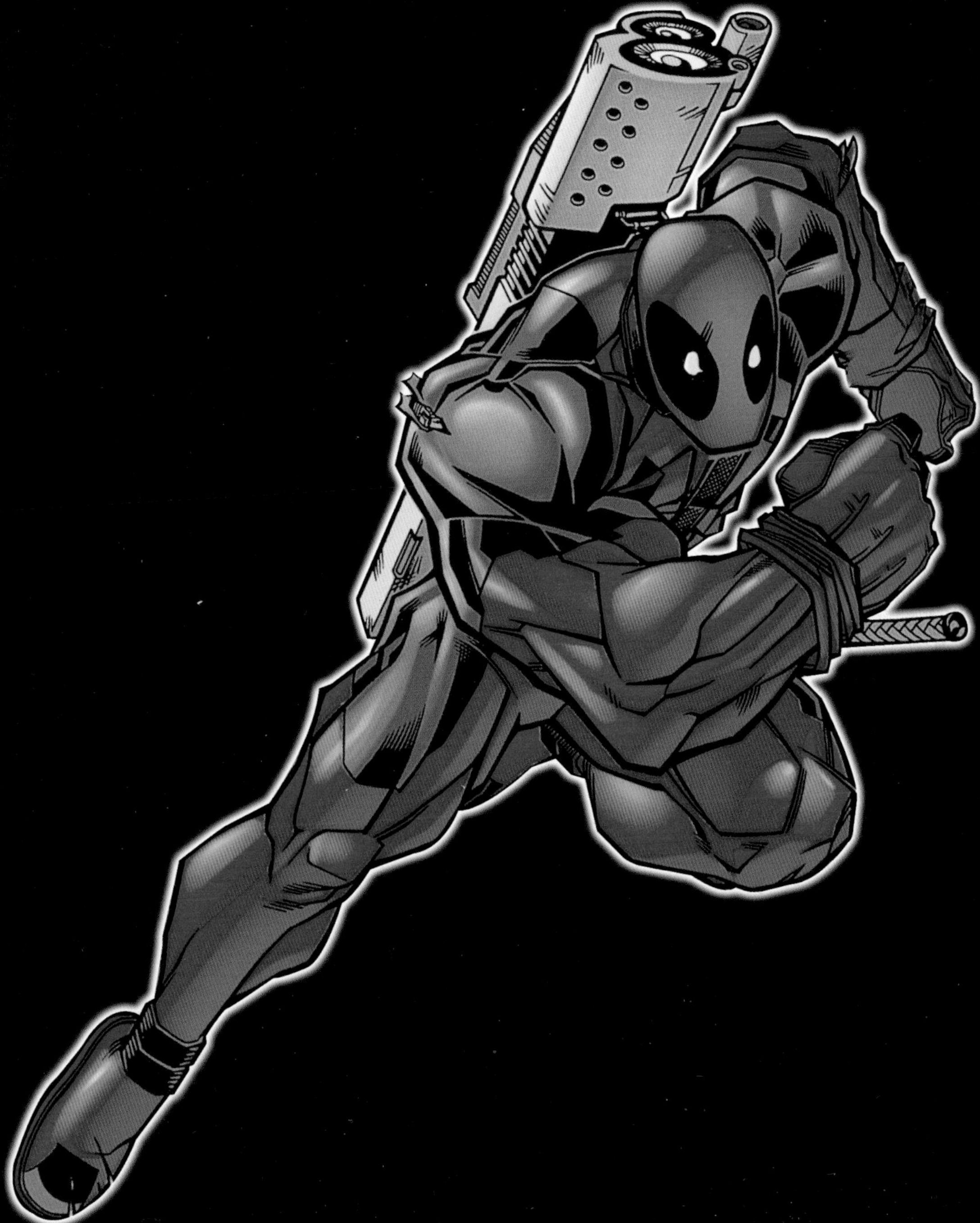

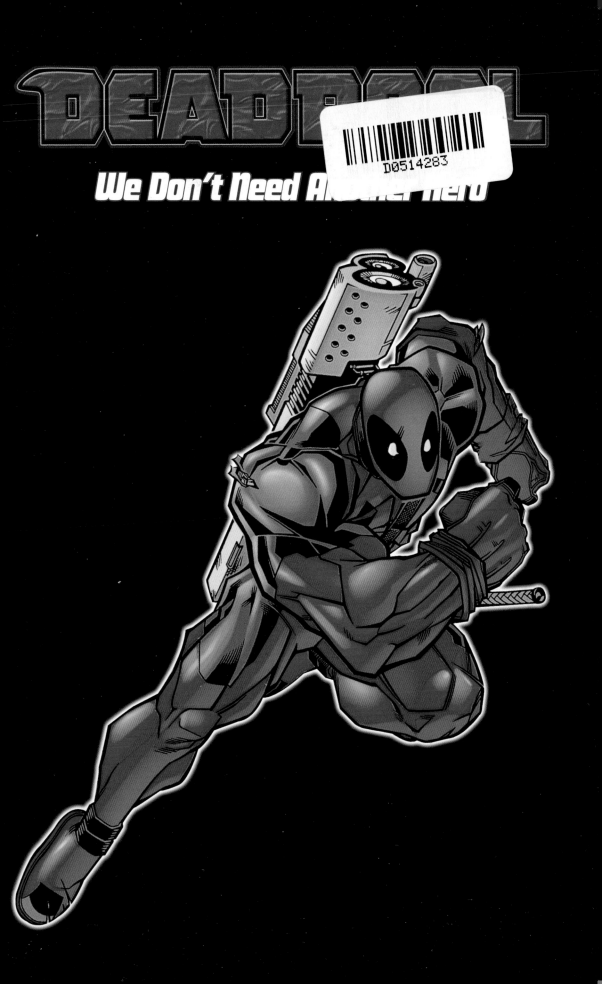

DEADPOOL ®

We Don't Need Another Hero

WRITERS: JOE KELLY, PETE WOODS

PENCILS: ED McGUINNESS, KEVIN LAU, SHANNON DENTON, JOHN FANG, AARON LOPRESTI, BERNARD CHANG

INKS: NATHAN MASSENGIL, NORMAN LEE

COLOURS: CHRISTIAN LICHTNER, AUDREY SHAH, DIGITAL CHAMELEON, MATTHEW PAINE, CHRIS SOTOMAYER AND LIQUID!

LETTERS: CHRIS ELIOPOULOS, RICHARD STARKINGS, COMICRAFT'S DAVE LANPHEAR, MIRANDA EMERSON, KOWA FUCHS, ALBERTDESCHESNE

EDITOR: MATT IDELSON

COVER ARTIST: STAZ JOHNSON
COVER COLOURS: JAMES OFFREDI

MARVEL, DEADPOOL: WE DON'T NEED ANOTHER HERO. Contains material originally published in magazine form as Deadpool #1-9, Deadpool #-1 and Daredevil/Deadpool Annual 1997. First printing 2009. Published by Panini Publishing, a division of Panini UK Limited. Mike Riddell, Managing Director. Alan O'Keefe, Managing Editor. Mark Irvine, Production Manager. Marco M. Lupoi, Publishing Director Europe. Brady Webb, Reprint Editor. Tim Warran-Smith, Designer. Office of publication: Brockbourne House, 77 Mount Ephraim, Tunbridge Wells, Kent TN4 8BS. MARVEL, DEADPOOL and all related characters and the distinctive likenesses thereof are trademarks of Marvel Entertainment, Inc. and its subsidiaries, and are used with permission. Copyright © 1997 & 2009 Marvel Entertainment, Inc. and its subsidiaries. No similarity between any of the names, characters, persons and/or institutions in this edition with those of any living or dead person or institution is intended, and any such similarity which may exist is purely coincidental. This publication may not be sold, except by authorised dealers, and is sold subject to the condition that it shall not be sold or distributed with any part of its cover or markings removed, nor in a mutilated condition. Licensed by Marvel Characters B.V. www.marvel.com. All rights reserved. Printed in Italy. ISBN: 978-1-84653-427-0

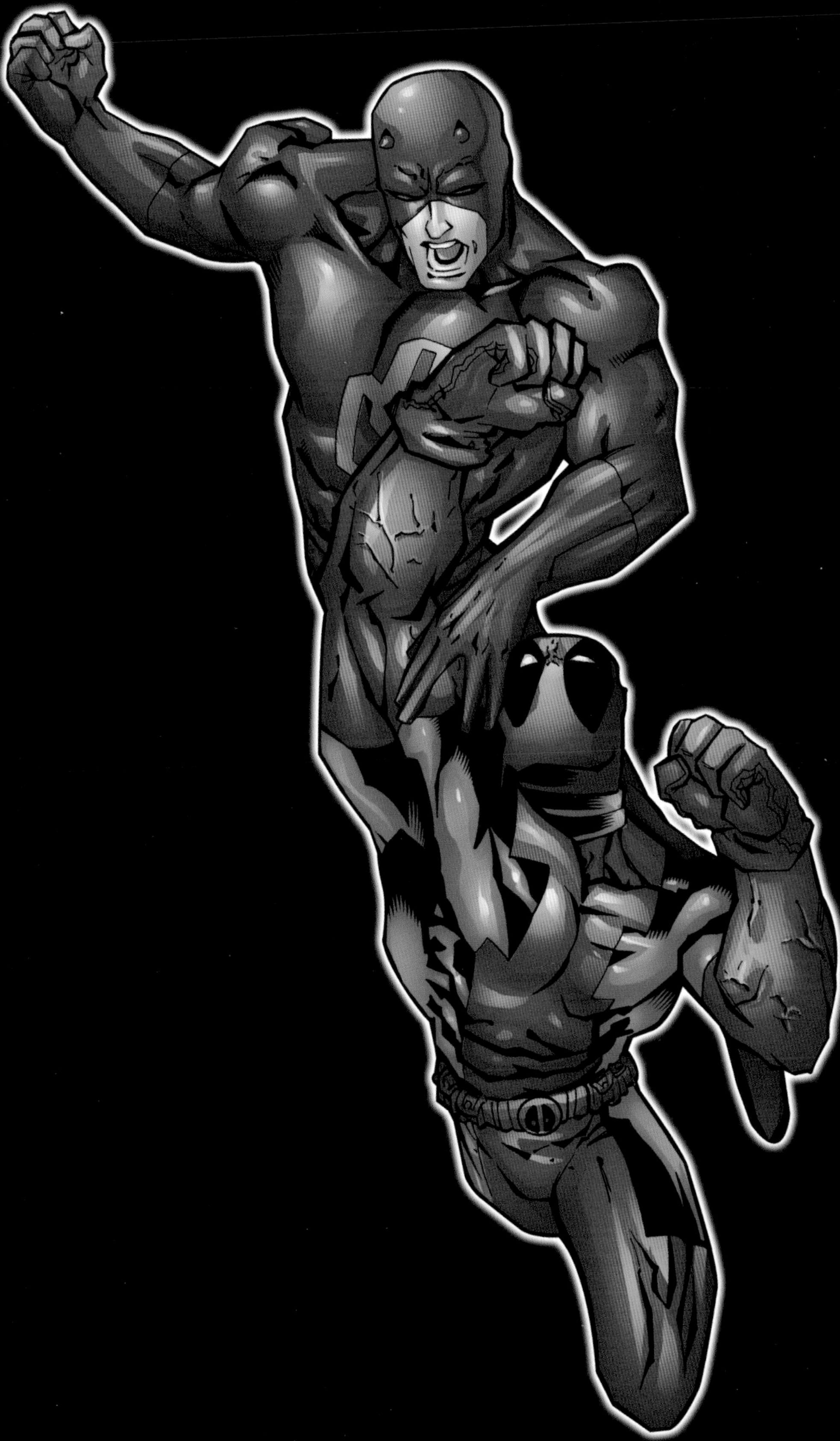

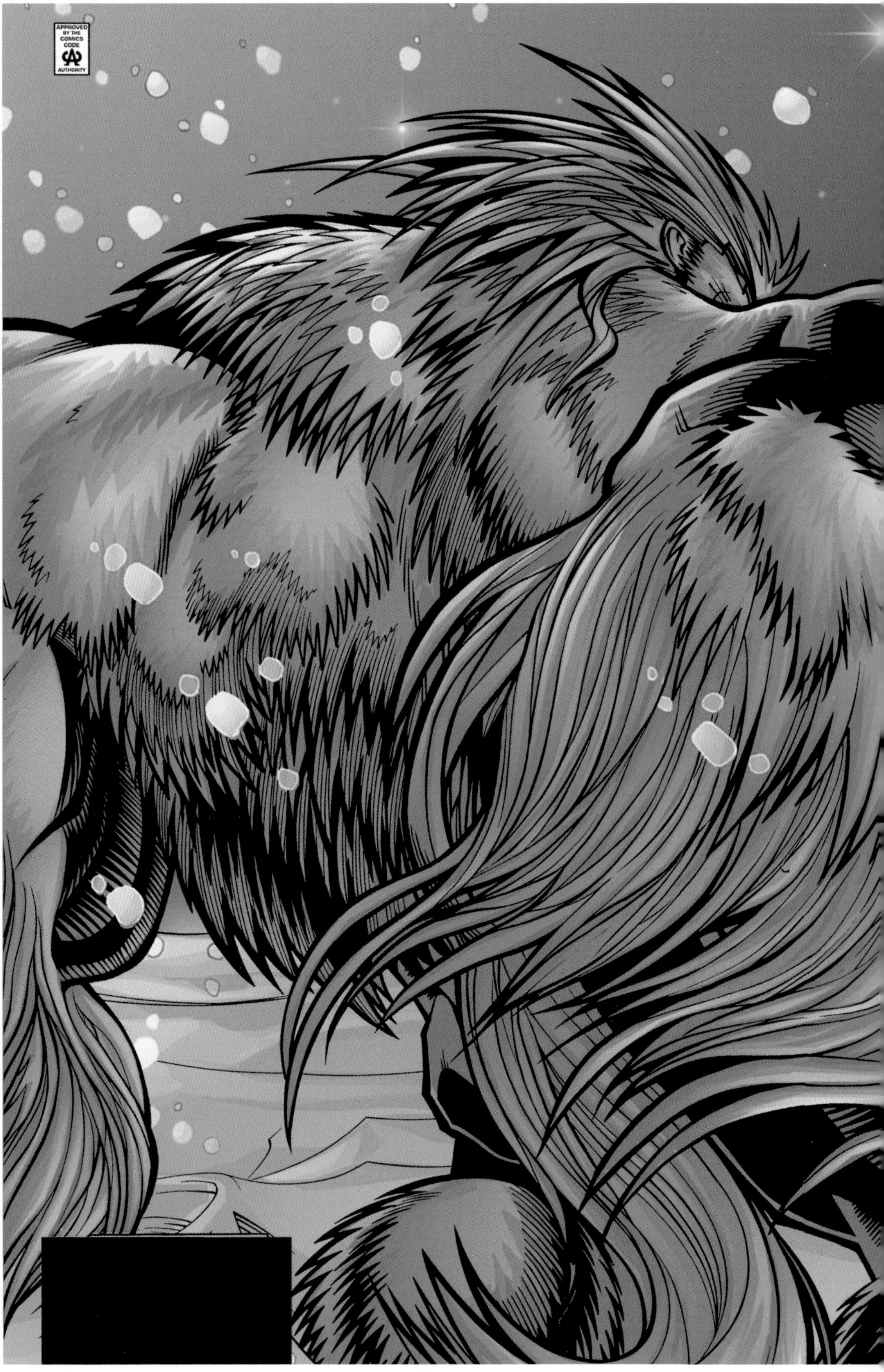
APPROVED BY THE COMICS CODE AUTHORITY

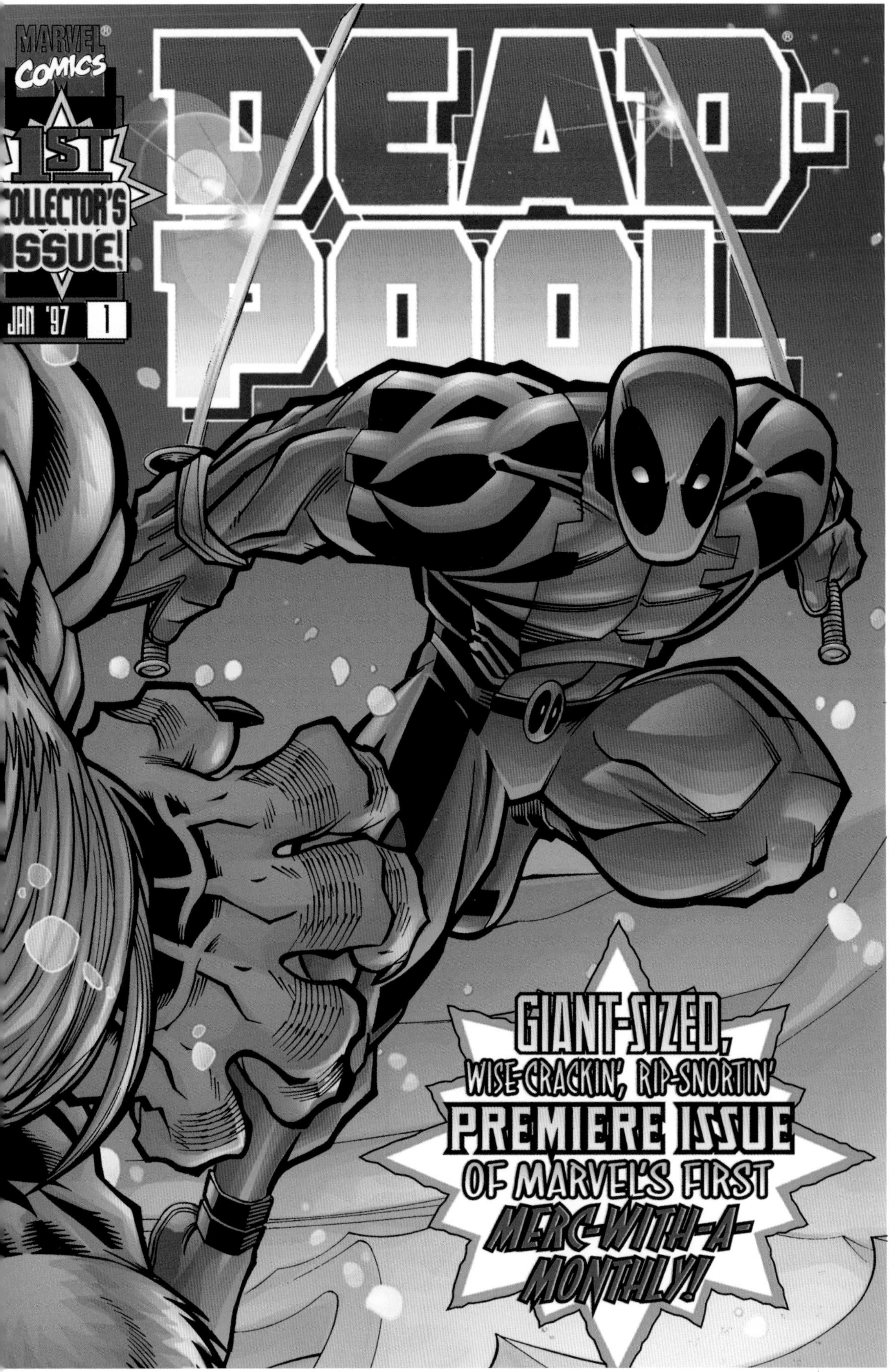

MARVEL COMICS
1ST COLLECTOR'S ISSUE!
JAN '97 1
DEAD-POOL
GIANT-SIZED, WISE-CRACKIN', RIP-SNORTIN' PREMIERE ISSUE OF MARVEL'S FIRST MERC-WITH-A-MONTHLY!

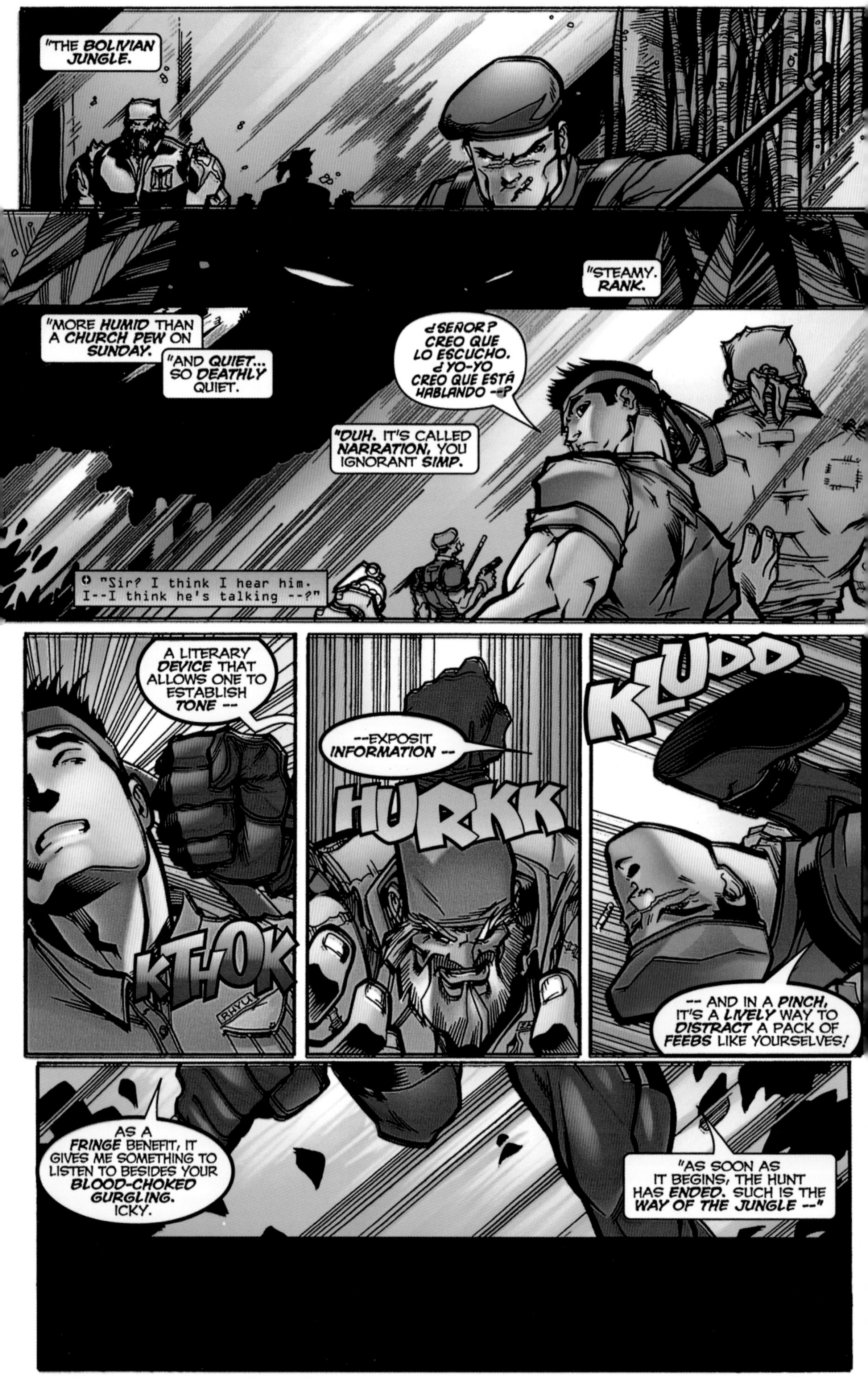
"THE BOLIVIAN JUNGLE.
"STEAMY. RANK.
"MORE HUMID THAN A CHURCH PEW ON SUNDAY.
"AND QUIET... SO DEATHLY QUIET.
¿SEÑOR? CREO QUE LO ESCUCHO. ¿YO-YO CREO QUE ESTÁ HABLANDO --?
"DUH. IT'S CALLED NARRATION, YOU IGNORANT SIMP.
"Sir? I think I hear him. I--I think he's talking --?"
A LITERARY DEVICE THAT ALLOWS ONE TO ESTABLISH TONE --
KTHOK
--EXPOSIT INFORMATION --
HURKK
KLUDD
-- AND IN A PINCH, IT'S A LIVELY WAY TO DISTRACT A PACK OF FEEBS LIKE YOURSELVES!
AS A FRINGE BENEFIT, IT GIVES ME SOMETHING TO LISTEN TO BESIDES YOUR BLOOD-CHOKED GURGLING. ICKY.
"AS SOON AS IT BEGINS, THE HUNT HAS ENDED. SUCH IS THE WAY OF THE JUNGLE --"

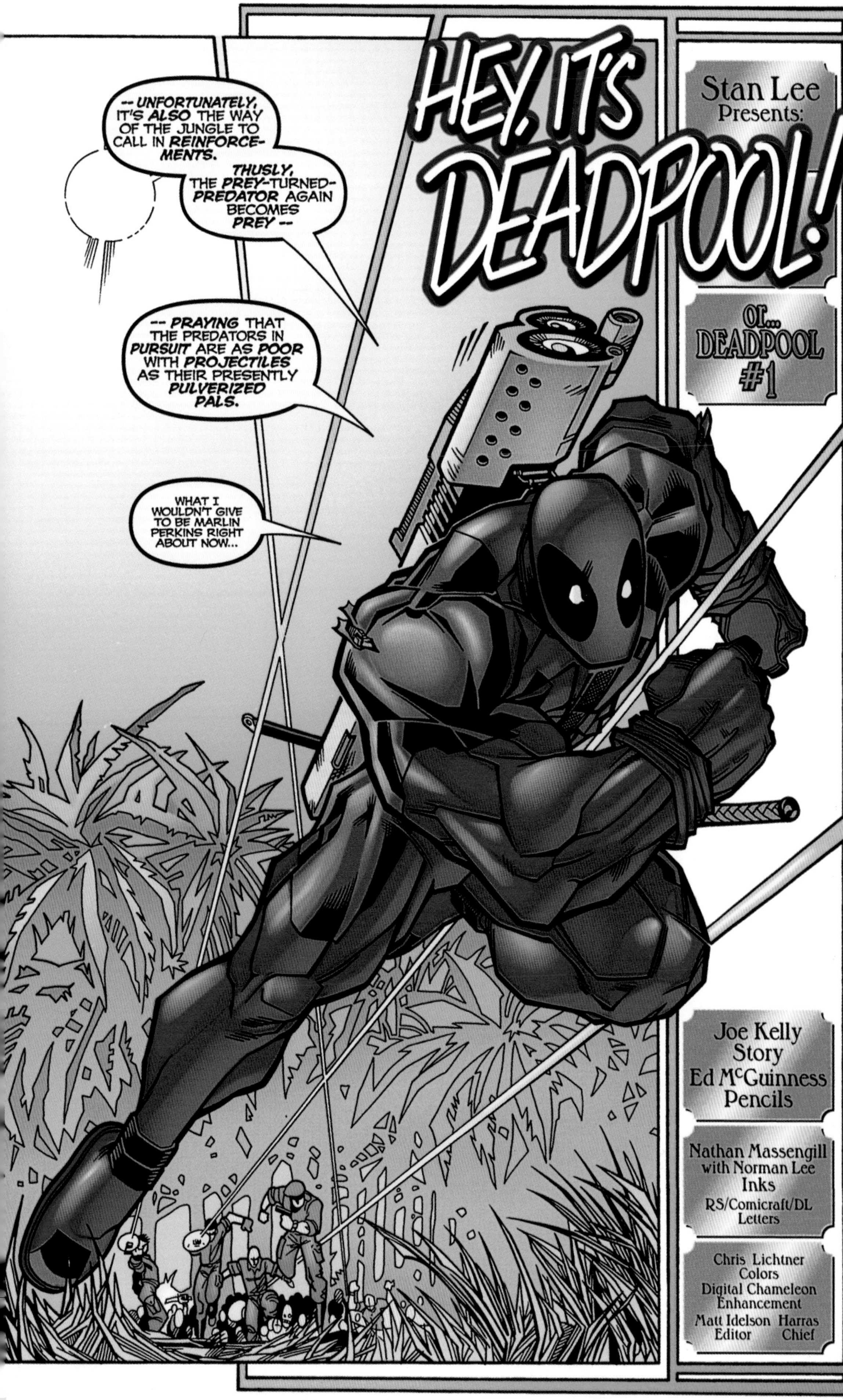

-- UNFORTUNATELY, IT'S ALSO THE WAY OF THE JUNGLE TO CALL IN REINFORCEMENTS.
THUSLY, THE PREY-TURNED-PREDATOR AGAIN BECOMES PREY --
-- PRAYING THAT THE PREDATORS IN PURSUIT ARE AS POOR WITH PROJECTILES AS THEIR PRESENTLY PULVERIZED PALS.
WHAT I WOULDN'T GIVE TO BE MARLIN PERKINS RIGHT ABOUT NOW...
HEY, IT'S DEADPOOL!
Stan Lee Presents:
or... DEADPOOL #1
Joe Kelly Story
Ed McGuinness Pencils
Nathan Massengill with Norman Lee Inks
RS/Comicraft/DL Letters
Chris Lichtner Colors
Digital Chameleon Enhancement
Matt Idelson Editor
Harras Chief

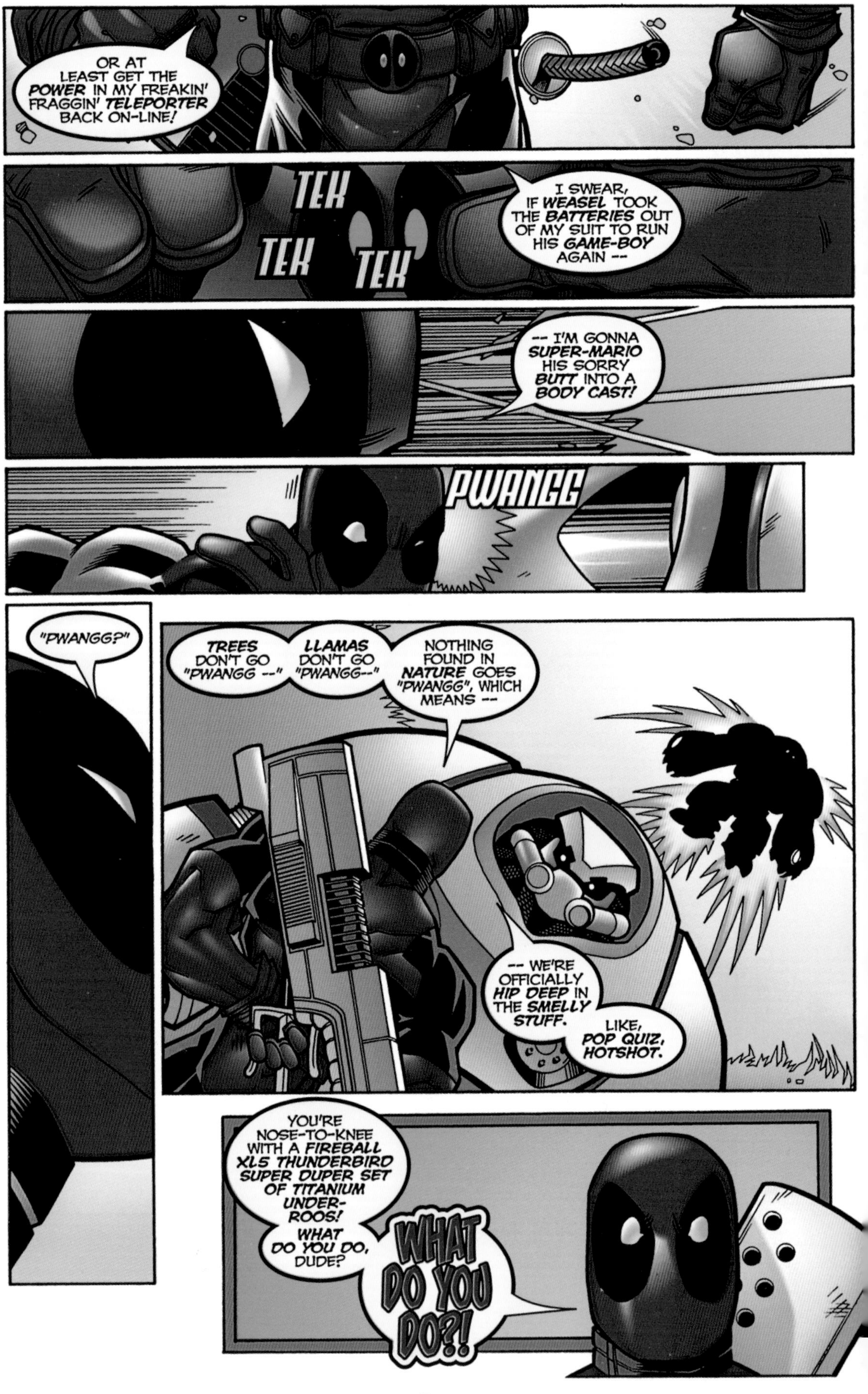

OR AT LEAST GET THE POWER IN MY FREAKIN' FRAGGIN' TELEPORTER BACK ON-LINE!
TEK
TEK
TEK
I SWEAR, IF WEASEL TOOK THE BATTERIES OUT OF MY SUIT TO RUN HIS GAME-BOY AGAIN --
-- I'M GONNA SUPER-MARIO HIS SORRY BUTT INTO A BODY CAST!
PWANGG
"PWANGG?"
TREES DON'T GO "PWANGG --"
LLAMAS DON'T GO "PWANGG--"
NOTHING FOUND IN NATURE GOES "PWANGG", WHICH MEANS --
-- WE'RE OFFICIALLY HIP DEEP IN THE SMELLY STUFF.
LIKE, POP QUIZ, HOTSHOT.
YOU'RE NOSE-TO-KNEE WITH A FIREBALL XLS THUNDERBIRD SUPER DUPER SET OF TITANIUM UNDER-ROOS!
WHAT DO YOU DO, DUDE?
WHAT DO YOU DO?!

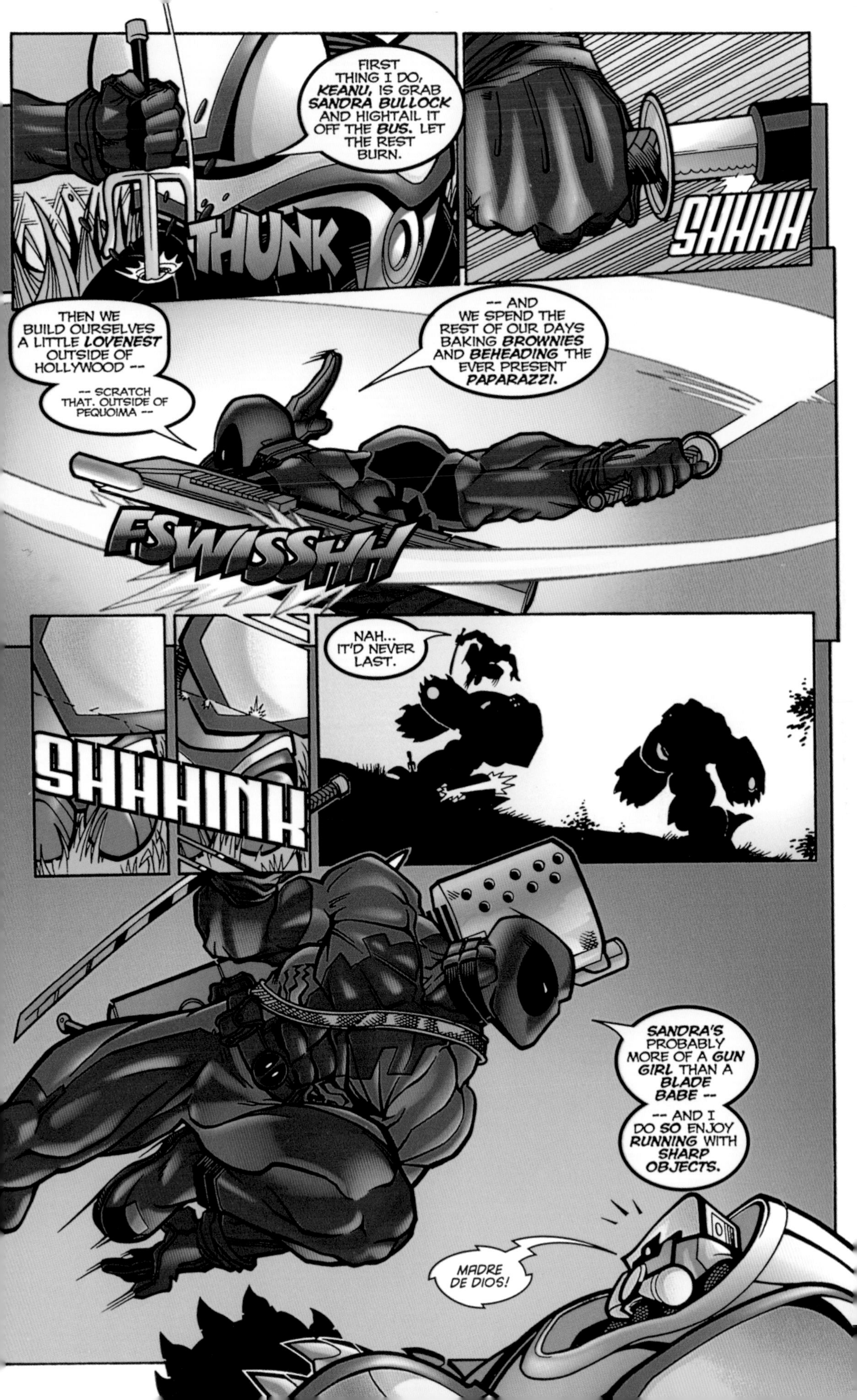
FIRST THING I DO, KEANU, IS GRAB SANDRA BULLOCK AND HIGHTAIL IT OFF THE BUS. LET THE REST BURN.
THUNK
SHHHH
THEN WE BUILD OURSELVES A LITTLE LOVENEST OUTSIDE OF HOLLYWOOD --
-- SCRATCH THAT. OUTSIDE OF PEQUOIMA --
-- AND WE SPEND THE REST OF OUR DAYS BAKING BROWNIES AND BEHEADING THE EVER PRESENT PAPARAZZI.
FSWISSHH
SHHHINK
NAH... IT'D NEVER LAST.
SANDRA'S PROBABLY MORE OF A GUN GIRL THAN A BLADE BABE --
-- AND I DO SO ENJOY RUNNING WITH SHARP OBJECTS.
MADRE DE DIOS!

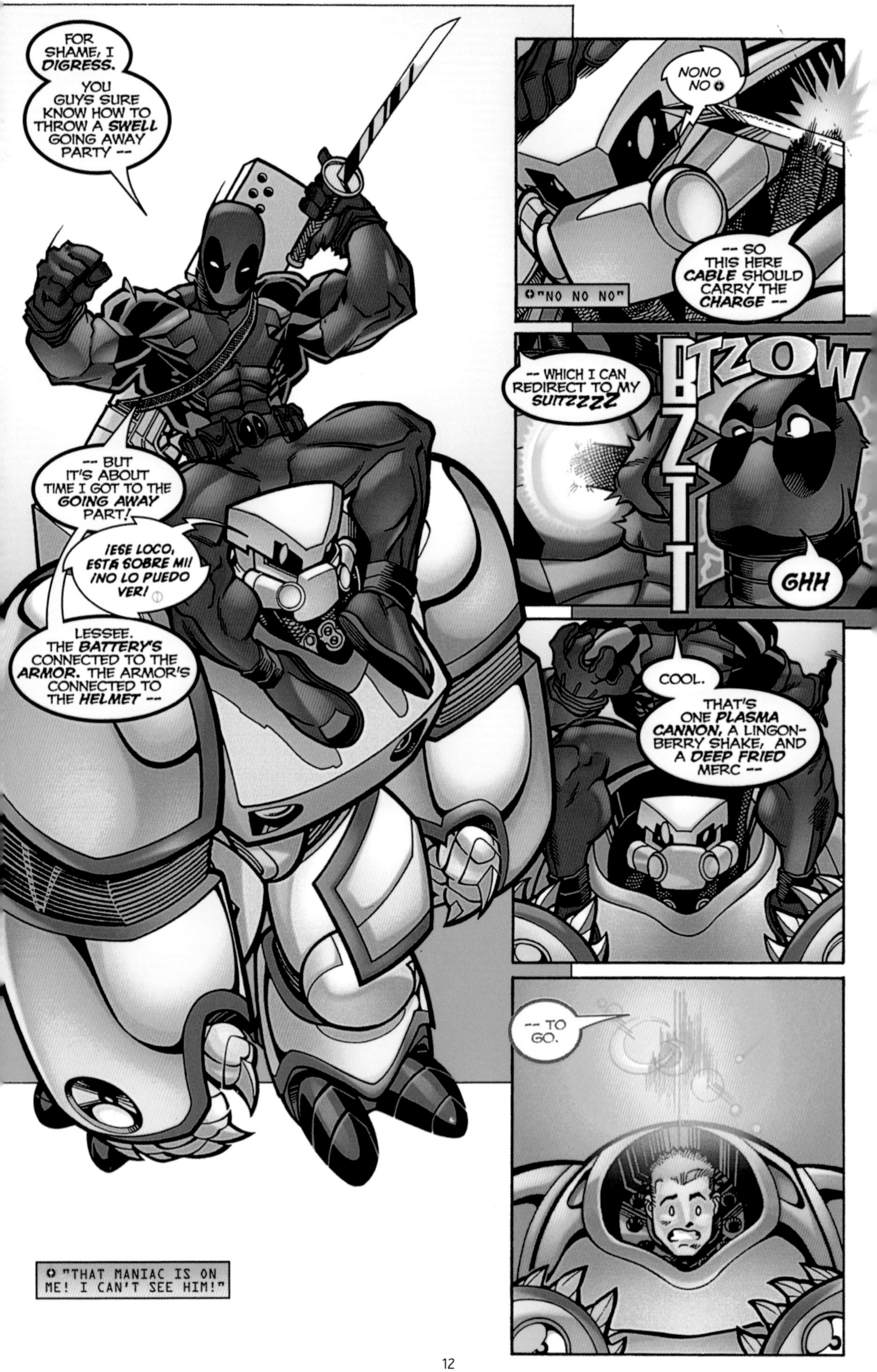
FOR SHAME, I DIGRESS.
YOU GUYS SURE KNOW HOW TO THROW A SWELL GOING AWAY PARTY --
-- BUT IT'S ABOUT TIME I GOT TO THE GOING AWAY PART!
¡ESE LOCO, ESTÁ SOBRE MÍ! ¡NO LO PUEDO VER!
LESSEE. THE BATTERY'S CONNECTED TO THE ARMOR. THE ARMOR'S CONNECTED TO THE HELMET --
"THAT MANIAC IS ON ME! I CAN'T SEE HIM!"
NONO NO
"NO NO NO"
-- SO THIS HERE CABLE SHOULD CARRY THE CHARGE --
-- WHICH I CAN REDIRECT TO MY SUITZZZZ
BZZT
TZOW
GHH
COOL.
THAT'S ONE PLASMA CANNON, A LINGON-BERRY SHAKE, AND A DEEP FRIED MERC --
-- TO GO.

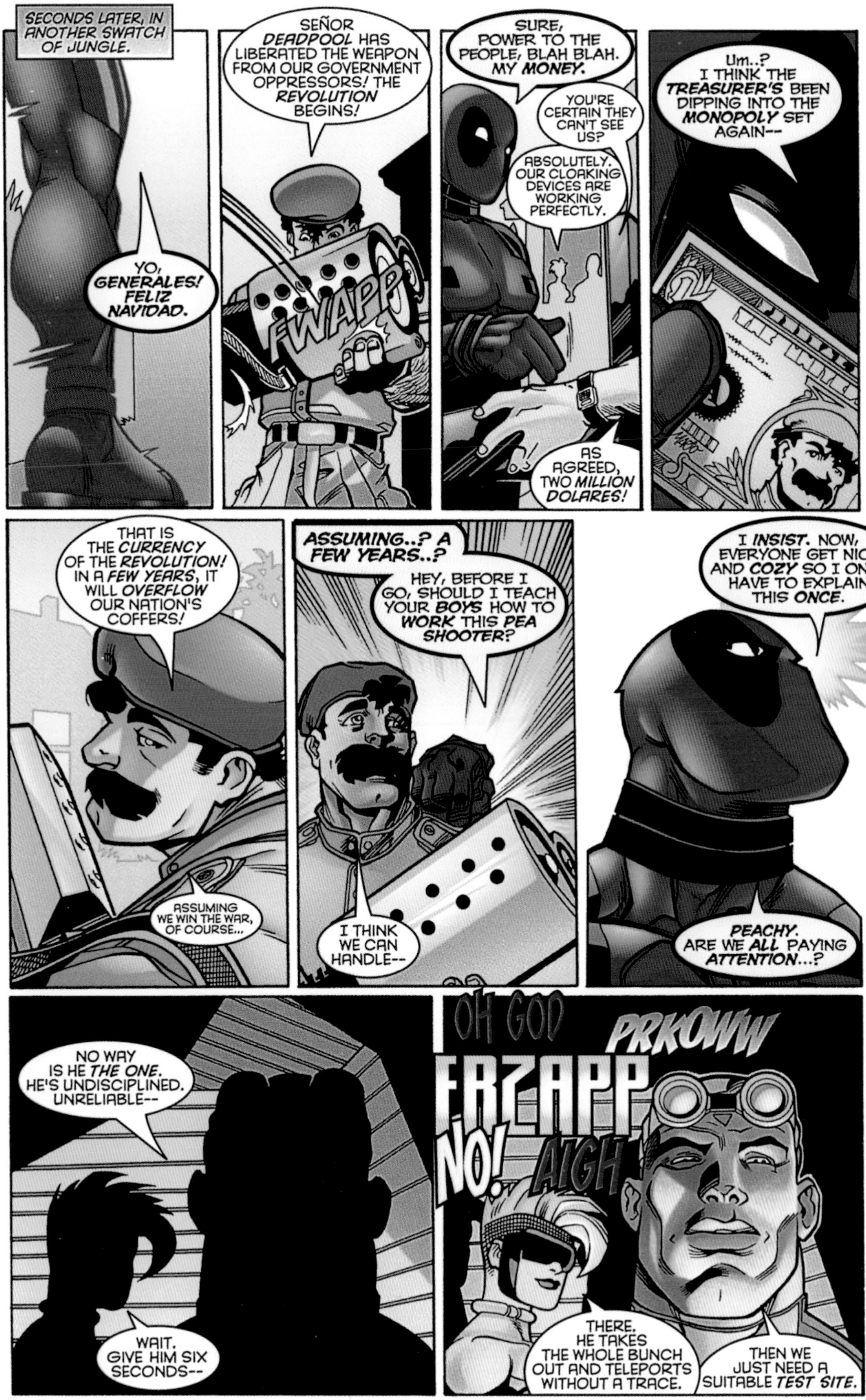

SECONDS LATER, IN ANOTHER SWATCH OF JUNGLE.
YO, GENERALES! FELIZ NAVIDAD.
SEÑOR DEADPOOL HAS LIBERATED THE WEAPON FROM OUR GOVERNMENT OPPRESSORS! THE REVOLUTION BEGINS!
FWAPP
SURE, POWER TO THE PEOPLE, BLAH BLAH. MY MONEY.
YOU'RE CERTAIN THEY CAN'T SEE US?
ABSOLUTELY. OUR CLOAKING DEVICES ARE WORKING PERFECTLY.
AS AGREED, TWO MILLION DOLARES!
Um..? I THINK THE TREASURER'S BEEN DIPPING INTO THE MONOPOLY SET AGAIN--
THAT IS THE CURRENCY OF THE REVOLUTION! IN A FEW YEARS, IT WILL OVERFLOW OUR NATION'S COFFERS!
ASSUMING WE WIN THE WAR, OF COURSE...
ASSUMING..? A FEW YEARS..?
HEY, BEFORE I GO, SHOULD I TEACH YOUR BOYS HOW TO WORK THIS PEA SHOOTER?
I THINK WE CAN HANDLE--
I INSIST. NOW, EVERYONE GET NICE AND COZY SO I ONLY HAVE TO EXPLAIN THIS ONCE.
PEACHY. ARE WE ALL PAYING ATTENTION...?
NO WAY IS HE THE ONE. HE'S UNDISCIPLINED. UNRELIABLE--
WAIT. GIVE HIM SIX SECONDS--
OH GOD
PRKOWW
FRZAPP
NO!
AIGH
THERE. HE TAKES THE WHOLE BUNCH OUT AND TELEPORTS WITHOUT A TRACE.
THEN WE JUST NEED A SUITABLE TEST SITE.

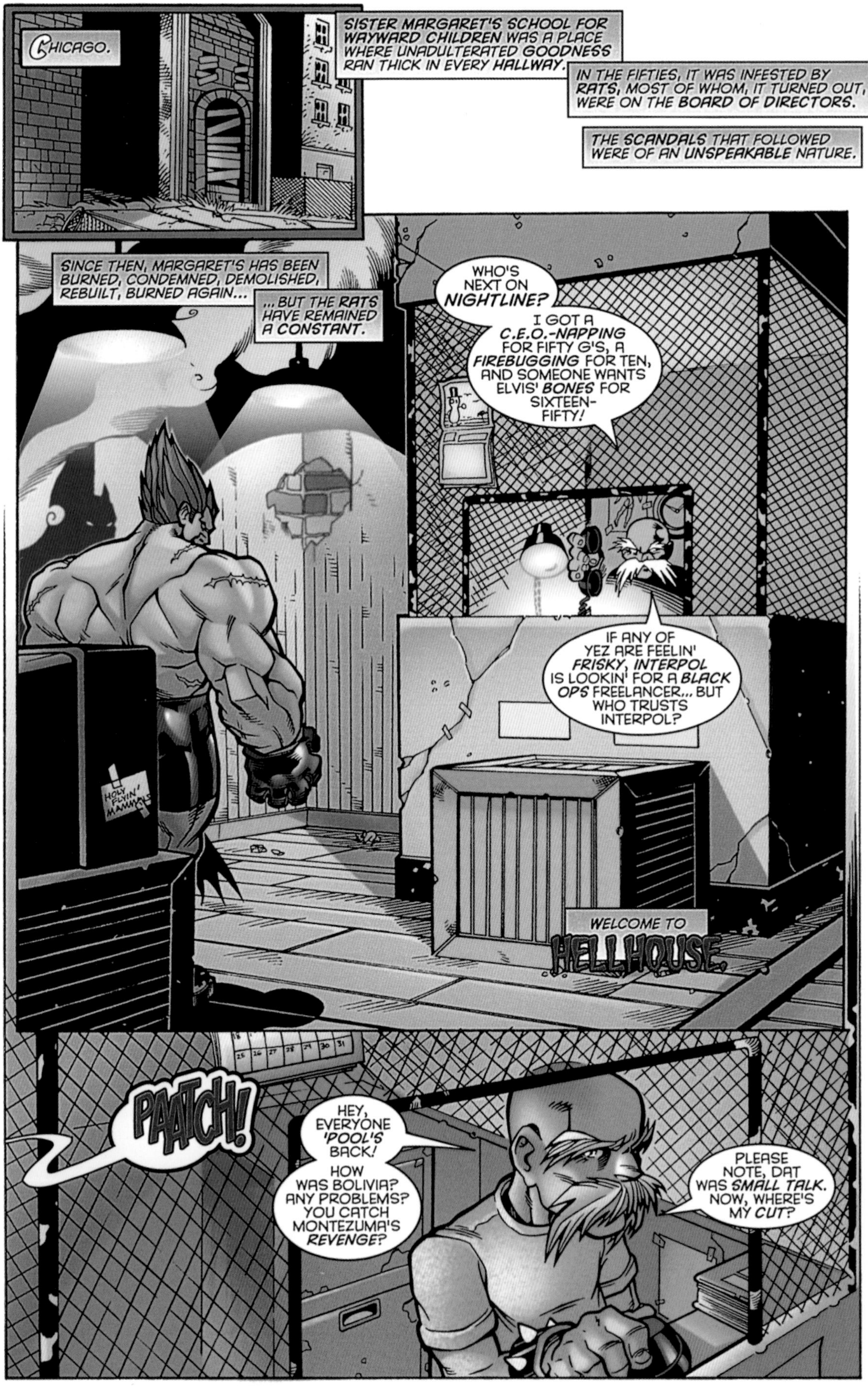
CHICAGO.
SISTER MARGARET'S SCHOOL FOR WAYWARD CHILDREN WAS A PLACE WHERE UNADULTERATED GOODNESS RAN THICK IN EVERY HALLWAY.
IN THE FIFTIES, IT WAS INFESTED BY RATS, MOST OF WHOM, IT TURNED OUT, WERE ON THE BOARD OF DIRECTORS.
THE SCANDALS THAT FOLLOWED WERE OF AN UNSPEAKABLE NATURE.
SINCE THEN, MARGARET'S HAS BEEN BURNED, CONDEMNED, DEMOLISHED, REBUILT, BURNED AGAIN...
...BUT THE RATS HAVE REMAINED A CONSTANT.
WHO'S NEXT ON NIGHTLINE?
I GOT A C.E.O.-NAPPING FOR FIFTY G'S, A FIREBUGGING FOR TEN, AND SOMEONE WANTS ELVIS' BONES FOR SIXTEEN-FIFTY!
IF ANY OF YEZ ARE FEELIN' FRISKY, INTERPOL IS LOOKIN' FOR A BLACK OPS FREELANCER... BUT WHO TRUSTS INTERPOL?
HOLY FLYIN' MAMMALS
WELCOME TO
HELLHOUSE.
PAATCH!
HEY, EVERYONE 'POOL'S BACK!
HOW WAS BOLIVIA? ANY PROBLEMS? YOU CATCH MONTEZUMA'S REVENGE?
PLEASE NOTE, DAT WAS SMALL TALK. NOW, WHERE'S MY CUT?

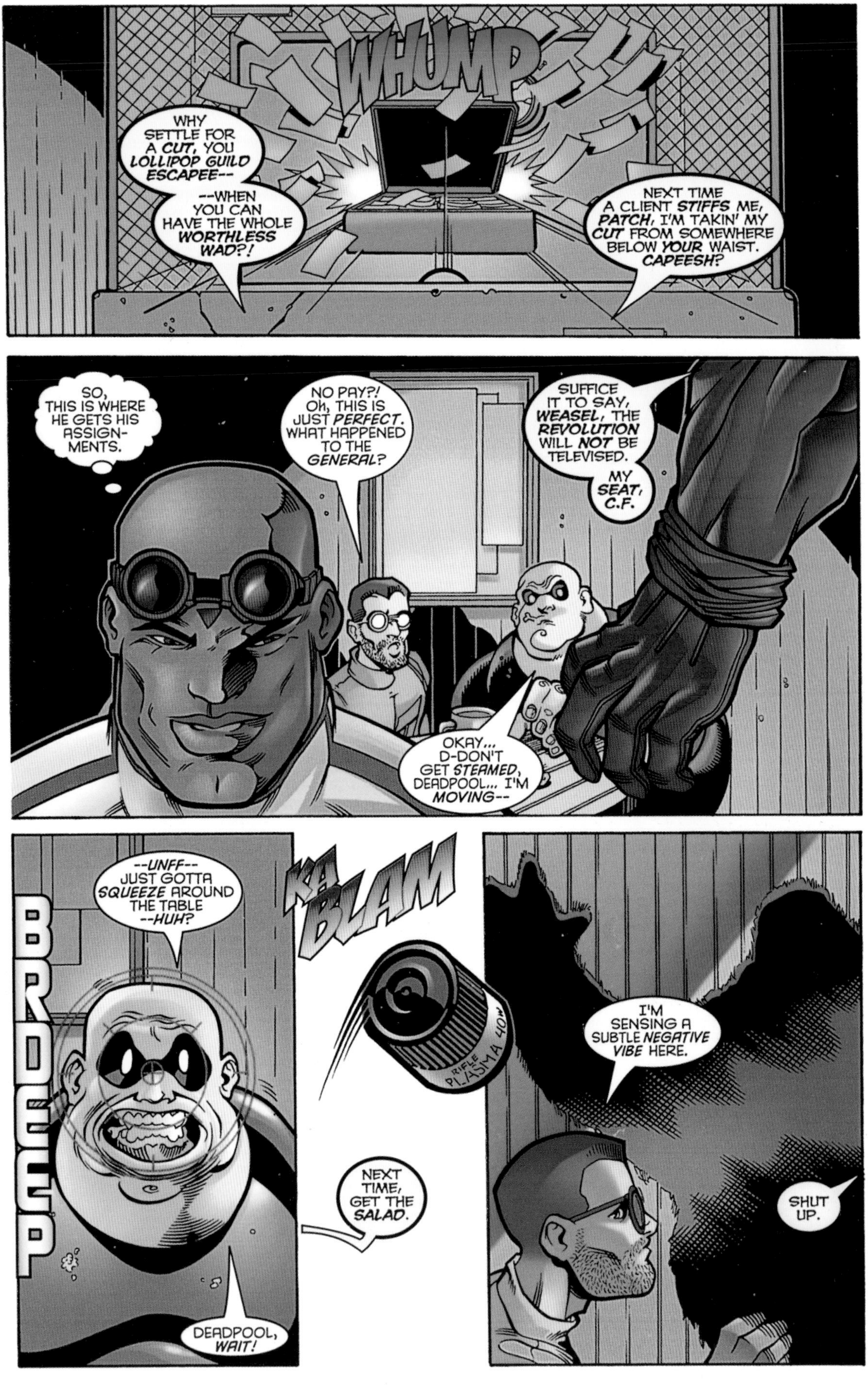
WHUMP
WHY SETTLE FOR A CUT, YOU LOLLIPOP GUILD ESCAPEE--
--WHEN YOU CAN HAVE THE WHOLE WORTHLESS WAD?!
NEXT TIME A CLIENT STIFFS ME, PATCH, I'M TAKIN' MY CUT FROM SOMEWHERE BELOW YOUR WAIST. CAPEESH?
SO, THIS IS WHERE HE GETS HIS ASSIGNMENTS.
NO PAY?! Oh, THIS IS JUST PERFECT. WHAT HAPPENED TO THE GENERAL?
SUFFICE IT TO SAY, WEASEL, THE REVOLUTION WILL NOT BE TELEVISED.
MY SEAT, C.F.
OKAY... D-DON'T GET STEAMED, DEADPOOL... I'M MOVING--
--UNFF-- JUST GOTTA SQUEEZE AROUND THE TABLE --HUH?
BREEEP
KA BLAM
RIFLE PLASMA 40W
NEXT TIME, GET THE SALAD.
DEADPOOL, WAIT!
I'M SENSING A SUBTLE NEGATIVE VIBE HERE.
SHUT UP.

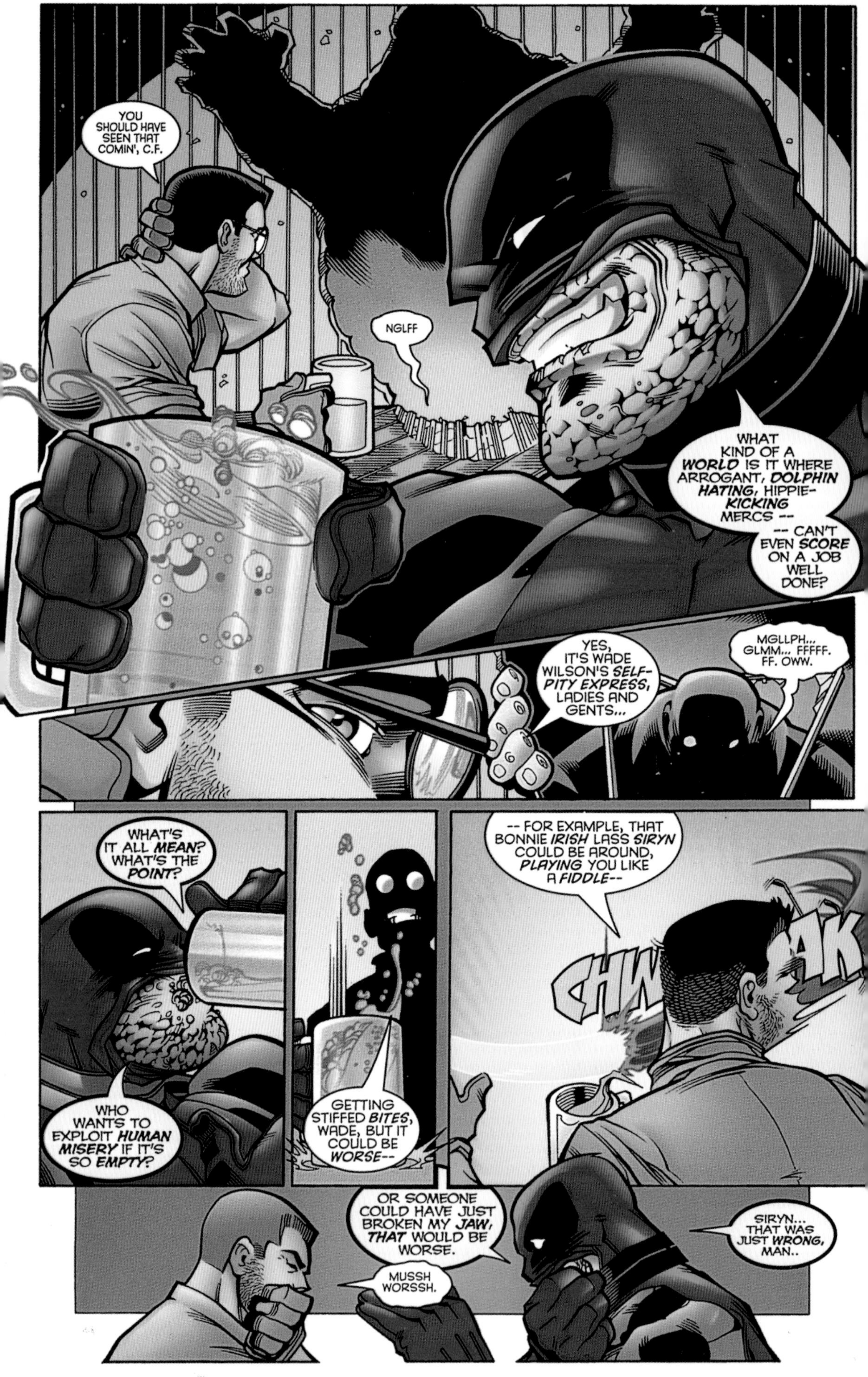

YOU SHOULD HAVE SEEN THAT COMIN', C.F.
NGLFF
WHAT KIND OF A WORLD IS IT WHERE ARROGANT, DOLPHIN HATING, HIPPIE-KICKING MERCS --
-- CAN'T EVEN SCORE ON A JOB WELL DONE?
YES, IT'S WADE WILSON'S SELF-PITY EXPRESS, LADIES AND GENTS...
MGLLPH... GLMM... FFFFF. FF. OWW.
WHAT'S IT ALL MEAN? WHAT'S THE POINT?
WHO WANTS TO EXPLOIT HUMAN MISERY IF IT'S SO EMPTY?
GETTING STIFFED BITES, WADE, BUT IT COULD BE WORSE--
-- FOR EXAMPLE, THAT BONNIE IRISH LASS SIRYN COULD BE AROUND, PLAYING YOU LIKE A FIDDLE--
CHWAK
OR SOMEONE COULD HAVE JUST BROKEN MY JAW, THAT WOULD BE WORSE.
MUSSH WORSSH.
SIRYN... THAT WAS JUST WRONG, MAN..

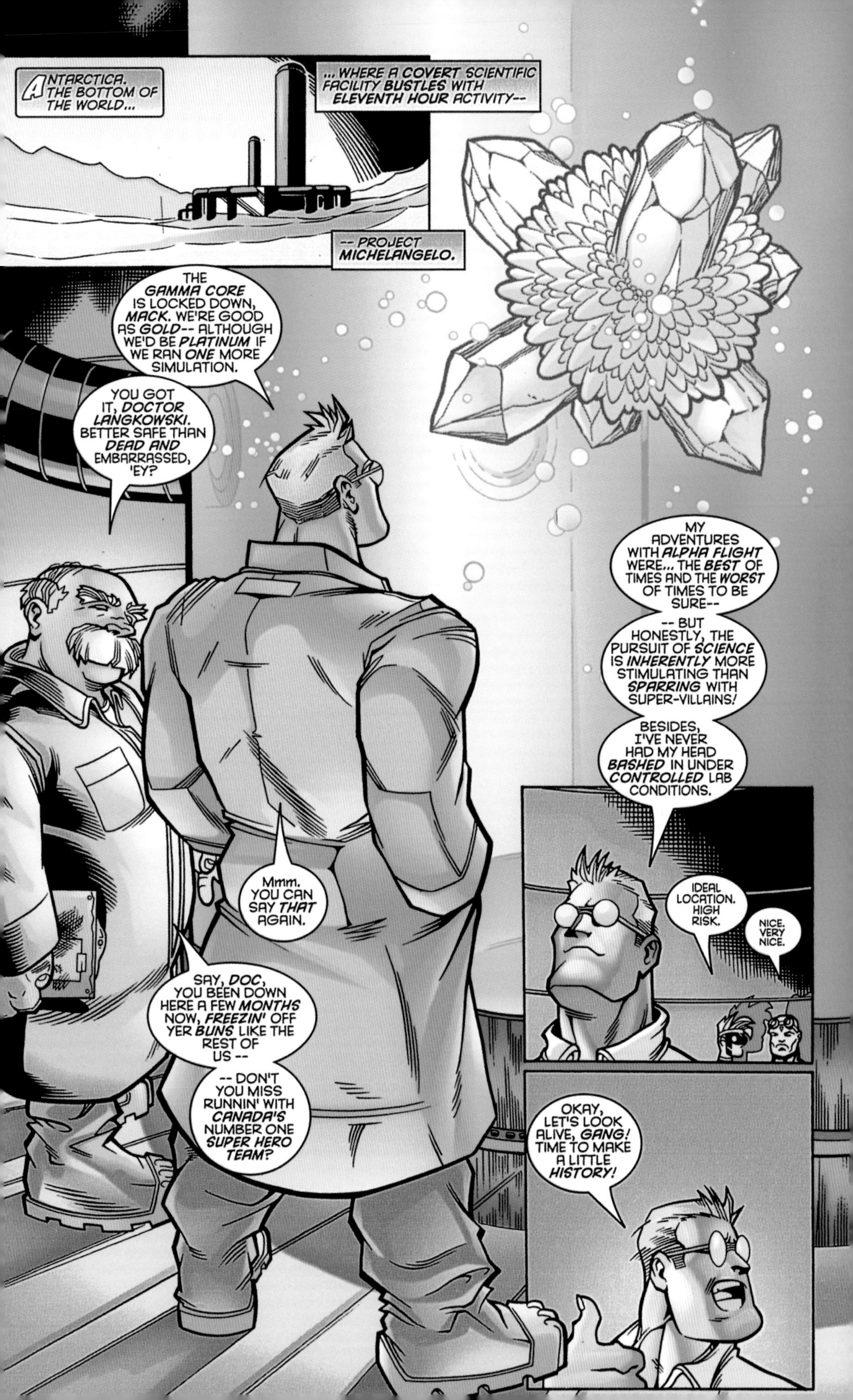
ANTARCTICA. THE BOTTOM OF THE WORLD...
...WHERE A COVERT SCIENTIFIC FACILITY BUSTLES WITH ELEVENTH HOUR ACTIVITY--
-- PROJECT MICHELANGELO.
THE GAMMA CORE IS LOCKED DOWN, MACK. WE'RE GOOD AS GOLD-- ALTHOUGH WE'D BE PLATINUM IF WE RAN ONE MORE SIMULATION.
YOU GOT IT, DOCTOR LANGKOWSKI. BETTER SAFE THAN DEAD AND EMBARRASSED, 'EY?
Mmm. YOU CAN SAY THAT AGAIN.
SAY, DOC, YOU BEEN DOWN HERE A FEW MONTHS NOW, FREEZIN' OFF YER BUNS LIKE THE REST OF US --
-- DON'T YOU MISS RUNNIN' WITH CANADA'S NUMBER ONE SUPER HERO TEAM?
MY ADVENTURES WITH ALPHA FLIGHT WERE... THE BEST OF TIMES AND THE WORST OF TIMES TO BE SURE--
-- BUT HONESTLY, THE PURSUIT OF SCIENCE IS INHERENTLY MORE STIMULATING THAN SPARRING WITH SUPER-VILLAINS!
BESIDES, I'VE NEVER HAD MY HEAD BASHED IN UNDER CONTROLLED LAB CONDITIONS.
IDEAL LOCATION. HIGH RISK.
NICE. VERY NICE.
OKAY, LET'S LOOK ALIVE, GANG! TIME TO MAKE A LITTLE HISTORY!

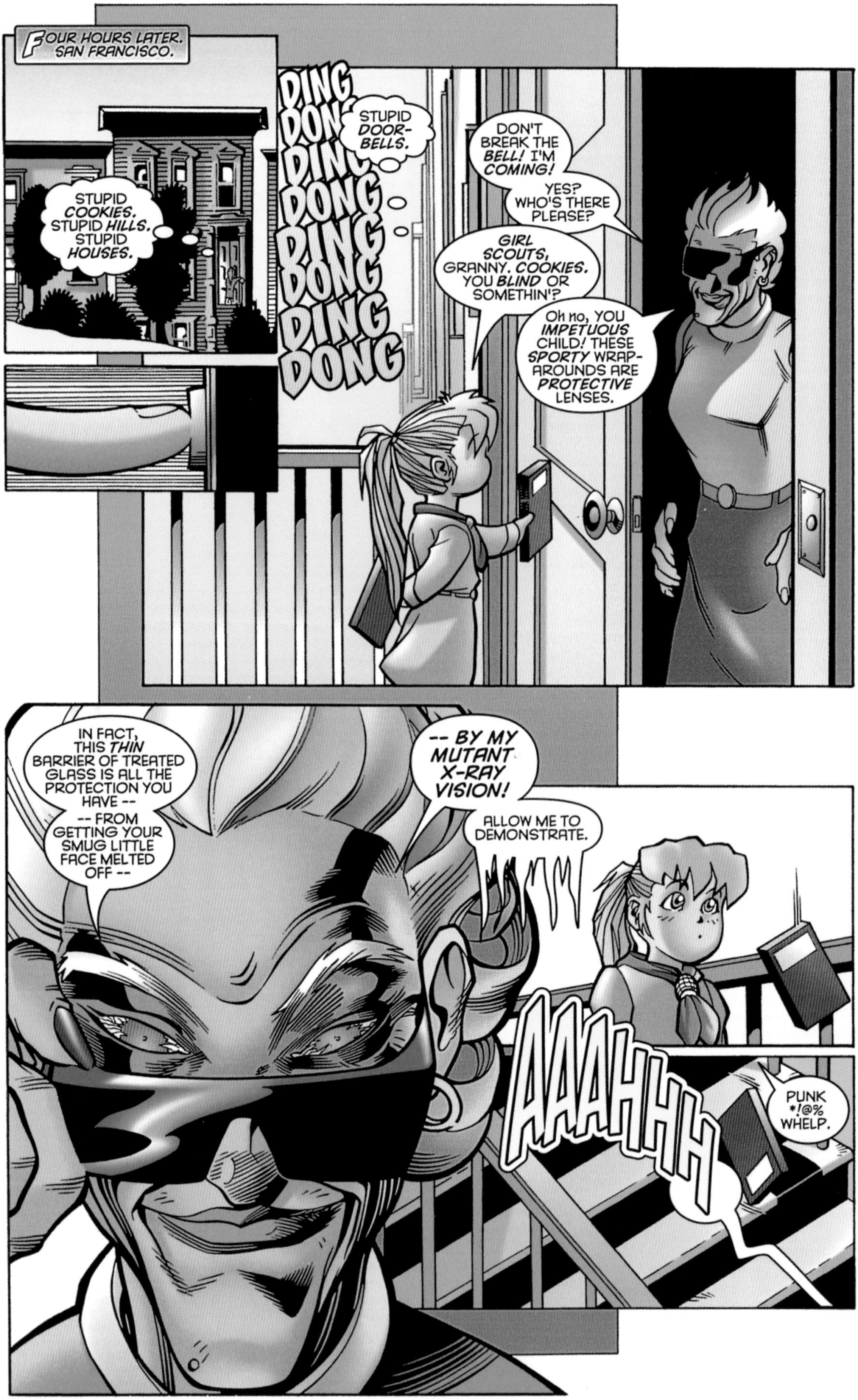
FOUR HOURS LATER. SAN FRANCISCO.
STUPID COOKIES. STUPID HILLS. STUPID HOUSES.
DING DONG DING DONG DING DONG DING DONG
STUPID DOOR-BELLS.
DON'T BREAK THE BELL! I'M COMING!
YES? WHO'S THERE PLEASE?
GIRL SCOUTS, GRANNY. COOKIES. YOU BLIND OR SOMETHIN'?
Oh no, YOU IMPETUOUS CHILD! THESE SPORTY WRAP-AROUNDS ARE PROTECTIVE LENSES.
IN FACT, THIS THIN BARRIER OF TREATED GLASS IS ALL THE PROTECTION YOU HAVE -- -- FROM GETTING YOUR SMUG LITTLE FACE MELTED OFF --
-- BY MY MUTANT X-RAY VISION!
ALLOW ME TO DEMONSTRATE.
AAAHHH
PUNK *!@% WHELP.

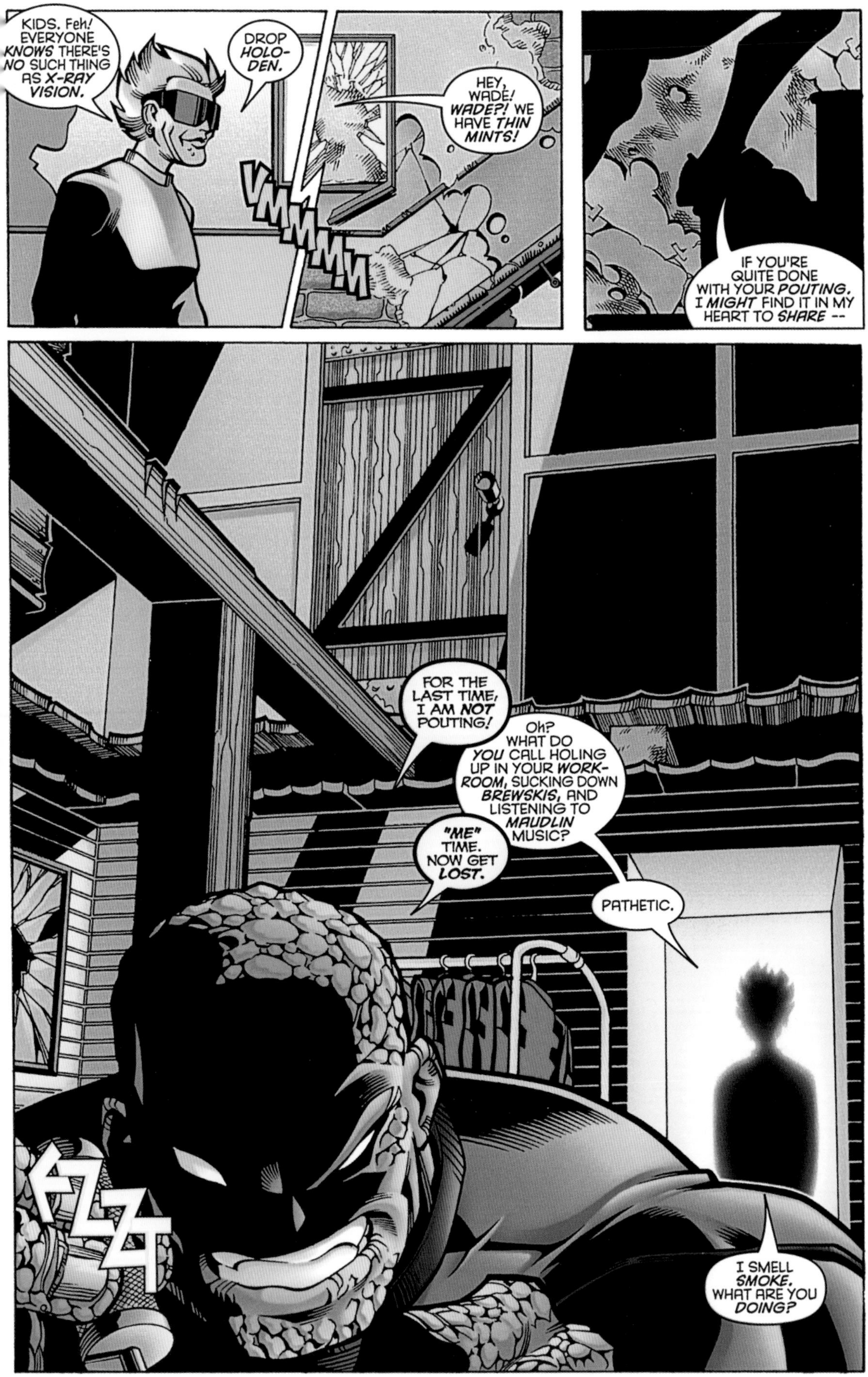
KIDS. Feh! EVERYONE KNOWS THERE'S NO SUCH THING AS X-RAY VISION.
DROP HOLO-DEN.
VMMMMM
HEY, WADE! WADE?! WE HAVE THIN MINTS!
IF YOU'RE QUITE DONE WITH YOUR POUTING, I MIGHT FIND IT IN MY HEART TO SHARE --
FOR THE LAST TIME, I AM NOT POUTING!
Oh? WHAT DO YOU CALL HOLING UP IN YOUR WORK-ROOM, SUCKING DOWN BREWSKIS, AND LISTENING TO MAUDLIN MUSIC?
"ME" TIME. NOW GET LOST.
PATHETIC.
FZZT
I SMELL SMOKE. WHAT ARE YOU DOING?

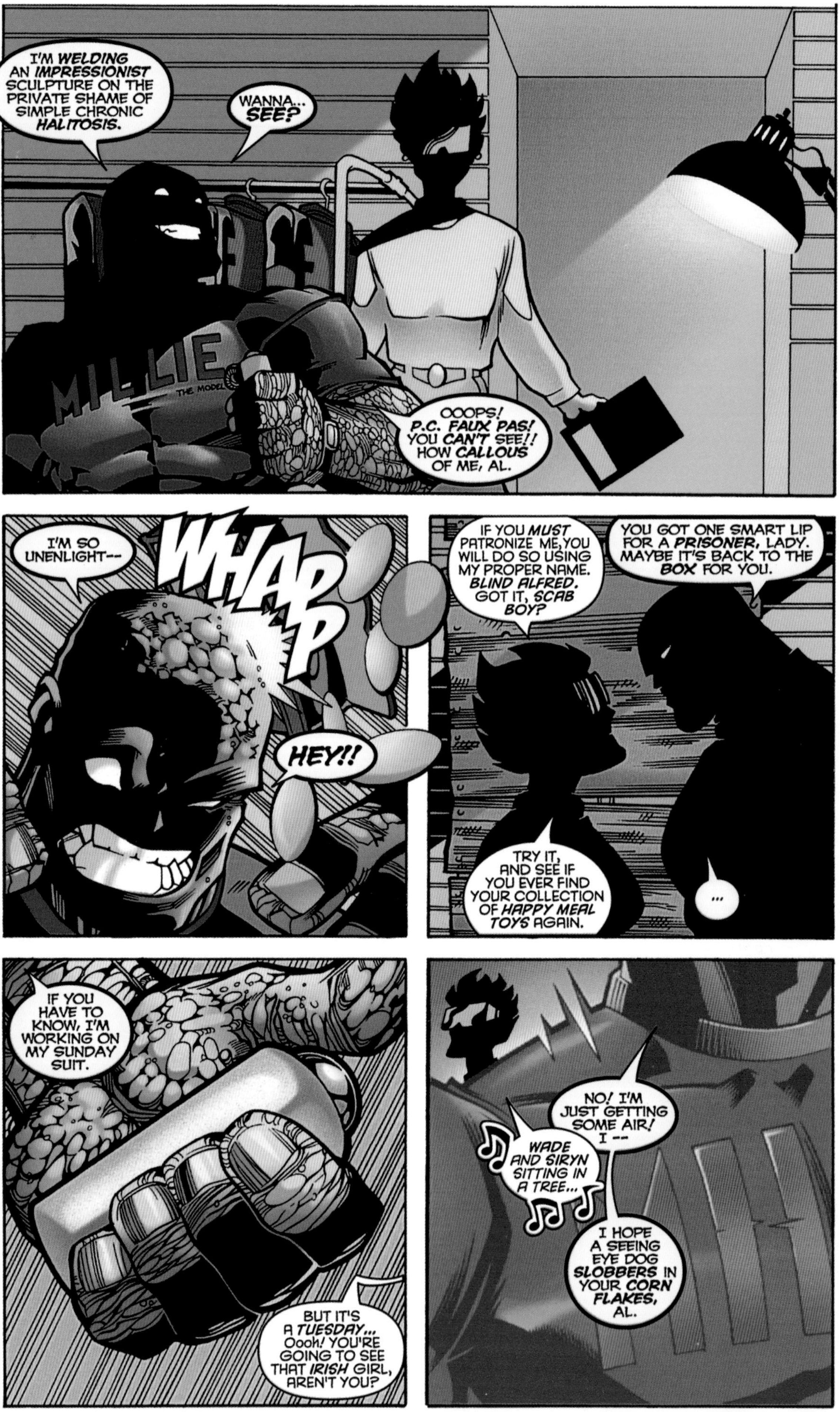
I'M WELDING AN IMPRESSIONIST SCULPTURE ON THE PRIVATE SHAME OF SIMPLE CHRONIC HALITOSIS.
WANNA... SEE?
MILLIE THE MODEL
OOOPS! P.C. FAUX PAS! YOU CAN'T SEE!! HOW CALLOUS OF ME, AL.
I'M SO UNENLIGHT--
WHAP
HEY!!
IF YOU MUST PATRONIZE ME, YOU WILL DO SO USING MY PROPER NAME. BLIND ALFRED. GOT IT, SCAB BOY?
YOU GOT ONE SMART LIP FOR A PRISONER, LADY. MAYBE IT'S BACK TO THE BOX FOR YOU.
TRY IT, AND SEE IF YOU EVER FIND YOUR COLLECTION OF HAPPY MEAL TOYS AGAIN.
...
IF YOU HAVE TO KNOW, I'M WORKING ON MY SUNDAY SUIT.
BUT IT'S A TUESDAY... Oooh! YOU'RE GOING TO SEE THAT IRISH GIRL, AREN'T YOU?
NO! I'M JUST GETTING SOME AIR! I --
WADE AND SIRYN SITTING IN A TREE...
I HOPE A SEEING EYE DOG SLOBBERS IN YOUR CORN FLAKES, AL.

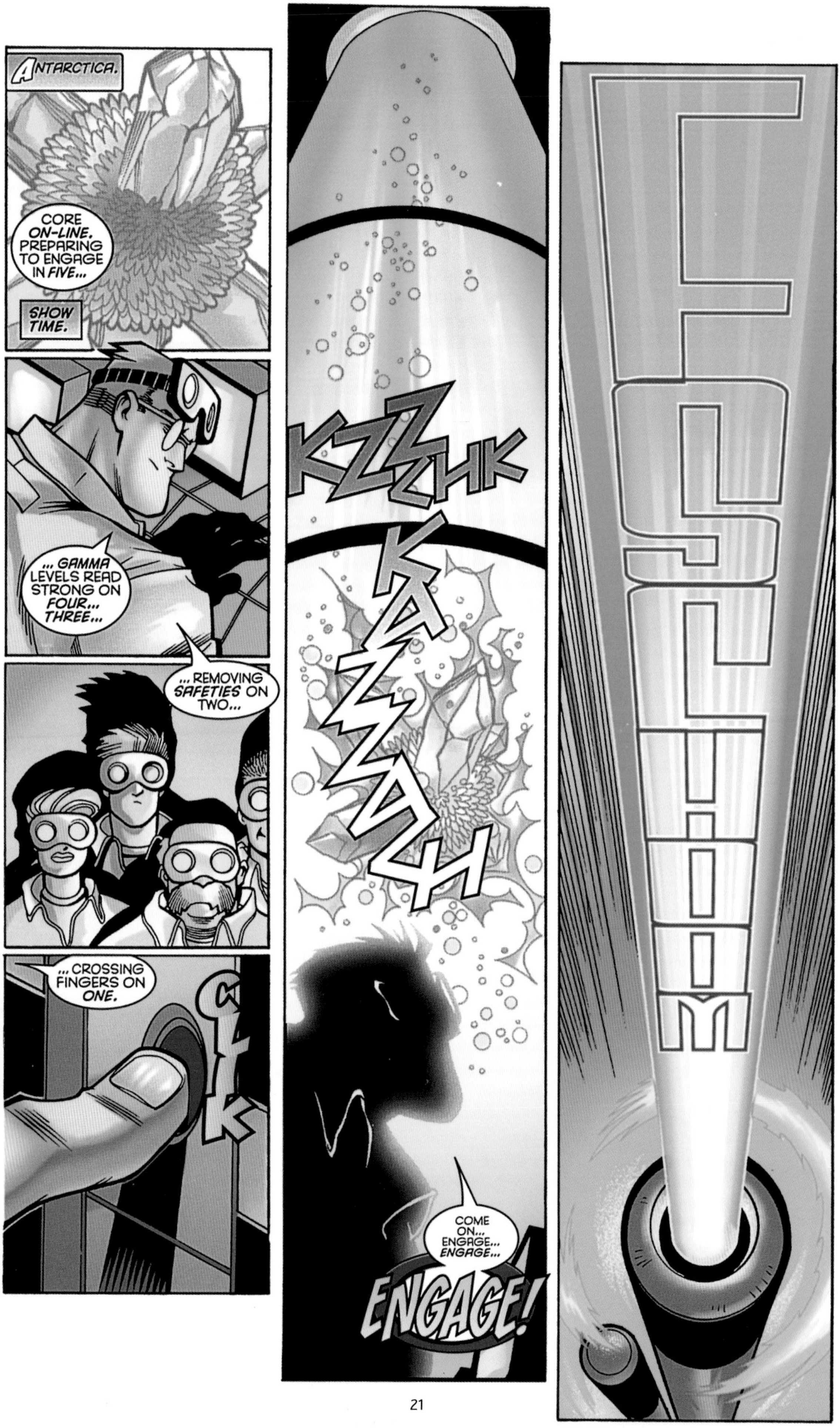
ANTARCTICA.
CORE ON-LINE. PREPARING TO ENGAGE IN FIVE...
SHOW TIME.
...GAMMA LEVELS READ STRONG ON FOUR... THREE...
...REMOVING SAFETIES ON TWO...
...CROSSING FINGERS ON ONE.
KZZZHK
COME ON... ENGAGE... ENGAGE...
ENGAGE!

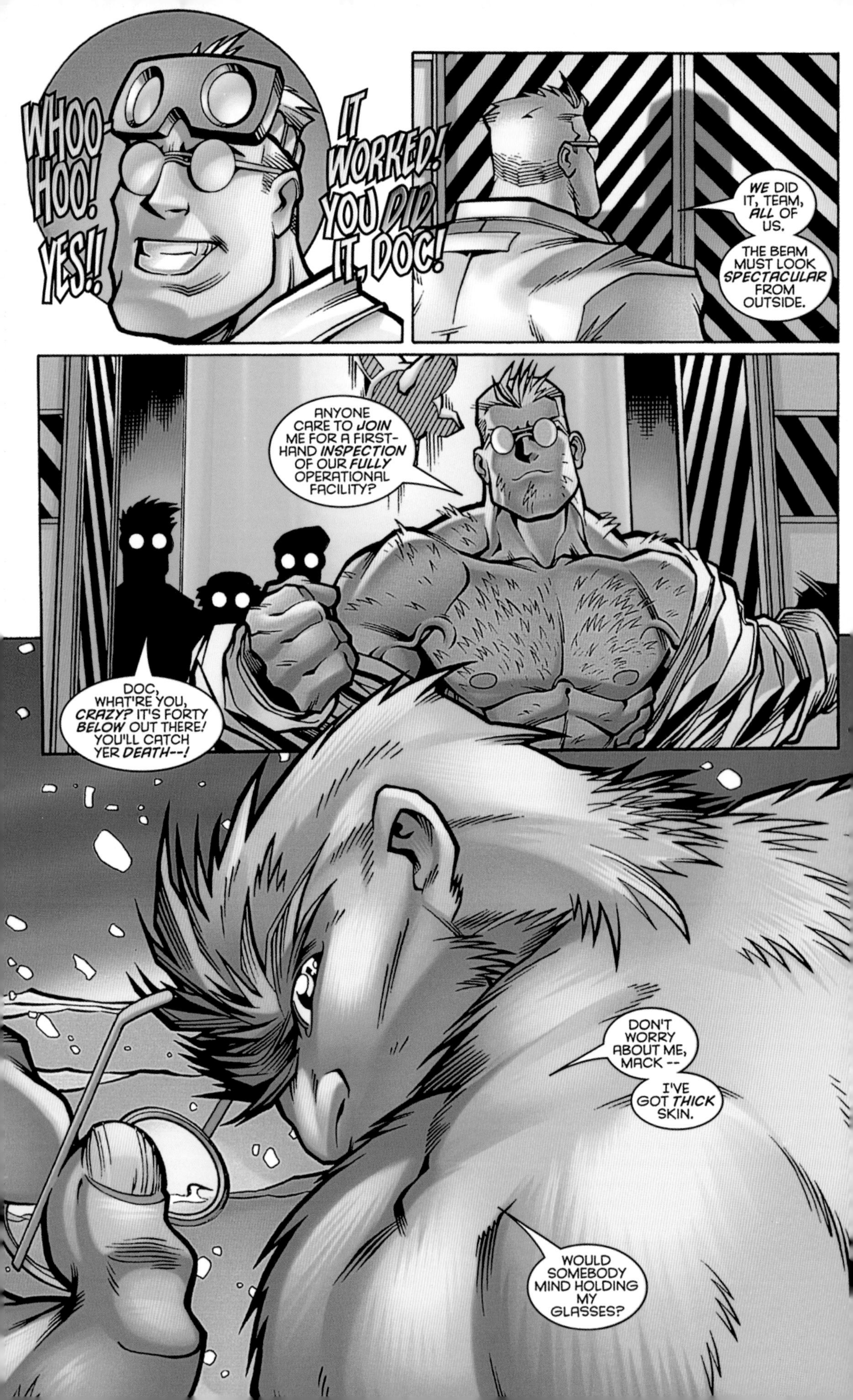
WHOO-HOO! YES!!
IT WORKED! YOU DID IT, DOC!
WE DID IT, TEAM, ALL OF US.
THE BEAM MUST LOOK SPECTACULAR FROM OUTSIDE.
ANYONE CARE TO JOIN ME FOR A FIRST-HAND INSPECTION OF OUR FULLY OPERATIONAL FACILITY?
DOC, WHAT'RE YOU, CRAZY? IT'S FORTY BELOW OUT THERE! YOU'LL CATCH YER DEATH--!
DON'T WORRY ABOUT ME, MACK --
I'VE GOT THICK SKIN.
WOULD SOMEBODY MIND HOLDING MY GLASSES?

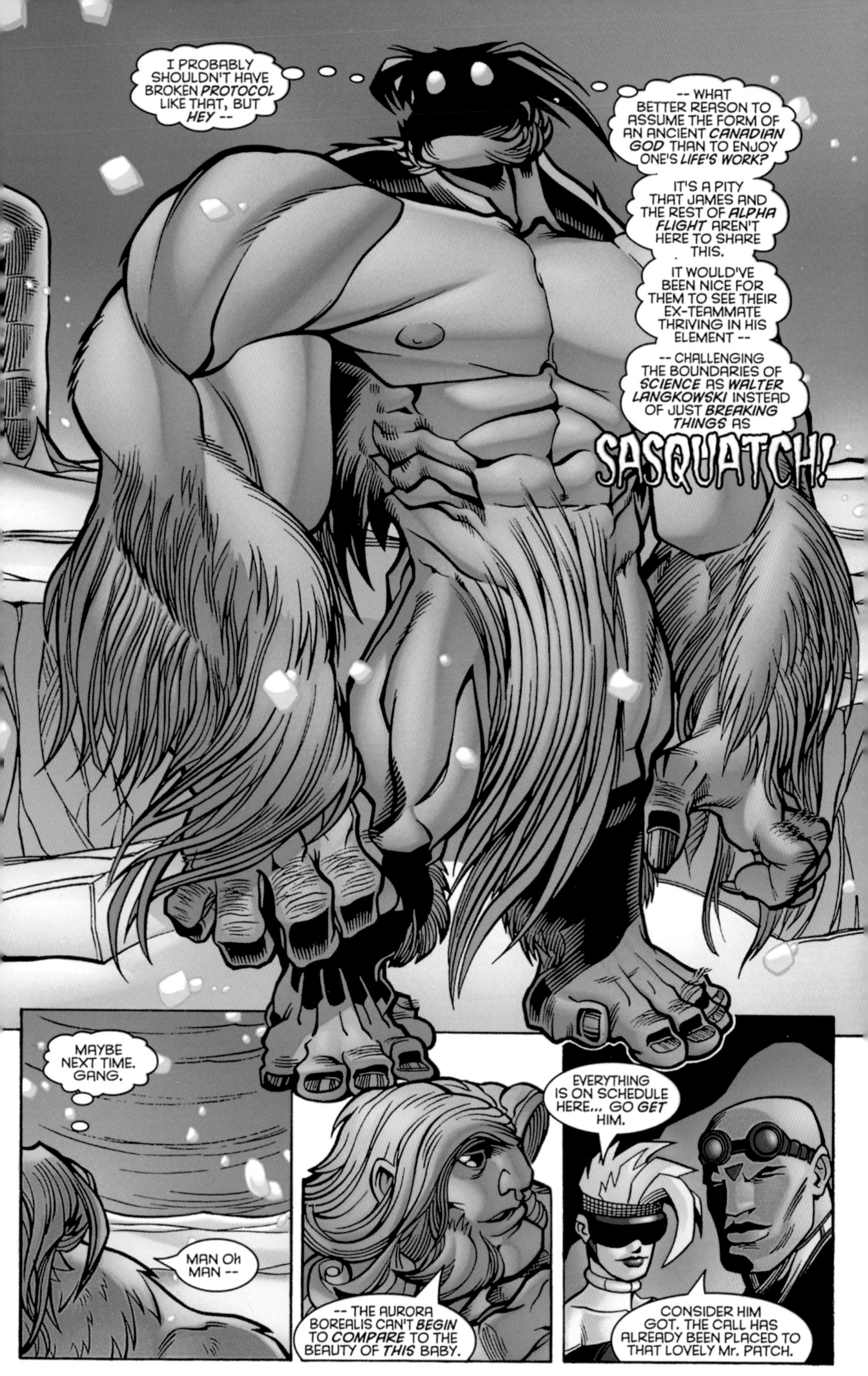

I PROBABLY SHOULDN'T HAVE BROKEN PROTOCOL LIKE THAT, BUT HEY --
-- WHAT BETTER REASON TO ASSUME THE FORM OF AN ANCIENT CANADIAN GOD THAN TO ENJOY ONE'S LIFE'S WORK?
IT'S A PITY THAT JAMES AND THE REST OF ALPHA FLIGHT AREN'T HERE TO SHARE THIS.
IT WOULD'VE BEEN NICE FOR THEM TO SEE THEIR EX-TEAMMATE THRIVING IN HIS ELEMENT --
-- CHALLENGING THE BOUNDARIES OF SCIENCE AS WALTER LANGKOWSKI INSTEAD OF JUST BREAKING THINGS AS
SASQUATCH!
MAYBE NEXT TIME, GANG.
MAN OH MAN --
-- THE AURORA BOREALIS CAN'T BEGIN TO COMPARE TO THE BEAUTY OF THIS BABY.
EVERYTHING IS ON SCHEDULE HERE... GO GET HIM.
CONSIDER HIM GOT. THE CALL HAS ALREADY BEEN PLACED TO THAT LOVELY Mr. PATCH.

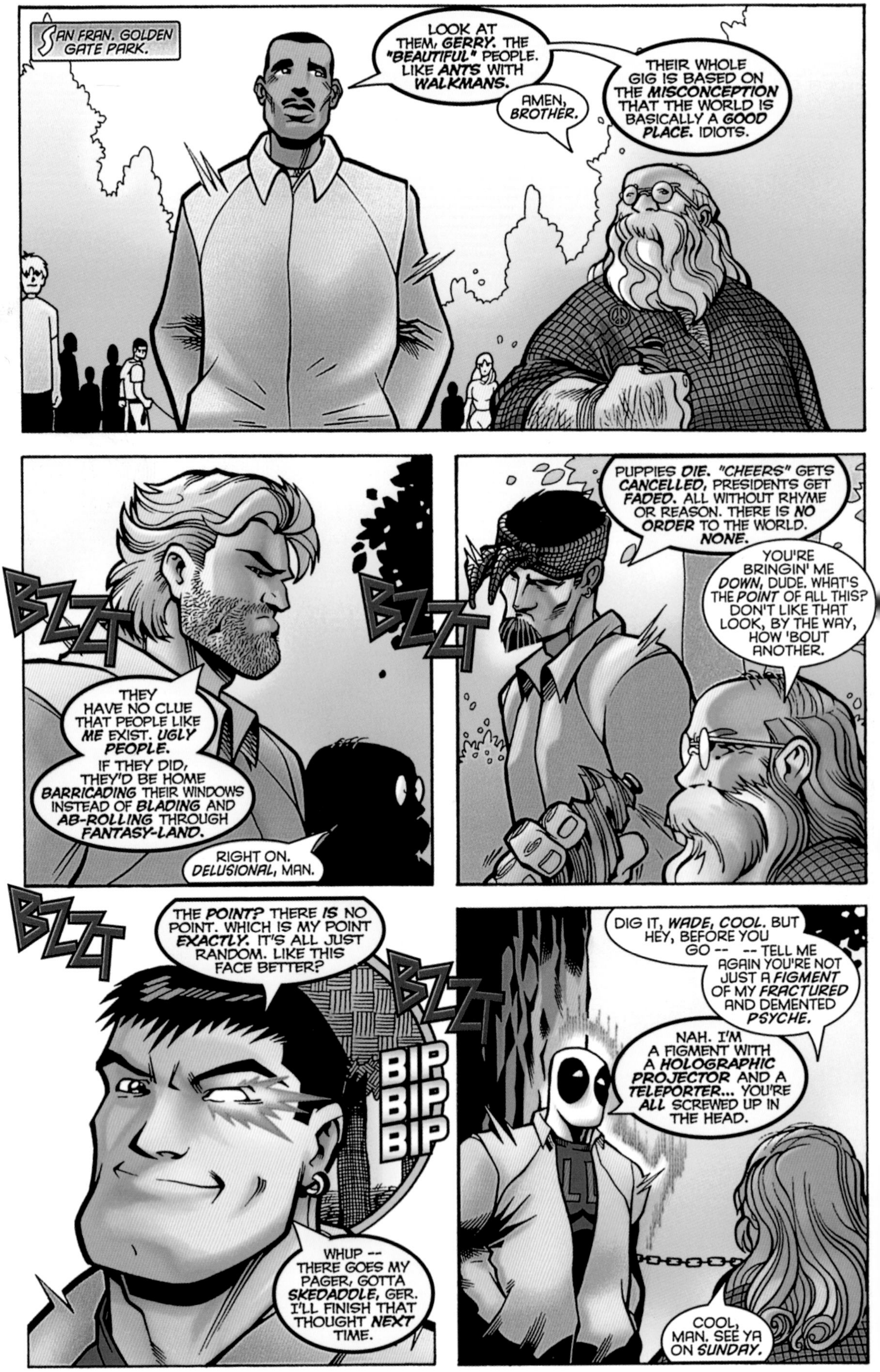
SAN FRAN. GOLDEN GATE PARK.
LOOK AT THEM, GERRY. THE "BEAUTIFUL" PEOPLE. LIKE ANTS WITH WALKMANS.
AMEN, BROTHER.
THEIR WHOLE GIG IS BASED ON THE MISCONCEPTION THAT THE WORLD IS BASICALLY A GOOD PLACE. IDIOTS.
BZZT
THEY HAVE NO CLUE THAT PEOPLE LIKE ME EXIST. UGLY PEOPLE.
IF THEY DID, THEY'D BE HOME BARRICADING THEIR WINDOWS INSTEAD OF BLADING AND AB-ROLLING THROUGH FANTASY-LAND.
RIGHT ON. DELUSIONAL, MAN.
BZZT
PUPPIES DIE. "CHEERS" GETS CANCELLED, PRESIDENTS GET FADED. ALL WITHOUT RHYME OR REASON. THERE IS NO ORDER TO THE WORLD. NONE.
YOU'RE BRINGIN' ME DOWN, DUDE. WHAT'S THE POINT OF ALL THIS? DON'T LIKE THAT LOOK, BY THE WAY, HOW 'BOUT ANOTHER.
BZZT
THE POINT? THERE IS NO POINT. WHICH IS MY POINT EXACTLY. IT'S ALL JUST RANDOM. LIKE THIS FACE BETTER?
BZZT
BIP BIP BIP
WHUP -- THERE GOES MY PAGER, GOTTA SKEDADDLE, GER. I'LL FINISH THAT THOUGHT NEXT TIME.
DIG IT, WADE, COOL. BUT HEY, BEFORE YOU GO -- -- TELL ME AGAIN YOU'RE NOT JUST A FIGMENT OF MY FRACTURED AND DEMENTED PSYCHE.
NAH. I'M A FIGMENT WITH A HOLOGRAPHIC PROJECTOR AND A TELEPORTER... YOU'RE ALL SCREWED UP IN THE HEAD.
COOL, MAN. SEE YA ON SUNDAY.

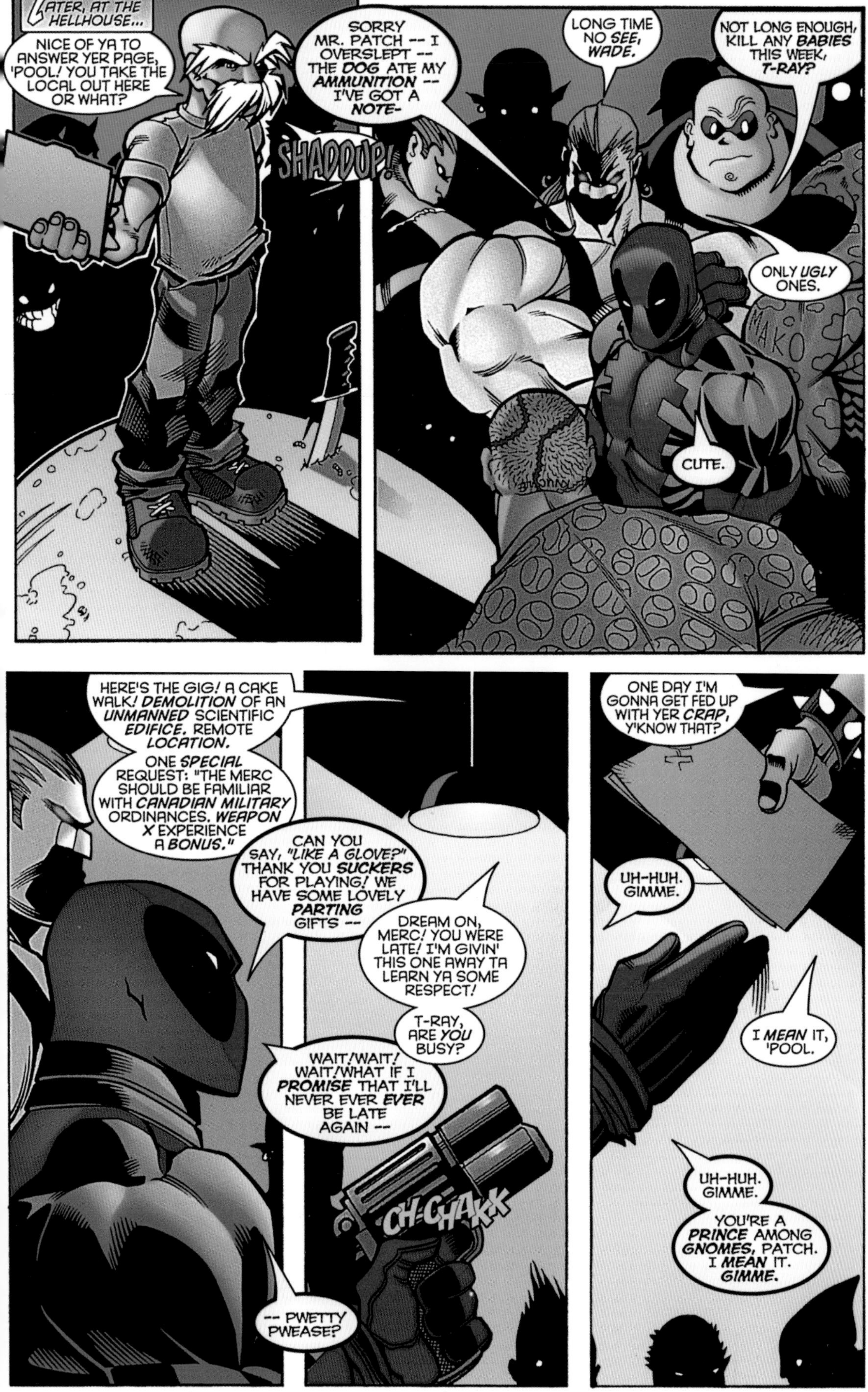
LATER, AT THE HELLHOUSE...
NICE OF YA TO ANSWER YER PAGE, 'POOL! YOU TAKE THE LOCAL OUT HERE OR WHAT?
SORRY MR. PATCH -- I OVERSLEPT -- THE DOG ATE MY AMMUNITION -- I'VE GOT A NOTE-
SHADDUP!
LONG TIME NO SEE, WADE.
NOT LONG ENOUGH. KILL ANY BABIES THIS WEEK, T-RAY?
ONLY UGLY ONES.
CUTE.
MAKO
HERE'S THE GIG! A CAKE WALK! DEMOLITION OF AN UNMANNED SCIENTIFIC EDIFICE. REMOTE LOCATION.
ONE SPECIAL REQUEST: "THE MERC SHOULD BE FAMILIAR WITH CANADIAN MILITARY ORDINANCES. WEAPON X EXPERIENCE A BONUS."
CAN YOU SAY, "LIKE A GLOVE?" THANK YOU SUCKERS FOR PLAYING! WE HAVE SOME LOVELY PARTING GIFTS --
DREAM ON, MERC! YOU WERE LATE! I'M GIVIN' THIS ONE AWAY TA LEARN YA SOME RESPECT!
T-RAY, ARE YOU BUSY?
WAIT! WAIT! WAIT! WHAT IF I PROMISE THAT I'LL NEVER EVER EVER BE LATE AGAIN --
CH-CHAKK
-- PWETTY PWEASE?
ONE DAY I'M GONNA GET FED UP WITH YER CRAP, Y'KNOW THAT?
UH-HUH. GIMME.
I MEAN IT, 'POOL.
UH-HUH. GIMME.
YOU'RE A PRINCE AMONG GNOMES, PATCH. I MEAN IT. GIMME.

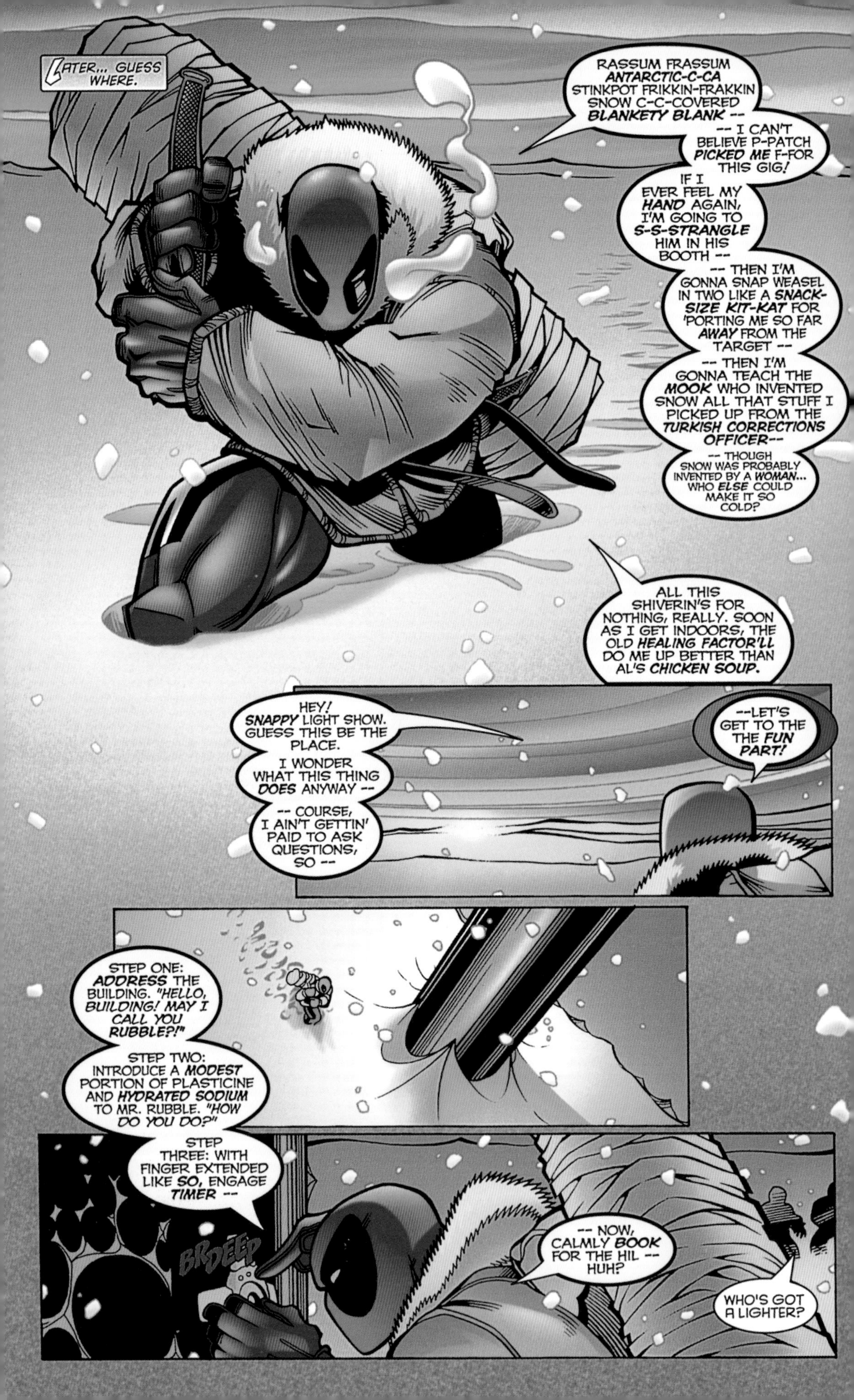
LATER... GUESS WHERE.
RASSUM FRASSUM ANTARCTIC-C-CA STINKPOT FRIKKIN-FRAKKIN SNOW C-C-COVERED BLANKETY BLANK --
-- I CAN'T BELIEVE P-PATCH PICKED ME F-FOR THIS GIG!
IF I EVER FEEL MY HAND AGAIN, I'M GOING TO S-S-STRANGLE HIM IN HIS BOOTH --
-- THEN I'M GONNA SNAP WEASEL IN TWO LIKE A SNACK-SIZE KIT-KAT FOR 'PORTING ME SO FAR AWAY FROM THE TARGET --
-- THEN I'M GONNA TEACH THE MOOK WHO INVENTED SNOW ALL THAT STUFF I PICKED UP FROM THE TURKISH CORRECTIONS OFFICER--
-- THOUGH SNOW WAS PROBABLY INVENTED BY A WOMAN... WHO ELSE COULD MAKE IT SO COLD?
ALL THIS SHIVERIN'S FOR NOTHING, REALLY. SOON AS I GET INDOORS, THE OLD HEALING FACTOR'LL DO ME UP BETTER THAN AL'S CHICKEN SOUP.
HEY! SNAPPY LIGHT SHOW. GUESS THIS BE THE PLACE.
I WONDER WHAT THIS THING DOES ANYWAY --
-- COURSE, I AIN'T GETTIN' PAID TO ASK QUESTIONS, SO --
--LET'S GET TO THE THE FUN PART!
STEP ONE: ADDRESS THE BUILDING. "HELLO, BUILDING! MAY I CALL YOU RUBBLE?!"
STEP TWO: INTRODUCE A MODEST PORTION OF PLASTICINE AND HYDRATED SODIUM TO MR. RUBBLE. "HOW DO YOU DO?"
STEP THREE: WITH FINGER EXTENDED LIKE SO, ENGAGE TIMER --
BRDEEP
-- NOW, CALMLY BOOK FOR THE HIL -- HUH?
WHO'S GOT A LIGHTER?

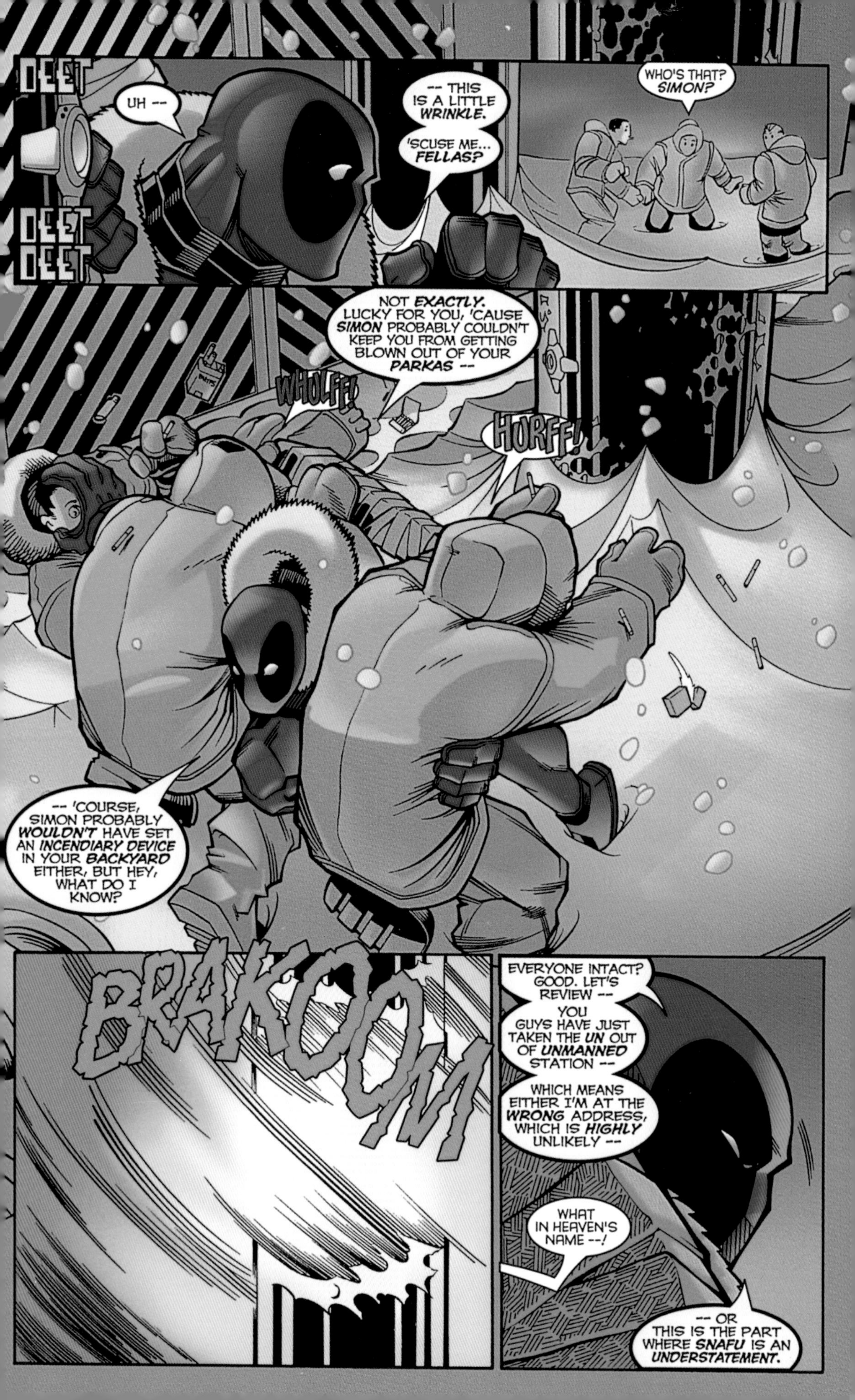
DEET
DEET
DEET
UH --
-- THIS IS A LITTLE WRINKLE.
'SCUSE ME... FELLAS?
WHO'S THAT? SIMON?
NOT EXACTLY. LUCKY FOR YOU, 'CAUSE SIMON PROBABLY COULDN'T KEEP YOU FROM GETTING BLOWN OUT OF YOUR PARKAS --
WHOLFF!
HURFF!
-- 'COURSE, SIMON PROBABLY WOULDN'T HAVE SET AN INCENDIARY DEVICE IN YOUR BACKYARD EITHER, BUT HEY, WHAT DO I KNOW?
BRAKOOM
EVERYONE INTACT? GOOD. LET'S REVIEW --
YOU GUYS HAVE JUST TAKEN THE UN OUT OF UNMANNED STATION --
WHICH MEANS EITHER I'M AT THE WRONG ADDRESS, WHICH IS HIGHLY UNLIKELY --
WHAT IN HEAVEN'S NAME --!
-- OR THIS IS THE PART WHERE SNAFU IS AN UNDERSTATEMENT.

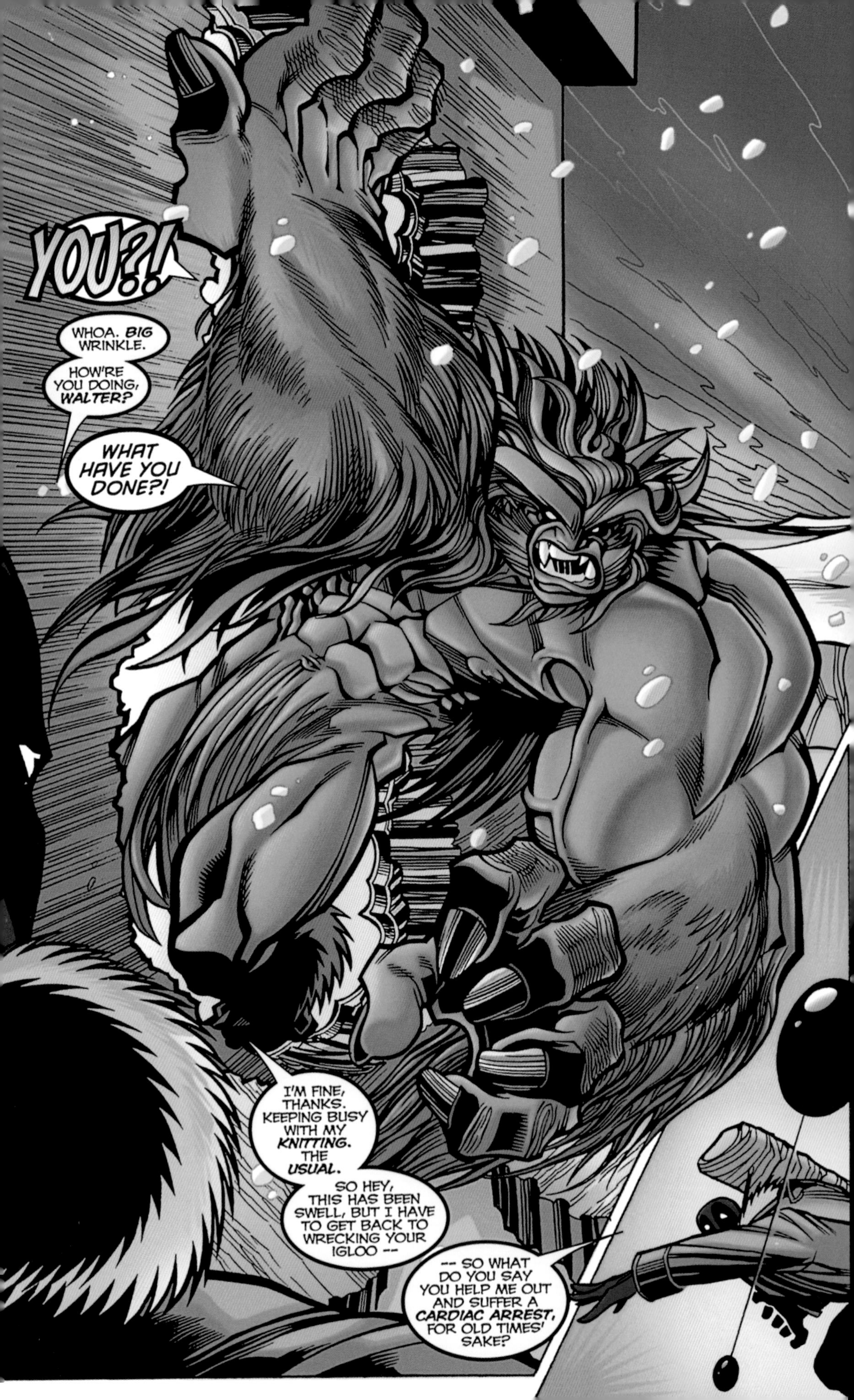
YOU?!
WHOA. BIG WRINKLE.
HOW'RE YOU DOING, WALTER?
WHAT HAVE YOU DONE?!
I'M FINE, THANKS. KEEPING BUSY WITH MY KNITTING. THE USUAL.
SO HEY, THIS HAS BEEN SWELL, BUT I HAVE TO GET BACK TO WRECKING YOUR IGLOO --
-- SO WHAT DO YOU SAY YOU HELP ME OUT AND SUFFER A CARDIAC ARREST, FOR OLD TIMES' SAKE?

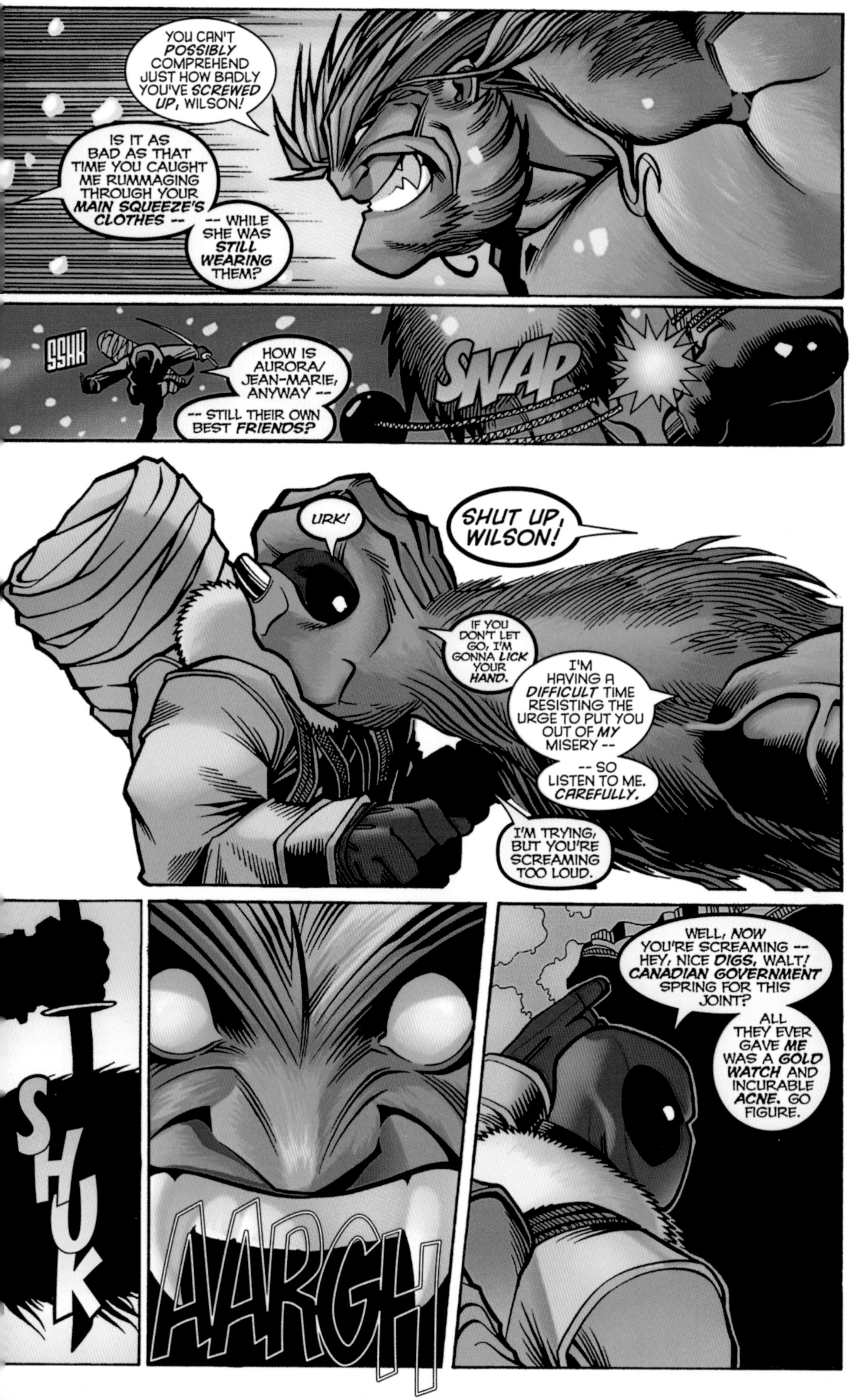
YOU CAN'T POSSIBLY COMPREHEND JUST HOW BADLY YOU'VE SCREWED UP, WILSON!
IS IT AS BAD AS THAT TIME YOU CAUGHT ME RUMMAGING THROUGH YOUR MAIN SQUEEZE'S CLOTHES --
-- WHILE SHE WAS STILL WEARING THEM?
SSHK
HOW IS AURORA/ JEAN-MARIE, ANYWAY --
-- STILL THEIR OWN BEST FRIENDS?
SNAP
URK!
SHUT UP, WILSON!
IF YOU DON'T LET GO, I'M GONNA LICK YOUR HAND.
I'M HAVING A DIFFICULT TIME RESISTING THE URGE TO PUT YOU OUT OF MY MISERY --
-- SO LISTEN TO ME. CAREFULLY.
I'M TRYING, BUT YOU'RE SCREAMING TOO LOUD.
SHUK
AARGH
WELL, NOW YOU'RE SCREAMING -- HEY, NICE DIGS, WALT! CANADIAN GOVERNMENT SPRING FOR THIS JOINT?
ALL THEY EVER GAVE ME WAS A GOLD WATCH AND INCURABLE ACNE. GO FIGURE.

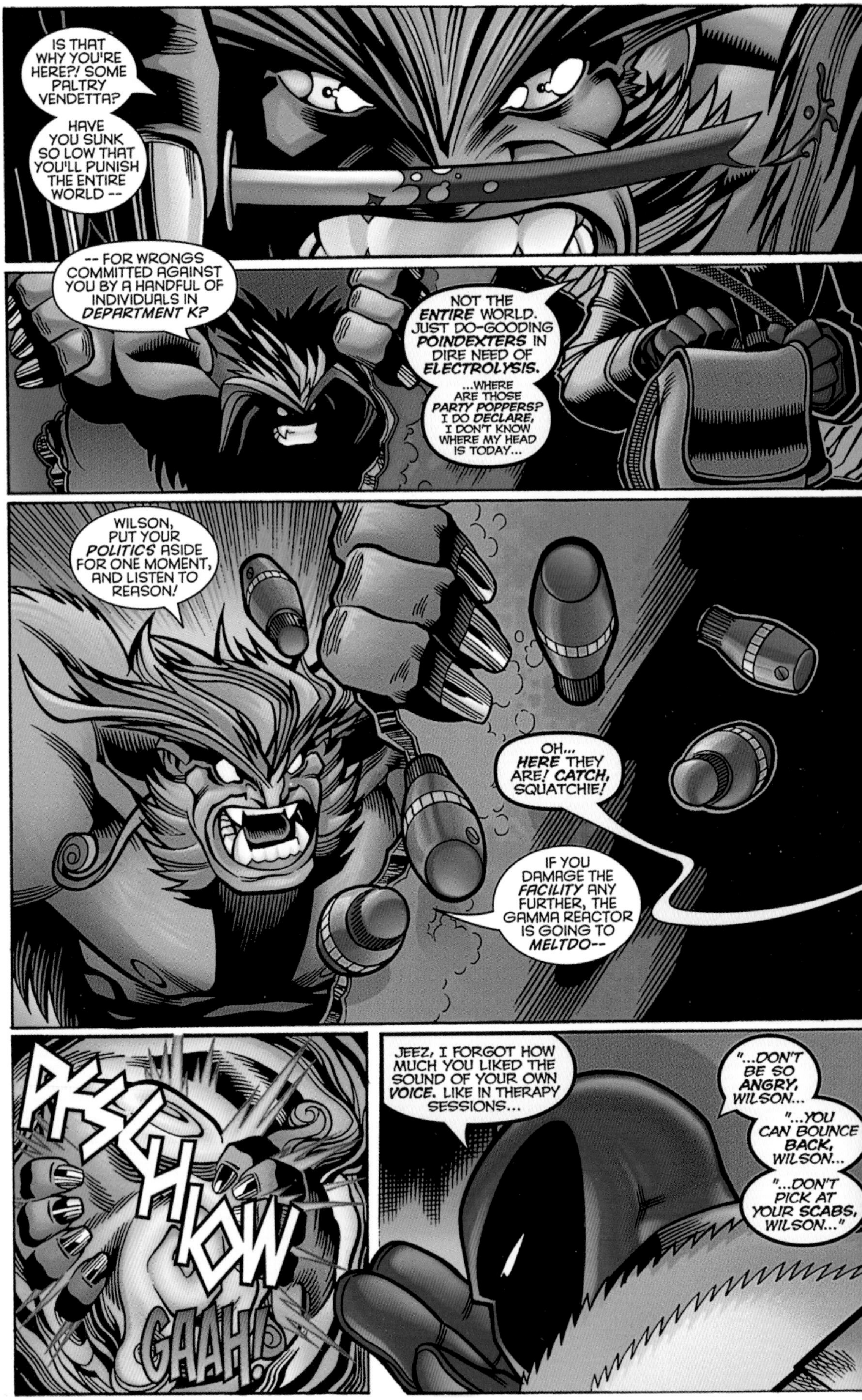
IS THAT WHY YOU'RE HERE?! SOME PALTRY VENDETTA?
HAVE YOU SUNK SO LOW THAT YOU'LL PUNISH THE ENTIRE WORLD --
-- FOR WRONGS COMMITTED AGAINST YOU BY A HANDFUL OF INDIVIDUALS IN DEPARTMENT K?
NOT THE ENTIRE WORLD. JUST DO-GOODING POINDEXTERS IN DIRE NEED OF ELECTROLYSIS.
...WHERE ARE THOSE PARTY POPPERS? I DO DECLARE, I DON'T KNOW WHERE MY HEAD IS TODAY...
WILSON, PUT YOUR POLITICS ASIDE FOR ONE MOMENT, AND LISTEN TO REASON!
OH... HERE THEY ARE! CATCH, SQUATCHIE!
IF YOU DAMAGE THE FACILITY ANY FURTHER, THE GAMMA REACTOR IS GOING TO MELTDO--
DRSCHKOW
GAAH!
JEEZ, I FORGOT HOW MUCH YOU LIKED THE SOUND OF YOUR OWN VOICE. LIKE IN THERAPY SESSIONS...
"...DON'T BE SO ANGRY, WILSON...
"...YOU CAN BOUNCE BACK, WILSON...
"...DON'T PICK AT YOUR SCABS, WILSON..."

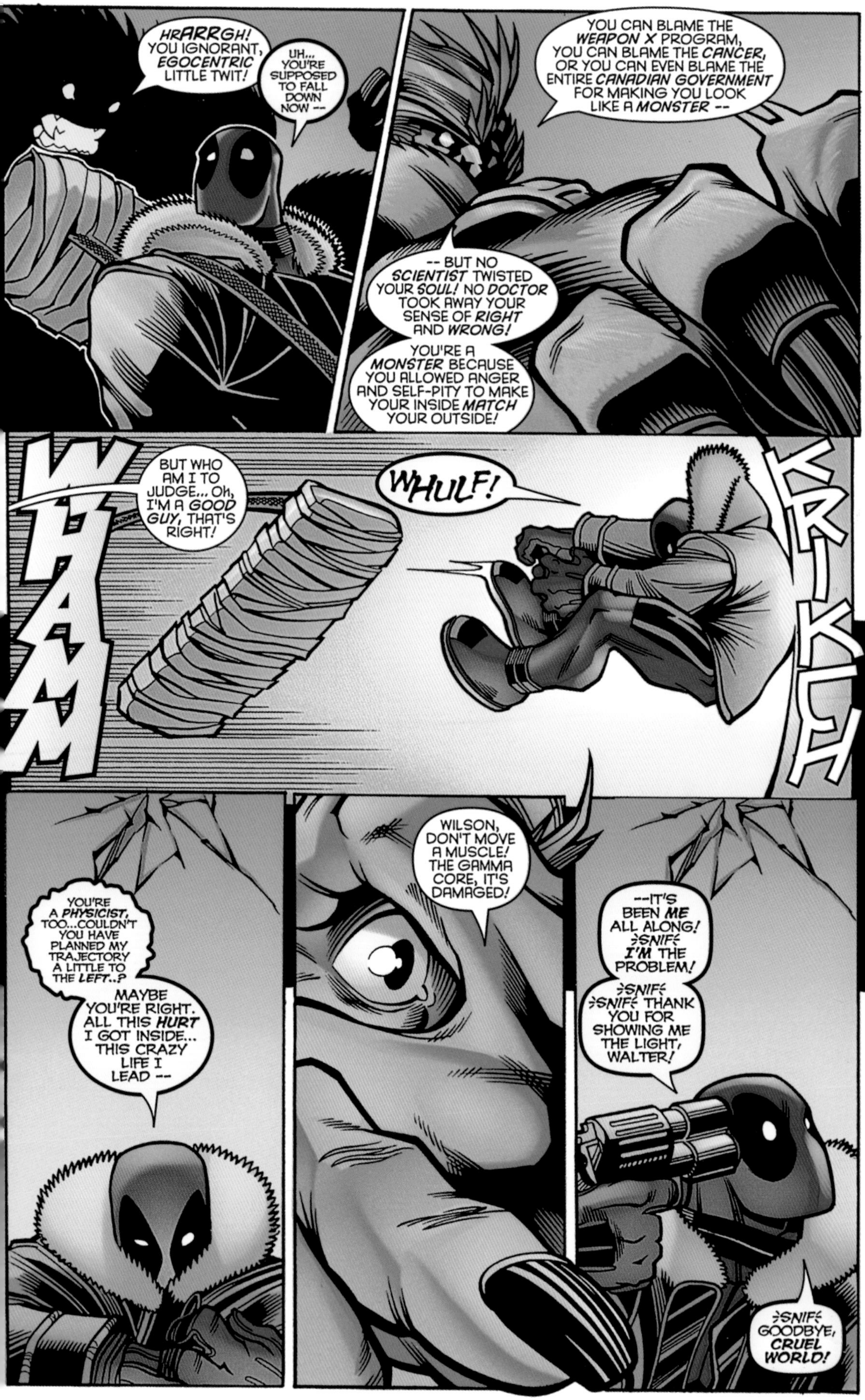
HRARRGH! YOU IGNORANT, EGOCENTRIC LITTLE TWIT!
UH... YOU'RE SUPPOSED TO FALL DOWN NOW --
YOU CAN BLAME THE WEAPON X PROGRAM, YOU CAN BLAME THE CANCER, OR YOU CAN EVEN BLAME THE ENTIRE CANADIAN GOVERNMENT FOR MAKING YOU LOOK LIKE A MONSTER --
-- BUT NO SCIENTIST TWISTED YOUR SOUL! NO DOCTOR TOOK AWAY YOUR SENSE OF RIGHT AND WRONG!
YOU'RE A MONSTER BECAUSE YOU ALLOWED ANGER AND SELF-PITY TO MAKE YOUR INSIDE MATCH YOUR OUTSIDE!
WHAM
BUT WHO AM I TO JUDGE... Oh, I'M A GOOD GUY, THAT'S RIGHT!
WHULF!
KRI-KUH
YOU'RE A PHYSICIST, TOO...COULDN'T YOU HAVE PLANNED MY TRAJECTORY A LITTLE TO THE LEFT..?
MAYBE YOU'RE RIGHT. ALL THIS HURT I GOT INSIDE... THIS CRAZY LIFE I LEAD --
WILSON, DON'T MOVE A MUSCLE! THE GAMMA CORE, IT'S DAMAGED!
--IT'S BEEN ME ALL ALONG! SNIF I'M THE PROBLEM!
SNIF SNIF THANK YOU FOR SHOWING ME THE LIGHT, WALTER!
SNIF GOODBYE, CRUEL WORLD!

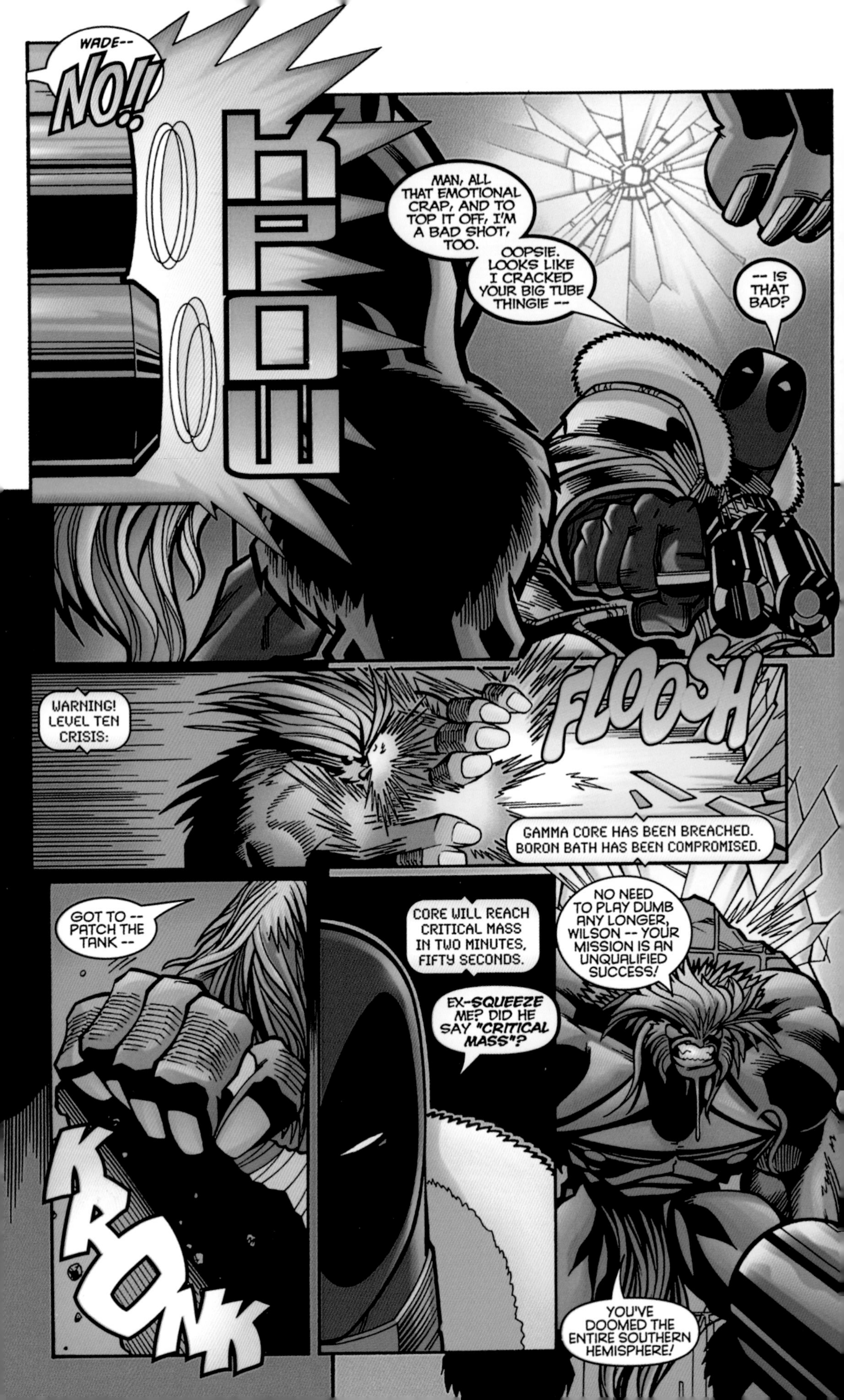
WADE--
NO!!
KPOW
MAN, ALL THAT EMOTIONAL CRAP, AND TO TOP IT OFF, I'M A BAD SHOT, TOO.
OOPSIE. LOOKS LIKE I CRACKED YOUR BIG TUBE THINGIE --
-- IS THAT BAD?
WARNING! LEVEL TEN CRISIS:
FLOOSH
GAMMA CORE HAS BEEN BREACHED. BORON BATH HAS BEEN COMPROMISED.
GOT TO -- PATCH THE TANK --
KRUNK
CORE WILL REACH CRITICAL MASS IN TWO MINUTES, FIFTY SECONDS.
EX-SQUEEZE ME? DID HE SAY "CRITICAL MASS"?
NO NEED TO PLAY DUMB ANY LONGER, WILSON -- YOUR MISSION IS AN UNQUALIFIED SUCCESS!
YOU'VE DOOMED THE ENTIRE SOUTHERN HEMISPHERE!

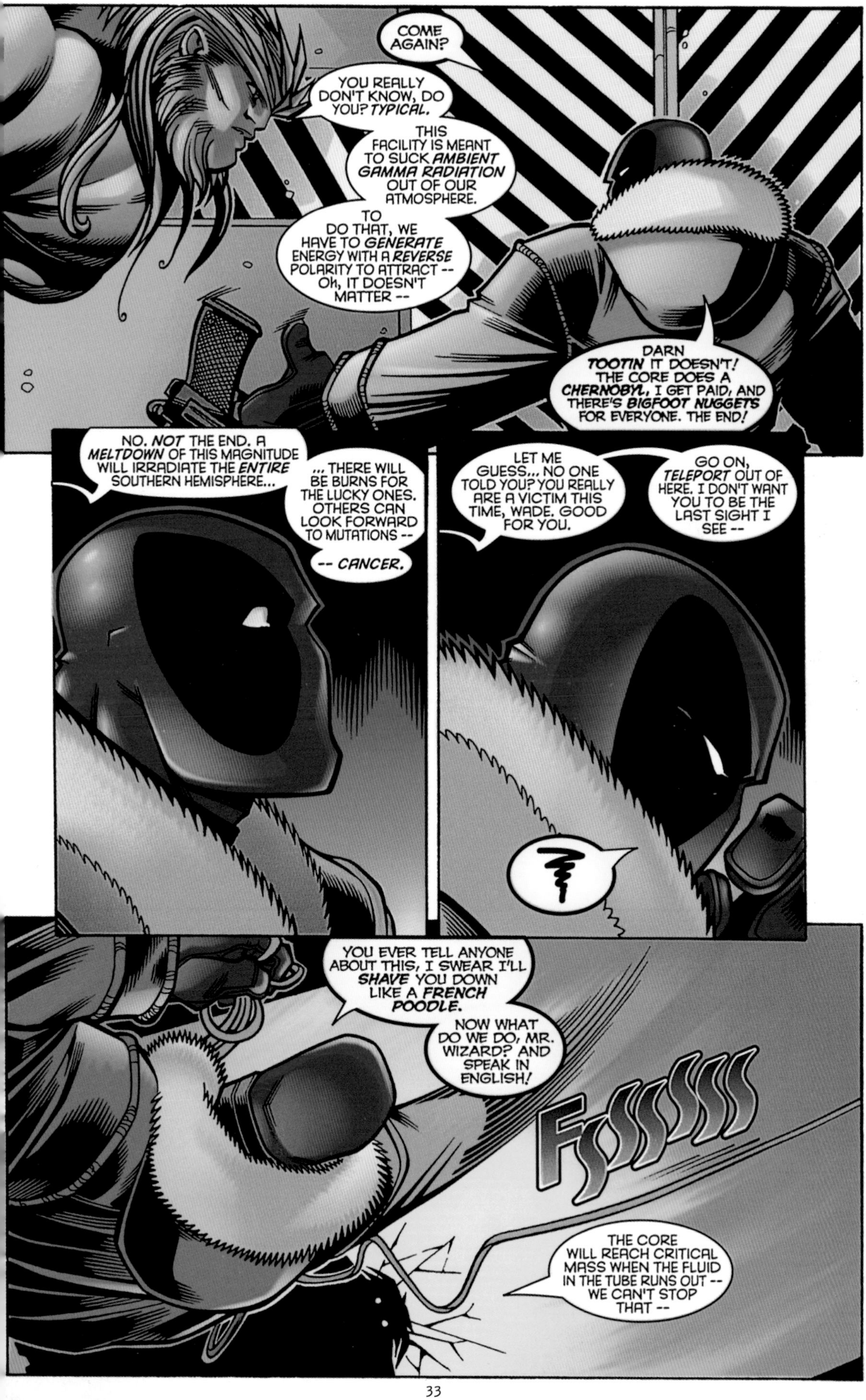
COME AGAIN?
YOU REALLY DON'T KNOW, DO YOU? TYPICAL.
THIS FACILITY IS MEANT TO SUCK AMBIENT GAMMA RADIATION OUT OF OUR ATMOSPHERE.
TO DO THAT, WE HAVE TO GENERATE ENERGY WITH A REVERSE POLARITY TO ATTRACT -- Oh, IT DOESN'T MATTER --
DARN TOOTIN IT DOESN'T! THE CORE DOES A CHERNOBYL, I GET PAID, AND THERE'S BIGFOOT NUGGETS FOR EVERYONE. THE END!
NO. NOT THE END. A MELTDOWN OF THIS MAGNITUDE WILL IRRADIATE THE ENTIRE SOUTHERN HEMISPHERE...
... THERE WILL BE BURNS FOR THE LUCKY ONES. OTHERS CAN LOOK FORWARD TO MUTATIONS --
-- CANCER.
LET ME GUESS... NO ONE TOLD YOU? YOU REALLY ARE A VICTIM THIS TIME, WADE. GOOD FOR YOU.
GO ON, TELEPORT OUT OF HERE. I DON'T WANT YOU TO BE THE LAST SIGHT I SEE --
YOU EVER TELL ANYONE ABOUT THIS, I SWEAR I'LL SHAVE YOU DOWN LIKE A FRENCH POODLE.
NOW WHAT DO WE DO, MR. WIZARD? AND SPEAK IN ENGLISH!
FSSSSSS
THE CORE WILL REACH CRITICAL MASS WHEN THE FLUID IN THE TUBE RUNS OUT -- WE CAN'T STOP THAT --

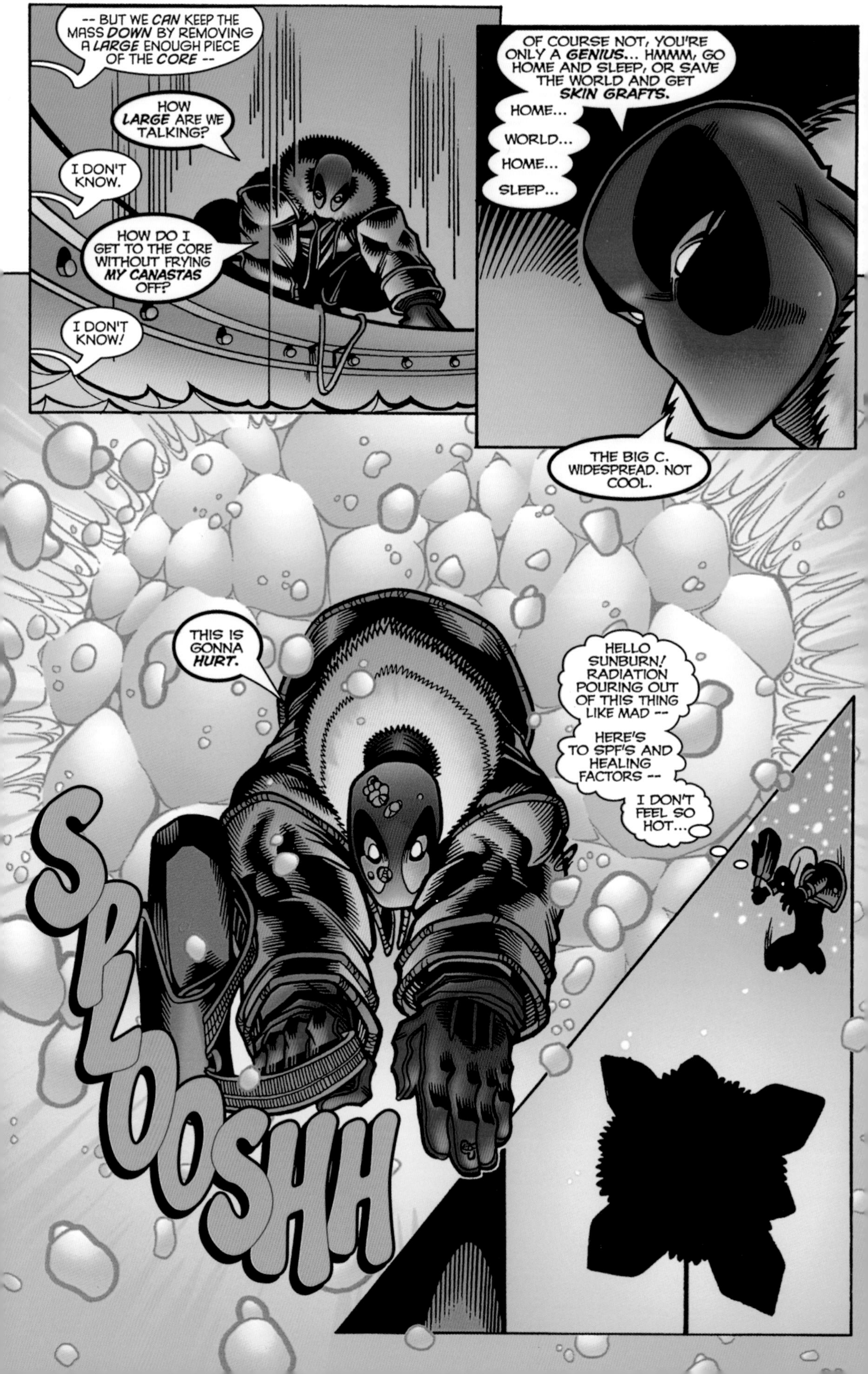
-- BUT WE CAN KEEP THE MASS DOWN BY REMOVING A LARGE ENOUGH PIECE OF THE CORE --
HOW LARGE ARE WE TALKING?
I DON'T KNOW.
HOW DO I GET TO THE CORE WITHOUT FRYING MY CANASTAS OFF?
I DON'T KNOW!
OF COURSE NOT, YOU'RE ONLY A GENIUS... HMMM, GO HOME AND SLEEP, OR SAVE THE WORLD AND GET SKIN GRAFTS.
HOME...
WORLD...
HOME...
SLEEP...
THE BIG C. WIDESPREAD. NOT COOL.
THIS IS GONNA HURT.
SPLOOSHH
HELLO SUNBURN! RADIATION POURING OUT OF THIS THING LIKE MAD --
HERE'S TO SPF'S AND HEALING FACTORS --
I DON'T FEEL SO HOT...

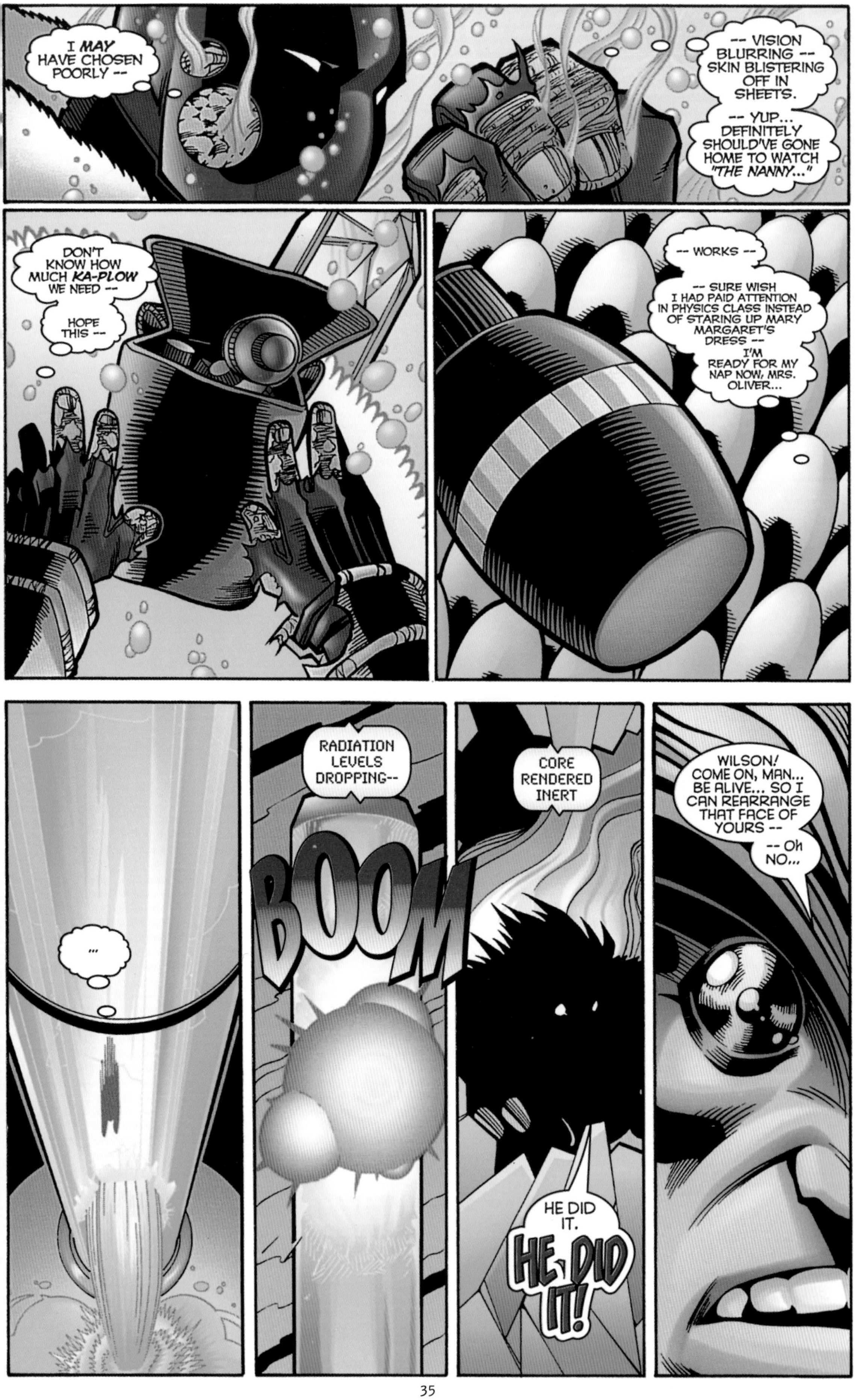

I MAY HAVE CHOSEN POORLY --
-- VISION BLURRING -- SKIN BLISTERING OFF IN SHEETS.
-- YUP... DEFINITELY SHOULD'VE GONE HOME TO WATCH "THE NANNY..."
DON'T KNOW HOW MUCH KA-PLOW WE NEED --
HOPE THIS --
-- WORKS --
-- SURE WISH I HAD PAID ATTENTION IN PHYSICS CLASS INSTEAD OF STARING UP MARY MARGARET'S DRESS --
I'M READY FOR MY NAP NOW, MRS. OLIVER...
...
RADIATION LEVELS DROPPING--
BOOM
CORE RENDERED INERT
HE DID IT.
HE DID IT!
WILSON! COME ON, MAN... BE ALIVE... SO I CAN REARRANGE THAT FACE OF YOURS --
-- Oh NO...

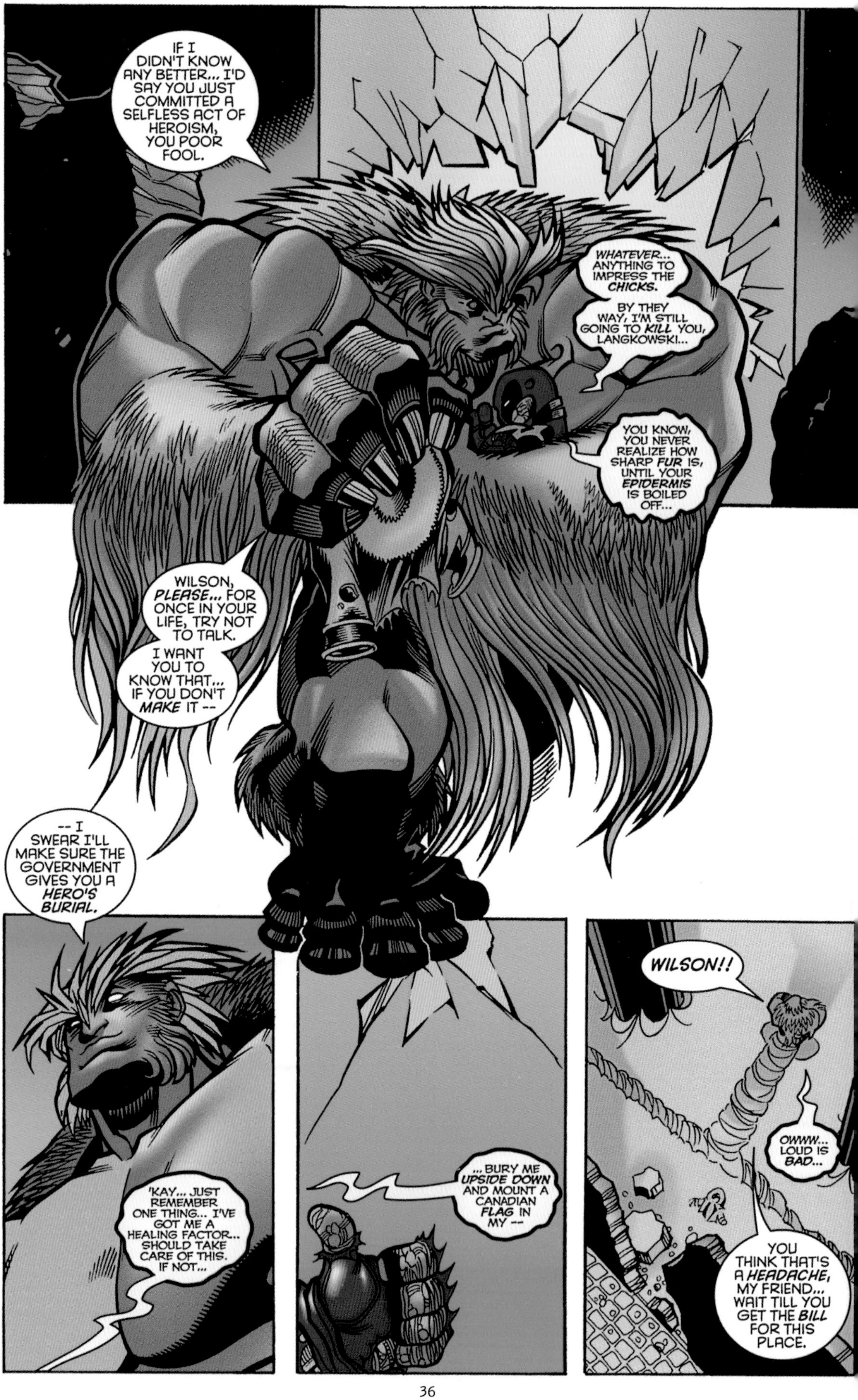
IF I DIDN'T KNOW ANY BETTER... I'D SAY YOU JUST COMMITTED A SELFLESS ACT OF HEROISM, YOU POOR FOOL.
WHATEVER... ANYTHING TO IMPRESS THE CHICKS.
BY THEY WAY, I'M STILL GOING TO KILL YOU, LANGKOWSKI...
YOU KNOW, YOU NEVER REALIZE HOW SHARP FUR IS, UNTIL YOUR EPIDERMIS IS BOILED OFF...
WILSON, PLEASE... FOR ONCE IN YOUR LIFE, TRY NOT TO TALK.
I WANT YOU TO KNOW THAT... IF YOU DON'T MAKE IT --
-- I SWEAR I'LL MAKE SURE THE GOVERNMENT GIVES YOU A HERO'S BURIAL.
'KAY... JUST REMEMBER ONE THING... I'VE GOT ME A HEALING FACTOR... SHOULD TAKE CARE OF THIS. IF NOT...
...BURY ME UPSIDE DOWN AND MOUNT A CANADIAN FLAG IN MY --
WILSON!!
OWWW... LOUD IS BAD...
YOU THINK THAT'S A HEADACHE, MY FRIEND... WAIT TILL YOU GET THE BILL FOR THIS PLACE.

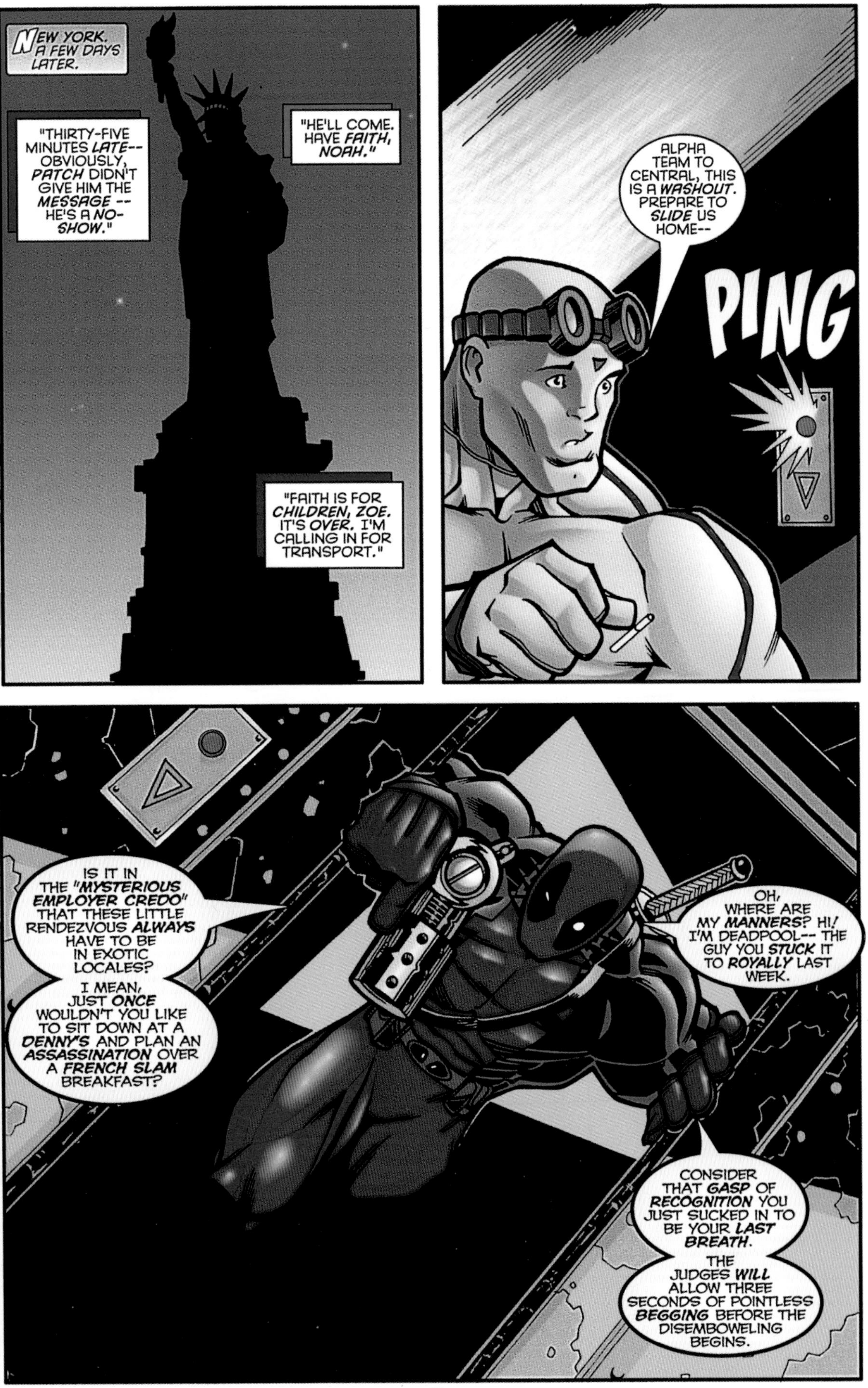
NEW YORK. A FEW DAYS LATER.
"THIRTY-FIVE MINUTES LATE-- OBVIOUSLY, PATCH DIDN'T GIVE HIM THE MESSAGE -- HE'S A NO-SHOW."
"HE'LL COME. HAVE FAITH, NOAH."
"FAITH IS FOR CHILDREN, ZOE. IT'S OVER. I'M CALLING IN FOR TRANSPORT."
ALPHA TEAM TO CENTRAL, THIS IS A WASHOUT. PREPARE TO SLIDE US HOME--
PING
IS IT IN THE "MYSTERIOUS EMPLOYER CREDO" THAT THESE LITTLE RENDEZVOUS ALWAYS HAVE TO BE IN EXOTIC LOCALES?
I MEAN, JUST ONCE WOULDN'T YOU LIKE TO SIT DOWN AT A DENNY'S AND PLAN AN ASSASSINATION OVER A FRENCH SLAM BREAKFAST?
OH, WHERE ARE MY MANNERS? HI! I'M DEADPOOL-- THE GUY YOU STUCK IT TO ROYALLY LAST WEEK.
CONSIDER THAT GASP OF RECOGNITION YOU JUST SUCKED IN TO BE YOUR LAST BREATH.
THE JUDGES WILL ALLOW THREE SECONDS OF POINTLESS BEGGING BEFORE THE DISEMBOWELING BEGINS.

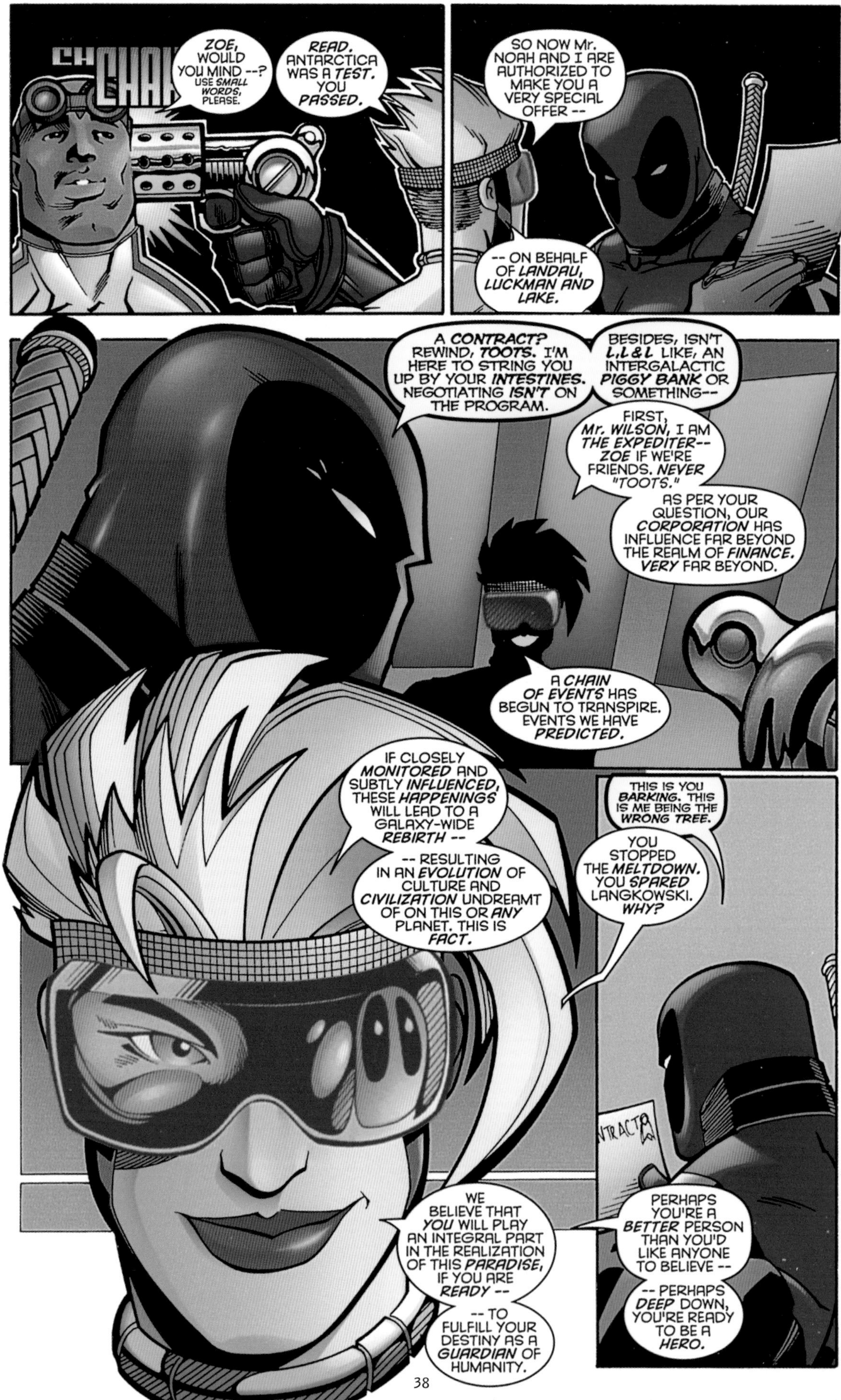
CHCHAK
ZOE, WOULD YOU MIND --? USE SMALL WORDS, PLEASE.
READ. ANTARCTICA WAS A TEST. YOU PASSED.
SO NOW Mr. NOAH AND I ARE AUTHORIZED TO MAKE YOU A VERY SPECIAL OFFER --
-- ON BEHALF OF LANDAU, LUCKMAN AND LAKE.
A CONTRACT? REWIND, TOOTS. I'M HERE TO STRING YOU UP BY YOUR INTESTINES. NEGOTIATING ISN'T ON THE PROGRAM.
BESIDES, ISN'T L,L&L LIKE, AN INTERGALACTIC PIGGY BANK OR SOMETHING--
FIRST, Mr. WILSON, I AM THE EXPEDITER-- ZOE IF WE'RE FRIENDS. NEVER "TOOTS."
AS PER YOUR QUESTION, OUR CORPORATION HAS INFLUENCE FAR BEYOND THE REALM OF FINANCE. VERY FAR BEYOND.
A CHAIN OF EVENTS HAS BEGUN TO TRANSPIRE. EVENTS WE HAVE PREDICTED.
IF CLOSELY MONITORED AND SUBTLY INFLUENCED, THESE HAPPENINGS WILL LEAD TO A GALAXY-WIDE REBIRTH --
-- RESULTING IN AN EVOLUTION OF CULTURE AND CIVILIZATION UNDREAMT OF ON THIS OR ANY PLANET. THIS IS FACT.
THIS IS YOU BARKING. THIS IS ME BEING THE WRONG TREE.
YOU STOPPED THE MELTDOWN. YOU SPARED LANGKOWSKI. WHY?
WE BELIEVE THAT YOU WILL PLAY AN INTEGRAL PART IN THE REALIZATION OF THIS PARADISE, IF YOU ARE READY --
-- TO FULFILL YOUR DESTINY AS A GUARDIAN OF HUMANITY.
PERHAPS YOU'RE A BETTER PERSON THAN YOU'D LIKE ANYONE TO BELIEVE --
-- PERHAPS DEEP DOWN, YOU'RE READY TO BE A HERO.

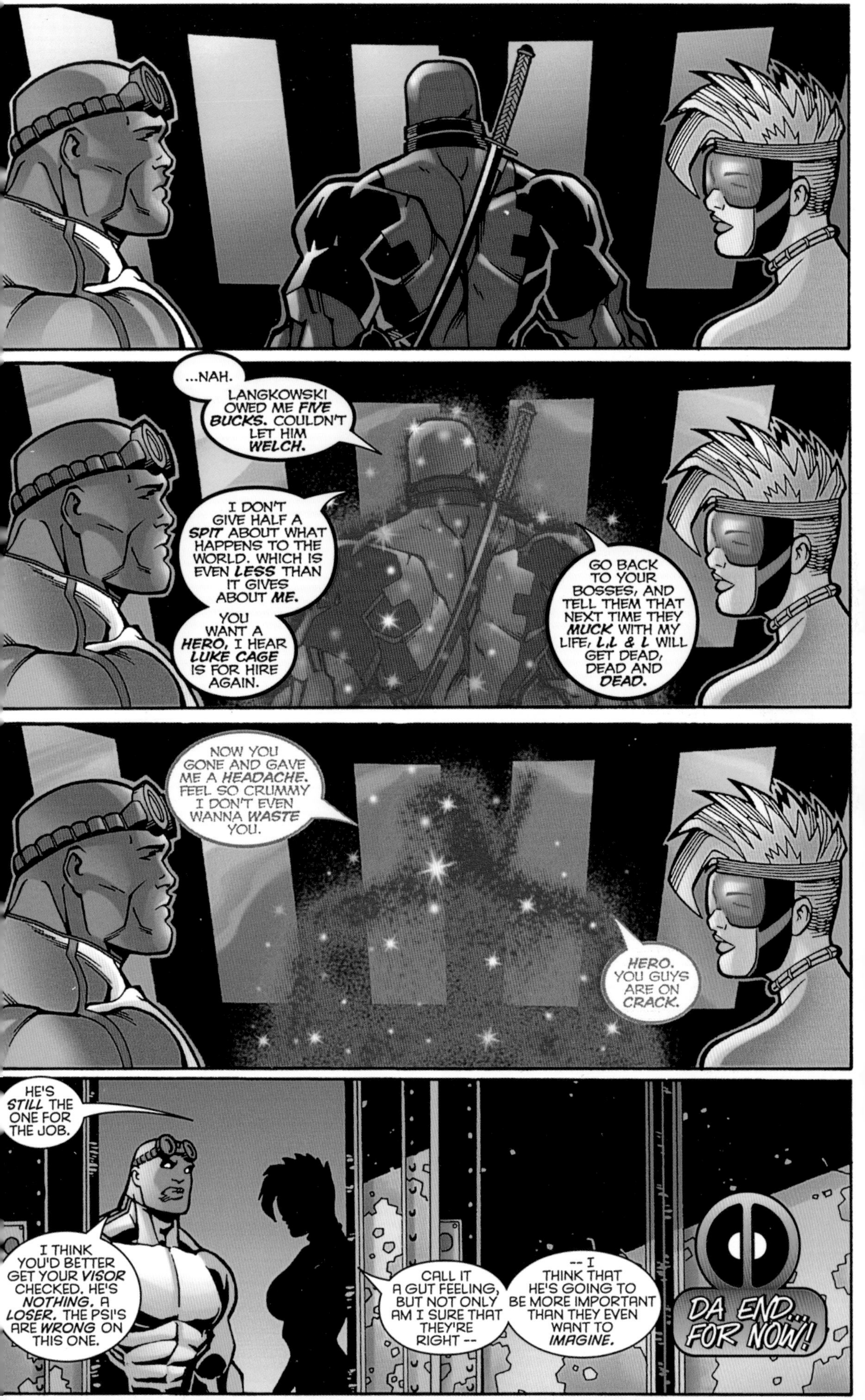
...NAH.
LANGKOWSKI OWED ME FIVE BUCKS. COULDN'T LET HIM WELCH.
I DON'T GIVE HALF A SPIT ABOUT WHAT HAPPENS TO THE WORLD. WHICH IS EVEN LESS THAN IT GIVES ABOUT ME.
YOU WANT A HERO, I HEAR LUKE CAGE IS FOR HIRE AGAIN.
GO BACK TO YOUR BOSSES, AND TELL THEM THAT NEXT TIME THEY MUCK WITH MY LIFE, L,L & L WILL GET DEAD, DEAD AND DEAD.
NOW YOU GONE AND GAVE ME A HEADACHE. FEEL SO CRUMMY I DON'T EVEN WANNA WASTE YOU.
HERO. YOU GUYS ARE ON CRACK.
HE'S STILL THE ONE FOR THE JOB.
I THINK YOU'D BETTER GET YOUR VISOR CHECKED. HE'S NOTHING. A LOSER. THE PSI'S ARE WRONG ON THIS ONE.
CALL IT A GUT FEELING, BUT NOT ONLY AM I SURE THAT THEY'RE RIGHT --
-- I THINK THAT HE'S GOING TO BE MORE IMPORTANT THAN THEY EVEN WANT TO IMAGINE.
DA END... FOR NOW!

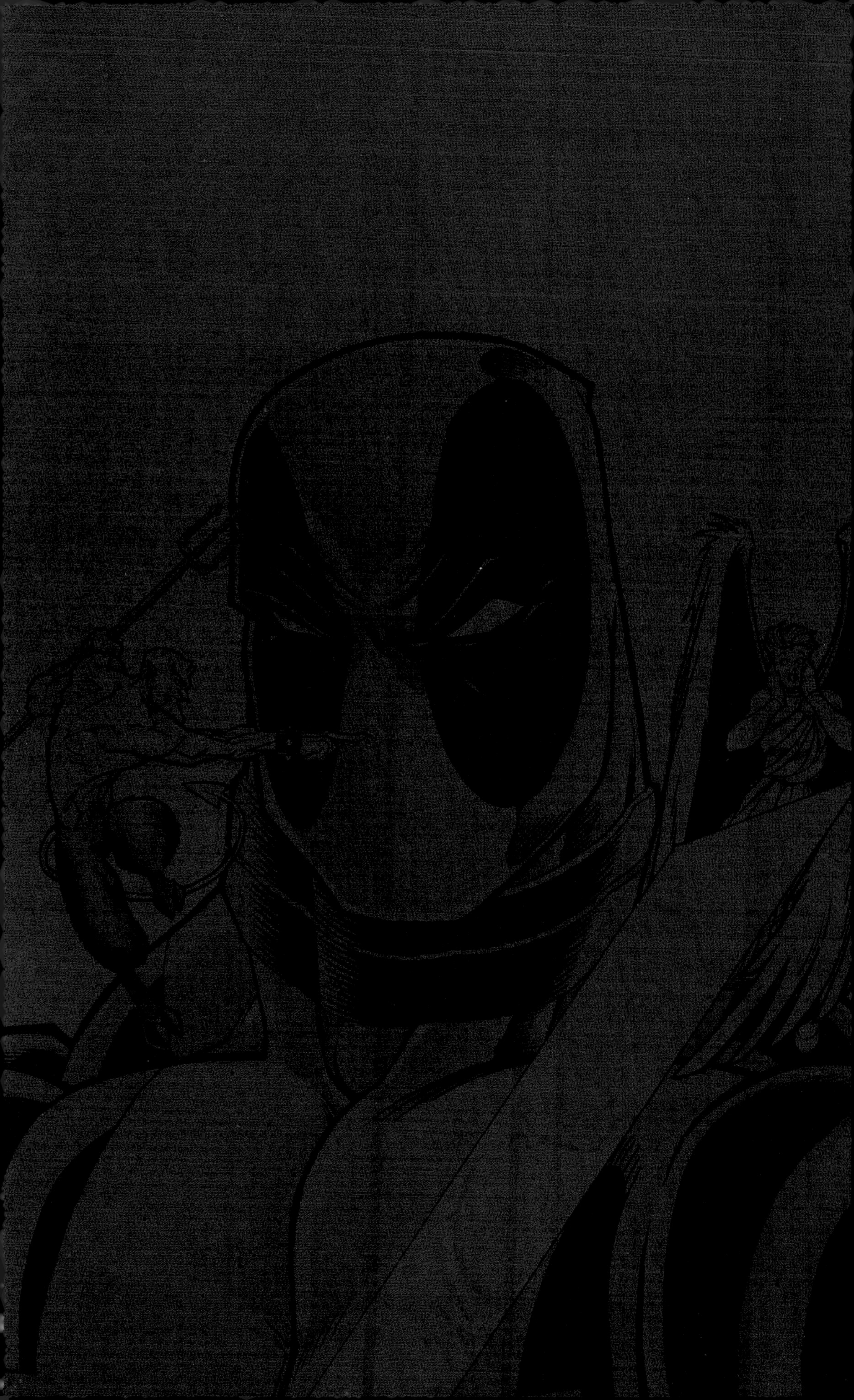

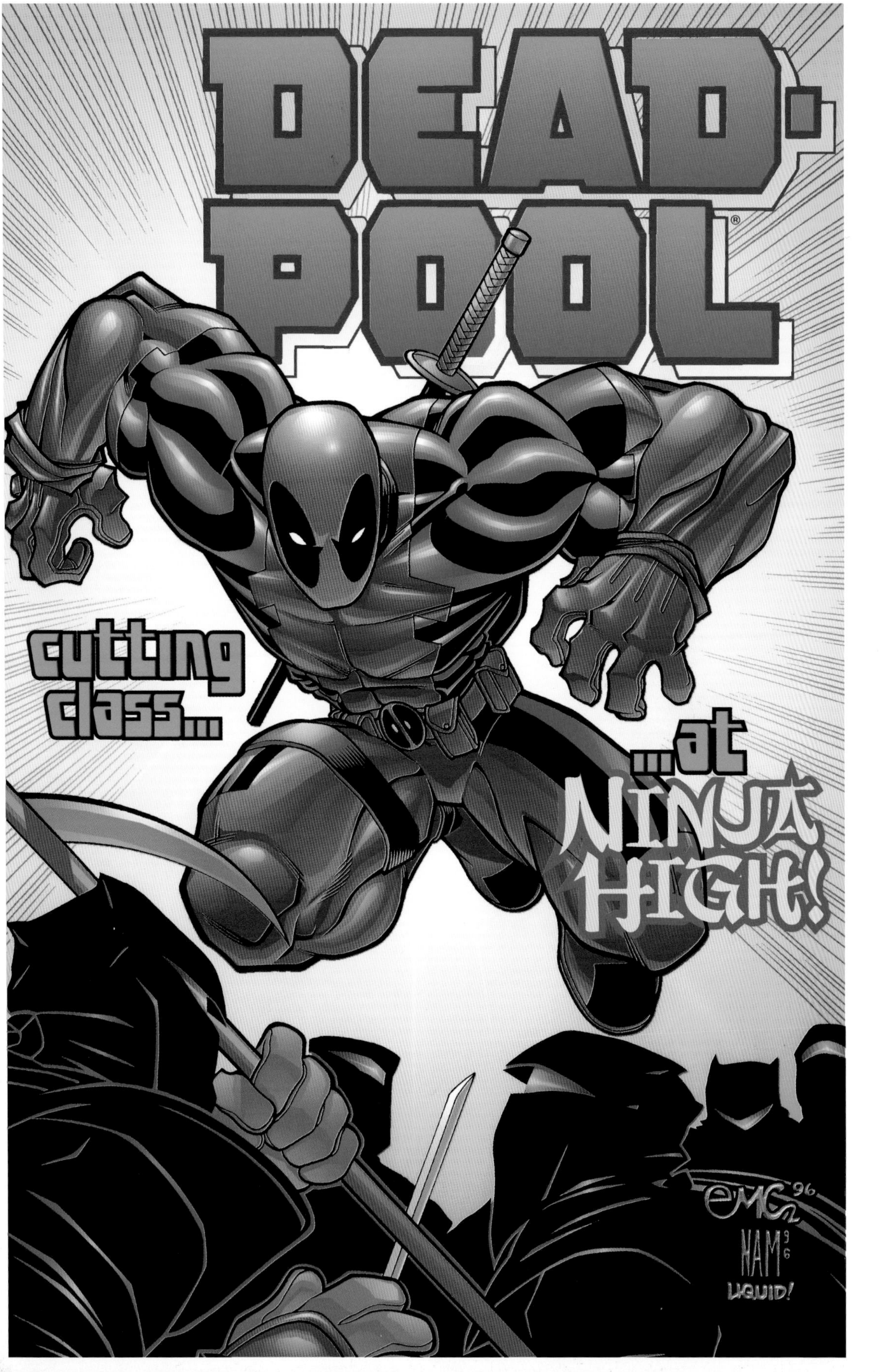
DEAD-
POOL
cutting
class...
...at
NINJA
HIGH!
LIQUID!

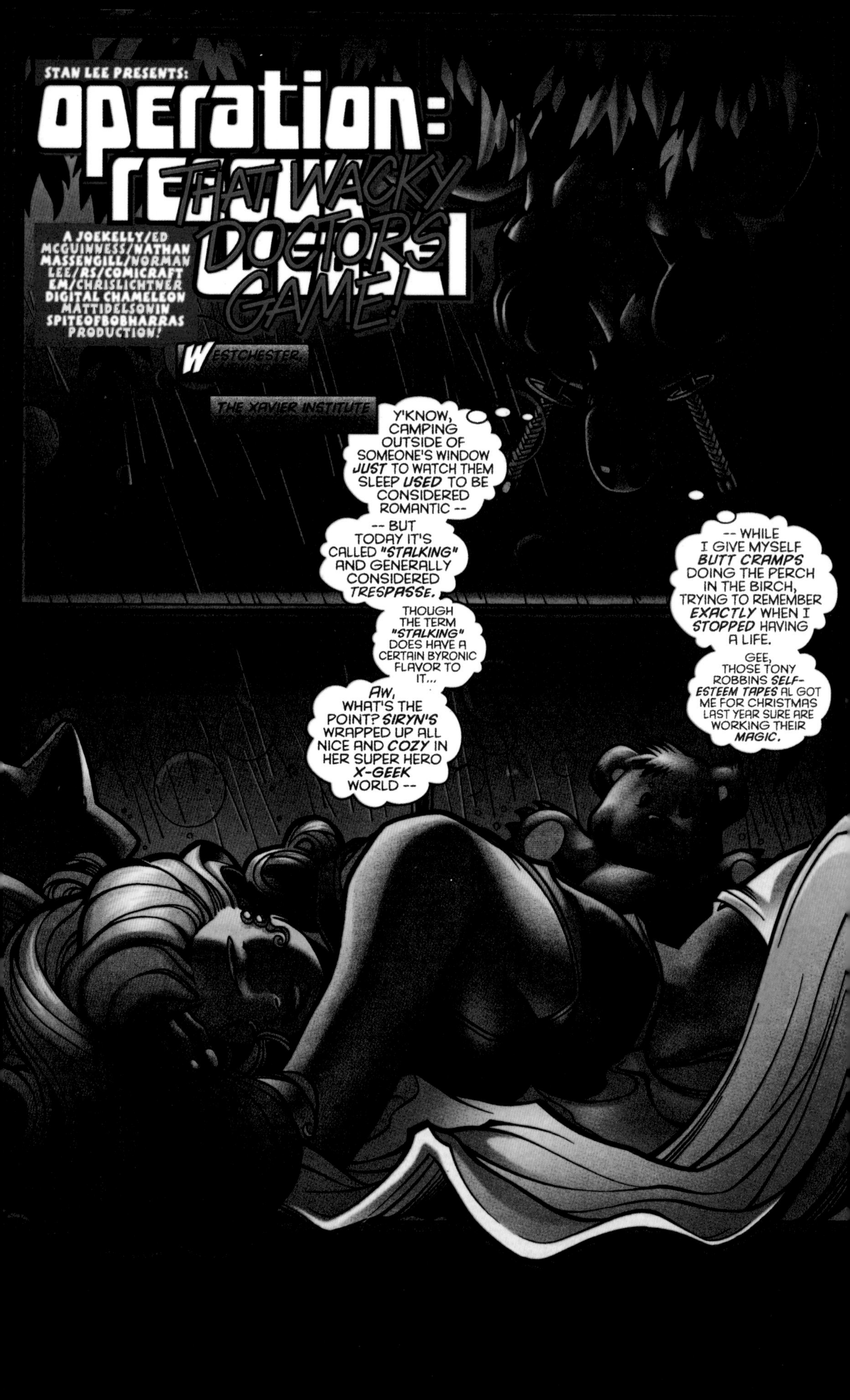
STAN LEE PRESENTS:
operation:
THAT WACKY DOCTOR'S GAME!
A JOEKELLY/ED MCGUINNESS/NATHAN MASSENGILL/NORMAN LEE/RS/COMICRAFT EM/CHRISLICHTNER DIGITAL CHAMELEON MATTIDELSONIN SPITEOFBOBHARRAS PRODUCTION!
WESTCHESTER,
THE XAVIER INSTITUTE
Y'KNOW, CAMPING OUTSIDE OF SOMEONE'S WINDOW JUST TO WATCH THEM SLEEP USED TO BE CONSIDERED ROMANTIC --
-- BUT TODAY IT'S CALLED "STALKING" AND GENERALLY CONSIDERED TRESPASSE.
THOUGH THE TERM "STALKING" DOES HAVE A CERTAIN BYRONIC FLAVOR TO IT...
AW, WHAT'S THE POINT? SIRYN'S WRAPPED UP ALL NICE AND COZY IN HER SUPER HERO X-GEEK WORLD --
-- WHILE I GIVE MYSELF BUTT CRAMPS DOING THE PERCH IN THE BIRCH, TRYING TO REMEMBER EXACTLY WHEN I STOPPED HAVING A LIFE.
GEE, THOSE TONY ROBBINS SELF-ESTEEM TAPES AL GOT ME FOR CHRISTMAS LAST YEAR SURE ARE WORKING THEIR MAGIC.

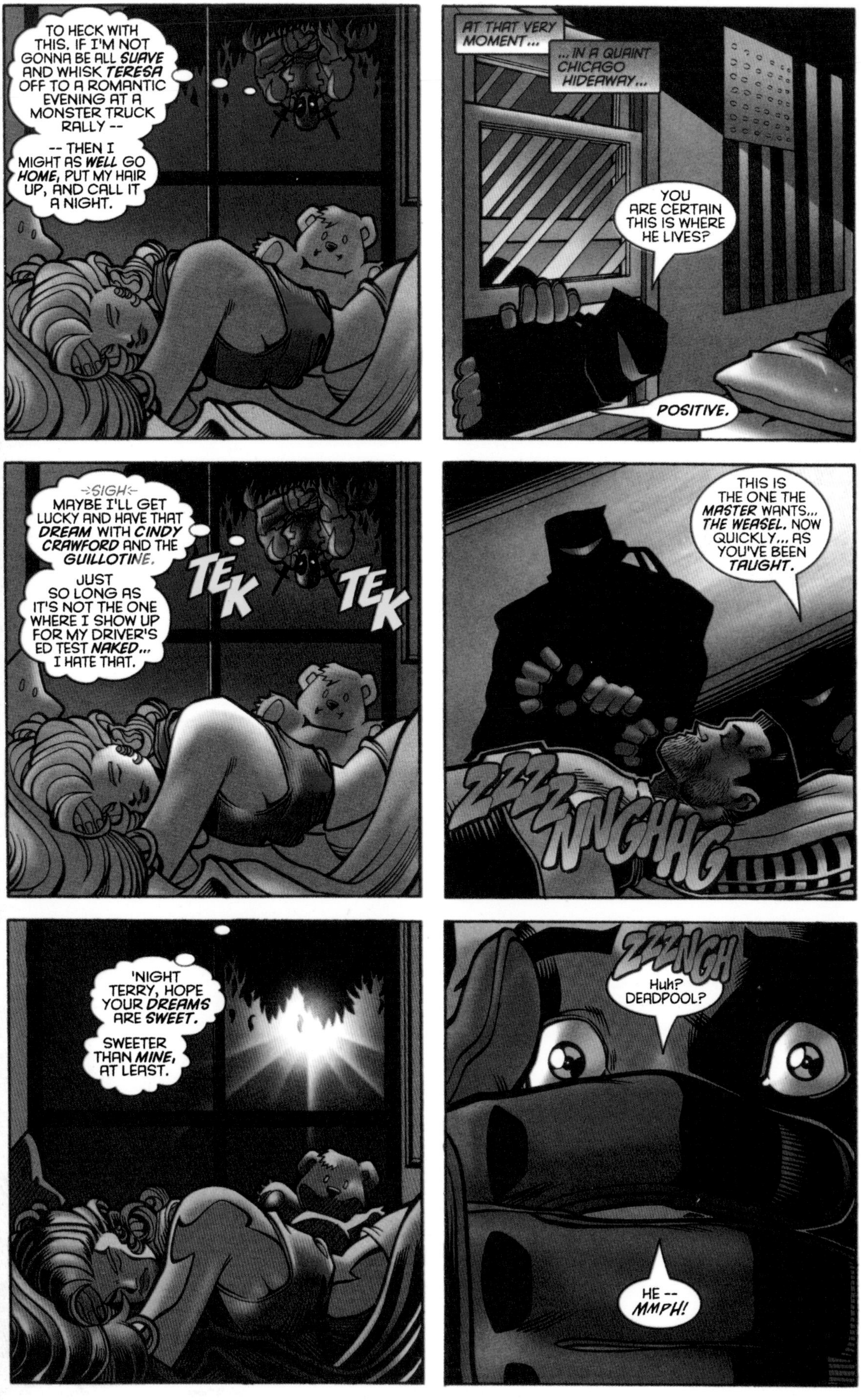

TO HECK WITH THIS. IF I'M NOT GONNA BE ALL SUAVE AND WHISK TERESA OFF TO A ROMANTIC EVENING AT A MONSTER TRUCK RALLY --
-- THEN I MIGHT AS WELL GO HOME, PUT MY HAIR UP, AND CALL IT A NIGHT.
AT THAT VERY MOMENT...
...IN A QUAINT CHICAGO HIDEAWAY...
YOU ARE CERTAIN THIS IS WHERE HE LIVES?
POSITIVE.
-SIGH-
MAYBE I'LL GET LUCKY AND HAVE THAT DREAM WITH CINDY CRAWFORD AND THE GUILLOTINE.
JUST SO LONG AS IT'S NOT THE ONE WHERE I SHOW UP FOR MY DRIVER'S ED TEST NAKED... I HATE THAT.
TEK
TEK
THIS IS THE ONE THE MASTER WANTS... THE WEASEL. NOW QUICKLY... AS YOU'VE BEEN TAUGHT.
ZZZZNNGHHG
'NIGHT TERRY, HOPE YOUR DREAMS ARE SWEET.
SWEETER THAN MINE, AT LEAST.
ZZZNGH
Huh? DEADPOOL?
HE -- MMPH!

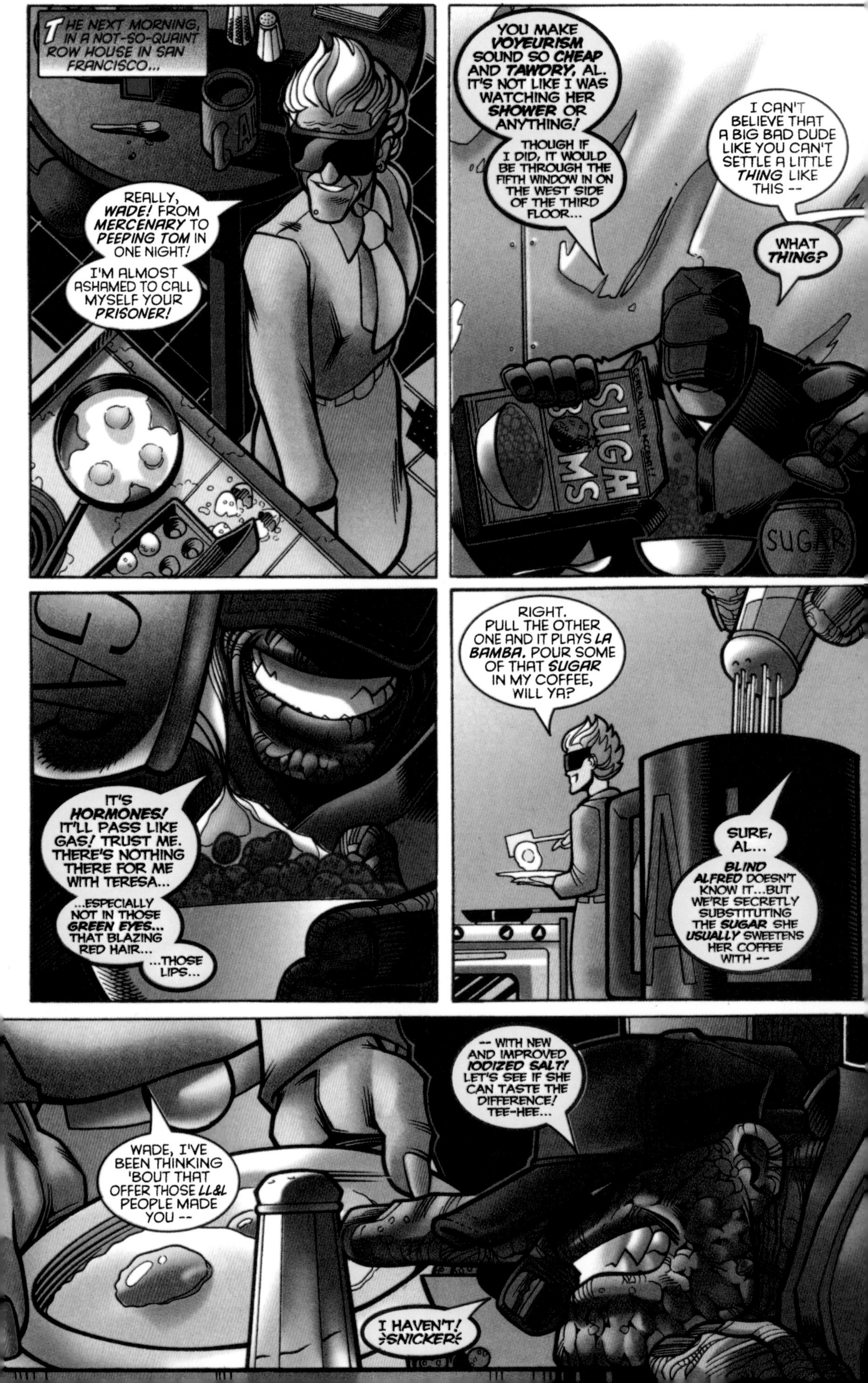
THE NEXT MORNING, IN A NOT-SO-QUAINT ROW HOUSE IN SAN FRANCISCO...
REALLY, WADE! FROM MERCENARY TO PEEPING TOM IN ONE NIGHT!
I'M ALMOST ASHAMED TO CALL MYSELF YOUR PRISONER!
YOU MAKE VOYEURISM SOUND SO CHEAP AND TAWDRY, AL. IT'S NOT LIKE I WAS WATCHING HER SHOWER OR ANYTHING!
THOUGH IF I DID, IT WOULD BE THROUGH THE FIFTH WINDOW IN ON THE WEST SIDE OF THE THIRD FLOOR...
I CAN'T BELIEVE THAT A BIG BAD DUDE LIKE YOU CAN'T SETTLE A LITTLE THING LIKE THIS --
WHAT THING?
SUGAR BOMS
SUGAR
IT'S HORMONES! IT'LL PASS LIKE GAS! TRUST ME. THERE'S NOTHING THERE FOR ME WITH TERESA...
...ESPECIALLY NOT IN THOSE GREEN EYES... THAT BLAZING RED HAIR... ...THOSE LIPS...
RIGHT. PULL THE OTHER ONE AND IT PLAYS LA BAMBA. POUR SOME OF THAT SUGAR IN MY COFFEE, WILL YA?
SURE, AL...
BLIND ALFRED DOESN'T KNOW IT...BUT WE'RE SECRETLY SUBSTITUTING THE SUGAR SHE USUALLY SWEETENS HER COFFEE WITH --
-- WITH NEW AND IMPROVED IODIZED SALT! LET'S SEE IF SHE CAN TASTE THE DIFFERENCE! TEE-HEE...
WADE, I'VE BEEN THINKING 'BOUT THAT OFFER THOSE LL&L PEOPLE MADE YOU --
I HAVEN'T! ≈SNICKER≈

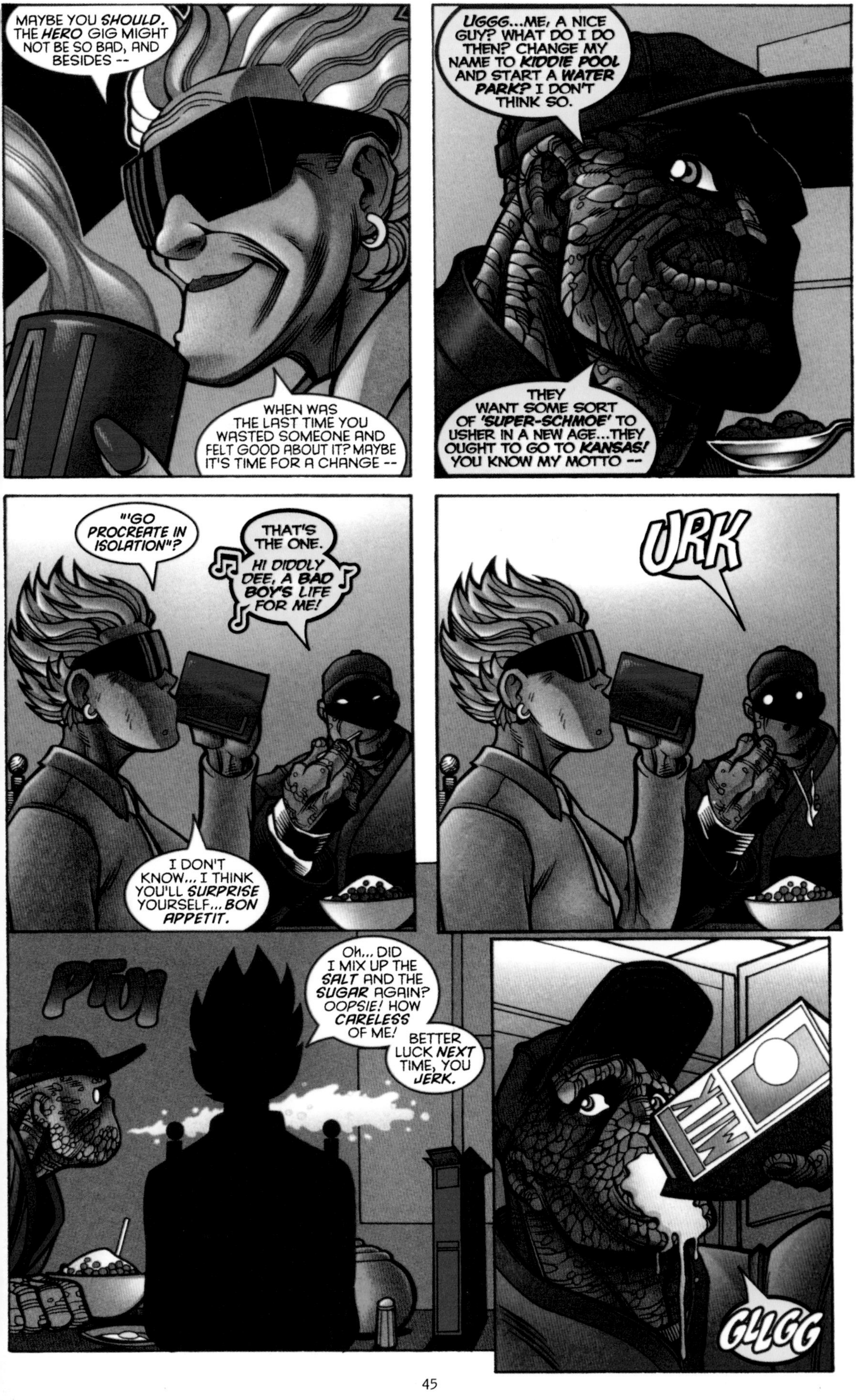
MAYBE YOU SHOULD. THE HERO GIG MIGHT NOT BE SO BAD, AND BESIDES --
WHEN WAS THE LAST TIME YOU WASTED SOMEONE AND FELT GOOD ABOUT IT? MAYBE IT'S TIME FOR A CHANGE --
UGGG...ME, A NICE GUY? WHAT DO I DO THEN? CHANGE MY NAME TO KIDDIE POOL AND START A WATER PARK? I DON'T THINK SO.
THEY WANT SOME SORT OF 'SUPER-SCHMOE' TO USHER IN A NEW AGE...THEY OUGHT TO GO TO KANSAS! YOU KNOW MY MOTTO --
"'GO PROCREATE IN ISOLATION"?
THAT'S THE ONE. HI DIDDLY DEE, A BAD BOY'S LIFE FOR ME!
I DON'T KNOW... I THINK YOU'LL SURPRISE YOURSELF... BON APPETIT.
URK
PTUI
OH... DID I MIX UP THE SALT AND THE SUGAR AGAIN? OOPSIE! HOW CARELESS OF ME!
BETTER LUCK NEXT TIME, YOU JERK.
GLLGG

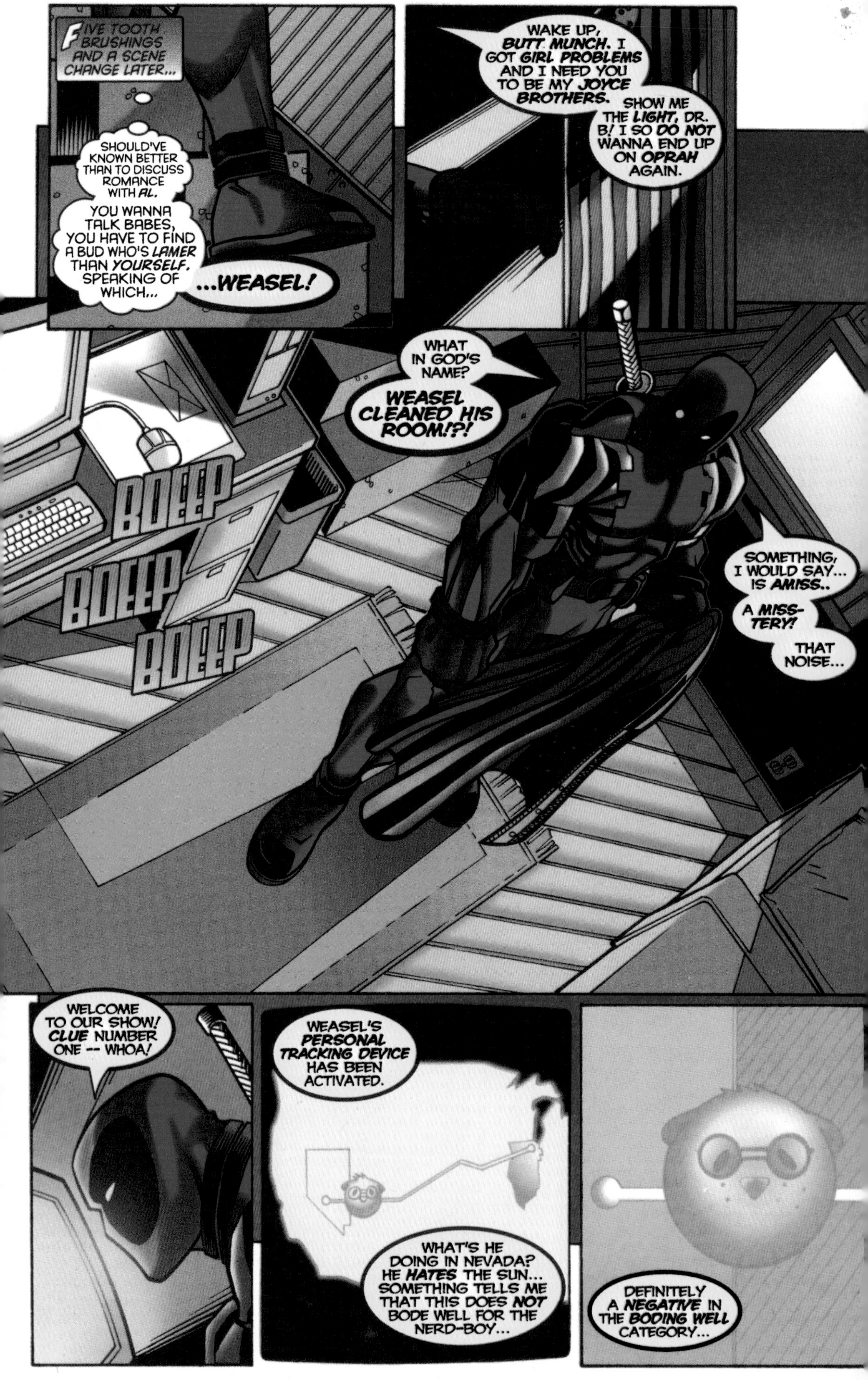
FIVE TOOTH BRUSHINGS AND A SCENE CHANGE LATER...
SHOULD'VE KNOWN BETTER THAN TO DISCUSS ROMANCE WITH AL.
YOU WANNA TALK BABES, YOU HAVE TO FIND A BUD WHO'S LAMER THAN YOURSELF. SPEAKING OF WHICH...
...WEASEL!
WAKE UP, BUTT MUNCH. I GOT GIRL PROBLEMS AND I NEED YOU TO BE MY JOYCE BROTHERS.
SHOW ME THE LIGHT, DR. B! I SO DO NOT WANNA END UP ON OPRAH AGAIN.
WHAT IN GOD'S NAME?
WEASEL CLEANED HIS ROOM!?!
BOEEP
BOEEP
BOEEP
SOMETHING, I WOULD SAY... IS AMISS..
A MISS-TERY!
THAT NOISE...
WELCOME TO OUR SHOW! CLUE NUMBER ONE -- WHOA!
WEASEL'S PERSONAL TRACKING DEVICE HAS BEEN ACTIVATED.
WHAT'S HE DOING IN NEVADA? HE HATES THE SUN... SOMETHING TELLS ME THAT THIS DOES NOT BODE WELL FOR THE NERD-BOY...
DEFINITELY A NEGATIVE IN THE BODING WELL CATEGORY...

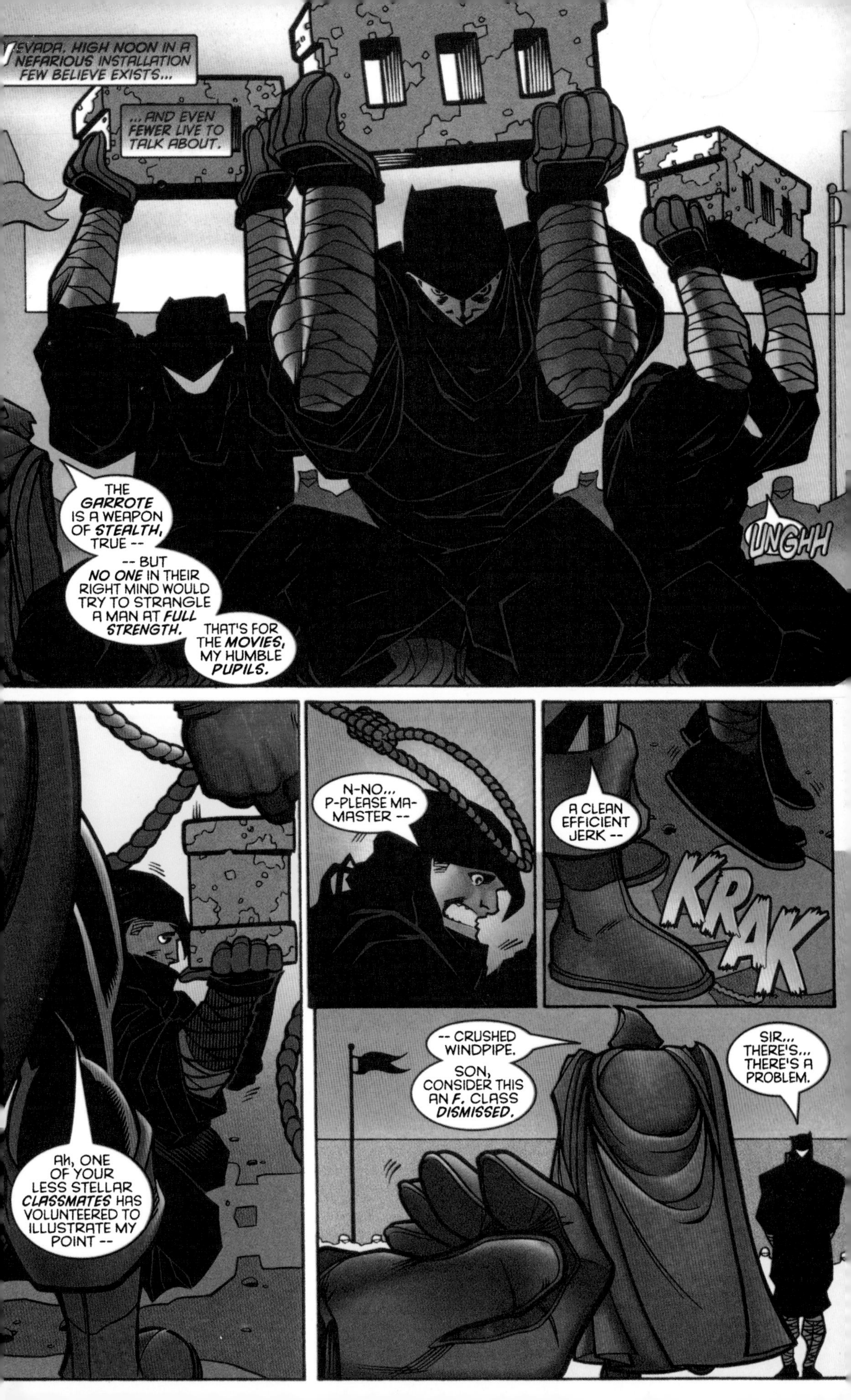
NEVADA. HIGH NOON IN A NEFARIOUS INSTALLATION FEW BELIEVE EXISTS...
...AND EVEN FEWER LIVE TO TALK ABOUT.
THE GARROTE IS A WEAPON OF STEALTH, TRUE --
-- BUT NO ONE IN THEIR RIGHT MIND WOULD TRY TO STRANGLE A MAN AT FULL STRENGTH.
THAT'S FOR THE MOVIES, MY HUMBLE PUPILS.
UNGHH
AH, ONE OF YOUR LESS STELLAR CLASSMATES HAS VOLUNTEERED TO ILLUSTRATE MY POINT --
N-NO... P-PLEASE MA-MASTER --
A CLEAN EFFICIENT JERK --
KRAK
-- CRUSHED WINDPIPE.
SON, CONSIDER THIS AN F. CLASS DISMISSED.
SIR... THERE'S... THERE'S A PROBLEM.

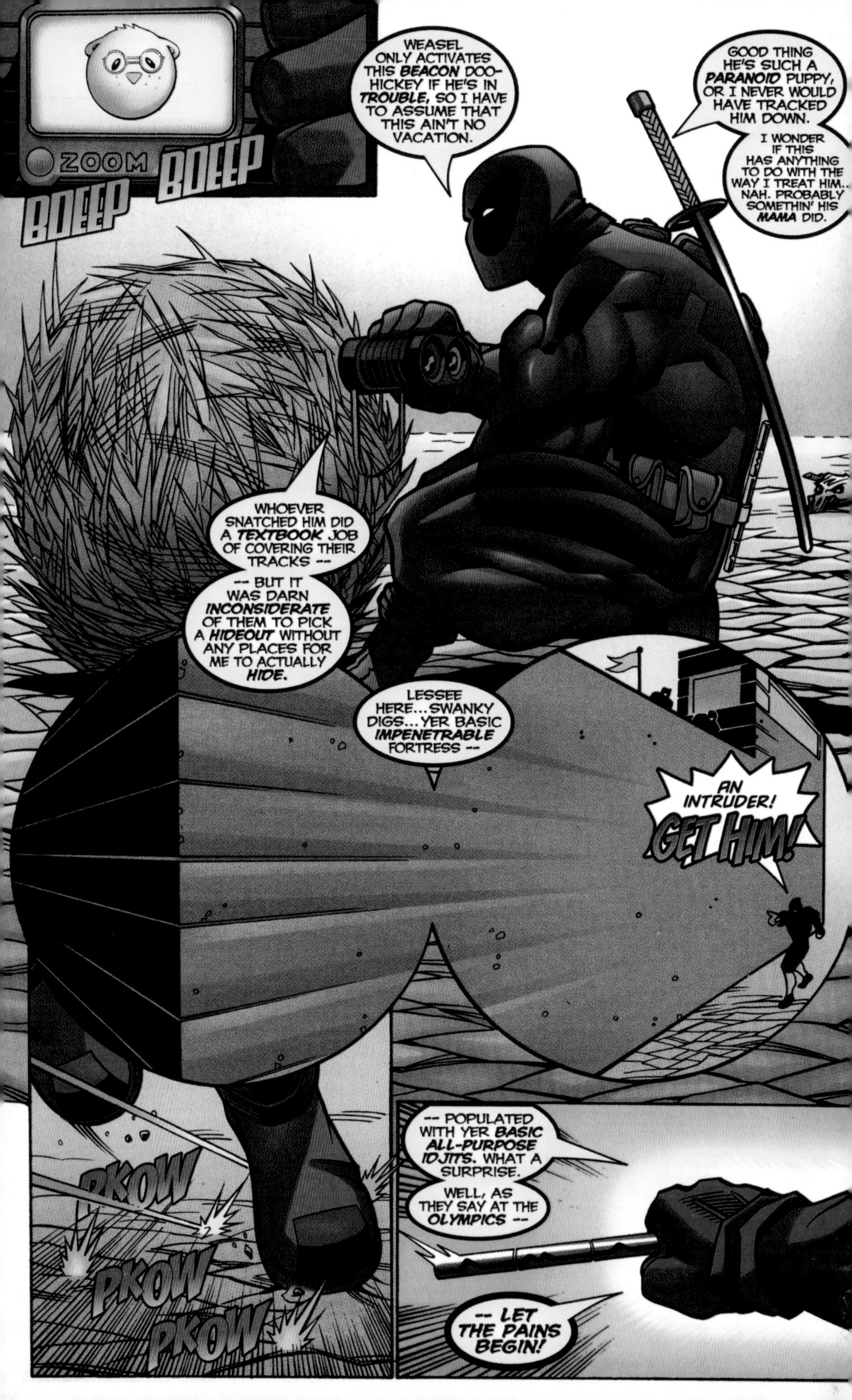
ZOOM
BOEEP BOEEP
WEASEL ONLY ACTIVATES THIS BEACON DOO-HICKEY IF HE'S IN TROUBLE, SO I HAVE TO ASSUME THAT THIS AIN'T NO VACATION.
GOOD THING HE'S SUCH A PARANOID PUPPY, OR I NEVER WOULD HAVE TRACKED HIM DOWN.
I WONDER IF THIS HAS ANYTHING TO DO WITH THE WAY I TREAT HIM.. NAH. PROBABLY SOMETHIN' HIS MAMA DID.
WHOEVER SNATCHED HIM DID A TEXTBOOK JOB OF COVERING THEIR TRACKS --
-- BUT IT WAS DARN INCONSIDERATE OF THEM TO PICK A HIDEOUT WITHOUT ANY PLACES FOR ME TO ACTUALLY HIDE.
LESSEE HERE...SWANKY DIGS...YER BASIC IMPENETRABLE FORTRESS --
AN INTRUDER! GET HIM!
PKOW PKOW PKOW
-- POPULATED WITH YER BASIC ALL-PURPOSE IDJITS. WHAT A SURPRISE.
WELL, AS THEY SAY AT THE OLYMPICS --
-- LET THE PAINS BEGIN!

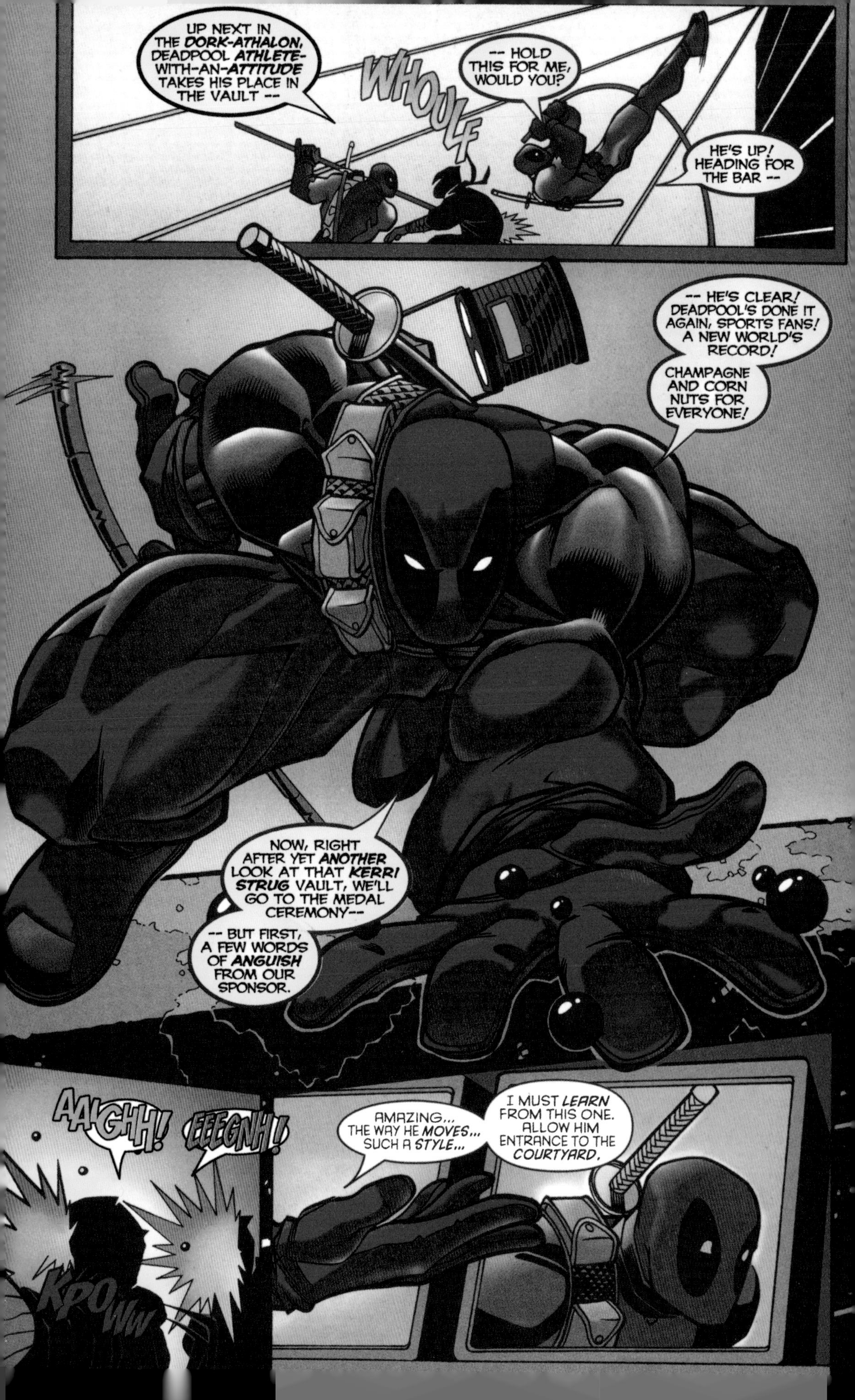
UP NEXT IN THE DORK-ATHALON, DEADPOOL ATHLETE-WITH-AN-ATTITUDE TAKES HIS PLACE IN THE VAULT --
WHOULF
-- HOLD THIS FOR ME, WOULD YOU?
HE'S UP! HEADING FOR THE BAR --
-- HE'S CLEAR! DEADPOOL'S DONE IT AGAIN, SPORTS FANS! A NEW WORLD'S RECORD!
CHAMPAGNE AND CORN NUTS FOR EVERYONE!
NOW, RIGHT AFTER YET ANOTHER LOOK AT THAT KERRI STRUG VAULT, WE'LL GO TO THE MEDAL CEREMONY--
-- BUT FIRST, A FEW WORDS OF ANGUISH FROM OUR SPONSOR.
AAIGHH!
EEEGNH!
KPOWW
AMAZING... THE WAY HE MOVES... SUCH A STYLE...
I MUST LEARN FROM THIS ONE. ALLOW HIM ENTRANCE TO THE COURTYARD.

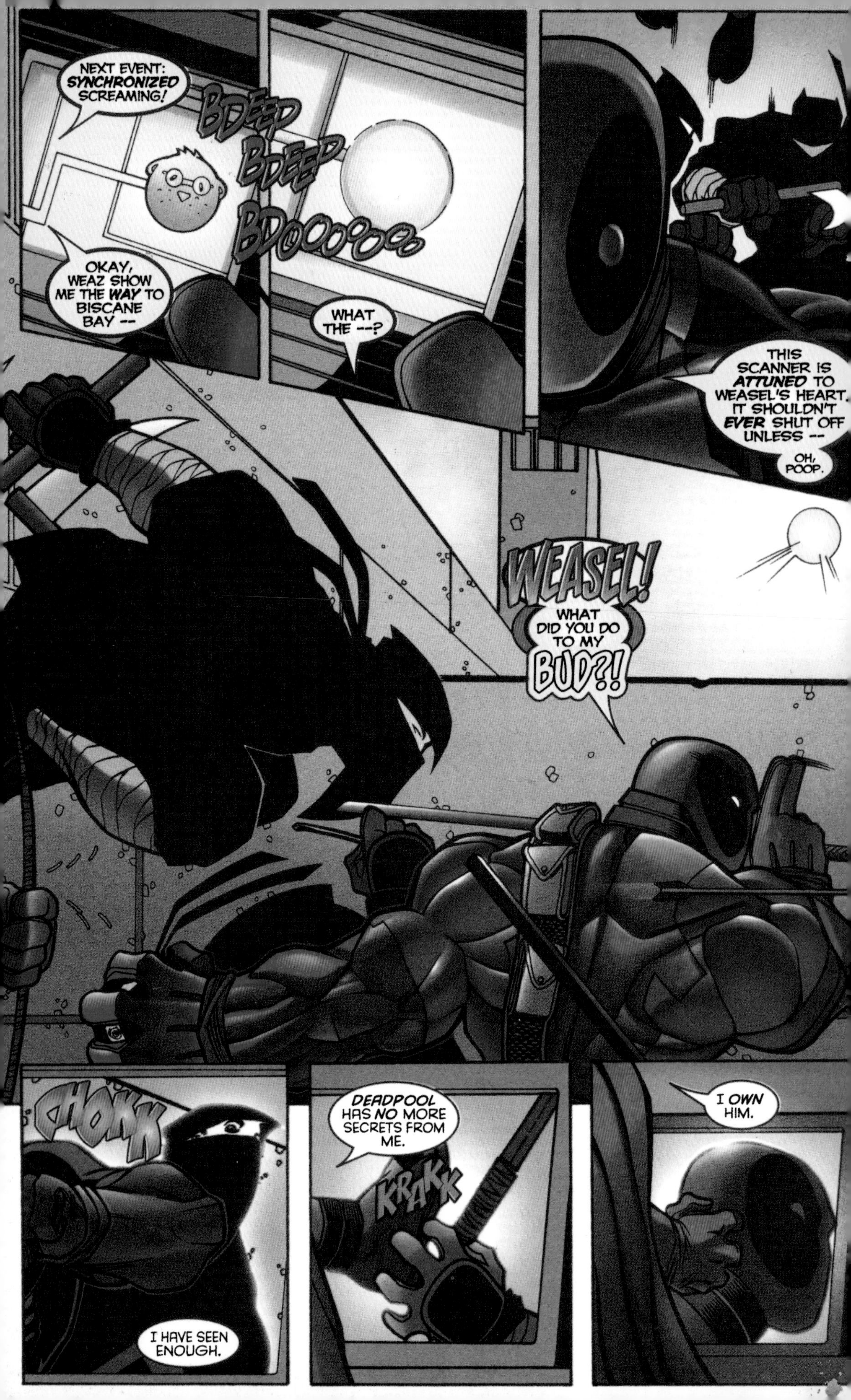
NEXT EVENT: SYNCHRONIZED SCREAMING!
BDEEP BDEEP BDOOOOOO
OKAY, WEAZ SHOW ME THE WAY TO BISCANE BAY --
WHAT THE --?
THIS SCANNER IS ATTUNED TO WEASEL'S HEART. IT SHOULDN'T EVER SHUT OFF UNLESS --
OH, POOP.
WEASEL!
WHAT DID YOU DO TO MY BUD?!
CHOKK
I HAVE SEEN ENOUGH.
DEADPOOL HAS NO MORE SECRETS FROM ME.
KRAKK
I OWN HIM.

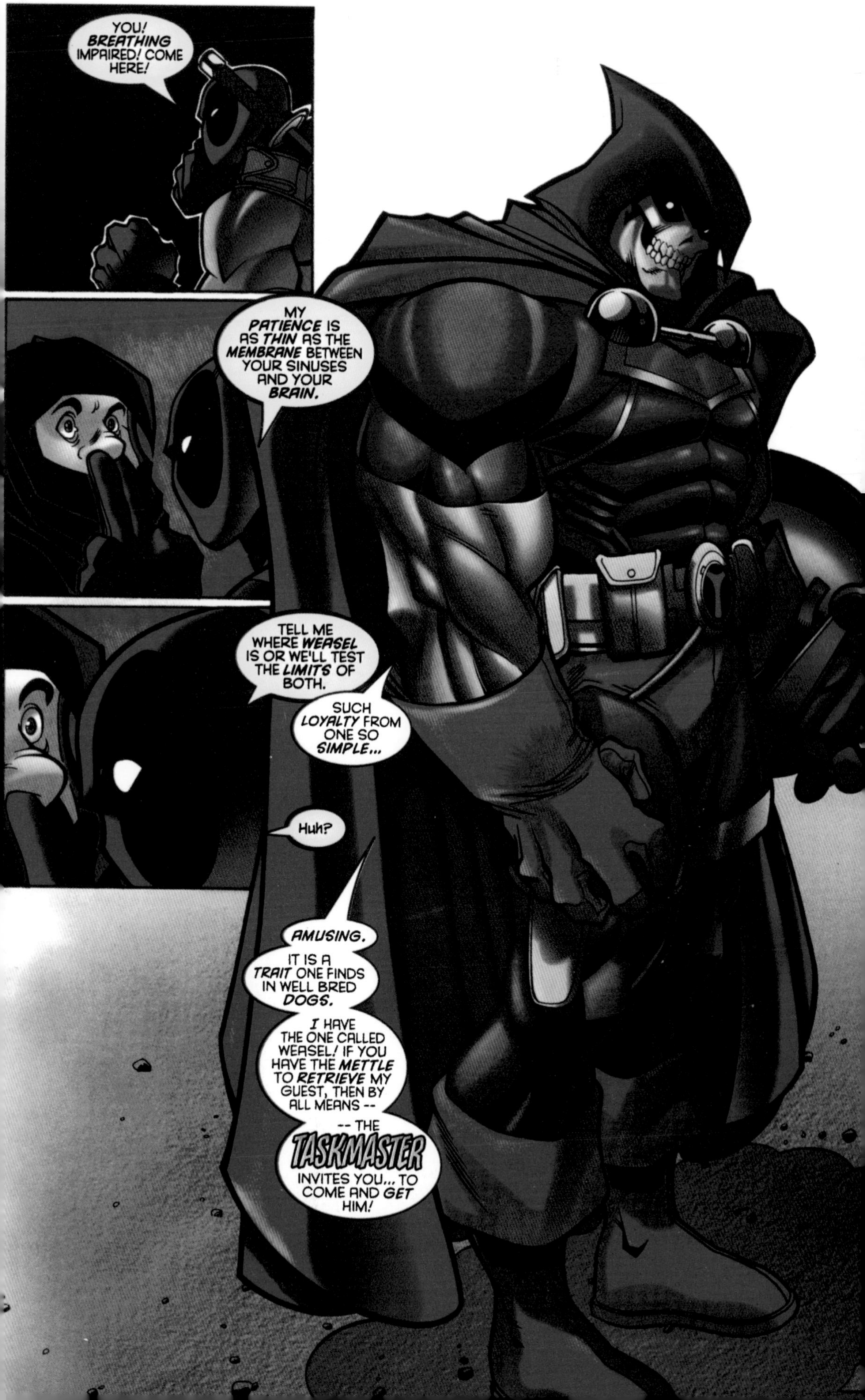
YOU! BREATHING IMPAIRED! COME HERE!
MY PATIENCE IS AS THIN AS THE MEMBRANE BETWEEN YOUR SINUSES AND YOUR BRAIN.
TELL ME WHERE WEASEL IS OR WE'LL TEST THE LIMITS OF BOTH.
SUCH LOYALTY FROM ONE SO SIMPLE...
Huh?
AMUSING.
IT IS A TRAIT ONE FINDS IN WELL BRED DOGS.
I HAVE THE ONE CALLED WEASEL! IF YOU HAVE THE METTLE TO RETRIEVE MY GUEST, THEN BY ALL MEANS --
-- THE TASKMASTER INVITES YOU... TO COME AND GET HIM!

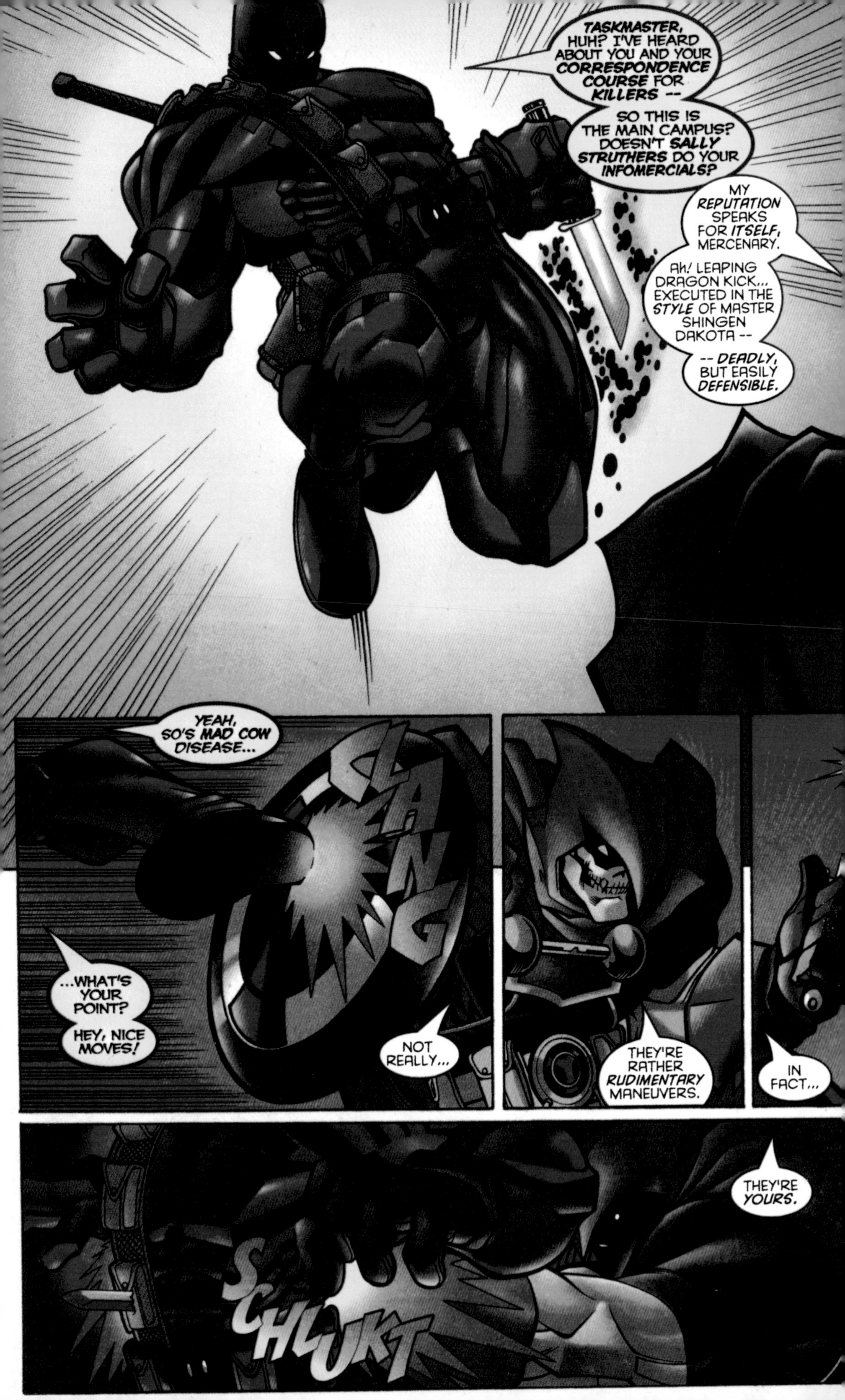
TASKMASTER, HUH? I'VE HEARD ABOUT YOU AND YOUR CORRESPONDENCE COURSE FOR KILLERS --
SO THIS IS THE MAIN CAMPUS? DOESN'T SALLY STRUTHERS DO YOUR INFOMERCIALS?
MY REPUTATION SPEAKS FOR ITSELF, MERCENARY.
AH! LEAPING DRAGON KICK... EXECUTED IN THE STYLE OF MASTER SHINGEN DAKOTA --
-- DEADLY, BUT EASILY DEFENSIBLE.
YEAH, SO'S MAD COW DISEASE...
...WHAT'S YOUR POINT?
HEY, NICE MOVES!
NOT REALLY...
THEY'RE RATHER RUDIMENTARY MANEUVERS.
IN FACT...
THEY'RE YOURS.
SCHLUKT

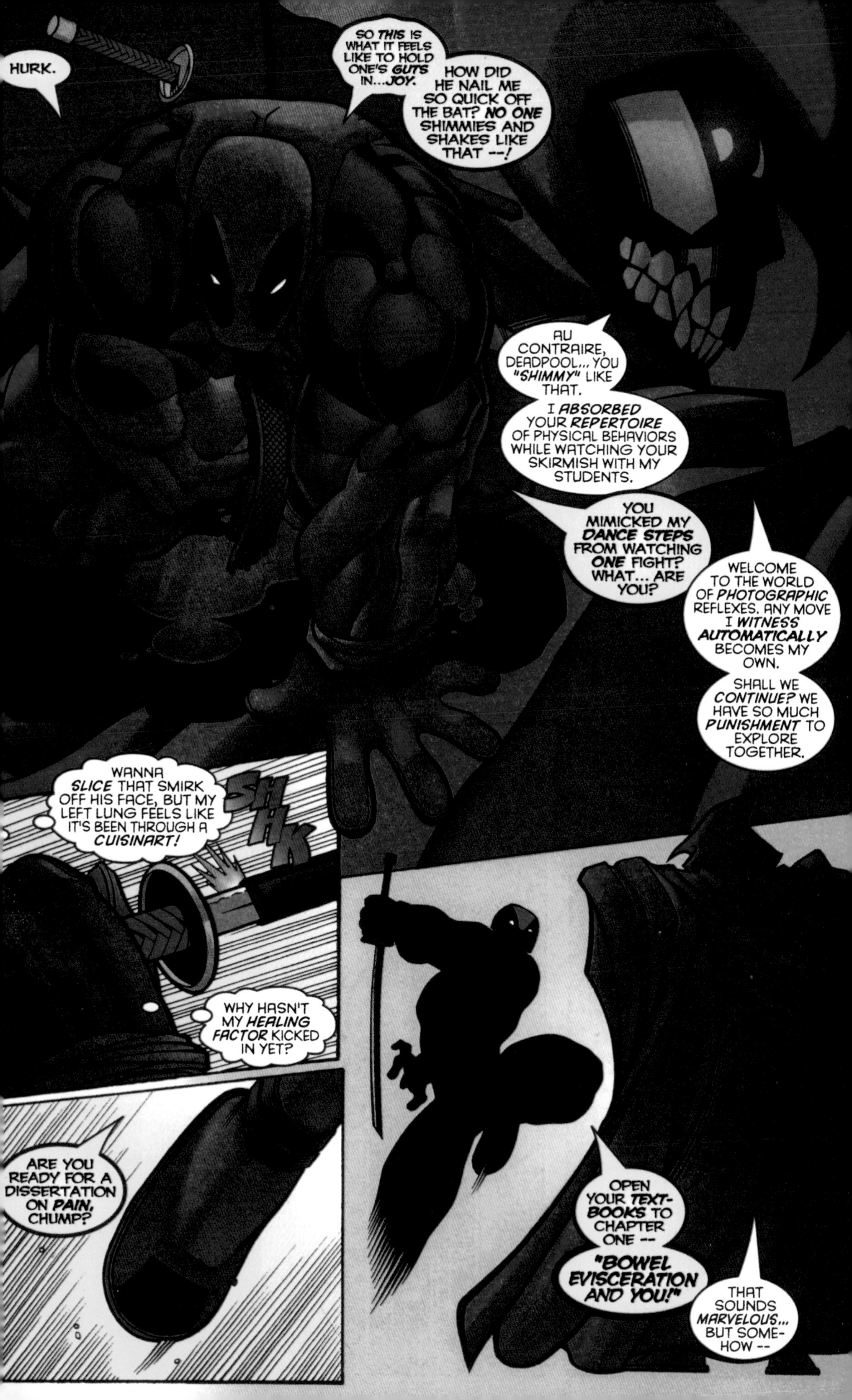
HURK.
SO THIS IS WHAT IT FEELS LIKE TO HOLD ONE'S GUTS IN...JOY.
HOW DID HE NAIL ME SO QUICK OFF THE BAT? NO ONE SHIMMIES AND SHAKES LIKE THAT --!
AU CONTRAIRE, DEADPOOL... YOU "SHIMMY" LIKE THAT.
I ABSORBED YOUR REPERTOIRE OF PHYSICAL BEHAVIORS WHILE WATCHING YOUR SKIRMISH WITH MY STUDENTS.
YOU MIMICKED MY DANCE STEPS FROM WATCHING ONE FIGHT? WHAT... ARE YOU?
WELCOME TO THE WORLD OF PHOTOGRAPHIC REFLEXES. ANY MOVE I WITNESS AUTOMATICALLY BECOMES MY OWN.
SHALL WE CONTINUE? WE HAVE SO MUCH PUNISHMENT TO EXPLORE TOGETHER.
WANNA SLICE THAT SMIRK OFF HIS FACE, BUT MY LEFT LUNG FEELS LIKE IT'S BEEN THROUGH A CUISINART!
SHHK
WHY HASN'T MY HEALING FACTOR KICKED IN YET?
ARE YOU READY FOR A DISSERTATION ON PAIN, CHUMP?
OPEN YOUR TEXT-BOOKS TO CHAPTER ONE --
"BOWEL EVISCERATION AND YOU!"
THAT SOUNDS MARVELOUS... BUT SOME-HOW --

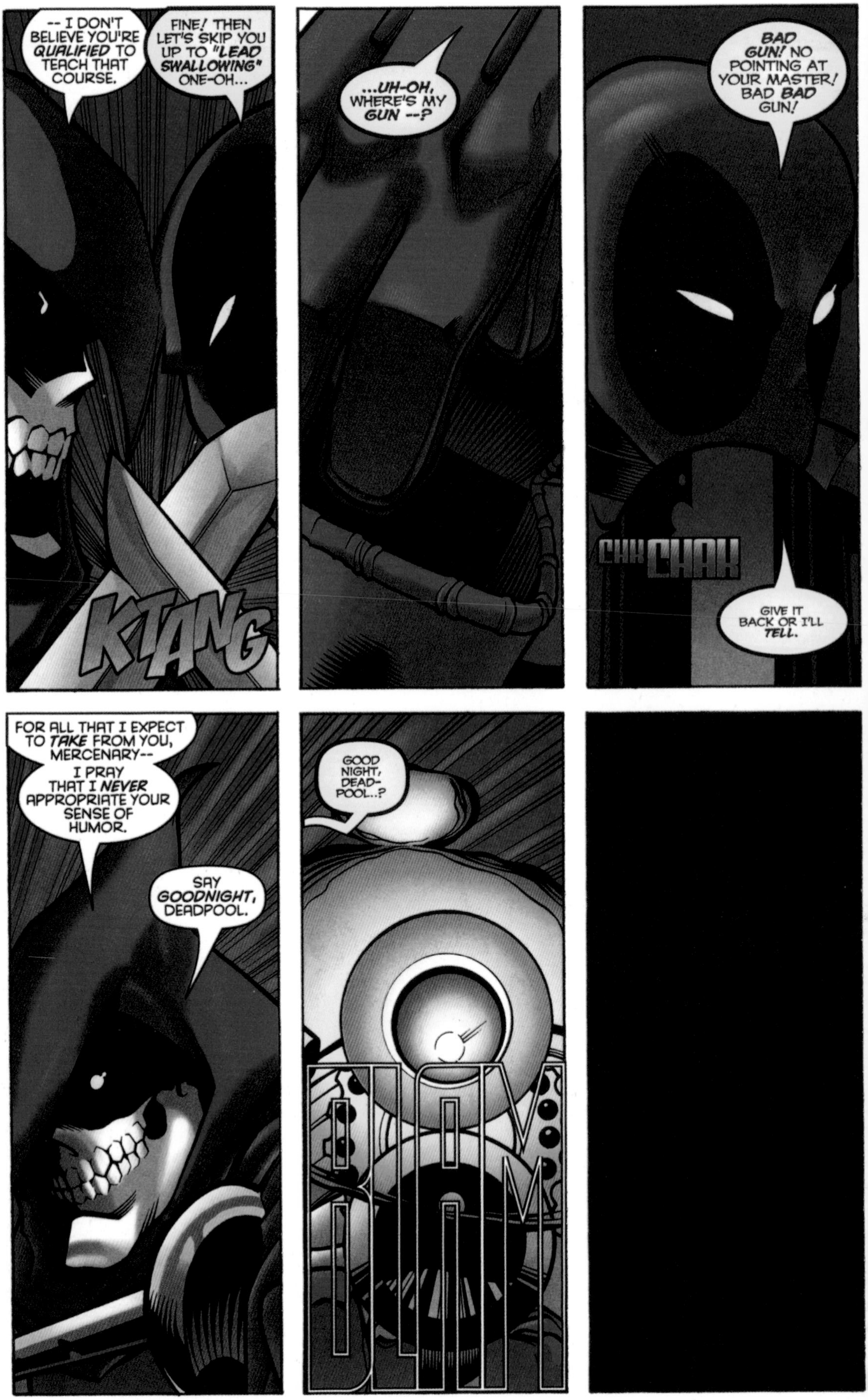
-- I DON'T BELIEVE YOU'RE QUALIFIED TO TEACH THAT COURSE.
FINE! THEN LET'S SKIP YOU UP TO "LEAD SWALLOWING" ONE-OH...
KTANG
...UH-OH, WHERE'S MY GUN --?
BAD GUN! NO POINTING AT YOUR MASTER! BAD BAD GUN!
CHK CHAK
GIVE IT BACK OR I'LL TELL.
FOR ALL THAT I EXPECT TO TAKE FROM YOU, MERCENARY--
I PRAY THAT I NEVER APPROPRIATE YOUR SENSE OF HUMOR.
SAY GOODNIGHT, DEADPOOL.
GOOD NIGHT, DEAD-POOL..?
BLAM

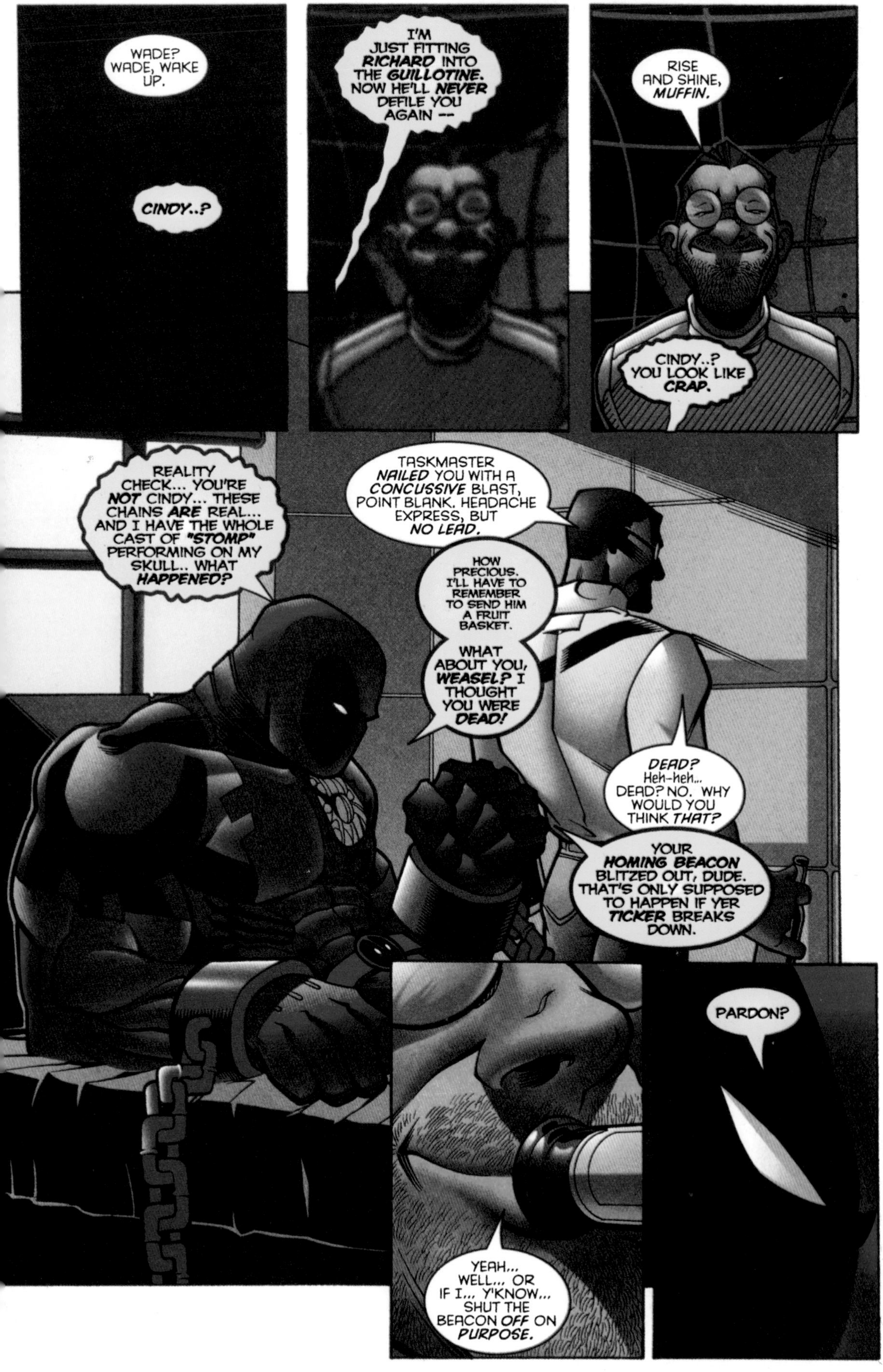
WADE? WADE, WAKE UP.
CINDY..?
I'M JUST FITTING RICHARD INTO THE GUILLOTINE. NOW HE'LL NEVER DEFILE YOU AGAIN --
RISE AND SHINE, MUFFIN.
CINDY..? YOU LOOK LIKE CRAP.
REALITY CHECK... YOU'RE NOT CINDY... THESE CHAINS ARE REAL... AND I HAVE THE WHOLE CAST OF "STOMP" PERFORMING ON MY SKULL.. WHAT HAPPENED?
TASKMASTER NAILED YOU WITH A CONCUSSIVE BLAST, POINT BLANK. HEADACHE EXPRESS, BUT NO LEAD.
HOW PRECIOUS. I'LL HAVE TO REMEMBER TO SEND HIM A FRUIT BASKET.
WHAT ABOUT YOU, WEASEL? I THOUGHT YOU WERE DEAD!
DEAD? Heh-heh... DEAD? NO. WHY WOULD YOU THINK THAT?
YOUR HOMING BEACON BLITZED OUT, DUDE. THAT'S ONLY SUPPOSED TO HAPPEN IF YER TICKER BREAKS DOWN.
YEAH... WELL... OR IF I... Y'KNOW... SHUT THE BEACON OFF ON PURPOSE.
PARDON?

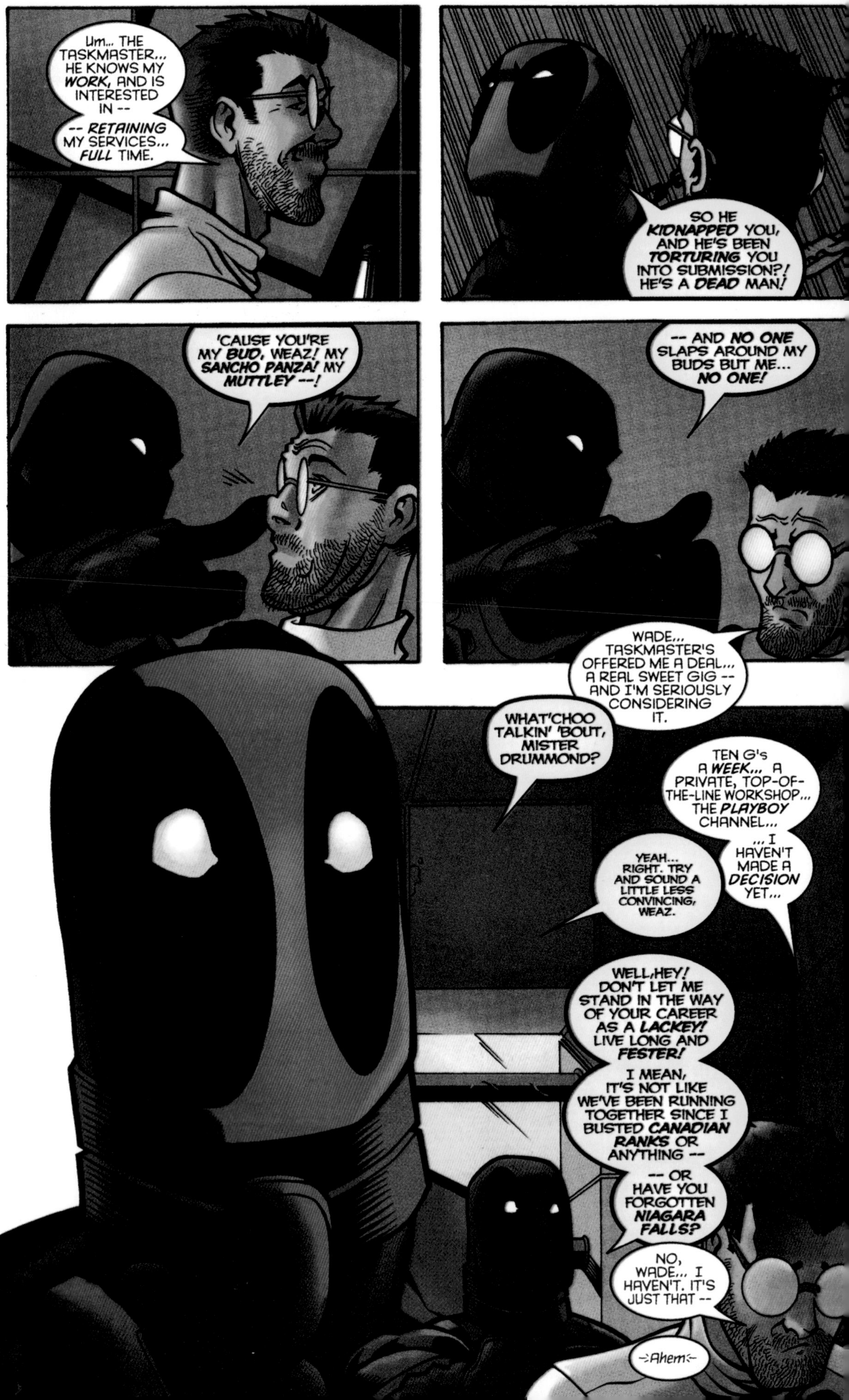
UM... THE TASKMASTER... HE KNOWS MY WORK, AND IS INTERESTED IN --
-- RETAINING MY SERVICES... FULL TIME.
SO HE KIDNAPPED YOU, AND HE'S BEEN TORTURING YOU INTO SUBMISSION?! HE'S A DEAD MAN!
'CAUSE YOU'RE MY BUD, WEAZ! MY SANCHO PANZA! MY MUTTLEY --!
-- AND NO ONE SLAPS AROUND MY BUDS BUT ME... NO ONE!
WADE... TASKMASTER'S OFFERED ME A DEAL... A REAL SWEET GIG -- AND I'M SERIOUSLY CONSIDERING IT.
WHAT'CHOO TALKIN' 'BOUT, MISTER DRUMMOND?
TEN G's A WEEK... A PRIVATE, TOP-OF-THE-LINE WORKSHOP... THE PLAYBOY CHANNEL...
... I HAVEN'T MADE A DECISION YET...
YEAH... RIGHT. TRY AND SOUND A LITTLE LESS CONVINCING, WEAZ.
WELL, HEY! DON'T LET ME STAND IN THE WAY OF YOUR CAREER AS A LACKEY! LIVE LONG AND FESTER!
I MEAN, IT'S NOT LIKE WE'VE BEEN RUNNING TOGETHER SINCE I BUSTED CANADIAN RANKS OR ANYTHING --
-- OR HAVE YOU FORGOTTEN NIAGARA FALLS?
NO, WADE... I HAVEN'T. IT'S JUST THAT --
Ahem

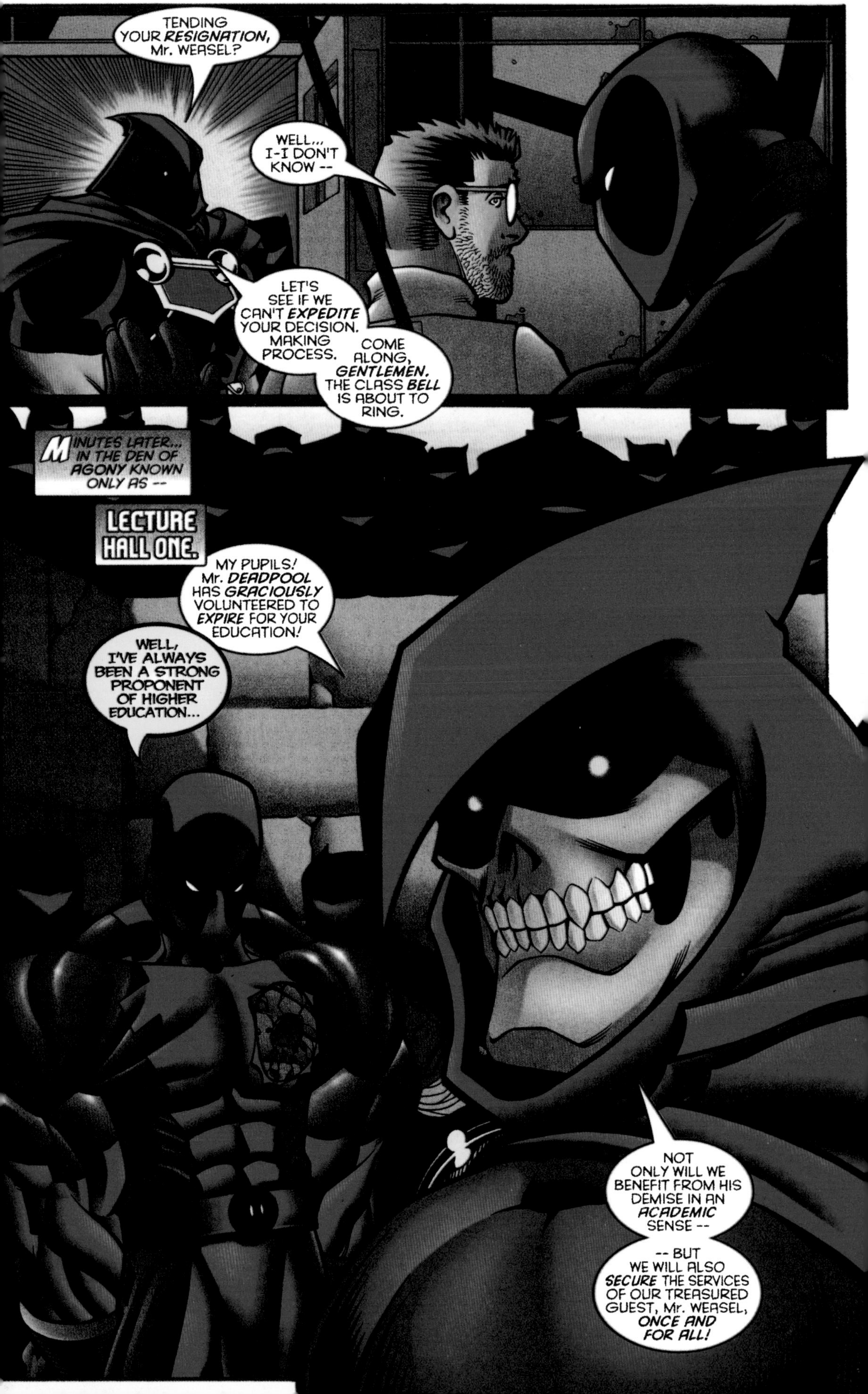
TENDING YOUR RESIGNATION, Mr. WEASEL?
WELL... I-I DON'T KNOW --
LET'S SEE IF WE CAN'T EXPEDITE YOUR DECISION. MAKING PROCESS.
COME ALONG, GENTLEMEN. THE CLASS BELL IS ABOUT TO RING.
MINUTES LATER... IN THE DEN OF AGONY KNOWN ONLY AS --
LECTURE HALL ONE.
MY PUPILS! Mr. DEADPOOL HAS GRACIOUSLY VOLUNTEERED TO EXPIRE FOR YOUR EDUCATION!
WELL, I'VE ALWAYS BEEN A STRONG PROPONENT OF HIGHER EDUCATION...
NOT ONLY WILL WE BENEFIT FROM HIS DEMISE IN AN ACADEMIC SENSE --
-- BUT WE WILL ALSO SECURE THE SERVICES OF OUR TREASURED GUEST, Mr. WEASEL, ONCE AND FOR ALL!

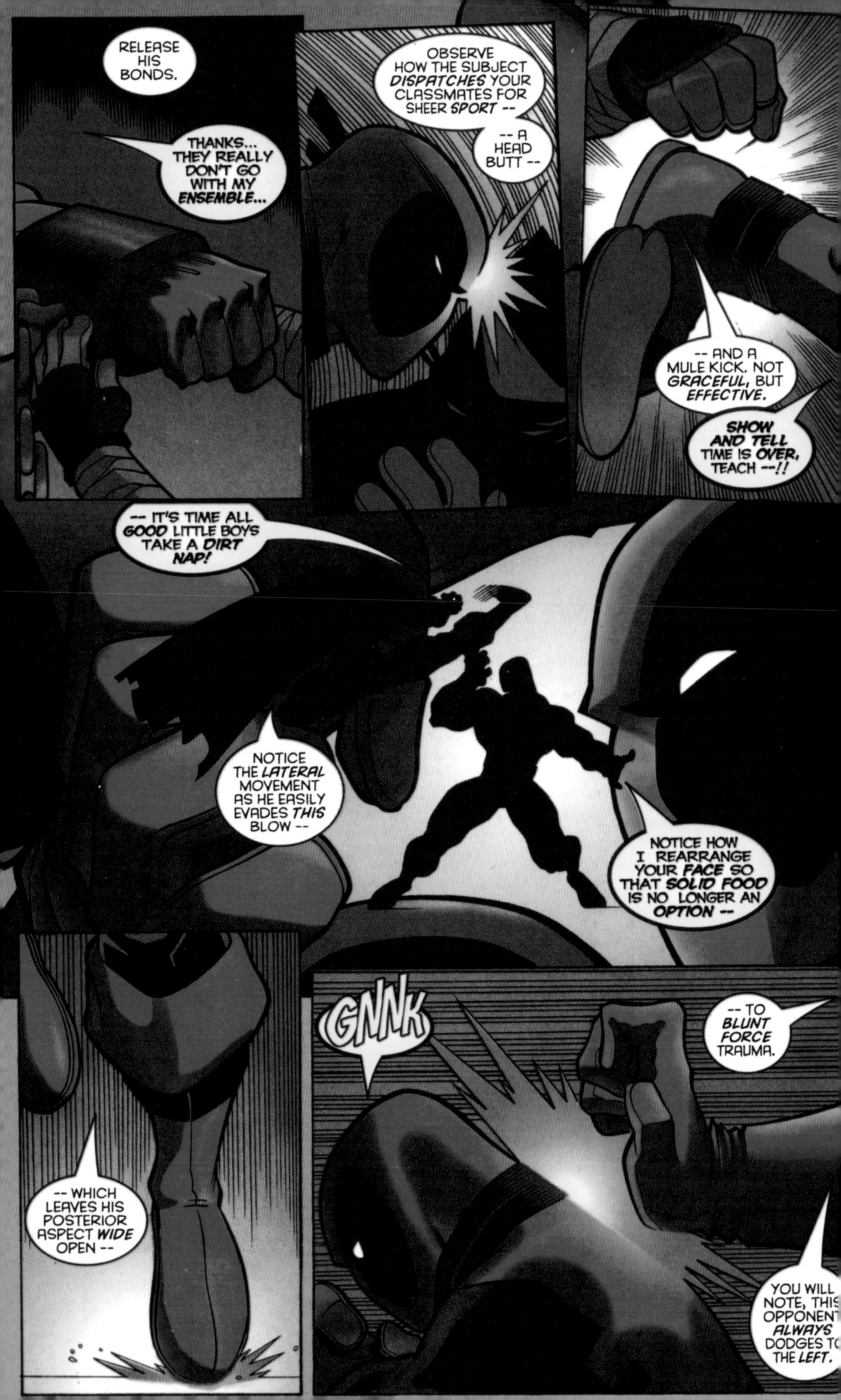

RELEASE HIS BONDS.
THANKS... THEY REALLY DON'T GO WITH MY ENSEMBLE...
OBSERVE HOW THE SUBJECT DISPATCHES YOUR CLASSMATES FOR SHEER SPORT --
-- A HEAD BUTT --
-- AND A MULE KICK. NOT GRACEFUL, BUT EFFECTIVE.
SHOW AND TELL TIME IS OVER, TEACH --!!
-- IT'S TIME ALL GOOD LITTLE BOYS TAKE A DIRT NAP!
NOTICE THE LATERAL MOVEMENT AS HE EASILY EVADES THIS BLOW --
NOTICE HOW I REARRANGE YOUR FACE SO THAT SOLID FOOD IS NO LONGER AN OPTION --
-- WHICH LEAVES HIS POSTERIOR ASPECT WIDE OPEN --
GNNK
-- TO BLUNT FORCE TRAUMA.
YOU WILL NOTE, THIS OPPONENT ALWAYS DODGES TO THE LEFT.

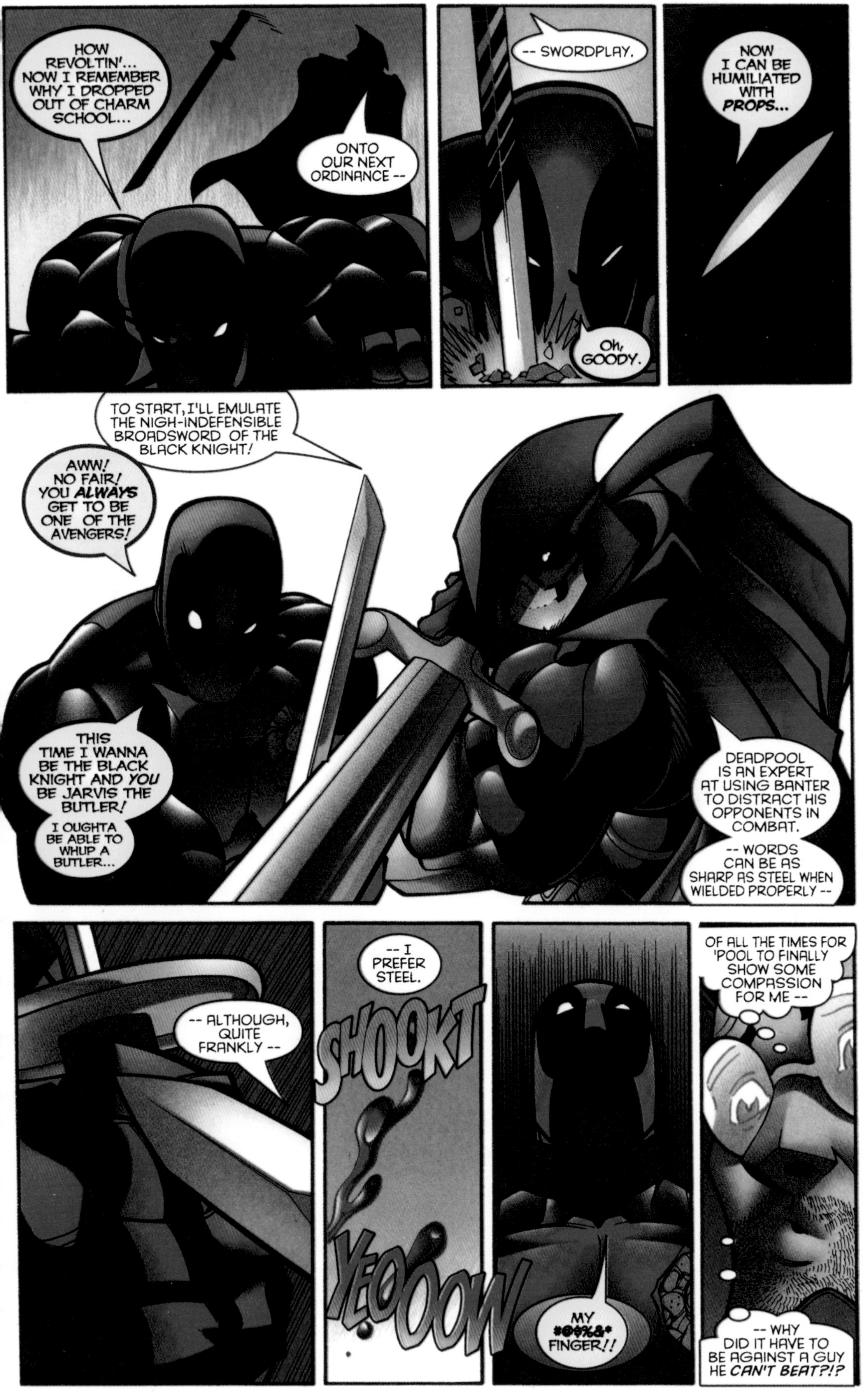
HOW REVOLTIN'... NOW I REMEMBER WHY I DROPPED OUT OF CHARM SCHOOL...
ONTO OUR NEXT ORDINANCE --
-- SWORDPLAY.
Oh, GOODY.
NOW I CAN BE HUMILIATED WITH PROPS...
TO START, I'LL EMULATE THE NIGH-INDEFENSIBLE BROADSWORD OF THE BLACK KNIGHT!
AWW! NO FAIR! YOU ALWAYS GET TO BE ONE OF THE AVENGERS!
THIS TIME I WANNA BE THE BLACK KNIGHT AND YOU BE JARVIS THE BUTLER!
I OUGHTA BE ABLE TO WHUP A BUTLER...
DEADPOOL IS AN EXPERT AT USING BANTER TO DISTRACT HIS OPPONENTS IN COMBAT.
-- WORDS CAN BE AS SHARP AS STEEL WHEN WIELDED PROPERLY --
-- ALTHOUGH, QUITE FRANKLY --
-- I PREFER STEEL.
SHOOKT
YEOOOW
MY #@$%&* FINGER!!
OF ALL THE TIMES FOR 'POOL TO FINALLY SHOW SOME COMPASSION FOR ME --
-- WHY DID IT HAVE TO BE AGAINST A GUY HE CAN'T BEAT?!?

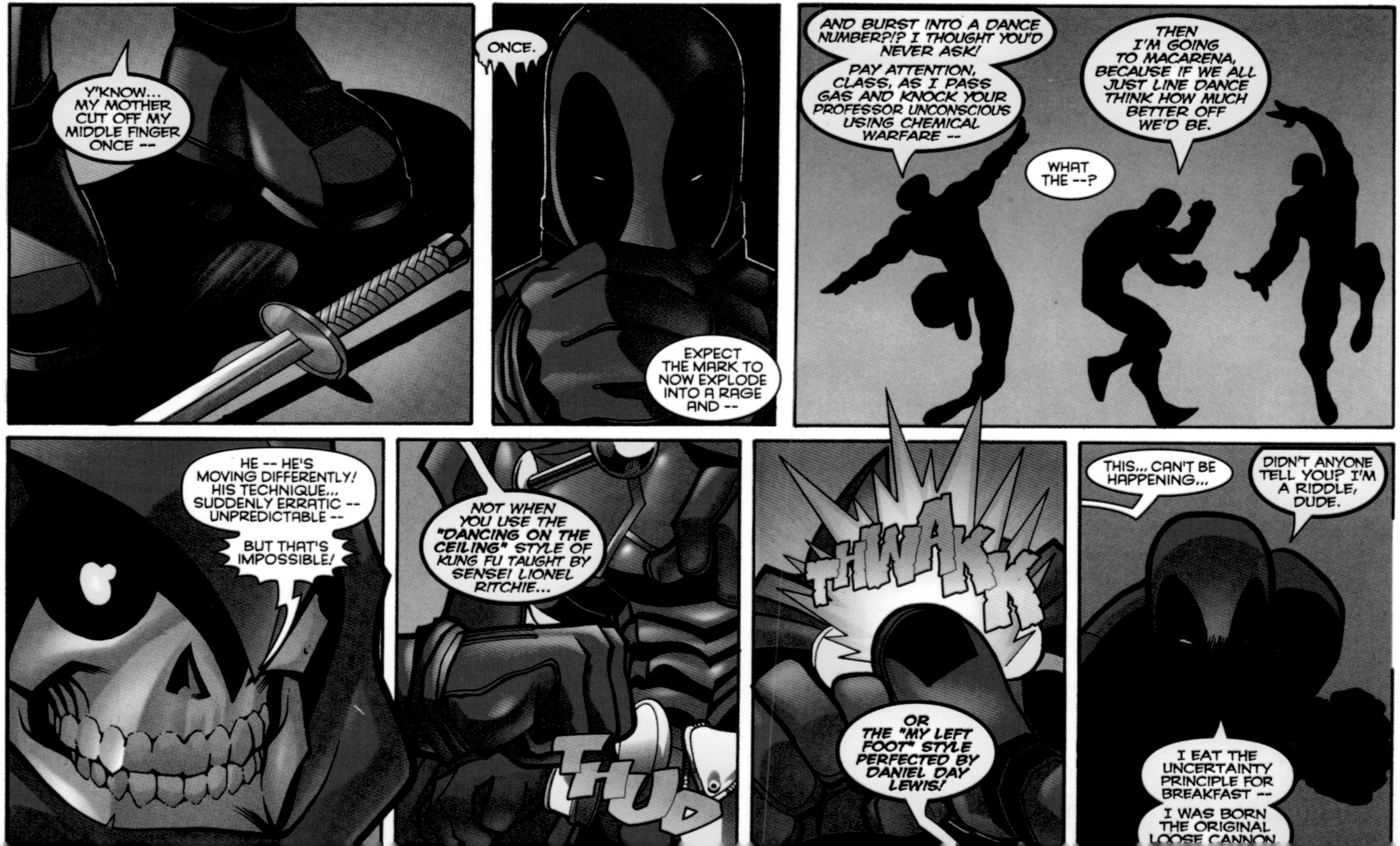
Y'KNOW... MY MOTHER CUT OFF MY MIDDLE FINGER ONCE --
ONCE.
EXPECT THE MARK TO NOW EXPLODE INTO A RAGE AND --
AND BURST INTO A DANCE NUMBER?!? I THOUGHT YOU'D NEVER ASK!
PAY ATTENTION, CLASS, AS I PASS GAS AND KNOCK YOUR PROFESSOR UNCONSCIOUS USING CHEMICAL WARFARE --
WHAT THE --?
THEN I'M GOING TO MACARENA, BECAUSE IF WE ALL JUST LINE DANCE THINK HOW MUCH BETTER OFF WE'D BE.
HE -- HE'S MOVING DIFFERENTLY! HIS TECHNIQUE... SUDDENLY ERRATIC -- UNPREDICTABLE --
BUT THAT'S IMPOSSIBLE!
NOT WHEN YOU USE THE "DANCING ON THE CEILING" STYLE OF KUNG FU TAUGHT BY SENSEI LIONEL RITCHIE...
THUD
THWAKK
OR THE "MY LEFT FOOT" STYLE PERFECTED BY DANIEL DAY LEWIS!
THIS... CAN'T BE HAPPENING...
DIDN'T ANYONE TELL YOU? I'M A RIDDLE, DUDE.
I EAT THE UNCERTAINTY PRINCIPLE FOR BREAKFAST --
I WAS BORN THE ORIGINAL LOOSE CANNON

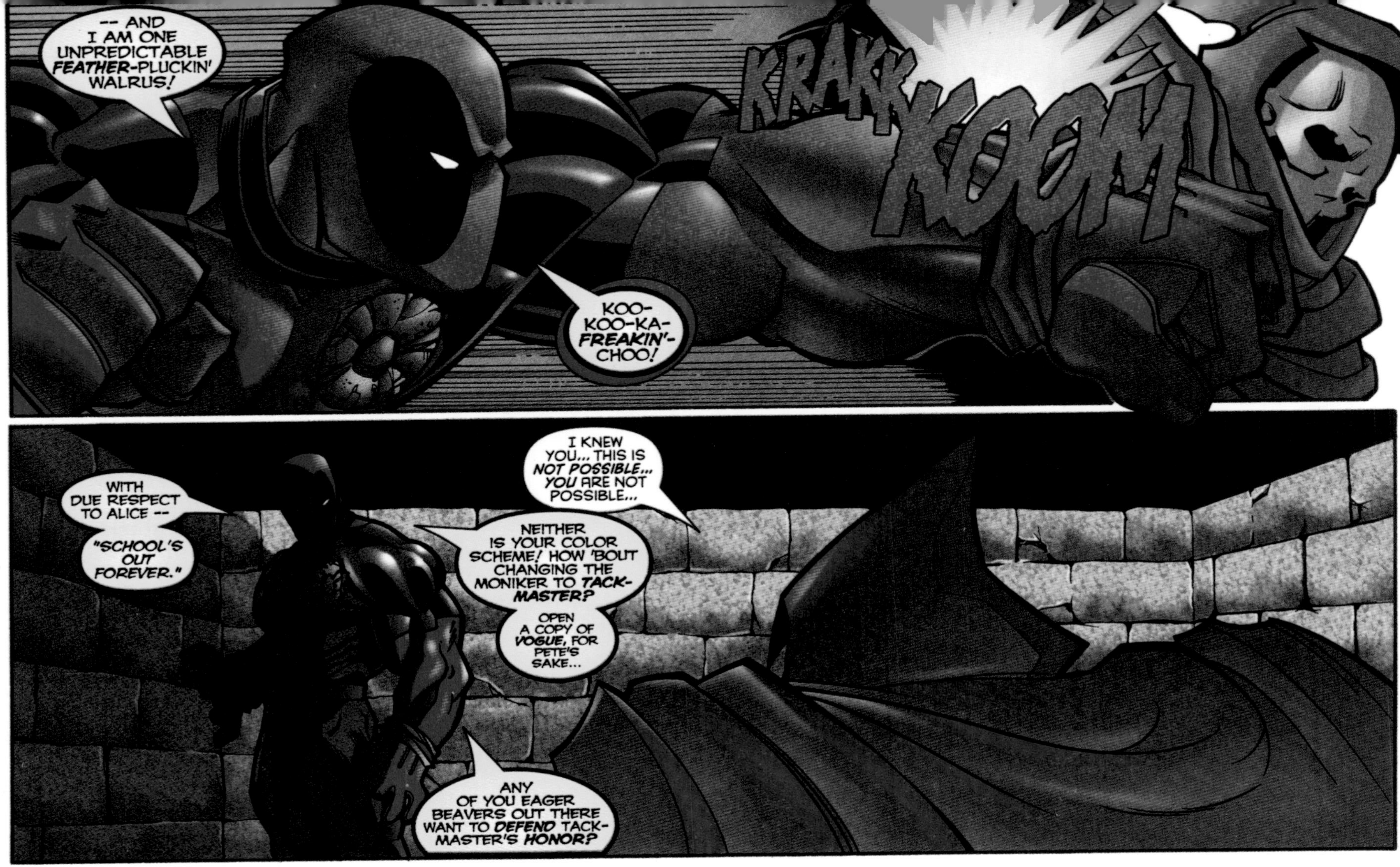
-- AND I AM ONE UNPREDICTABLE *FEATHER*-PLUCKIN' WALRUS!
KRAKK KOOM
KOO-KOO-KA-*FREAKIN'*-CHOO!
WITH DUE RESPECT TO ALICE -- *"SCHOOL'S OUT FOREVER."*
I KNEW YOU... THIS IS *NOT POSSIBLE*... *YOU* ARE NOT POSSIBLE...
NEITHER IS YOUR COLOR SCHEME! HOW 'BOUT CHANGING THE MONIKER TO *TACK-MASTER?*
OPEN A COPY OF *VOGUE*, FOR PETE'S SAKE...
ANY OF YOU EAGER BEAVERS OUT THERE WANT TO *DEFEND* TACK-MASTER'S *HONOR?*

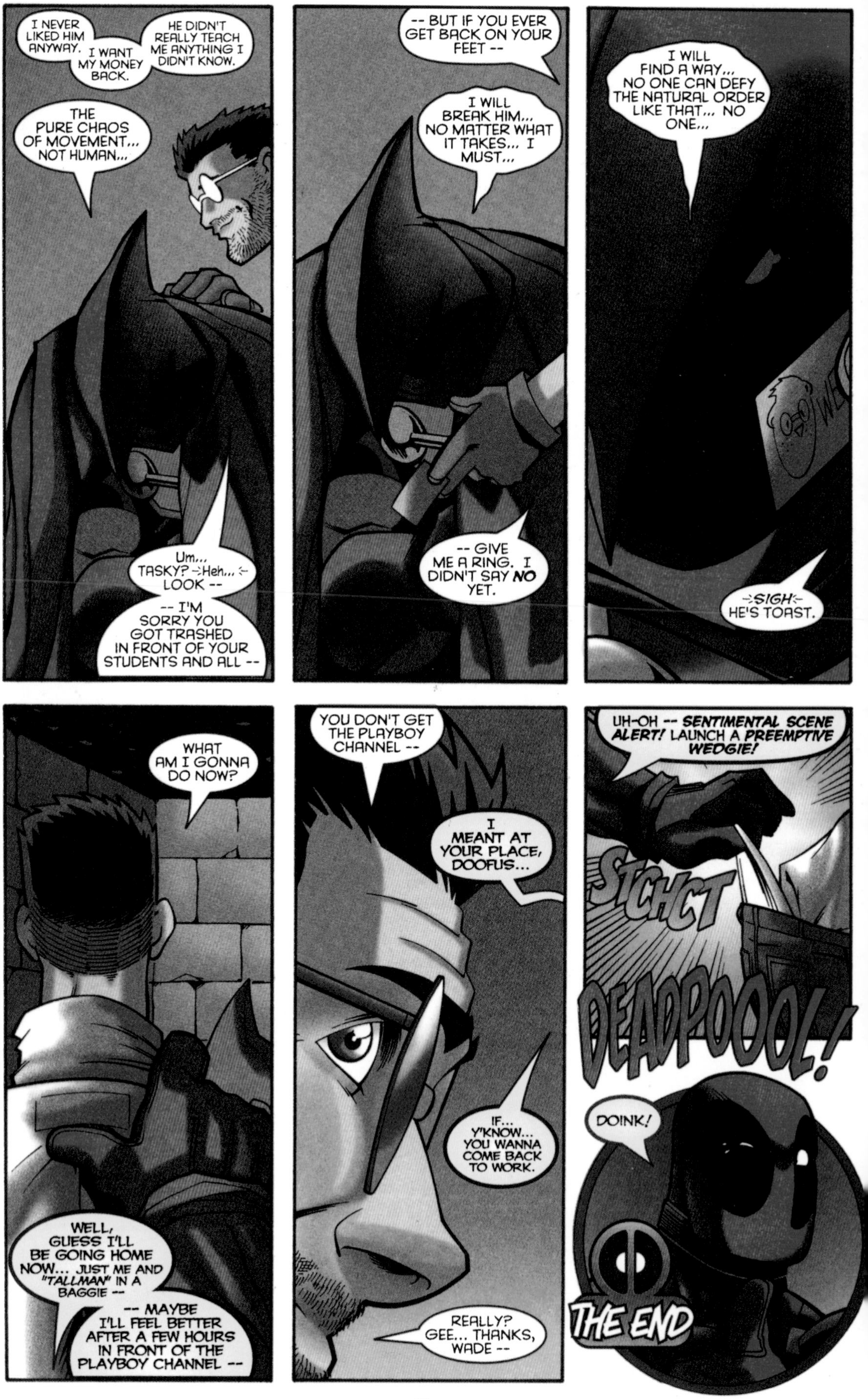
I NEVER LIKED HIM ANYWAY.
I WANT MY MONEY BACK.
HE DIDN'T REALLY TEACH ME ANYTHING I DIDN'T KNOW.
THE PURE CHAOS OF MOVEMENT... NOT HUMAN...
Um... TASKY? ~Heh...~ LOOK --
-- I'M SORRY YOU GOT TRASHED IN FRONT OF YOUR STUDENTS AND ALL --
-- BUT IF YOU EVER GET BACK ON YOUR FEET --
I WILL BREAK HIM... NO MATTER WHAT IT TAKES... I MUST...
-- GIVE ME A RING. I DIDN'T SAY NO YET.
I WILL FIND A WAY... NO ONE CAN DEFY THE NATURAL ORDER LIKE THAT... NO ONE...
~SIGH~ HE'S TOAST.
WHAT AM I GONNA DO NOW?
WELL, GUESS I'LL BE GOING HOME NOW... JUST ME AND "TALLMAN" IN A BAGGIE --
-- MAYBE I'LL FEEL BETTER AFTER A FEW HOURS IN FRONT OF THE PLAYBOY CHANNEL --
YOU DON'T GET THE PLAYBOY CHANNEL --
I MEANT AT YOUR PLACE, DOOFUS...
IF... Y'KNOW... YOU WANNA COME BACK TO WORK.
REALLY? GEE... THANKS, WADE --
UH-OH -- SENTIMENTAL SCENE ALERT! LAUNCH A PREEMPTIVE WEDGIE!
STCHCT
DEADPOOOL!
DOINK!
THE END

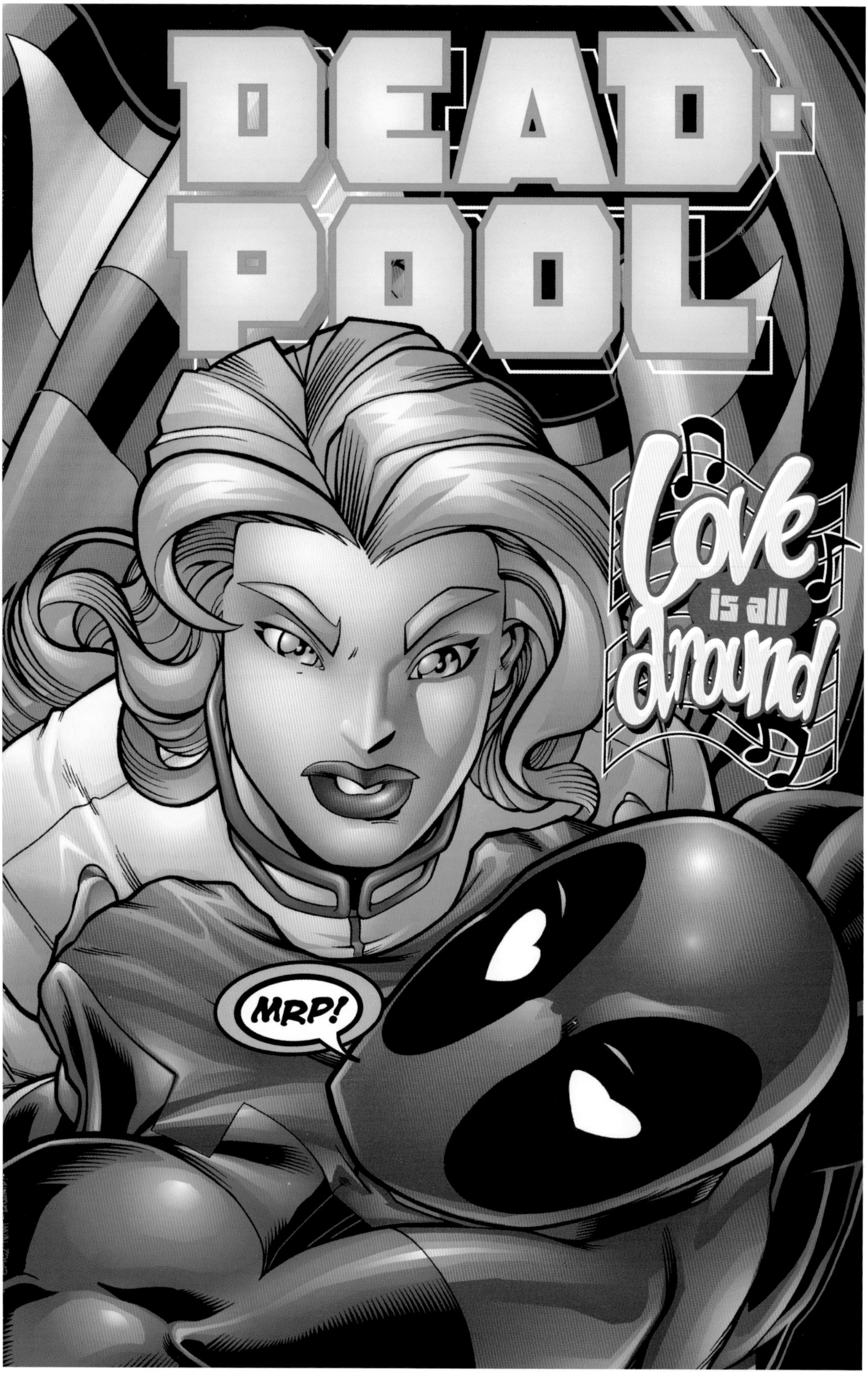
DEAD-POOL
Love is all around!
MRP!

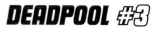

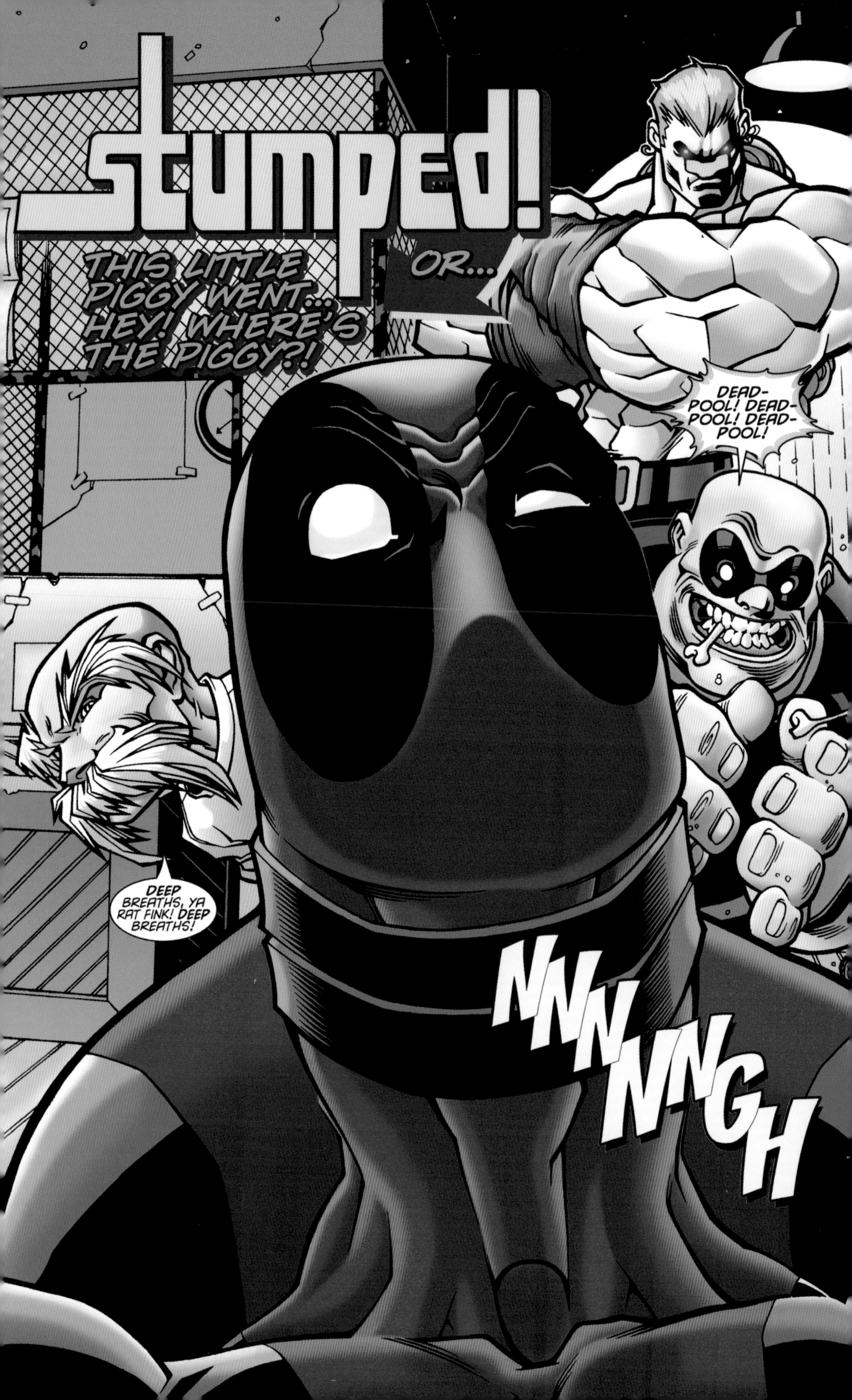

STUMPED!
OR...
THIS LITTLE PIGGY WENT... HEY! WHERE'S THE PIGGY?!
DEAD-POOL! DEAD-POOL! DEAD-POOL!
DEEP BREATHS, YA RAT FINK! DEEP BREATHS!
NNNNNNGH

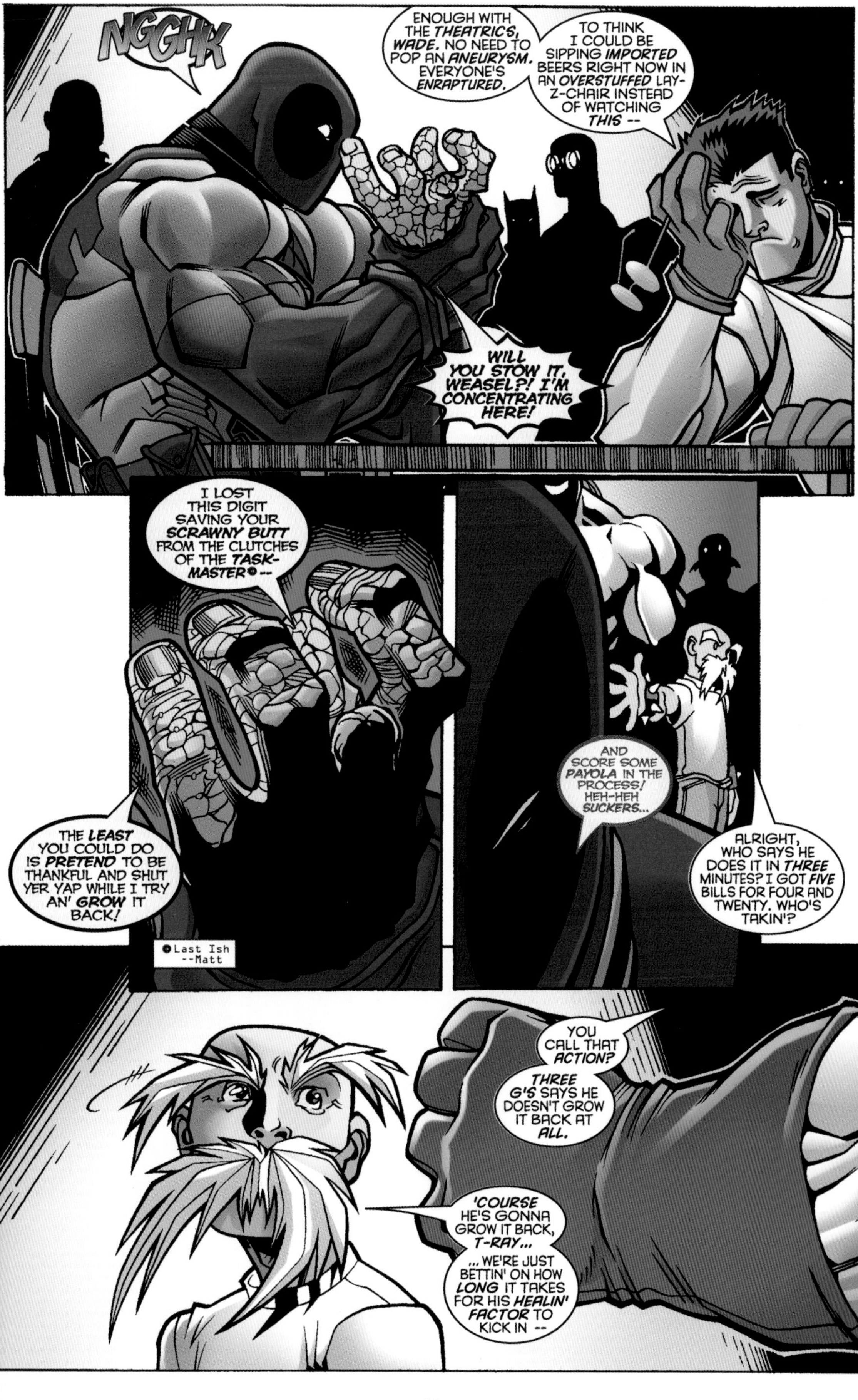
NGGHK
ENOUGH WITH THE THEATRICS, WADE. NO NEED TO POP AN ANEURYSM. EVERYONE'S ENRAPTURED.
TO THINK I COULD BE SIPPING IMPORTED BEERS RIGHT NOW IN AN OVERSTUFFED LAY-Z-CHAIR INSTEAD OF WATCHING THIS --
WILL YOU STOW IT, WEASEL?! I'M CONCENTRATING HERE!
I LOST THIS DIGIT SAVING YOUR SCRAWNY BUTT FROM THE CLUTCHES OF THE TASK-MASTER* --
THE LEAST YOU COULD DO IS PRETEND TO BE THANKFUL AND SHUT YER YAP WHILE I TRY AN' GROW IT BACK!
*Last Ish --Matt
AND SCORE SOME PAYOLA IN THE PROCESS! HEH-HEH SUCKERS...
ALRIGHT, WHO SAYS HE DOES IT IN THREE MINUTES? I GOT FIVE BILLS FOR FOUR AND TWENTY. WHO'S TAKIN'?
YOU CALL THAT ACTION?
THREE G'S SAYS HE DOESN'T GROW IT BACK AT ALL.
'COURSE HE'S GONNA GROW IT BACK, T-RAY...
...WE'RE JUST BETTIN' ON HOW LONG IT TAKES FOR HIS HEALIN' FACTOR TO KICK IN --

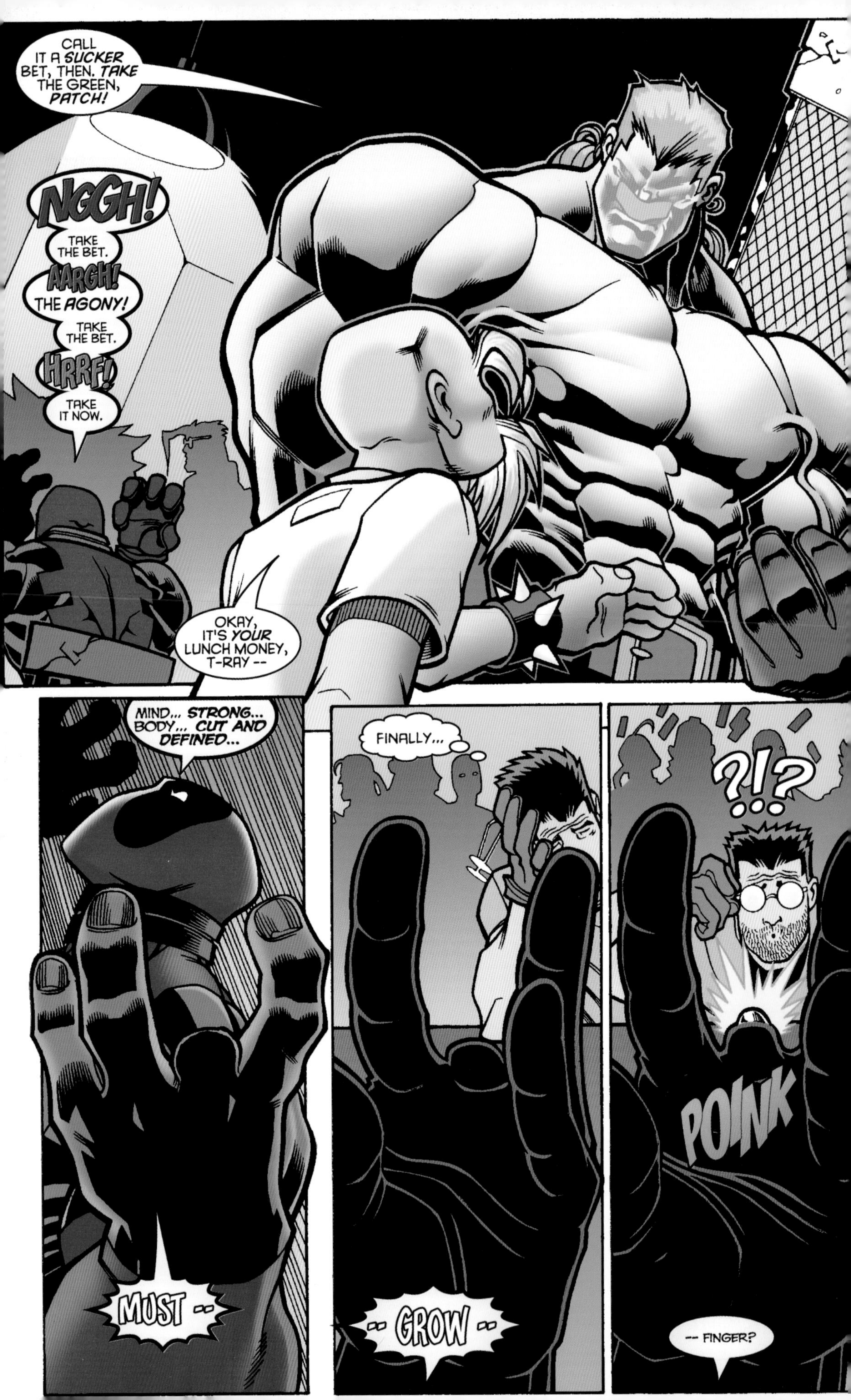

CALL IT A SUCKER BET, THEN. TAKE THE GREEN, PATCH!
NGGH!
TAKE THE BET.
AARGH! THE AGONY!
TAKE THE BET.
HRRF!
TAKE IT NOW.
OKAY, IT'S YOUR LUNCH MONEY, T-RAY --
MIND... STRONG... BODY... CUT AND DEFINED...
MUST --
FINALLY...
-- GROW --
?!?
POINK
-- FINGER?

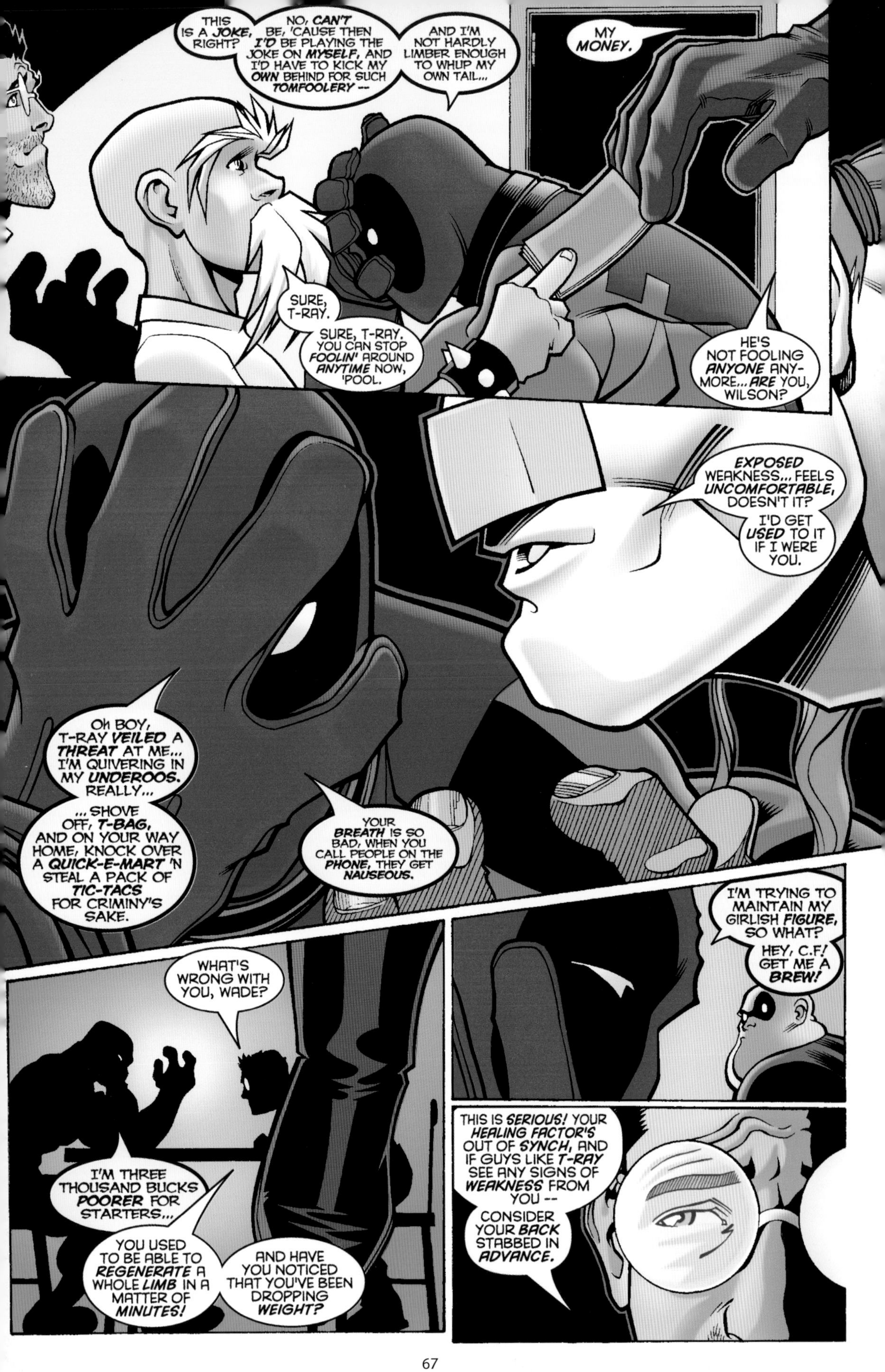
THIS IS A JOKE, RIGHT?
NO, CAN'T BE, 'CAUSE THEN I'D BE PLAYING THE JOKE ON MYSELF, AND I'D HAVE TO KICK MY OWN BEHIND FOR SUCH TOMFOOLERY --
AND I'M NOT HARDLY LIMBER ENOUGH TO WHUP MY OWN TAIL...
MY MONEY.
SURE, T-RAY.
SURE, T-RAY. YOU CAN STOP FOOLIN' AROUND ANYTIME NOW, 'POOL.
HE'S NOT FOOLING ANYONE ANY-MORE... ARE YOU, WILSON?
EXPOSED WEAKNESS... FEELS UNCOMFORTABLE, DOESN'T IT?
I'D GET USED TO IT IF I WERE YOU.
Oh BOY, T-RAY VEILED A THREAT AT ME... I'M QUIVERING IN MY UNDEROOS. REALLY...
... SHOVE OFF, T-BAG, AND ON YOUR WAY HOME, KNOCK OVER A QUICK-E-MART 'N STEAL A PACK OF TIC-TACS FOR CRIMINY'S SAKE.
YOUR BREATH IS SO BAD, WHEN YOU CALL PEOPLE ON THE PHONE, THEY GET NAUSEOUS.
I'M TRYING TO MAINTAIN MY GIRLISH FIGURE, SO WHAT?
HEY, C.F.! GET ME A BREW!
WHAT'S WRONG WITH YOU, WADE?
I'M THREE THOUSAND BUCKS POORER FOR STARTERS...
YOU USED TO BE ABLE TO REGENERATE A WHOLE LIMB IN A MATTER OF MINUTES!
AND HAVE YOU NOTICED THAT YOU'VE BEEN DROPPING WEIGHT?
THIS IS SERIOUS! YOUR HEALING FACTOR'S OUT OF SYNCH, AND IF GUYS LIKE T-RAY SEE ANY SIGNS OF WEAKNESS FROM YOU --
CONSIDER YOUR BACK STABBED IN ADVANCE.

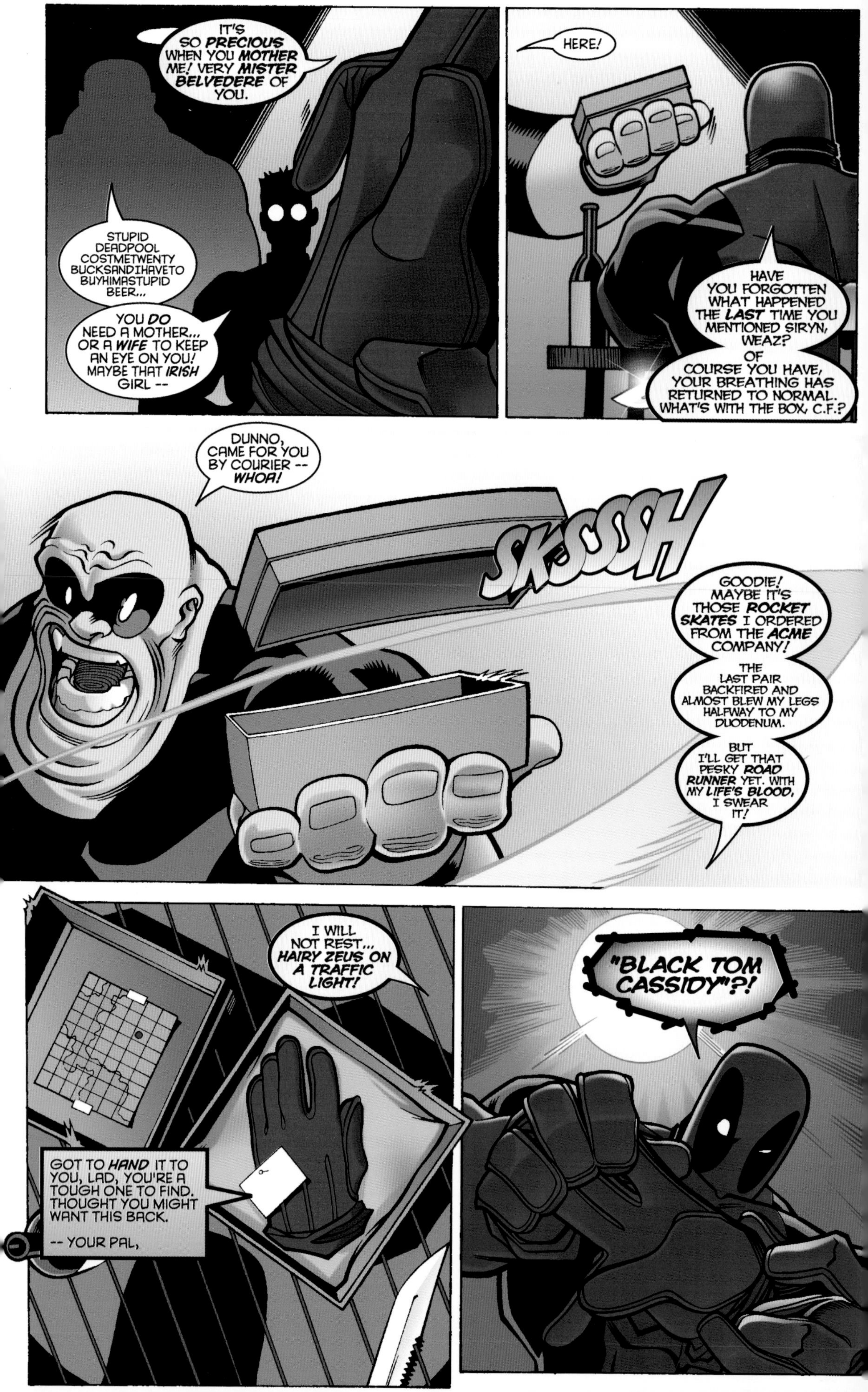
IT'S SO PRECIOUS WHEN YOU MOTHER ME! VERY MISTER BELVEDERE OF YOU.
STUPID DEADPOOL COSTMETWENTY BUCKSANDIHAVETO BUYHIMASTUPID BEER...
YOU DO NEED A MOTHER... OR A WIFE TO KEEP AN EYE ON YOU! MAYBE THAT IRISH GIRL --
HERE!
HAVE YOU FORGOTTEN WHAT HAPPENED THE LAST TIME YOU MENTIONED SIRYN, WEAZ?
OF COURSE YOU HAVE, YOUR BREATHING HAS RETURNED TO NORMAL. WHAT'S WITH THE BOX, C.F.?
DUNNO, CAME FOR YOU BY COURIER -- WHOA!
SKSSSH
GOODIE! MAYBE IT'S THOSE ROCKET SKATES I ORDERED FROM THE ACME COMPANY!
THE LAST PAIR BACKFIRED AND ALMOST BLEW MY LEGS HALFWAY TO MY DUODENUM.
BUT I'LL GET THAT PESKY ROAD RUNNER YET. WITH MY LIFE'S BLOOD, I SWEAR IT!
I WILL NOT REST... HAIRY ZEUS ON A TRAFFIC LIGHT!
GOT TO HAND IT TO YOU, LAD, YOU'RE A TOUGH ONE TO FIND. THOUGHT YOU MIGHT WANT THIS BACK.
-- YOUR PAL,
"BLACK TOM CASSIDY"?!

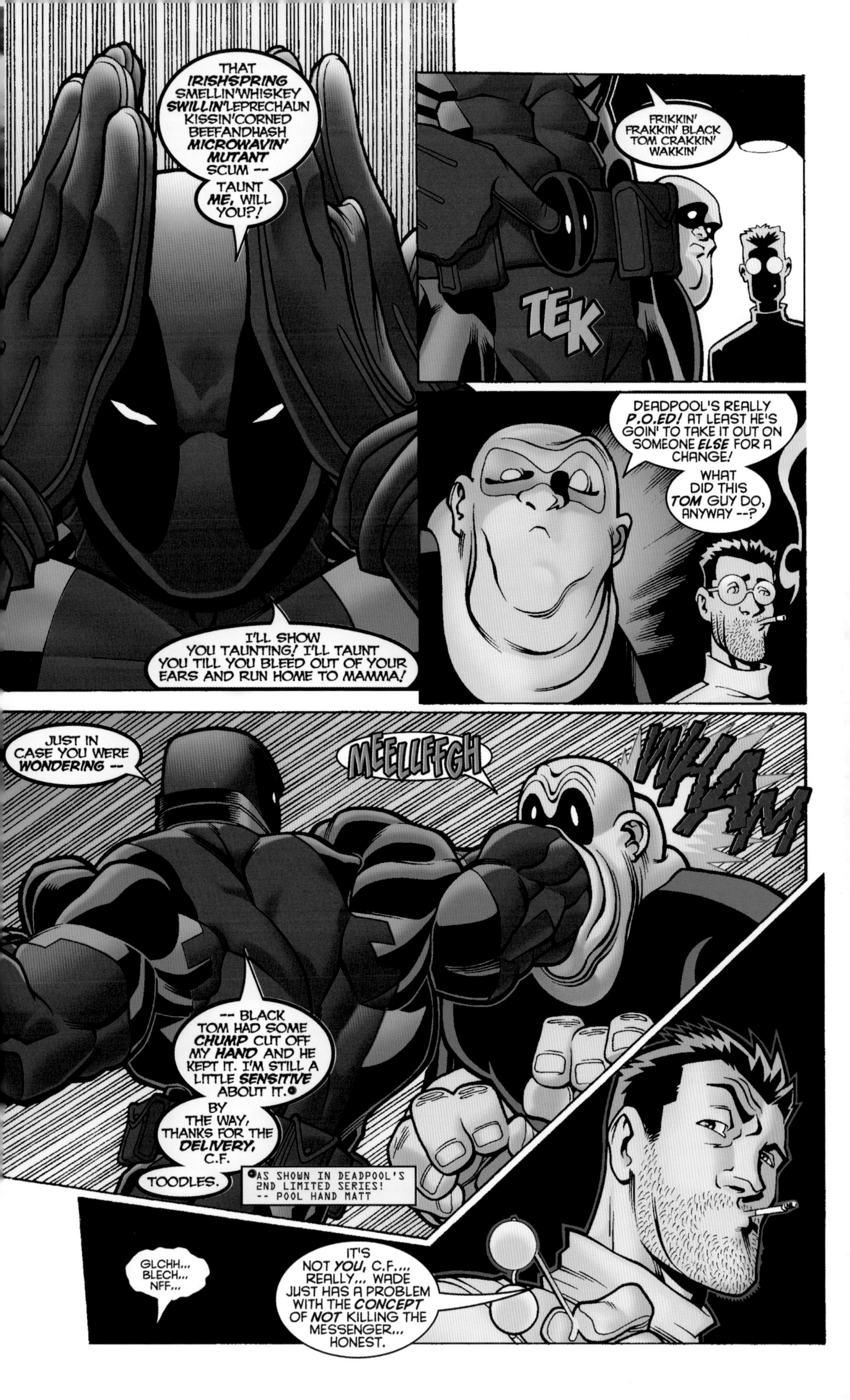
THAT IRISHSPRING SMELLIN'WHISKEY SWILLIN'LEPRECHAUN KISSIN'CORNED BEEFANDHASH MICROWAVIN' MUTANT SCUM --
TAUNT ME, WILL YOU?!
FRIKKIN' FRAKKIN' BLACK TOM CRAKKIN' WAKKIN'
I'LL SHOW YOU TAUNTING! I'LL TAUNT YOU TILL YOU BLEED OUT OF YOUR EARS AND RUN HOME TO MAMMA!
TEK
DEADPOOL'S REALLY P.O.ED! AT LEAST HE'S GOIN' TO TAKE IT OUT ON SOMEONE ELSE FOR A CHANGE!
WHAT DID THIS TOM GUY DO, ANYWAY --?
JUST IN CASE YOU WERE WONDERING --
MEELLFFGH
WHAM
-- BLACK TOM HAD SOME CHUMP CUT OFF MY HAND AND HE KEPT IT. I'M STILL A LITTLE SENSITIVE ABOUT IT.
BY THE WAY, THANKS FOR THE DELIVERY, C.F.
TOODLES.
AS SHOWN IN DEADPOOL'S 2ND LIMITED SERIES! -- POOL HAND MATT
GLCHH... BLECH... NFF...
IT'S NOT YOU, C.F.... REALLY... WADE JUST HAS A PROBLEM WITH THE CONCEPT OF NOT KILLING THE MESSENGER... HONEST.

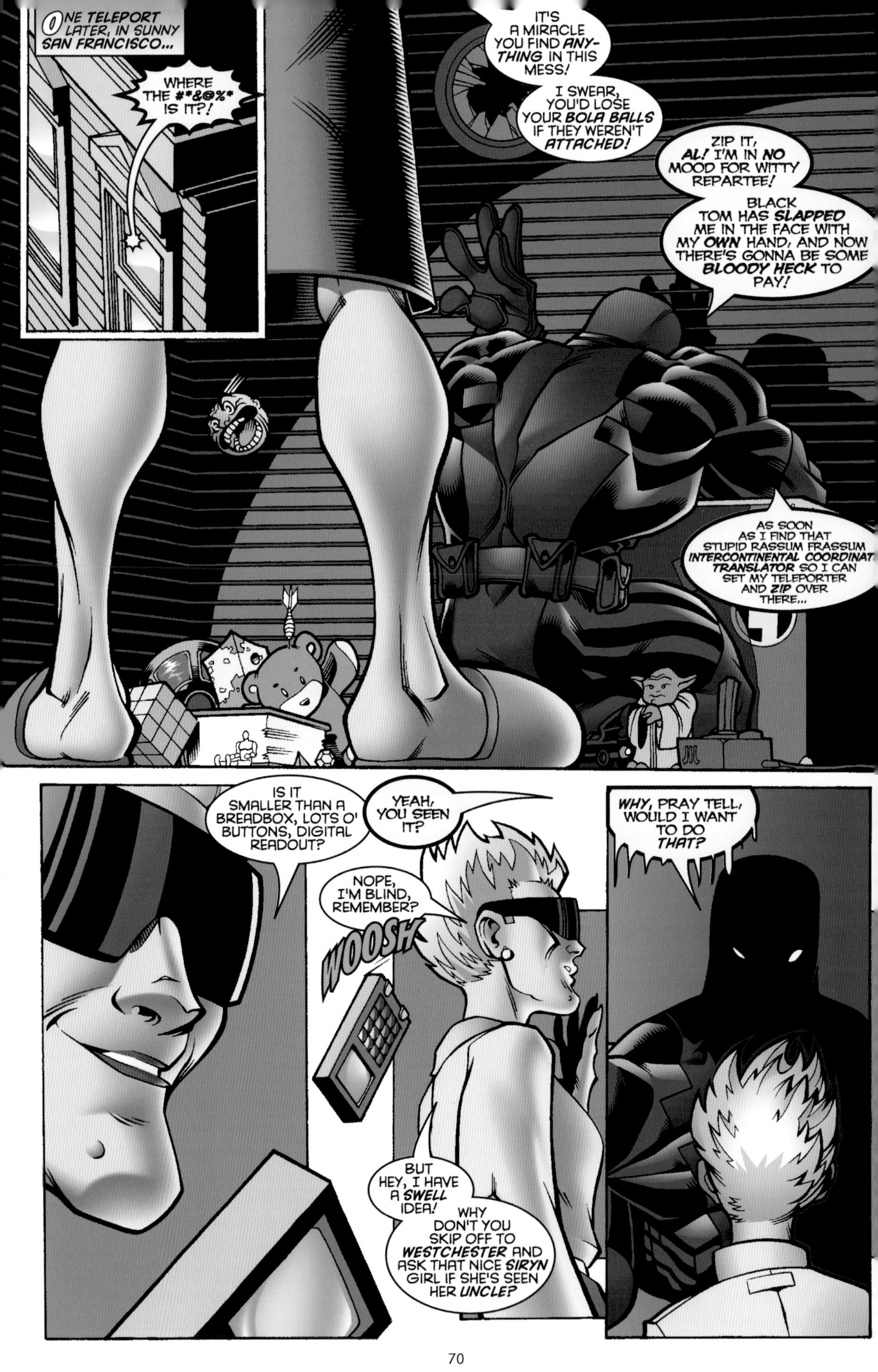
ONE TELEPORT LATER, IN SUNNY SAN FRANCISCO...
WHERE THE #*&@%* IS IT?!
IT'S A MIRACLE YOU FIND ANYTHING IN THIS MESS!
I SWEAR, YOU'D LOSE YOUR BOLA BALLS IF THEY WEREN'T ATTACHED!
ZIP IT, AL! I'M IN NO MOOD FOR WITTY REPARTEE!
BLACK TOM HAS SLAPPED ME IN THE FACE WITH MY OWN HAND, AND NOW THERE'S GONNA BE SOME BLOODY HECK TO PAY!
AS SOON AS I FIND THAT STUPID RASSUM FRASSUM INTERCONTINENTAL COORDINAT TRANSLATOR SO I CAN SET MY TELEPORTER AND ZIP OVER THERE...
IS IT SMALLER THAN A BREADBOX, LOTS O' BUTTONS, DIGITAL READOUT?
YEAH, YOU SEEN IT?
NOPE, I'M BLIND, REMEMBER?
WOOSH
BUT HEY, I HAVE A SWELL IDEA!
WHY DON'T YOU SKIP OFF TO WESTCHESTER AND ASK THAT NICE SIRYN GIRL IF SHE'S SEEN HER UNCLE?
WHY, PRAY TELL, WOULD I WANT TO DO THAT?

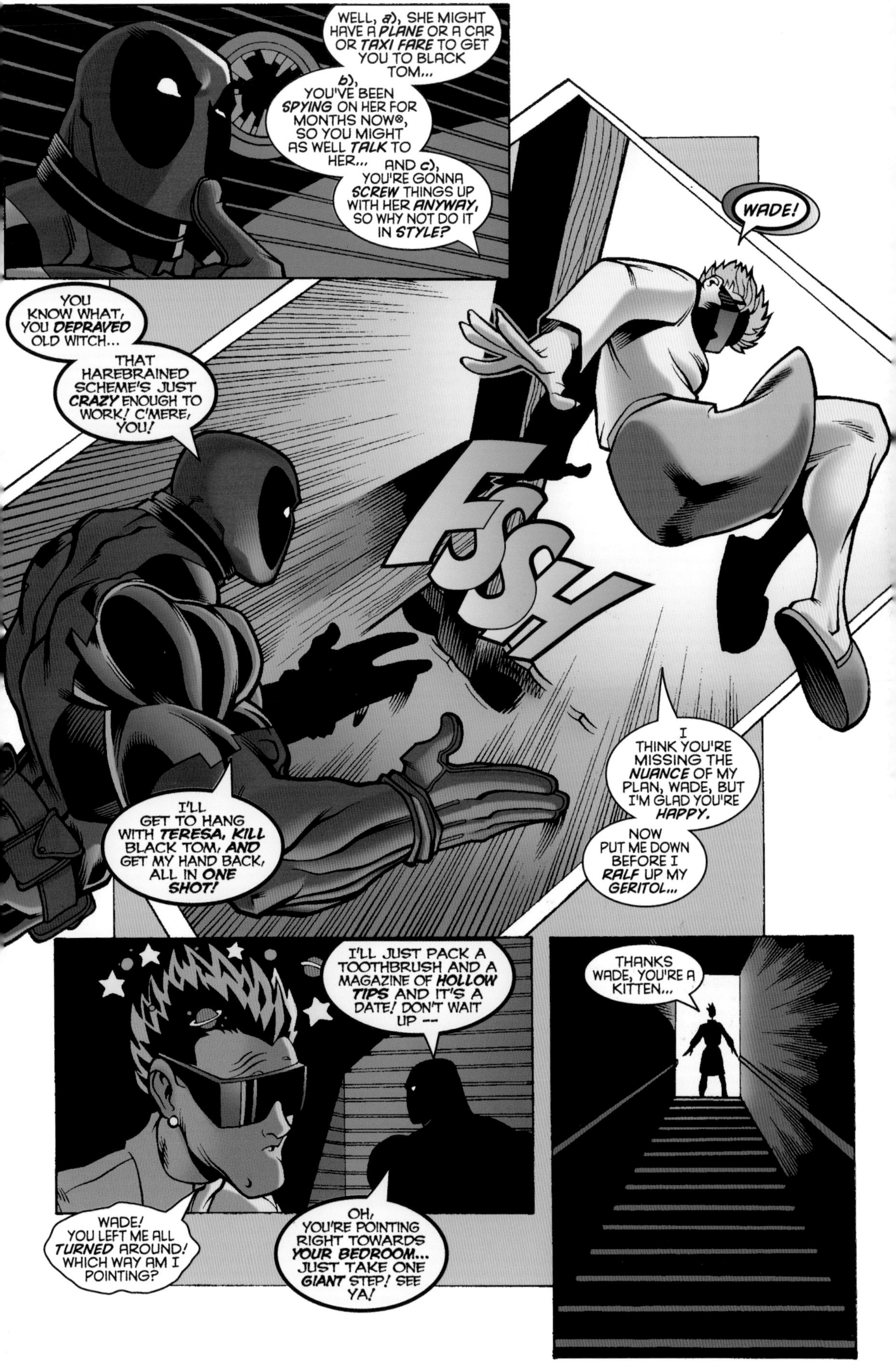
WELL, a), SHE MIGHT HAVE A PLANE OR A CAR OR TAXI FARE TO GET YOU TO BLACK TOM...
b), YOU'VE BEEN SPYING ON HER FOR MONTHS NOW®, SO YOU MIGHT AS WELL TALK TO HER...
AND c), YOU'RE GONNA SCREW THINGS UP WITH HER ANYWAY, SO WHY NOT DO IT IN STYLE?
WADE!
YOU KNOW WHAT, YOU DEPRAVED OLD WITCH...
THAT HAREBRAINED SCHEME'S JUST CRAZY ENOUGH TO WORK! C'MERE, YOU!
FSSH!
I'LL GET TO HANG WITH TERESA, KILL BLACK TOM, AND GET MY HAND BACK, ALL IN ONE SHOT!
I THINK YOU'RE MISSING THE NUANCE OF MY PLAN, WADE, BUT I'M GLAD YOU'RE HAPPY.
NOW PUT ME DOWN BEFORE I RALF UP MY GERITOL...
I'LL JUST PACK A TOOTHBRUSH AND A MAGAZINE OF HOLLOW TIPS AND IT'S A DATE! DON'T WAIT UP --
WADE! YOU LEFT ME ALL TURNED AROUND! WHICH WAY AM I POINTING?
OH, YOU'RE POINTING RIGHT TOWARDS YOUR BEDROOM... JUST TAKE ONE GIANT STEP! SEE YA!
THANKS WADE, YOU'RE A KITTEN...

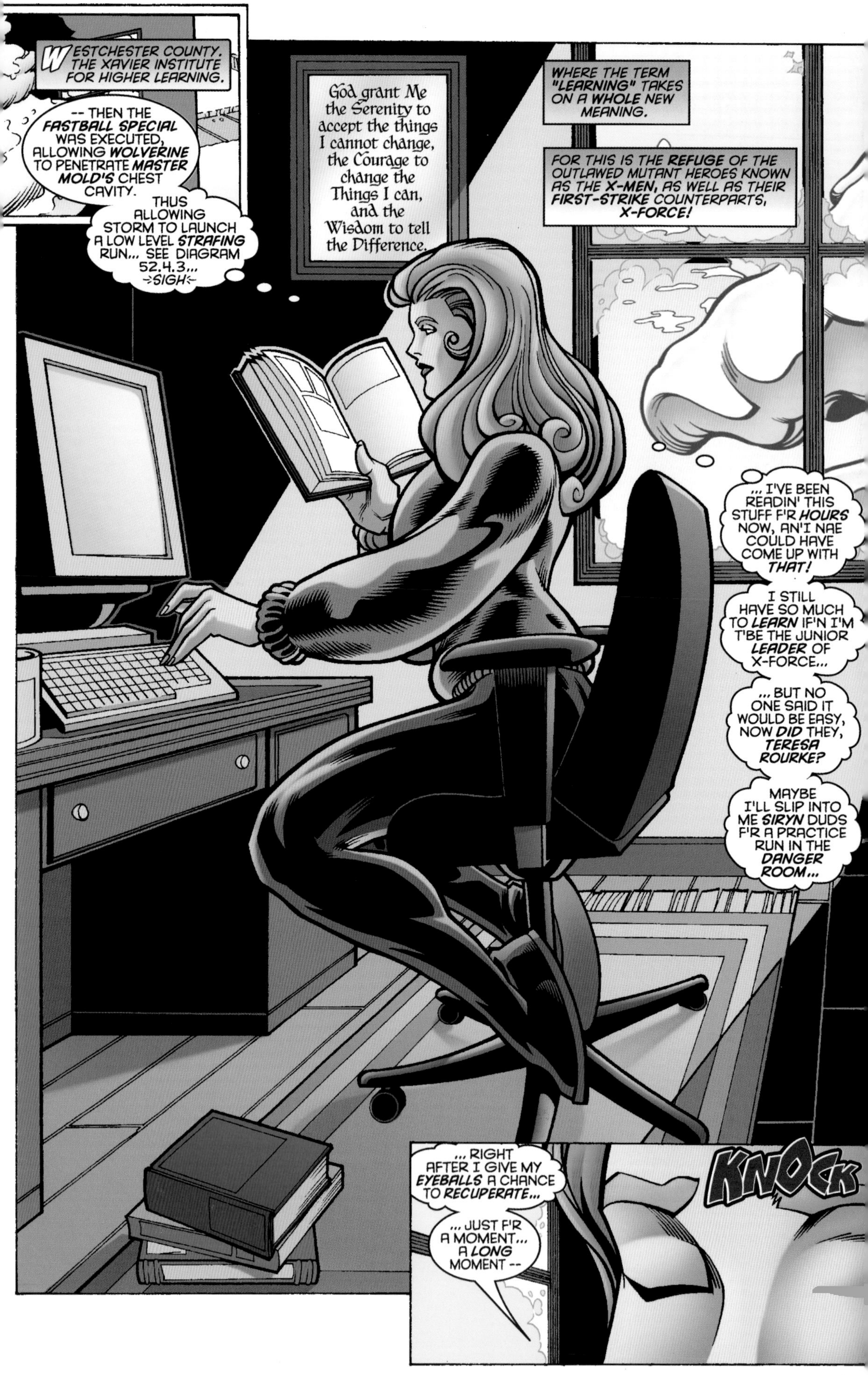
WESTCHESTER COUNTY. THE XAVIER INSTITUTE FOR HIGHER LEARNING.
-- THEN THE FASTBALL SPECIAL WAS EXECUTED, ALLOWING WOLVERINE TO PENETRATE MASTER MOLD'S CHEST CAVITY.
THUS ALLOWING STORM TO LAUNCH A LOW LEVEL STRAFING RUN... SEE DIAGRAM 52.4.3... ⇒SIGH⇐
God grant Me the Serenity to accept the things I cannot change, the Courage to change the Things I can, and the Wisdom to tell the Difference.
WHERE THE TERM "LEARNING" TAKES ON A WHOLE NEW MEANING.
FOR THIS IS THE REFUGE OF THE OUTLAWED MUTANT HEROES KNOWN AS THE X-MEN, AS WELL AS THEIR FIRST-STRIKE COUNTERPARTS, X-FORCE!
... I'VE BEEN READIN' THIS STUFF F'R HOURS NOW, AN'I NAE COULD HAVE COME UP WITH THAT!
I STILL HAVE SO MUCH TO LEARN IF'N I'M T'BE THE JUNIOR LEADER OF X-FORCE...
... BUT NO ONE SAID IT WOULD BE EASY, NOW DID THEY, TERESA ROURKE?
MAYBE I'LL SLIP INTO ME SIRYN DUDS F'R A PRACTICE RUN IN THE DANGER ROOM...
... RIGHT AFTER I GIVE MY EYEBALLS A CHANCE TO RECUPERATE...
... JUST F'R A MOMENT... A LONG MOMENT --
KNOCK

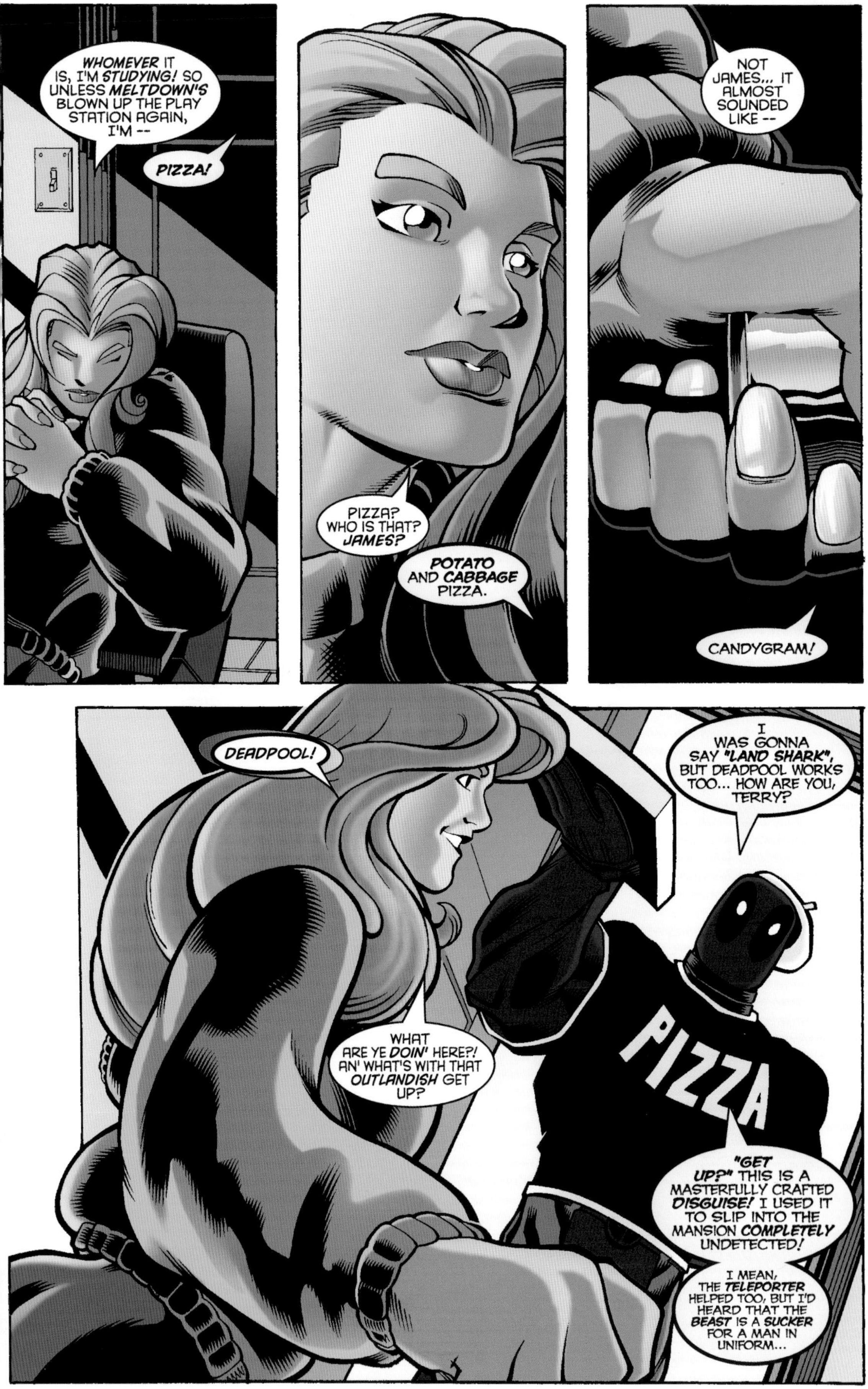
WHOMEVER IT IS, I'M STUDYING! SO UNLESS MELTDOWN'S BLOWN UP THE PLAY STATION AGAIN, I'M --
PIZZA!
PIZZA? WHO IS THAT? JAMES?
POTATO AND CABBAGE PIZZA.
NOT JAMES... IT ALMOST SOUNDED LIKE --
CANDYGRAM!
DEADPOOL!
I WAS GONNA SAY "LAND SHARK", BUT DEADPOOL WORKS TOO... HOW ARE YOU, TERRY?
WHAT ARE YE DOIN' HERE?! AN' WHAT'S WITH THAT OUTLANDISH GET UP?
PIZZA
"GET UP?" THIS IS A MASTERFULLY CRAFTED DISGUISE! I USED IT TO SLIP INTO THE MANSION COMPLETELY UNDETECTED!
I MEAN, THE TELEPORTER HELPED TOO, BUT I'D HEARD THAT THE BEAST IS A SUCKER FOR A MAN IN UNIFORM...

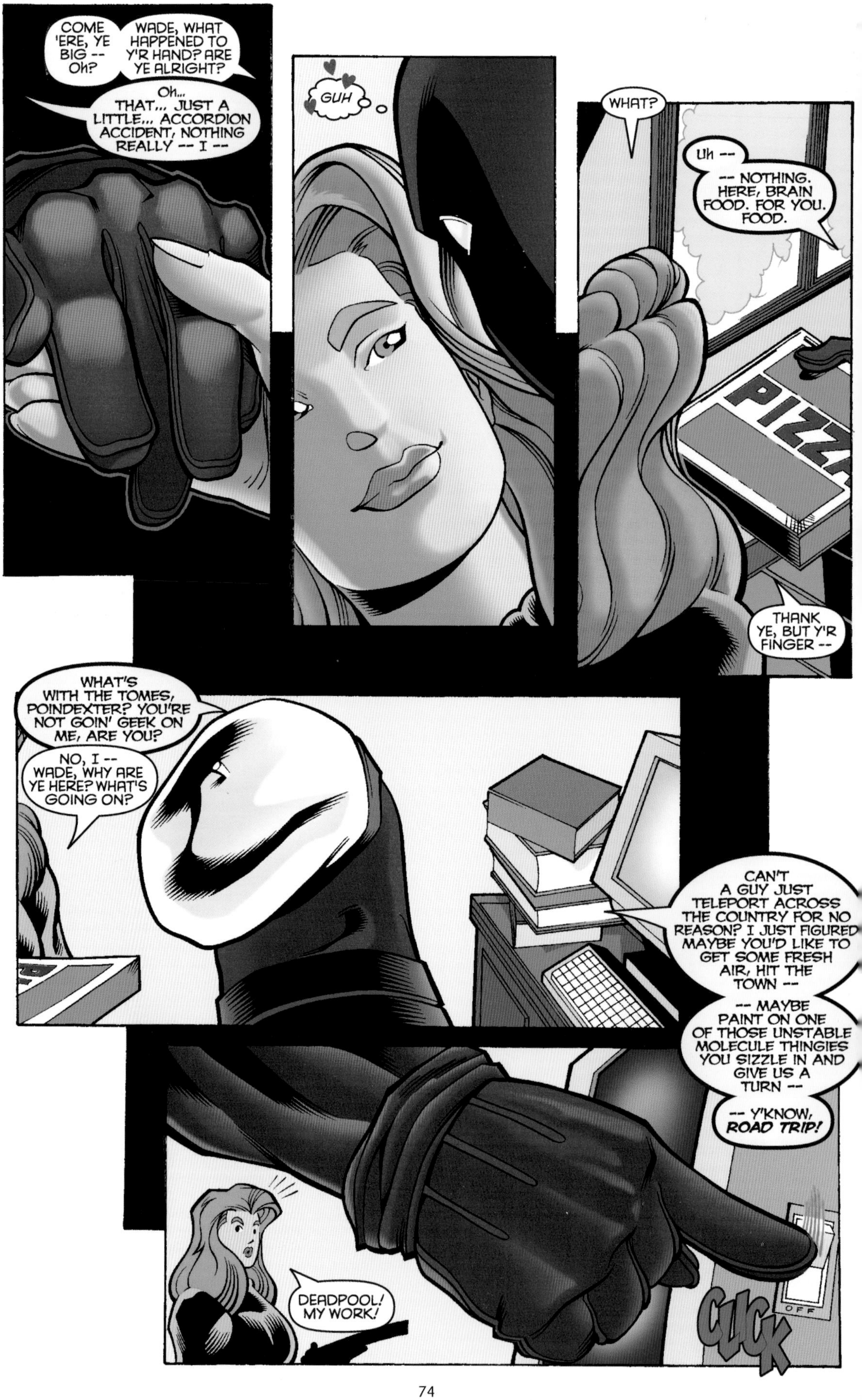
COME 'ERE, YE BIG -- Oh?
WADE, WHAT HAPPENED TO Y'R HAND? ARE YE ALRIGHT?
Oh... THAT... JUST A LITTLE... ACCORDION ACCIDENT, NOTHING REALLY -- I --
GUH
WHAT?
Uh --
-- NOTHING. HERE, BRAIN FOOD. FOR YOU. FOOD.
PIZZ
THANK YE, BUT Y'R FINGER --
WHAT'S WITH THE TOMES, POINDEXTER? YOU'RE NOT GOIN' GEEK ON ME, ARE YOU?
NO, I -- WADE, WHY ARE YE HERE? WHAT'S GOING ON?
CAN'T A GUY JUST TELEPORT ACROSS THE COUNTRY FOR NO REASON? I JUST FIGURED MAYBE YOU'D LIKE TO GET SOME FRESH AIR, HIT THE TOWN --
-- MAYBE PAINT ON ONE OF THOSE UNSTABLE MOLECULE THINGIES YOU SIZZLE IN AND GIVE US A TURN --
-- Y'KNOW, ROAD TRIP!
DEADPOOL! MY WORK!
OFF
CLICK

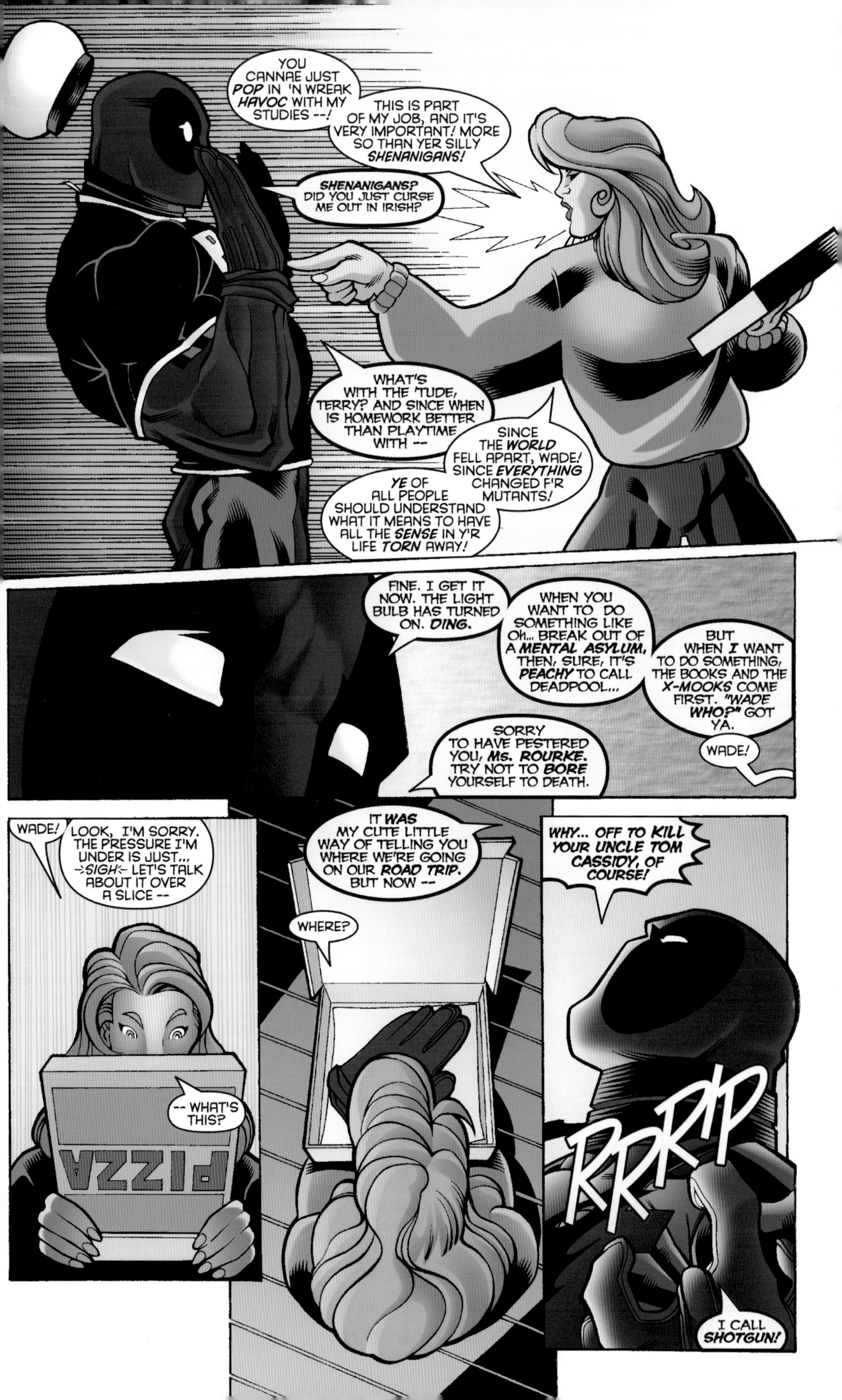
YOU CANNAE JUST POP IN 'N WREAK HAVOC WITH MY STUDIES --!
THIS IS PART OF MY JOB, AND IT'S VERY IMPORTANT! MORE SO THAN YER SILLY SHENANIGANS!
SHENANIGANS? DID YOU JUST CURSE ME OUT IN IRISH?
WHAT'S WITH THE 'TUDE, TERRY? AND SINCE WHEN IS HOMEWORK BETTER THAN PLAYTIME WITH --
SINCE THE WORLD FELL APART, WADE! SINCE EVERYTHING CHANGED F'R MUTANTS!
YE OF ALL PEOPLE SHOULD UNDERSTAND WHAT IT MEANS TO HAVE ALL THE SENSE IN Y'R LIFE TORN AWAY!
FINE. I GET IT NOW. THE LIGHT BULB HAS TURNED ON. DING.
WHEN YOU WANT TO DO SOMETHING LIKE Oh... BREAK OUT OF A MENTAL ASYLUM, THEN, SURE, IT'S PEACHY TO CALL DEADPOOL...
BUT WHEN I WANT TO DO SOMETHING, THE BOOKS AND THE X-MOOKS COME FIRST. "WADE WHO?" GOT YA.
SORRY TO HAVE PESTERED YOU, Ms. ROURKE. TRY NOT TO BORE YOURSELF TO DEATH.
WADE!
WADE!
LOOK, I'M SORRY. THE PRESSURE I'M UNDER IS JUST... -SIGH- LET'S TALK ABOUT IT OVER A SLICE --
-- WHAT'S THIS?
PIZZA
IT WAS MY CUTE LITTLE WAY OF TELLING YOU WHERE WE'RE GOING ON OUR ROAD TRIP. BUT NOW --
WHERE?
WHY... OFF TO KILL YOUR UNCLE TOM CASSIDY, OF COURSE!
RRRIP
I CALL SHOTGUN!

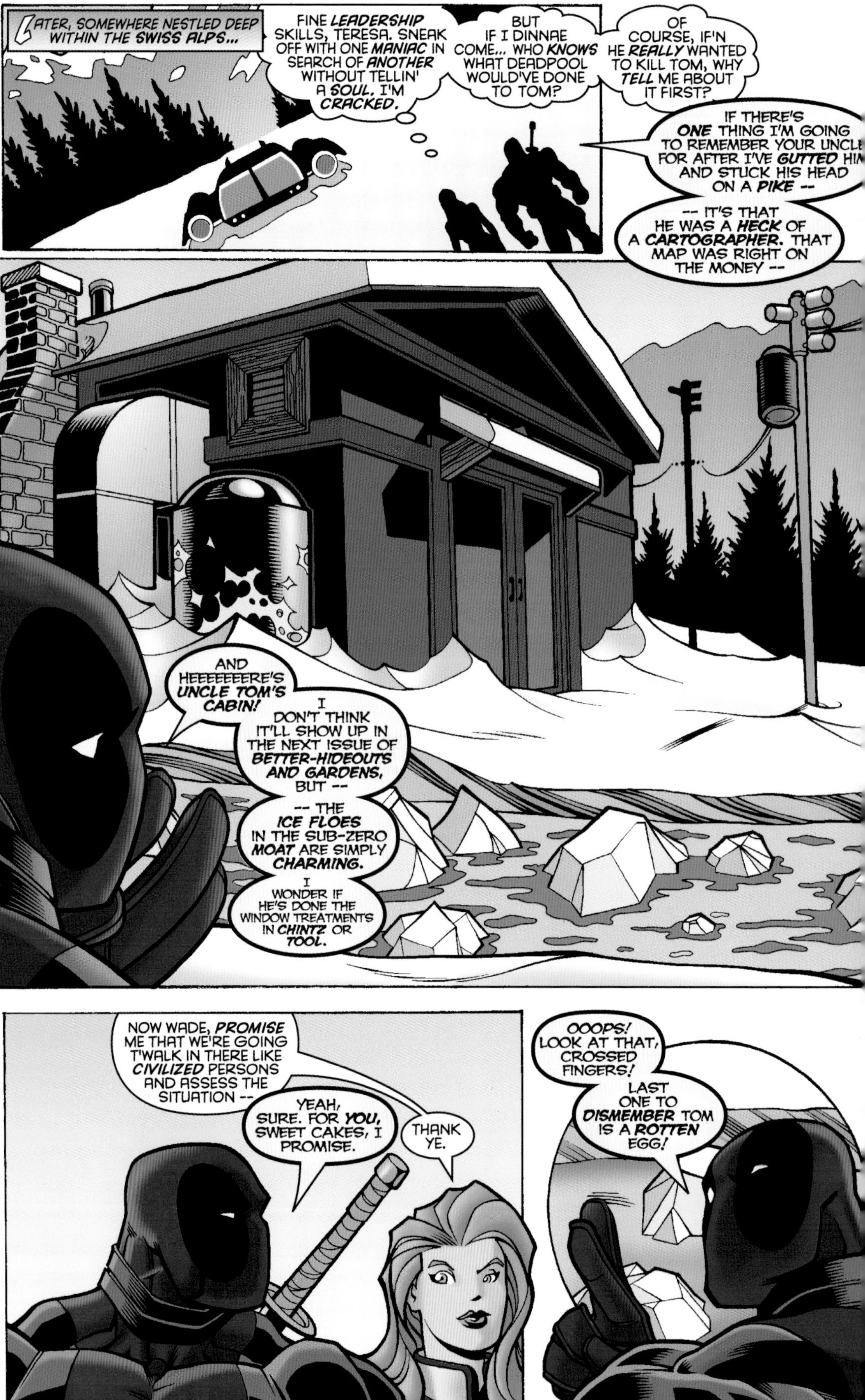
LATER, SOMEWHERE NESTLED DEEP WITHIN THE SWISS ALPS...
FINE LEADERSHIP SKILLS, TERESA. SNEAK OFF WITH ONE MANIAC IN SEARCH OF ANOTHER WITHOUT TELLIN' A SOUL. I'M CRACKED.
BUT IF I DINNAE COME... WHO KNOWS WHAT DEADPOOL WOULD'VE DONE TO TOM?
OF COURSE, IF'N HE REALLY WANTED TO KILL TOM, WHY TELL ME ABOUT IT FIRST?
IF THERE'S ONE THING I'M GOING TO REMEMBER YOUR UNCLE FOR AFTER I'VE GUTTED HIM AND STUCK HIS HEAD ON A PIKE --
-- IT'S THAT HE WAS A HECK OF A CARTOGRAPHER. THAT MAP WAS RIGHT ON THE MONEY --
AND HEEEEEEERE'S UNCLE TOM'S CABIN!
I DON'T THINK IT'LL SHOW UP IN THE NEXT ISSUE OF BETTER-HIDEOUTS AND GARDENS, BUT --
-- THE ICE FLOES IN THE SUB-ZERO MOAT ARE SIMPLY CHARMING.
I WONDER IF HE'S DONE THE WINDOW TREATMENTS IN CHINTZ OR TOOL.
NOW WADE, PROMISE ME THAT WE'RE GOING T'WALK IN THERE LIKE CIVILIZED PERSONS AND ASSESS THE SITUATION --
YEAH, SURE. FOR YOU, SWEET CAKES, I PROMISE.
THANK YE.
OOOPS! LOOK AT THAT, CROSSED FINGERS!
LAST ONE TO DISMEMBER TOM IS A ROTTEN EGG!

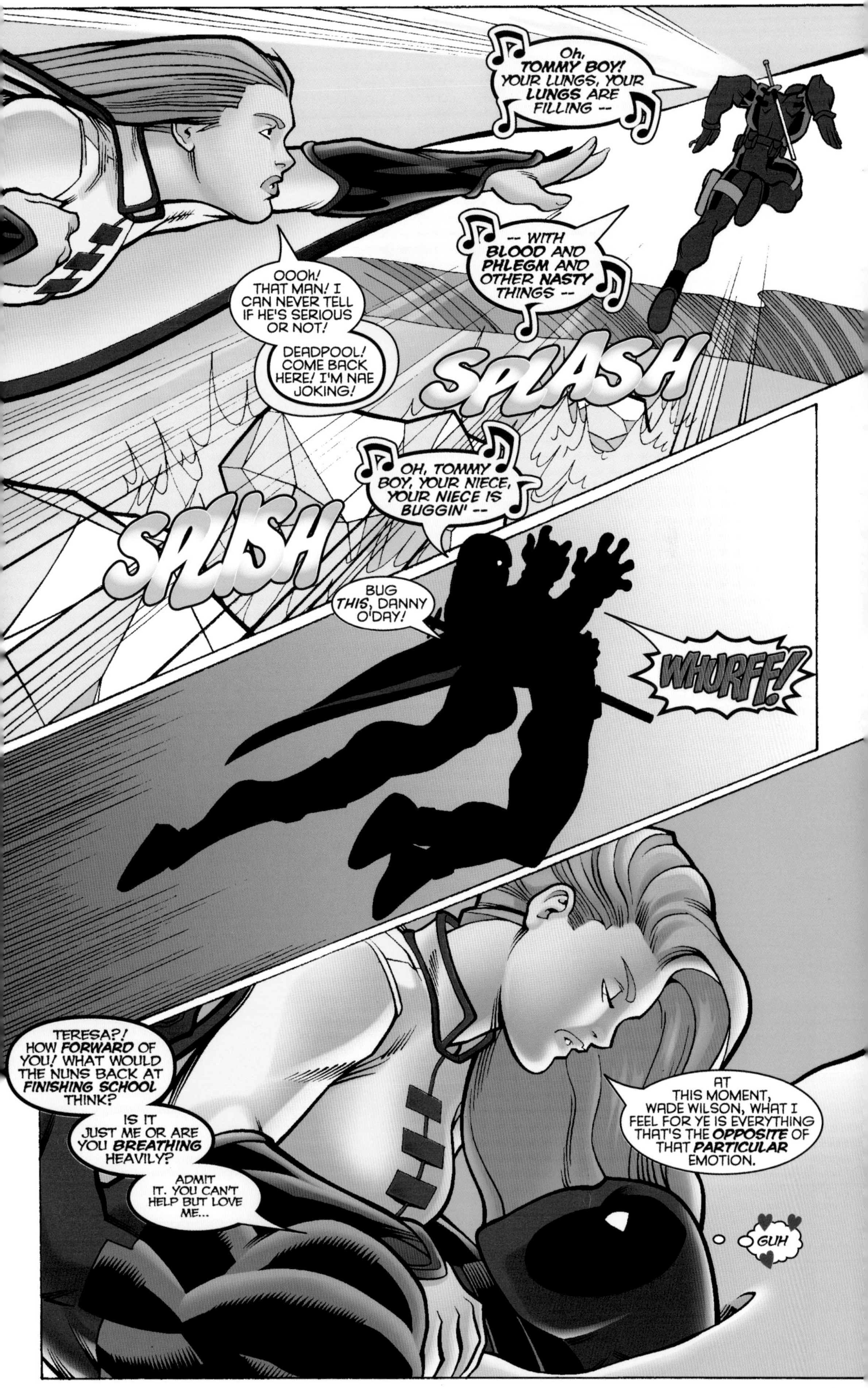

Oh, TOMMY BOY! YOUR LUNGS, YOUR LUNGS ARE FILLING --
-- WITH BLOOD AND PHLEGM AND OTHER NASTY THINGS --
OOOh! THAT MAN! I CAN NEVER TELL IF HE'S SERIOUS OR NOT!
DEADPOOL! COME BACK HERE! I'M NAE JOKING!
SPLASH
OH, TOMMY BOY, YOUR NIECE, YOUR NIECE IS BUGGIN' --
SPLISH
BUG THIS, DANNY O'DAY!
WHURFF!
TERESA?! HOW FORWARD OF YOU! WHAT WOULD THE NUNS BACK AT FINISHING SCHOOL THINK?
IS IT JUST ME OR ARE YOU BREATHING HEAVILY?
ADMIT IT. YOU CAN'T HELP BUT LOVE ME...
AT THIS MOMENT, WADE WILSON, WHAT I FEEL FOR YE IS EVERYTHING THAT'S THE OPPOSITE OF THAT PARTICULAR EMOTION.
GUH

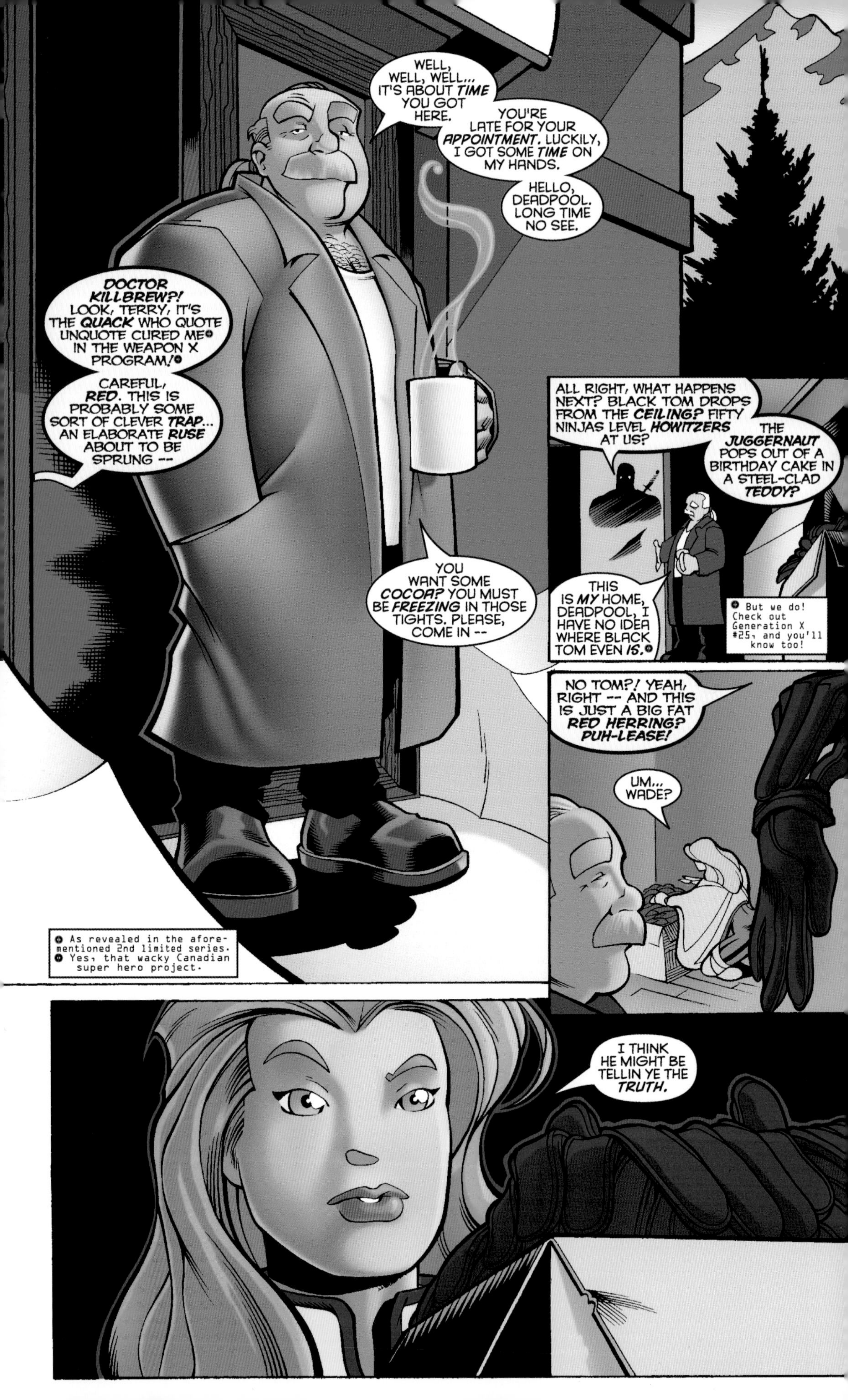

WELL, WELL, WELL... IT'S ABOUT TIME YOU GOT HERE.
YOU'RE LATE FOR YOUR APPOINTMENT. LUCKILY, I GOT SOME TIME ON MY HANDS.
HELLO, DEADPOOL. LONG TIME NO SEE.
DOCTOR KILLBREW?! LOOK, TERRY, IT'S THE QUACK WHO QUOTE UNQUOTE CURED ME IN THE WEAPON X PROGRAM!
CAREFUL, RED. THIS IS PROBABLY SOME SORT OF CLEVER TRAP... AN ELABORATE RUSE ABOUT TO BE SPRUNG --
YOU WANT SOME COCOA? YOU MUST BE FREEZING IN THOSE TIGHTS. PLEASE, COME IN --
As revealed in the afore-mentioned 2nd limited series.
Yes, that wacky Canadian super hero project.
ALL RIGHT, WHAT HAPPENS NEXT? BLACK TOM DROPS FROM THE CEILING? FIFTY NINJAS LEVEL HOWITZERS AT US?
THE JUGGERNAUT POPS OUT OF A BIRTHDAY CAKE IN A STEEL-CLAD TEDDY?
THIS IS MY HOME, DEADPOOL, I HAVE NO IDEA WHERE BLACK TOM EVEN IS.
But we do! Check out Generation X #25, and you'll know too!
NO TOM?! YEAH, RIGHT -- AND THIS IS JUST A BIG FAT RED HERRING? PUH-LEASE!
UM... WADE?
I THINK HE MIGHT BE TELLIN YE THE TRUTH.

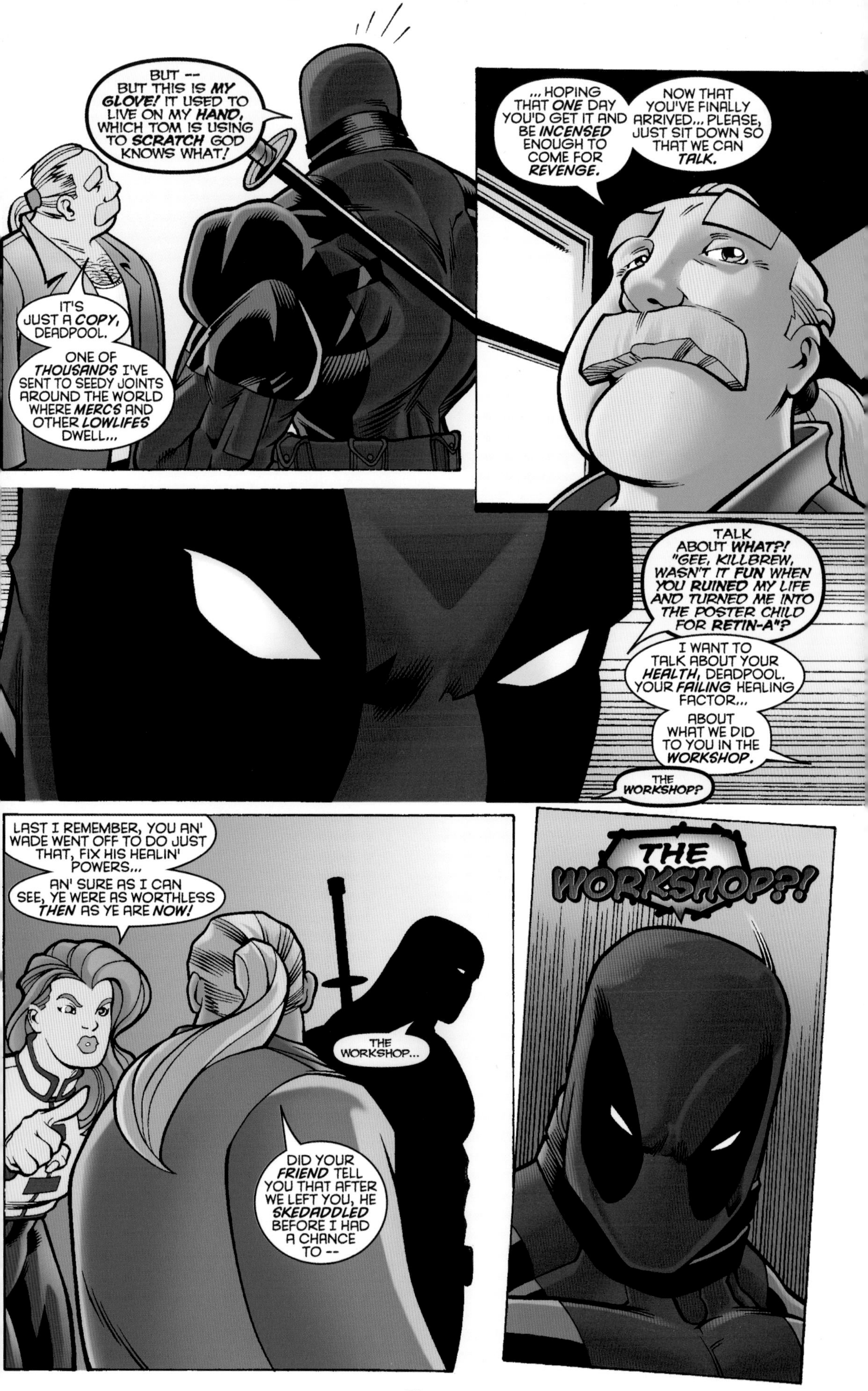
BUT -- BUT THIS IS MY GLOVE! IT USED TO LIVE ON MY HAND, WHICH TOM IS USING TO SCRATCH GOD KNOWS WHAT!
IT'S JUST A COPY, DEADPOOL.
ONE OF THOUSANDS I'VE SENT TO SEEDY JOINTS AROUND THE WORLD WHERE MERCS AND OTHER LOWLIFES DWELL...
...HOPING THAT ONE DAY YOU'D GET IT AND BE INCENSED ENOUGH TO COME FOR REVENGE.
NOW THAT YOU'VE FINALLY ARRIVED... PLEASE, JUST SIT DOWN SO THAT WE CAN TALK.
TALK ABOUT WHAT?! "GEE, KILLBREW, WASN'T IT FUN WHEN YOU RUINED MY LIFE AND TURNED ME INTO THE POSTER CHILD FOR RETIN-A"?
I WANT TO TALK ABOUT YOUR HEALTH, DEADPOOL. YOUR FAILING HEALING FACTOR...
ABOUT WHAT WE DID TO YOU IN THE WORKSHOP.
THE WORKSHOP?
LAST I REMEMBER, YOU AN' WADE WENT OFF TO DO JUST THAT, FIX HIS HEALIN' POWERS...
AN' SURE AS I CAN SEE, YE WERE AS WORTHLESS THEN AS YE ARE NOW!
THE WORKSHOP...
DID YOUR FRIEND TELL YOU THAT AFTER WE LEFT YOU, HE SKEDADDLED BEFORE I HAD A CHANCE TO --
THE WORKSHOP?!

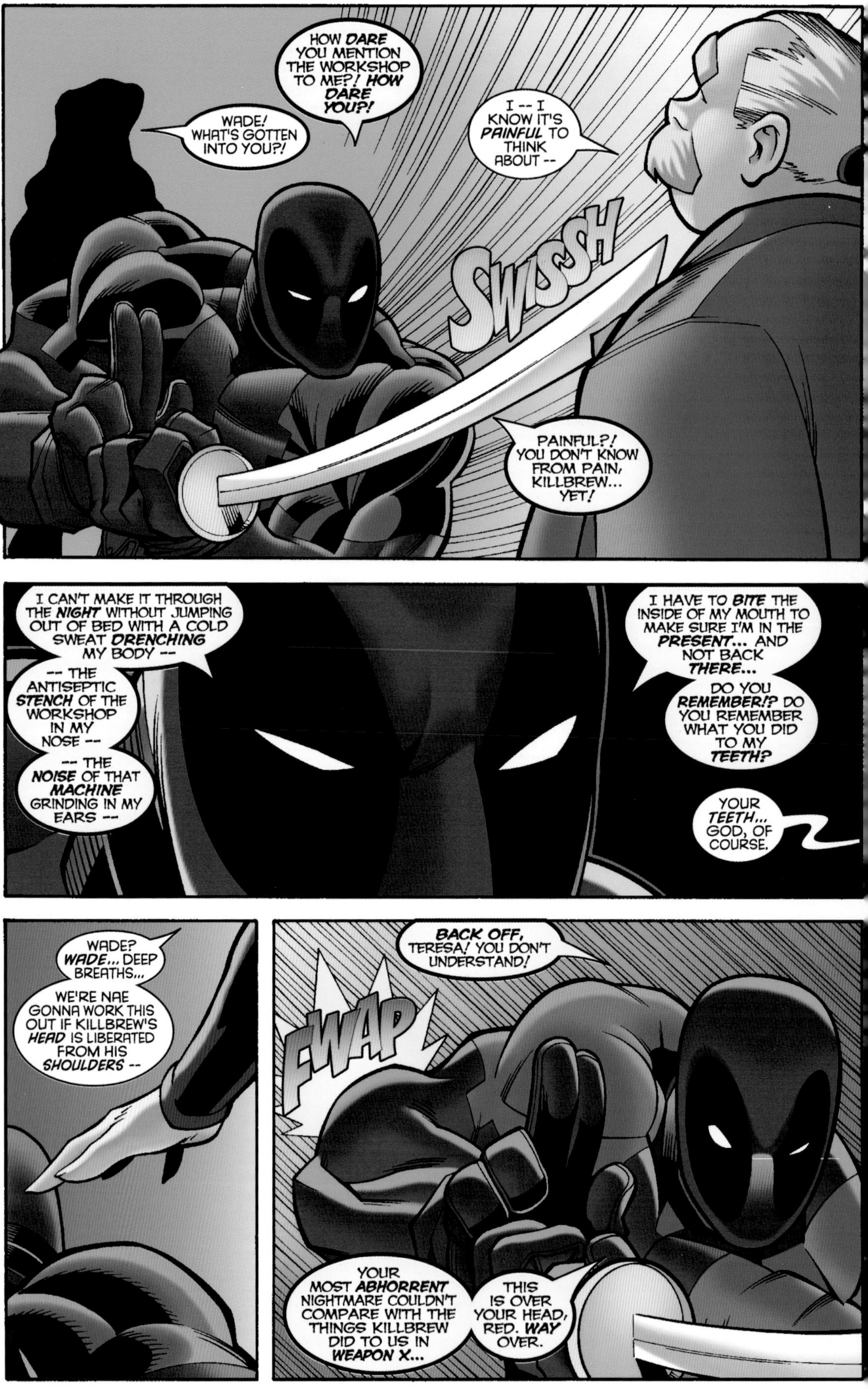
WADE! WHAT'S GOTTEN INTO YOU?!
HOW DARE YOU MENTION THE WORKSHOP TO ME?! HOW DARE YOU?!
I -- I KNOW IT'S PAINFUL TO THINK ABOUT --
SWISSH
PAINFUL?! YOU DON'T KNOW FROM PAIN, KILLBREW... YET!
I CAN'T MAKE IT THROUGH THE NIGHT WITHOUT JUMPING OUT OF BED WITH A COLD SWEAT DRENCHING MY BODY --
-- THE ANTISEPTIC STENCH OF THE WORKSHOP IN MY NOSE --
-- THE NOISE OF THAT MACHINE GRINDING IN MY EARS --
I HAVE TO BITE THE INSIDE OF MY MOUTH TO MAKE SURE I'M IN THE PRESENT... AND NOT BACK THERE...
DO YOU REMEMBER!? DO YOU REMEMBER WHAT YOU DID TO MY TEETH?
YOUR TEETH... GOD, OF COURSE.
WADE? WADE... DEEP BREATHS...
WE'RE NAE GONNA WORK THIS OUT IF KILLBREW'S HEAD IS LIBERATED FROM HIS SHOULDERS --
BACK OFF, TERESA! YOU DON'T UNDERSTAND!
FWAP
YOUR MOST ABHORRENT NIGHTMARE COULDN'T COMPARE WITH THE THINGS KILLBREW DID TO US IN WEAPON X...
THIS IS OVER YOUR HEAD, RED. WAY OVER.

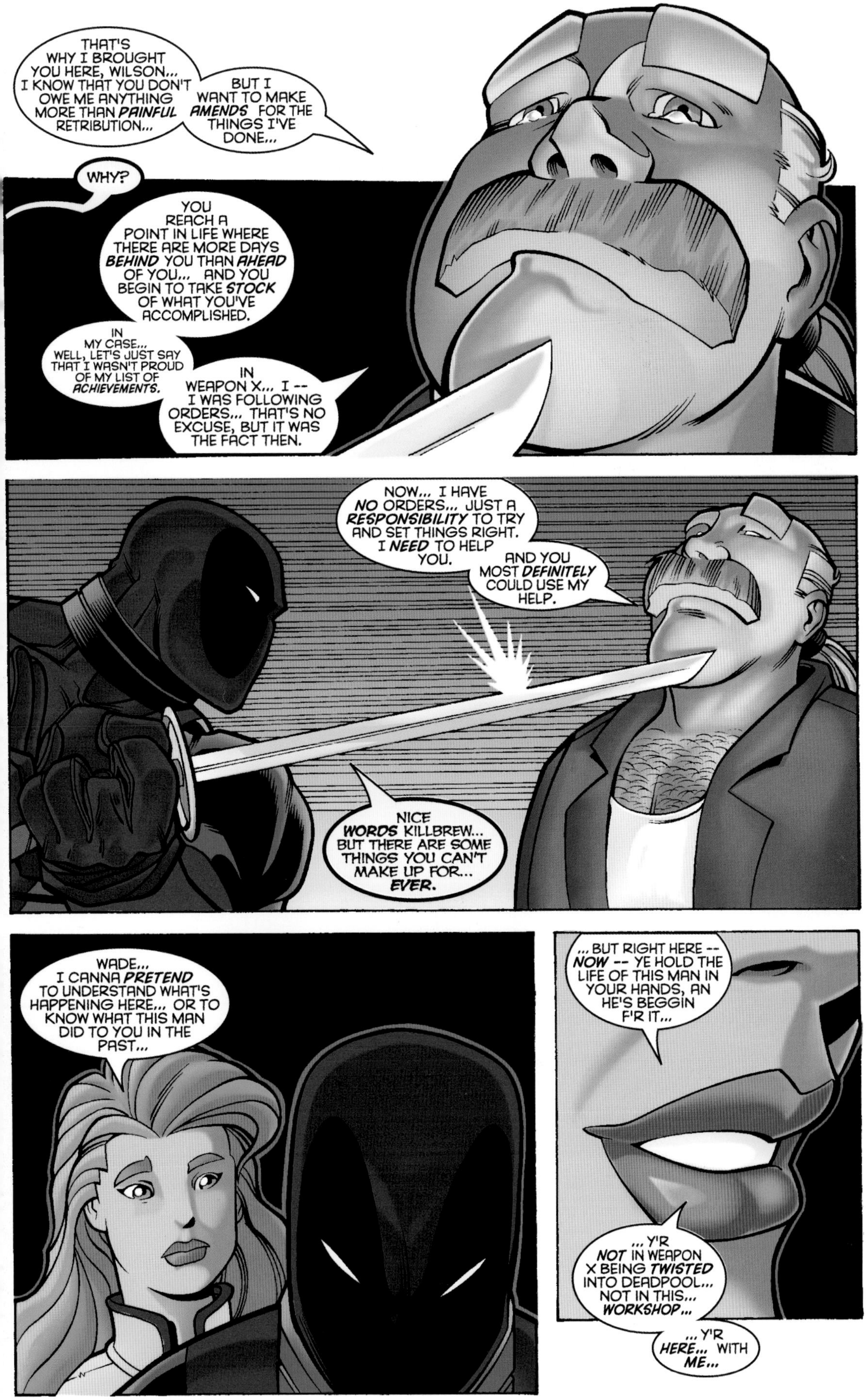
THAT'S WHY I BROUGHT YOU HERE, WILSON... I KNOW THAT YOU DON'T OWE ME ANYTHING MORE THAN PAINFUL RETRIBUTION...
BUT I WANT TO MAKE AMENDS FOR THE THINGS I'VE DONE...
WHY?
YOU REACH A POINT IN LIFE WHERE THERE ARE MORE DAYS BEHIND YOU THAN AHEAD OF YOU... AND YOU BEGIN TO TAKE STOCK OF WHAT YOU'VE ACCOMPLISHED.
IN MY CASE... WELL, LET'S JUST SAY THAT I WASN'T PROUD OF MY LIST OF ACHIEVEMENTS.
IN WEAPON X... I -- I WAS FOLLOWING ORDERS... THAT'S NO EXCUSE, BUT IT WAS THE FACT THEN.
NOW... I HAVE NO ORDERS... JUST A RESPONSIBILITY TO TRY AND SET THINGS RIGHT. I NEED TO HELP YOU.
AND YOU MOST DEFINITELY COULD USE MY HELP.
NICE WORDS KILLBREW... BUT THERE ARE SOME THINGS YOU CAN'T MAKE UP FOR... EVER.
WADE... I CANNA PRETEND TO UNDERSTAND WHAT'S HAPPENING HERE... OR TO KNOW WHAT THIS MAN DID TO YOU IN THE PAST...
... BUT RIGHT HERE -- NOW -- YE HOLD THE LIFE OF THIS MAN IN YOUR HANDS, AN HE'S BEGGIN F'R IT...
... Y'R NOT IN WEAPON X BEING TWISTED INTO DEADPOOL... NOT IN THIS... WORKSHOP...
... Y'R HERE... WITH ME...

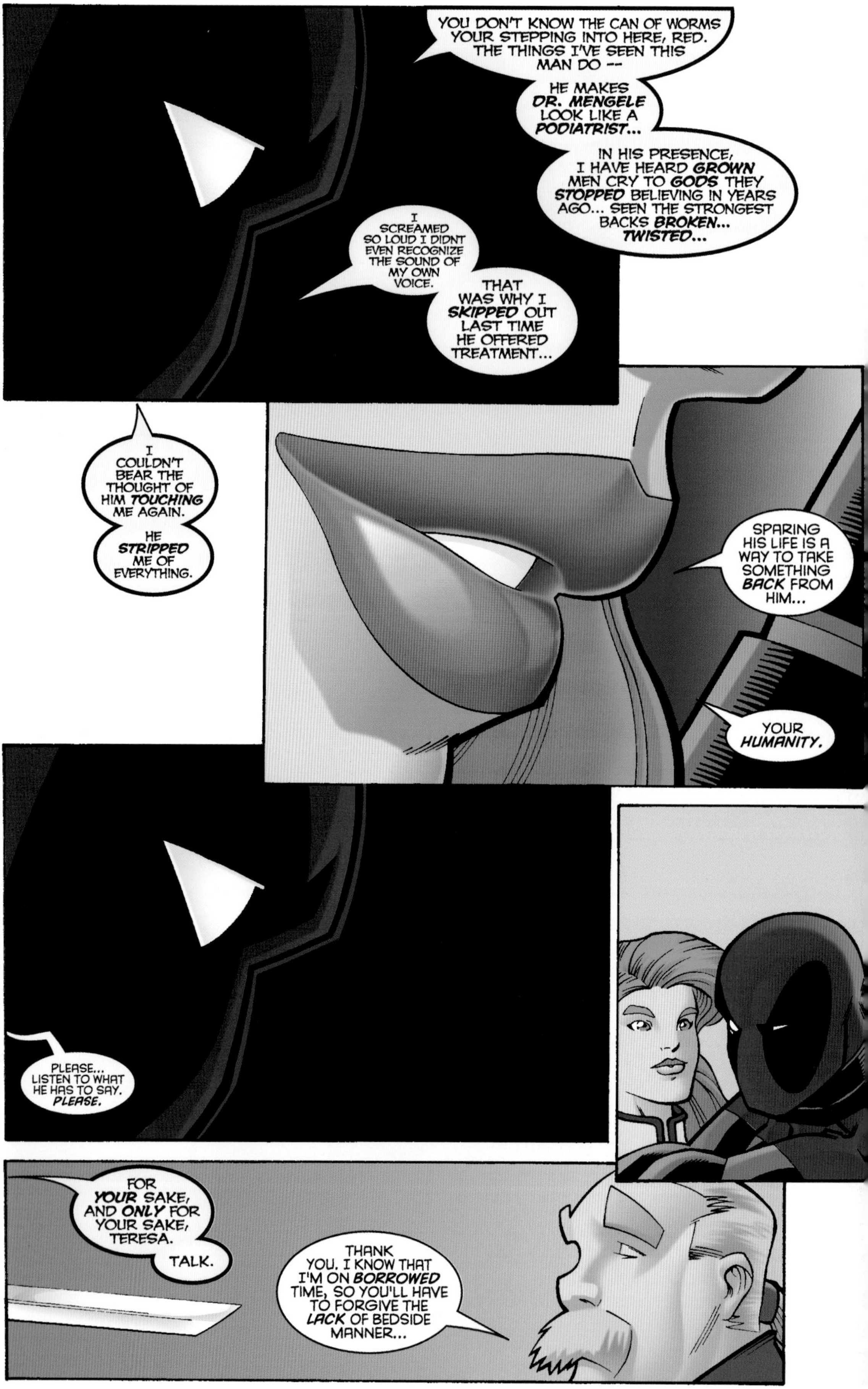
YOU DON'T KNOW THE CAN OF WORMS YOUR STEPPING INTO HERE, RED. THE THINGS I'VE SEEN THIS MAN DO --
HE MAKES DR. MENGELE LOOK LIKE A PODIATRIST...
IN HIS PRESENCE, I HAVE HEARD GROWN MEN CRY TO GODS THEY STOPPED BELIEVING IN YEARS AGO... SEEN THE STRONGEST BACKS BROKEN... TWISTED...
I SCREAMED SO LOUD I DIDNT EVEN RECOGNIZE THE SOUND OF MY OWN VOICE.
THAT WAS WHY I SKIPPED OUT LAST TIME HE OFFERED TREATMENT...
I COULDN'T BEAR THE THOUGHT OF HIM TOUCHING ME AGAIN.
HE STRIPPED ME OF EVERYTHING.
SPARING HIS LIFE IS A WAY TO TAKE SOMETHING BACK FROM HIM...
YOUR HUMANITY.
PLEASE... LISTEN TO WHAT HE HAS TO SAY. PLEASE.
FOR YOUR SAKE, AND ONLY FOR YOUR SAKE, TERESA.
TALK.
THANK YOU. I KNOW THAT I'M ON BORROWED TIME, SO YOU'LL HAVE TO FORGIVE THE LACK OF BEDSIDE MANNER...

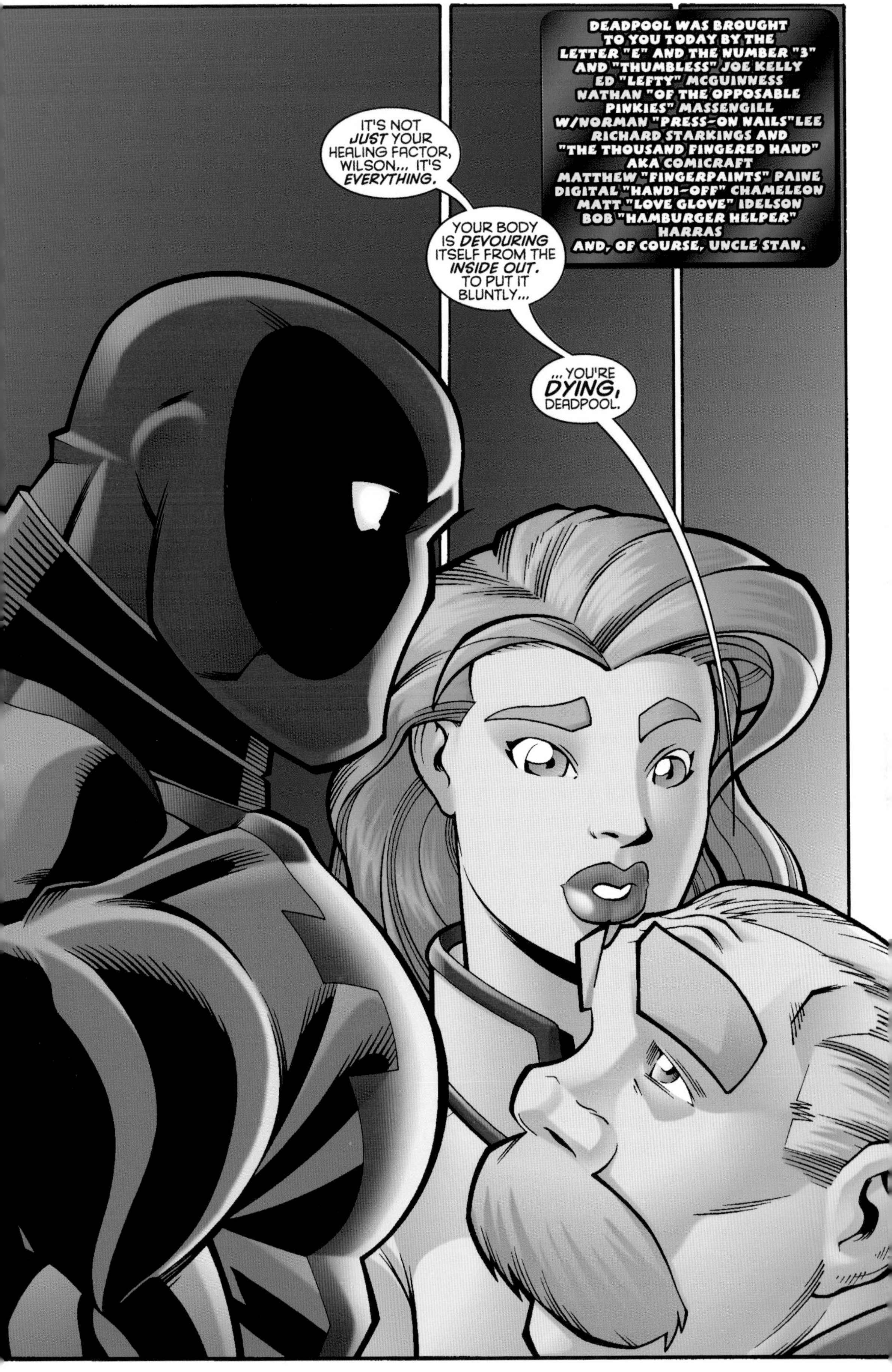
DEADPOOL WAS BROUGHT TO YOU TODAY BY THE LETTER "E" AND THE NUMBER "3" AND "THUMBLESS" JOE KELLY ED "LEFTY" MCGUINNESS NATHAN "OF THE OPPOSABLE PINKIES" MASSENGILL W/NORMAN "PRESS-ON NAILS" LEE RICHARD STARKINGS AND "THE THOUSAND FINGERED HAND" AKA COMICRAFT MATTHEW "FINGERPAINTS" PAINE DIGITAL "HANDI-OFF" CHAMELEON MATT "LOVE GLOVE" IDELSON BOB "HAMBURGER HELPER" HARRAS AND, OF COURSE, UNCLE STAN.
IT'S NOT JUST YOUR HEALING FACTOR, WILSON... IT'S EVERYTHING.
YOUR BODY IS DEVOURING ITSELF FROM THE INSIDE OUT. TO PUT IT BLUNTLY...
...YOU'RE DYING, DEADPOOL.

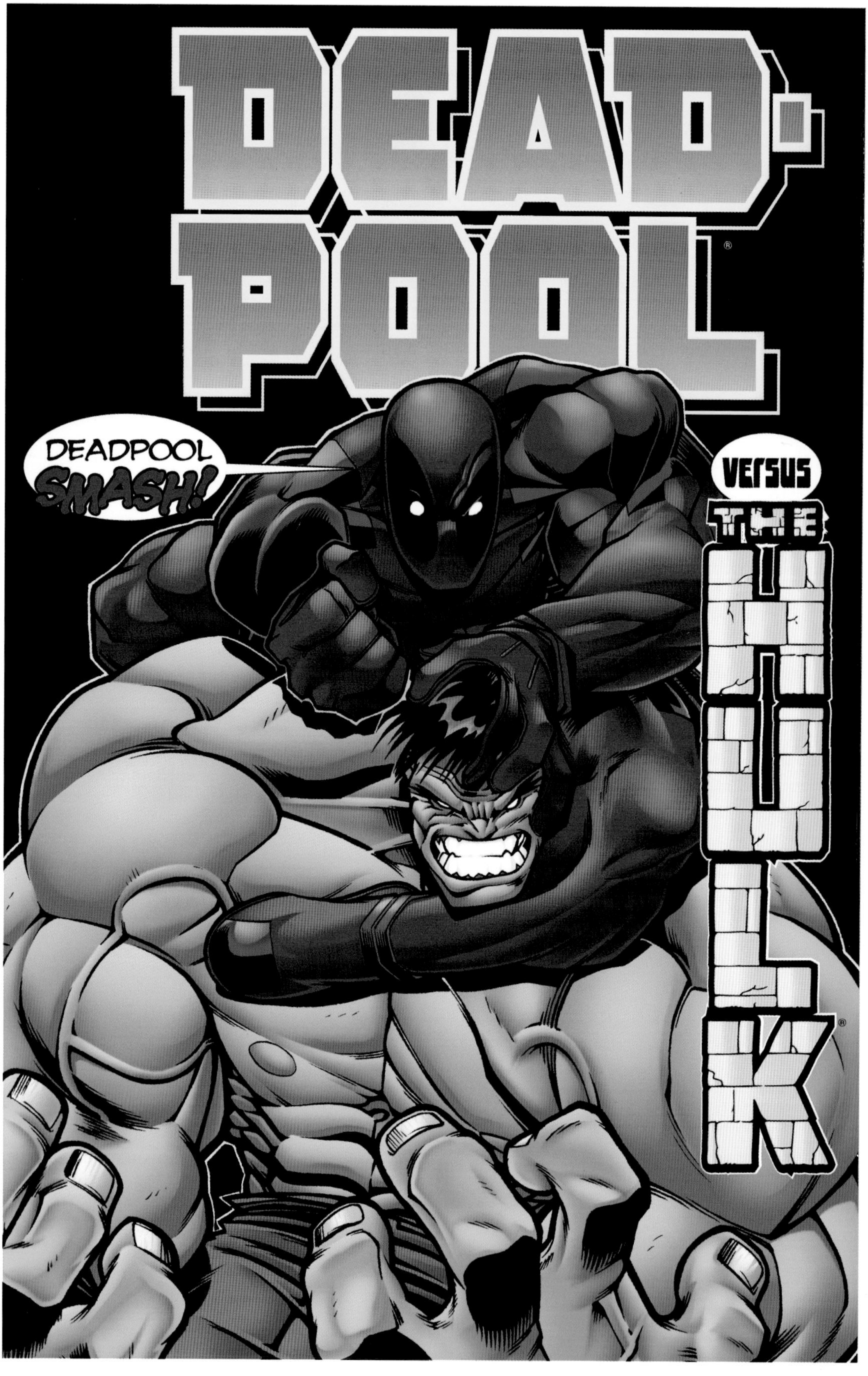
DEAD-POOL
DEADPOOL SMASH!
VERSUS
THE HULK

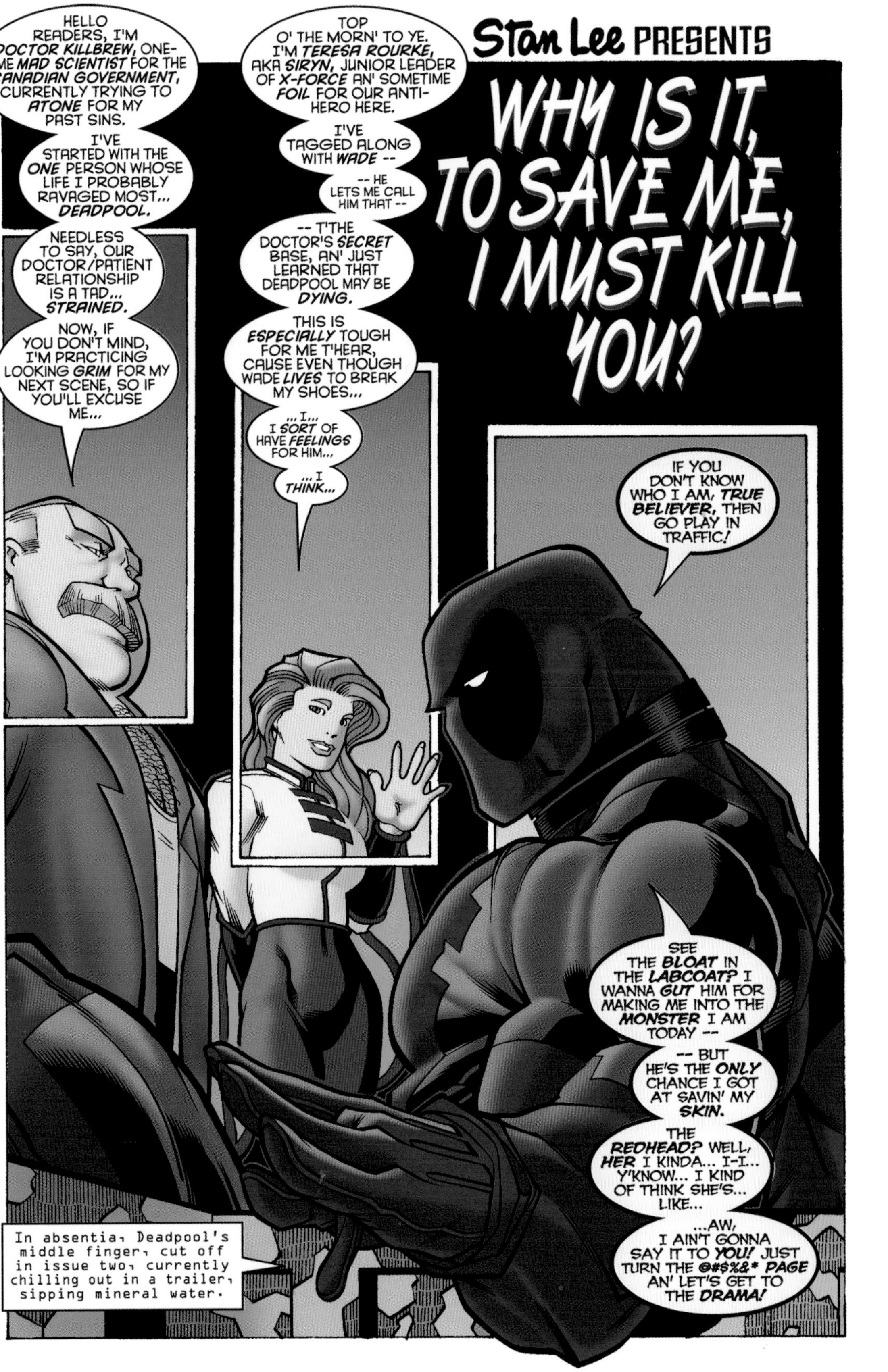
Stan Lee PRESENTS
WHY IS IT, TO SAVE ME, I MUST KILL YOU?
HELLO READERS, I'M DOCTOR KILLBREW, ONE-TIME MAD SCIENTIST FOR THE CANADIAN GOVERNMENT, CURRENTLY TRYING TO ATONE FOR MY PAST SINS.
I'VE STARTED WITH THE ONE PERSON WHOSE LIFE I PROBABLY RAVAGED MOST... DEADPOOL.
NEEDLESS TO SAY, OUR DOCTOR/PATIENT RELATIONSHIP IS A TAD... STRAINED.
NOW, IF YOU DON'T MIND, I'M PRACTICING LOOKING GRIM FOR MY NEXT SCENE, SO IF YOU'LL EXCUSE ME...
TOP O' THE MORN' TO YE. I'M TERESA ROURKE, AKA SIRYN, JUNIOR LEADER OF X-FORCE AN' SOMETIME FOIL FOR OUR ANTI-HERO HERE.
I'VE TAGGED ALONG WITH WADE --
-- HE LETS ME CALL HIM THAT --
-- T'THE DOCTOR'S SECRET BASE, AN' JUST LEARNED THAT DEADPOOL MAY BE DYING.
THIS IS ESPECIALLY TOUGH FOR ME T'HEAR, CAUSE EVEN THOUGH WADE LIVES TO BREAK MY SHOES...
... I... I SORT OF HAVE FEELINGS FOR HIM...
... I THINK...
IF YOU DON'T KNOW WHO I AM, TRUE BELIEVER, THEN GO PLAY IN TRAFFIC!
SEE THE BLOAT IN THE LABCOAT? I WANNA GUT HIM FOR MAKING ME INTO THE MONSTER I AM TODAY --
-- BUT HE'S THE ONLY CHANCE I GOT AT SAVIN' MY SKIN.
THE REDHEAD? WELL, HER I KINDA... I-I... Y'KNOW... I KIND OF THINK SHE'S... LIKE...
...AW, I AIN'T GONNA SAY IT TO YOU! JUST TURN THE @#$%&* PAGE AN' LET'S GET TO THE DRAMA!
In absentia, Deadpool's middle finger, cut off in issue two, currently chilling out in a trailer, sipping mineral water.

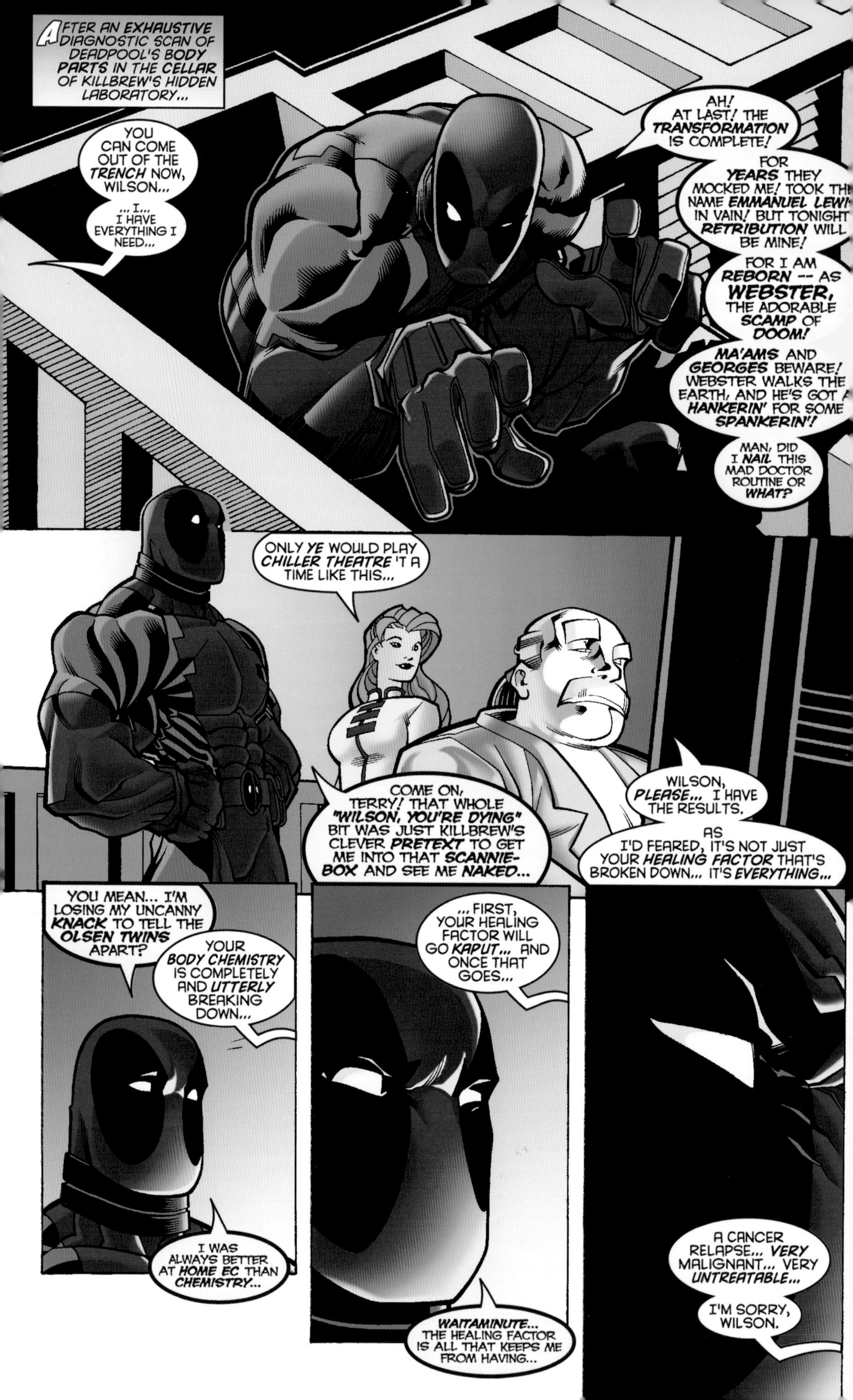

AFTER AN EXHAUSTIVE DIAGNOSTIC SCAN OF DEADPOOL'S BODY PARTS IN THE CELLAR OF KILLBREW'S HIDDEN LABORATORY...
YOU CAN COME OUT OF THE TRENCH NOW, WILSON...
... I... I HAVE EVERYTHING I NEED...
AH! AT LAST! THE TRANSFORMATION IS COMPLETE!
FOR YEARS THEY MOCKED ME! TOOK THE NAME EMMANUEL LEWIS IN VAIN! BUT TONIGHT RETRIBUTION WILL BE MINE!
FOR I AM REBORN -- AS WEBSTER, THE ADORABLE SCAMP OF DOOM!
MA'AMS AND GEORGES BEWARE! WEBSTER WALKS THE EARTH, AND HE'S GOT A HANKERIN' FOR SOME SPANKERIN'!
MAN, DID I NAIL THIS MAD DOCTOR ROUTINE OR WHAT?
ONLY YE WOULD PLAY CHILLER THEATRE 'T A TIME LIKE THIS...
COME ON, TERRY! THAT WHOLE "WILSON, YOU'RE DYING" BIT WAS JUST KILLBREW'S CLEVER PRETEXT TO GET ME INTO THAT SCANNIE-BOX AND SEE ME NAKED...
WILSON, PLEASE... I HAVE THE RESULTS.
AS I'D FEARED, IT'S NOT JUST YOUR HEALING FACTOR THAT'S BROKEN DOWN... IT'S EVERYTHING...
YOU MEAN... I'M LOSING MY UNCANNY KNACK TO TELL THE OLSEN TWINS APART?
YOUR BODY CHEMISTRY IS COMPLETELY AND UTTERLY BREAKING DOWN...
I WAS ALWAYS BETTER AT HOME EC THAN CHEMISTRY...
... FIRST, YOUR HEALING FACTOR WILL GO KAPUT... AND ONCE THAT GOES...
WAITAMINUTE... THE HEALING FACTOR IS ALL THAT KEEPS ME FROM HAVING...
A CANCER RELAPSE... VERY MALIGNANT... VERY UNTREATABLE...
I'M SORRY, WILSON.

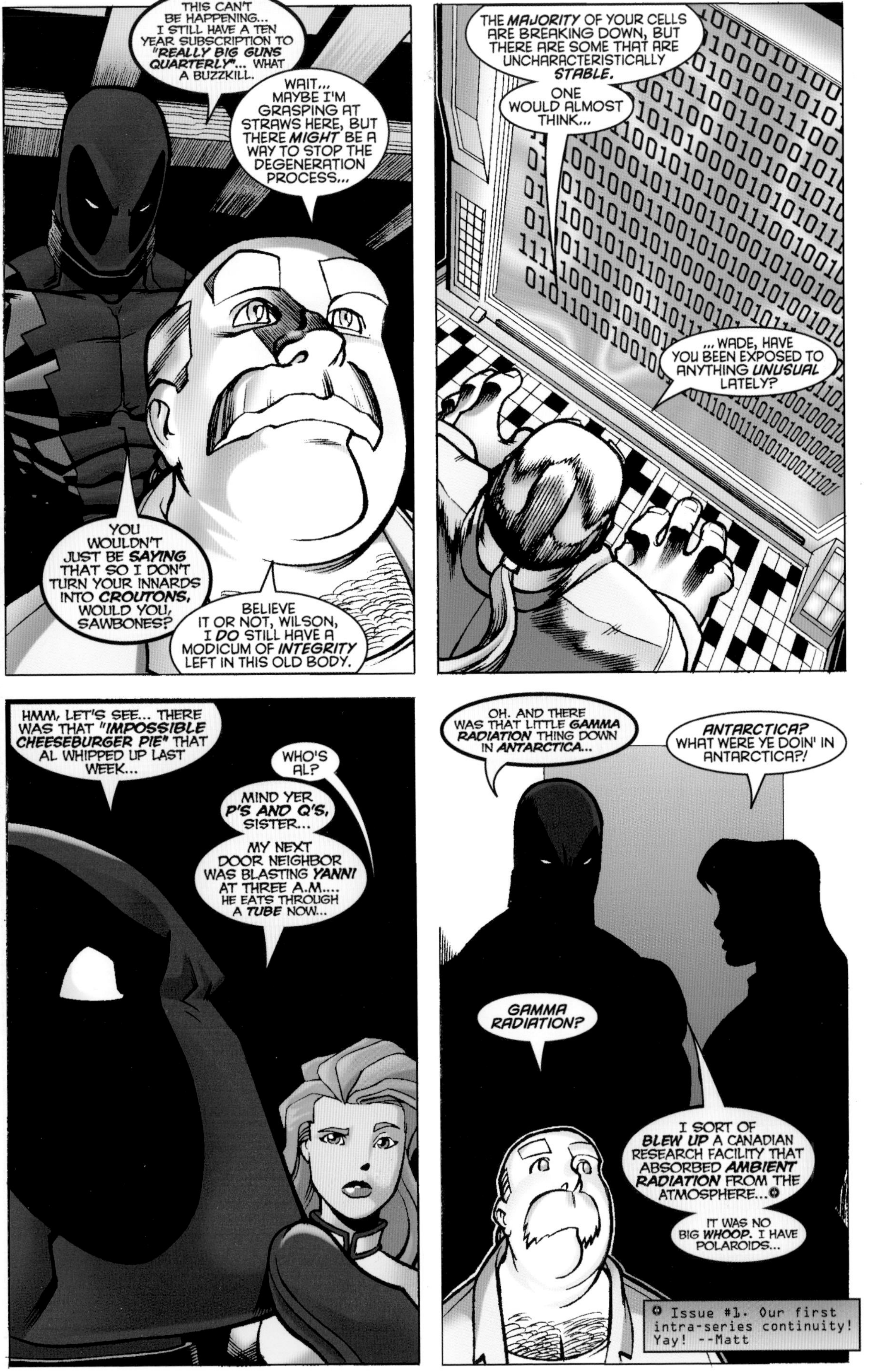
THIS CAN'T BE HAPPENING... I STILL HAVE A TEN YEAR SUBSCRIPTION TO "REALLY BIG GUNS QUARTERLY"... WHAT A BUZZKILL.
WAIT... MAYBE I'M GRASPING AT STRAWS HERE, BUT THERE MIGHT BE A WAY TO STOP THE DEGENERATION PROCESS...
YOU WOULDN'T JUST BE SAYING THAT SO I DON'T TURN YOUR INNARDS INTO CROUTONS, WOULD YOU, SAWBONES?
BELIEVE IT OR NOT, WILSON, I DO STILL HAVE A MODICUM OF INTEGRITY LEFT IN THIS OLD BODY.
THE MAJORITY OF YOUR CELLS ARE BREAKING DOWN, BUT THERE ARE SOME THAT ARE UNCHARACTERISTICALLY STABLE.
ONE WOULD ALMOST THINK...
...WADE, HAVE YOU BEEN EXPOSED TO ANYTHING UNUSUAL LATELY?
HMM, LET'S SEE... THERE WAS THAT "IMPOSSIBLE CHEESEBURGER PIE" THAT AL WHIPPED UP LAST WEEK...
WHO'S AL?
MIND YER P'S AND Q'S, SISTER...
MY NEXT DOOR NEIGHBOR WAS BLASTING YANNI AT THREE A.M.... HE EATS THROUGH A TUBE NOW...
OH. AND THERE WAS THAT LITTLE GAMMA RADIATION THING DOWN IN ANTARCTICA...
ANTARCTICA? WHAT WERE YE DOIN' IN ANTARCTICA?!
GAMMA RADIATION?
I SORT OF BLEW UP A CANADIAN RESEARCH FACILITY THAT ABSORBED AMBIENT RADIATION FROM THE ATMOSPHERE...
IT WAS NO BIG WHOOP. I HAVE POLAROIDS...
Issue #1. Our first intra-series continuity! Yay! --Matt

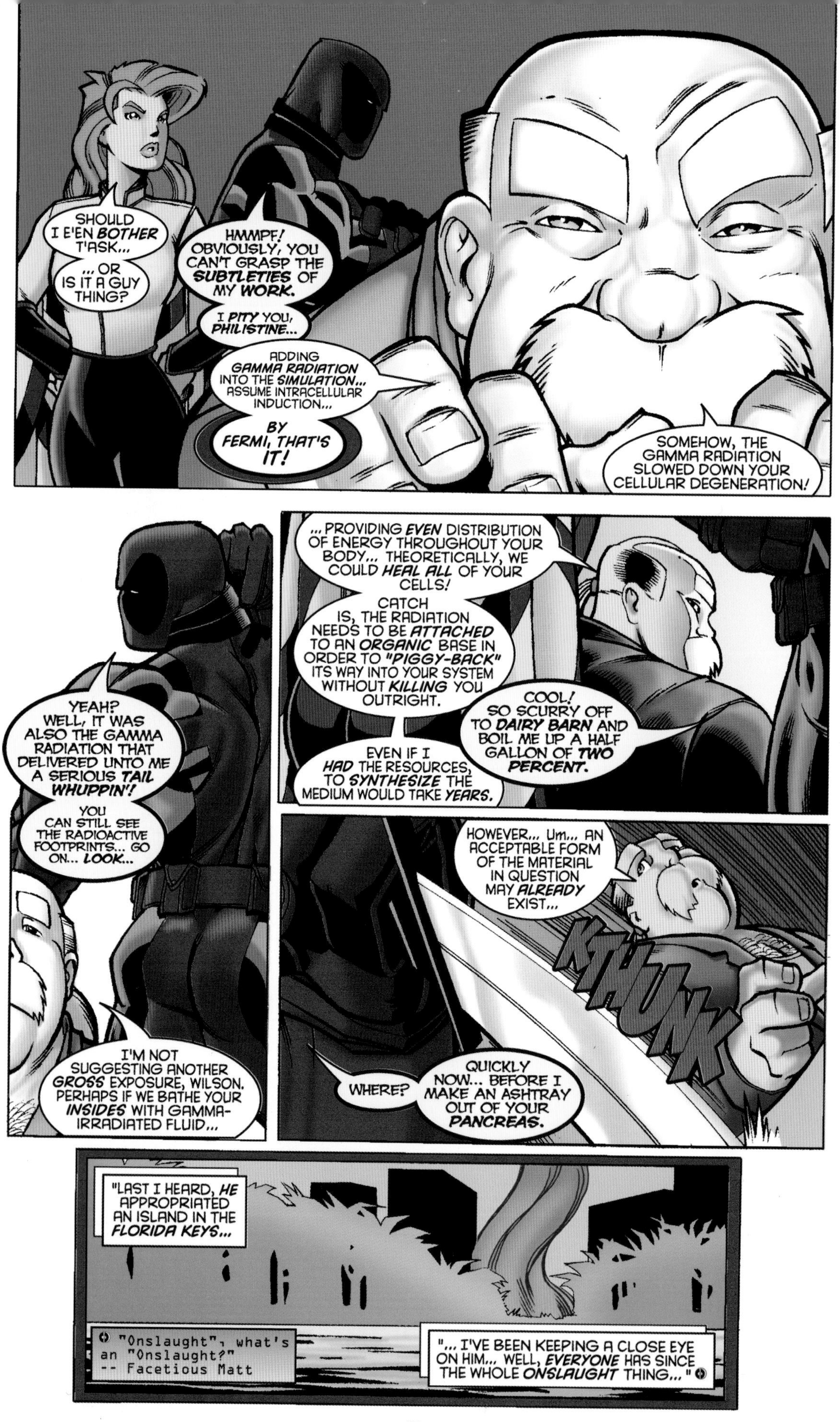
SHOULD I E'EN BOTHER T'ASK...
... OR IS IT A GUY THING?
HMMPF! OBVIOUSLY, YOU CAN'T GRASP THE SUBTLETIES OF MY WORK.
I PITY YOU, PHILISTINE...
ADDING GAMMA RADIATION INTO THE SIMULATION... ASSUME INTRACELLULAR INDUCTION...
BY FERMI, THAT'S IT!
SOMEHOW, THE GAMMA RADIATION SLOWED DOWN YOUR CELLULAR DEGENERATION!
... PROVIDING EVEN DISTRIBUTION OF ENERGY THROUGHOUT YOUR BODY... THEORETICALLY, WE COULD HEAL ALL OF YOUR CELLS!
CATCH IS, THE RADIATION NEEDS TO BE ATTACHED TO AN ORGANIC BASE IN ORDER TO "PIGGY-BACK" ITS WAY INTO YOUR SYSTEM WITHOUT KILLING YOU OUTRIGHT.
EVEN IF I HAD THE RESOURCES, TO SYNTHESIZE THE MEDIUM WOULD TAKE YEARS.
COOL! SO SCURRY OFF TO DAIRY BARN AND BOIL ME UP A HALF GALLON OF TWO PERCENT.
YEAH? WELL, IT WAS ALSO THE GAMMA RADIATION THAT DELIVERED UNTO ME A SERIOUS TAIL WHUPPIN'!
YOU CAN STILL SEE THE RADIOACTIVE FOOTPRINTS... GO ON... LOOK...
I'M NOT SUGGESTING ANOTHER GROSS EXPOSURE, WILSON. PERHAPS IF WE BATHE YOUR INSIDES WITH GAMMA-IRRADIATED FLUID...
HOWEVER... Um... AN ACCEPTABLE FORM OF THE MATERIAL IN QUESTION MAY ALREADY EXIST...
KTHUNK
WHERE?
QUICKLY NOW... BEFORE I MAKE AN ASHTRAY OUT OF YOUR PANCREAS.
"LAST I HEARD, HE APPROPRIATED AN ISLAND IN THE FLORIDA KEYS...
"Onslaught", what's an "Onslaught?" -- Facetious Matt
"... I'VE BEEN KEEPING A CLOSE EYE ON HIM... WELL, EVERYONE HAS SINCE THE WHOLE ONSLAUGHT THING..."

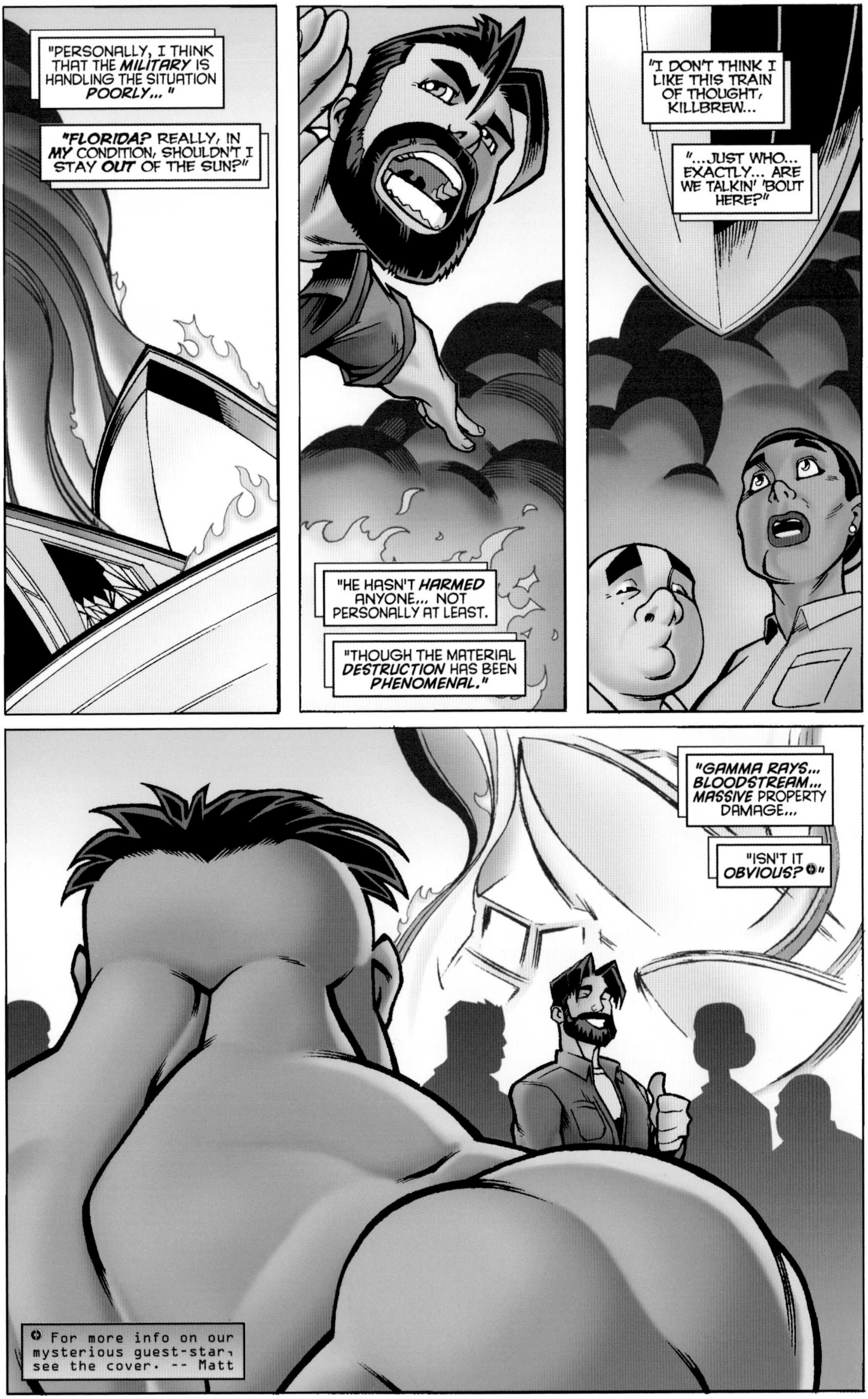
"PERSONALLY, I THINK THAT THE MILITARY IS HANDLING THE SITUATION POORLY..."
"FLORIDA? REALLY, IN MY CONDITION, SHOULDN'T I STAY OUT OF THE SUN?"
"HE HASN'T HARMED ANYONE... NOT PERSONALLY AT LEAST.
"THOUGH THE MATERIAL DESTRUCTION HAS BEEN PHENOMENAL."
"I DON'T THINK I LIKE THIS TRAIN OF THOUGHT, KILLBREW...
"...JUST WHO... EXACTLY... ARE WE TALKIN' 'BOUT HERE?"
"GAMMA RAYS... BLOODSTREAM... MASSIVE PROPERTY DAMAGE...
"ISN'T IT OBVIOUS?"
For more info on our mysterious guest-star, see the cover. -- Matt

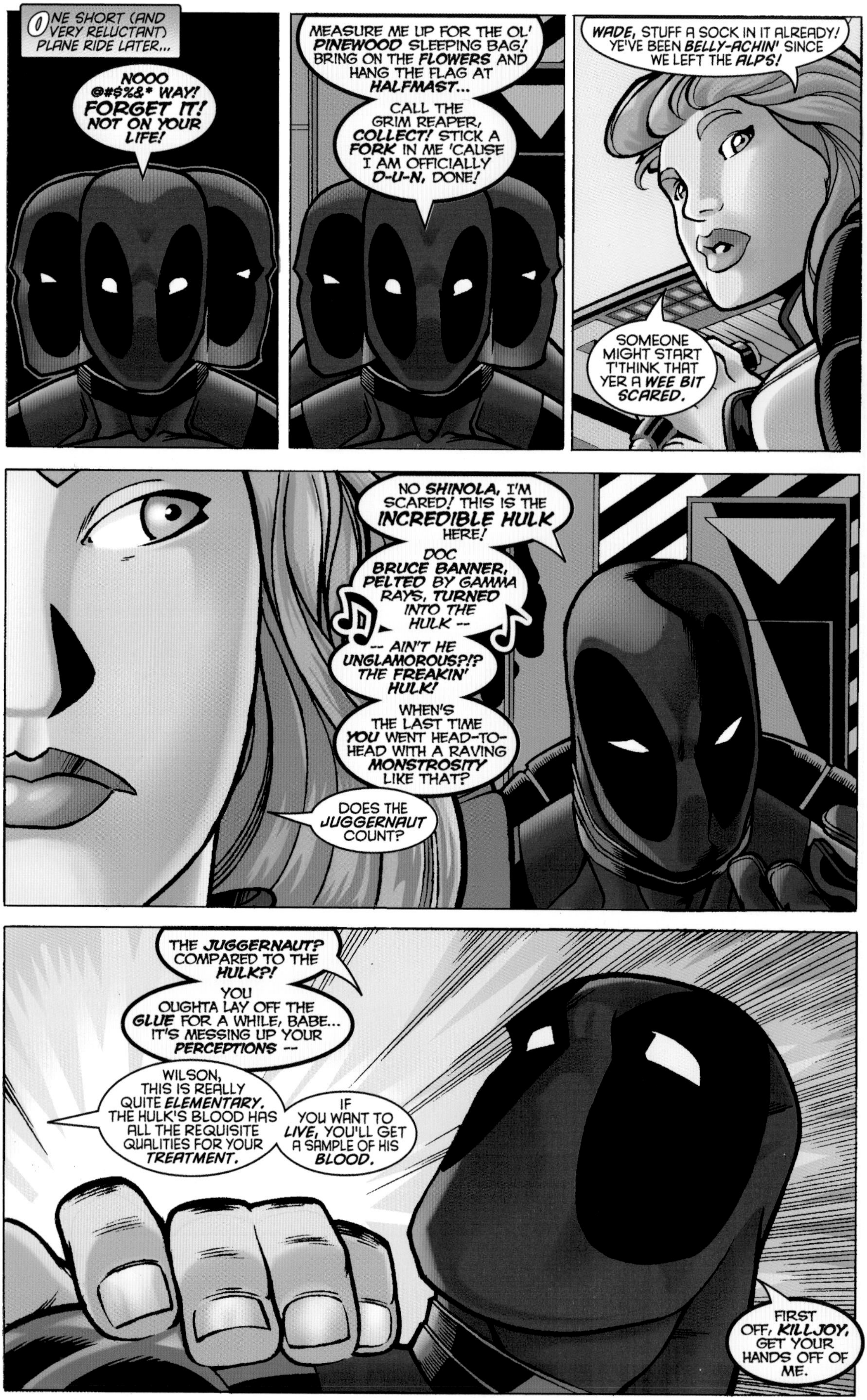
ONE SHORT (AND VERY RELUCTANT) PLANE RIDE LATER...
NOOO @#$%&* WAY! FORGET IT! NOT ON YOUR LIFE!
MEASURE ME UP FOR THE OL' PINEWOOD SLEEPING BAG! BRING ON THE FLOWERS AND HANG THE FLAG AT HALFMAST...
CALL THE GRIM REAPER, COLLECT! STICK A FORK IN ME 'CAUSE I AM OFFICIALLY D-U-N, DONE!
WADE, STUFF A SOCK IN IT ALREADY! YE'VE BEEN BELLY-ACHIN' SINCE WE LEFT THE ALPS!
SOMEONE MIGHT START T'THINK THAT YER A WEE BIT SCARED.
NO SHINOLA, I'M SCARED! THIS IS THE INCREDIBLE HULK HERE!
DOC BRUCE BANNER, PELTED BY GAMMA RAYS, TURNED INTO THE HULK --
-- AIN'T HE UNGLAMOROUS?!? THE FREAKIN' HULK!
WHEN'S THE LAST TIME YOU WENT HEAD-TO-HEAD WITH A RAVING MONSTROSITY LIKE THAT?
DOES THE JUGGERNAUT COUNT?
THE JUGGERNAUT? COMPARED TO THE HULK?!
YOU OUGHTA LAY OFF THE GLUE FOR A WHILE, BABE... IT'S MESSING UP YOUR PERCEPTIONS --
WILSON, THIS IS REALLY QUITE ELEMENTARY. THE HULK'S BLOOD HAS ALL THE REQUISITE QUALITIES FOR YOUR TREATMENT.
IF YOU WANT TO LIVE, YOU'LL GET A SAMPLE OF HIS BLOOD.
FIRST OFF, KILLJOY, GET YOUR HANDS OFF OF ME.

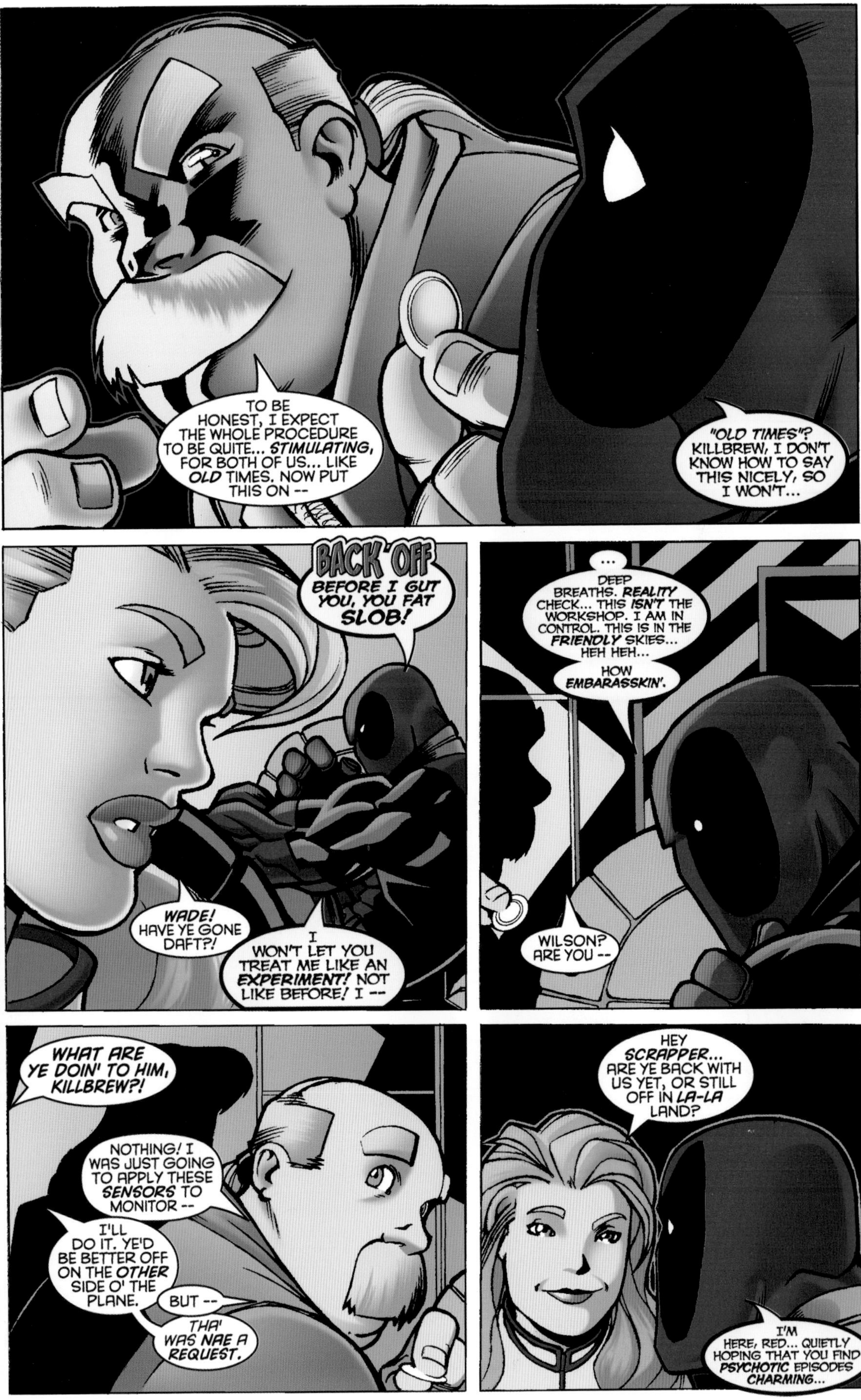
TO BE HONEST, I EXPECT THE WHOLE PROCEDURE TO BE QUITE... STIMULATING, FOR BOTH OF US... LIKE OLD TIMES. NOW PUT THIS ON --
"OLD TIMES"? KILLBREW, I DON'T KNOW HOW TO SAY THIS NICELY, SO I WON'T...
BACK OFF
BEFORE I GUT YOU, YOU FAT SLOB!
WADE! HAVE YE GONE DAFT?!
I WON'T LET YOU TREAT ME LIKE AN EXPERIMENT! NOT LIKE BEFORE! I --
...
DEEP BREATHS. REALITY CHECK... THIS ISN'T THE WORKSHOP. I AM IN CONTROL. THIS IS IN THE FRIENDLY SKIES... HEH HEH...
HOW EMBARASSKIN'.
WILSON? ARE YOU --
WHAT ARE YE DOIN' TO HIM, KILLBREW?!
NOTHING! I WAS JUST GOING TO APPLY THESE SENSORS TO MONITOR --
I'LL DO IT. YE'D BE BETTER OFF ON THE OTHER SIDE O' THE PLANE.
BUT --
THA' WAS NAE A REQUEST.
HEY SCRAPPER... ARE YE BACK WITH US YET, OR STILL OFF IN LA-LA LAND?
I'M HERE, RED... QUIETLY HOPING THAT YOU FIND PSYCHOTIC EPISODES CHARMING...

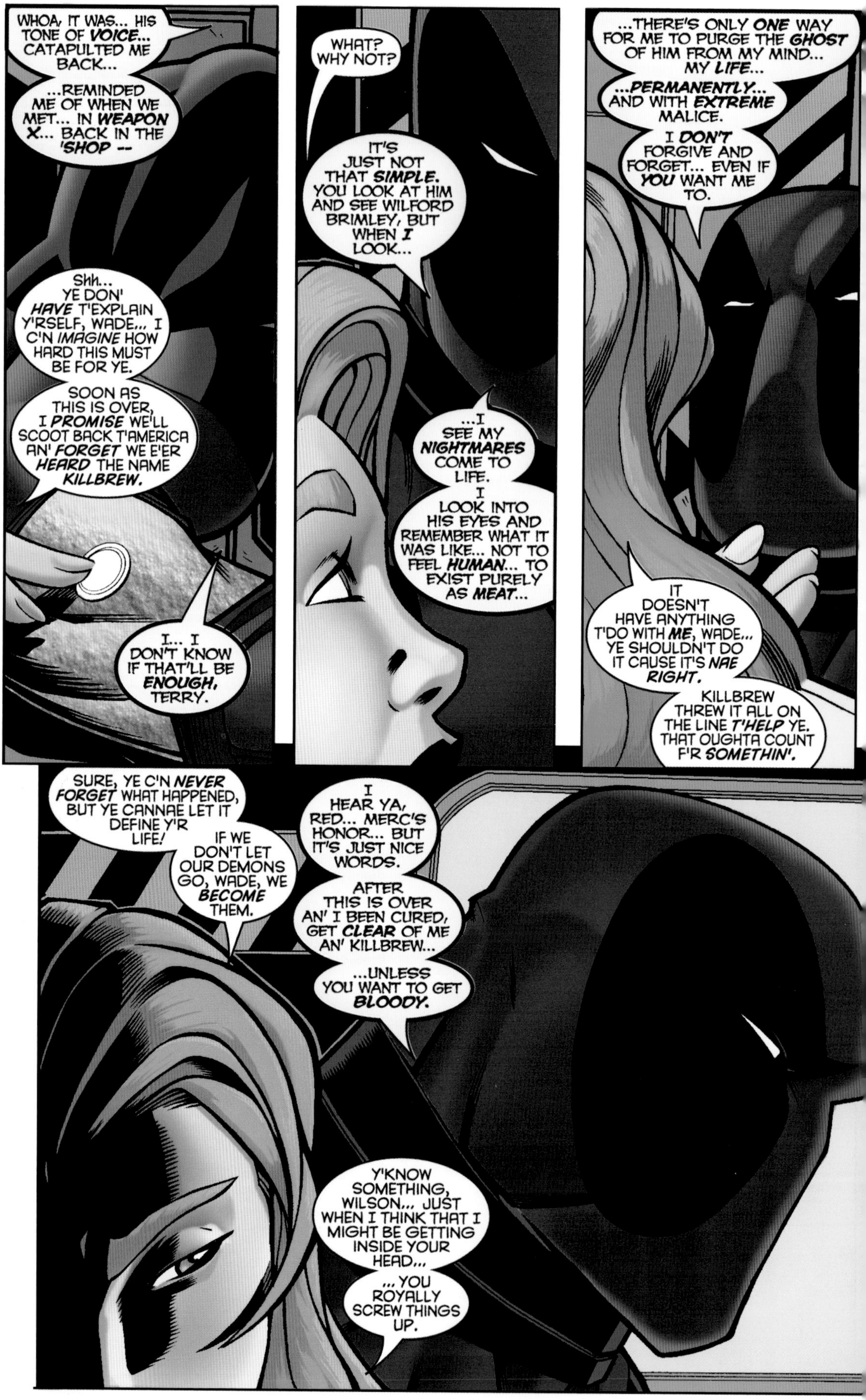
WHOA, IT WAS... HIS TONE OF VOICE... CATAPULTED ME BACK...
...REMINDED ME OF WHEN WE MET... IN WEAPON X... BACK IN THE 'SHOP --
Shh... YE DON' HAVE T'EXPLAIN Y'RSELF, WADE... I C'N IMAGINE HOW HARD THIS MUST BE FOR YE.
SOON AS THIS IS OVER, I PROMISE WE'LL SCOOT BACK T'AMERICA AN' FORGET WE E'ER HEARD THE NAME KILLBREW.
I... I DON'T KNOW IF THAT'LL BE ENOUGH, TERRY.
WHAT? WHY NOT?
IT'S JUST NOT THAT SIMPLE. YOU LOOK AT HIM AND SEE WILFORD BRIMLEY, BUT WHEN I LOOK...
...I SEE MY NIGHTMARES COME TO LIFE.
I LOOK INTO HIS EYES AND REMEMBER WHAT IT WAS LIKE... NOT TO FEEL HUMAN... TO EXIST PURELY AS MEAT...
...THERE'S ONLY ONE WAY FOR ME TO PURGE THE GHOST OF HIM FROM MY MIND... MY LIFE...
...PERMANENTLY... AND WITH EXTREME MALICE.
I DON'T FORGIVE AND FORGET... EVEN IF YOU WANT ME TO.
IT DOESN'T HAVE ANYTHING T'DO WITH ME, WADE... YE SHOULDN'T DO IT CAUSE IT'S NAE RIGHT.
KILLBREW THREW IT ALL ON THE LINE T'HELP YE. THAT OUGHTA COUNT F'R SOMETHIN'.
SURE, YE C'N NEVER FORGET WHAT HAPPENED, BUT YE CANNAE LET IT DEFINE Y'R LIFE!
IF WE DON'T LET OUR DEMONS GO, WADE, WE BECOME THEM.
I HEAR YA, RED... MERC'S HONOR... BUT IT'S JUST NICE WORDS.
AFTER THIS IS OVER AN' I BEEN CURED, GET CLEAR OF ME AN' KILLBREW...
...UNLESS YOU WANT TO GET BLOODY.
Y'KNOW SOMETHING, WILSON... JUST WHEN I THINK THAT I MIGHT BE GETTING INSIDE YOUR HEAD...
...YOU ROYALLY SCREW THINGS UP.

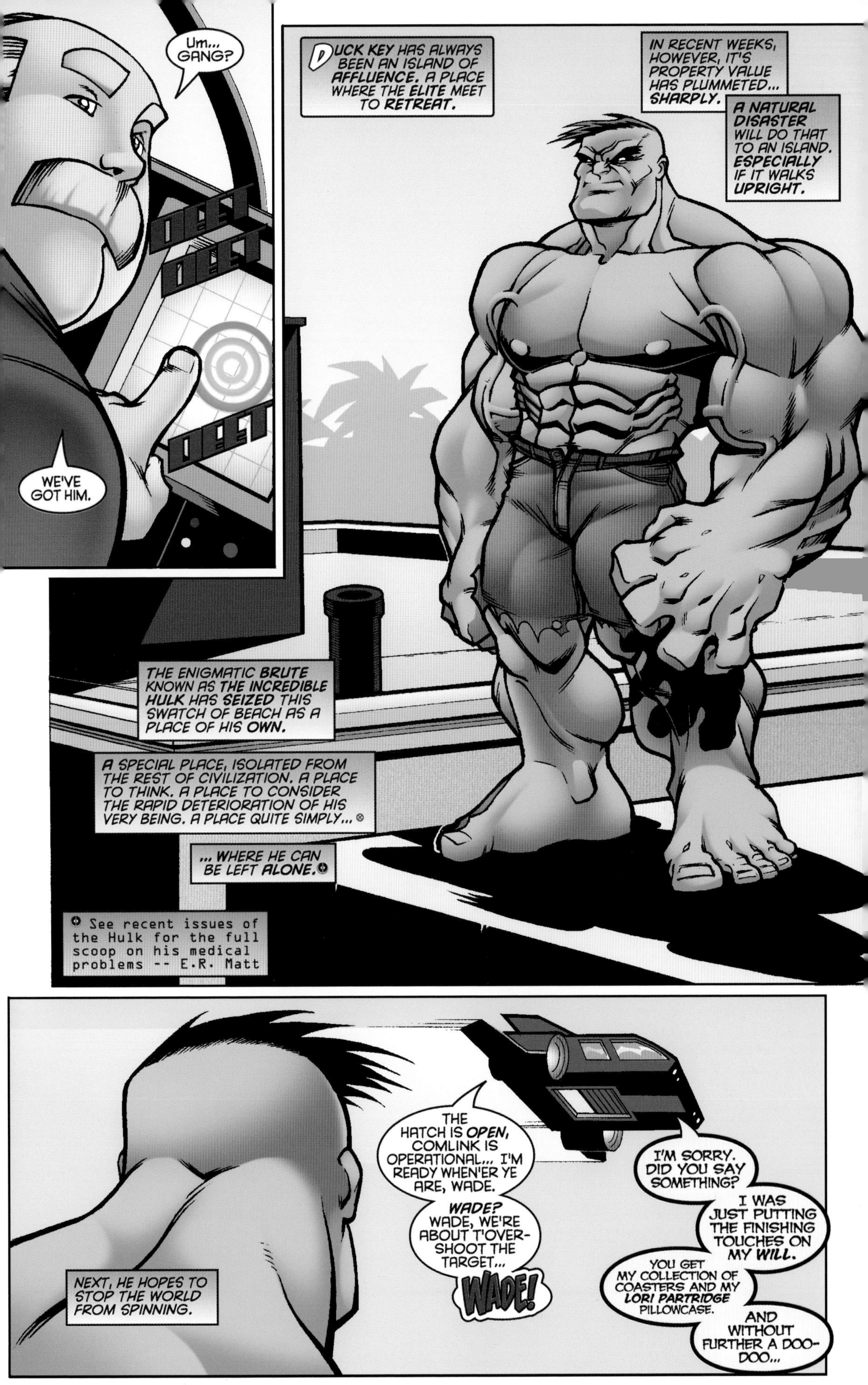
Um... GANG?
DEET
DEET
DEET
WE'VE GOT HIM.
DUCK KEY HAS ALWAYS BEEN AN ISLAND OF AFFLUENCE. A PLACE WHERE THE ELITE MEET TO RETREAT.
IN RECENT WEEKS, HOWEVER, IT'S PROPERTY VALUE HAS PLUMMETED... SHARPLY.
A NATURAL DISASTER WILL DO THAT TO AN ISLAND. ESPECIALLY IF IT WALKS UPRIGHT.
THE ENIGMATIC BRUTE KNOWN AS THE INCREDIBLE HULK HAS SEIZED THIS SWATCH OF BEACH AS A PLACE OF HIS OWN.
A SPECIAL PLACE, ISOLATED FROM THE REST OF CIVILIZATION. A PLACE TO THINK. A PLACE TO CONSIDER THE RAPID DETERIORATION OF HIS VERY BEING. A PLACE QUITE SIMPLY...
... WHERE HE CAN BE LEFT ALONE.
See recent issues of the Hulk for the full scoop on his medical problems -- E.R. Matt
NEXT, HE HOPES TO STOP THE WORLD FROM SPINNING.
THE HATCH IS OPEN, COMLINK IS OPERATIONAL... I'M READY WHEN'ER YE ARE, WADE.
WADE? WADE, WE'RE ABOUT T'OVER-SHOOT THE TARGET...
WADE!
I'M SORRY. DID YOU SAY SOMETHING?
I WAS JUST PUTTING THE FINISHING TOUCHES ON MY WILL.
YOU GET MY COLLECTION OF COASTERS AND MY LORI PARTRIDGE PILLOWCASE.
AND WITHOUT FURTHER A DOO-DOO...

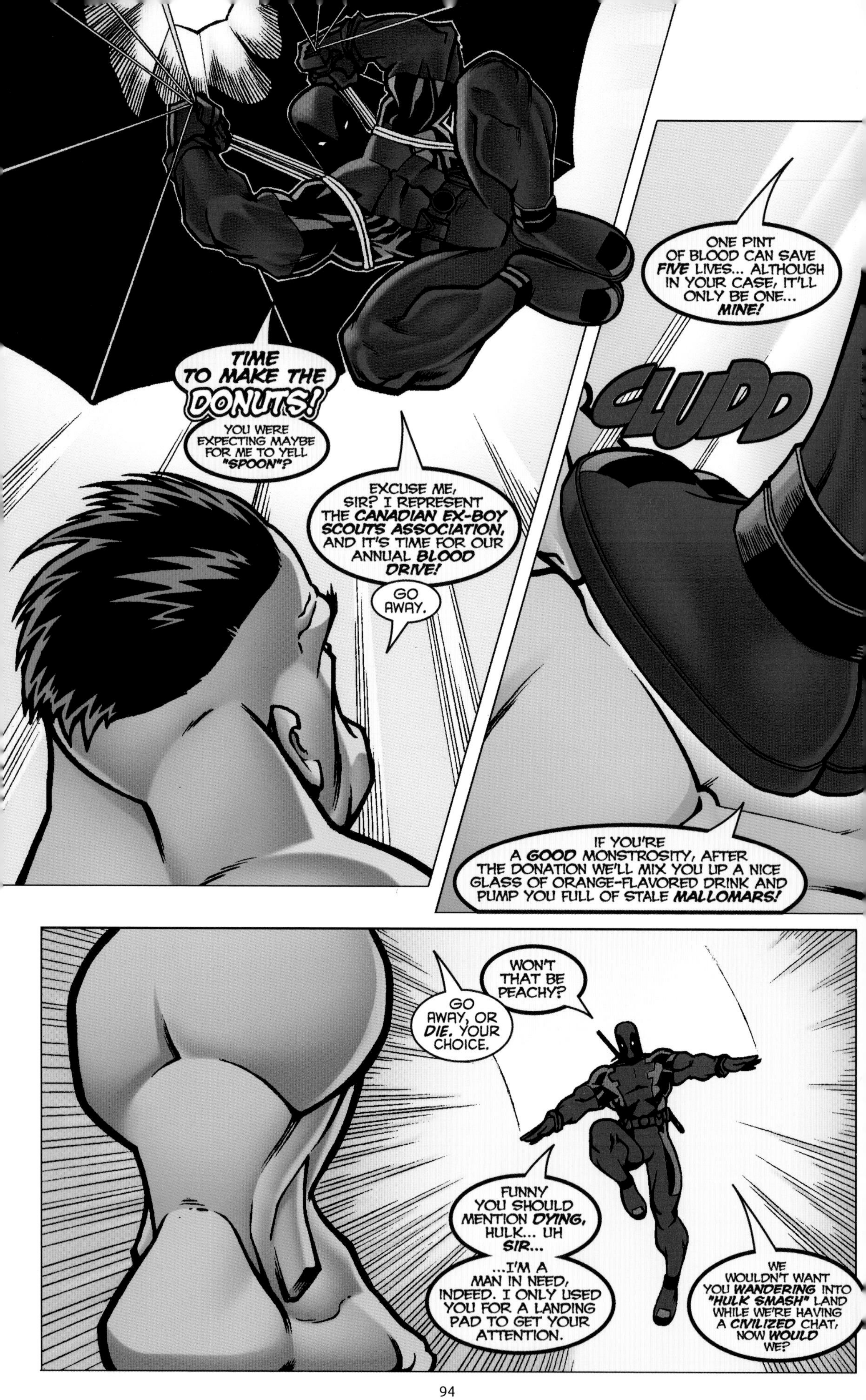
TIME TO MAKE THE DONUTS!
YOU WERE EXPECTING MAYBE FOR ME TO YELL "SPOON"?
EXCUSE ME, SIR? I REPRESENT THE CANADIAN EX-BOY SCOUTS ASSOCIATION, AND IT'S TIME FOR OUR ANNUAL BLOOD DRIVE!
GO AWAY.
ONE PINT OF BLOOD CAN SAVE FIVE LIVES... ALTHOUGH IN YOUR CASE, IT'LL ONLY BE ONE... MINE!
CLUDD
IF YOU'RE A GOOD MONSTROSITY, AFTER THE DONATION WE'LL MIX YOU UP A NICE GLASS OF ORANGE-FLAVORED DRINK AND PUMP YOU FULL OF STALE MALLOMARS!
WON'T THAT BE PEACHY?
GO AWAY, OR DIE. YOUR CHOICE.
FUNNY YOU SHOULD MENTION DYING, HULK... UH SIR...
...I'M A MAN IN NEED, INDEED. I ONLY USED YOU FOR A LANDING PAD TO GET YOUR ATTENTION.
WE WOULDN'T WANT YOU WANDERING INTO "HULK SMASH" LAND WHILE WE'RE HAVING A CIVILIZED CHAT, NOW WOULD WE?

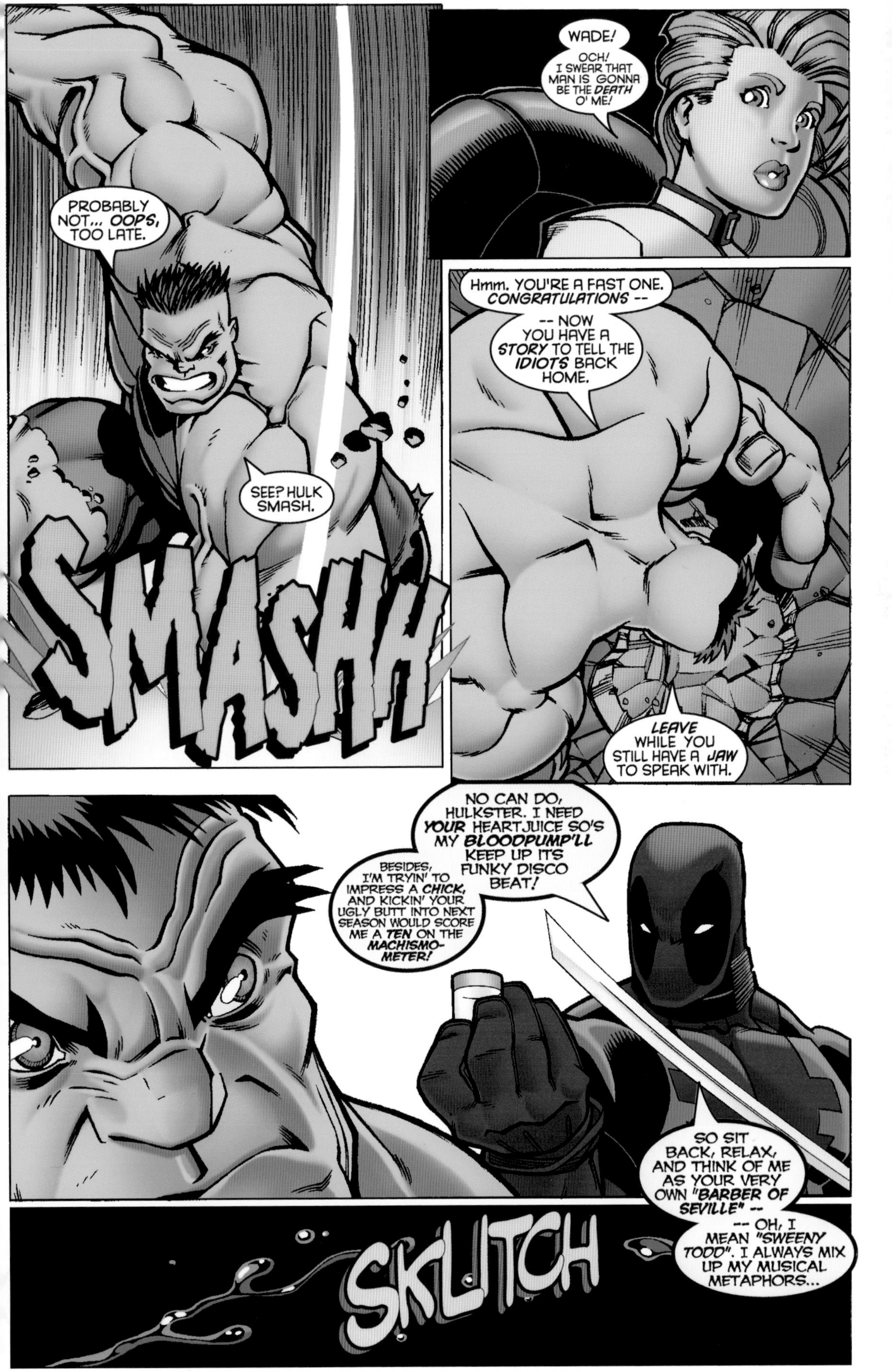
PROBABLY NOT... OOPS, TOO LATE.
SEE? HULK SMASH.
SMASHH
WADE!
OCH! I SWEAR THAT MAN IS GONNA BE THE DEATH O' ME!
Hmm. YOU'RE A FAST ONE. CONGRATULATIONS --
-- NOW YOU HAVE A STORY TO TELL THE IDIOTS BACK HOME.
LEAVE WHILE YOU STILL HAVE A JAW TO SPEAK WITH.
NO CAN DO, HULKSTER. I NEED YOUR HEARTJUICE SO'S MY BLOODPUMP'LL KEEP UP ITS FUNKY DISCO BEAT!
BESIDES, I'M TRYIN' TO IMPRESS A CHICK, AND KICKIN' YOUR UGLY BUTT INTO NEXT SEASON WOULD SCORE ME A TEN ON THE MACHISMO-METER!
SO SIT BACK, RELAX, AND THINK OF ME AS YOUR VERY OWN "BARBER OF SEVILLE" --
-- OH, I MEAN "SWEENY TODD". I ALWAYS MIX UP MY MUSICAL METAPHORS...
SKLITCH

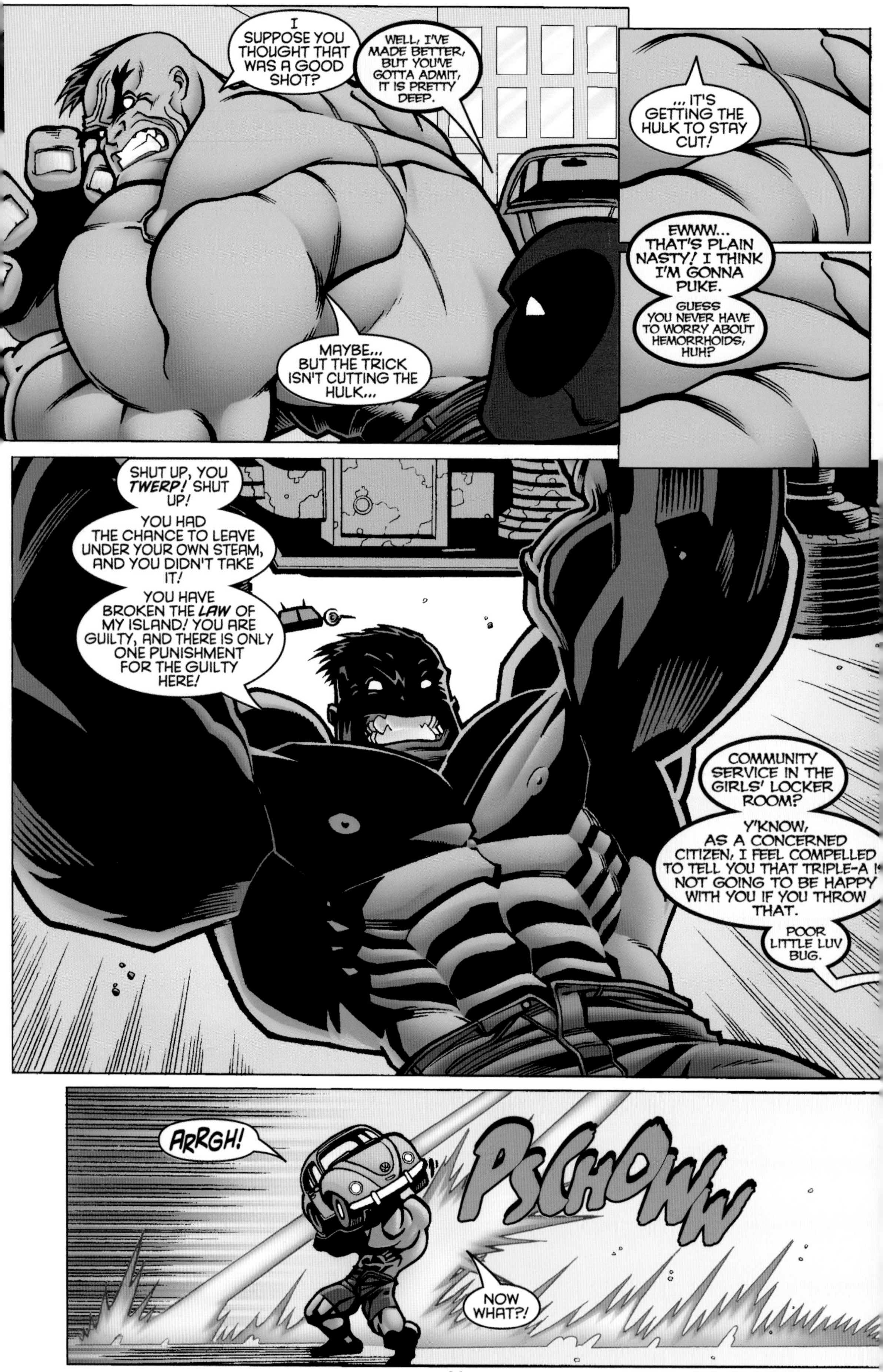
I SUPPOSE YOU THOUGHT THAT WAS A GOOD SHOT?
WELL, I'VE MADE BETTER, BUT YOU'VE GOTTA ADMIT, IT IS PRETTY DEEP.
MAYBE... BUT THE TRICK ISN'T CUTTING THE HULK...
... IT'S GETTING THE HULK TO STAY CUT!
EWWW... THAT'S PLAIN NASTY! I THINK I'M GONNA PUKE.
GUESS YOU NEVER HAVE TO WORRY ABOUT HEMORRHOIDS, HUH?
SHUT UP, YOU TWERP! SHUT UP!
YOU HAD THE CHANCE TO LEAVE UNDER YOUR OWN STEAM, AND YOU DIDN'T TAKE IT!
YOU HAVE BROKEN THE LAW OF MY ISLAND! YOU ARE GUILTY, AND THERE IS ONLY ONE PUNISHMENT FOR THE GUILTY HERE!
COMMUNITY SERVICE IN THE GIRLS' LOCKER ROOM?
Y'KNOW, AS A CONCERNED CITIZEN, I FEEL COMPELLED TO TELL YOU THAT TRIPLE-A I
NOT GOING TO BE HAPPY WITH YOU IF YOU THROW THAT.
POOR LITTLE LUV BUG.
ARRGH!
PSCHOWW
NOW WHAT?!

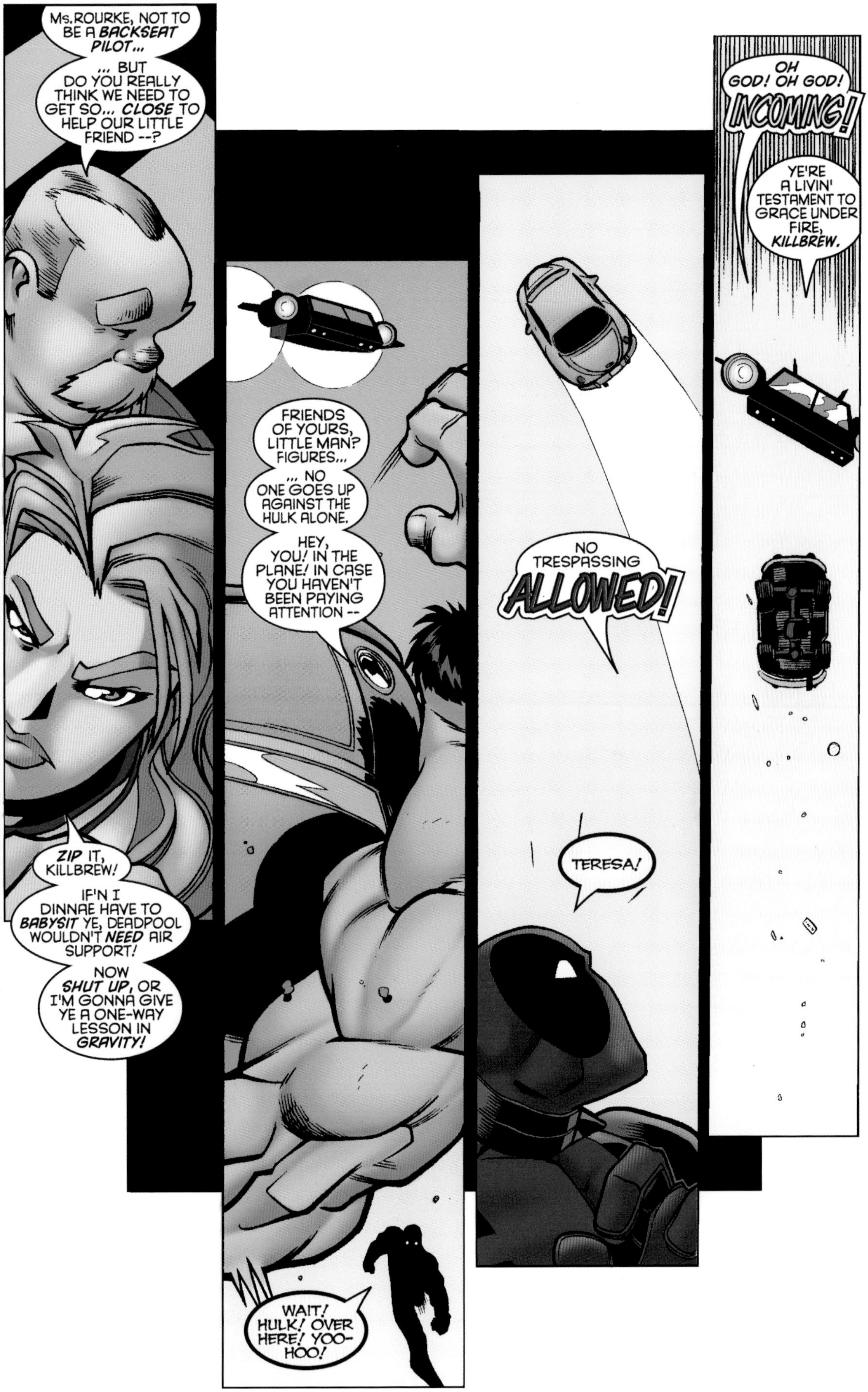
Ms. ROURKE, NOT TO BE A BACKSEAT PILOT...
... BUT DO YOU REALLY THINK WE NEED TO GET SO... CLOSE TO HELP OUR LITTLE FRIEND --?
ZIP IT, KILLBREW!
IF'N I DINNAE HAVE TO BABYSIT YE, DEADPOOL WOULDN'T NEED AIR SUPPORT!
NOW SHUT UP, OR I'M GONNA GIVE YE A ONE-WAY LESSON IN GRAVITY!
FRIENDS OF YOURS, LITTLE MAN? FIGURES...
... NO ONE GOES UP AGAINST THE HULK ALONE.
HEY, YOU! IN THE PLANE! IN CASE YOU HAVEN'T BEEN PAYING ATTENTION --
WAIT! HULK! OVER HERE! YOO-HOO!
NO TRESPASSING ALLOWED!
TERESA!
OH GOD! OH GOD! INCOMING!
YE'RE A LIVIN' TESTAMENT TO GRACE UNDER FIRE, KILLBREW.

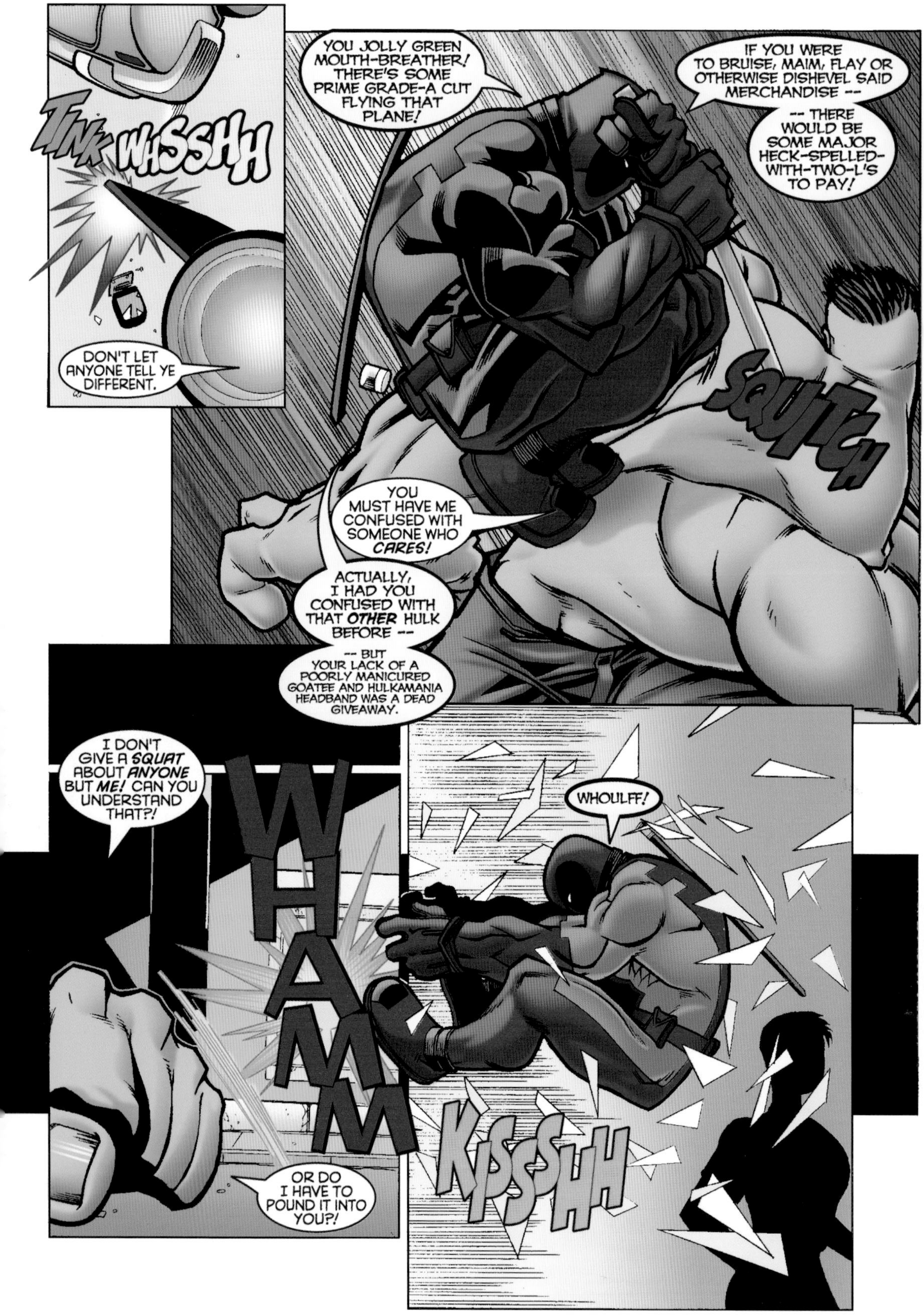
TINK WHSSHH
DON'T LET ANYONE TELL YE DIFFERENT.
YOU JOLLY GREEN MOUTH-BREATHER! THERE'S SOME PRIME GRADE-A CUT FLYING THAT PLANE!
IF YOU WERE TO BRUISE, MAIM, FLAY OR OTHERWISE DISHEVEL SAID MERCHANDISE --
-- THERE WOULD BE SOME MAJOR HECK-SPELLED-WITH-TWO-L'S TO PAY!
SQUITCH
YOU MUST HAVE ME CONFUSED WITH SOMEONE WHO CARES!
ACTUALLY, I HAD YOU CONFUSED WITH THAT OTHER HULK BEFORE --
-- BUT YOUR LACK OF A POORLY MANICURED GOATEE AND HULKAMANIA HEADBAND WAS A DEAD GIVEAWAY.
I DON'T GIVE A SQUAT ABOUT ANYONE BUT ME! CAN YOU UNDERSTAND THAT?!
WHAMM
WHOULFF!
OR DO I HAVE TO POUND IT INTO YOU?!
KISSHH

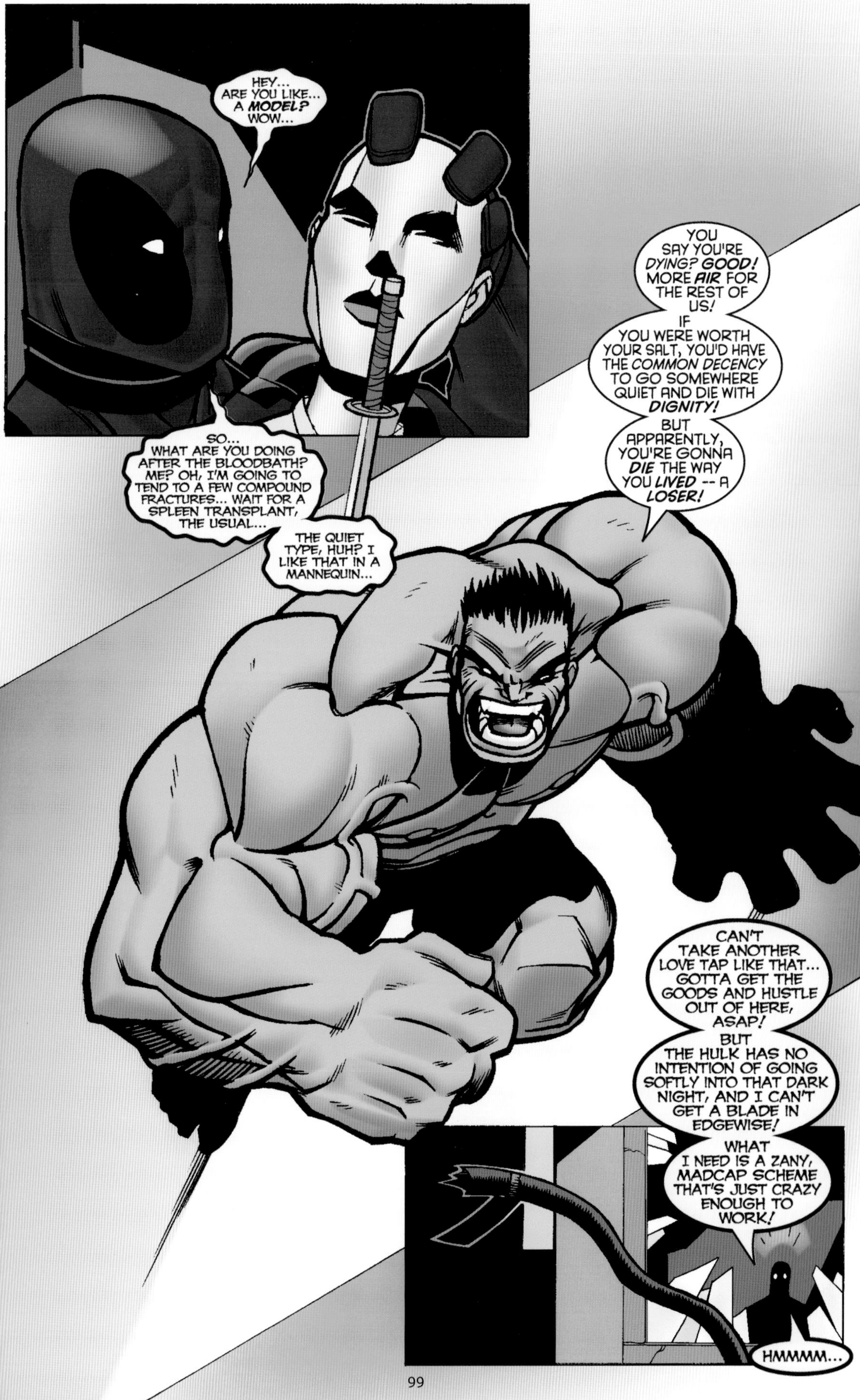
HEY... ARE YOU LIKE... A MODEL? WOW...
YOU SAY YOU'RE DYING? GOOD! MORE AIR FOR THE REST OF US!
IF YOU WERE WORTH YOUR SALT, YOU'D HAVE THE COMMON DECENCY TO GO SOMEWHERE QUIET AND DIE WITH DIGNITY!
BUT APPARENTLY, YOU'RE GONNA DIE THE WAY YOU LIVED -- A LOSER!
SO... WHAT ARE YOU DOING AFTER THE BLOODBATH? ME? OH, I'M GOING TO TEND TO A FEW COMPOUND FRACTURES... WAIT FOR A SPLEEN TRANSPLANT, THE USUAL...
THE QUIET TYPE, HUH? I LIKE THAT IN A MANNEQUIN...
CAN'T TAKE ANOTHER LOVE TAP LIKE THAT... GOTTA GET THE GOODS AND HUSTLE OUT OF HERE, ASAP!
BUT THE HULK HAS NO INTENTION OF GOING SOFTLY INTO THAT DARK NIGHT, AND I CAN'T GET A BLADE IN EDGEWISE!
WHAT I NEED IS A ZANY, MADCAP SCHEME THAT'S JUST CRAZY ENOUGH TO WORK!
HMMMM...

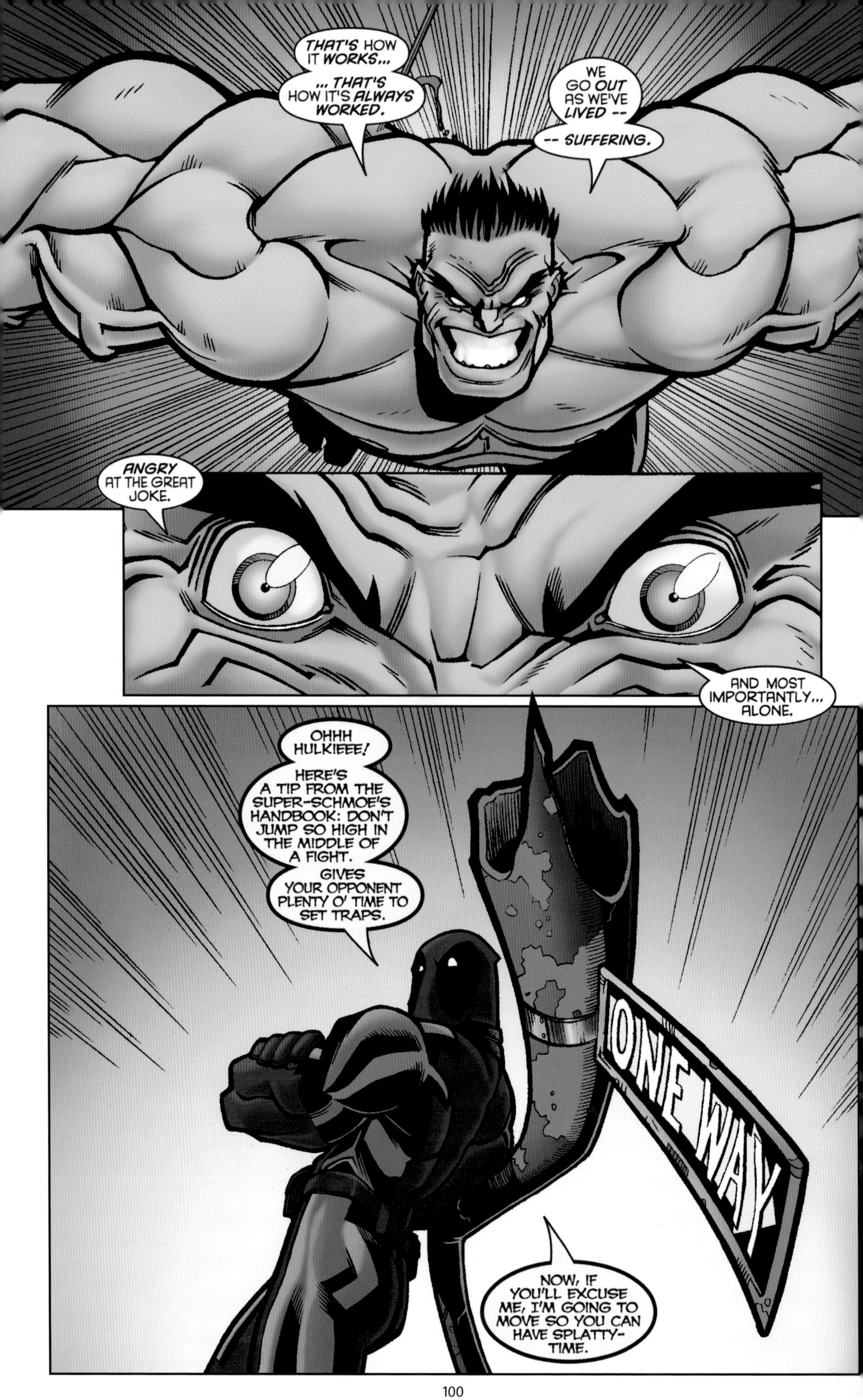
THAT'S HOW IT WORKS...
... THAT'S HOW IT'S ALWAYS WORKED.
WE GO OUT AS WE'VE LIVED --
-- SUFFERING.
ANGRY AT THE GREAT JOKE.
AND MOST IMPORTANTLY... ALONE.
OHHH HULKIEEE!
HERE'S A TIP FROM THE SUPER-SCHMOE'S HANDBOOK: DON'T JUMP SO HIGH IN THE MIDDLE OF A FIGHT.
GIVES YOUR OPPONENT PLENTY O' TIME TO SET TRAPS.
ONE WAY
NOW, IF YOU'LL EXCUSE ME, I'M GOING TO MOVE SO YOU CAN HAVE SPLATTY-TIME.

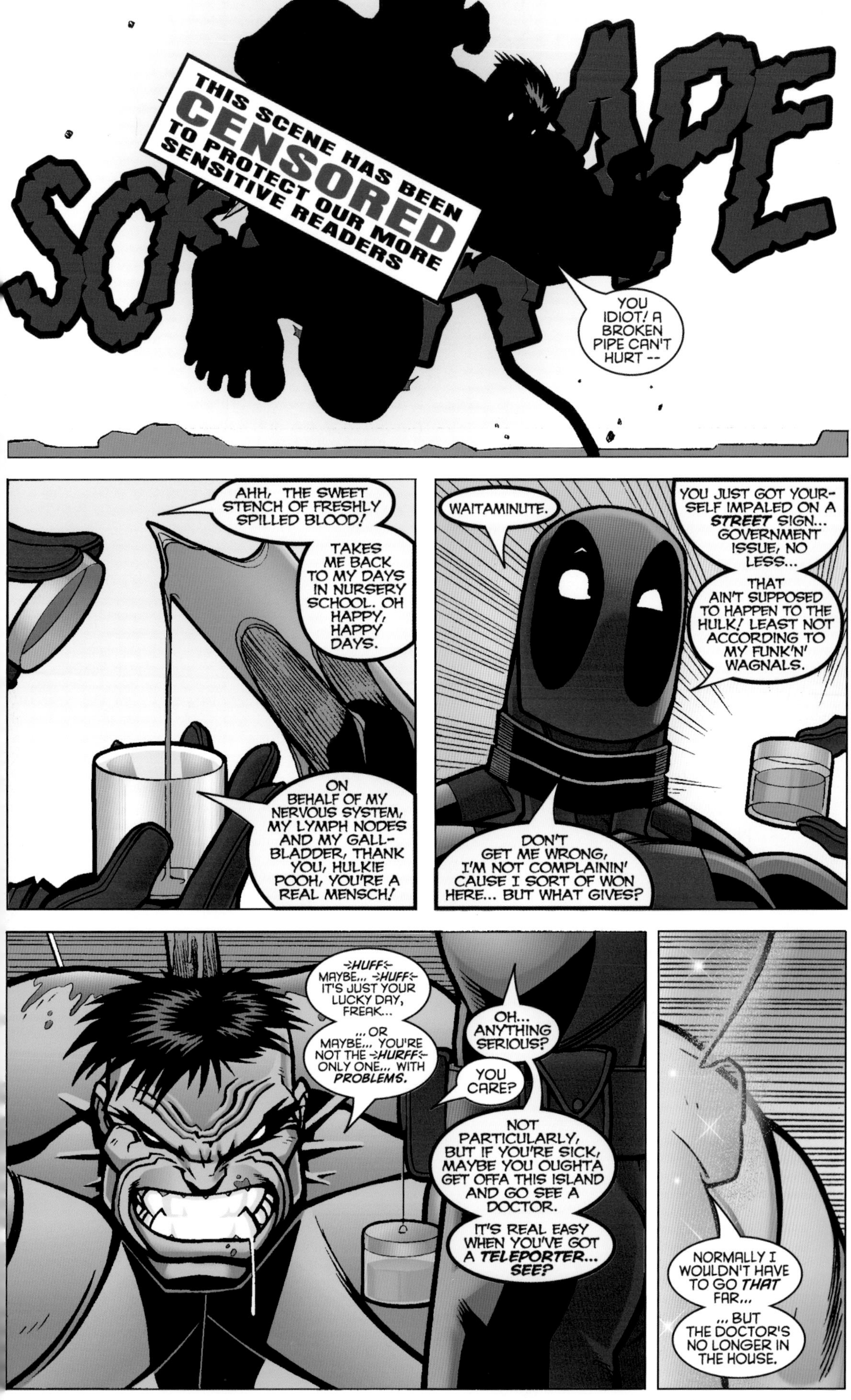
THIS SCENE HAS BEEN CENSORED TO PROTECT OUR MORE SENSITIVE READERS
YOU IDIOT! A BROKEN PIPE CAN'T HURT --
AHH, THE SWEET STENCH OF FRESHLY SPILLED BLOOD!
TAKES ME BACK TO MY DAYS IN NURSERY SCHOOL. OH HAPPY, HAPPY DAYS.
ON BEHALF OF MY NERVOUS SYSTEM, MY LYMPH NODES AND MY GALL-BLADDER, THANK YOU, HULKIE POOH, YOU'RE A REAL MENSCH!
WAITAMINUTE.
YOU JUST GOT YOUR-SELF IMPALED ON A STREET SIGN... GOVERNMENT ISSUE, NO LESS...
THAT AIN'T SUPPOSED TO HAPPEN TO THE HULK! LEAST NOT ACCORDING TO MY FUNK'N' WAGNALS.
DON'T GET ME WRONG, I'M NOT COMPLAININ' CAUSE I SORT OF WON HERE... BUT WHAT GIVES?
HUFF MAYBE... HUFF IT'S JUST YOUR LUCKY DAY, FREAK...
...OR MAYBE... YOU'RE NOT THE HURFF ONLY ONE... WITH PROBLEMS.
OH... ANYTHING SERIOUS?
YOU CARE?
NOT PARTICULARLY, BUT IF YOU'RE SICK, MAYBE YOU OUGHTA GET OFFA THIS ISLAND AND GO SEE A DOCTOR.
IT'S REAL EASY WHEN YOU'VE GOT A TELEPORTER... SEE?
NORMALLY I WOULDN'T HAVE TO GO THAT FAR...
... BUT THE DOCTOR'S NO LONGER IN THE HOUSE.

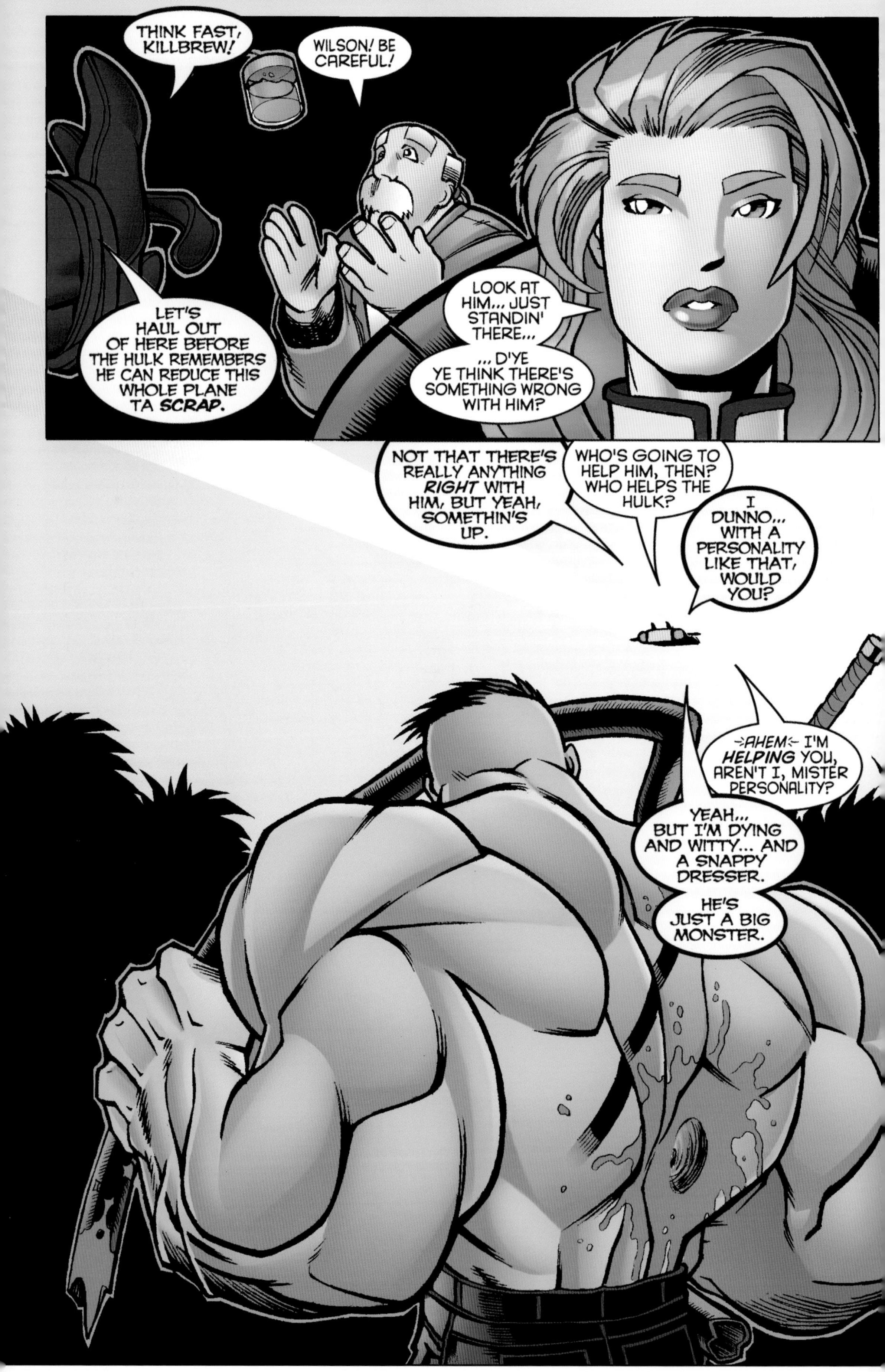
THINK FAST, KILLBREW!
WILSON! BE CAREFUL!
LET'S HAUL OUT OF HERE BEFORE THE HULK REMEMBERS HE CAN REDUCE THIS WHOLE PLANE TA *SCRAP*.
LOOK AT HIM... JUST STANDIN' THERE...
... D'YE YE THINK THERE'S SOMETHING WRONG WITH HIM?
NOT THAT THERE'S REALLY ANYTHING *RIGHT* WITH HIM, BUT YEAH, SOMETHIN'S UP.
WHO'S GOING TO HELP HIM, THEN? WHO HELPS THE HULK?
I DUNNO... WITH A PERSONALITY LIKE THAT, WOULD YOU?
=AHEM= I'M *HELPING* YOU, AREN'T I, MISTER PERSONALITY?
YEAH... BUT I'M DYING AND WITTY... AND A SNAPPY DRESSER.
HE'S JUST A BIG MONSTER.

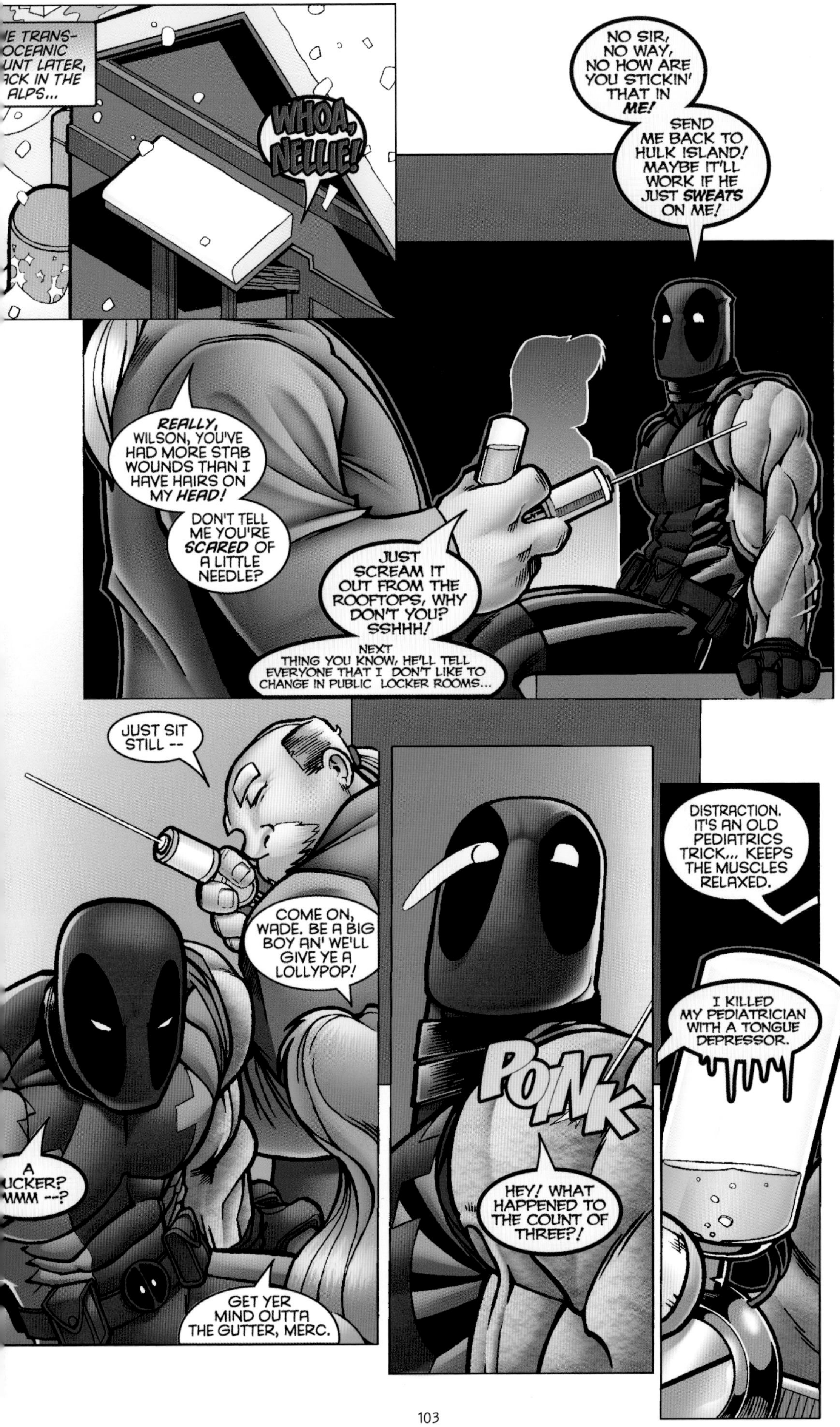
E TRANS-OCEANIC UNT LATER, ACK IN THE ALPS...
WHOA, NELLIE!
NO SIR, NO WAY, NO HOW ARE YOU STICKIN' THAT IN ME!
SEND ME BACK TO HULK ISLAND! MAYBE IT'LL WORK IF HE JUST SWEATS ON ME!
REALLY, WILSON, YOU'VE HAD MORE STAB WOUNDS THAN I HAVE HAIRS ON MY HEAD!
DON'T TELL ME YOU'RE SCARED OF A LITTLE NEEDLE?
JUST SCREAM IT OUT FROM THE ROOFTOPS, WHY DON'T YOU? SSHHH!
NEXT THING YOU KNOW, HE'LL TELL EVERYONE THAT I DON'T LIKE TO CHANGE IN PUBLIC LOCKER ROOMS...
JUST SIT STILL --
COME ON, WADE. BE A BIG BOY AN' WE'LL GIVE YE A LOLLYPOP!
A UCKER? MMM --?
GET YER MIND OUTTA THE GUTTER, MERC.
DISTRACTION. IT'S AN OLD PEDIATRICS TRICK... KEEPS THE MUSCLES RELAXED.
POINK
HEY! WHAT HAPPENED TO THE COUNT OF THREE?!
I KILLED MY PEDIATRICIAN WITH A TONGUE DEPRESSOR.

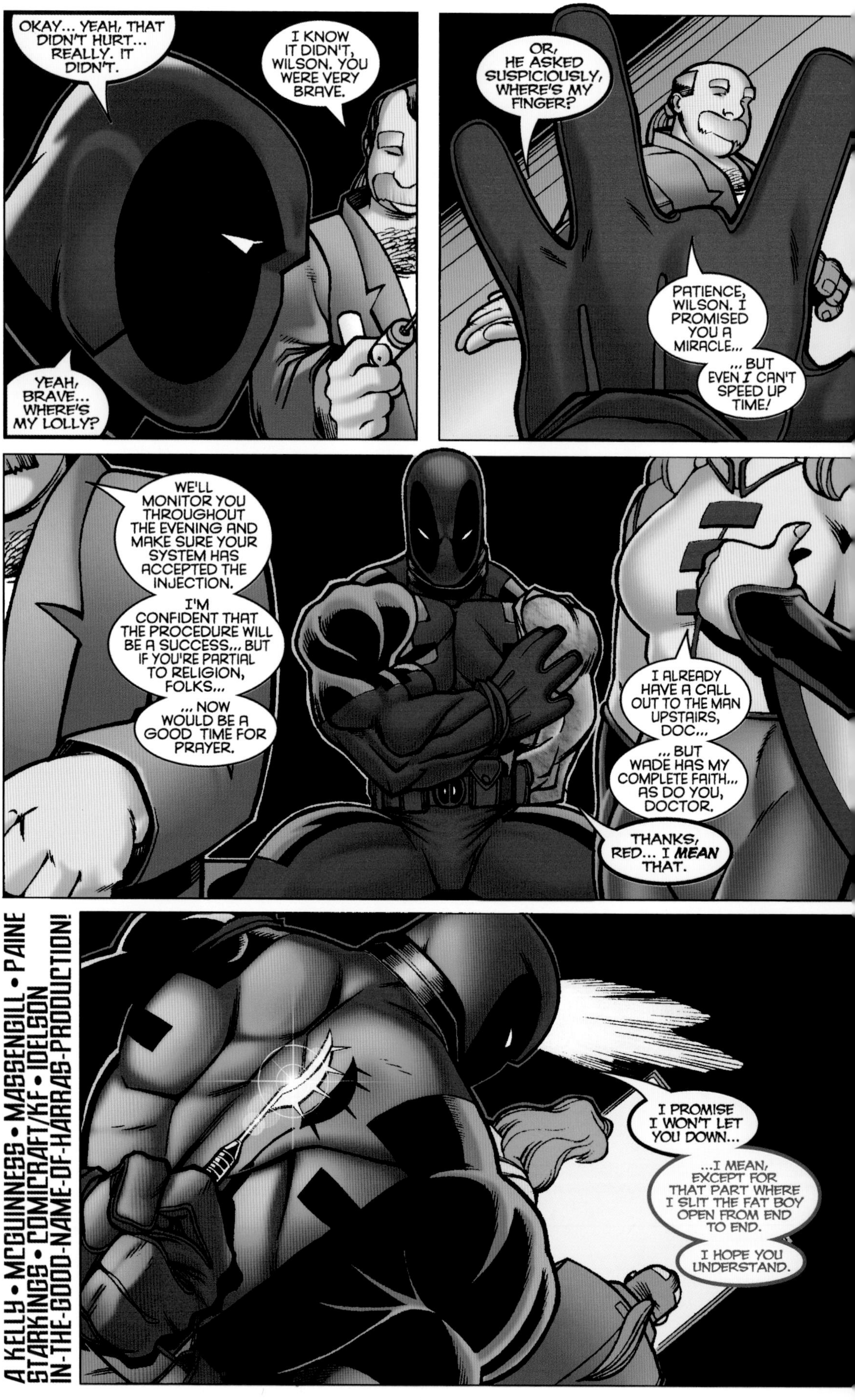
OKAY... YEAH, THAT DIDN'T HURT... REALLY. IT DIDN'T.
I KNOW IT DIDN'T, WILSON. YOU WERE VERY BRAVE.
YEAH, BRAVE... WHERE'S MY LOLLY?
OR, HE ASKED SUSPICIOUSLY, WHERE'S MY FINGER?
PATIENCE, WILSON. I PROMISED YOU A MIRACLE...
...BUT EVEN *I* CAN'T SPEED UP TIME!
WE'LL MONITOR YOU THROUGHOUT THE EVENING AND MAKE SURE YOUR SYSTEM HAS ACCEPTED THE INJECTION.
I'M CONFIDENT THAT THE PROCEDURE WILL BE A SUCCESS... BUT IF YOU'RE PARTIAL TO RELIGION, FOLKS...
...NOW WOULD BE A GOOD TIME FOR PRAYER.
I ALREADY HAVE A CALL OUT TO THE MAN UPSTAIRS, DOC...
...BUT WADE HAS MY COMPLETE FAITH... AS DO YOU, DOCTOR.
THANKS, RED... I ***MEAN*** THAT.
I PROMISE I WON'T LET YOU DOWN...
...I MEAN, EXCEPT FOR THAT PART WHERE I SLIT THE FAT BOY OPEN FROM END TO END.
I HOPE YOU UNDERSTAND.
A KELLY • MCGUINNESS • MASSENGILL • PAINE
STARKINGS • COMICRAFT/KF • IDELSON
IN-THE-GOOD-NAME-OF-HARRAS-PRODUCTION!

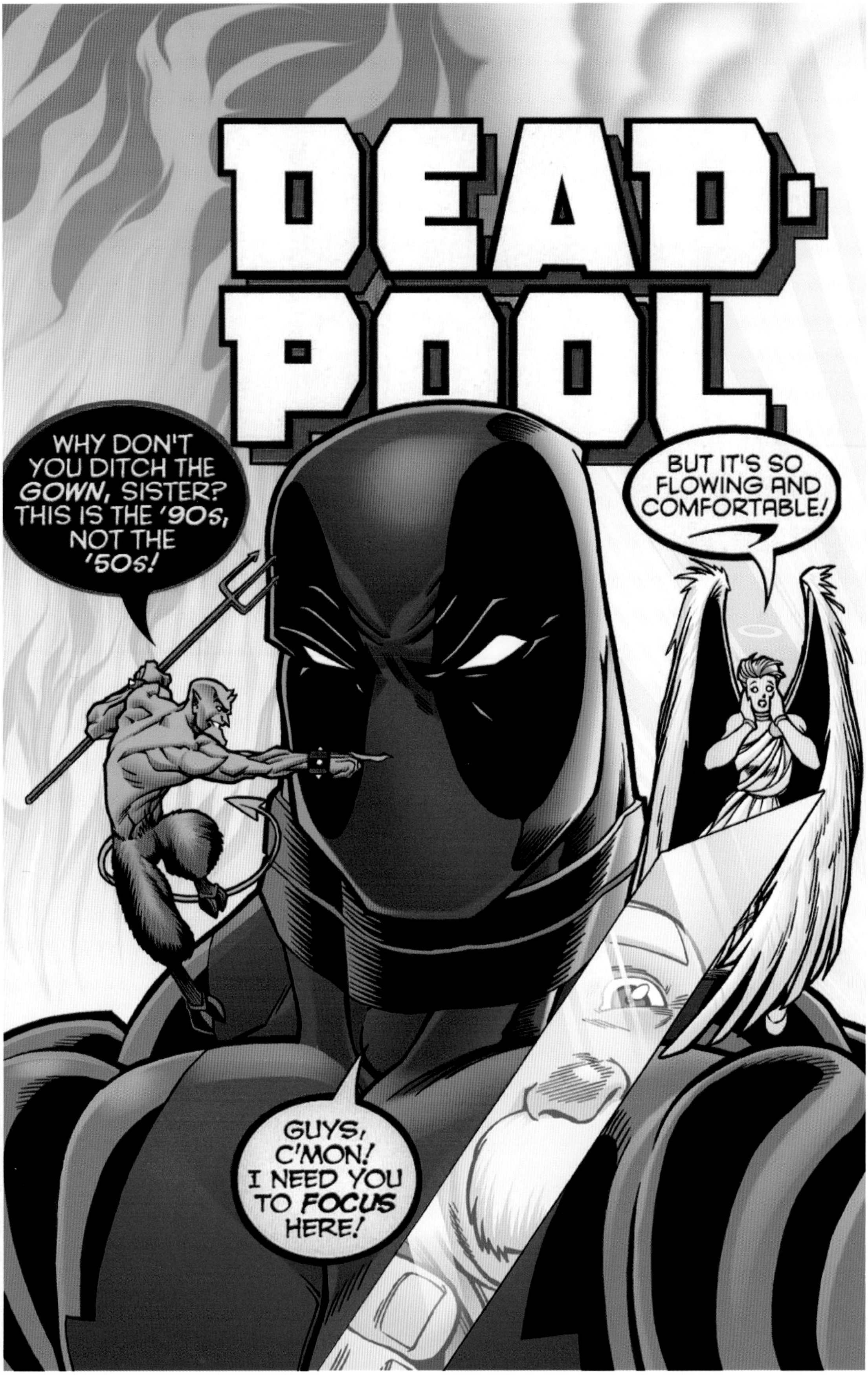
DEAD-POOL
WHY DON'T YOU DITCH THE *GOWN*, SISTER? THIS IS THE *'90s*, NOT THE *'50s!*
BUT IT'S SO FLOWING AND COMFORTABLE!
GUYS, C'MON! I NEED YOU TO *FOCUS* HERE!

IN A SECLUDED SCIENTIFIC FACILITY TUCKED AWAY IN THE SWISS ALPS, A BOLD EXPERIMENT HAS JUST COME TO FRUITION...

OH... THIS IS GOOD, WILSON... BETTER THAN GOOD... THE RESULTS OF THIS MOST RECENT SCAN ARE SPECTACULAR!

THE TRANSFUSION OF GAMMA IRRADIATED BLOOD INTO YOUR SYSTEM APPEARS TO HAVE BEEN A SUCCESS!

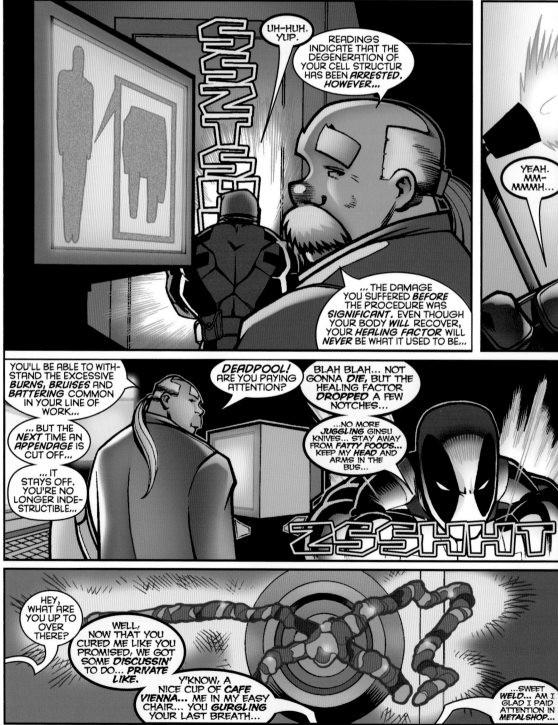

UH-HUH. YUP.

READINGS INDICATE THAT THE DEGENERATION OF YOUR CELL STRUCTUR HAS BEEN ARRESTED. HOWEVER...

YEAH. MM-MMMH...

... THE DAMAGE YOU SUFFERED BEFORE THE PROCEDURE WAS SIGNIFICANT. EVEN THOUGH YOUR BODY WILL RECOVER, YOUR HEALING FACTOR WILL NEVER BE WHAT IT USED TO BE...

YOU'LL BE ABLE TO WITHSTAND THE EXCESSIVE BURNS, BRUISES AND BATTERING COMMON IN YOUR LINE OF WORK...

... BUT THE NEXT TIME AN APPENDAGE IS CUT OFF...

... IT STAYS OFF. YOU'RE NO LONGER INDESTRUCTIBLE...

DEADPOOL! ARE YOU PAYING ATTENTION?

BLAH BLAH... NOT GONNA DIE, BUT THE HEALING FACTOR DROPPED A FEW NOTCHES...

...NO MORE JUGGLING GINSU KNIVES... STAY AWAY FROM FATTY FOODS... KEEP MY HEAD AND ARMS IN THE BUS...

HEY, WHAT ARE YOU UP TO OVER THERE?

WELL, NOW THAT YOU CURED ME LIKE YOU PROMISED, WE GOT SOME DISCUSSIN' TO DO... PRIVATE LIKE.

Y'KNOW, A NICE CUP OF CAFE VIENNA... ME IN MY EASY CHAIR... YOU GURGLING YOUR LAST BREATH...

...SWEET WELD... AM I GLAD I PAID ATTENTION IN METALSHOP!

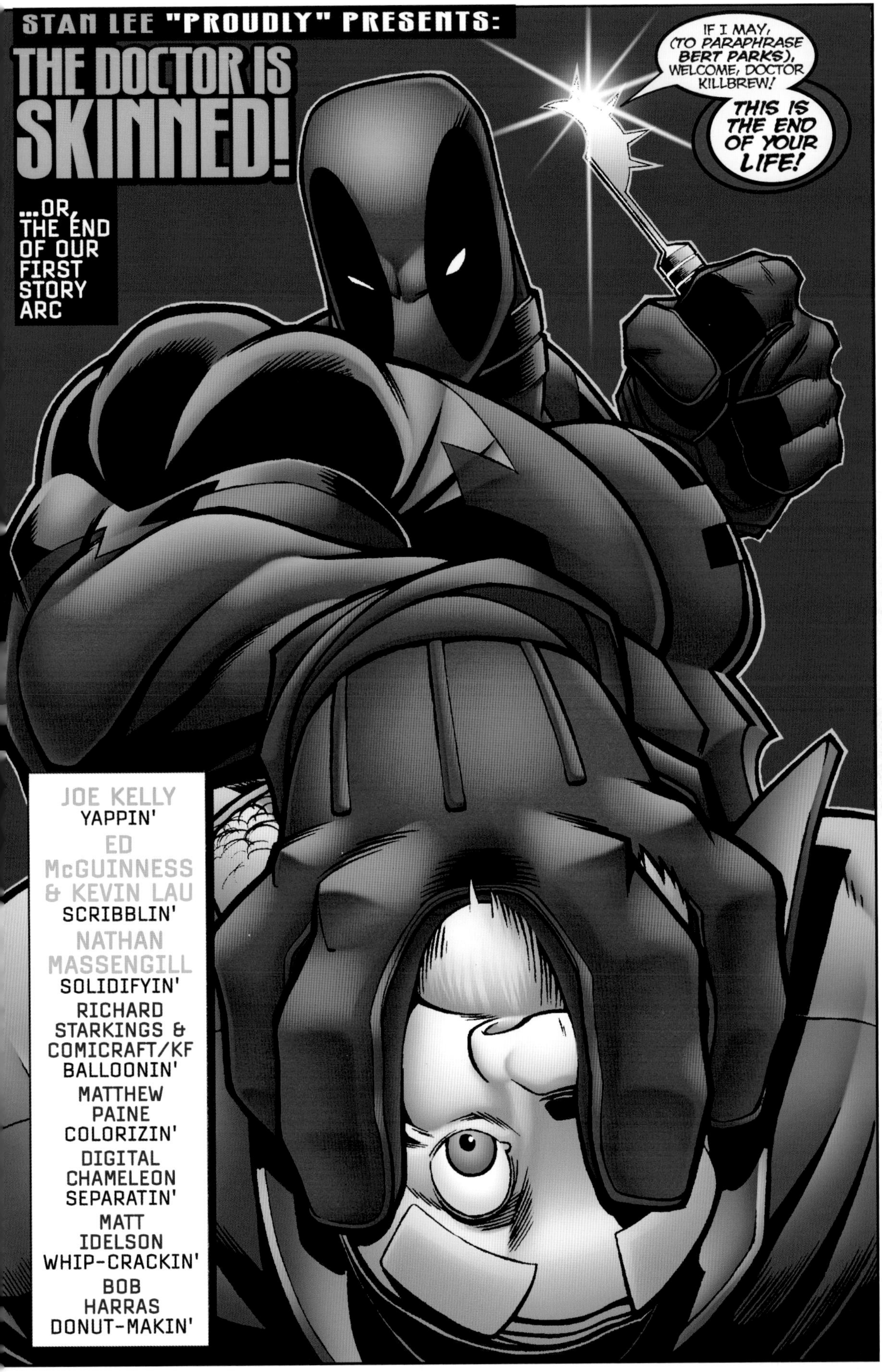
STAN LEE "PROUDLY" PRESENTS:
THE DOCTOR IS SKINNED!
...OR, THE END OF OUR FIRST STORY ARC
IF I MAY, (TO PARAPHRASE BERT PARKS), WELCOME, DOCTOR KILLBREW!
THIS IS THE END OF YOUR LIFE!
JOE KELLY YAPPIN'
ED McGUINNESS & KEVIN LAU SCRIBBLIN'
NATHAN MASSENGILL SOLIDIFYIN'
RICHARD STARKINGS & COMICRAFT/KF BALLOONIN'
MATTHEW PAINE COLORIZIN'
DIGITAL CHAMELEON SEPARATIN'
MATT IDELSON WHIP-CRACKIN'
BOB HARRAS DONUT-MAKIN'

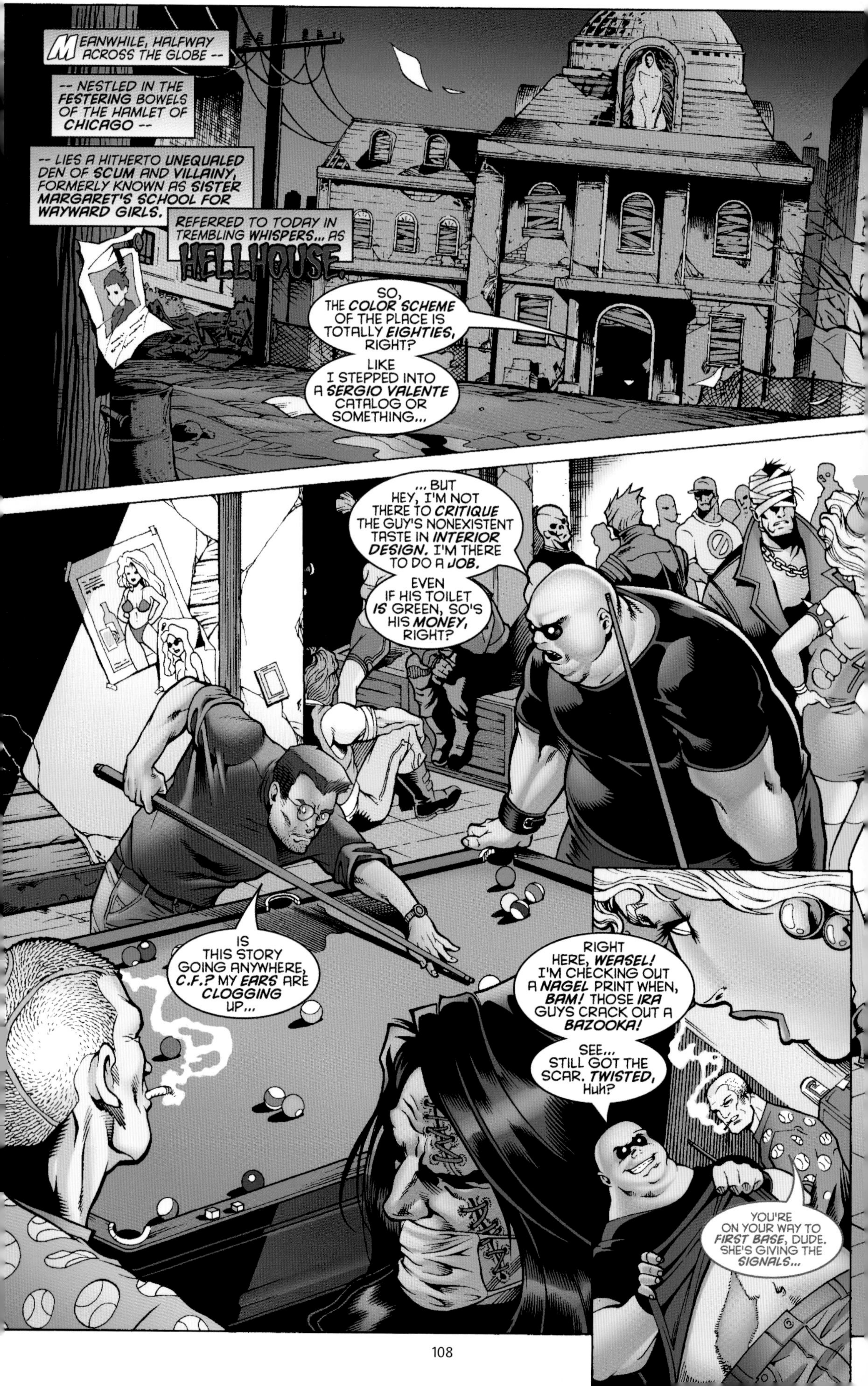
MEANWHILE, HALFWAY ACROSS THE GLOBE --
-- NESTLED IN THE FESTERING BOWELS OF THE HAMLET OF CHICAGO --
-- LIES A HITHERTO UNEQUALED DEN OF SCUM AND VILLAINY, FORMERLY KNOWN AS SISTER MARGARET'S SCHOOL FOR WAYWARD GIRLS.
REFERRED TO TODAY IN TREMBLING WHISPERS... AS
HELLHOUSE.
SO, THE COLOR SCHEME OF THE PLACE IS TOTALLY EIGHTIES, RIGHT?
LIKE I STEPPED INTO A SERGIO VALENTE CATALOG OR SOMETHING...
... BUT HEY, I'M NOT THERE TO CRITIQUE THE GUY'S NONEXISTENT TASTE IN INTERIOR DESIGN. I'M THERE TO DO A JOB.
EVEN IF HIS TOILET IS GREEN, SO'S HIS MONEY, RIGHT?
IS THIS STORY GOING ANYWHERE, C.F.? MY EARS ARE CLOGGING UP...
RIGHT HERE, WEASEL! I'M CHECKING OUT A NAGEL PRINT WHEN, BAM! THOSE IRA GUYS CRACK OUT A BAZOOKA!
SEE... STILL GOT THE SCAR. TWISTED, Huh?
YOU'RE ON YOUR WAY TO FIRST BASE, DUDE. SHE'S GIVING THE SIGNALS...

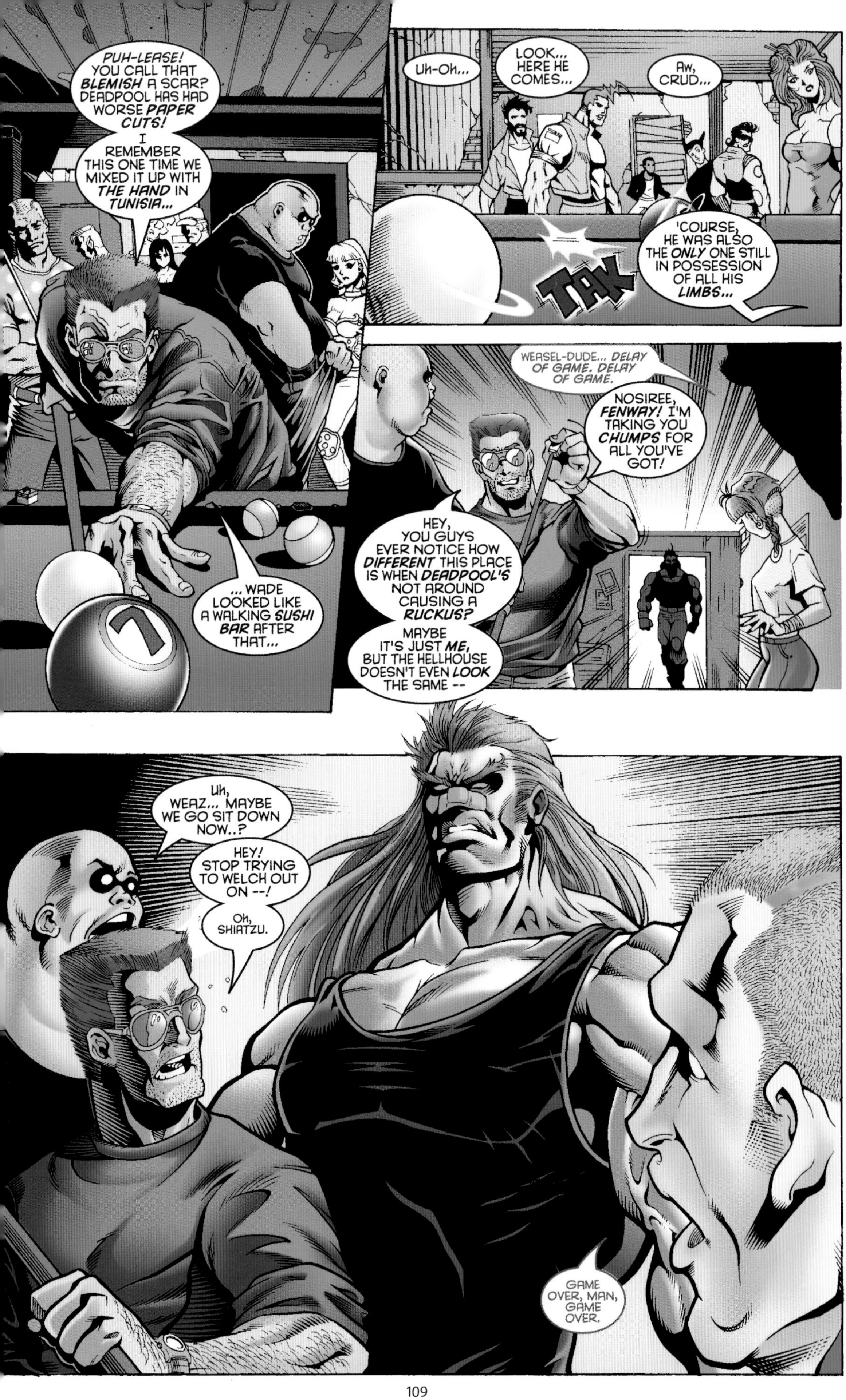
PUH-LEASE! YOU CALL THAT BLEMISH A SCAR? DEADPOOL HAS HAD WORSE PAPER CUTS!
I REMEMBER THIS ONE TIME WE MIXED IT UP WITH THE HAND IN TUNISIA...
...WADE LOOKED LIKE A WALKING SUSHI BAR AFTER THAT...
Uh-Oh...
LOOK... HERE HE COMES...
AW, CRUD...
TAK
'COURSE, HE WAS ALSO THE ONLY ONE STILL IN POSSESSION OF ALL HIS LIMBS...
WEASEL-DUDE... DELAY OF GAME. DELAY OF GAME.
NOSIREE, FENWAY! I'M TAKING YOU CHUMPS FOR ALL YOU'VE GOT!
HEY, YOU GUYS EVER NOTICE HOW DIFFERENT THIS PLACE IS WHEN DEADPOOL'S NOT AROUND CAUSING A RUCKUS?
MAYBE IT'S JUST ME, BUT THE HELLHOUSE DOESN'T EVEN LOOK THE SAME --
Uh, WEAZ... MAYBE WE GO SIT DOWN NOW..?
HEY! STOP TRYING TO WELCH OUT ON --!
Oh, SHIATZU.
GAME OVER, MAN, GAME OVER.

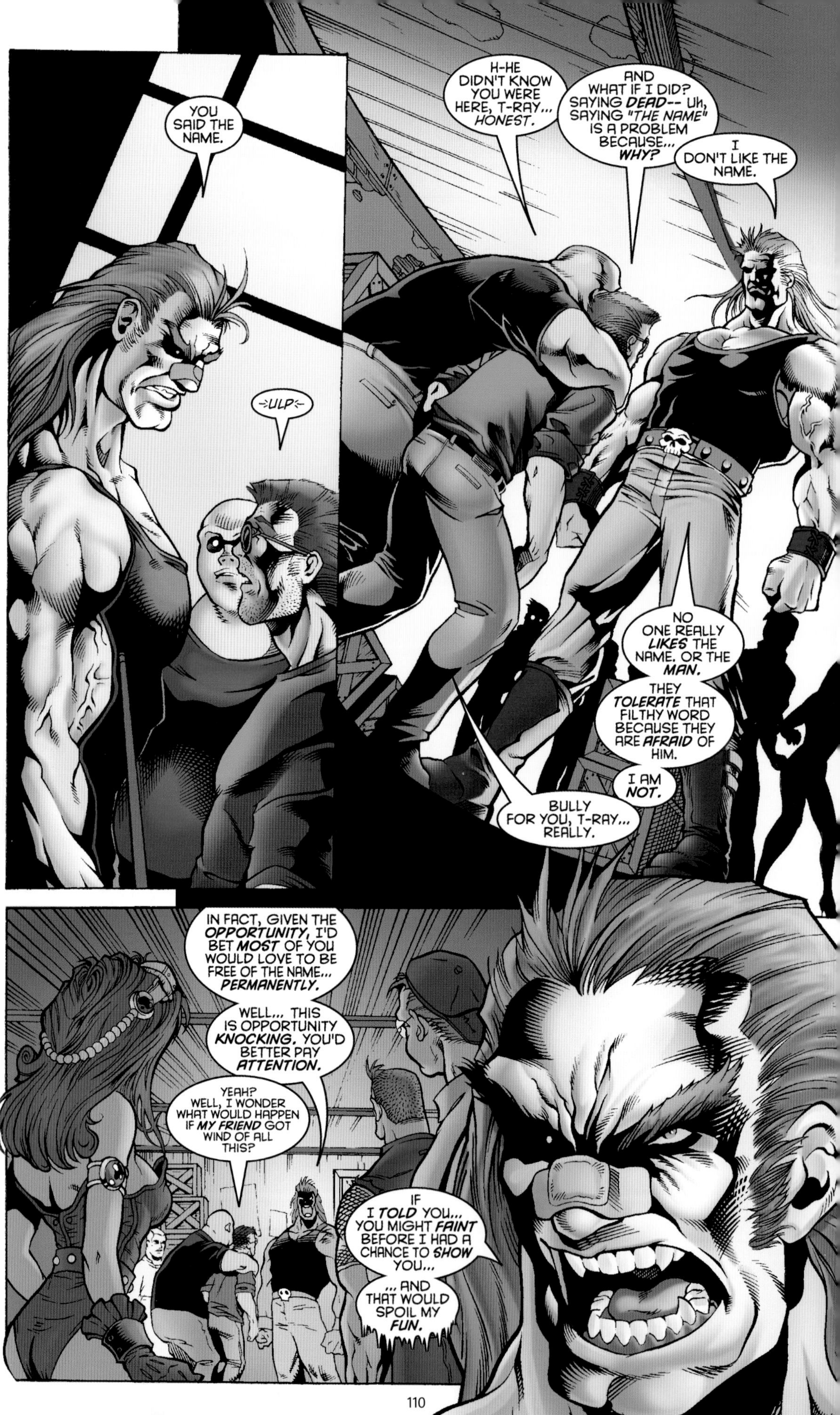

YOU SAID THE NAME.
-ULP-
H-HE DIDN'T KNOW YOU WERE HERE, T-RAY... HONEST.
AND WHAT IF I DID? SAYING DEAD-- Uh, SAYING "THE NAME" IS A PROBLEM BECAUSE... WHY?
I DON'T LIKE THE NAME.
NO ONE REALLY LIKES THE NAME. OR THE MAN.
THEY TOLERATE THAT FILTHY WORD BECAUSE THEY ARE AFRAID OF HIM.
I AM NOT.
BULLY FOR YOU, T-RAY... REALLY.
IN FACT, GIVEN THE OPPORTUNITY, I'D BET MOST OF YOU WOULD LOVE TO BE FREE OF THE NAME... PERMANENTLY.
WELL... THIS IS OPPORTUNITY KNOCKING. YOU'D BETTER PAY ATTENTION.
YEAH? WELL, I WONDER WHAT WOULD HAPPEN IF MY FRIEND GOT WIND OF ALL THIS?
IF I TOLD YOU... YOU MIGHT FAINT BEFORE I HAD A CHANCE TO SHOW YOU...
... AND THAT WOULD SPOIL MY FUN.

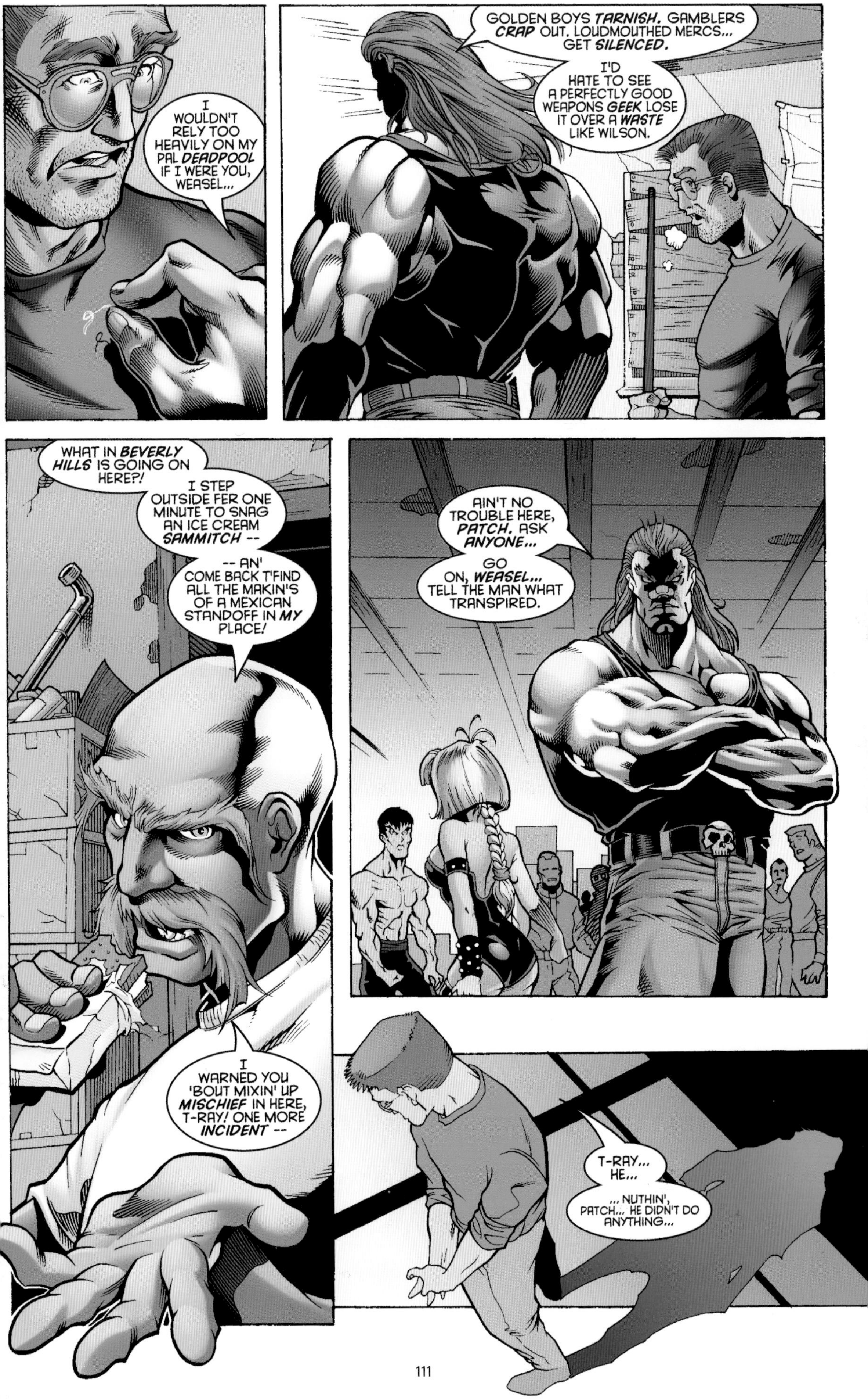
I WOULDN'T RELY TOO HEAVILY ON MY PAL DEADPOOL IF I WERE YOU, WEASEL...
GOLDEN BOYS TARNISH. GAMBLERS CRAP OUT. LOUDMOUTHED MERCS... GET SILENCED.
I'D HATE TO SEE A PERFECTLY GOOD WEAPONS GEEK LOSE IT OVER A WASTE LIKE WILSON.
WHAT IN BEVERLY HILLS IS GOING ON HERE?!
I STEP OUTSIDE FER ONE MINUTE TO SNAG AN ICE CREAM SAMMITCH --
-- AN' COME BACK T'FIND ALL THE MAKIN'S OF A MEXICAN STANDOFF IN MY PLACE!
AIN'T NO TROUBLE HERE, PATCH. ASK ANYONE...
GO ON, WEASEL... TELL THE MAN WHAT TRANSPIRED.
I WARNED YOU 'BOUT MIXIN' UP MISCHIEF IN HERE, T-RAY! ONE MORE INCIDENT --
T-RAY... HE...
... NUTHIN', PATCH... HE DIDN'T DO ANYTHING...

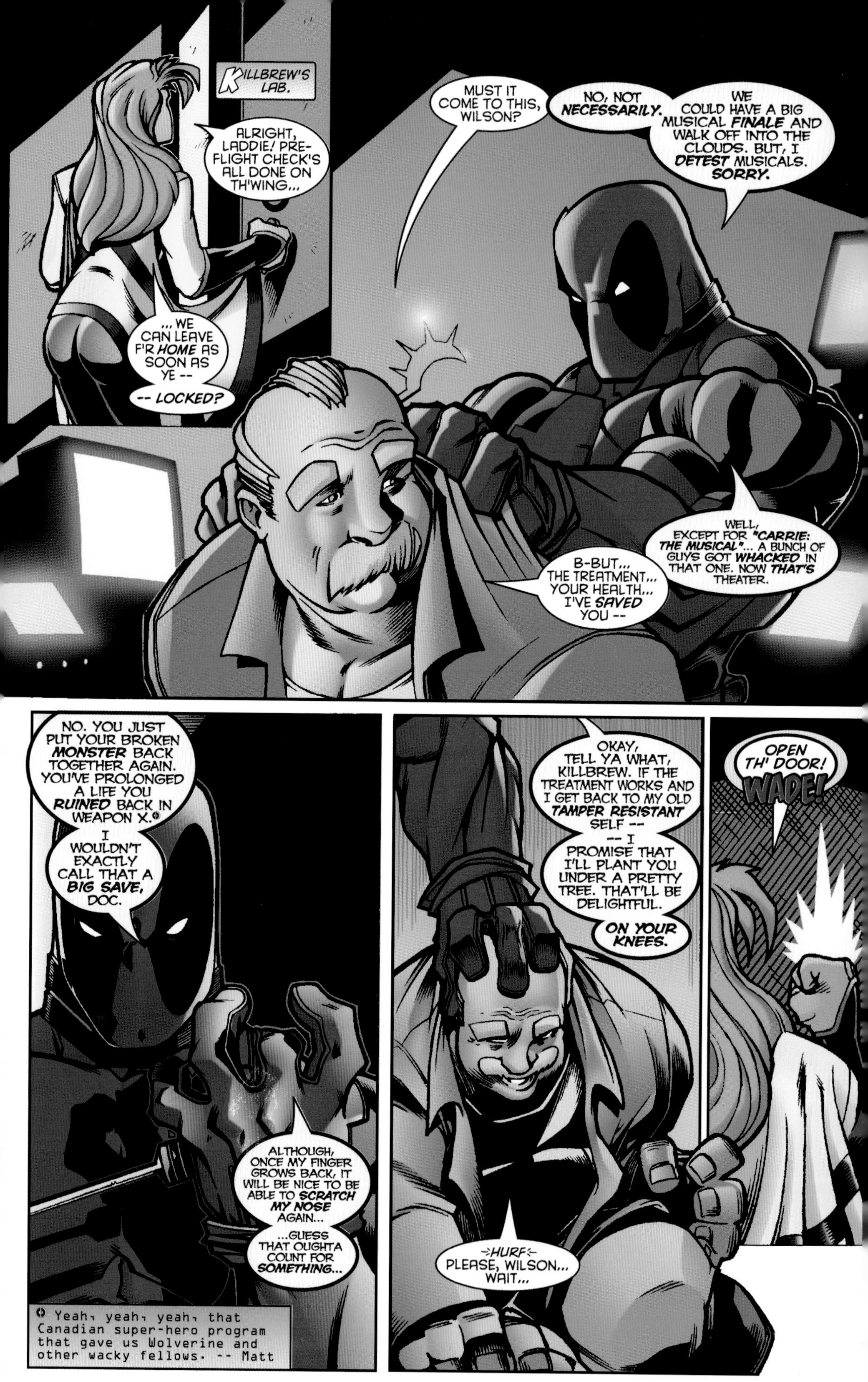
KILLBREW'S LAB.
ALRIGHT, LADDIE! PRE-FLIGHT CHECK'S ALL DONE ON TH'WING...
...WE CAN LEAVE F'R HOME AS SOON AS YE --
-- LOCKED?
MUST IT COME TO THIS, WILSON?
NO, NOT NECESSARILY.
WE COULD HAVE A BIG MUSICAL FINALE AND WALK OFF INTO THE CLOUDS. BUT, I DETEST MUSICALS. SORRY.
WELL, EXCEPT FOR "CARRIE: THE MUSICAL"... A BUNCH OF GUYS GOT WHACKED IN THAT ONE. NOW THAT'S THEATER.
B-BUT... THE TREATMENT... YOUR HEALTH... I'VE SAVED YOU --
NO. YOU JUST PUT YOUR BROKEN MONSTER BACK TOGETHER AGAIN. YOU'VE PROLONGED A LIFE YOU RUINED BACK IN WEAPON X.
I WOULDN'T EXACTLY CALL THAT A BIG SAVE, DOC.
ALTHOUGH, ONCE MY FINGER GROWS BACK, IT WILL BE NICE TO BE ABLE TO SCRATCH MY NOSE AGAIN...
...GUESS THAT OUGHTA COUNT FOR SOMETHING...
Yeah, yeah, yeah, that Canadian super-hero program that gave us Wolverine and other wacky fellows. -- Matt
OKAY, TELL YA WHAT, KILLBREW. IF THE TREATMENT WORKS AND I GET BACK TO MY OLD TAMPER RESISTANT SELF --
-- I PROMISE THAT I'LL PLANT YOU UNDER A PRETTY TREE. THAT'LL BE DELIGHTFUL.
ON YOUR KNEES.
HURF
PLEASE, WILSON... WAIT...
OPEN TH' DOOR! WADE!

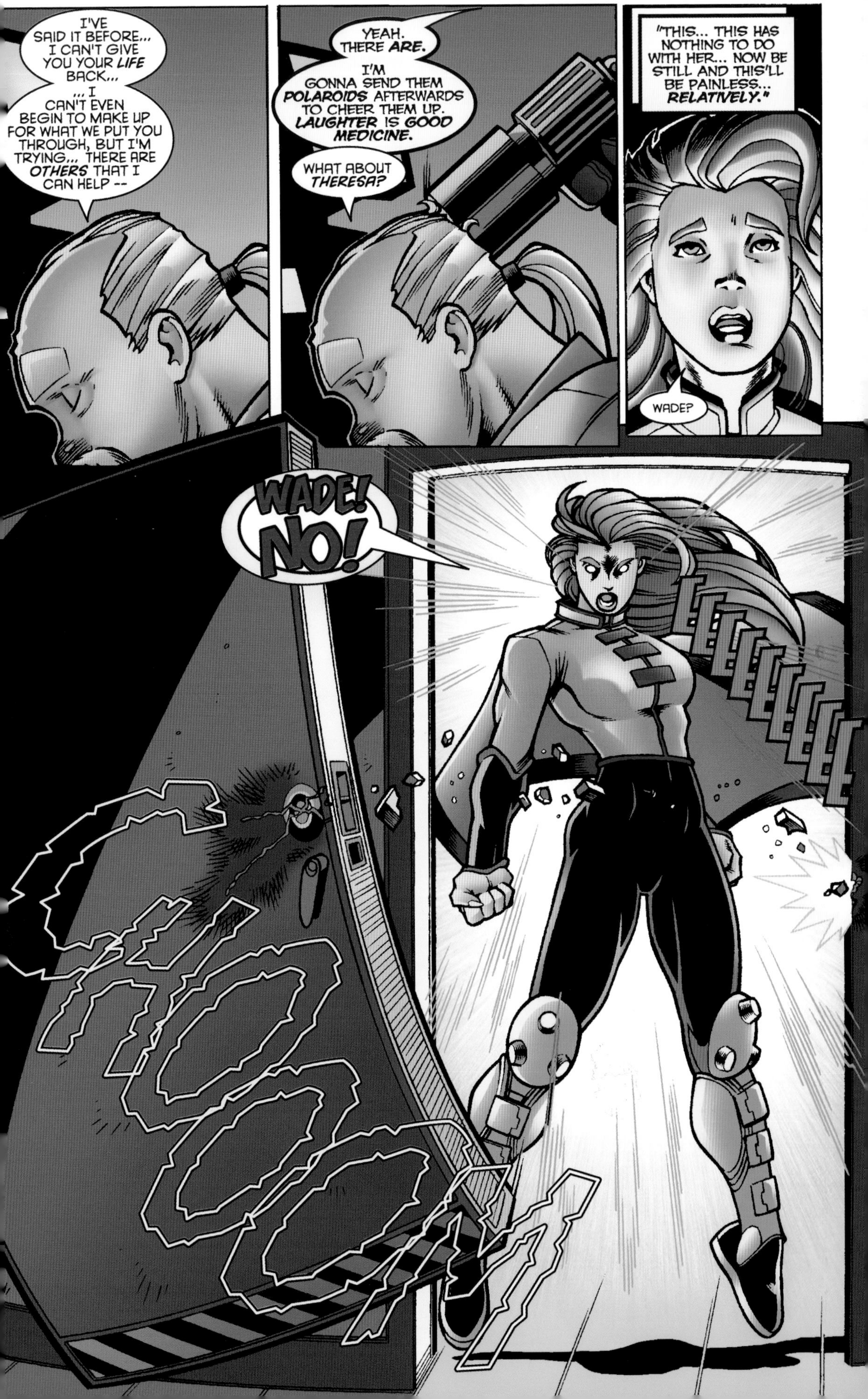

I'VE SAID IT BEFORE... I CAN'T GIVE YOU YOUR *LIFE* BACK...
... I CAN'T EVEN BEGIN TO MAKE UP FOR WHAT WE PUT YOU THROUGH, BUT I'M TRYING... THERE ARE *OTHERS* THAT I CAN HELP --
YEAH. THERE *ARE*.
I'M GONNA SEND THEM *POLAROIDS* AFTERWARDS TO CHEER THEM UP. *LAUGHTER* IS *GOOD MEDICINE*.
WHAT ABOUT *THERESA?*
"THIS... THIS HAS NOTHING TO DO WITH HER... NOW BE STILL AND THIS'LL BE PAINLESS... *RELATIVELY.*"
WADE?
WADE! NO!

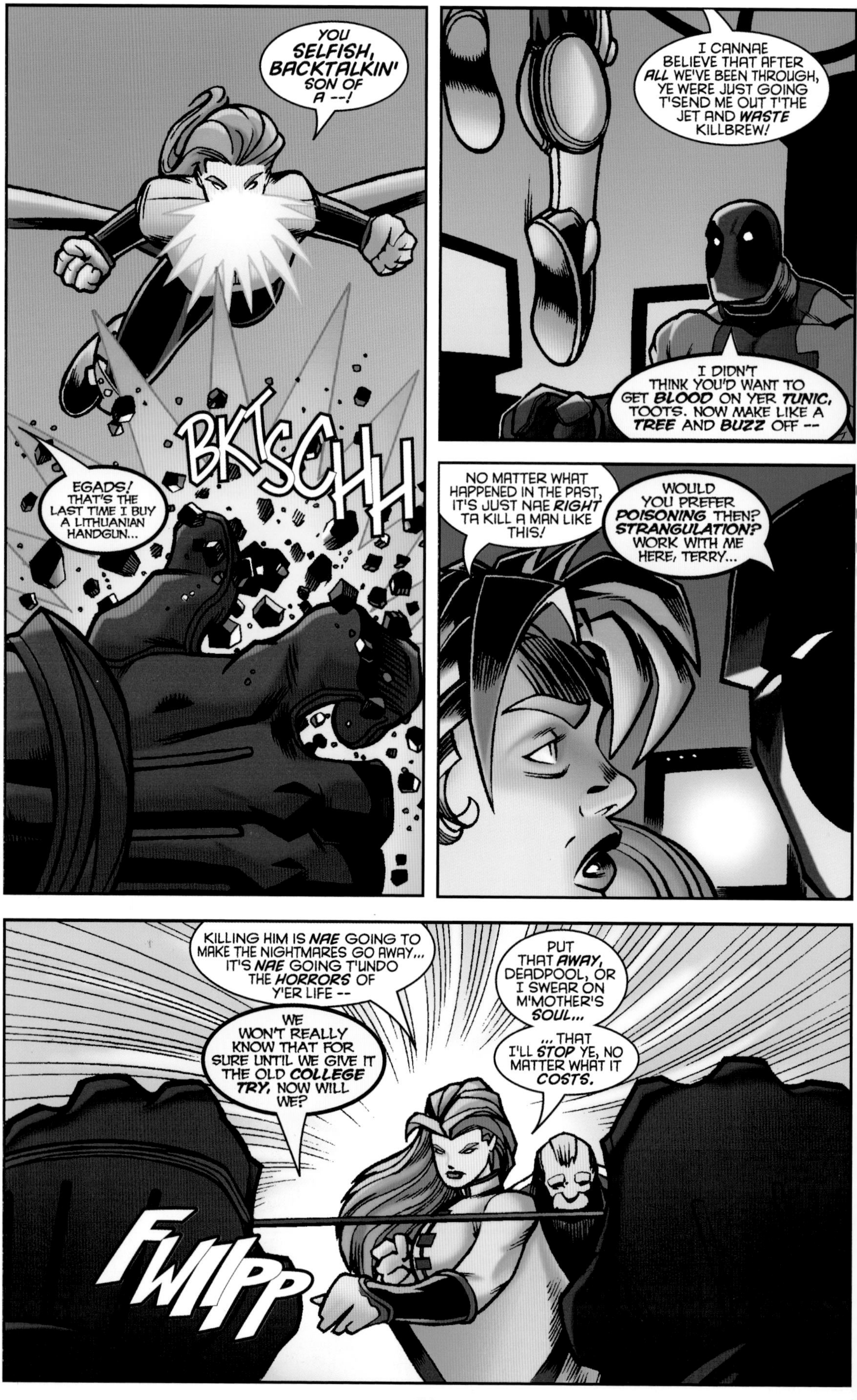

YOU SELFISH, BACKTALKIN' SON OF A --!
I CANNAE BELIEVE THAT AFTER ALL WE'VE BEEN THROUGH, YE WERE JUST GOING T'SEND ME OUT T'THE JET AND WASTE KILLBREW!
I DIDN'T THINK YOU'D WANT TO GET BLOOD ON YER TUNIC, TOOTS. NOW MAKE LIKE A TREE AND BUZZ OFF --
BKTSCHH
EGADS! THAT'S THE LAST TIME I BUY A LITHUANIAN HANDGUN...
NO MATTER WHAT HAPPENED IN THE PAST, IT'S JUST NAE RIGHT TA KILL A MAN LIKE THIS!
WOULD YOU PREFER POISONING THEN? STRANGULATION? WORK WITH ME HERE, TERRY...
KILLING HIM IS NAE GOING TO MAKE THE NIGHTMARES GO AWAY... IT'S NAE GOING T'UNDO THE HORRORS OF Y'ER LIFE --
WE WON'T REALLY KNOW THAT FOR SURE UNTIL WE GIVE IT THE OLD COLLEGE TRY, NOW WILL WE?
PUT THAT AWAY, DEADPOOL, OR I SWEAR ON M'MOTHER'S SOUL...
... THAT I'LL STOP YE, NO MATTER WHAT IT COSTS.
FWIPP

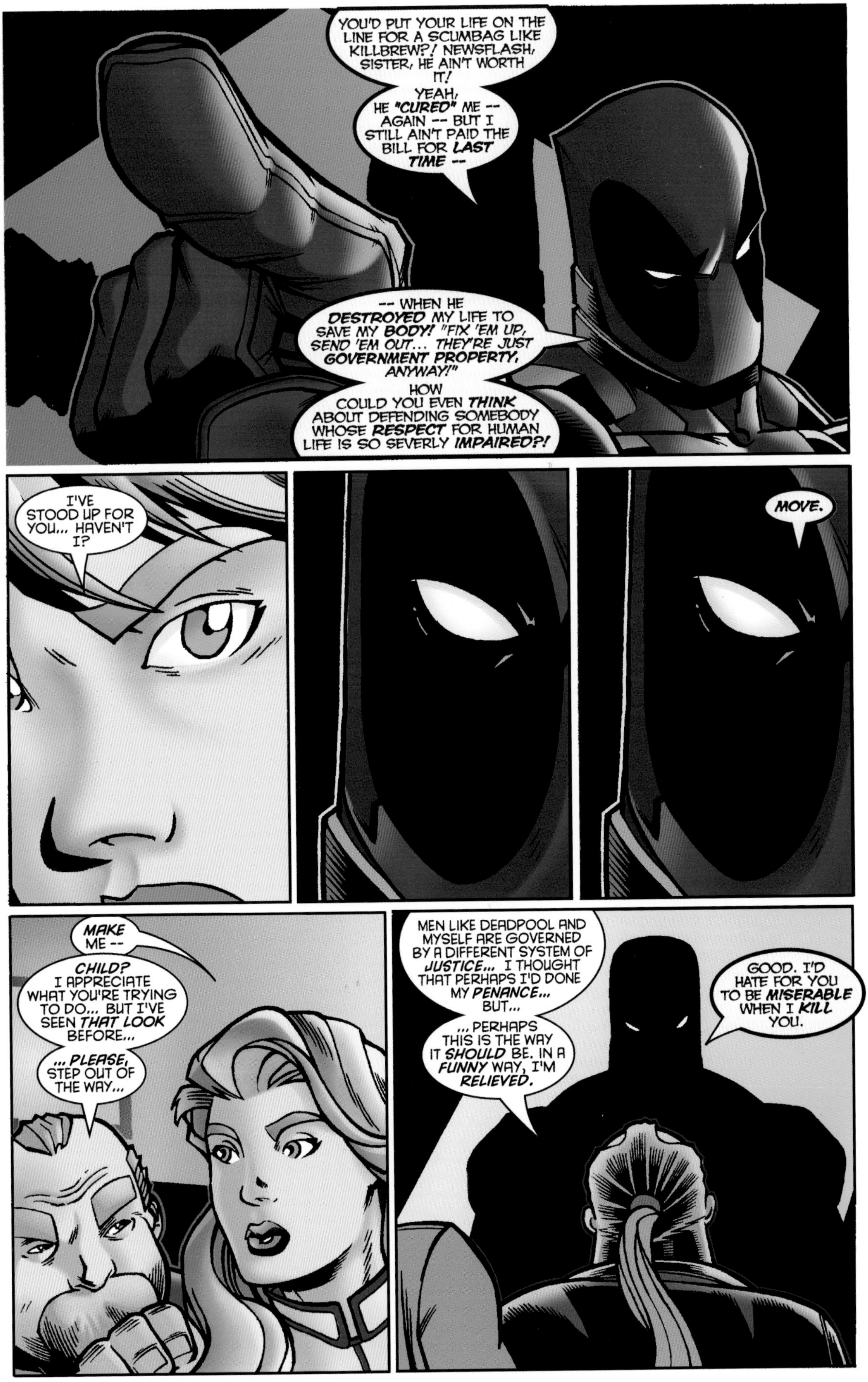
YOU'D PUT YOUR LIFE ON THE LINE FOR A SCUMBAG LIKE KILLBREW?! NEWSFLASH, SISTER, HE AIN'T WORTH IT!
YEAH, HE "CURED" ME -- AGAIN -- BUT I STILL AIN'T PAID THE BILL FOR LAST TIME --
-- WHEN HE DESTROYED MY LIFE TO SAVE MY BODY! "FIX 'EM UP, SEND 'EM OUT... THEY'RE JUST GOVERNMENT PROPERTY, ANYWAY!"
HOW COULD YOU EVEN THINK ABOUT DEFENDING SOMEBODY WHOSE RESPECT FOR HUMAN LIFE IS SO SEVERLY IMPAIRED?!
I'VE STOOD UP FOR YOU... HAVEN'T I?
MOVE.
MAKE ME --
CHILD? I APPRECIATE WHAT YOU'RE TRYING TO DO... BUT I'VE SEEN THAT LOOK BEFORE...
...PLEASE, STEP OUT OF THE WAY...
MEN LIKE DEADPOOL AND MYSELF ARE GOVERNED BY A DIFFERENT SYSTEM OF JUSTICE... I THOUGHT THAT PERHAPS I'D DONE MY PENANCE... BUT...
...PERHAPS THIS IS THE WAY IT SHOULD BE. IN A FUNNY WAY, I'M RELIEVED.
GOOD. I'D HATE FOR YOU TO BE MISERABLE WHEN I KILL YOU.

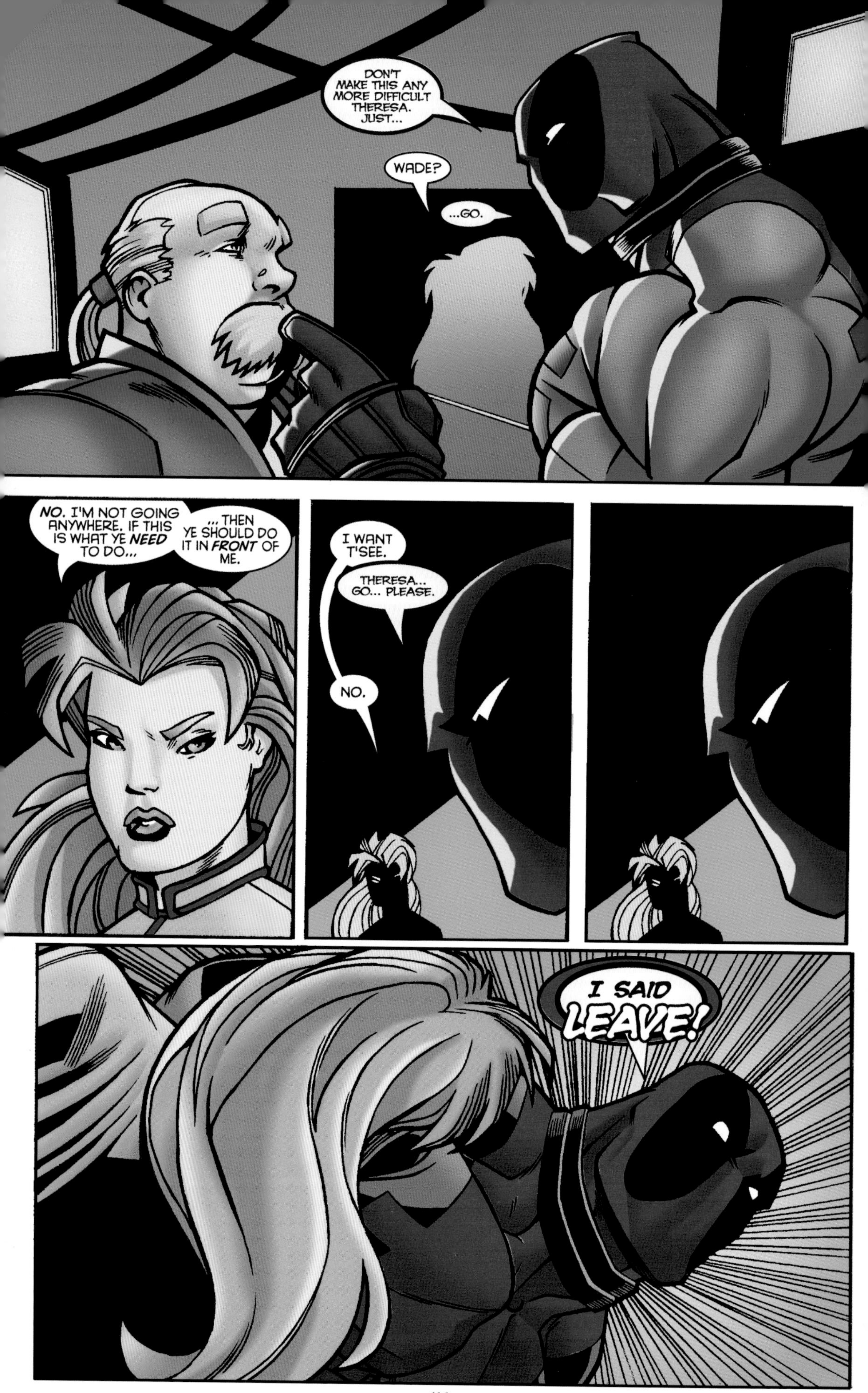
DON'T MAKE THIS ANY MORE DIFFICULT THERESA. JUST...
WADE?
...GO.
NO. I'M NOT GOING ANYWHERE. IF THIS IS WHAT YE NEED TO DO...
... THEN YE SHOULD DO IT IN FRONT OF ME.
I WANT T'SEE.
THERESA... GO... PLEASE.
NO.
I SAID LEAVE!

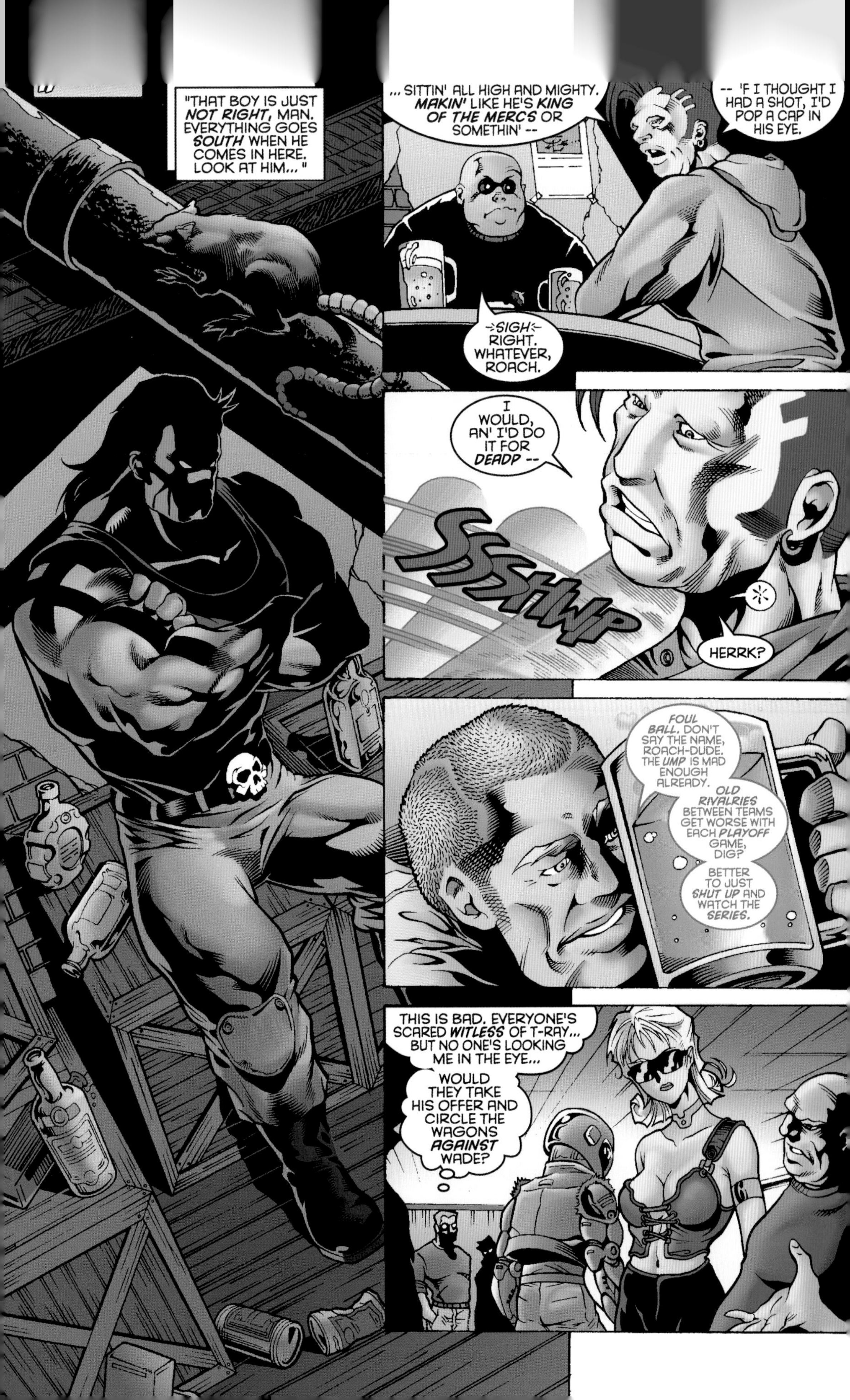
"THAT BOY IS JUST NOT RIGHT, MAN. EVERYTHING GOES SOUTH WHEN HE COMES IN HERE. LOOK AT HIM... "
... SITTIN' ALL HIGH AND MIGHTY. MAKIN' LIKE HE'S KING OF THE MERCS OR SOMETHIN' --
-- 'F I THOUGHT I HAD A SHOT, I'D POP A CAP IN HIS EYE.
SIGH RIGHT. WHATEVER, ROACH.
I WOULD, AN' I'D DO IT FOR DEADP --
SSSHWP
HERRK?
FOUL BALL. DON'T SAY THE NAME, ROACH-DUDE. THE UMP IS MAD ENOUGH ALREADY.
OLD RIVALRIES BETWEEN TEAMS GET WORSE WITH EACH PLAYOFF GAME, DIG?
BETTER TO JUST SHUT UP AND WATCH THE SERIES.
THIS IS BAD. EVERYONE'S SCARED WITLESS OF T-RAY... BUT NO ONE'S LOOKING ME IN THE EYE...
WOULD THEY TAKE HIS OFFER AND CIRCLE THE WAGONS AGAINST WADE?

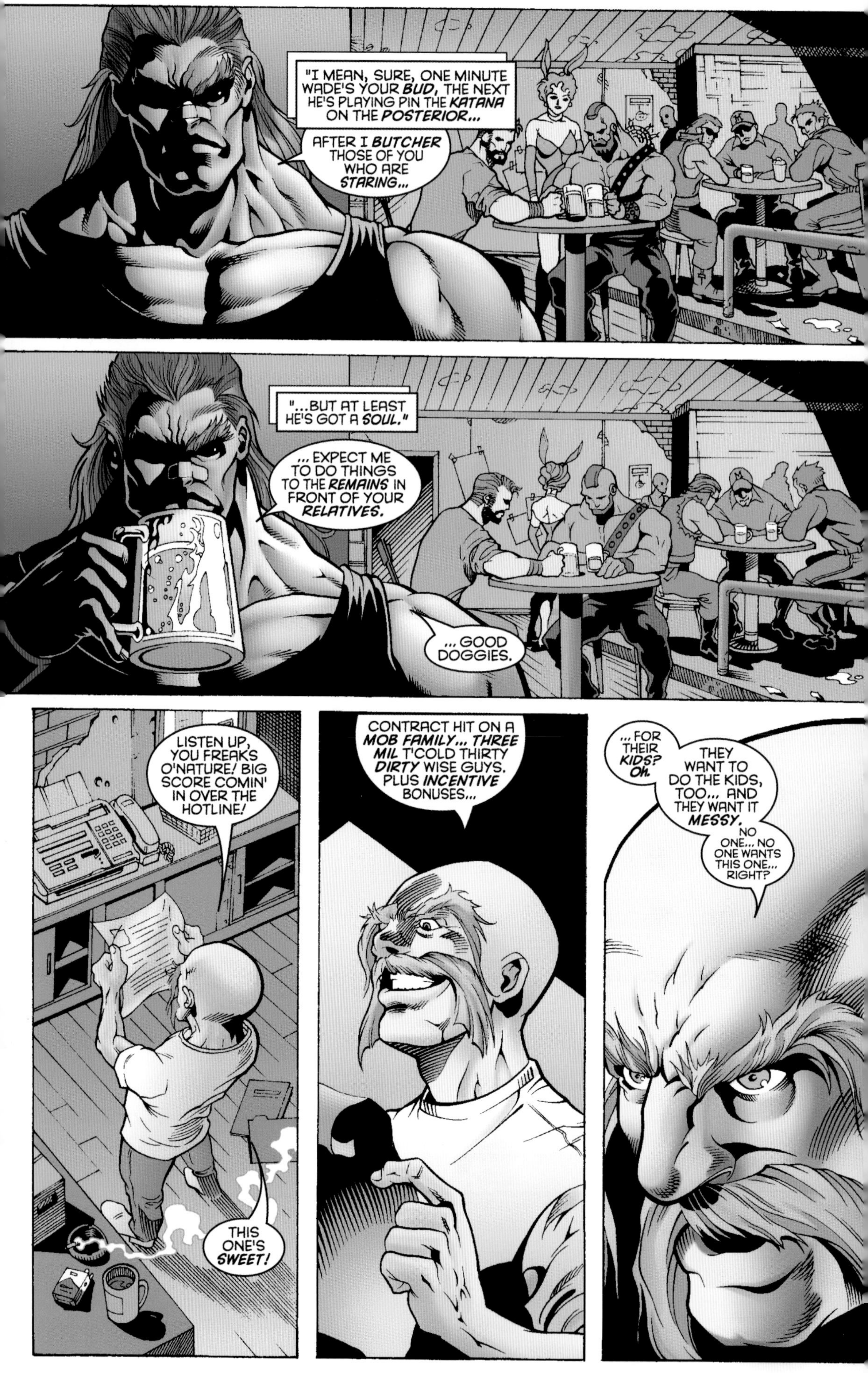
"I MEAN, SURE, ONE MINUTE WADE'S YOUR BUD, THE NEXT HE'S PLAYING PIN THE KATANA ON THE POSTERIOR...
AFTER I BUTCHER THOSE OF YOU WHO ARE STARING...
"...BUT AT LEAST HE'S GOT A SOUL."
...EXPECT ME TO DO THINGS TO THE REMAINS IN FRONT OF YOUR RELATIVES.
...GOOD DOGGIES.
LISTEN UP, YOU FREAKS O'NATURE! BIG SCORE COMIN' IN OVER THE HOTLINE!
THIS ONE'S SWEET!
CONTRACT HIT ON A MOB FAMILY... THREE MIL T'COLD THIRTY DIRTY WISE GUYS. PLUS INCENTIVE BONUSES...
...FOR THEIR KIDS? OH.
THEY WANT TO DO THE KIDS, TOO... AND THEY WANT IT MESSY.
NO ONE... NO ONE WANTS THIS ONE... RIGHT?

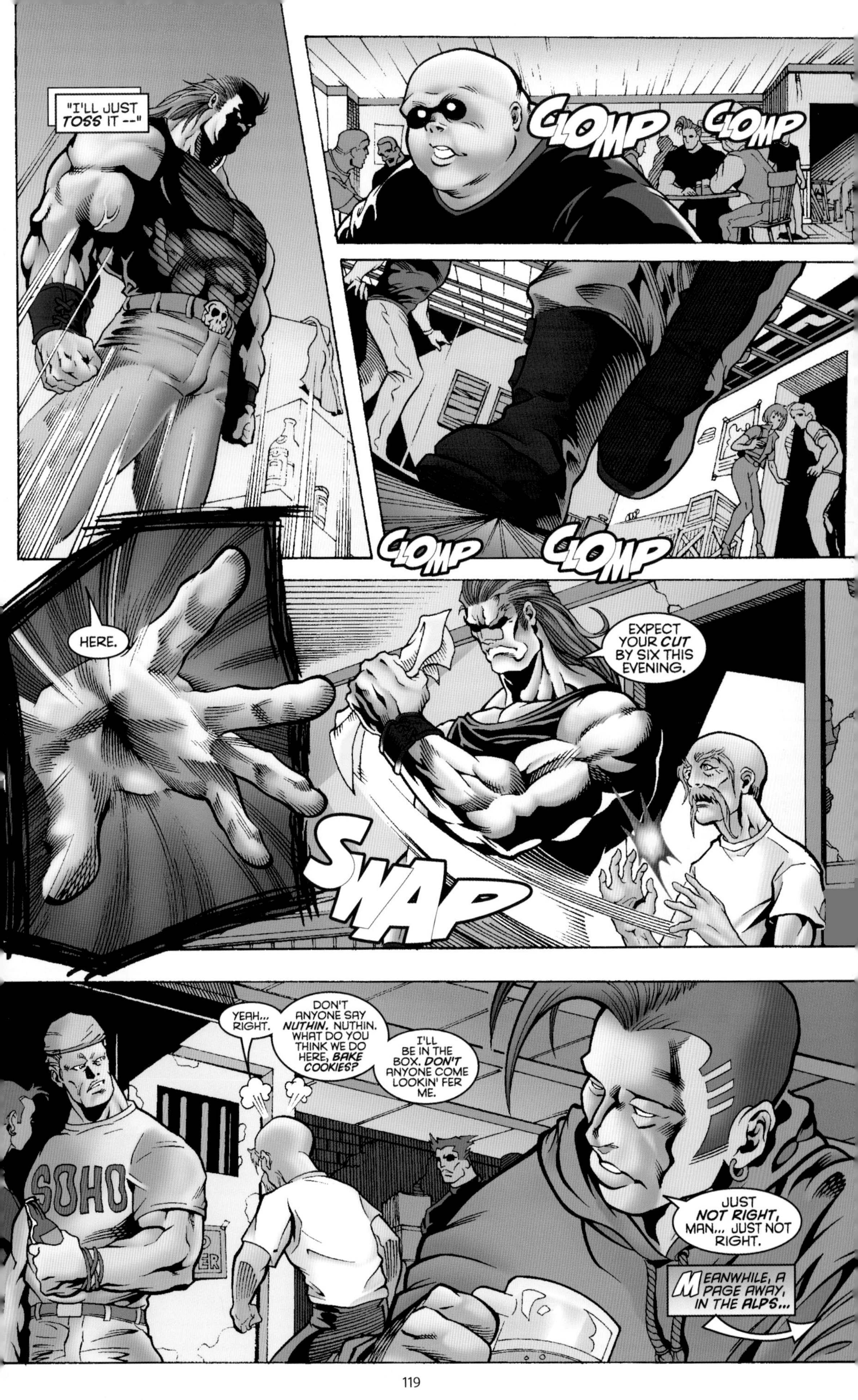
"I'LL JUST TOSS IT --"
CLOMP CLOMP
CLOMP CLOMP
HERE.
EXPECT YOUR CUT BY SIX THIS EVENING.
SWAP
YEAH... RIGHT.
DON'T ANYONE SAY NUTHIN. NUTHIN. WHAT DO YOU THINK WE DO HERE, BAKE COOKIES?
I'LL BE IN THE BOX. DON'T ANYONE COME LOOKIN' FER ME.
SOHO
JUST NOT RIGHT, MAN... JUST NOT RIGHT.
MEANWHILE, A PAGE AWAY, IN THE ALPS...

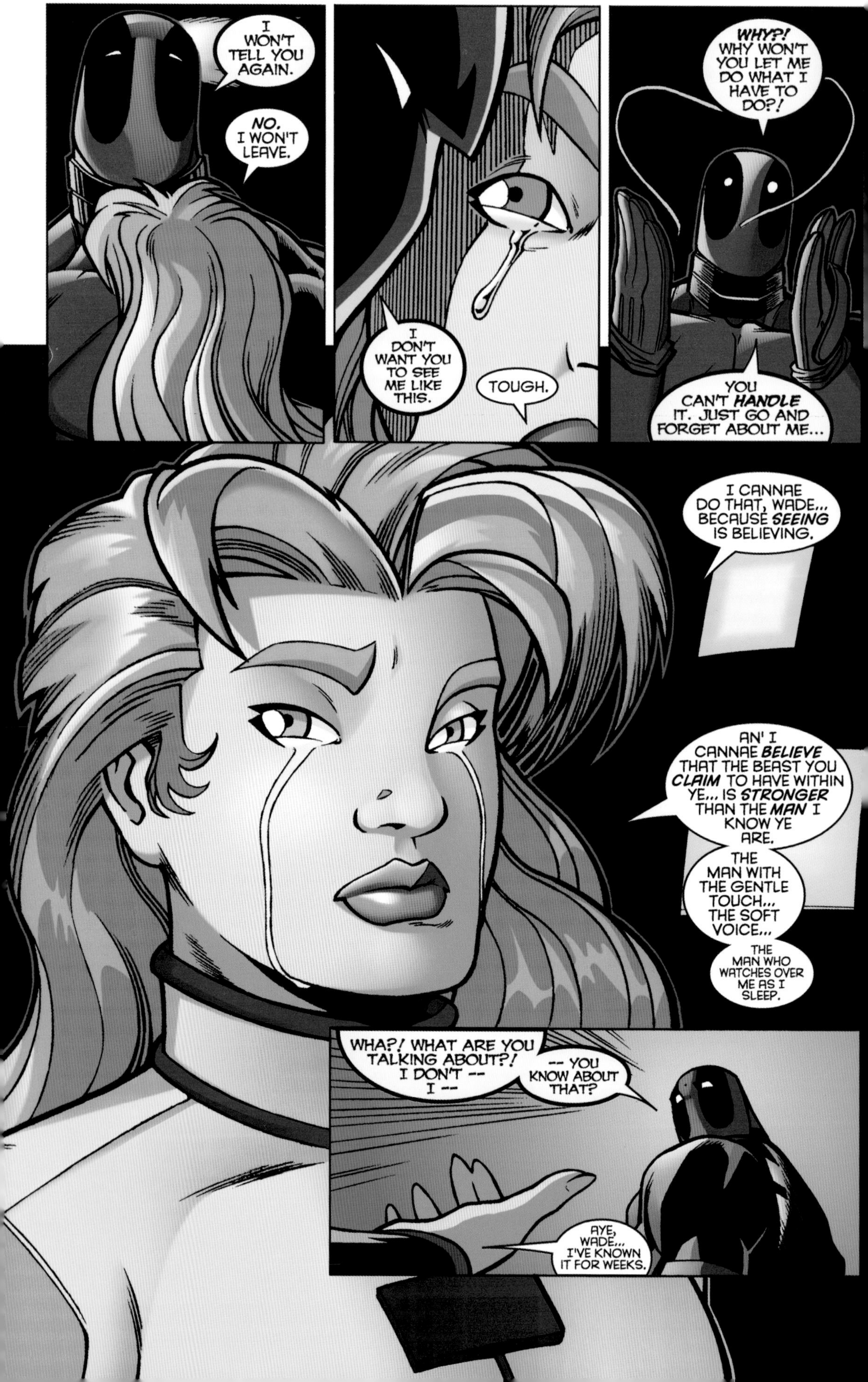
I WON'T TELL YOU AGAIN.
NO. I WON'T LEAVE.
I DON'T WANT YOU TO SEE ME LIKE THIS.
TOUGH.
WHY?! WHY WON'T YOU LET ME DO WHAT I HAVE TO DO?!
YOU CAN'T HANDLE IT. JUST GO AND FORGET ABOUT ME...
I CANNAE DO THAT, WADE... BECAUSE SEEING IS BELIEVING.
AN' I CANNAE BELIEVE THAT THE BEAST YOU CLAIM TO HAVE WITHIN YE... IS STRONGER THAN THE MAN I KNOW YE ARE.
THE MAN WITH THE GENTLE TOUCH... THE SOFT VOICE...
THE MAN WHO WATCHES OVER ME AS I SLEEP.
WHA?! WHAT ARE YOU TALKING ABOUT?! I DON'T -- I --
-- YOU KNOW ABOUT THAT?
AYE, WADE... I'VE KNOWN IT FOR WEEKS.

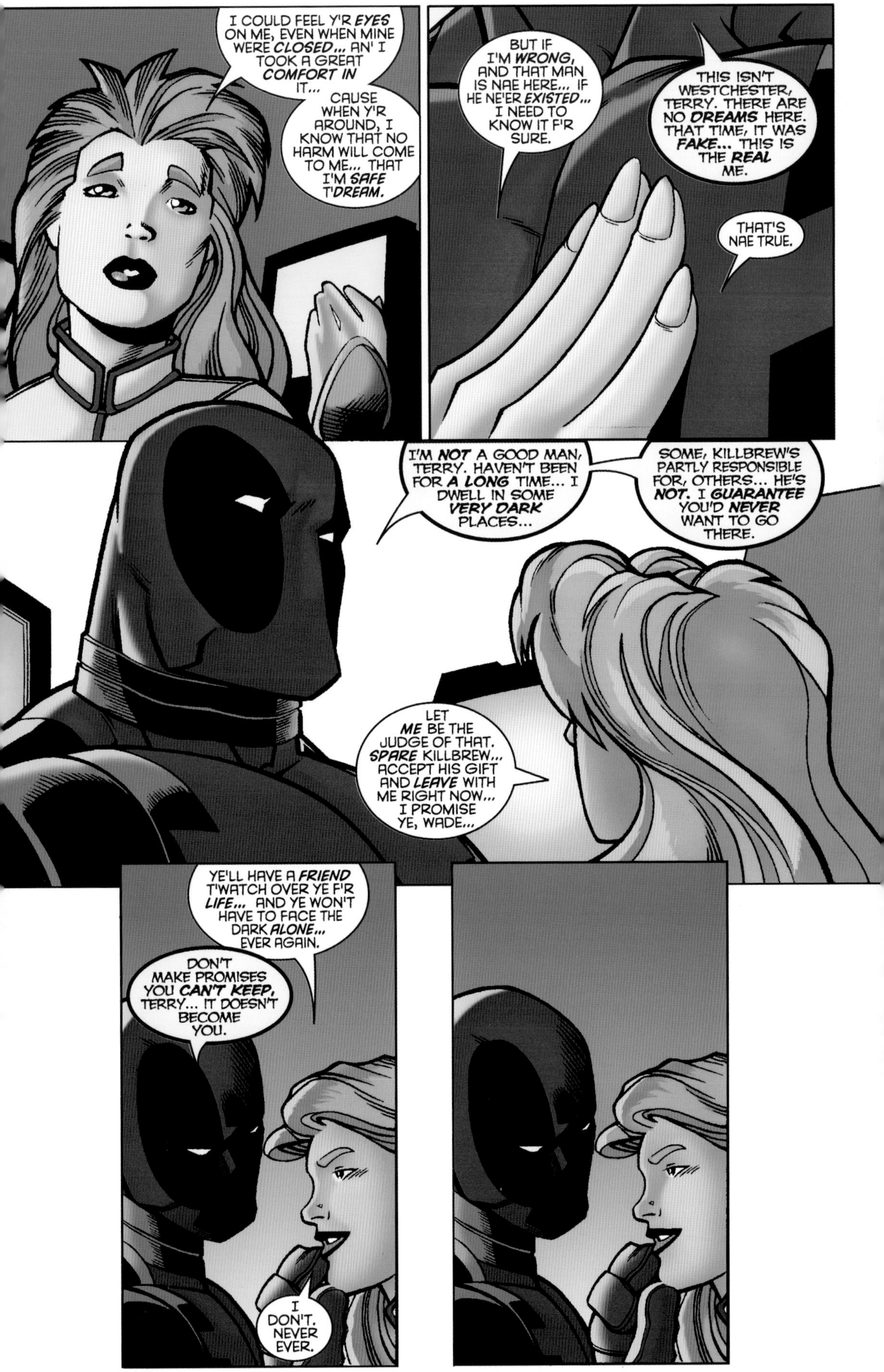
I COULD FEEL Y'R EYES ON ME, EVEN WHEN MINE WERE CLOSED... AN' I TOOK A GREAT COMFORT IN IT...
CAUSE WHEN Y'R AROUND, I KNOW THAT NO HARM WILL COME TO ME... THAT I'M SAFE T'DREAM.
BUT IF I'M WRONG, AND THAT MAN IS NAE HERE... IF HE NE'ER EXISTED... I NEED TO KNOW IT F'R SURE.
THIS ISN'T WESTCHESTER, TERRY. THERE ARE NO DREAMS HERE. THAT TIME, IT WAS FAKE... THIS IS THE REAL ME.
THAT'S NAE TRUE.
I'M NOT A GOOD MAN, TERRY. HAVEN'T BEEN FOR A LONG TIME... I DWELL IN SOME VERY DARK PLACES...
SOME, KILLBREW'S PARTLY RESPONSIBLE FOR, OTHERS... HE'S NOT. I GUARANTEE YOU'D NEVER WANT TO GO THERE.
LET ME BE THE JUDGE OF THAT. SPARE KILLBREW... ACCEPT HIS GIFT AND LEAVE WITH ME RIGHT NOW... I PROMISE YE, WADE...
YE'LL HAVE A FRIEND T'WATCH OVER YE F'R LIFE... AND YE WON'T HAVE TO FACE THE DARK ALONE... EVER AGAIN.
DON'T MAKE PROMISES YOU CAN'T KEEP, TERRY... IT DOESN'T BECOME YOU.
I DON'T. NEVER EVER.

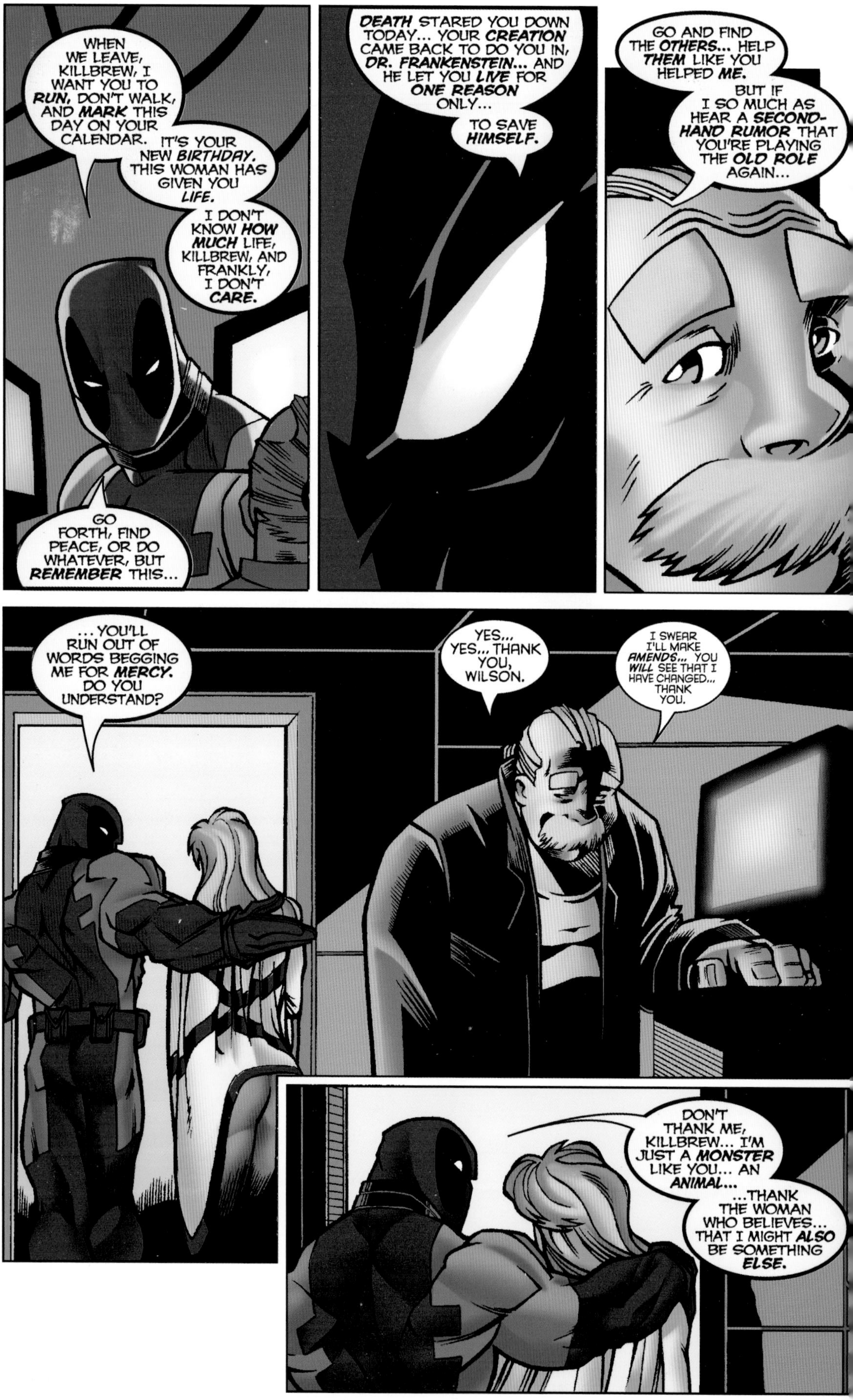

WHEN WE LEAVE, KILLBREW, I WANT YOU TO RUN, DON'T WALK, AND MARK THIS DAY ON YOUR CALENDAR.
IT'S YOUR NEW BIRTHDAY. THIS WOMAN HAS GIVEN YOU LIFE.
I DON'T KNOW HOW MUCH LIFE, KILLBREW, AND FRANKLY, I DON'T CARE.
GO FORTH, FIND PEACE, OR DO WHATEVER, BUT REMEMBER THIS...
DEATH STARED YOU DOWN TODAY... YOUR CREATION CAME BACK TO DO YOU IN, DR. FRANKENSTEIN... AND HE LET YOU LIVE FOR ONE REASON ONLY...
TO SAVE HIMSELF.
GO AND FIND THE OTHERS... HELP THEM LIKE YOU HELPED ME.
BUT IF I SO MUCH AS HEAR A SECOND-HAND RUMOR THAT YOU'RE PLAYING THE OLD ROLE AGAIN...
...YOU'LL RUN OUT OF WORDS BEGGING ME FOR MERCY. DO YOU UNDERSTAND?
YES... YES... THANK YOU, WILSON.
I SWEAR I'LL MAKE AMENDS... YOU WILL SEE THAT I HAVE CHANGED... THANK YOU.
DON'T THANK ME, KILLBREW... I'M JUST A MONSTER LIKE YOU... AN ANIMAL...
...THANK THE WOMAN WHO BELIEVES... THAT I MIGHT ALSO BE SOMETHING ELSE.

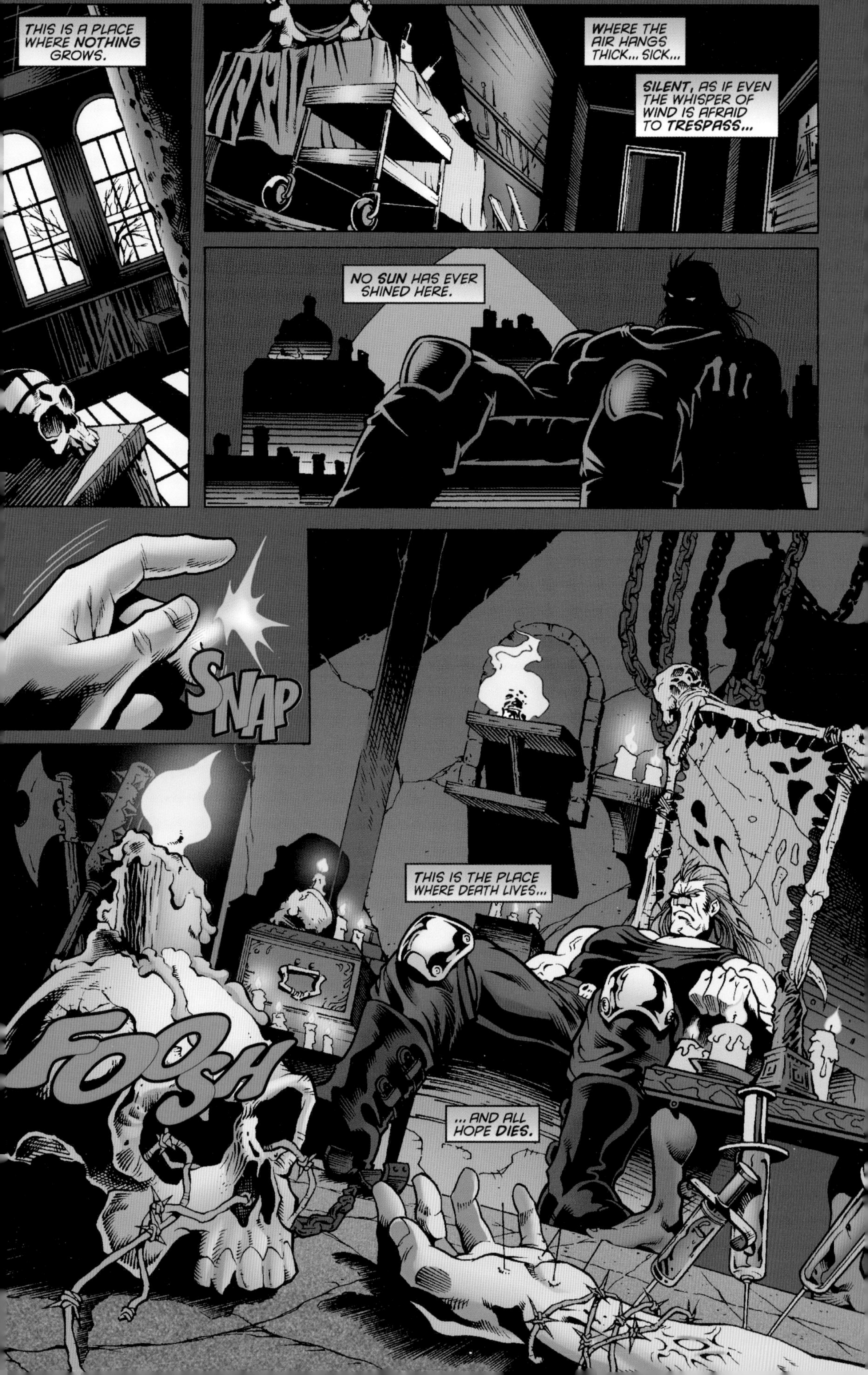
THIS IS A PLACE WHERE NOTHING GROWS.
WHERE THE AIR HANGS THICK... SICK...
SILENT, AS IF EVEN THE WHISPER OF WIND IS AFRAID TO TRESPASS...
NO SUN HAS EVER SHINED HERE.
SNAP
THIS IS THE PLACE WHERE DEATH LIVES...
FOOSH
...AND ALL HOPE DIES.

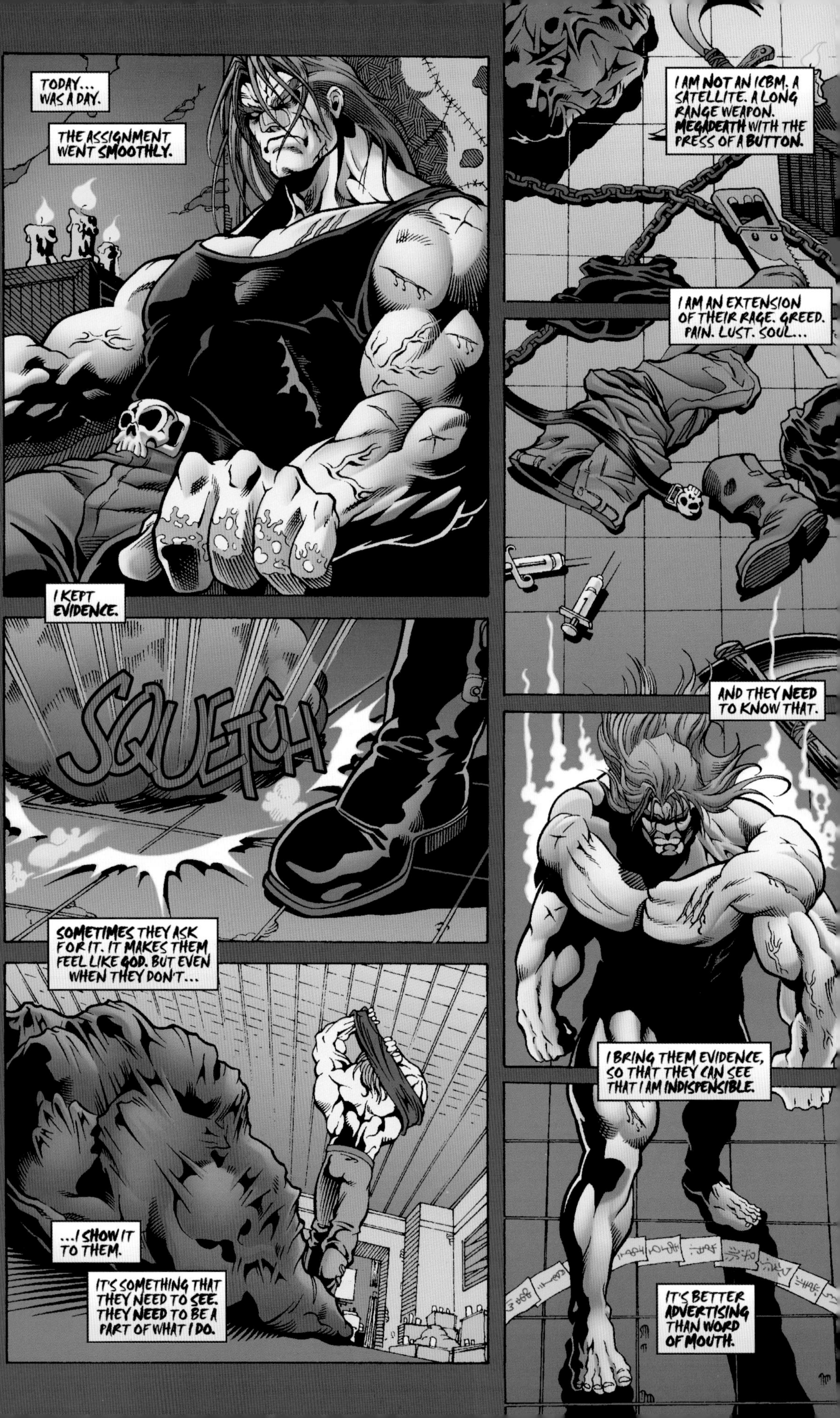
TODAY... WAS A DAY.
THE ASSIGNMENT WENT SMOOTHLY.
I KEPT EVIDENCE.
SQUETCH
SOMETIMES THEY ASK FOR IT. IT MAKES THEM FEEL LIKE GOD. BUT EVEN WHEN THEY DON'T...
...I SHOW IT TO THEM.
IT'S SOMETHING THAT THEY NEED TO SEE. THEY NEED TO BE A PART OF WHAT I DO.
I AM NOT AN ICBM. A SATELLITE. A LONG RANGE WEAPON. MEGADEATH WITH THE PRESS OF A BUTTON.
I AM AN EXTENSION OF THEIR RAGE. GREED. PAIN. LUST. SOUL...
AND THEY NEED TO KNOW THAT.
I BRING THEM EVIDENCE, SO THAT THEY CAN SEE THAT I AM INDISPENSIBLE.
IT'S BETTER ADVERTISING THAN WORD OF MOUTH.

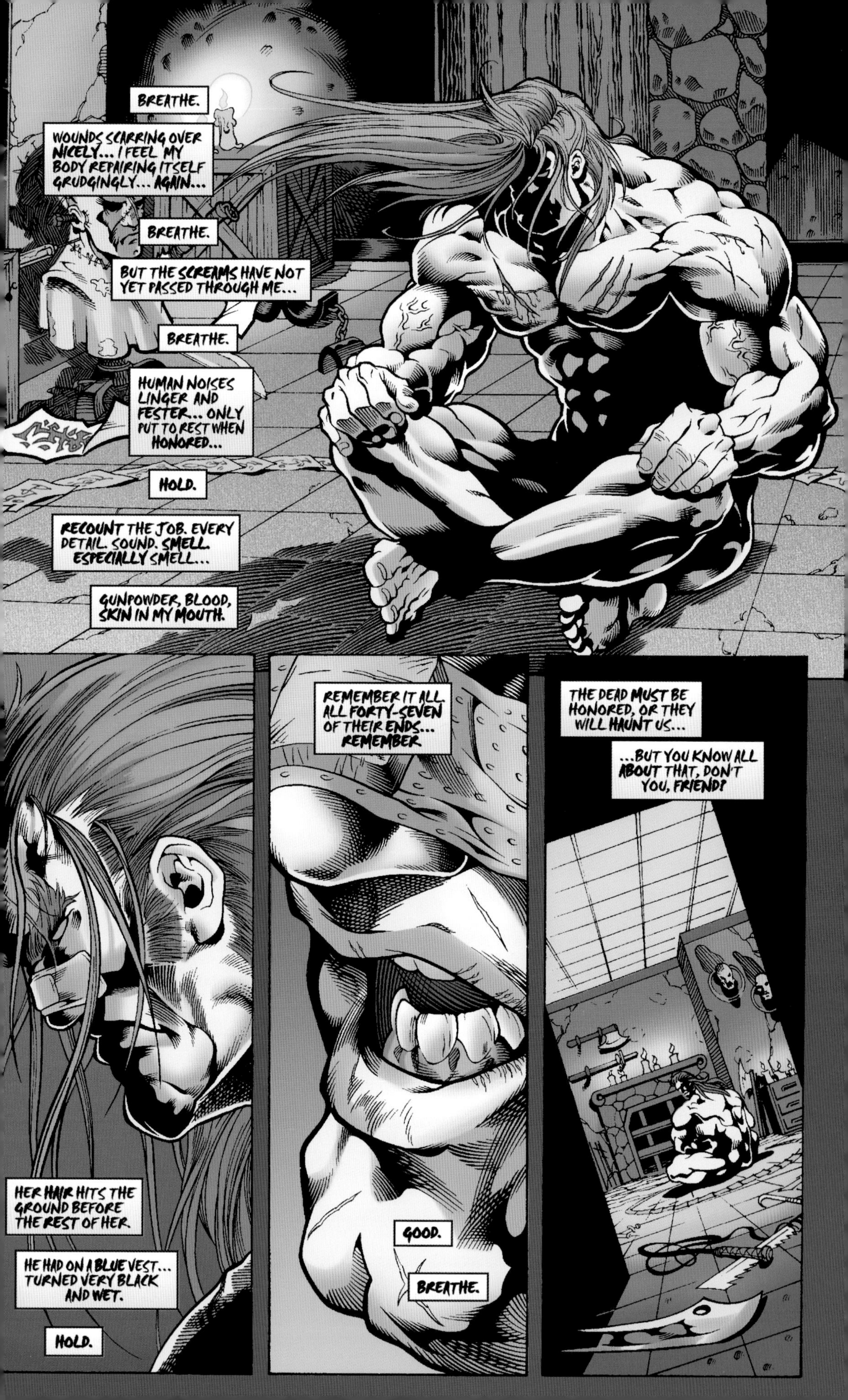
BREATHE.
WOUNDS SCARRING OVER NICELY... I FEEL MY BODY REPAIRING ITSELF GRUDGINGLY... AGAIN...
BREATHE.
BUT THE SCREAMS HAVE NOT YET PASSED THROUGH ME...
BREATHE.
HUMAN NOISES LINGER AND FESTER... ONLY PUT TO REST WHEN HONORED...
HOLD.
RECOUNT THE JOB. EVERY DETAIL. SOUND. SMELL. ESPECIALLY SMELL...
GUNPOWDER, BLOOD, SKIN IN MY MOUTH.
HER HAIR HITS THE GROUND BEFORE THE REST OF HER.
HE HAD ON A BLUE VEST... TURNED VERY BLACK AND WET.
HOLD.
REMEMBER IT ALL. ALL FORTY-SEVEN OF THEIR ENDS... REMEMBER
GOOD.
BREATHE.
THE DEAD MUST BE HONORED, OR THEY WILL HAUNT US...
...BUT YOU KNOW ALL ABOUT THAT, DON'T YOU, FRIEND?

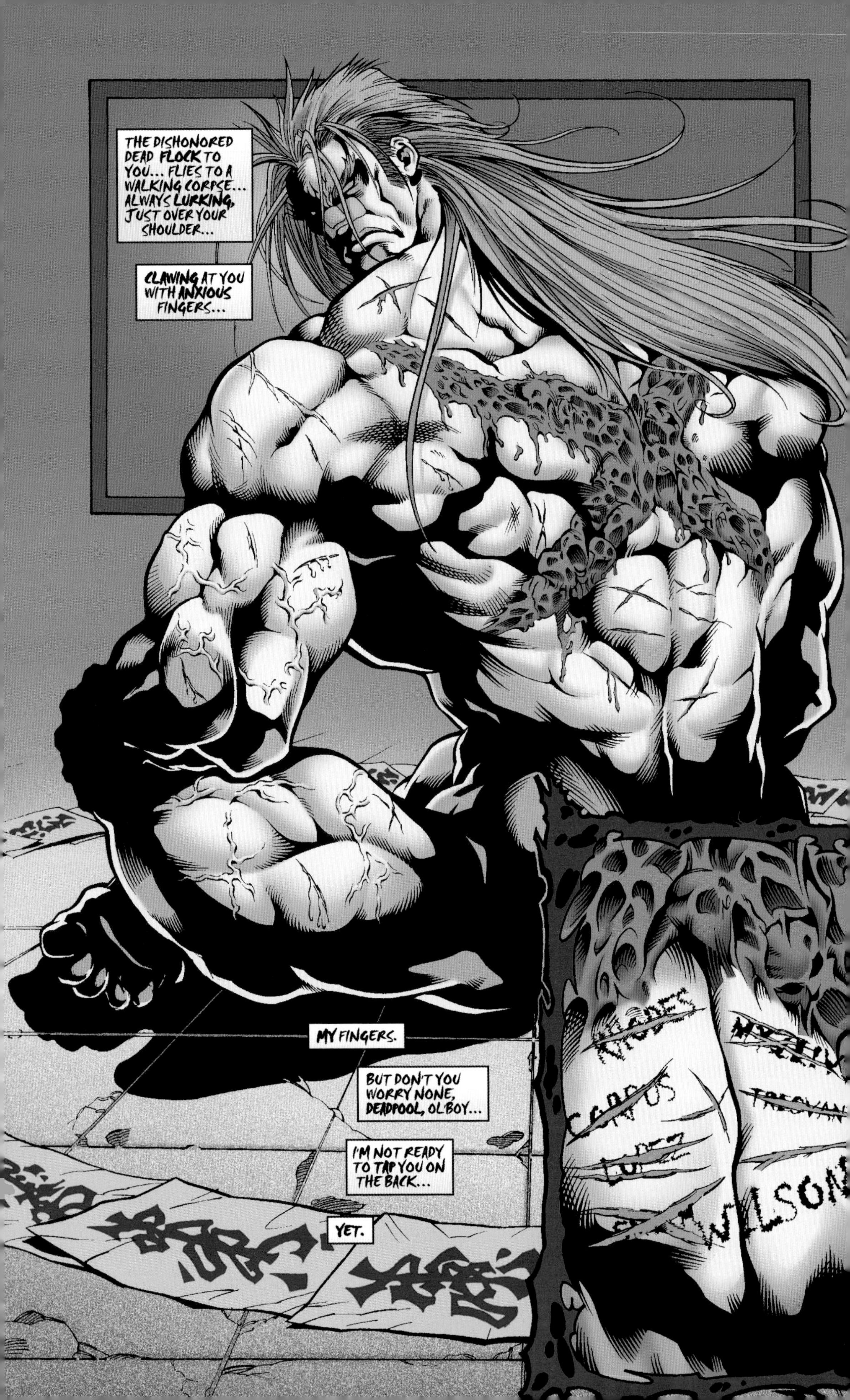
THE DISHONORED DEAD FLOCK TO YOU... FLIES TO A WALKING CORPSE... ALWAYS LURKING, JUST OVER YOUR SHOULDER...
CLAWING AT YOU WITH ANXIOUS FINGERS...
MY FINGERS.
BUT DON'T YOU WORRY NONE, DEADPOOL, OL' BOY...
I'M NOT READY TO TAP YOU ON THE BACK...
YET.
WILSON

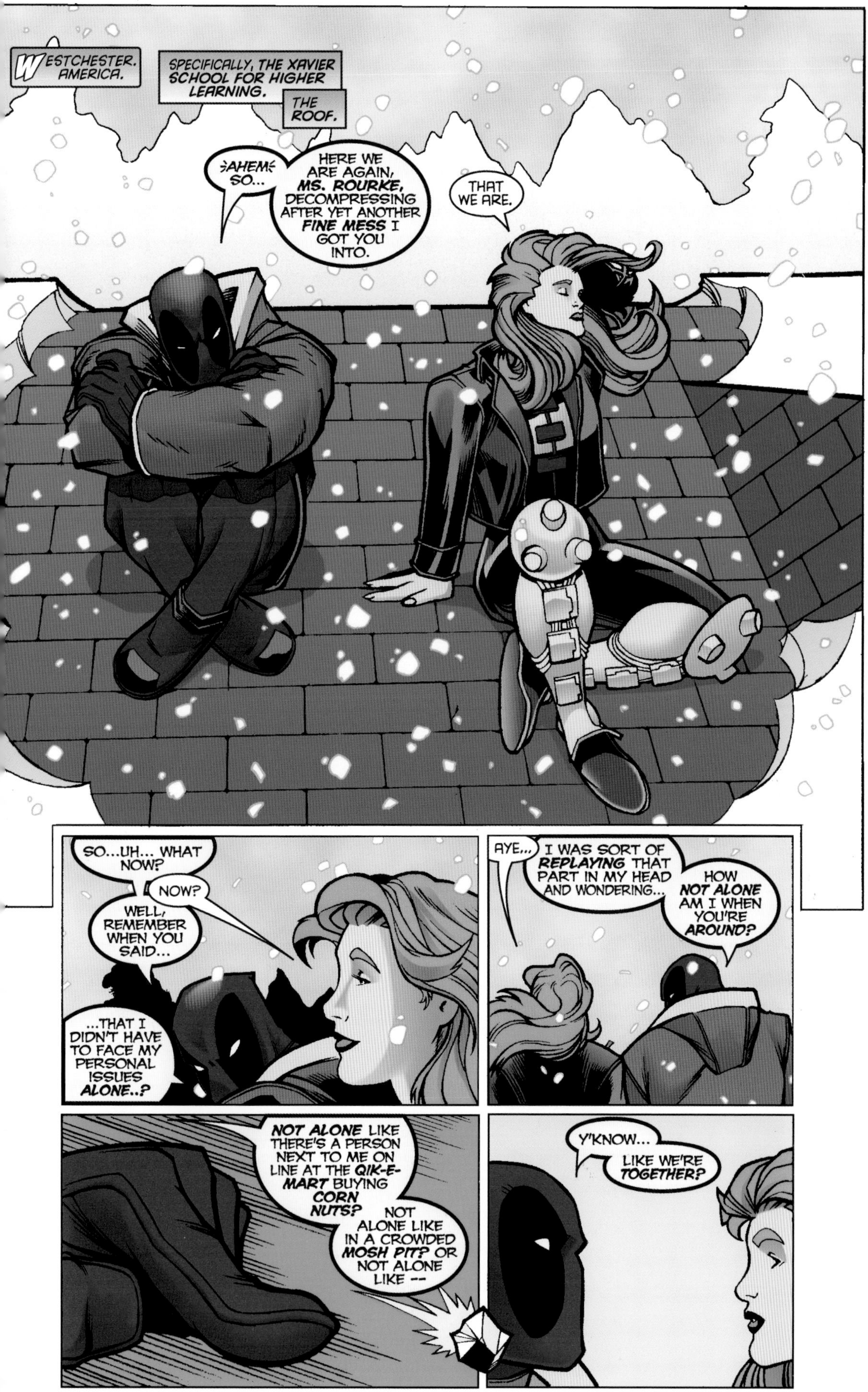
WESTCHESTER. AMERICA.
SPECIFICALLY, THE XAVIER SCHOOL FOR HIGHER LEARNING.
THE ROOF.
AHEM SO...
HERE WE ARE AGAIN, MS. ROURKE, DECOMPRESSING AFTER YET ANOTHER FINE MESS I GOT YOU INTO.
THAT WE ARE.
SO...UH... WHAT NOW?
NOW?
WELL, REMEMBER WHEN YOU SAID...
...THAT I DIDN'T HAVE TO FACE MY PERSONAL ISSUES ALONE..?
AYE...
I WAS SORT OF REPLAYING THAT PART IN MY HEAD AND WONDERING...
HOW NOT ALONE AM I WHEN YOU'RE AROUND?
NOT ALONE LIKE THERE'S A PERSON NEXT TO ME ON LINE AT THE QIK-E-MART BUYING CORN NUTS?
NOT ALONE LIKE IN A CROWDED MOSH PIT? OR NOT ALONE LIKE --
Y'KNOW...
LIKE WE'RE TOGETHER?

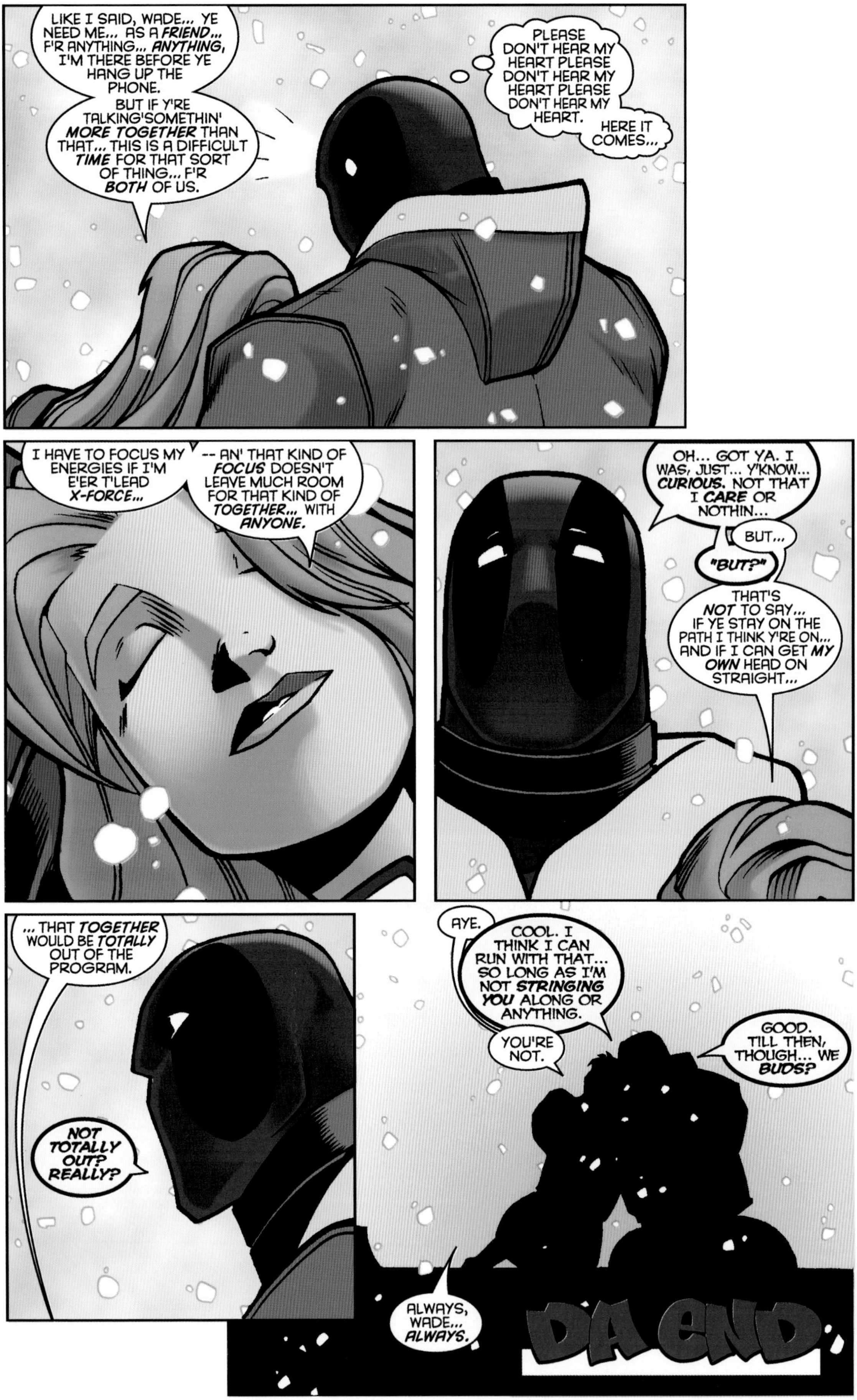
LIKE I SAID, WADE... YE NEED ME... AS A FRIEND... F'R ANYTHING... ANYTHING, I'M THERE BEFORE YE HANG UP THE PHONE.
BUT IF Y'RE TALKING'SOMETHIN' MORE TOGETHER THAN THAT... THIS IS A DIFFICULT TIME FOR THAT SORT OF THING... F'R BOTH OF US.
PLEASE DON'T HEAR MY HEART PLEASE DON'T HEAR MY HEART PLEASE DON'T HEAR MY HEART.
HERE IT COMES...
I HAVE TO FOCUS MY ENERGIES IF I'M E'ER T'LEAD X-FORCE...
-- AN' THAT KIND OF FOCUS DOESN'T LEAVE MUCH ROOM FOR THAT KIND OF TOGETHER... WITH ANYONE.
OH... GOT YA. I WAS, JUST... Y'KNOW... CURIOUS. NOT THAT I CARE OR NOTHIN...
BUT...
"BUT?"
THAT'S NOT TO SAY... IF YE STAY ON THE PATH I THINK Y'RE ON... AND IF I CAN GET MY OWN HEAD ON STRAIGHT...
...THAT TOGETHER WOULD BE TOTALLY OUT OF THE PROGRAM.
NOT TOTALLY OUT? REALLY?
AYE.
COOL. I THINK I CAN RUN WITH THAT... SO LONG AS I'M NOT STRINGING YOU ALONG OR ANYTHING.
YOU'RE NOT.
GOOD. TILL THEN, THOUGH... WE BUDS?
ALWAYS, WADE... ALWAYS.
DA END

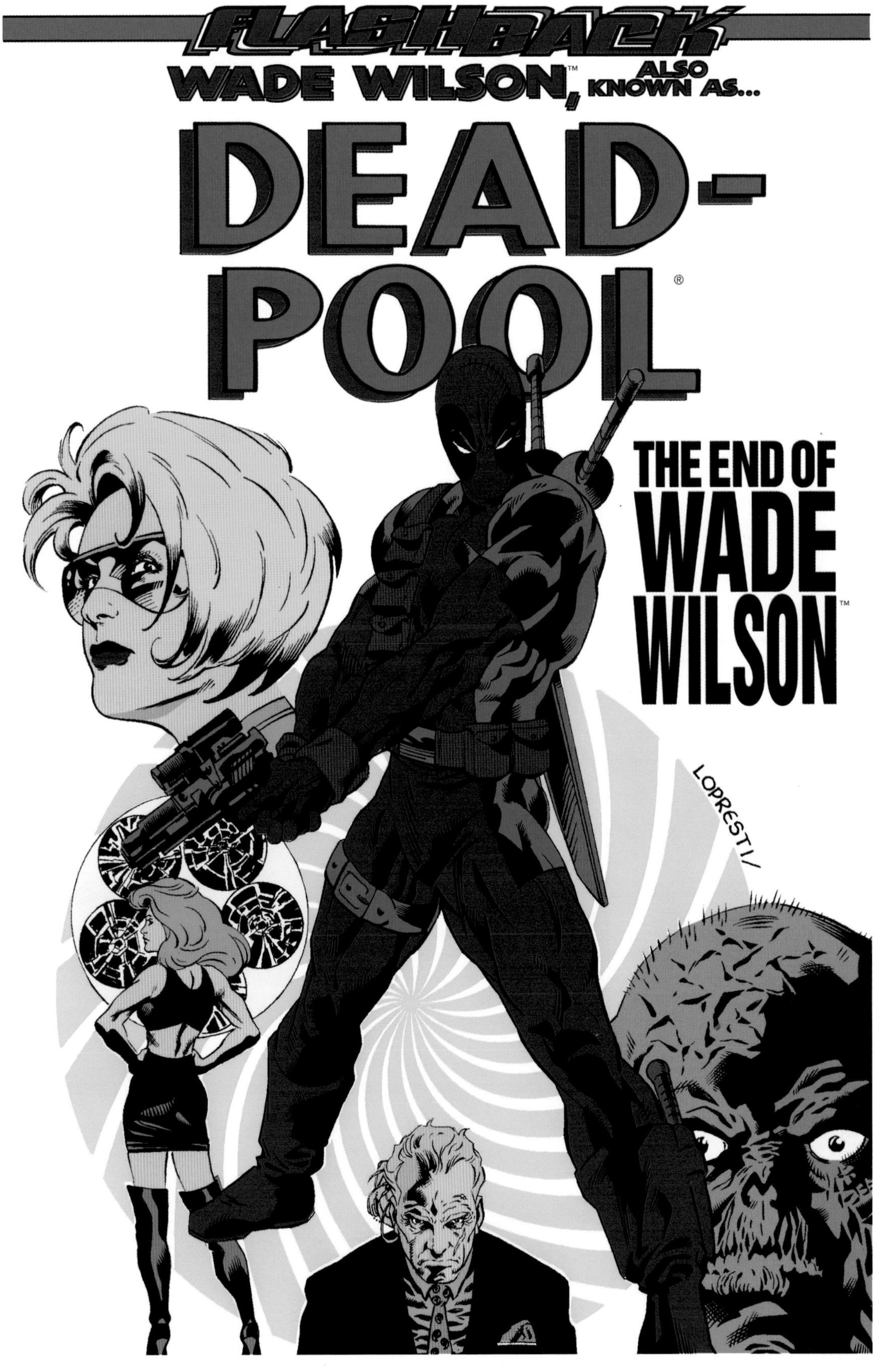
FLASHBACK
WADE WILSON™, ALSO KNOWN AS...
DEAD-POOL®
THE END OF WADE WILSON™
LOPRESTI/

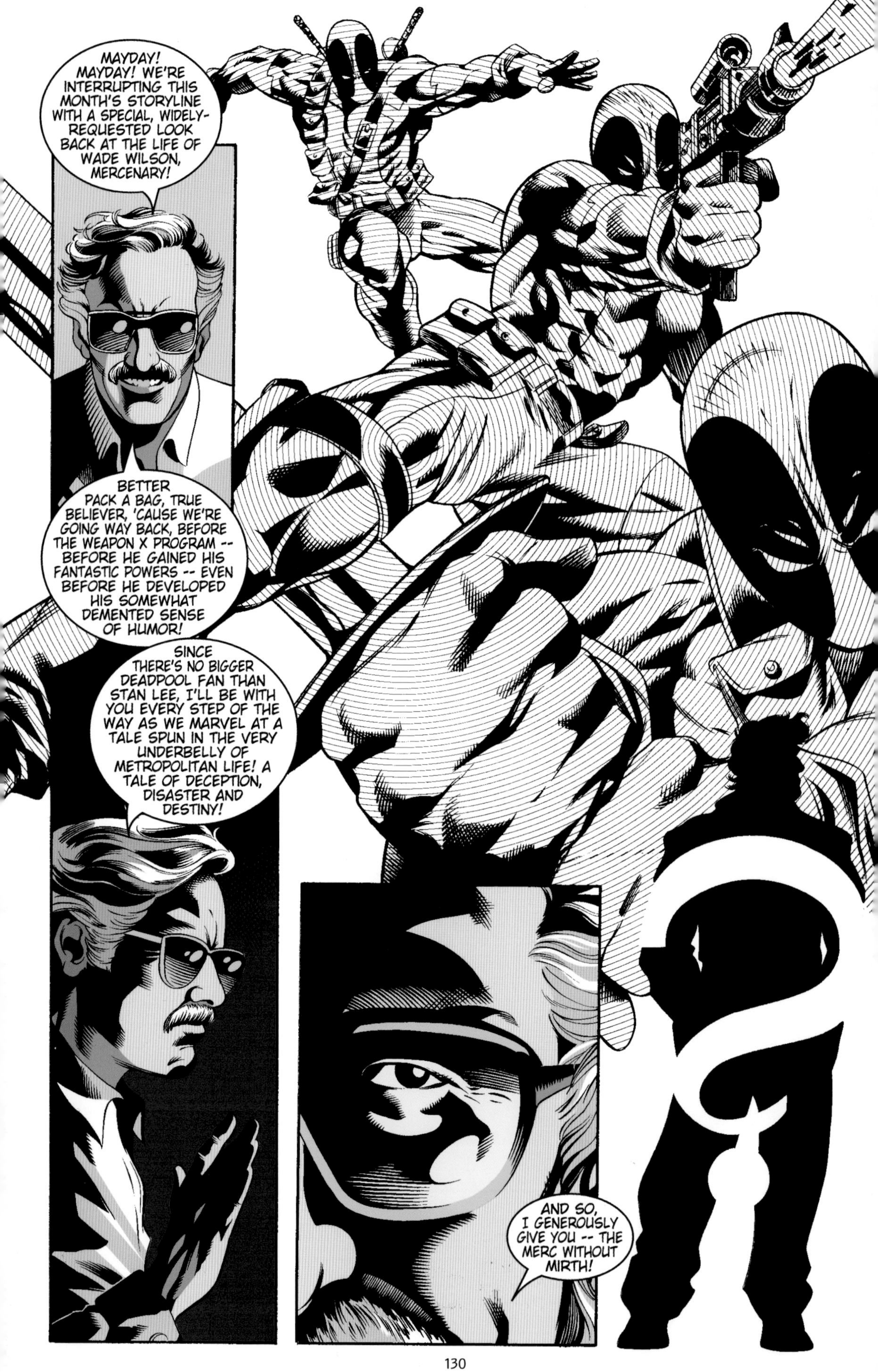
MAYDAY! MAYDAY! WE'RE INTERRUPTING THIS MONTH'S STORYLINE WITH A SPECIAL, WIDELY-REQUESTED LOOK BACK AT THE LIFE OF WADE WILSON, MERCENARY!
BETTER PACK A BAG, TRUE BELIEVER, 'CAUSE WE'RE GOING WAY BACK, BEFORE THE WEAPON X PROGRAM -- BEFORE HE GAINED HIS FANTASTIC POWERS -- EVEN BEFORE HE DEVELOPED HIS SOMEWHAT DEMENTED SENSE OF HUMOR!
SINCE THERE'S NO BIGGER DEADPOOL FAN THAN STAN LEE, I'LL BE WITH YOU EVERY STEP OF THE WAY AS WE MARVEL AT A TALE SPUN IN THE VERY UNDERBELLY OF METROPOLITAN LIFE! A TALE OF DECEPTION, DISASTER AND DESTINY!
AND SO, I GENEROUSLY GIVE YOU -- THE MERC WITHOUT MIRTH!

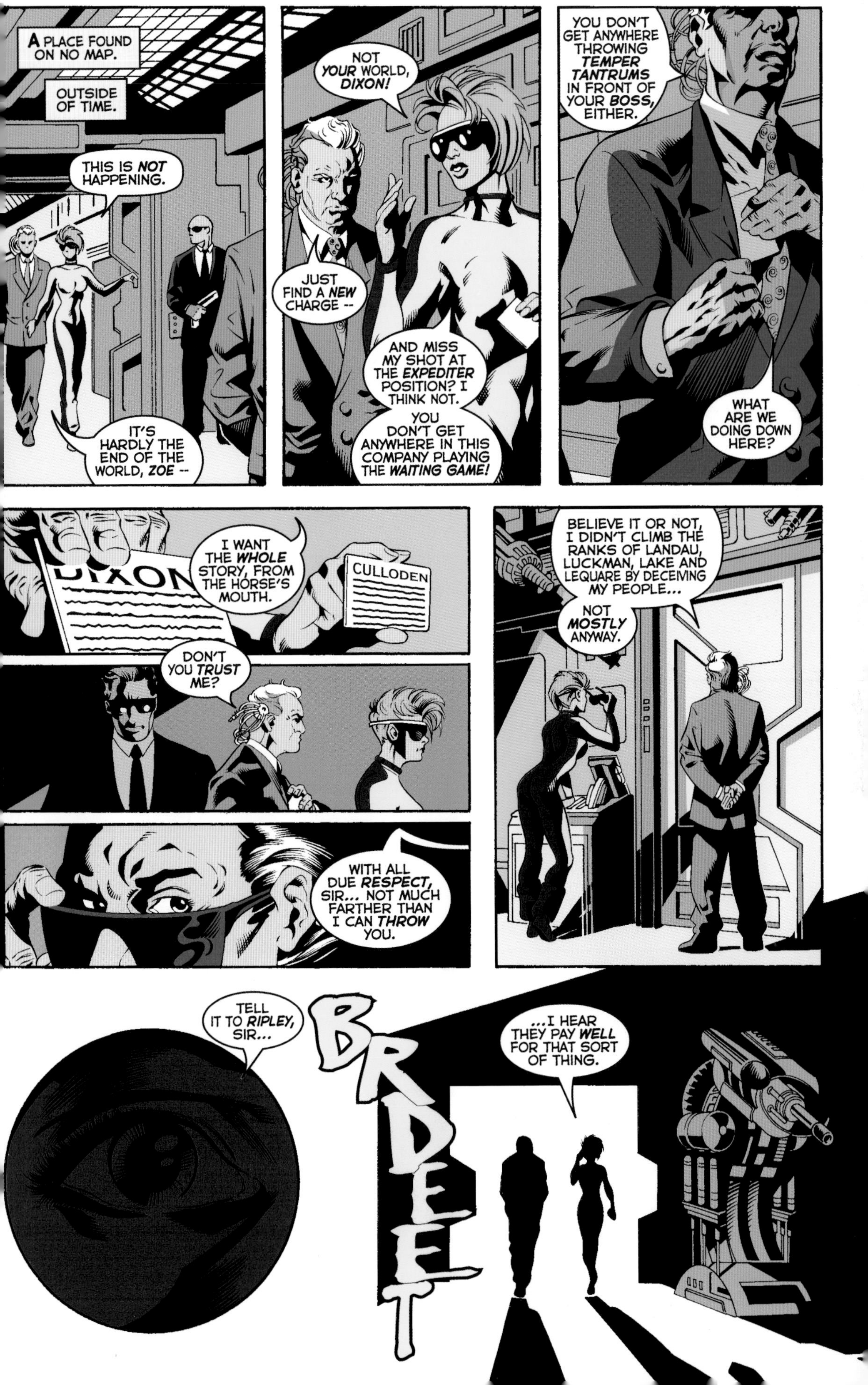
A PLACE FOUND ON NO MAP.
OUTSIDE OF TIME.
THIS IS NOT HAPPENING.
IT'S HARDLY THE END OF THE WORLD, ZOE --
NOT YOUR WORLD, DIXON!
JUST FIND A NEW CHARGE --
AND MISS MY SHOT AT THE EXPEDITER POSITION? I THINK NOT.
YOU DON'T GET ANYWHERE IN THIS COMPANY PLAYING THE WAITING GAME!
YOU DON'T GET ANYWHERE THROWING TEMPER TANTRUMS IN FRONT OF YOUR BOSS, EITHER.
WHAT ARE WE DOING DOWN HERE?
DIXON
I WANT THE WHOLE STORY, FROM THE HORSE'S MOUTH.
CULLODEN
DON'T YOU TRUST ME?
WITH ALL DUE RESPECT, SIR... NOT MUCH FARTHER THAN I CAN THROW YOU.
BELIEVE IT OR NOT, I DIDN'T CLIMB THE RANKS OF LANDAU, LUCKMAN, LAKE AND LEQUARE BY DECEIVING MY PEOPLE...
NOT MOSTLY ANYWAY.
TELL IT TO RIPLEY, SIR...
BRDEEET
...I HEAR THEY PAY WELL FOR THAT SORT OF THING.

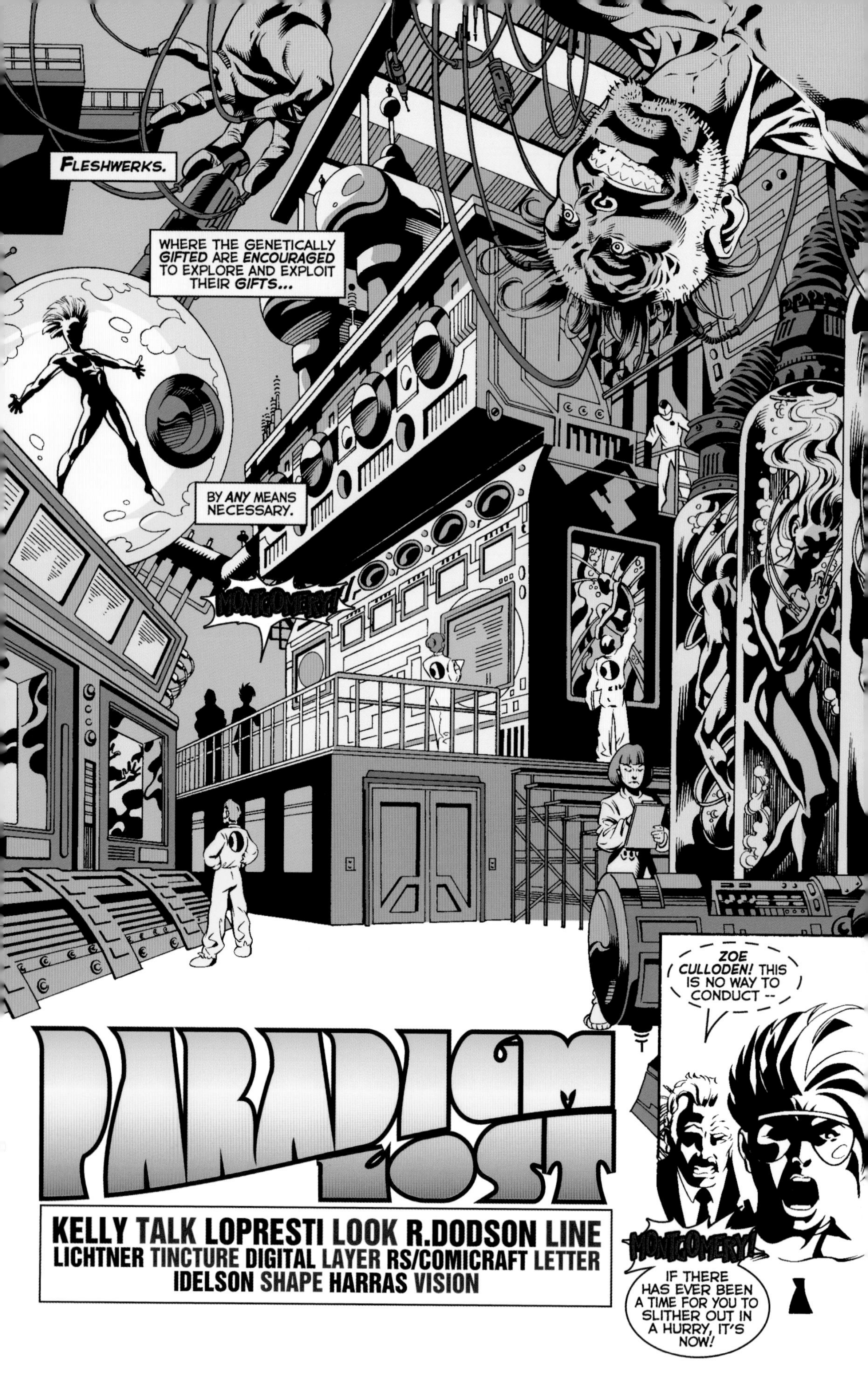
FLESHWERKS.
WHERE THE GENETICALLY GIFTED ARE ENCOURAGED TO EXPLORE AND EXPLOIT THEIR GIFTS...
BY ANY MEANS NECESSARY.
MONTGOMERY!
PARADIGM LOST
KELLY TALK LOPRESTI LOOK R.DODSON LINE
LICHTNER TINCTURE DIGITAL LAYER RS/COMICRAFT LETTER
IDELSON SHAPE HARRAS VISION
ZOE CULLODEN! THIS IS NO WAY TO CONDUCT --
MONTGOMERY!
IF THERE HAS EVER BEEN A TIME FOR YOU TO SLITHER OUT IN A HURRY, IT'S NOW!

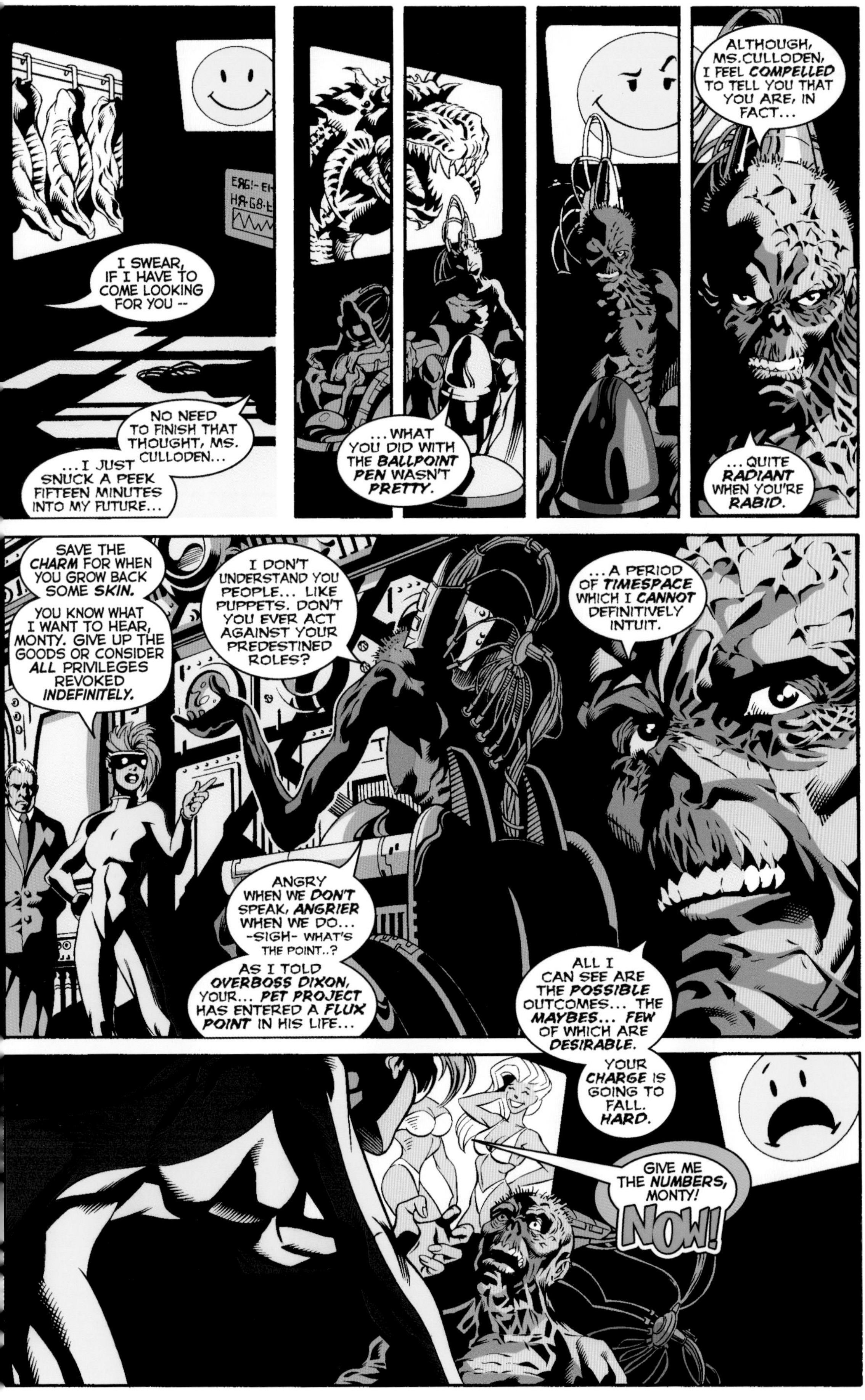
I SWEAR, IF I HAVE TO COME LOOKING FOR YOU --
NO NEED TO FINISH THAT THOUGHT, MS. CULLODEN...
...I JUST SNUCK A PEEK FIFTEEN MINUTES INTO MY FUTURE...
...WHAT YOU DID WITH THE BALLPOINT PEN WASN'T PRETTY.
ALTHOUGH, MS.CULLODEN, I FEEL COMPELLED TO TELL YOU THAT YOU ARE, IN FACT...
...QUITE RADIANT WHEN YOU'RE RABID.
SAVE THE CHARM FOR WHEN YOU GROW BACK SOME SKIN.
YOU KNOW WHAT I WANT TO HEAR, MONTY. GIVE UP THE GOODS OR CONSIDER ALL PRIVILEGES REVOKED INDEFINITELY.
I DON'T UNDERSTAND YOU PEOPLE... LIKE PUPPETS. DON'T YOU EVER ACT AGAINST YOUR PREDESTINED ROLES?
ANGRY WHEN WE DON'T SPEAK, ANGRIER WHEN WE DO... -SIGH- WHAT'S THE POINT..?
AS I TOLD OVERBOSS DIXON, YOUR... PET PROJECT HAS ENTERED A FLUX POINT IN HIS LIFE...
...A PERIOD OF TIMESPACE WHICH I CANNOT DEFINITIVELY INTUIT.
ALL I CAN SEE ARE THE POSSIBLE OUTCOMES... THE MAYBES... FEW OF WHICH ARE DESIRABLE.
YOUR CHARGE IS GOING TO FALL. HARD.
GIVE ME THE NUMBERS, MONTY!
NOW!

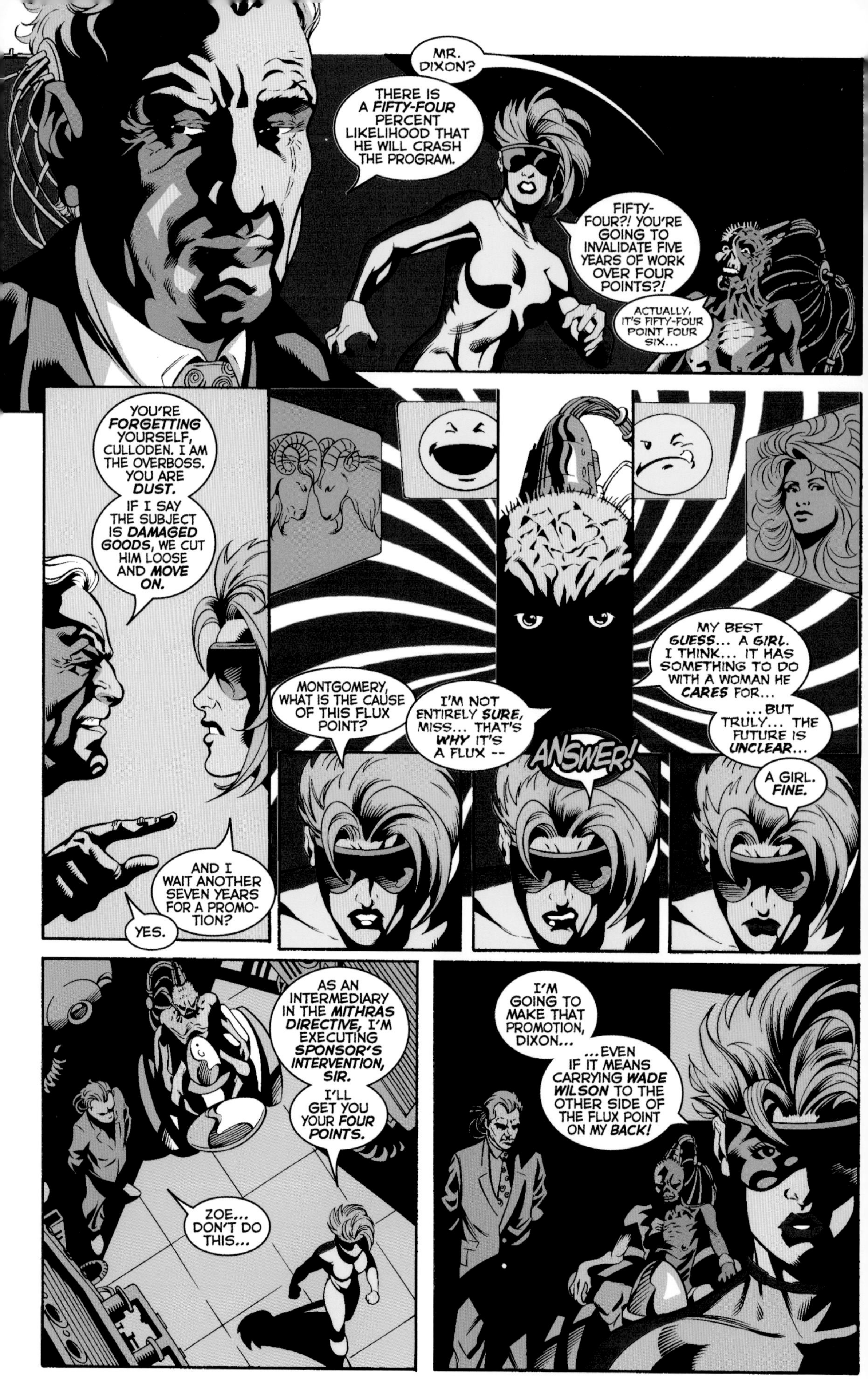
MR. DIXON?
THERE IS A FIFTY-FOUR PERCENT LIKELIHOOD THAT HE WILL CRASH THE PROGRAM.
FIFTY-FOUR?! YOU'RE GOING TO INVALIDATE FIVE YEARS OF WORK OVER FOUR POINTS?!
ACTUALLY, IT'S FIFTY-FOUR POINT FOUR SIX...
YOU'RE FORGETTING YOURSELF, CULLODEN. I AM THE OVERBOSS. YOU ARE DUST.
IF I SAY THE SUBJECT IS DAMAGED GOODS, WE CUT HIM LOOSE AND MOVE ON.
AND I WAIT ANOTHER SEVEN YEARS FOR A PROMOTION?
YES.
MONTGOMERY, WHAT IS THE CAUSE OF THIS FLUX POINT?
I'M NOT ENTIRELY SURE, MISS... THAT'S WHY IT'S A FLUX --
ANSWER!
MY BEST GUESS... A GIRL. I THINK... IT HAS SOMETHING TO DO WITH A WOMAN HE CARES FOR...
...BUT TRULY... THE FUTURE IS UNCLEAR...
A GIRL. FINE.
AS AN INTERMEDIARY IN THE MITHRAS DIRECTIVE, I'M EXECUTING SPONSOR'S INTERVENTION, SIR.
I'LL GET YOU YOUR FOUR POINTS.
ZOE... DON'T DO THIS...
I'M GOING TO MAKE THAT PROMOTION, DIXON...
...EVEN IF IT MEANS CARRYING WADE WILSON TO THE OTHER SIDE OF THE FLUX POINT ON MY BACK!

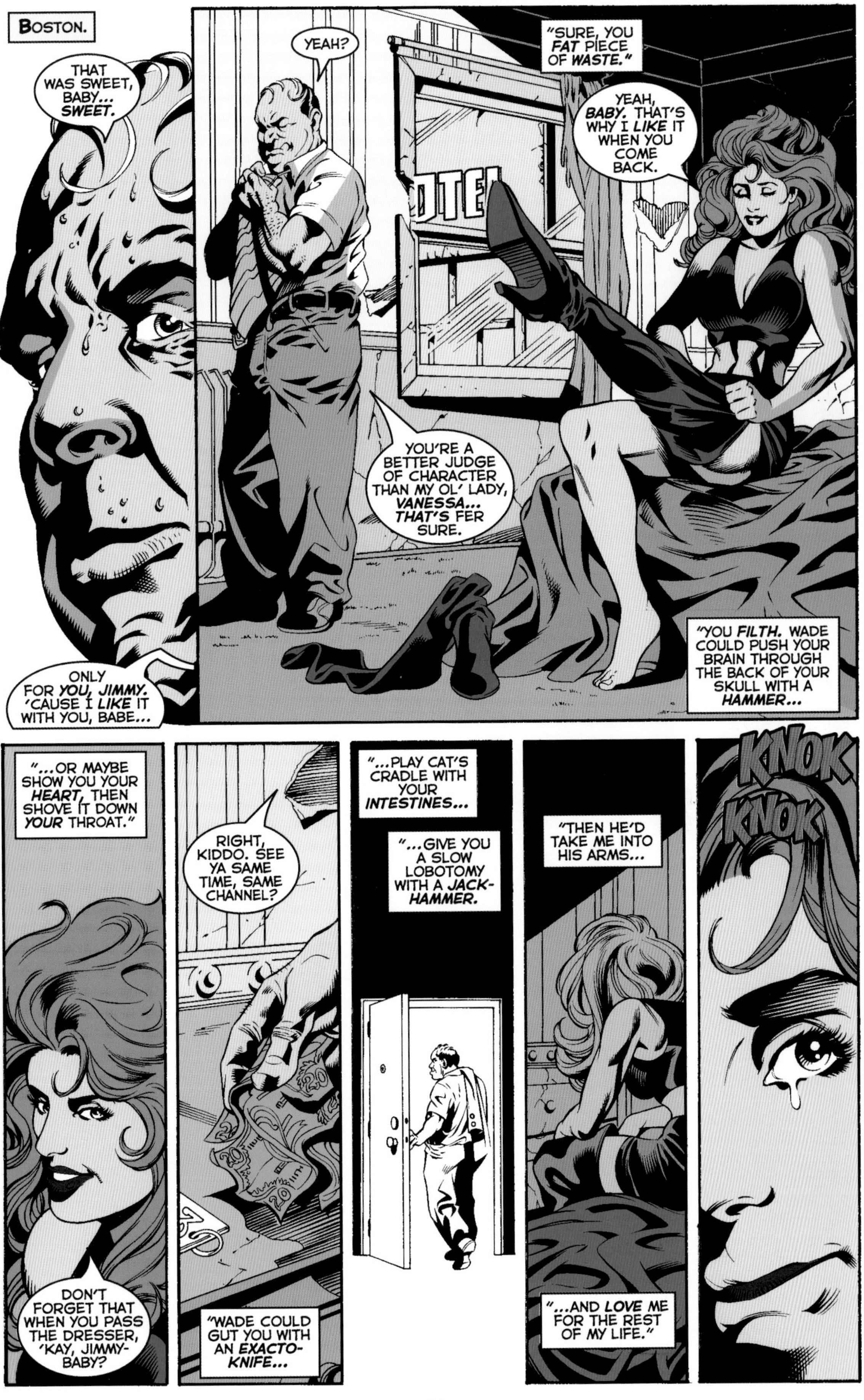
BOSTON.
THAT WAS SWEET, BABY... SWEET.
YEAH?
"SURE, YOU FAT PIECE OF WASTE."
YEAH, BABY. THAT'S WHY I LIKE IT WHEN YOU COME BACK.
YOU'RE A BETTER JUDGE OF CHARACTER THAN MY OL' LADY, VANESSA... THAT'S FER SURE.
ONLY FOR YOU, JIMMY. 'CAUSE I LIKE IT WITH YOU, BABE...
"YOU FILTH. WADE COULD PUSH YOUR BRAIN THROUGH THE BACK OF YOUR SKULL WITH A HAMMER...
"...OR MAYBE SHOW YOU YOUR HEART, THEN SHOVE IT DOWN YOUR THROAT."
DON'T FORGET THAT WHEN YOU PASS THE DRESSER, 'KAY, JIMMY-BABY?
RIGHT, KIDDO. SEE YA SAME TIME, SAME CHANNEL?
"WADE COULD GUT YOU WITH AN EXACTO-KNIFE...
"...PLAY CAT'S CRADLE WITH YOUR INTESTINES...
"...GIVE YOU A SLOW LOBOTOMY WITH A JACK-HAMMER.
"THEN HE'D TAKE ME INTO HIS ARMS...
"...AND LOVE ME FOR THE REST OF MY LIFE."
KNOK
KNOK

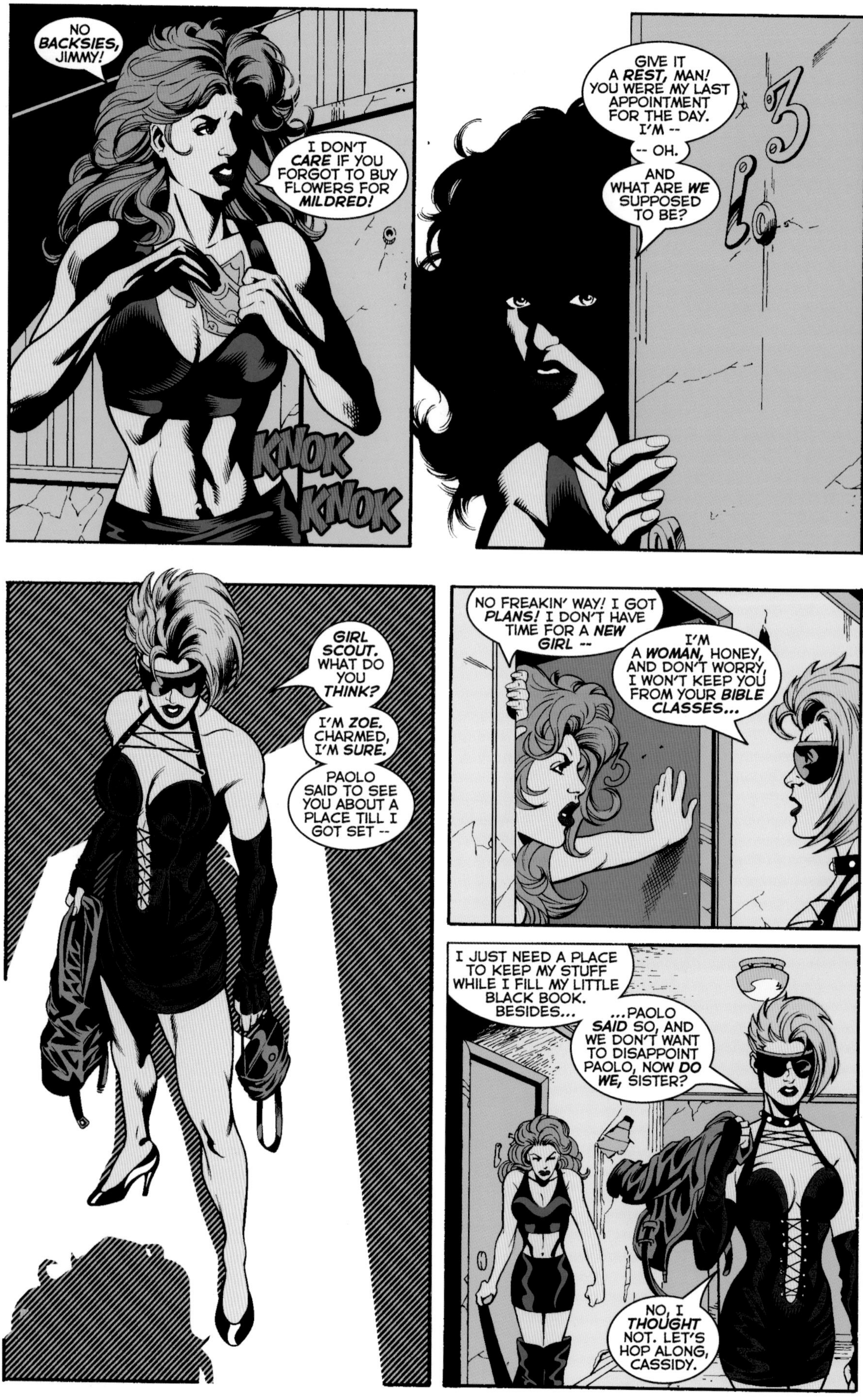

NO BACKSIES, JIMMY!
I DON'T CARE IF YOU FORGOT TO BUY FLOWERS FOR MILDRED!
KNOK KNOK
GIVE IT A REST, MAN! YOU WERE MY LAST APPOINTMENT FOR THE DAY. I'M --
-- OH.
AND WHAT ARE WE SUPPOSED TO BE?
GIRL SCOUT. WHAT DO YOU THINK?
I'M ZOE. CHARMED, I'M SURE.
PAOLO SAID TO SEE YOU ABOUT A PLACE TILL I GOT SET --
NO FREAKIN' WAY! I GOT PLANS! I DON'T HAVE TIME FOR A NEW GIRL --
I'M A WOMAN, HONEY, AND DON'T WORRY, I WON'T KEEP YOU FROM YOUR BIBLE CLASSES...
I JUST NEED A PLACE TO KEEP MY STUFF WHILE I FILL MY LITTLE BLACK BOOK. BESIDES...
...PAOLO SAID SO, AND WE DON'T WANT TO DISAPPOINT PAOLO, NOW DO WE, SISTER?
NO, I THOUGHT NOT. LET'S HOP ALONG, CASSIDY.

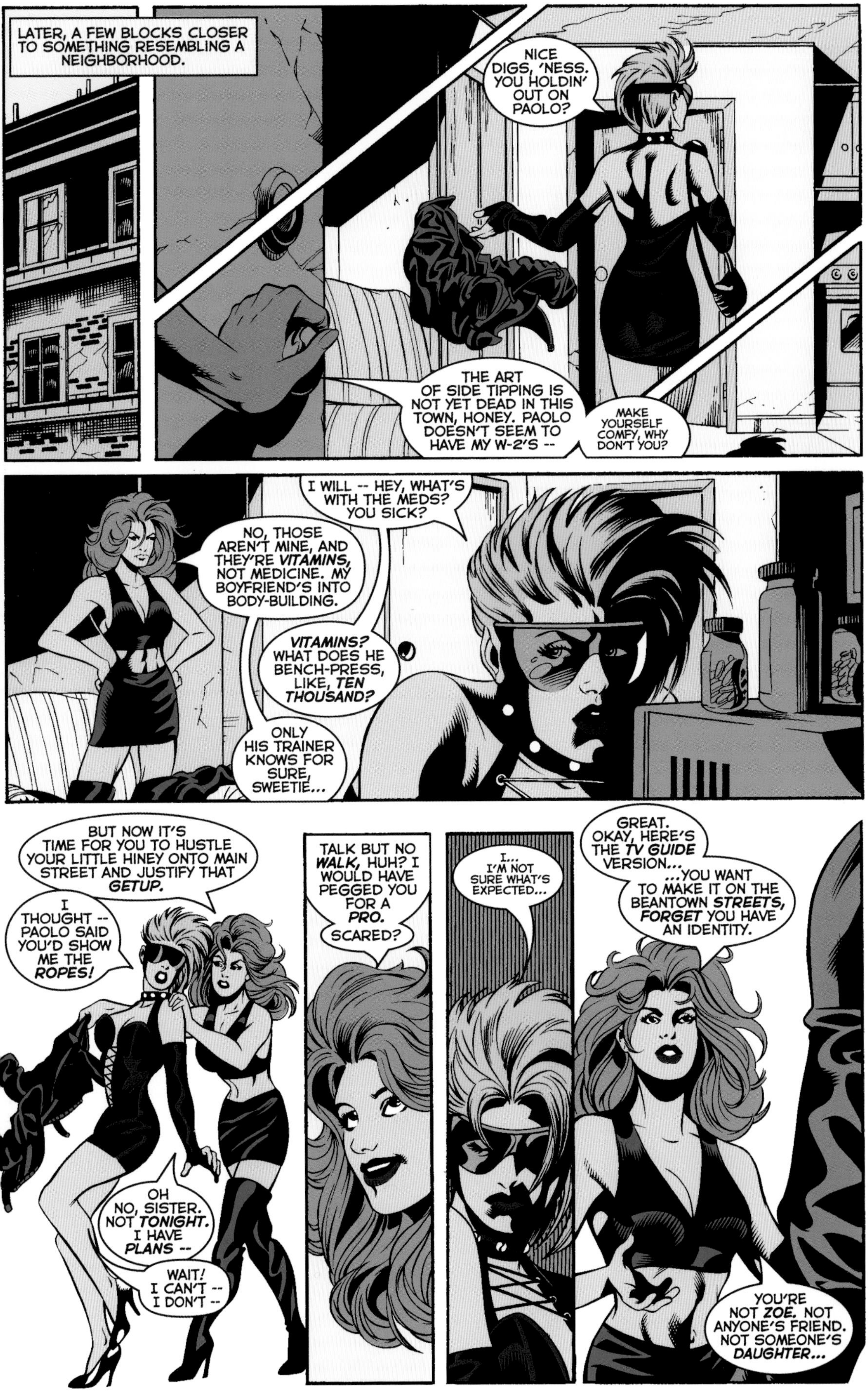
LATER, A FEW BLOCKS CLOSER TO SOMETHING RESEMBLING A NEIGHBORHOOD.
NICE DIGS, 'NESS. YOU HOLDIN' OUT ON PAOLO?
THE ART OF SIDE TIPPING IS NOT YET DEAD IN THIS TOWN, HONEY. PAOLO DOESN'T SEEM TO HAVE MY W-2'S --
MAKE YOURSELF COMFY, WHY DON'T YOU?
I WILL -- HEY, WHAT'S WITH THE MEDS? YOU SICK?
NO, THOSE AREN'T MINE, AND THEY'RE VITAMINS, NOT MEDICINE. MY BOYFRIEND'S INTO BODY-BUILDING.
VITAMINS? WHAT DOES HE BENCH-PRESS, LIKE, TEN THOUSAND?
ONLY HIS TRAINER KNOWS FOR SURE, SWEETIE...
BUT NOW IT'S TIME FOR YOU TO HUSTLE YOUR LITTLE HINEY ONTO MAIN STREET AND JUSTIFY THAT GETUP.
I THOUGHT -- PAOLO SAID YOU'D SHOW ME THE ROPES!
OH NO, SISTER. NOT TONIGHT. I HAVE PLANS --
WAIT! I CAN'T -- I DON'T --
TALK BUT NO WALK, HUH? I WOULD HAVE PEGGED YOU FOR A PRO.
SCARED?
I... I'M NOT SURE WHAT'S EXPECTED...
GREAT. OKAY, HERE'S THE TV GUIDE VERSION...
...YOU WANT TO MAKE IT ON THE BEANTOWN STREETS, FORGET YOU HAVE AN IDENTITY.
YOU'RE NOT ZOE. NOT ANYONE'S FRIEND. NOT SOMEONE'S DAUGHTER...

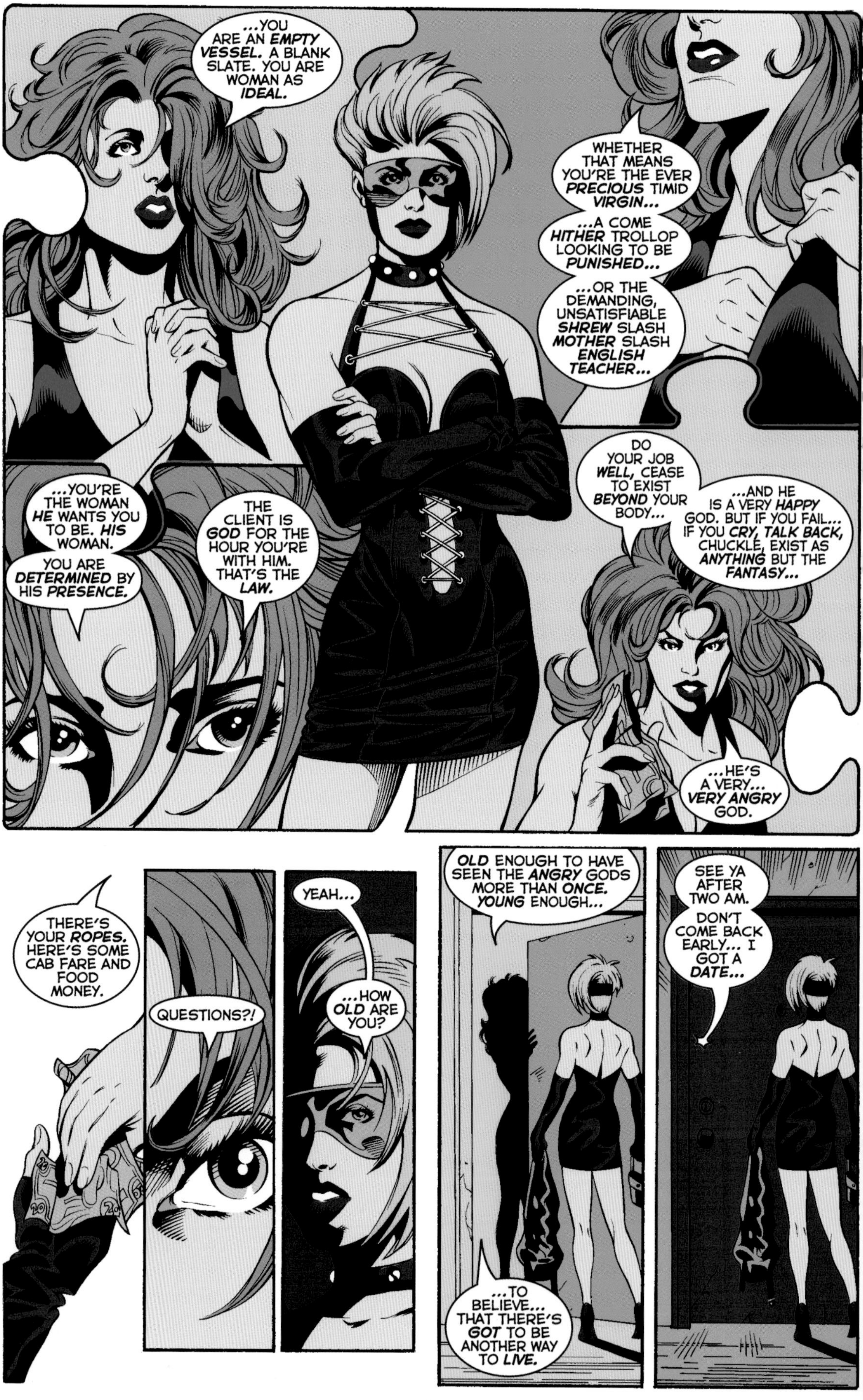
...YOU ARE AN EMPTY VESSEL. A BLANK SLATE. YOU ARE WOMAN AS IDEAL.
WHETHER THAT MEANS YOU'RE THE EVER PRECIOUS TIMID VIRGIN...
...A COME HITHER TROLLOP LOOKING TO BE PUNISHED...
...OR THE DEMANDING, UNSATISFIABLE SHREW SLASH MOTHER SLASH ENGLISH TEACHER...
...YOU'RE THE WOMAN HE WANTS YOU TO BE. HIS WOMAN.
YOU ARE DETERMINED BY HIS PRESENCE.
THE CLIENT IS GOD FOR THE HOUR YOU'RE WITH HIM. THAT'S THE LAW.
DO YOUR JOB WELL, CEASE TO EXIST BEYOND YOUR BODY...
...AND HE IS A VERY HAPPY GOD. BUT IF YOU FAIL... IF YOU CRY, TALK BACK, CHUCKLE, EXIST AS ANYTHING BUT THE FANTASY...
...HE'S A VERY... VERY ANGRY GOD.
THERE'S YOUR ROPES. HERE'S SOME CAB FARE AND FOOD MONEY.
QUESTIONS?!
YEAH...
...HOW OLD ARE YOU?
OLD ENOUGH TO HAVE SEEN THE ANGRY GODS MORE THAN ONCE. YOUNG ENOUGH...
...TO BELIEVE... THAT THERE'S GOT TO BE ANOTHER WAY TO LIVE.
SEE YA AFTER TWO AM.
DON'T COME BACK EARLY... I GOT A DATE...

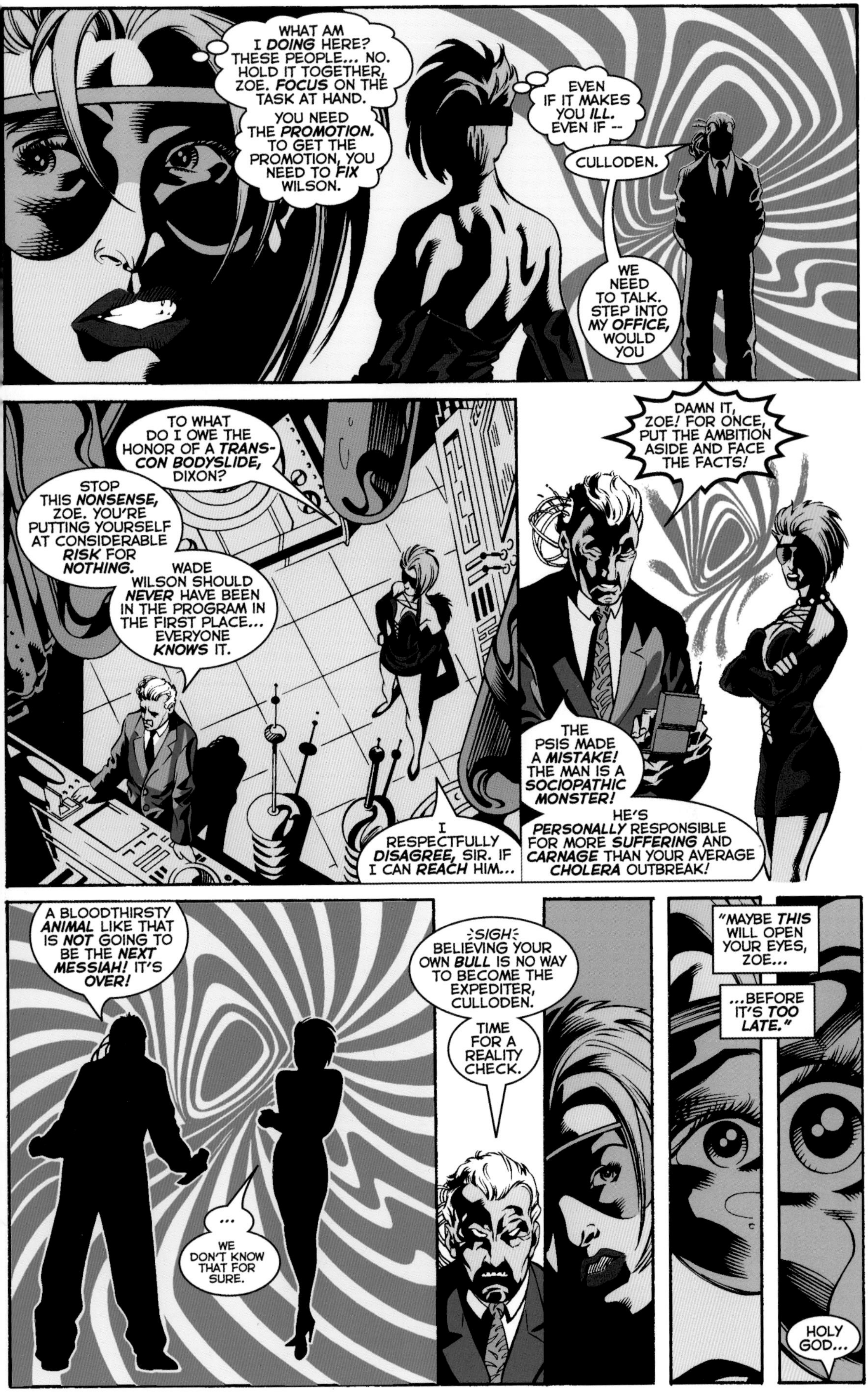
WHAT AM I DOING HERE? THESE PEOPLE... NO. HOLD IT TOGETHER, ZOE. FOCUS ON THE TASK AT HAND.
YOU NEED THE PROMOTION. TO GET THE PROMOTION, YOU NEED TO FIX WILSON.
EVEN IF IT MAKES YOU ILL. EVEN IF --
CULLODEN.
WE NEED TO TALK. STEP INTO MY OFFICE, WOULD YOU
TO WHAT DO I OWE THE HONOR OF A TRANS-CON BODYSLIDE, DIXON?
STOP THIS NONSENSE, ZOE. YOU'RE PUTTING YOURSELF AT CONSIDERABLE RISK FOR NOTHING.
WADE WILSON SHOULD NEVER HAVE BEEN IN THE PROGRAM IN THE FIRST PLACE... EVERYONE KNOWS IT.
I RESPECTFULLY DISAGREE, SIR. IF I CAN REACH HIM...
DAMN IT, ZOE! FOR ONCE, PUT THE AMBITION ASIDE AND FACE THE FACTS!
THE PSIS MADE A MISTAKE! THE MAN IS A SOCIOPATHIC MONSTER!
HE'S PERSONALLY RESPONSIBLE FOR MORE SUFFERING AND CARNAGE THAN YOUR AVERAGE CHOLERA OUTBREAK!
A BLOODTHIRSTY ANIMAL LIKE THAT IS NOT GOING TO BE THE NEXT MESSIAH! IT'S OVER!
...
WE DON'T KNOW THAT FOR SURE.
SIGH
BELIEVING YOUR OWN BULL IS NO WAY TO BECOME THE EXPEDITER, CULLODEN.
TIME FOR A REALITY CHECK.
"MAYBE THIS WILL OPEN YOUR EYES, ZOE...
...BEFORE IT'S TOO LATE."
HOLY GOD...

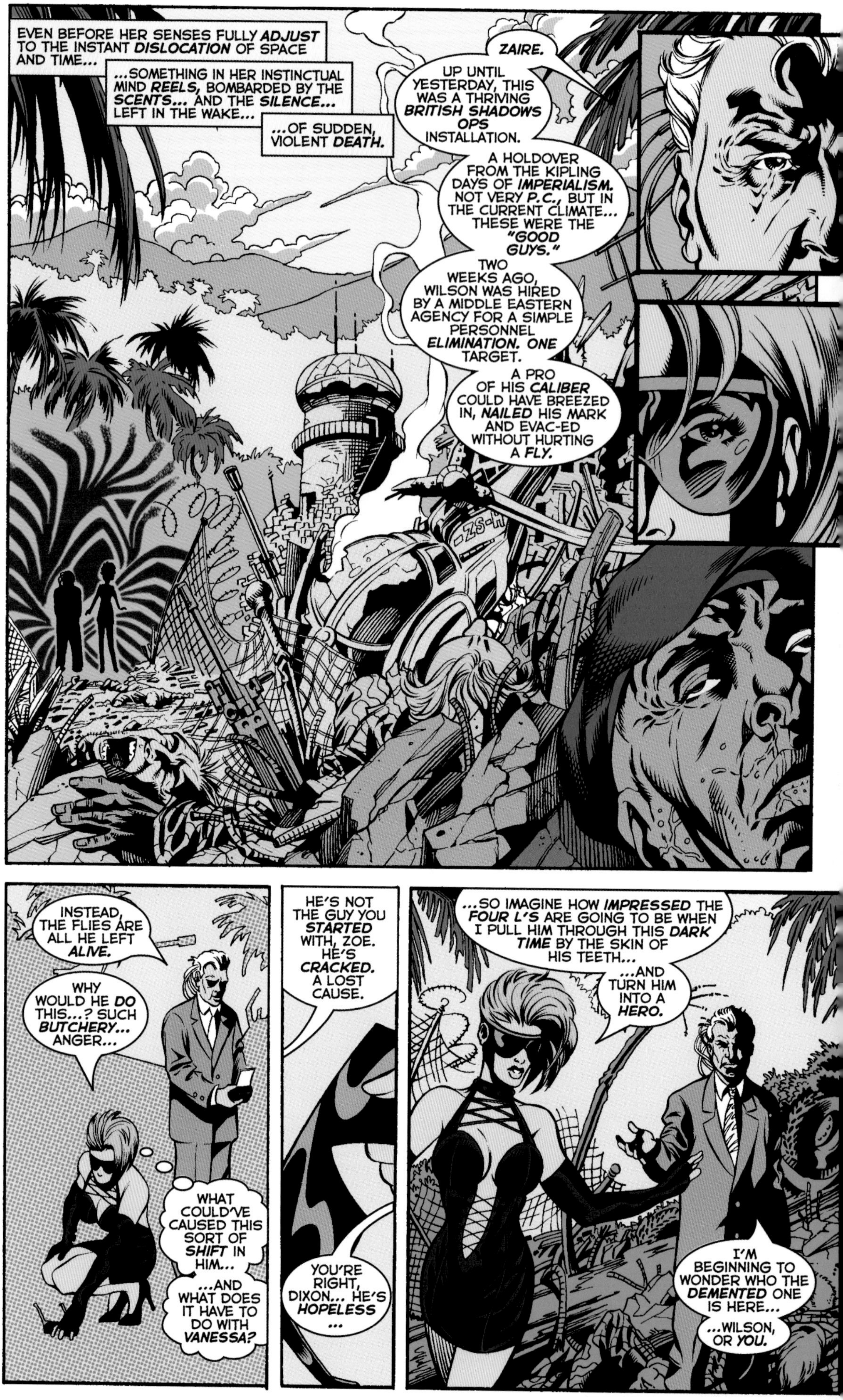
EVEN BEFORE HER SENSES FULLY ADJUST TO THE INSTANT DISLOCATION OF SPACE AND TIME...
...SOMETHING IN HER INSTINCTUAL MIND REELS, BOMBARDED BY THE SCENTS... AND THE SILENCE... LEFT IN THE WAKE...
...OF SUDDEN, VIOLENT DEATH.
ZAIRE.
UP UNTIL YESTERDAY, THIS WAS A THRIVING BRITISH SHADOWS OPS INSTALLATION.
A HOLDOVER FROM THE KIPLING DAYS OF IMPERIALISM. NOT VERY P.C., BUT IN THE CURRENT CLIMATE... THESE WERE THE "GOOD GUYS."
TWO WEEKS AGO, WILSON WAS HIRED BY A MIDDLE EASTERN AGENCY FOR A SIMPLE PERSONNEL ELIMINATION. ONE TARGET.
A PRO OF HIS CALIBER COULD HAVE BREEZED IN, NAILED HIS MARK AND EVAC-ED WITHOUT HURTING A FLY.
INSTEAD, THE FLIES ARE ALL HE LEFT ALIVE.
WHY WOULD HE DO THIS...? SUCH BUTCHERY... ANGER...
WHAT COULD'VE CAUSED THIS SORT OF SHIFT IN HIM...
...AND WHAT DOES IT HAVE TO DO WITH VANESSA?
HE'S NOT THE GUY YOU STARTED WITH, ZOE. HE'S CRACKED. A LOST CAUSE.
YOU'RE RIGHT, DIXON... HE'S HOPELESS...
...SO IMAGINE HOW IMPRESSED THE FOUR L'S ARE GOING TO BE WHEN I PULL HIM THROUGH THIS DARK TIME BY THE SKIN OF HIS TEETH...
...AND TURN HIM INTO A HERO.
I'M BEGINNING TO WONDER WHO THE DEMENTED ONE IS HERE...
...WILSON, OR YOU.

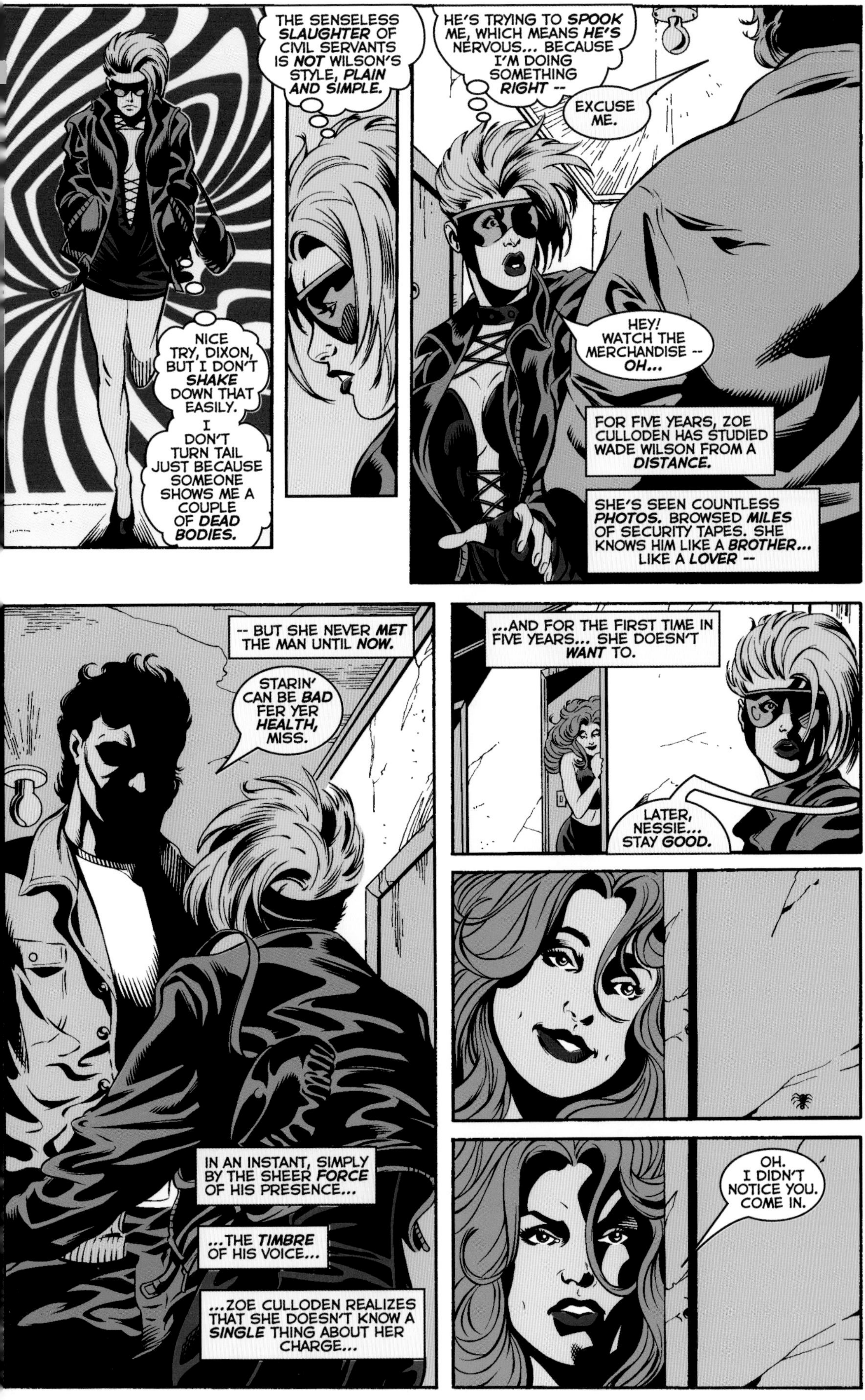
NICE TRY, DIXON, BUT I DON'T SHAKE DOWN THAT EASILY.
I DON'T TURN TAIL JUST BECAUSE SOMEONE SHOWS ME A COUPLE OF DEAD BODIES.
THE SENSELESS SLAUGHTER OF CIVIL SERVANTS IS NOT WILSON'S STYLE, PLAIN AND SIMPLE.
HE'S TRYING TO SPOOK ME, WHICH MEANS HE'S NERVOUS... BECAUSE I'M DOING SOMETHING RIGHT --
EXCUSE ME.
HEY! WATCH THE MERCHANDISE -- OH...
FOR FIVE YEARS, ZOE CULLODEN HAS STUDIED WADE WILSON FROM A DISTANCE.
SHE'S SEEN COUNTLESS PHOTOS. BROWSED MILES OF SECURITY TAPES. SHE KNOWS HIM LIKE A BROTHER... LIKE A LOVER --
-- BUT SHE NEVER MET THE MAN UNTIL NOW.
STARIN' CAN BE BAD FER YER HEALTH, MISS.
IN AN INSTANT, SIMPLY BY THE SHEER FORCE OF HIS PRESENCE...
...THE TIMBRE OF HIS VOICE...
...ZOE CULLODEN REALIZES THAT SHE DOESN'T KNOW A SINGLE THING ABOUT HER CHARGE...
...AND FOR THE FIRST TIME IN FIVE YEARS... SHE DOESN'T WANT TO.
LATER, NESSIE... STAY GOOD.
OH. I DIDN'T NOTICE YOU. COME IN.

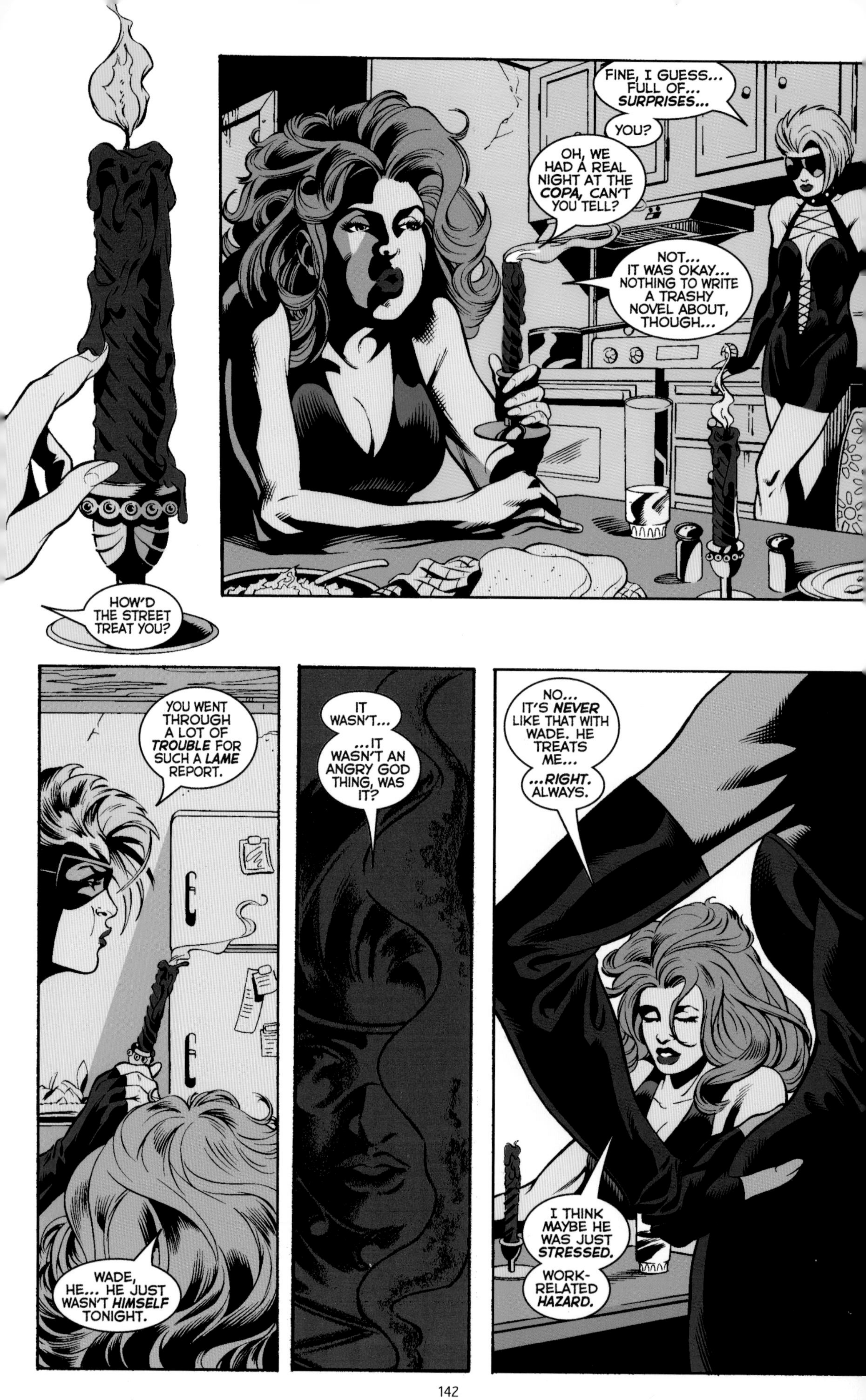
HOW'D THE STREET TREAT YOU?
FINE, I GUESS... FULL OF... SURPRISES...
YOU?
OH, WE HAD A REAL NIGHT AT THE COPA, CAN'T YOU TELL?
NOT... IT WAS OKAY... NOTHING TO WRITE A TRASHY NOVEL ABOUT, THOUGH...
YOU WENT THROUGH A LOT OF TROUBLE FOR SUCH A LAME REPORT.
WADE, HE... HE JUST WASN'T HIMSELF TONIGHT.
IT WASN'T...
...IT WASN'T AN ANGRY GOD THING, WAS IT?
NO... IT'S NEVER LIKE THAT WITH WADE. HE TREATS ME...
...RIGHT. ALWAYS.
I THINK MAYBE HE WAS JUST STRESSED.
WORK-RELATED HAZARD.

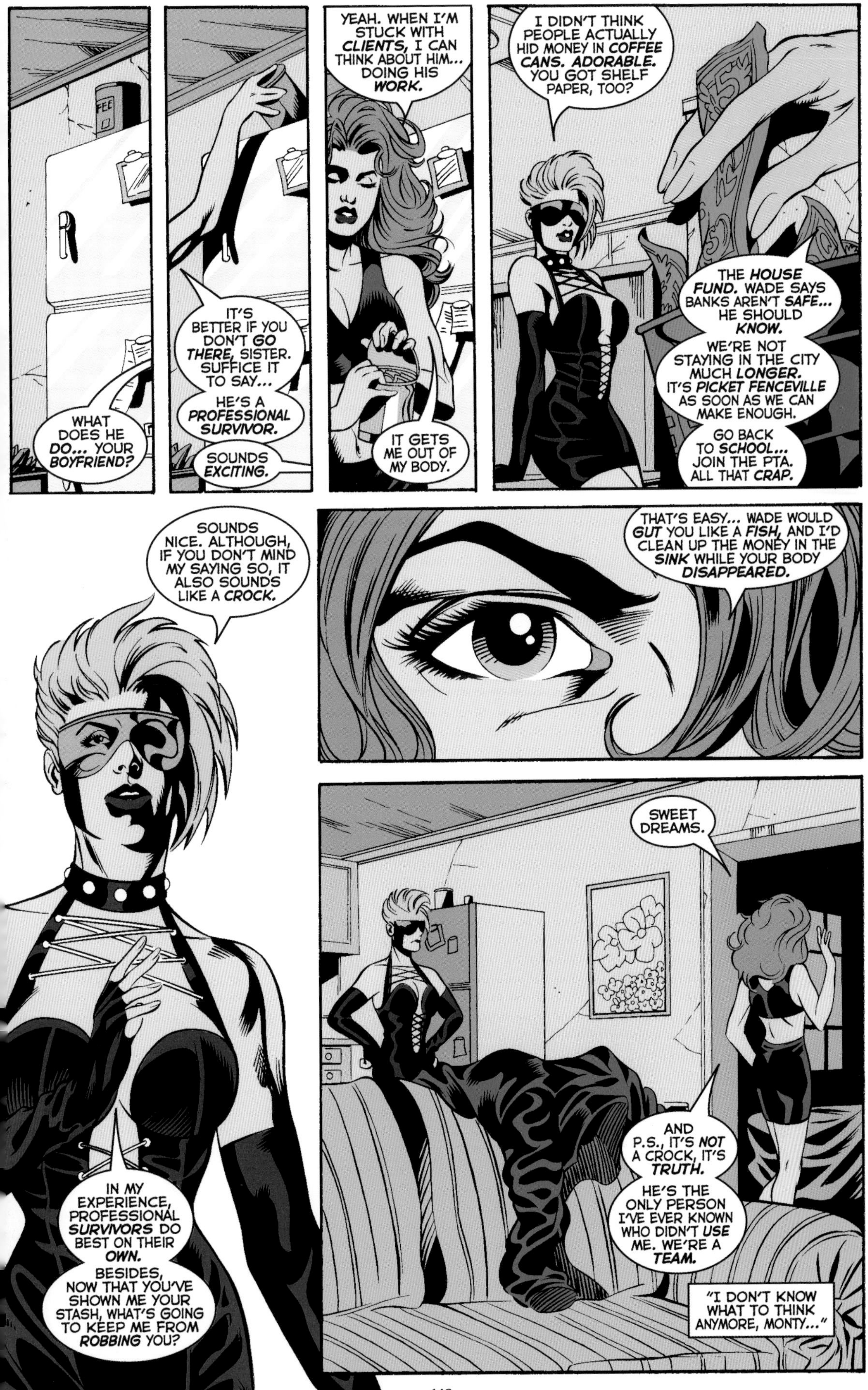
WHAT DOES HE DO... YOUR BOYFRIEND?
IT'S BETTER IF YOU DON'T GO THERE, SISTER. SUFFICE IT TO SAY...
HE'S A PROFESSIONAL SURVIVOR.
SOUNDS EXCITING.
YEAH. WHEN I'M STUCK WITH CLIENTS, I CAN THINK ABOUT HIM... DOING HIS WORK.
IT GETS ME OUT OF MY BODY.
I DIDN'T THINK PEOPLE ACTUALLY HID MONEY IN COFFEE CANS. ADORABLE. YOU GOT SHELF PAPER, TOO?
THE HOUSE FUND. WADE SAYS BANKS AREN'T SAFE... HE SHOULD KNOW.
WE'RE NOT STAYING IN THE CITY MUCH LONGER. IT'S PICKET FENCEVILLE AS SOON AS WE CAN MAKE ENOUGH.
GO BACK TO SCHOOL... JOIN THE PTA. ALL THAT CRAP.
SOUNDS NICE. ALTHOUGH, IF YOU DON'T MIND MY SAYING SO, IT ALSO SOUNDS LIKE A CROCK.
IN MY EXPERIENCE, PROFESSIONAL SURVIVORS DO BEST ON THEIR OWN.
BESIDES, NOW THAT YOU'VE SHOWN ME YOUR STASH, WHAT'S GOING TO KEEP ME FROM ROBBING YOU?
THAT'S EASY... WADE WOULD GUT YOU LIKE A FISH, AND I'D CLEAN UP THE MONEY IN THE SINK WHILE YOUR BODY DISAPPEARED.
SWEET DREAMS.
AND P.S., IT'S NOT A CROCK, IT'S TRUTH.
HE'S THE ONLY PERSON I'VE EVER KNOWN WHO DIDN'T USE ME. WE'RE A TEAM.
"I DON'T KNOW WHAT TO THINK ANYMORE, MONTY..."

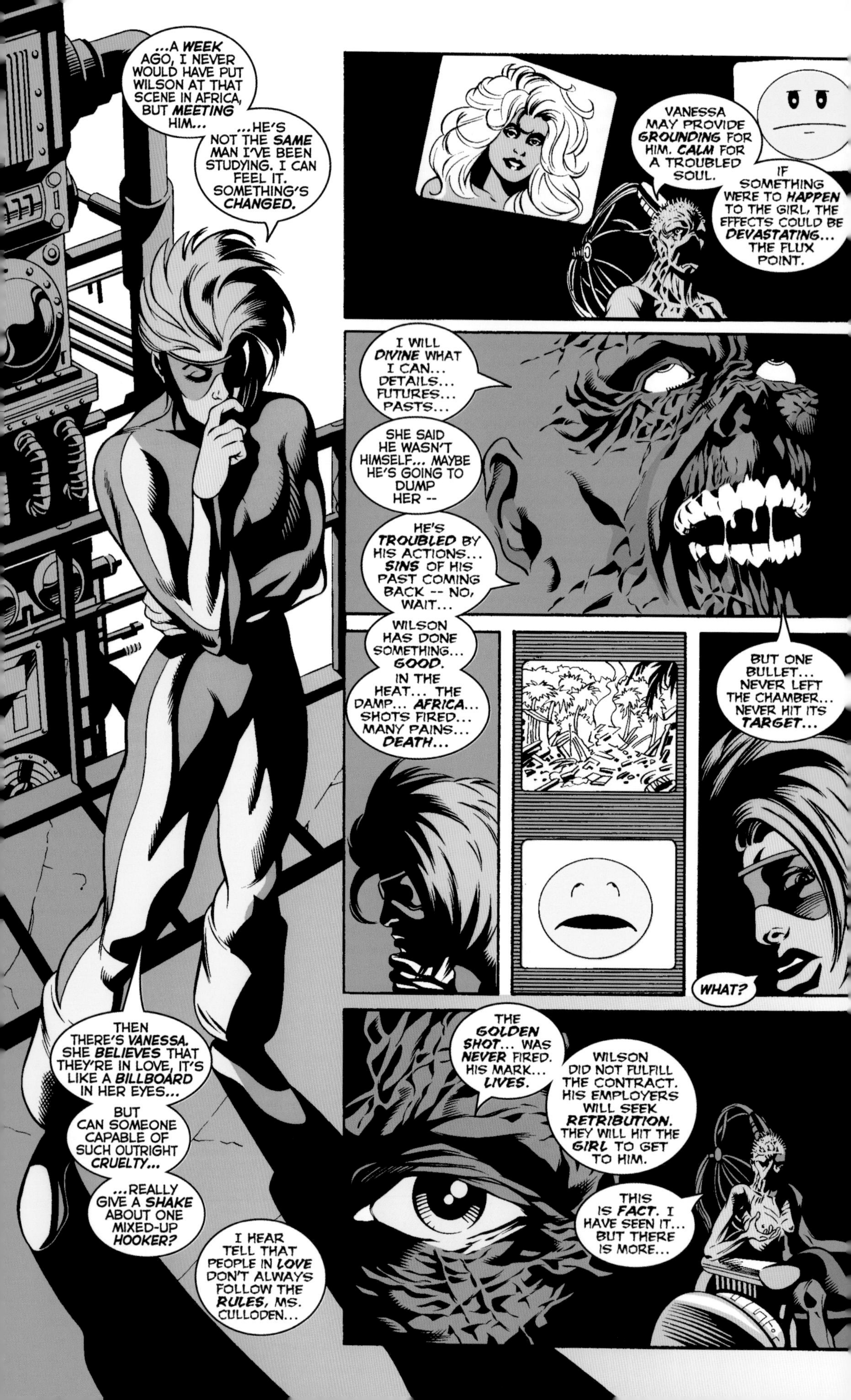
...A WEEK AGO, I NEVER WOULD HAVE PUT WILSON AT THAT SCENE IN AFRICA, BUT MEETING HIM...
...HE'S NOT THE SAME MAN I'VE BEEN STUDYING. I CAN FEEL IT. SOMETHING'S CHANGED.
VANESSA MAY PROVIDE GROUNDING FOR HIM. CALM FOR A TROUBLED SOUL.
IF SOMETHING WERE TO HAPPEN TO THE GIRL, THE EFFECTS COULD BE DEVASTATING... THE FLUX POINT.
I WILL DIVINE WHAT I CAN... DETAILS... FUTURES... PASTS...
SHE SAID HE WASN'T HIMSELF... MAYBE HE'S GOING TO DUMP HER --
HE'S TROUBLED BY HIS ACTIONS... SINS OF HIS PAST COMING BACK -- NO, WAIT...
WILSON HAS DONE SOMETHING... GOOD.
IN THE HEAT... THE DAMP... AFRICA... SHOTS FIRED... MANY PAINS... DEATH...
BUT ONE BULLET... NEVER LEFT THE CHAMBER... NEVER HIT ITS TARGET...
WHAT?
THE GOLDEN SHOT... WAS NEVER FIRED. HIS MARK... LIVES.
WILSON DID NOT FULFILL THE CONTRACT. HIS EMPLOYERS WILL SEEK RETRIBUTION. THEY WILL HIT THE GIRL TO GET TO HIM.
THIS IS FACT. I HAVE SEEN IT... BUT THERE IS MORE...
THEN THERE'S VANESSA. SHE BELIEVES THAT THEY'RE IN LOVE, IT'S LIKE A BILLBOARD IN HER EYES...
BUT CAN SOMEONE CAPABLE OF SUCH OUTRIGHT CRUELTY...
...REALLY GIVE A SHAKE ABOUT ONE MIXED-UP HOOKER?
I HEAR TELL THAT PEOPLE IN LOVE DON'T ALWAYS FOLLOW THE RULES, MS. CULLODEN...

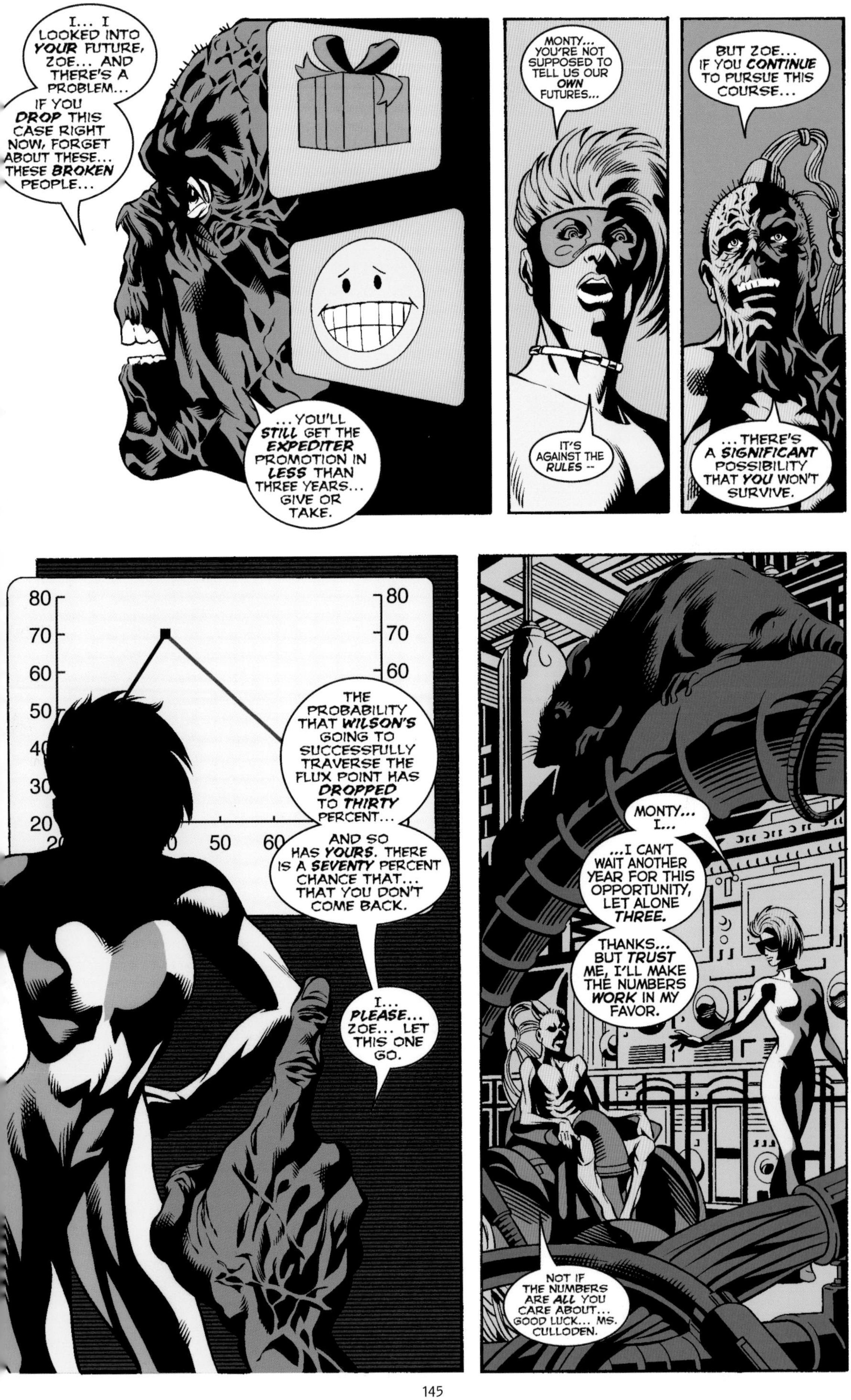
I... I LOOKED INTO YOUR FUTURE, ZOE... AND THERE'S A PROBLEM...
IF YOU DROP THIS CASE RIGHT NOW, FORGET ABOUT THESE... THESE BROKEN PEOPLE...
...YOU'LL STILL GET THE EXPEDITER PROMOTION IN LESS THAN THREE YEARS... GIVE OR TAKE.
MONTY... YOU'RE NOT SUPPOSED TO TELL US OUR OWN FUTURES...
IT'S AGAINST THE RULES --
BUT ZOE... IF YOU CONTINUE TO PURSUE THIS COURSE...
...THERE'S A SIGNIFICANT POSSIBILITY THAT YOU WON'T SURVIVE.
80
70
60
50
20
50
THE PROBABILITY THAT WILSON'S GOING TO SUCCESSFULLY TRAVERSE THE FLUX POINT HAS DROPPED TO THIRTY PERCENT...
AND SO HAS YOURS. THERE IS A SEVENTY PERCENT CHANCE THAT... THAT YOU DON'T COME BACK.
I... PLEASE... ZOE... LET THIS ONE GO.
MONTY... I...
...I CAN'T WAIT ANOTHER YEAR FOR THIS OPPORTUNITY, LET ALONE THREE.
THANKS... BUT TRUST ME, I'LL MAKE THE NUMBERS WORK IN MY FAVOR.
NOT IF THE NUMBERS ARE ALL YOU CARE ABOUT... GOOD LUCK... MS. CULLODEN.

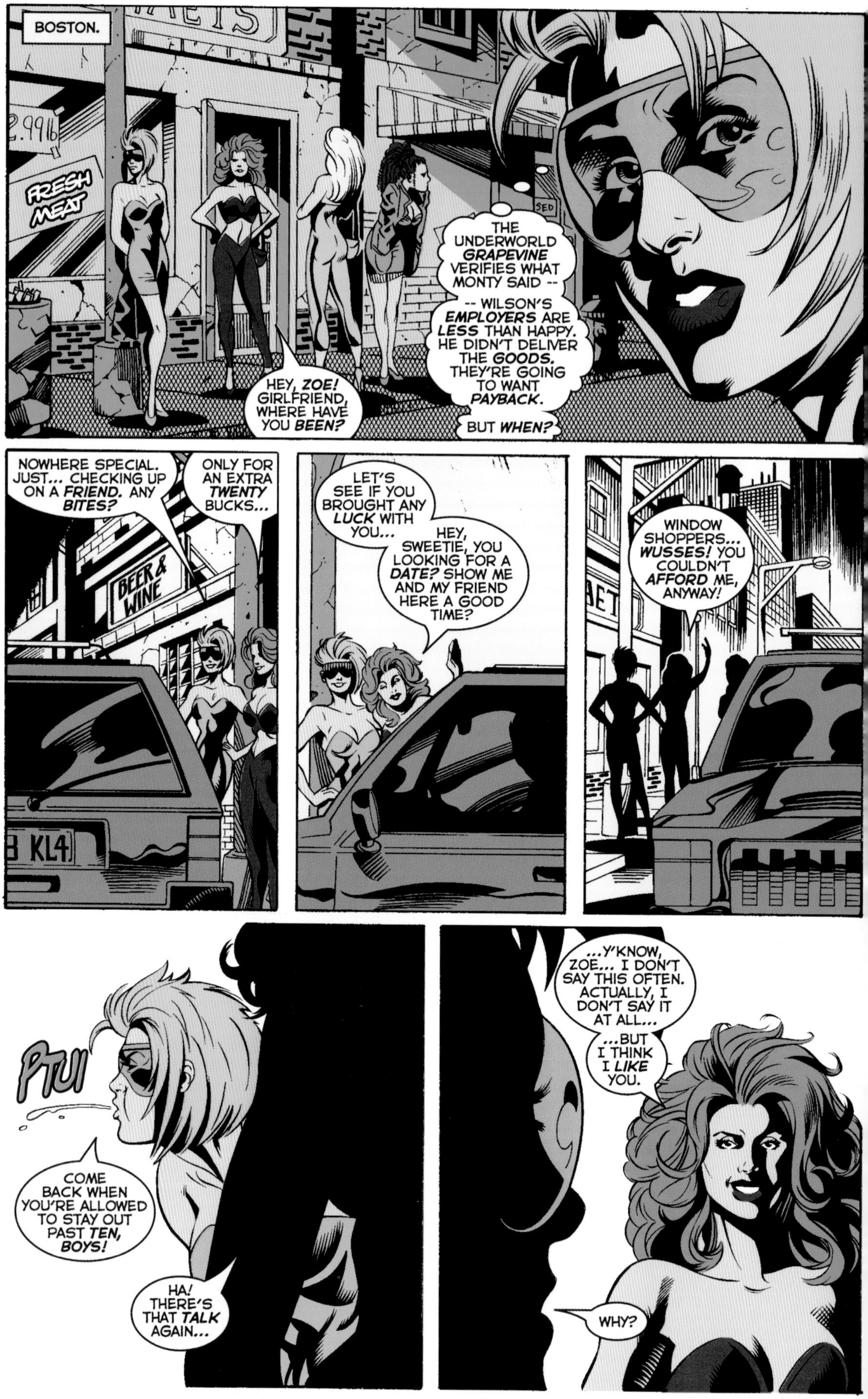
BOSTON.
FRESH MEAT
2.99lb
THE UNDERWORLD GRAPEVINE VERIFIES WHAT MONTY SAID --
-- WILSON'S EMPLOYERS ARE LESS THAN HAPPY. HE DIDN'T DELIVER THE GOODS. THEY'RE GOING TO WANT PAYBACK.
BUT WHEN?
HEY, ZOE! GIRLFRIEND, WHERE HAVE YOU BEEN?
NOWHERE SPECIAL. JUST... CHECKING UP ON A FRIEND. ANY BITES?
ONLY FOR AN EXTRA TWENTY BUCKS...
BEER & WINE
LET'S SEE IF YOU BROUGHT ANY LUCK WITH YOU...
HEY, SWEETIE, YOU LOOKING FOR A DATE? SHOW ME AND MY FRIEND HERE A GOOD TIME?
WINDOW SHOPPERS... WUSSES! YOU COULDN'T AFFORD ME, ANYWAY!
PTUI
COME BACK WHEN YOU'RE ALLOWED TO STAY OUT PAST TEN, BOYS!
HA! THERE'S THAT TALK AGAIN...
...Y'KNOW, ZOE... I DON'T SAY THIS OFTEN. ACTUALLY, I DON'T SAY IT AT ALL...
...BUT I THINK I LIKE YOU.
WHY?

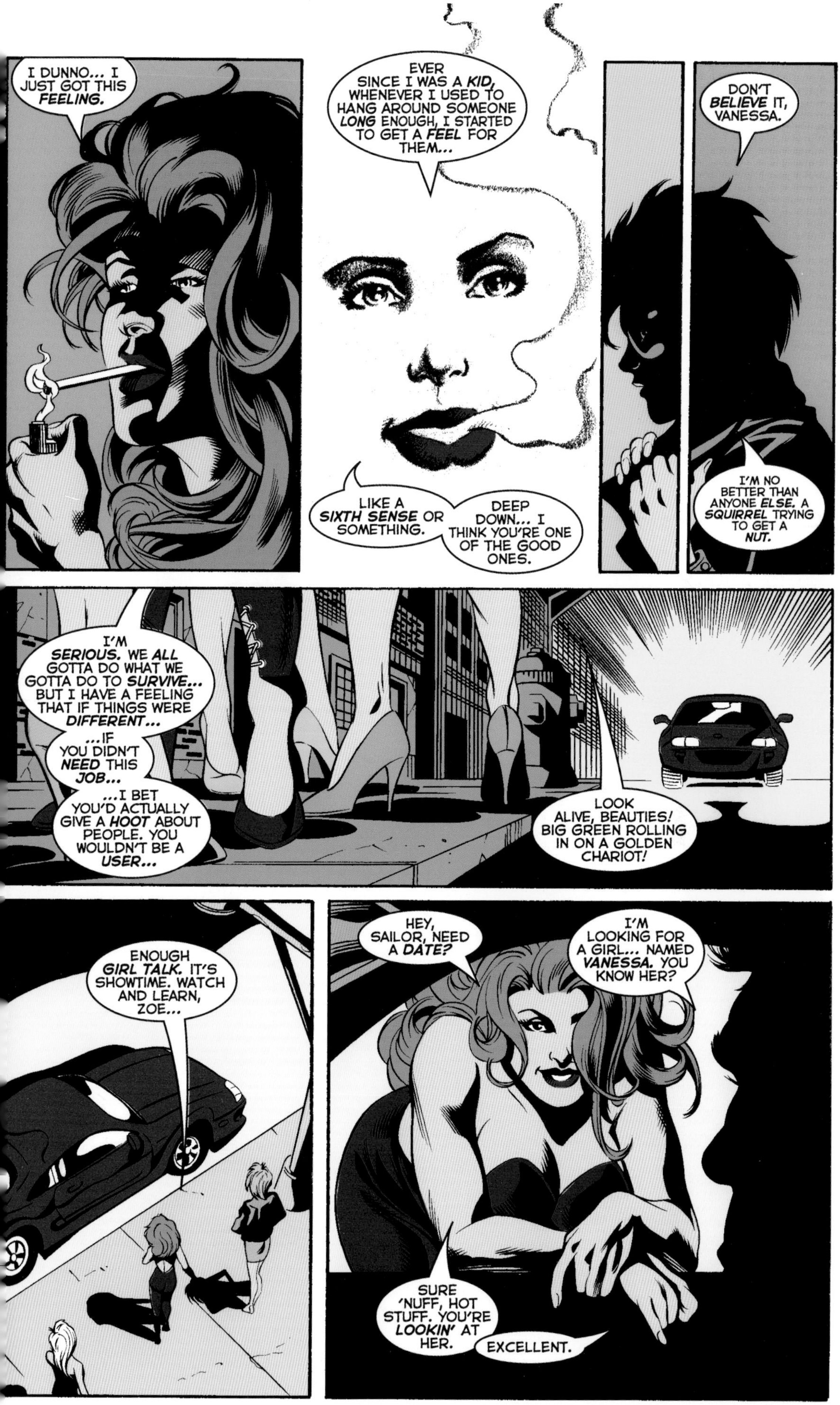
I DUNNO... I JUST GOT THIS FEELING.
EVER SINCE I WAS A KID, WHENEVER I USED TO HANG AROUND SOMEONE LONG ENOUGH, I STARTED TO GET A FEEL FOR THEM...
LIKE A SIXTH SENSE OR SOMETHING.
DEEP DOWN... I THINK YOU'RE ONE OF THE GOOD ONES.
DON'T BELIEVE IT, VANESSA.
I'M NO BETTER THAN ANYONE ELSE. A SQUIRREL TRYING TO GET A NUT.
I'M SERIOUS. WE ALL GOTTA DO WHAT WE GOTTA DO TO SURVIVE... BUT I HAVE A FEELING THAT IF THINGS WERE DIFFERENT...
...IF YOU DIDN'T NEED THIS JOB...
...I BET YOU'D ACTUALLY GIVE A HOOT ABOUT PEOPLE. YOU WOULDN'T BE A USER...
LOOK ALIVE, BEAUTIES! BIG GREEN ROLLING IN ON A GOLDEN CHARIOT!
ENOUGH GIRL TALK. IT'S SHOWTIME. WATCH AND LEARN, ZOE...
HEY, SAILOR, NEED A DATE?
I'M LOOKING FOR A GIRL... NAMED VANESSA. YOU KNOW HER?
SURE 'NUFF, HOT STUFF. YOU'RE LOOKIN' AT HER.
EXCELLENT.

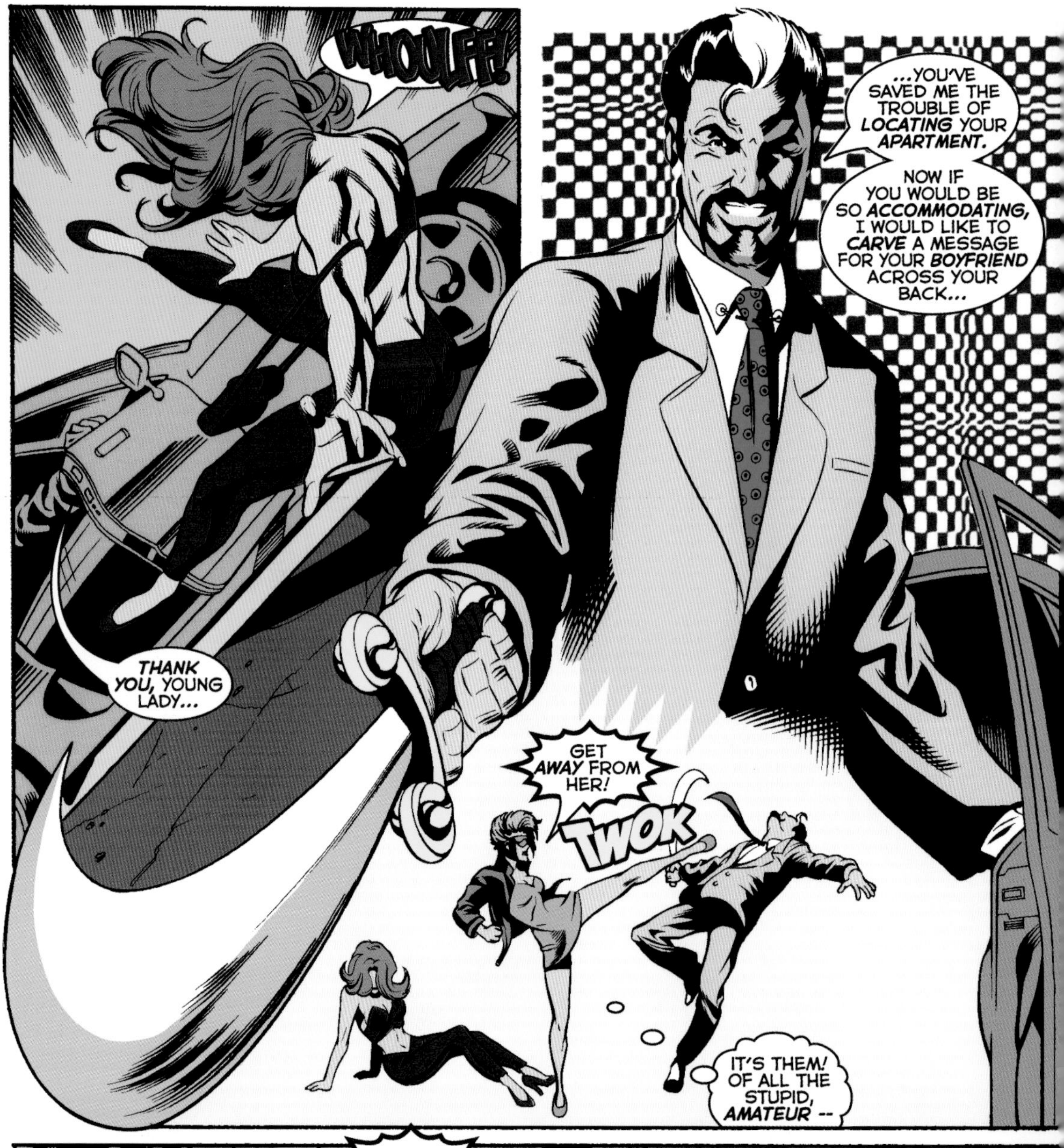
WHOULFF!
...YOU'VE SAVED ME THE TROUBLE OF LOCATING YOUR APARTMENT.
NOW IF YOU WOULD BE SO ACCOMMODATING, I WOULD LIKE TO CARVE A MESSAGE FOR YOUR BOYFRIEND ACROSS YOUR BACK...
THANK YOU, YOUNG LADY...
GET AWAY FROM HER!
TWOK
IT'S THEM! OF ALL THE STUPID, AMATEUR --

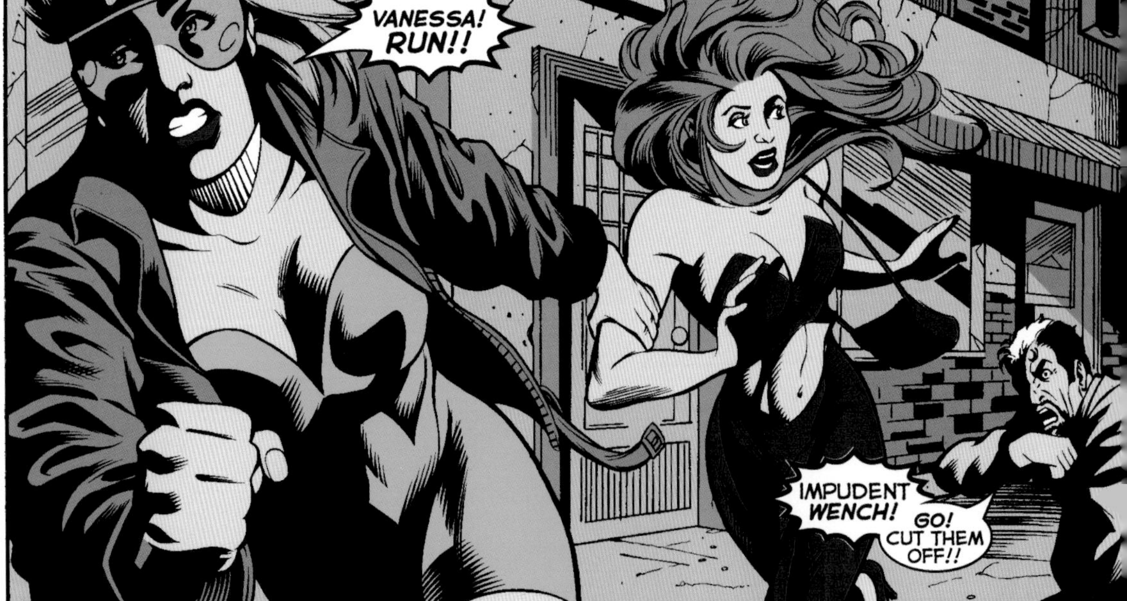
VANESSA! RUN!!
IMPUDENT WENCH!
GO! CUT THEM OFF!!

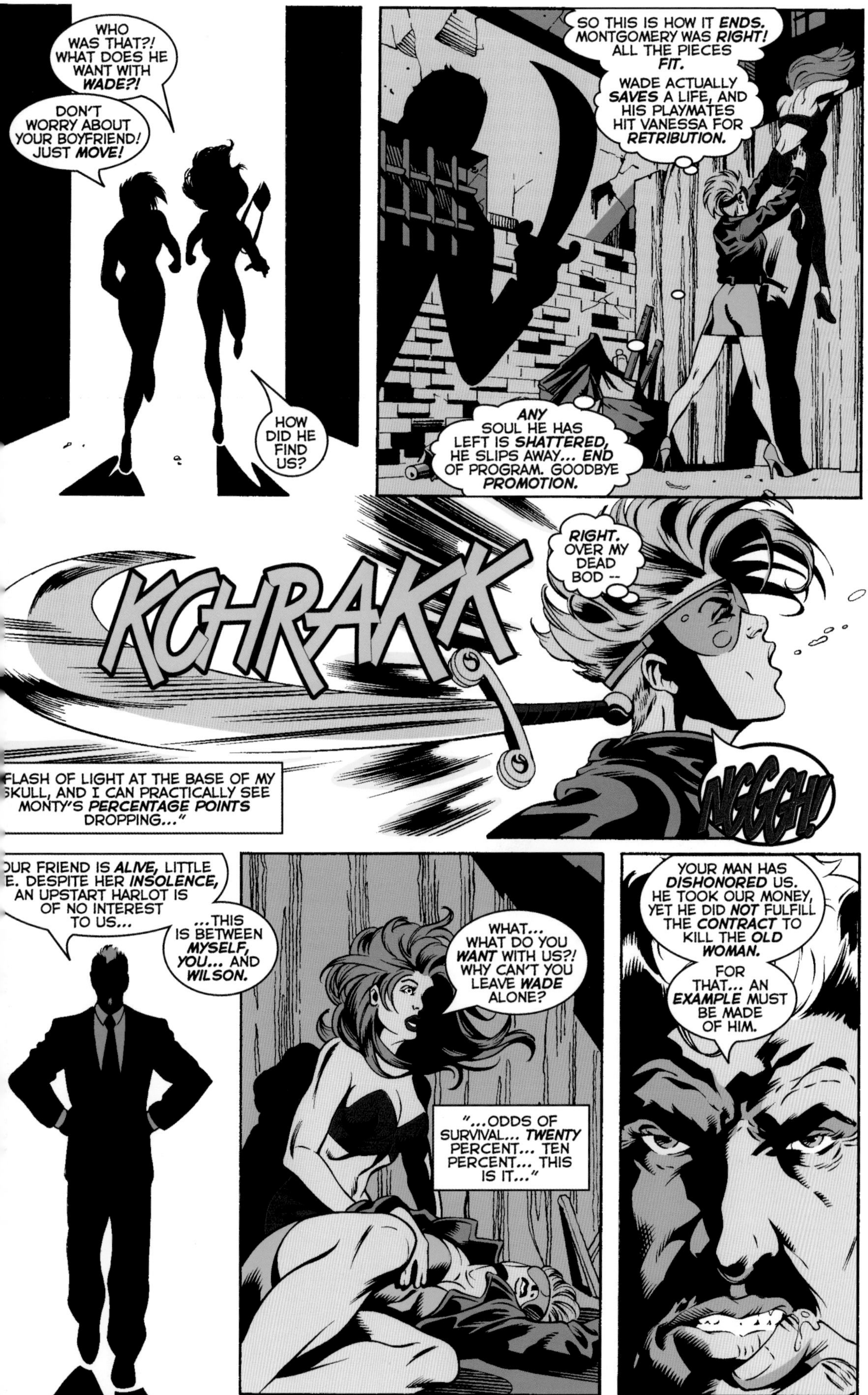
WHO WAS THAT?! WHAT DOES HE WANT WITH WADE?!
DON'T WORRY ABOUT YOUR BOYFRIEND! JUST MOVE!
HOW DID HE FIND US?
SO THIS IS HOW IT ENDS. MONTGOMERY WAS RIGHT! ALL THE PIECES FIT.
WADE ACTUALLY SAVES A LIFE, AND HIS PLAYMATES HIT VANESSA FOR RETRIBUTION.
ANY SOUL HE HAS LEFT IS SHATTERED, HE SLIPS AWAY... END OF PROGRAM. GOODBYE PROMOTION.
KCHRAKK
RIGHT. OVER MY DEAD BOD --
FLASH OF LIGHT AT THE BASE OF MY SKULL, AND I CAN PRACTICALLY SEE MONTY'S PERCENTAGE POINTS DROPPING..."
NGGGH!
OUR FRIEND IS ALIVE, LITTLE E. DESPITE HER INSOLENCE, AN UPSTART HARLOT IS OF NO INTEREST TO US...
...THIS IS BETWEEN MYSELF, YOU... AND WILSON.
WHAT... WHAT DO YOU WANT WITH US?! WHY CAN'T YOU LEAVE WADE ALONE?
"...ODDS OF SURVIVAL... TWENTY PERCENT... TEN PERCENT... THIS IS IT..."
YOUR MAN HAS DISHONORED US. HE TOOK OUR MONEY, YET HE DID NOT FULFILL THE CONTRACT TO KILL THE OLD WOMAN.
FOR THAT... AN EXAMPLE MUST BE MADE OF HIM.

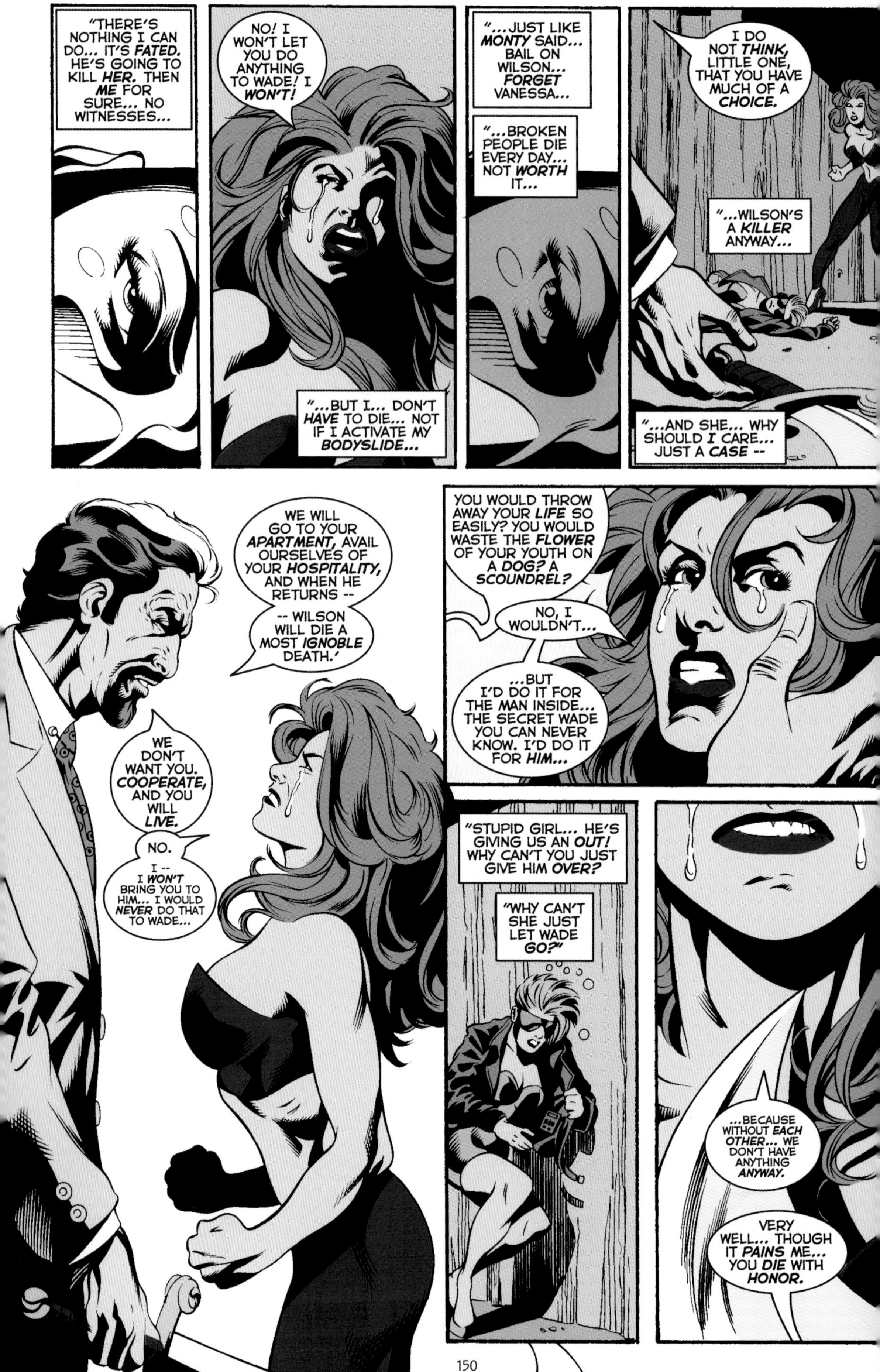
"THERE'S NOTHING I CAN DO... IT'S FATED. HE'S GOING TO KILL HER. THEN ME FOR SURE... NO WITNESSES...
NO! I WON'T LET YOU DO ANYTHING TO WADE! I WON'T!
"...BUT I... DON'T HAVE TO DIE... NOT IF I ACTIVATE MY BODYSLIDE...
"...JUST LIKE MONTY SAID... BAIL ON WILSON... FORGET VANESSA...
"...BROKEN PEOPLE DIE EVERY DAY... NOT WORTH IT...
I DO NOT THINK, LITTLE ONE, THAT YOU HAVE MUCH OF A CHOICE.
"...WILSON'S A KILLER ANYWAY...
"...AND SHE... WHY SHOULD I CARE... JUST A CASE --
WE WILL GO TO YOUR APARTMENT, AVAIL OURSELVES OF YOUR HOSPITALITY, AND WHEN HE RETURNS --
-- WILSON WILL DIE A MOST IGNOBLE DEATH.'
WE DON'T WANT YOU. COOPERATE, AND YOU WILL LIVE.
NO.
I -- I WON'T BRING YOU TO HIM... I WOULD NEVER DO THAT TO WADE...
YOU WOULD THROW AWAY YOUR LIFE SO EASILY? YOU WOULD WASTE THE FLOWER OF YOUR YOUTH ON A DOG? A SCOUNDREL?
NO, I WOULDN'T...
...BUT I'D DO IT FOR THE MAN INSIDE... THE SECRET WADE YOU CAN NEVER KNOW. I'D DO IT FOR HIM...
"STUPID GIRL... HE'S GIVING US AN OUT! WHY CAN'T YOU JUST GIVE HIM OVER?
"WHY CAN'T SHE JUST LET WADE GO?"
...BECAUSE WITHOUT EACH OTHER... WE DON'T HAVE ANYTHING ANYWAY.
VERY WELL... THOUGH IT PAINS ME... YOU DIE WITH HONOR.

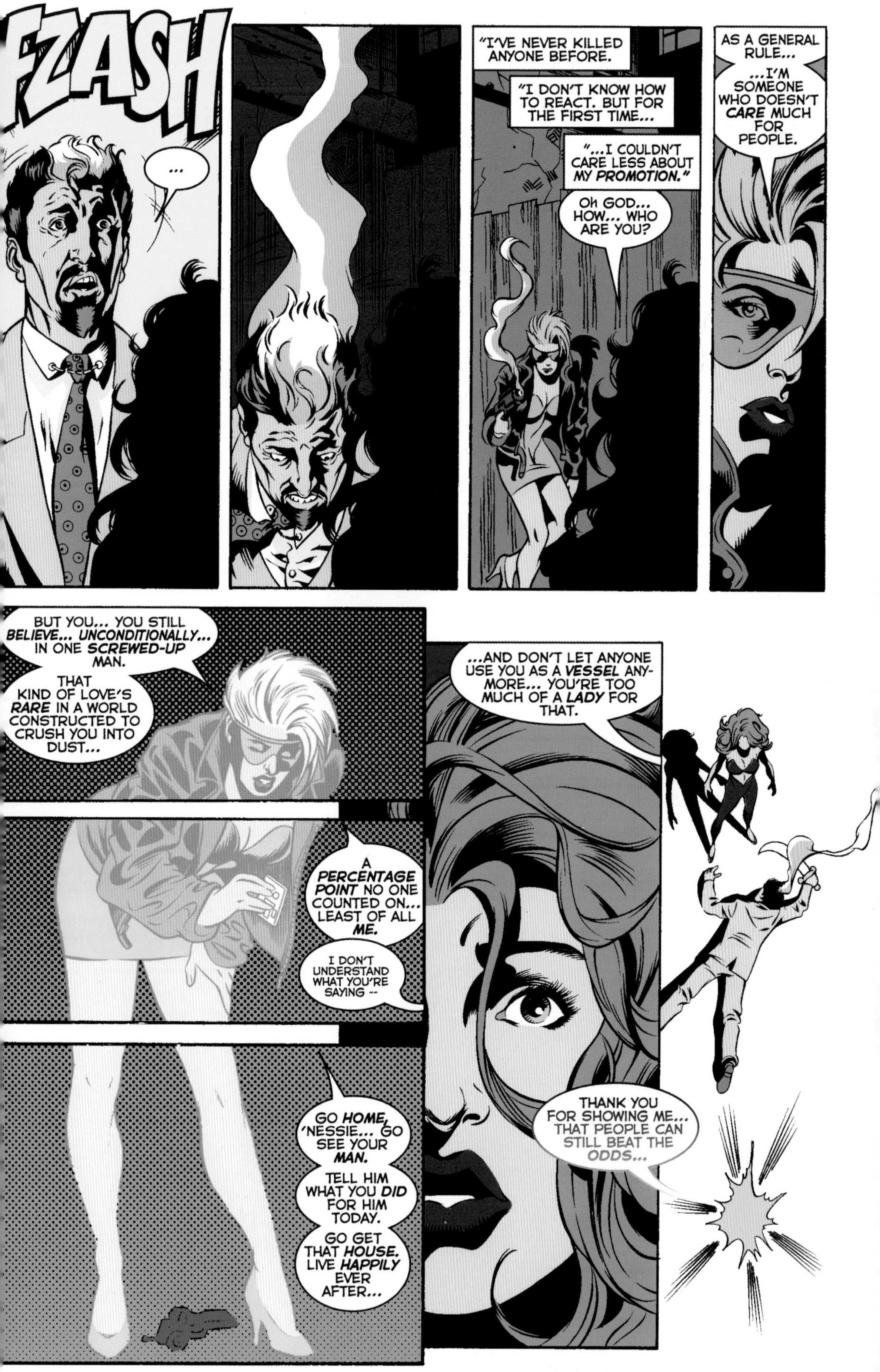
FZASH
...
"I'VE NEVER KILLED ANYONE BEFORE.
"I DON'T KNOW HOW TO REACT. BUT FOR THE FIRST TIME...
"...I COULDN'T CARE LESS ABOUT MY PROMOTION."
Oh GOD... HOW... WHO ARE YOU?
AS A GENERAL RULE...
...I'M SOMEONE WHO DOESN'T CARE MUCH FOR PEOPLE.
BUT YOU... YOU STILL BELIEVE... UNCONDITIONALLY... IN ONE SCREWED-UP MAN.
THAT KIND OF LOVE'S RARE IN A WORLD CONSTRUCTED TO CRUSH YOU INTO DUST...
A PERCENTAGE POINT NO ONE COUNTED ON... LEAST OF ALL ME.
I DON'T UNDERSTAND WHAT YOU'RE SAYING --
GO HOME, 'NESSIE... GO SEE YOUR MAN.
TELL HIM WHAT YOU DID FOR HIM TODAY.
GO GET THAT HOUSE. LIVE HAPPILY EVER AFTER...
...AND DON'T LET ANYONE USE YOU AS A VESSEL ANY-MORE... YOU'RE TOO MUCH OF A LADY FOR THAT.
THANK YOU FOR SHOWING ME... THAT PEOPLE CAN STILL BEAT THE ODDS...

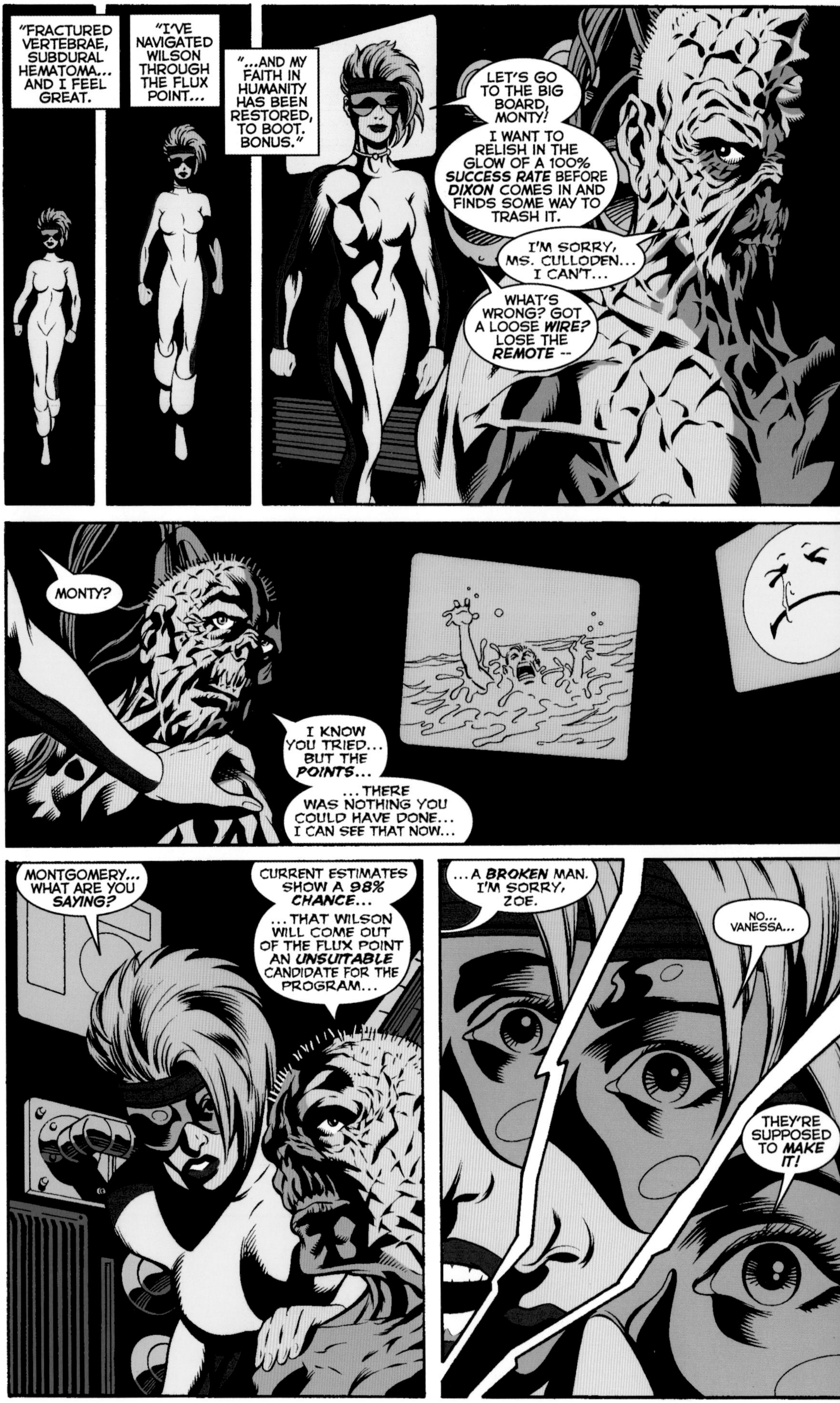
"FRACTURED VERTEBRAE, SUBDURAL HEMATOMA... AND I FEEL GREAT.
"I'VE NAVIGATED WILSON THROUGH THE FLUX POINT...
"...AND MY FAITH IN HUMANITY HAS BEEN RESTORED, TO BOOT. BONUS."
LET'S GO TO THE BIG BOARD, MONTY!
I WANT TO RELISH IN THE GLOW OF A 100% SUCCESS RATE BEFORE DIXON COMES IN AND FINDS SOME WAY TO TRASH IT.
I'M SORRY, MS. CULLODEN... I CAN'T...
WHAT'S WRONG? GOT A LOOSE WIRE? LOSE THE REMOTE --
MONTY?
I KNOW YOU TRIED... BUT THE POINTS...
...THERE WAS NOTHING YOU COULD HAVE DONE... I CAN SEE THAT NOW...
MONTGOMERY... WHAT ARE YOU SAYING?
CURRENT ESTIMATES SHOW A 98% CHANCE...
...THAT WILSON WILL COME OUT OF THE FLUX POINT AN UNSUITABLE CANDIDATE FOR THE PROGRAM...
...A BROKEN MAN. I'M SORRY, ZOE.
NO... VANESSA...
THEY'RE SUPPOSED TO MAKE IT!

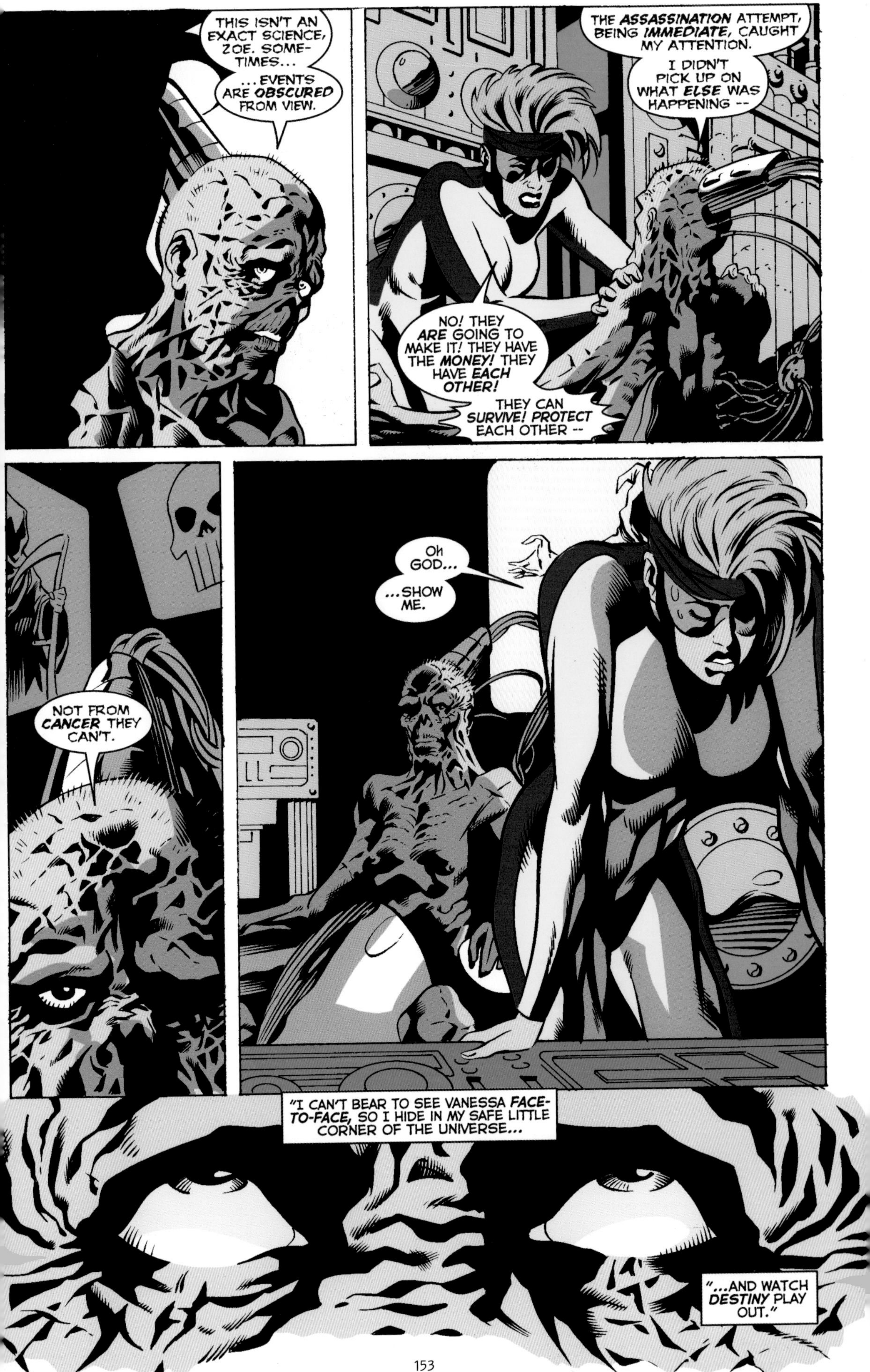
THIS ISN'T AN EXACT SCIENCE, ZOE. SOME-TIMES...
...EVENTS ARE OBSCURED FROM VIEW.
THE ASSASSINATION ATTEMPT, BEING IMMEDIATE, CAUGHT MY ATTENTION.
I DIDN'T PICK UP ON WHAT ELSE WAS HAPPENING --
NO! THEY ARE GOING TO MAKE IT! THEY HAVE THE MONEY! THEY HAVE EACH OTHER!
THEY CAN SURVIVE! PROTECT EACH OTHER --
NOT FROM CANCER THEY CAN'T.
Oh GOD...
...SHOW ME.
"I CAN'T BEAR TO SEE VANESSA FACE-TO-FACE, SO I HIDE IN MY SAFE LITTLE CORNER OF THE UNIVERSE...
"...AND WATCH DESTINY PLAY OUT."

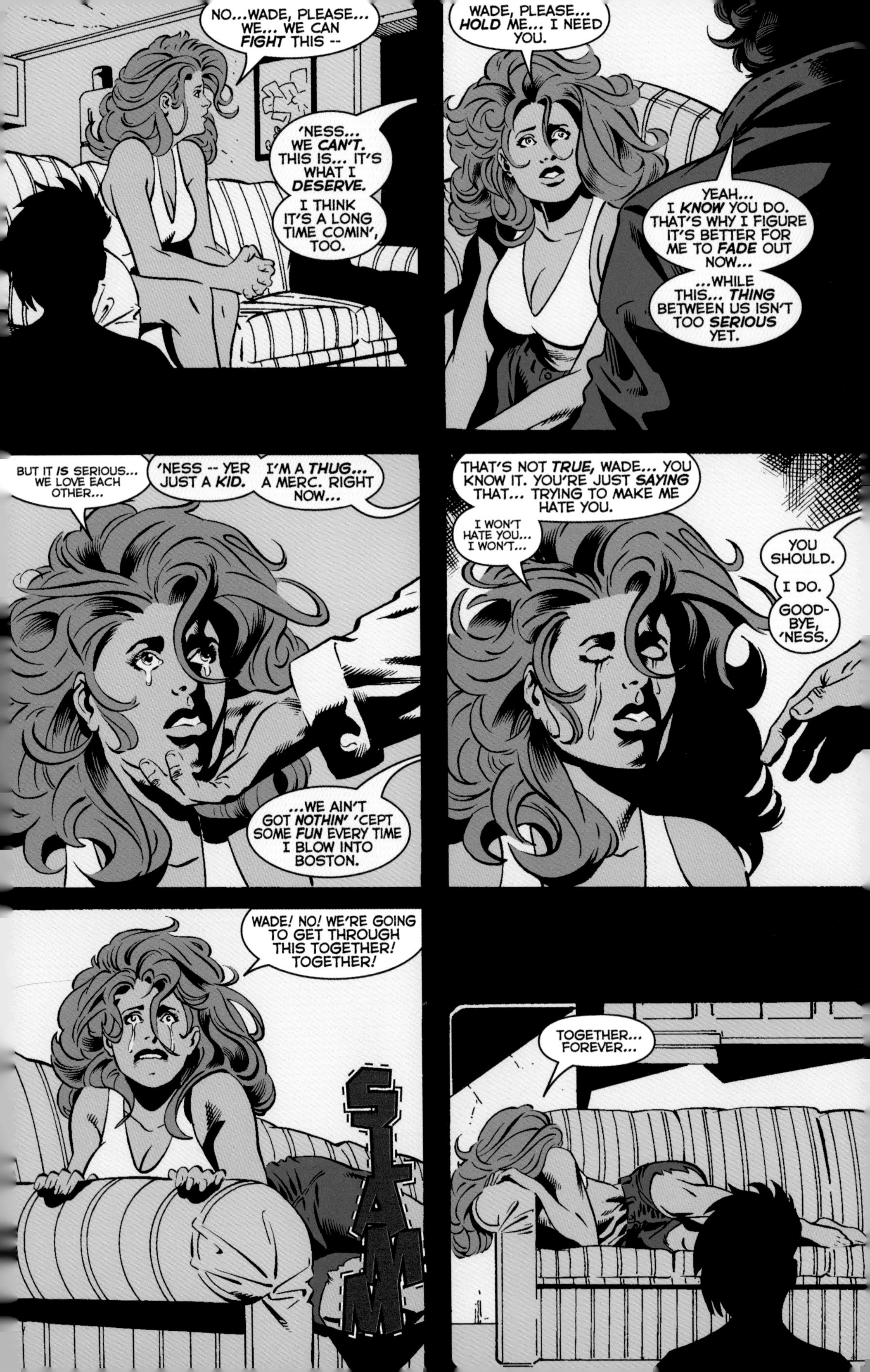

NO...WADE, PLEASE... WE... WE CAN FIGHT THIS --
'NESS... WE CAN'T. THIS IS... IT'S WHAT I DESERVE.
I THINK IT'S A LONG TIME COMIN', TOO.
WADE, PLEASE... HOLD ME... I NEED YOU.
YEAH... I KNOW YOU DO. THAT'S WHY I FIGURE IT'S BETTER FOR ME TO FADE OUT NOW...
...WHILE THIS... THING BETWEEN US ISN'T TOO SERIOUS YET.
BUT IT IS SERIOUS... WE LOVE EACH OTHER...
'NESS -- YER JUST A KID.
I'M A THUG... A MERC. RIGHT NOW...
...WE AIN'T GOT NOTHIN' 'CEPT SOME FUN EVERY TIME I BLOW INTO BOSTON.
THAT'S NOT TRUE, WADE... YOU KNOW IT. YOU'RE JUST SAYING THAT... TRYING TO MAKE ME HATE YOU.
I WON'T HATE YOU... I WON'T...
YOU SHOULD.
I DO.
GOOD-BYE, 'NESS.
WADE! NO! WE'RE GOING TO GET THROUGH THIS TOGETHER! TOGETHER!
SLAM
TOGETHER... FOREVER...

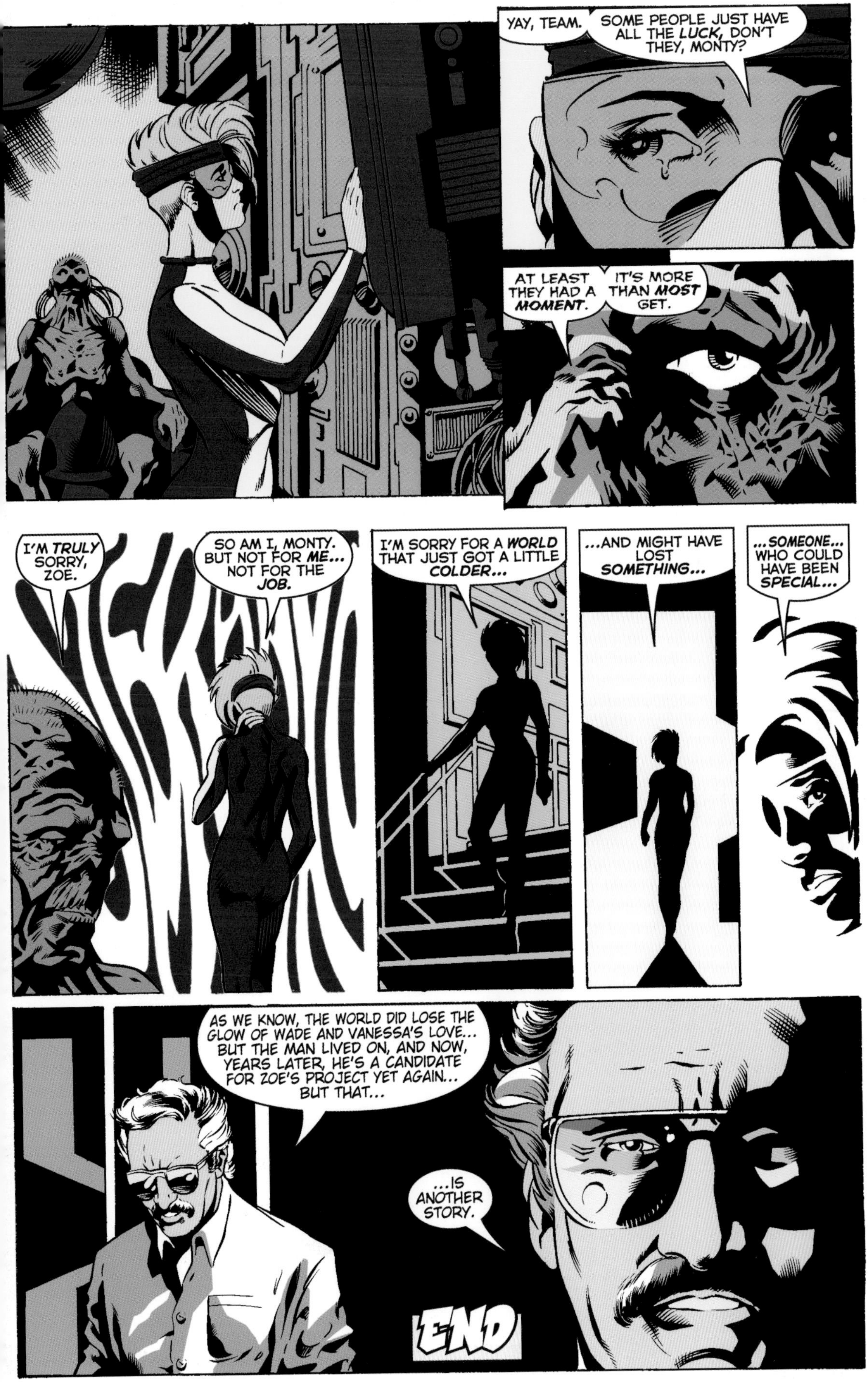
YAY, TEAM.
SOME PEOPLE JUST HAVE ALL THE LUCK, DON'T THEY, MONTY?
AT LEAST THEY HAD A MOMENT.
IT'S MORE THAN MOST GET.
I'M TRULY SORRY, ZOE.
SO AM I, MONTY. BUT NOT FOR ME... NOT FOR THE JOB.
I'M SORRY FOR A WORLD THAT JUST GOT A LITTLE COLDER...
...AND MIGHT HAVE LOST SOMETHING...
...SOMEONE... WHO COULD HAVE BEEN SPECIAL...
AS WE KNOW, THE WORLD DID LOSE THE GLOW OF WADE AND VANESSA'S LOVE... BUT THE MAN LIVED ON, AND NOW, YEARS LATER, HE'S A CANDIDATE FOR ZOE'S PROJECT YET AGAIN... BUT THAT...
...IS ANOTHER STORY.
END

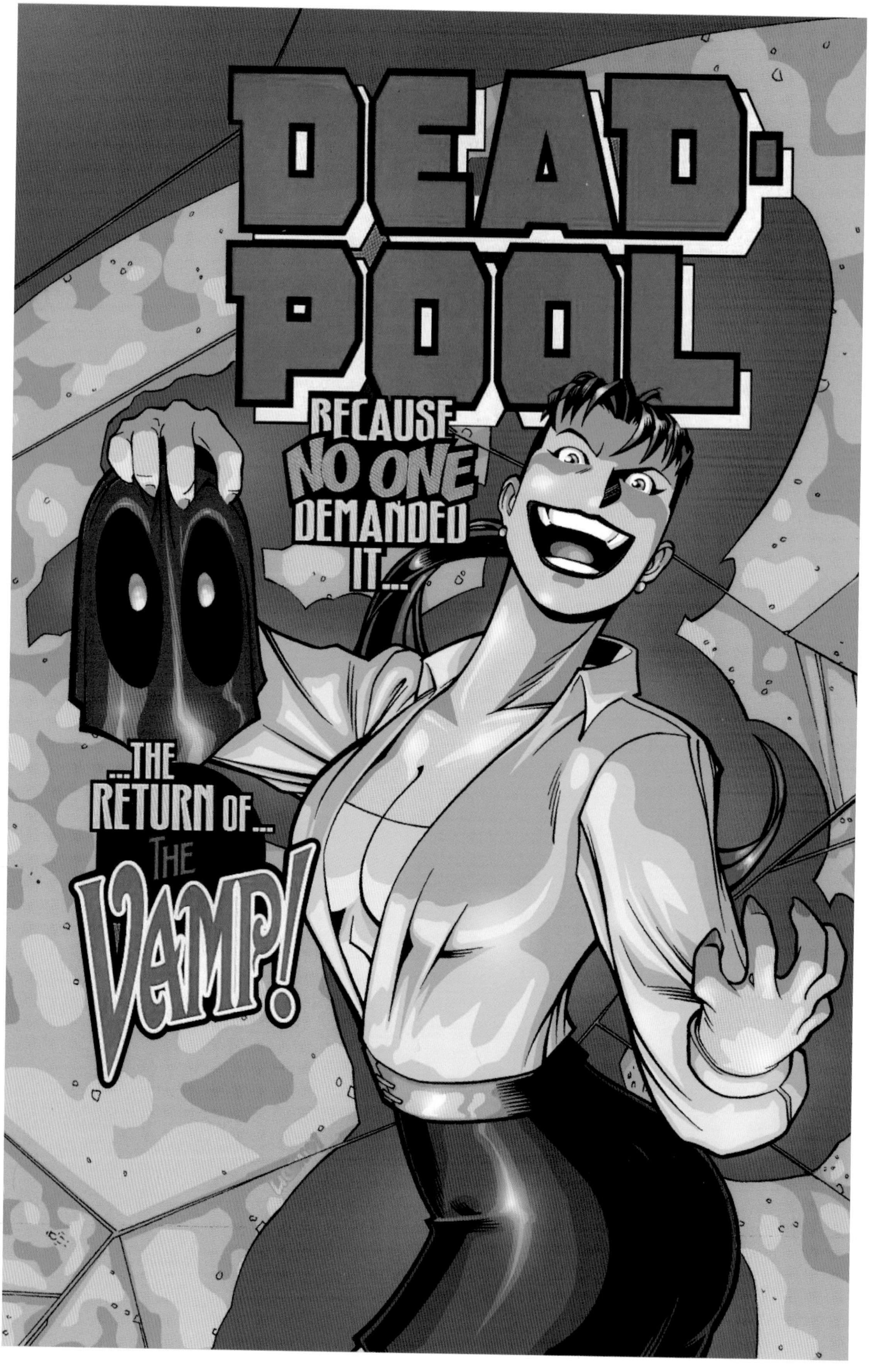
DEAD-POOL
BECAUSE NO ONE DEMANDED IT...
...THE RETURN OF... THE VAMP!

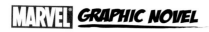

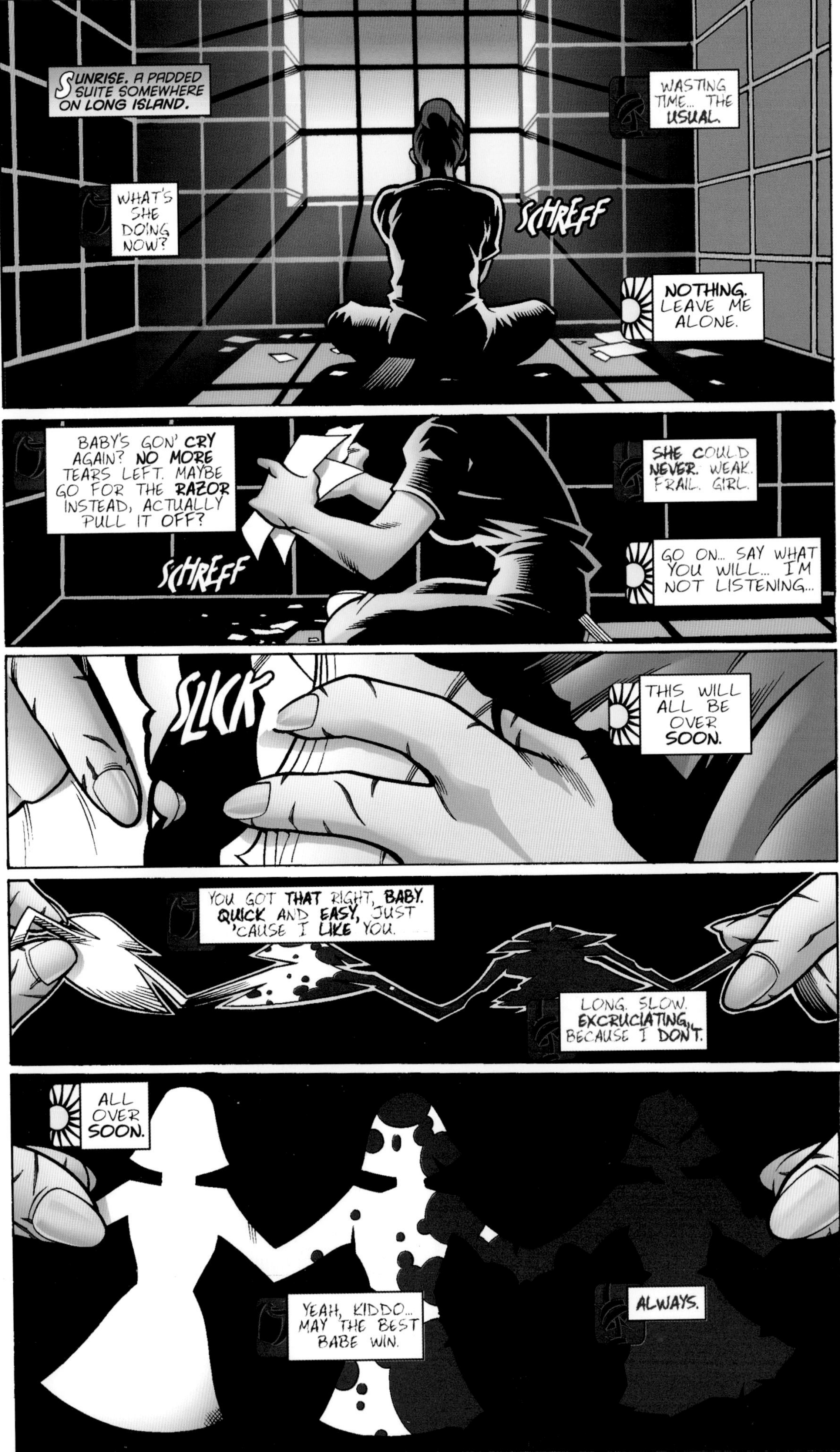
SUNRISE. A PADDED SUITE SOMEWHERE ON LONG ISLAND.
WASTING TIME... THE USUAL.
WHAT'S SHE DOING NOW?
SCHREFF
NOTHING. LEAVE ME ALONE.
BABY'S GON' CRY AGAIN? NO MORE TEARS LEFT. MAYBE GO FOR THE RAZOR INSTEAD, ACTUALLY PULL IT OFF?
SHE COULD NEVER. WEAK. FRAIL. GIRL.
SCHREFF
GO ON... SAY WHAT YOU WILL... I'M NOT LISTENING...
SLICK
THIS WILL ALL BE OVER SOON.
YOU GOT THAT RIGHT, BABY. QUICK AND EASY, JUST 'CAUSE I LIKE YOU.
LONG. SLOW. EXCRUCIATING, BECAUSE I DON'T.
ALL OVER SOON.
YEAH, KIDDO... MAY THE BEST BABE WIN.
ALWAYS.

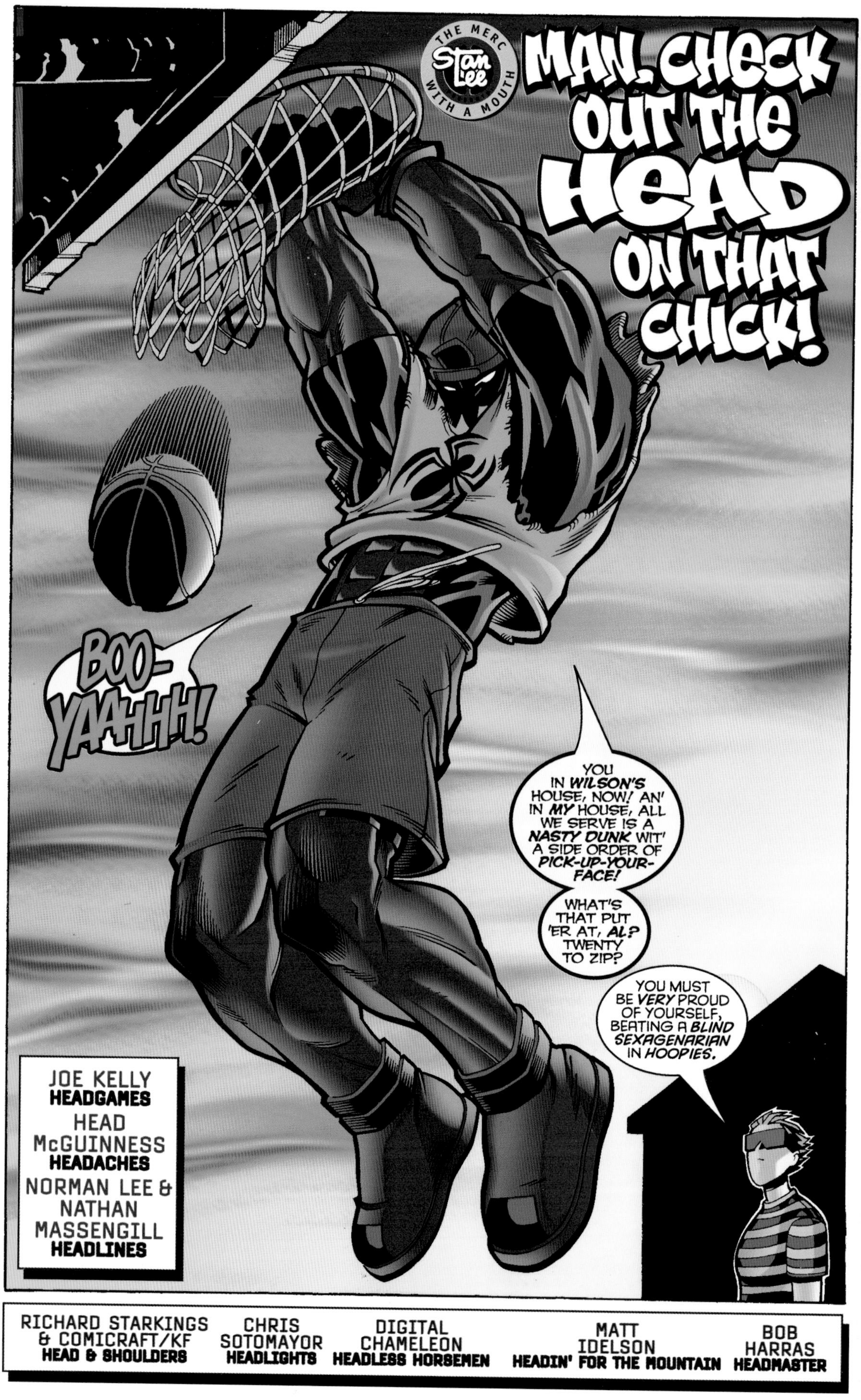
THE MERC WITH A MOUTH
Stan Lee
MAN, CHECK OUT THE HEAD ON THAT CHICK!
BOO-YAAHHH!
YOU IN WILSON'S HOUSE, NOW! AN' IN MY HOUSE, ALL WE SERVE IS A NASTY DUNK WIT' A SIDE ORDER OF PICK-UP-YOUR-FACE!
WHAT'S THAT PUT 'ER AT, AL? TWENTY TO ZIP?
YOU MUST BE VERY PROUD OF YOURSELF, BEATING A BLIND SEXAGENARIAN IN HOOPIES.
JOE KELLY HEADGAMES
HEAD McGUINNESS HEADACHES
NORMAN LEE & NATHAN MASSENGILL HEADLINES
RICHARD STARKINGS & COMICRAFT/KF HEAD & SHOULDERS
CHRIS SOTOMAYOR HEADLIGHTS
DIGITAL CHAMELEON HEADLESS HORSEMEN
MATT IDELSON HEADIN' FOR THE MOUNTAIN
BOB HARRAS HEADMASTER

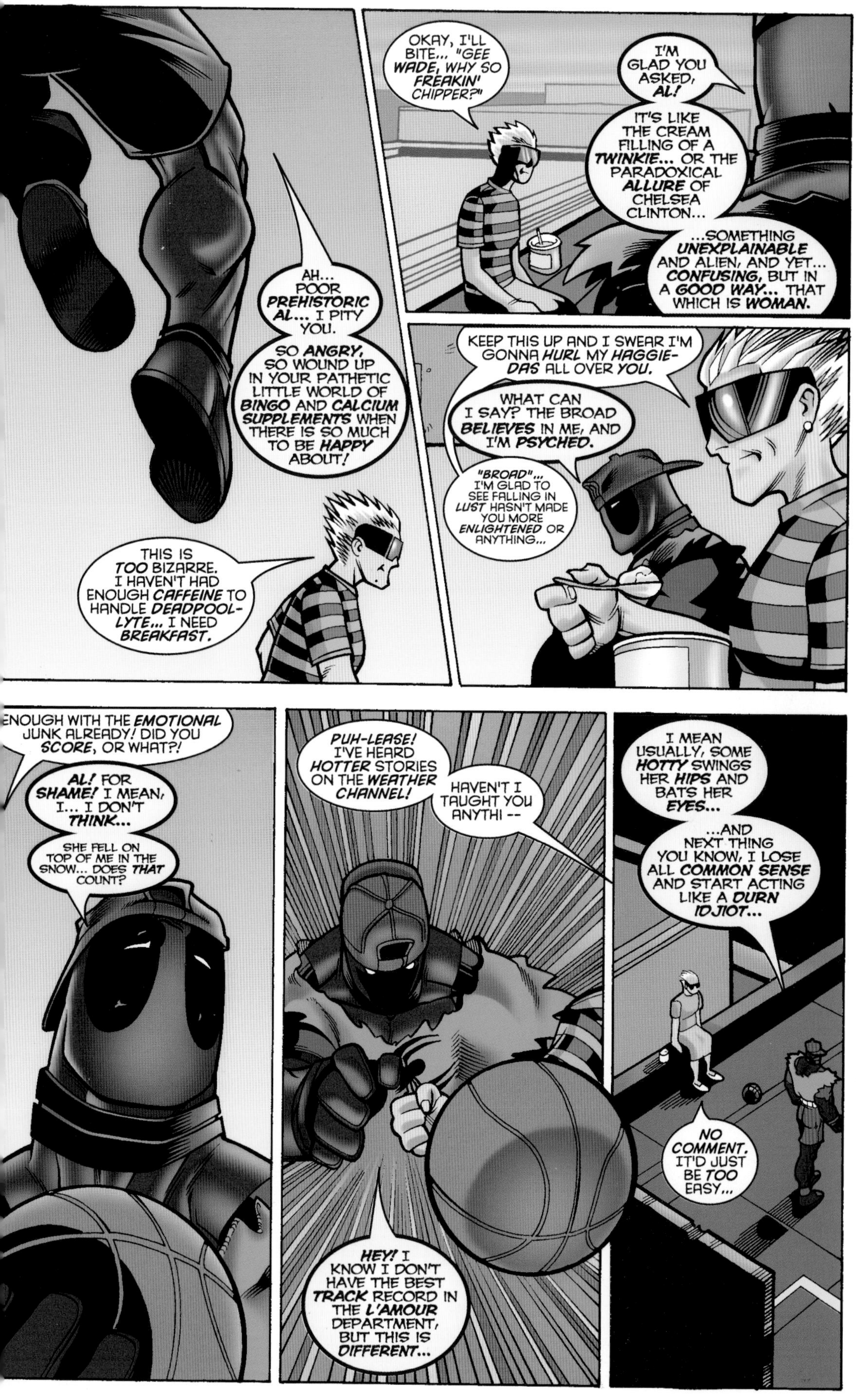
AH... POOR PREHISTORIC AL... I PITY YOU.
SO ANGRY, SO WOUND UP IN YOUR PATHETIC LITTLE WORLD OF BINGO AND CALCIUM SUPPLEMENTS WHEN THERE IS SO MUCH TO BE HAPPY ABOUT!
THIS IS TOO BIZARRE. I HAVEN'T HAD ENOUGH CAFFEINE TO HANDLE DEADPOOL-LYTE... I NEED BREAKFAST.
OKAY, I'LL BITE... "GEE WADE, WHY SO FREAKIN' CHIPPER?"
I'M GLAD YOU ASKED, AL!
IT'S LIKE THE CREAM FILLING OF A TWINKIE... OR THE PARADOXICAL ALLURE OF CHELSEA CLINTON...
...SOMETHING UNEXPLAINABLE AND ALIEN, AND YET... CONFUSING, BUT IN A GOOD WAY... THAT WHICH IS WOMAN.
KEEP THIS UP AND I SWEAR I'M GONNA HURL MY HAGGIE-DAS ALL OVER YOU.
WHAT CAN I SAY? THE BROAD BELIEVES IN ME, AND I'M PSYCHED.
"BROAD"... I'M GLAD TO SEE FALLING IN LUST HASN'T MADE YOU MORE ENLIGHTENED OR ANYTHING...
ENOUGH WITH THE EMOTIONAL JUNK ALREADY! DID YOU SCORE, OR WHAT?!
AL! FOR SHAME! I MEAN, I... I DON'T THINK...
SHE FELL ON TOP OF ME IN THE SNOW... DOES THAT COUNT?
PUH-LEASE! I'VE HEARD HOTTER STORIES ON THE WEATHER CHANNEL!
HAVEN'T I TAUGHT YOU ANYTHI --
HEY! I KNOW I DON'T HAVE THE BEST TRACK RECORD IN THE L'AMOUR DEPARTMENT, BUT THIS IS DIFFERENT...
I MEAN USUALLY, SOME HOTTY SWINGS HER HIPS AND BATS HER EYES...
...AND NEXT THING YOU KNOW, I LOSE ALL COMMON SENSE AND START ACTING LIKE A DURN IDJIOT...
NO COMMENT. IT'D JUST BE TOO EASY...

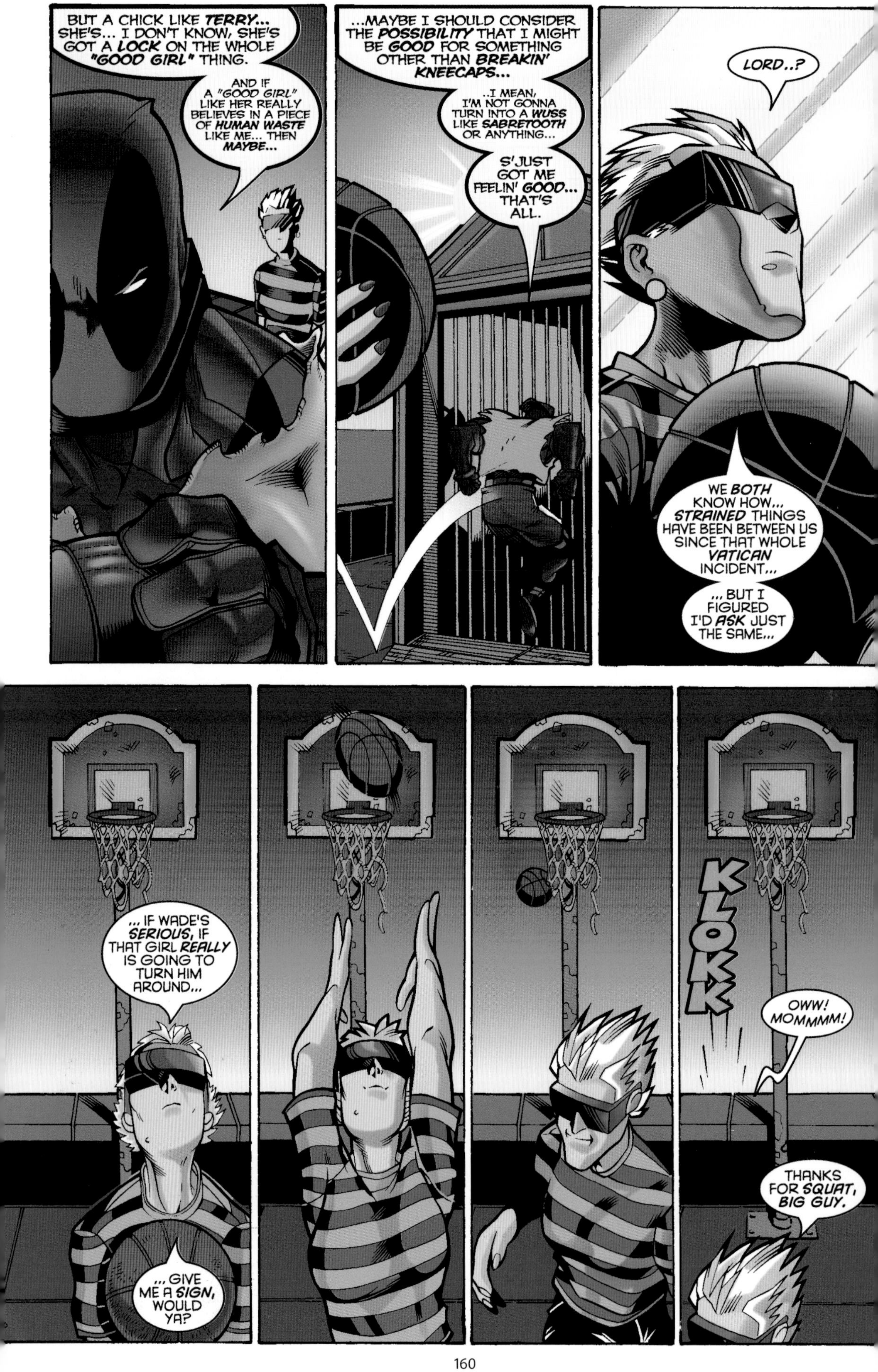
BUT A CHICK LIKE TERRY... SHE'S... I DON'T KNOW, SHE'S GOT A LOCK ON THE WHOLE "GOOD GIRL" THING.
AND IF A "GOOD GIRL" LIKE HER REALLY BELIEVES IN A PIECE OF HUMAN WASTE LIKE ME... THEN MAYBE...
...MAYBE I SHOULD CONSIDER THE POSSIBILITY THAT I MIGHT BE GOOD FOR SOMETHING OTHER THAN BREAKIN' KNEECAPS...
..I MEAN, I'M NOT GONNA TURN INTO A WUSS LIKE SABRETOOTH OR ANYTHING...
S'JUST GOT ME FEELIN' GOOD... THAT'S ALL.
LORD..?
WE BOTH KNOW HOW... STRAINED THINGS HAVE BEEN BETWEEN US SINCE THAT WHOLE VATICAN INCIDENT...
...BUT I FIGURED I'D ASK JUST THE SAME...
...IF WADE'S SERIOUS, IF THAT GIRL REALLY IS GOING TO TURN HIM AROUND...
...GIVE ME A SIGN, WOULD YA?
KLOKK
OWW! MOMMMM!
THANKS FOR SQUAT, BIG GUY.

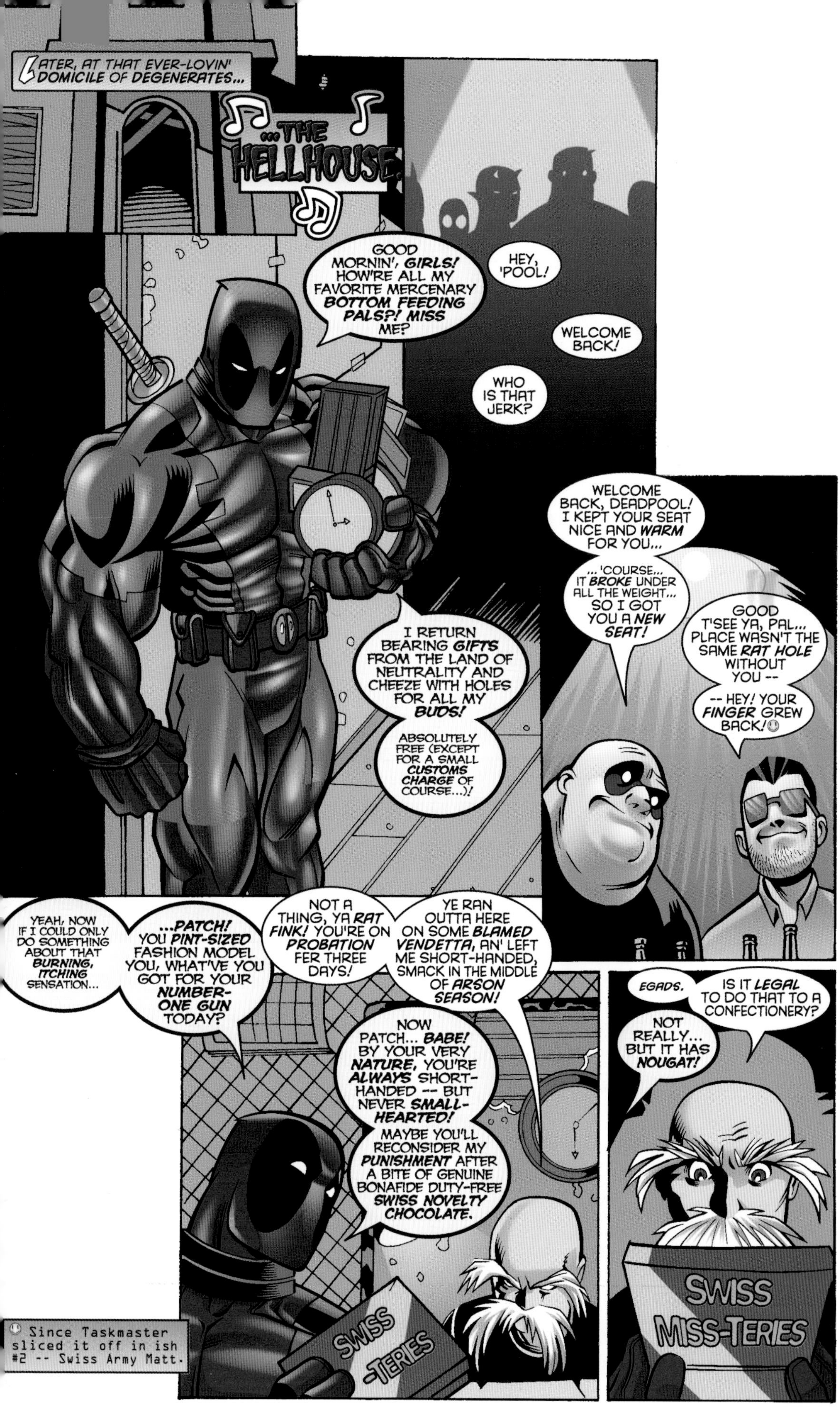
LATER, AT THAT EVER-LOVIN' DOMICILE OF DEGENERATES...
...THE HELLHOUSE.
GOOD MORNIN', GIRLS! HOW'RE ALL MY FAVORITE MERCENARY BOTTOM FEEDING PALS?! MISS ME?
HEY, 'POOL!
WELCOME BACK!
WHO IS THAT JERK?
I RETURN BEARING GIFTS FROM THE LAND OF NEUTRALITY AND CHEEZE WITH HOLES FOR ALL MY BUDS!
ABSOLUTELY FREE (EXCEPT FOR A SMALL CUSTOMS CHARGE OF COURSE...)!
WELCOME BACK, DEADPOOL! I KEPT YOUR SEAT NICE AND WARM FOR YOU...
...'COURSE... IT BROKE UNDER ALL THE WEIGHT... SO I GOT YOU A NEW SEAT!
GOOD T'SEE YA, PAL... PLACE WASN'T THE SAME RAT HOLE WITHOUT YOU --
-- HEY! YOUR FINGER GREW BACK!
YEAH, NOW IF I COULD ONLY DO SOMETHING ABOUT THAT BURNING, ITCHING SENSATION...
...PATCH! YOU PINT-SIZED FASHION MODEL YOU, WHAT'VE YOU GOT FOR YOUR NUMBER-ONE GUN TODAY?
NOT A THING, YA RAT FINK! YOU'RE ON PROBATION FER THREE DAYS!
YE RAN OUTTA HERE ON SOME BLAMED VENDETTA, AN' LEFT ME SHORT-HANDED, SMACK IN THE MIDDLE OF ARSON SEASON!
NOW PATCH... BABE! BY YOUR VERY NATURE, YOU'RE ALWAYS SHORT-HANDED -- BUT NEVER SMALL-HEARTED!
MAYBE YOU'LL RECONSIDER MY PUNISHMENT AFTER A BITE OF GENUINE BONAFIDE DUTY-FREE SWISS NOVELTY CHOCOLATE.
SWISS -TERIES
EGADS.
IS IT LEGAL TO DO THAT TO A CONFECTIONERY?
NOT REALLY... BUT IT HAS NOUGAT!
SWISS MISS-TERIES
Since Taskmaster sliced it off in ish #2 -- Swiss Army Matt.

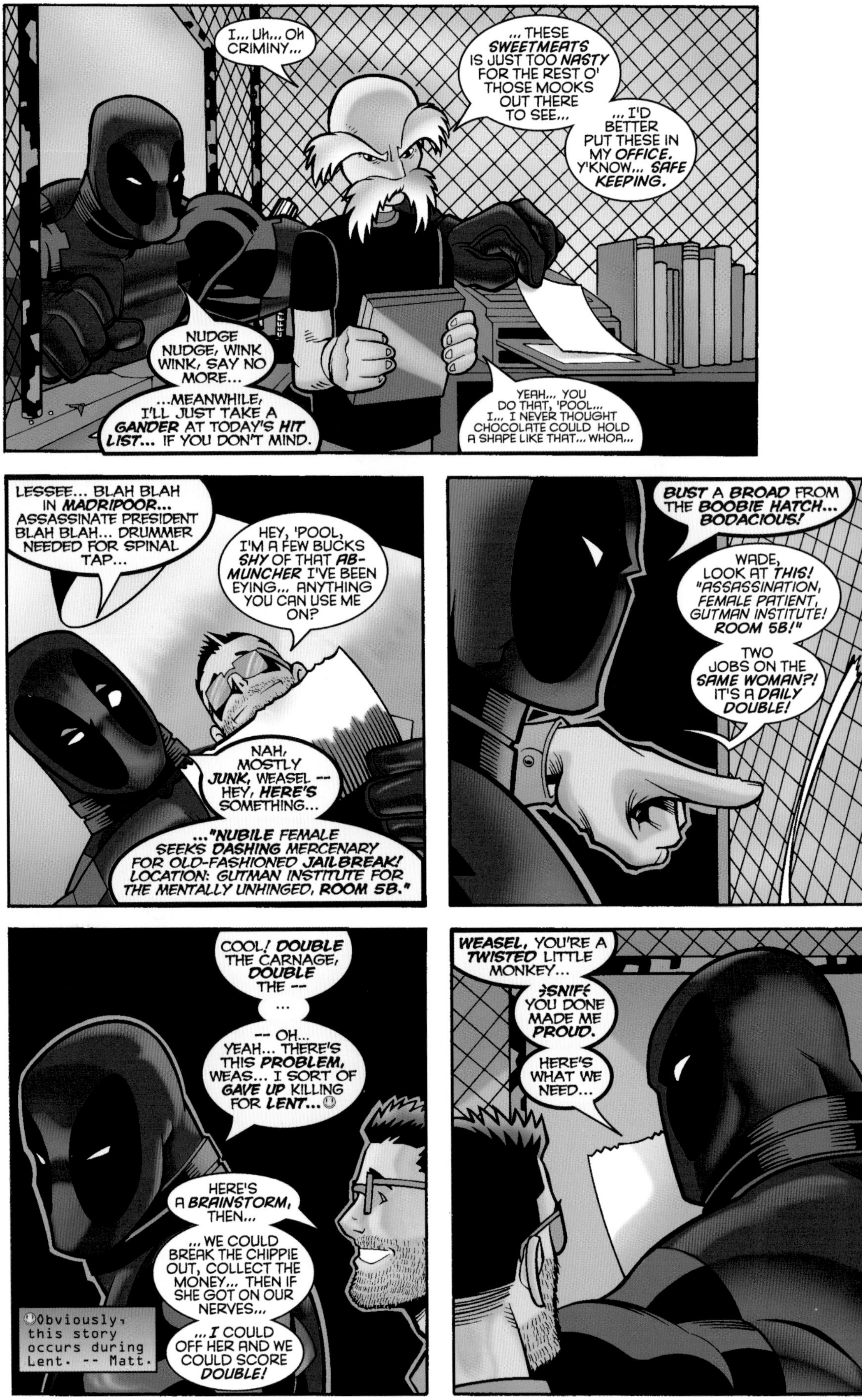
I... Uh... Oh CRIMINY...
...THESE SWEETMEATS IS JUST TOO NASTY FOR THE REST O' THOSE MOOKS OUT THERE TO SEE...
...I'D BETTER PUT THESE IN MY OFFICE. Y'KNOW... SAFE KEEPING.
NUDGE NUDGE, WINK WINK, SAY NO MORE...
...MEANWHILE, I'LL JUST TAKE A GANDER AT TODAY'S HIT LIST... IF YOU DON'T MIND.
YEAH... YOU DO THAT, 'POOL... I... I NEVER THOUGHT CHOCOLATE COULD HOLD A SHAPE LIKE THAT... WHOA...
LESSEE... BLAH BLAH IN MADRIPOOR... ASSASSINATE PRESIDENT BLAH BLAH... DRUMMER NEEDED FOR SPINAL TAP...
HEY, 'POOL, I'M A FEW BUCKS SHY OF THAT AB-MUNCHER I'VE BEEN EYING... ANYTHING YOU CAN USE ME ON?
NAH, MOSTLY JUNK, WEASEL -- HEY, HERE'S SOMETHING...
..."NUBILE FEMALE SEEKS DASHING MERCENARY FOR OLD-FASHIONED JAILBREAK! LOCATION: GUTMAN INSTITUTE FOR THE MENTALLY UNHINGED, ROOM 5B."
BUST A BROAD FROM THE BOOBIE HATCH... BODACIOUS!
WADE, LOOK AT THIS! "ASSASSINATION, FEMALE PATIENT, GUTMAN INSTITUTE! ROOM 5B!"
TWO JOBS ON THE SAME WOMAN?! IT'S A DAILY DOUBLE!
COOL! DOUBLE THE CARNAGE, DOUBLE THE --
...
-- OH... YEAH... THERE'S THIS PROBLEM, WEAS... I SORT OF GAVE UP KILLING FOR LENT...
HERE'S A BRAINSTORM, THEN...
...WE COULD BREAK THE CHIPPIE OUT, COLLECT THE MONEY... THEN IF SHE GOT ON OUR NERVES...
...I COULD OFF HER AND WE COULD SCORE DOUBLE!
Obviously, this story occurs during Lent. -- Matt.
WEASEL, YOU'RE A TWISTED LITTLE MONKEY...
SNIF YOU DONE MADE ME PROUD.
HERE'S WHAT WE NEED...

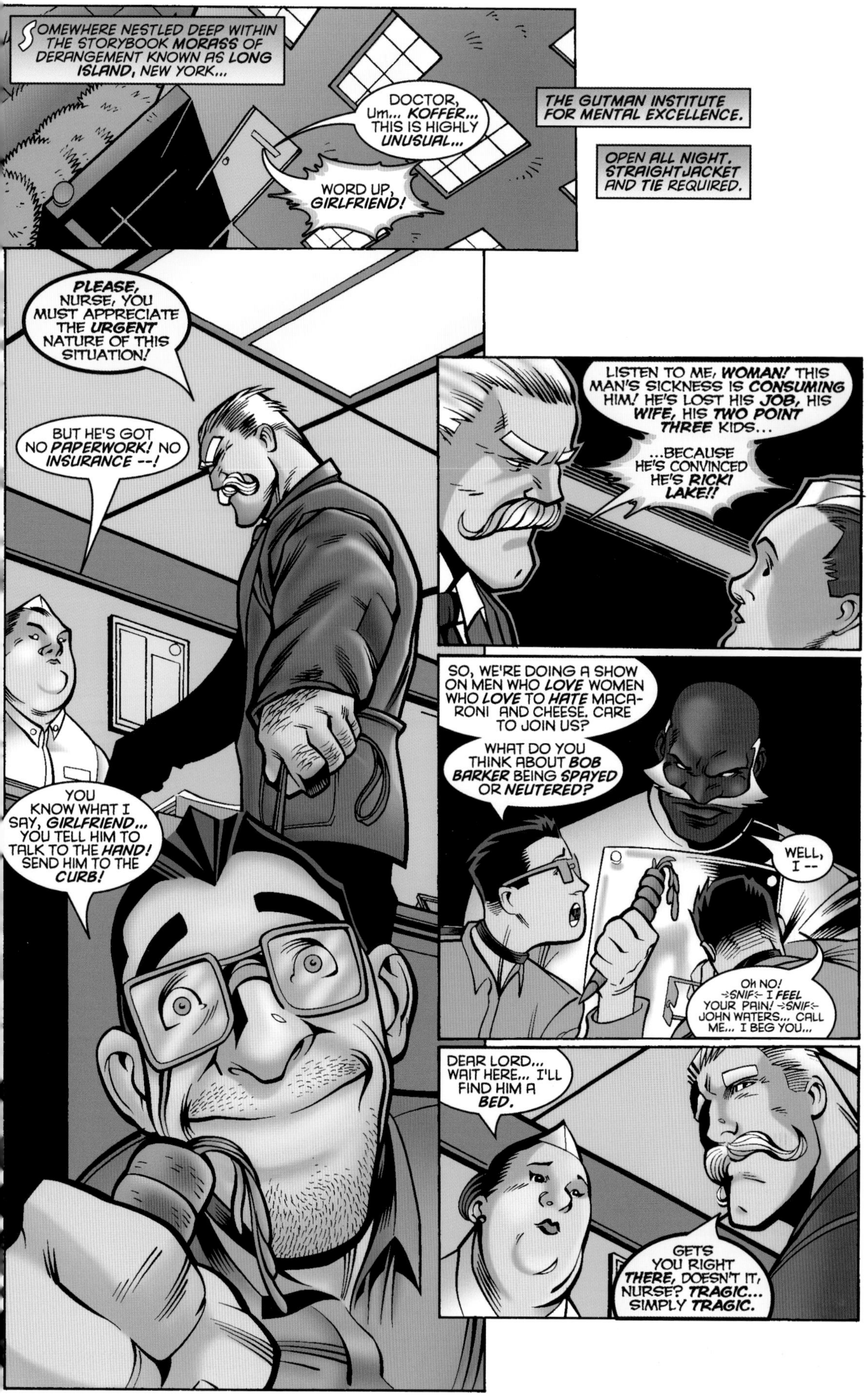
SOMEWHERE NESTLED DEEP WITHIN THE STORYBOOK MORASS OF DERANGEMENT KNOWN AS LONG ISLAND, NEW YORK...
DOCTOR, Um... KOFFER... THIS IS HIGHLY UNUSUAL...
WORD UP, GIRLFRIEND!
THE GUTMAN INSTITUTE FOR MENTAL EXCELLENCE.
OPEN ALL NIGHT. STRAIGHTJACKET AND TIE REQUIRED.
PLEASE, NURSE, YOU MUST APPRECIATE THE URGENT NATURE OF THIS SITUATION!
BUT HE'S GOT NO PAPERWORK! NO INSURANCE --!
YOU KNOW WHAT I SAY, GIRLFRIEND... YOU TELL HIM TO TALK TO THE HAND! SEND HIM TO THE CURB!
LISTEN TO ME, WOMAN! THIS MAN'S SICKNESS IS CONSUMING HIM! HE'S LOST HIS JOB, HIS WIFE, HIS TWO POINT THREE KIDS...
...BECAUSE HE'S CONVINCED HE'S RICKI LAKE!!
SO, WE'RE DOING A SHOW ON MEN WHO LOVE WOMEN WHO LOVE TO HATE MACARONI AND CHEESE. CARE TO JOIN US?
WHAT DO YOU THINK ABOUT BOB BARKER BEING SPAYED OR NEUTERED?
WELL, I --
Oh NO! ->SNIF<- I FEEL YOUR PAIN! ->SNIF<- JOHN WATERS... CALL ME... I BEG YOU...
DEAR LORD... WAIT HERE... I'LL FIND HIM A BED.
GETS YOU RIGHT THERE, DOESN'T IT, NURSE? TRAGIC... SIMPLY TRAGIC.

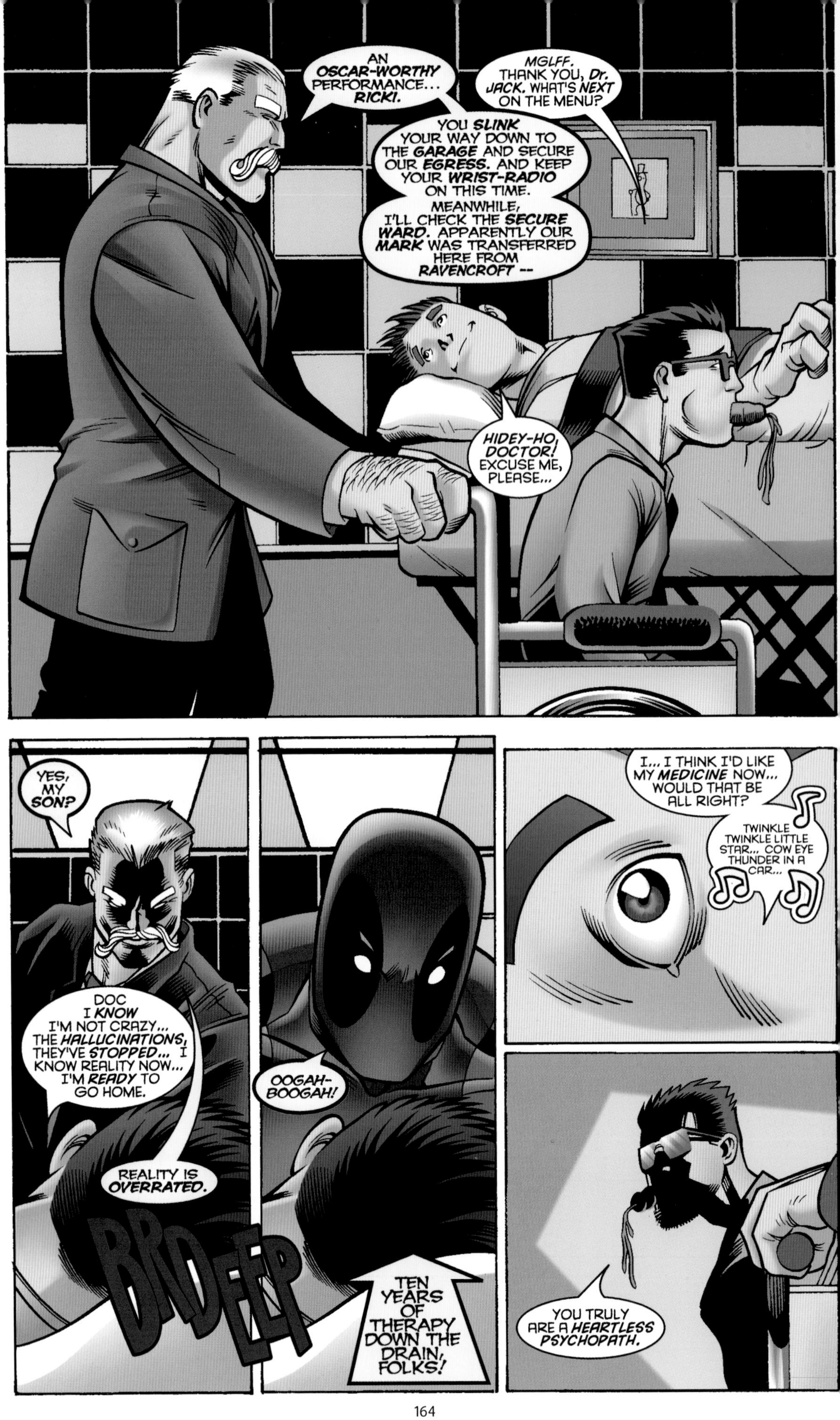

AN OSCAR-WORTHY PERFORMANCE... RICKI.
MGLFF. THANK YOU, Dr. JACK. WHAT'S NEXT ON THE MENU?
YOU SLINK YOUR WAY DOWN TO THE GARAGE AND SECURE OUR EGRESS. AND KEEP YOUR WRIST-RADIO ON THIS TIME.
MEANWHILE, I'LL CHECK THE SECURE WARD. APPARENTLY OUR MARK WAS TRANSFERRED HERE FROM RAVENCROFT --
HIDEY-HO, DOCTOR! EXCUSE ME, PLEASE...
YES, MY SON?
DOC I KNOW I'M NOT CRAZY... THE HALLUCINATIONS, THEY'VE STOPPED... I KNOW REALITY NOW... I'M READY TO GO HOME.
REALITY IS OVERRATED.
BRDEEP
OOGAH-BOOGAH!
TEN YEARS OF THERAPY DOWN THE DRAIN, FOLKS!
I... I THINK I'D LIKE MY MEDICINE NOW... WOULD THAT BE ALL RIGHT?
TWINKLE TWINKLE LITTLE STAR... COW EYE THUNDER IN A CAR...
YOU TRULY ARE A HEARTLESS PSYCHOPATH.

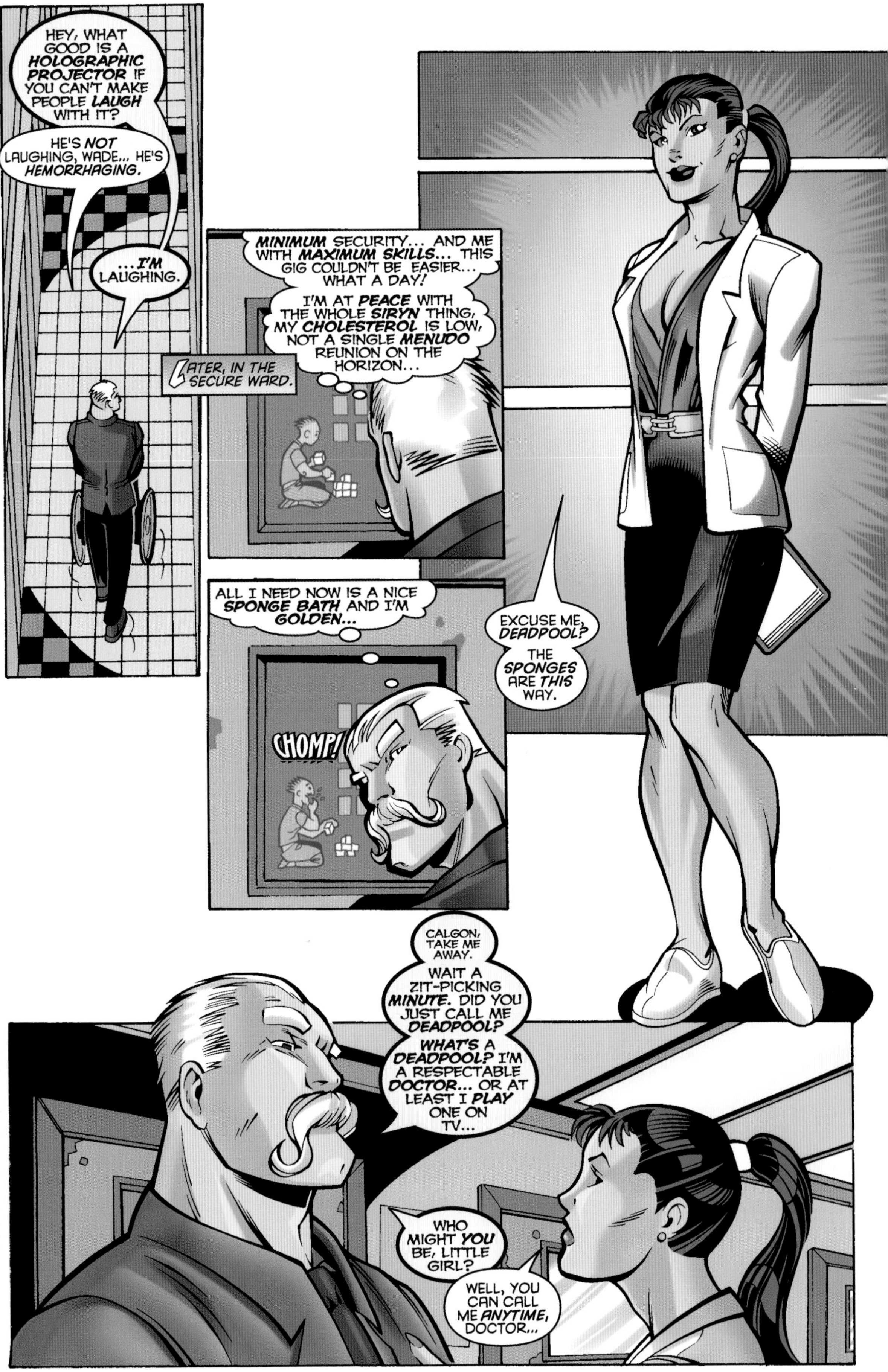
HEY, WHAT GOOD IS A HOLOGRAPHIC PROJECTOR IF YOU CAN'T MAKE PEOPLE LAUGH WITH IT?
HE'S NOT LAUGHING, WADE... HE'S HEMORRHAGING.
...I'M LAUGHING.
LATER, IN THE SECURE WARD.
MINIMUM SECURITY... AND ME WITH MAXIMUM SKILLS... THIS GIG COULDN'T BE EASIER... WHAT A DAY!
I'M AT PEACE WITH THE WHOLE SIRYN THING, MY CHOLESTEROL IS LOW, NOT A SINGLE MENUDO REUNION ON THE HORIZON...
ALL I NEED NOW IS A NICE SPONGE BATH AND I'M GOLDEN...
CHOMP!
EXCUSE ME, DEADPOOL?
THE SPONGES ARE THIS WAY.
CALGON, TAKE ME AWAY.
WAIT A ZIT-PICKING MINUTE. DID YOU JUST CALL ME DEADPOOL?
WHAT'S A DEADPOOL? I'M A RESPECTABLE DOCTOR... OR AT LEAST I PLAY ONE ON TV...
WHO MIGHT YOU BE, LITTLE GIRL?
WELL, YOU CAN CALL ME ANYTIME, DOCTOR...

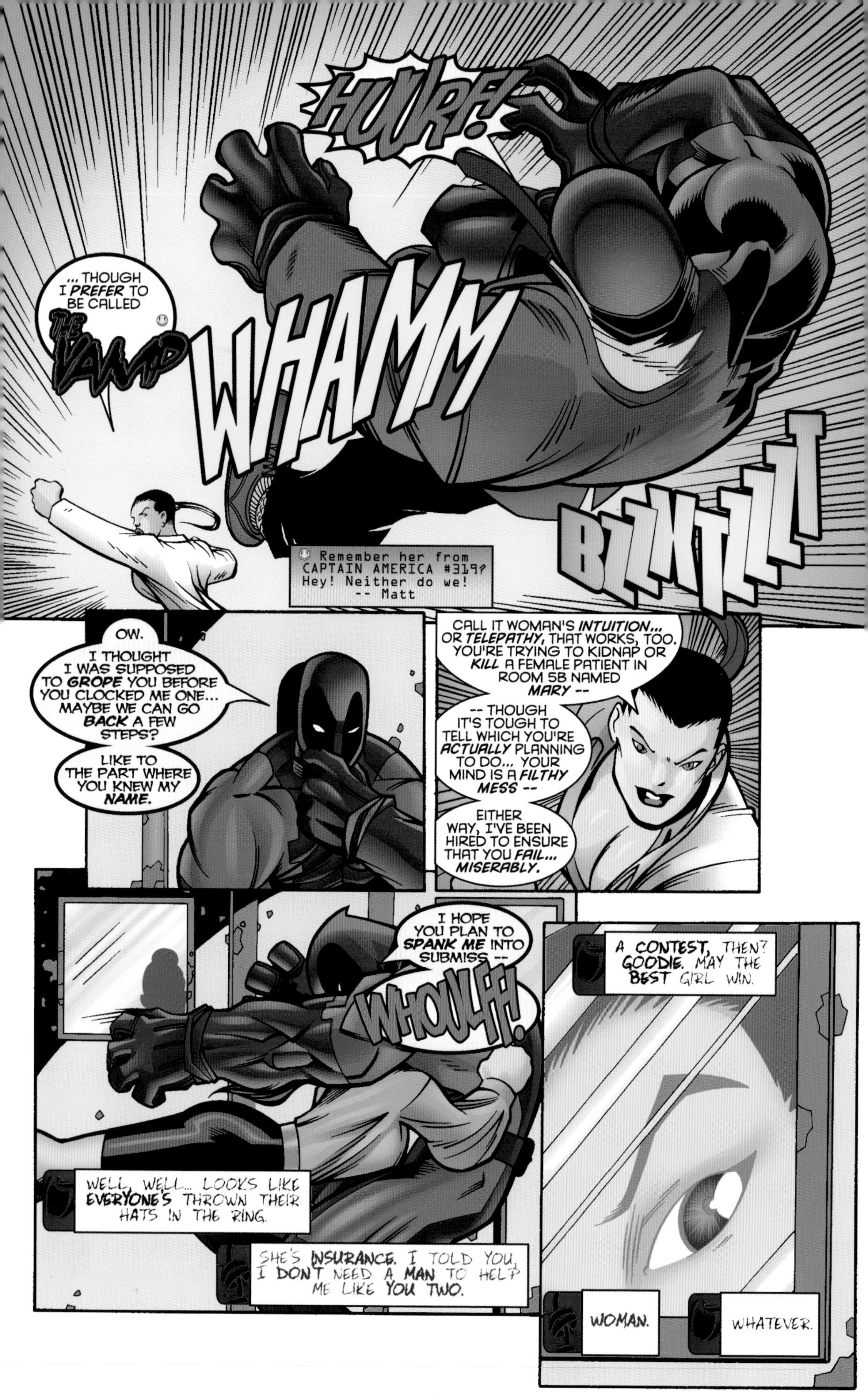
HUURF!
...THOUGH I PREFER TO BE CALLED THE VAMP
WHAMM
BZZKTZZZT
Remember her from CAPTAIN AMERICA #319? Hey! Neither do we! -- Matt
OW.
I THOUGHT I WAS SUPPOSED TO GROPE YOU BEFORE YOU CLOCKED ME ONE... MAYBE WE CAN GO BACK A FEW STEPS?
LIKE TO THE PART WHERE YOU KNEW MY NAME.
CALL IT WOMAN'S INTUITION... OR TELEPATHY, THAT WORKS, TOO. YOU'RE TRYING TO KIDNAP OR KILL A FEMALE PATIENT IN ROOM 5B NAMED MARY --
-- THOUGH IT'S TOUGH TO TELL WHICH YOU'RE ACTUALLY PLANNING TO DO... YOUR MIND IS A FILTHY MESS --
EITHER WAY, I'VE BEEN HIRED TO ENSURE THAT YOU FAIL... MISERABLY.
I HOPE YOU PLAN TO SPANK ME INTO SUBMISS --
WHOUFF!
WELL, WELL... LOOKS LIKE EVERYONE'S THROWN THEIR HATS IN THE RING.
SHE'S INSURANCE. I TOLD YOU, I DON'T NEED A MAN TO HELP ME LIKE YOU TWO.
A CONTEST, THEN? GOODIE. MAY THE BEST GIRL WIN.
WOMAN.
WHATEVER.

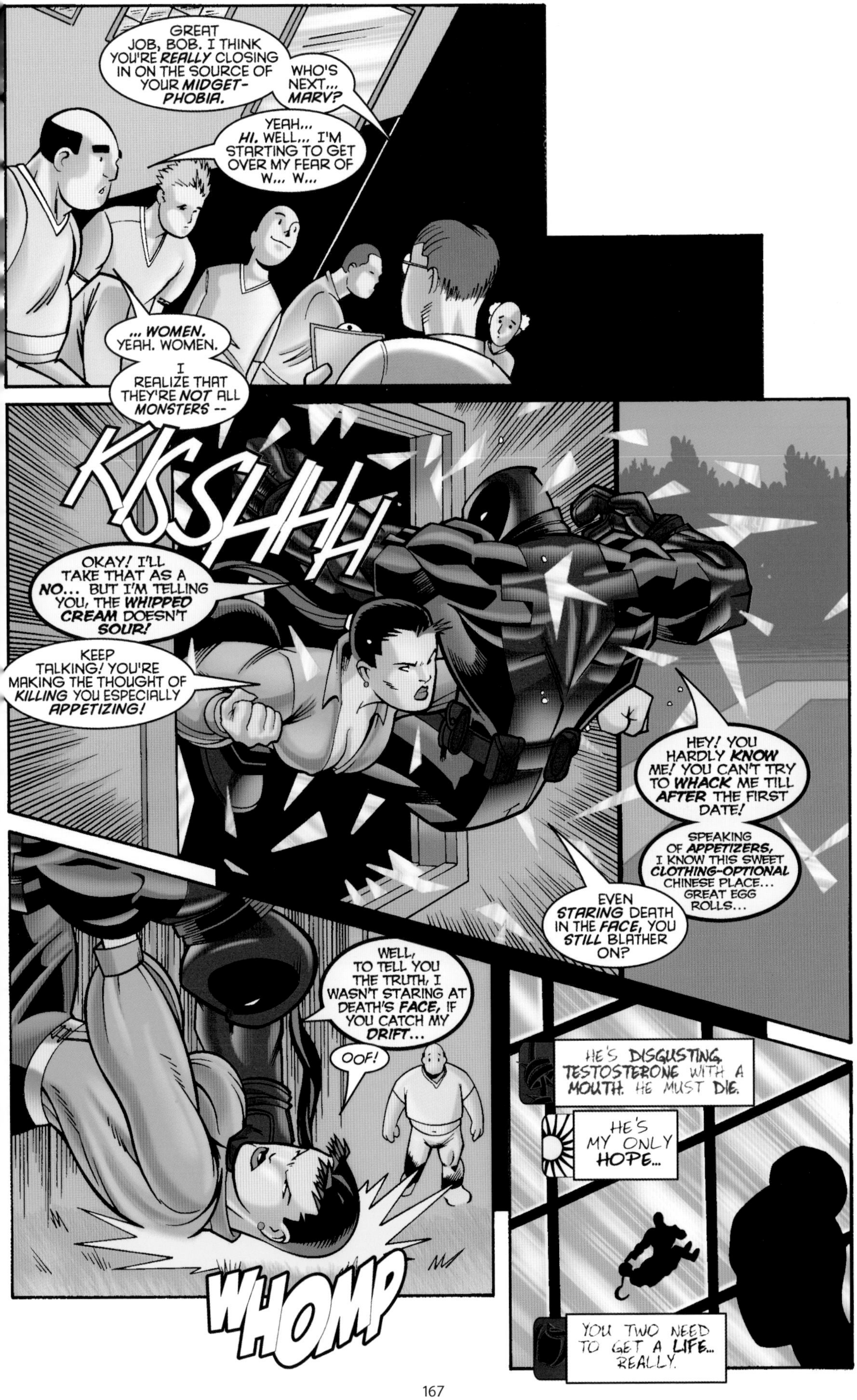
GREAT JOB, BOB. I THINK YOU'RE REALLY CLOSING IN ON THE SOURCE OF YOUR MIDGET-PHOBIA.
WHO'S NEXT,... MARV?
YEAH,... HI. WELL... I'M STARTING TO GET OVER MY FEAR OF W... W...
... WOMEN. YEAH. WOMEN.
I REALIZE THAT THEY'RE NOT ALL MONSTERS --
KISSHHH
OKAY! I'LL TAKE THAT AS A NO... BUT I'M TELLING YOU, THE WHIPPED CREAM DOESN'T SOUR!
KEEP TALKING! YOU'RE MAKING THE THOUGHT OF KILLING YOU ESPECIALLY APPETIZING!
HEY! YOU HARDLY KNOW ME! YOU CAN'T TRY TO WHACK ME TILL AFTER THE FIRST DATE!
SPEAKING OF APPETIZERS, I KNOW THIS SWEET CLOTHING-OPTIONAL CHINESE PLACE... GREAT EGG ROLLS...
EVEN STARING DEATH IN THE FACE, YOU STILL BLATHER ON?
WELL, TO TELL YOU THE TRUTH, I WASN'T STARING AT DEATH'S FACE, IF YOU CATCH MY DRIFT...
OOF!
WHOMP
HE'S DISGUSTING TESTOSTERONE WITH A MOUTH. HE MUST DIE.
HE'S MY ONLY HOPE...
YOU TWO NEED TO GET A LIFE... REALLY.

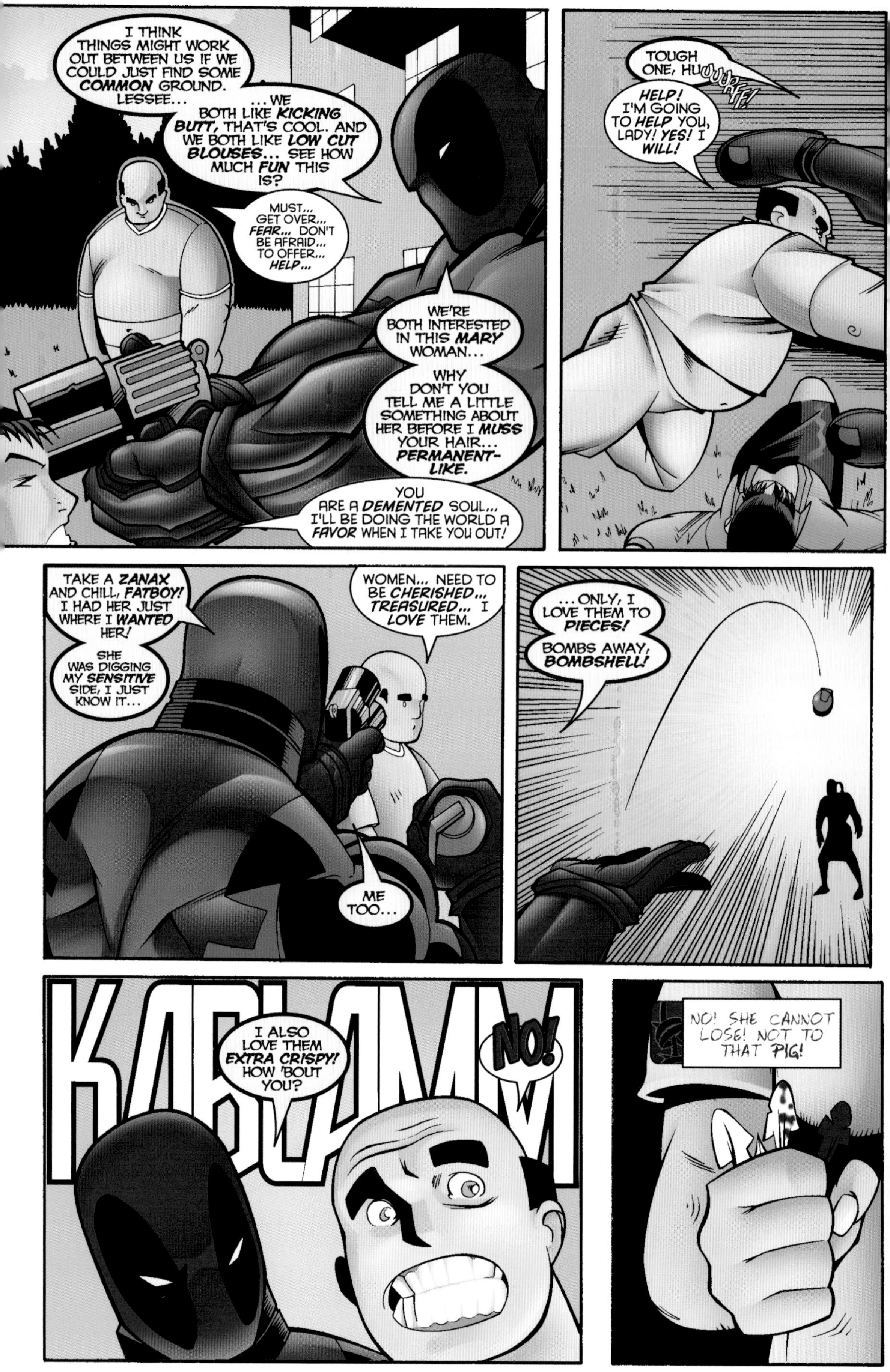
I THINK THINGS MIGHT WORK OUT BETWEEN US IF WE COULD JUST FIND SOME COMMON GROUND. LESSEE...
...WE BOTH LIKE KICKING BUTT, THAT'S COOL. AND WE BOTH LIKE LOW CUT BLOUSES... SEE HOW MUCH FUN THIS IS?
MUST... GET OVER... FEAR... DON'T BE AFRAID... TO OFFER... HELP...
WE'RE BOTH INTERESTED IN THIS MARY WOMAN...
WHY DON'T YOU TELL ME A LITTLE SOMETHING ABOUT HER BEFORE I MUSS YOUR HAIR... PERMANENT-LIKE.
YOU ARE A DEMENTED SOUL... I'LL BE DOING THE WORLD A FAVOR WHEN I TAKE YOU OUT!
TOUGH ONE, HUUUURFF!
HELP! I'M GOING TO HELP YOU, LADY! YES! I WILL!
TAKE A ZANAX AND CHILL, FATBOY! I HAD HER JUST WHERE I WANTED HER!
SHE WAS DIGGING MY SENSITIVE SIDE, I JUST KNOW IT...
WOMEN... NEED TO BE CHERISHED... TREASURED... I LOVE THEM.
ME TOO...
...ONLY, I LOVE THEM TO PIECES!
BOMBS AWAY, BOMBSHELL!
KABLOMM
I ALSO LOVE THEM EXTRA CRISPY! HOW 'BOUT YOU?
NO!
NO! SHE CANNOT LOSE! NOT TO THAT PIG!

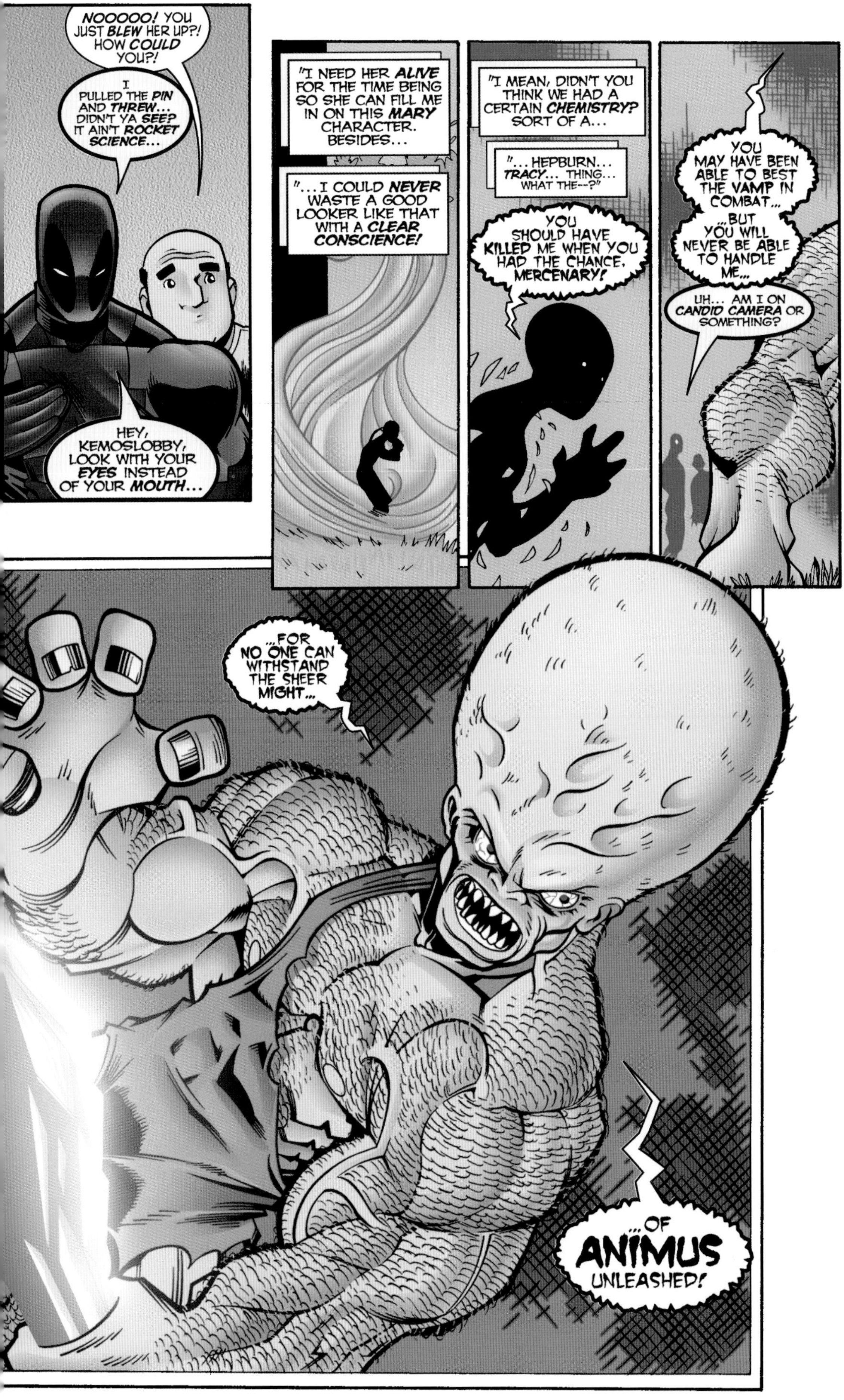
NOOOOO! YOU JUST BLEW HER UP?! HOW COULD YOU?!
I PULLED THE PIN AND THREW... DIDN'T YA SEE? IT AIN'T ROCKET SCIENCE...
HEY, KEMOSLOBBY, LOOK WITH YOUR EYES INSTEAD OF YOUR MOUTH...
"I NEED HER ALIVE FOR THE TIME BEING SO SHE CAN FILL ME IN ON THIS MARY CHARACTER. BESIDES...
"...I COULD NEVER WASTE A GOOD LOOKER LIKE THAT WITH A CLEAR CONSCIENCE!
"I MEAN, DIDN'T YOU THINK WE HAD A CERTAIN CHEMISTRY? SORT OF A...
"...HEPBURN... TRACY... THING... WHAT THE--?"
YOU SHOULD HAVE KILLED ME WHEN YOU HAD THE CHANCE, MERCENARY!
YOU MAY HAVE BEEN ABLE TO BEST THE VAMP IN COMBAT...
...BUT YOU WILL NEVER BE ABLE TO HANDLE ME...
UH... AM I ON CANDID CAMERA OR SOMETHING?
...FOR NO ONE CAN WITHSTAND THE SHEER MIGHT...
...OF ANIMUS UNLEASHED!

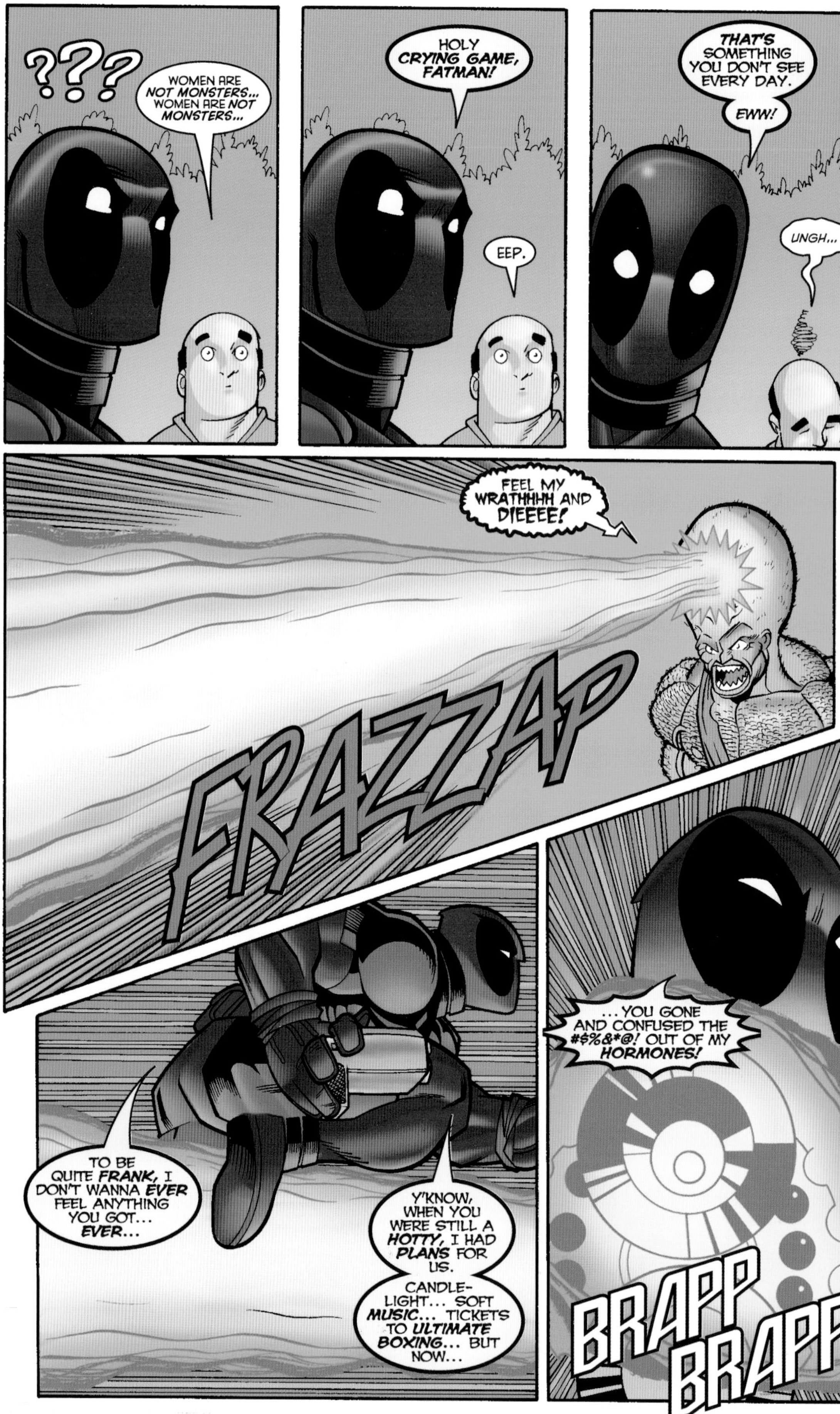
???
WOMEN ARE NOT MONSTERS... WOMEN ARE NOT MONSTERS...
HOLY CRYING GAME, FATMAN!
EEP.
THAT'S SOMETHING YOU DON'T SEE EVERY DAY.
EWW!
UNGH...
FEEL MY WRATHHHH AND DIEEEE!
FRAZZAP
TO BE QUITE FRANK, I DON'T WANNA EVER FEEL ANYTHING YOU GOT... EVER...
Y'KNOW, WHEN YOU WERE STILL A HOTTY, I HAD PLANS FOR US.
CANDLE-LIGHT... SOFT MUSIC... TICKETS TO ULTIMATE BOXING... BUT NOW...
...YOU GONE AND CONFUSED THE #$%&*@! OUT OF MY HORMONES!
BRAPP BRAPP

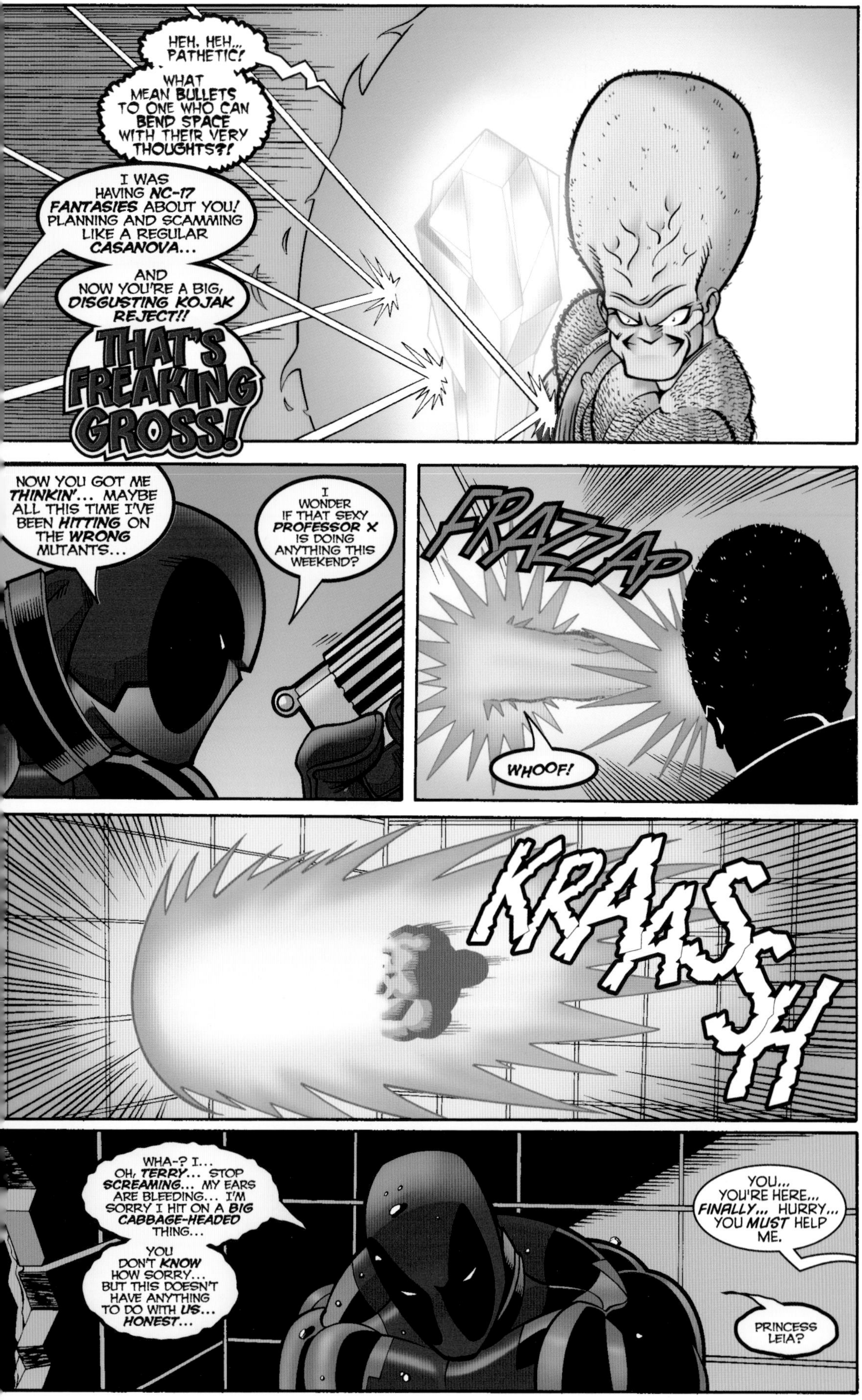
HEH, HEH... PATHETIC!
WHAT MEAN BULLETS TO ONE WHO CAN BEND SPACE WITH THEIR VERY THOUGHTS?!
I WAS HAVING NC-17 FANTASIES ABOUT YOU! PLANNING AND SCAMMING LIKE A REGULAR CASANOVA...
AND NOW YOU'RE A BIG, DISGUSTING KOJAK REJECT!!
THAT'S FREAKING GROSS!
NOW YOU GOT ME THINKIN'... MAYBE ALL THIS TIME I'VE BEEN HITTING ON THE WRONG MUTANTS...
I WONDER IF THAT SEXY PROFESSOR X IS DOING ANYTHING THIS WEEKEND?
FRAZZAP
WHOOF!
KRAASH
WHA-? I... OH, TERRY... STOP SCREAMING... MY EARS ARE BLEEDING... I'M SORRY I HIT ON A BIG CABBAGE-HEADED THING...
YOU DON'T KNOW HOW SORRY... BUT THIS DOESN'T HAVE ANYTHING TO DO WITH US... HONEST...
YOU... YOU'RE HERE... FINALLY... HURRY... YOU MUST HELP ME.
PRINCESS LEIA?

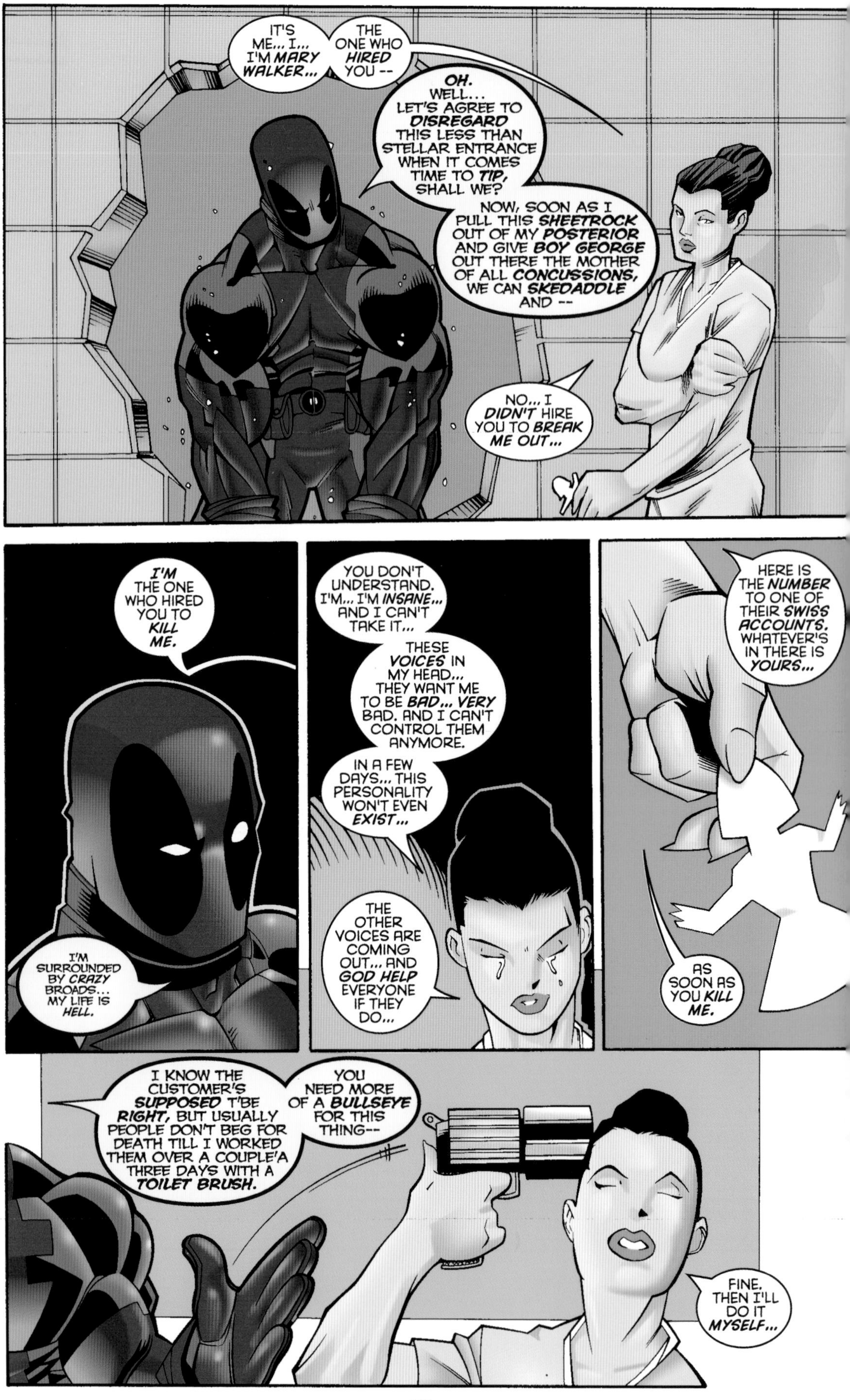
IT'S ME... I... I'M MARY WALKER...
THE ONE WHO HIRED YOU --
OH. WELL... LET'S AGREE TO DISREGARD THIS LESS THAN STELLAR ENTRANCE WHEN IT COMES TIME TO TIP, SHALL WE?
NOW, SOON AS I PULL THIS SHEETROCK OUT OF MY POSTERIOR AND GIVE BOY GEORGE OUT THERE THE MOTHER OF ALL CONCUSSIONS, WE CAN SKEDADDLE AND --
NO... I DIDN'T HIRE YOU TO BREAK ME OUT...
I'M THE ONE WHO HIRED YOU TO KILL ME.
I'M SURROUNDED BY CRAZY BROADS... MY LIFE IS HELL.
YOU DON'T UNDERSTAND. I'M... I'M INSANE... AND I CAN'T TAKE IT...
THESE VOICES IN MY HEAD... THEY WANT ME TO BE BAD... VERY BAD. AND I CAN'T CONTROL THEM ANYMORE.
IN A FEW DAYS... THIS PERSONALITY WON'T EVEN EXIST...
THE OTHER VOICES ARE COMING OUT... AND GOD HELP EVERYONE IF THEY DO...
HERE IS THE NUMBER TO ONE OF THEIR SWISS ACCOUNTS. WHATEVER'S IN THERE IS YOURS...
AS SOON AS YOU KILL ME.
I KNOW THE CUSTOMER'S SUPPOSED T'BE RIGHT, BUT USUALLY PEOPLE DON'T BEG FOR DEATH TILL I WORKED THEM OVER A COUPLE'A THREE DAYS WITH A TOILET BRUSH.
YOU NEED MORE OF A BULLSEYE FOR THIS THING--
FINE. THEN I'LL DO IT MYSELF...

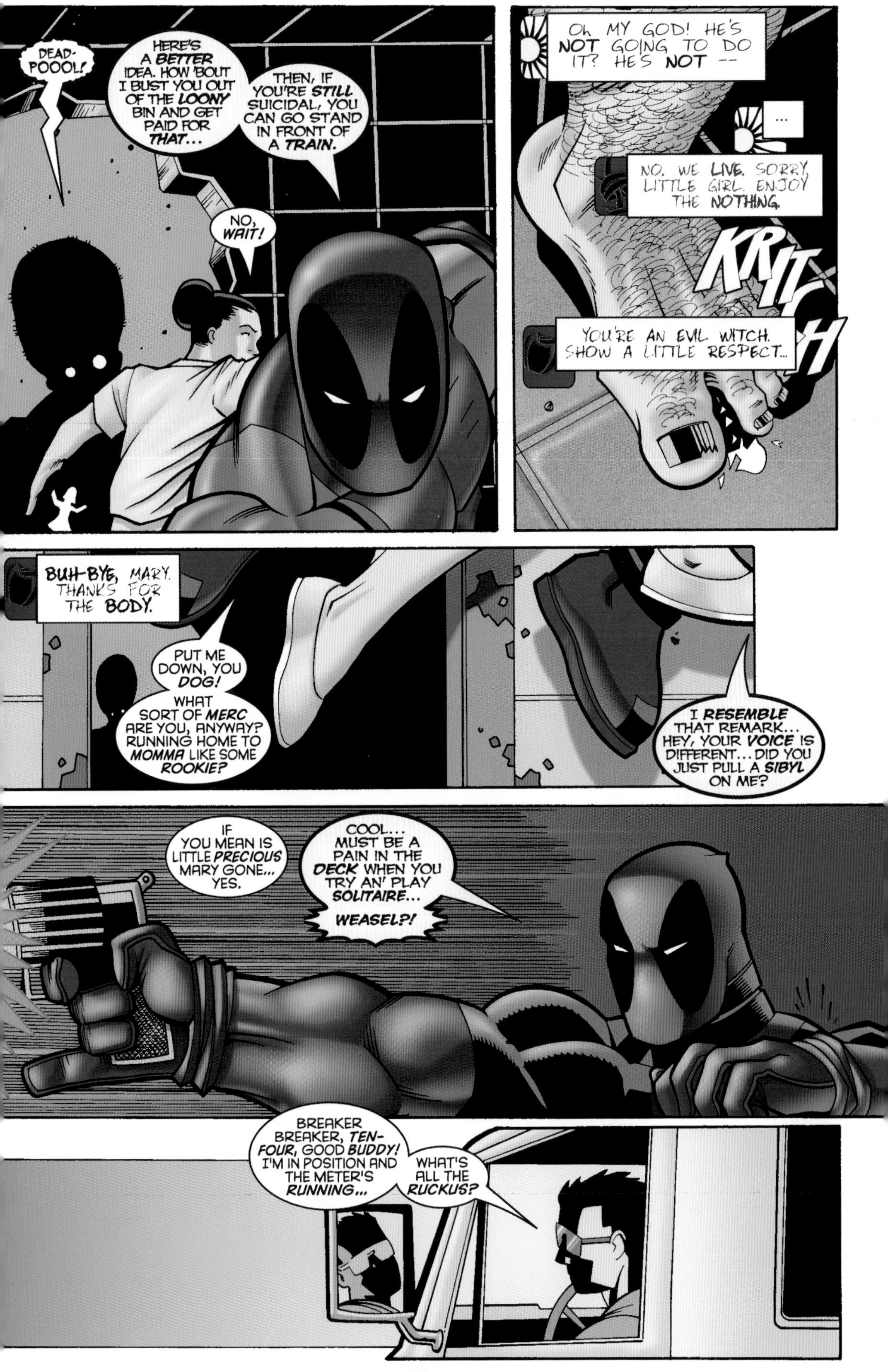
DEAD-POOOL!
HERE'S A BETTER IDEA. HOW 'BOUT I BUST YOU OUT OF THE LOONY BIN AND GET PAID FOR THAT...
THEN, IF YOU'RE STILL SUICIDAL, YOU CAN GO STAND IN FRONT OF A TRAIN.
NO, WAIT!
Oh MY GOD! HE'S NOT GOING TO DO IT? HE'S NOT --
...
NO. WE LIVE. SORRY, LITTLE GIRL. ENJOY THE NOTHING.
KRITCH
YOU'RE AN EVIL WITCH. SHOW A LITTLE RESPECT...
BUH-BYE, MARY. THANKS FOR THE BODY.
PUT ME DOWN, YOU DOG!
WHAT SORT OF MERC ARE YOU, ANYWAY? RUNNING HOME TO MOMMA LIKE SOME ROOKIE?
I RESEMBLE THAT REMARK... HEY, YOUR VOICE IS DIFFERENT... DID YOU JUST PULL A SIBYL ON ME?
IF YOU MEAN IS LITTLE PRECIOUS MARY GONE... YES.
COOL... MUST BE A PAIN IN THE DECK WHEN YOU TRY AN' PLAY SOLITAIRE...
WEASEL?!
BREAKER BREAKER, TEN-FOUR, GOOD BUDDY! I'M IN POSITION AND THE METER'S RUNNING...
WHAT'S ALL THE RUCKUS?

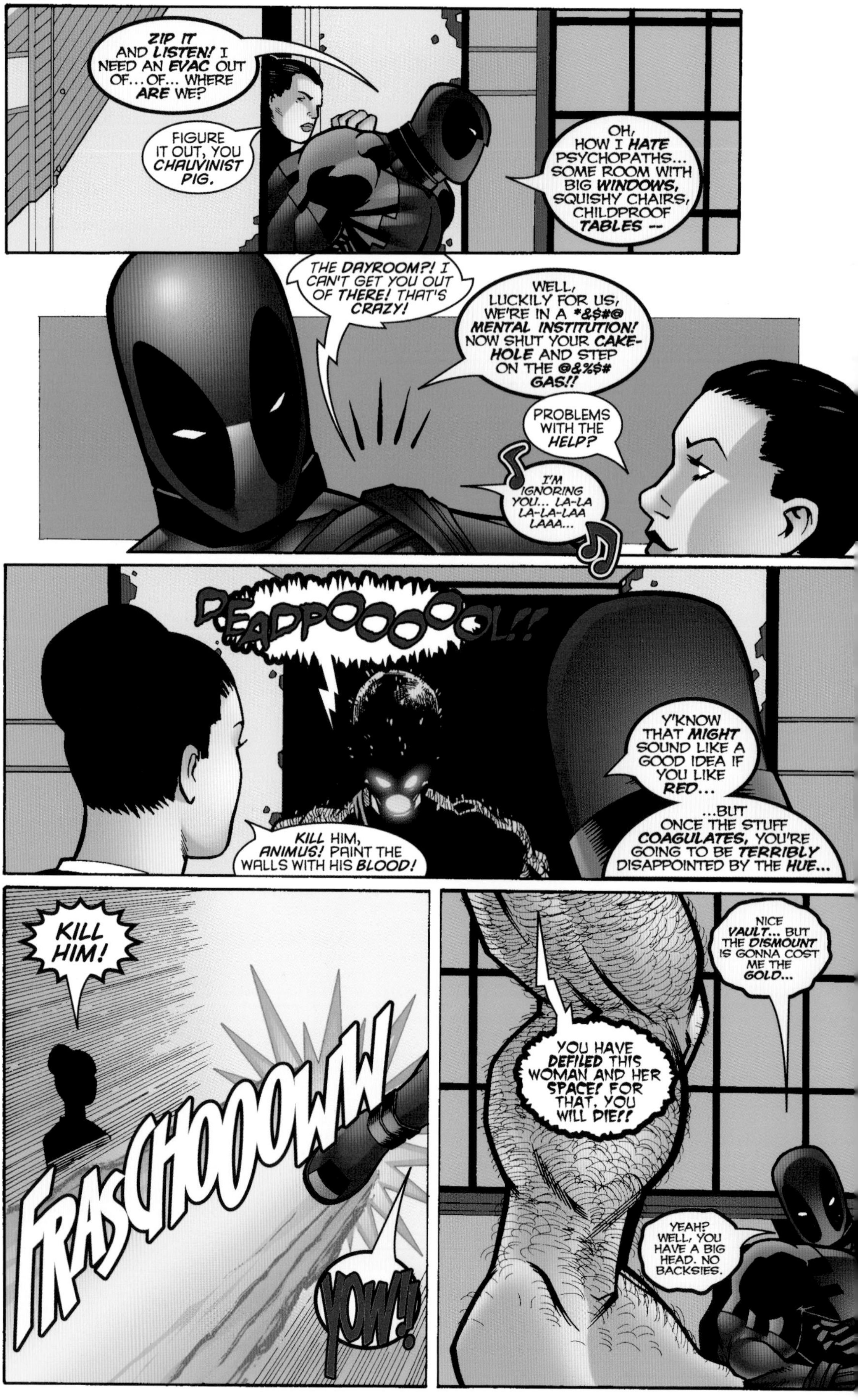
ZIP IT AND LISTEN! I NEED AN EVAC OUT OF... OF... WHERE ARE WE?
FIGURE IT OUT, YOU CHAUVINIST PIG.
OH, HOW I HATE PSYCHOPATHS... SOME ROOM WITH BIG WINDOWS, SQUISHY CHAIRS, CHILDPROOF TABLES --
THE DAYROOM?! I CAN'T GET YOU OUT OF THERE! THAT'S CRAZY!
WELL, LUCKILY FOR US, WE'RE IN A *&$#@ MENTAL INSTITUTION! NOW SHUT YOUR CAKE-HOLE AND STEP ON THE @&%$# GAS!!
PROBLEMS WITH THE HELP?
I'M IGNORING YOU... LA-LA LA-LA-LAA LAAA...
DEADPOOOOOOOL!!
KILL HIM, ANIMUS! PAINT THE WALLS WITH HIS BLOOD!
Y'KNOW THAT MIGHT SOUND LIKE A GOOD IDEA IF YOU LIKE RED...
...BUT ONCE THE STUFF COAGULATES, YOU'RE GOING TO BE TERRIBLY DISAPPOINTED BY THE HUE...
KILL HIM!
FRASCHOOOWW
YOW!!
YOU HAVE DEFILED THIS WOMAN AND HER SPACE! FOR THAT, YOU WILL DIE!!
NICE VAULT... BUT THE DISMOUNT IS GONNA COST ME THE GOLD...
YEAH? WELL, YOU HAVE A BIG HEAD. NO BACKSIES.

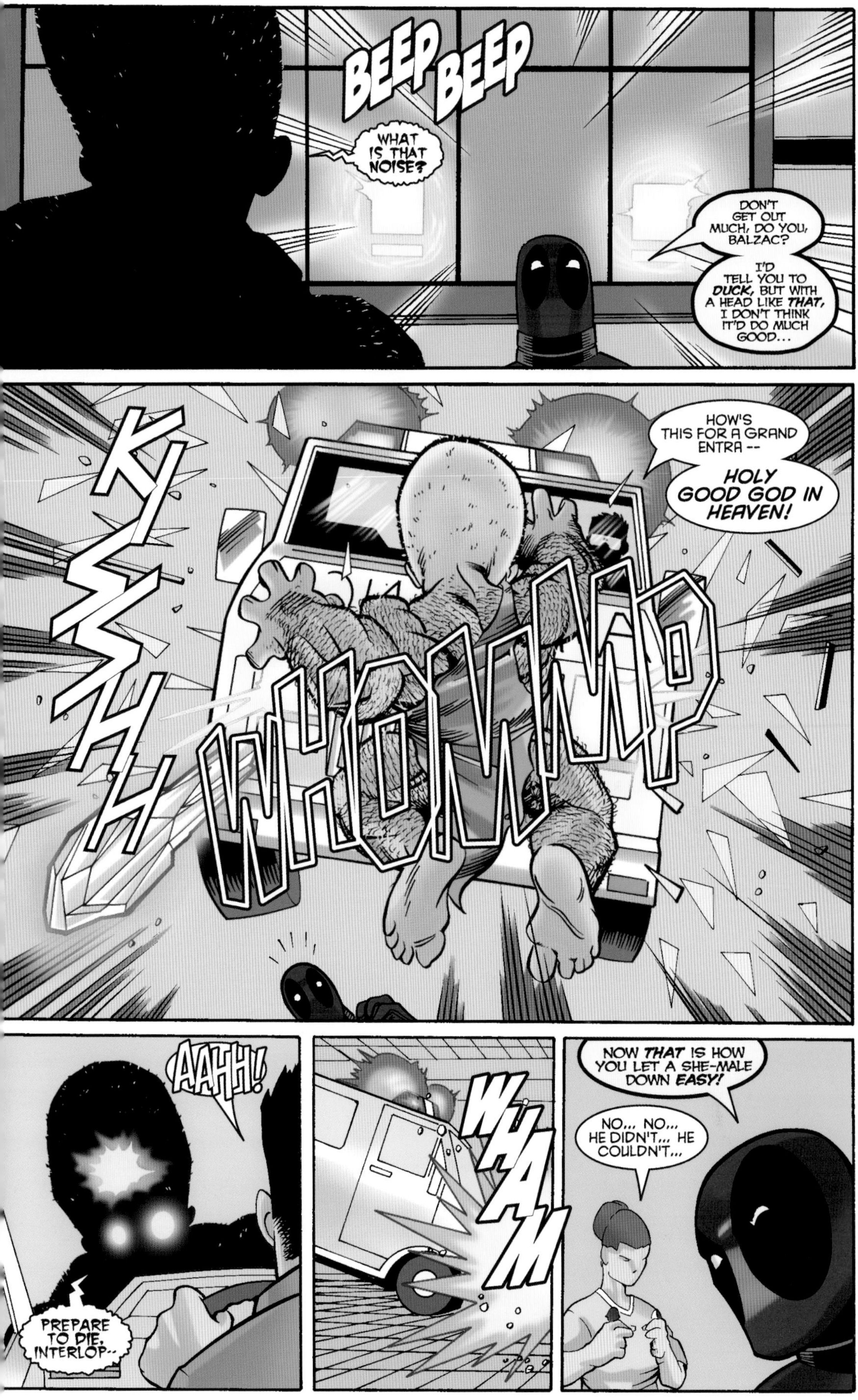
BEEP BEEP
WHAT IS THAT NOISE?
DON'T GET OUT MUCH, DO YOU, BALZAC?
I'D TELL YOU TO DUCK, BUT WITH A HEAD LIKE THAT, I DON'T THINK IT'D DO MUCH GOOD...
HOW'S THIS FOR A GRAND ENTRA --
HOLY GOOD GOD IN HEAVEN!
KSHHH
WHOMMP
AAHH!
PREPARE TO DIE, INTERLOP--
WHAM
NOW THAT IS HOW YOU LET A SHE-MALE DOWN EASY!
NO... NO... HE DIDN'T... HE COULDN'T...

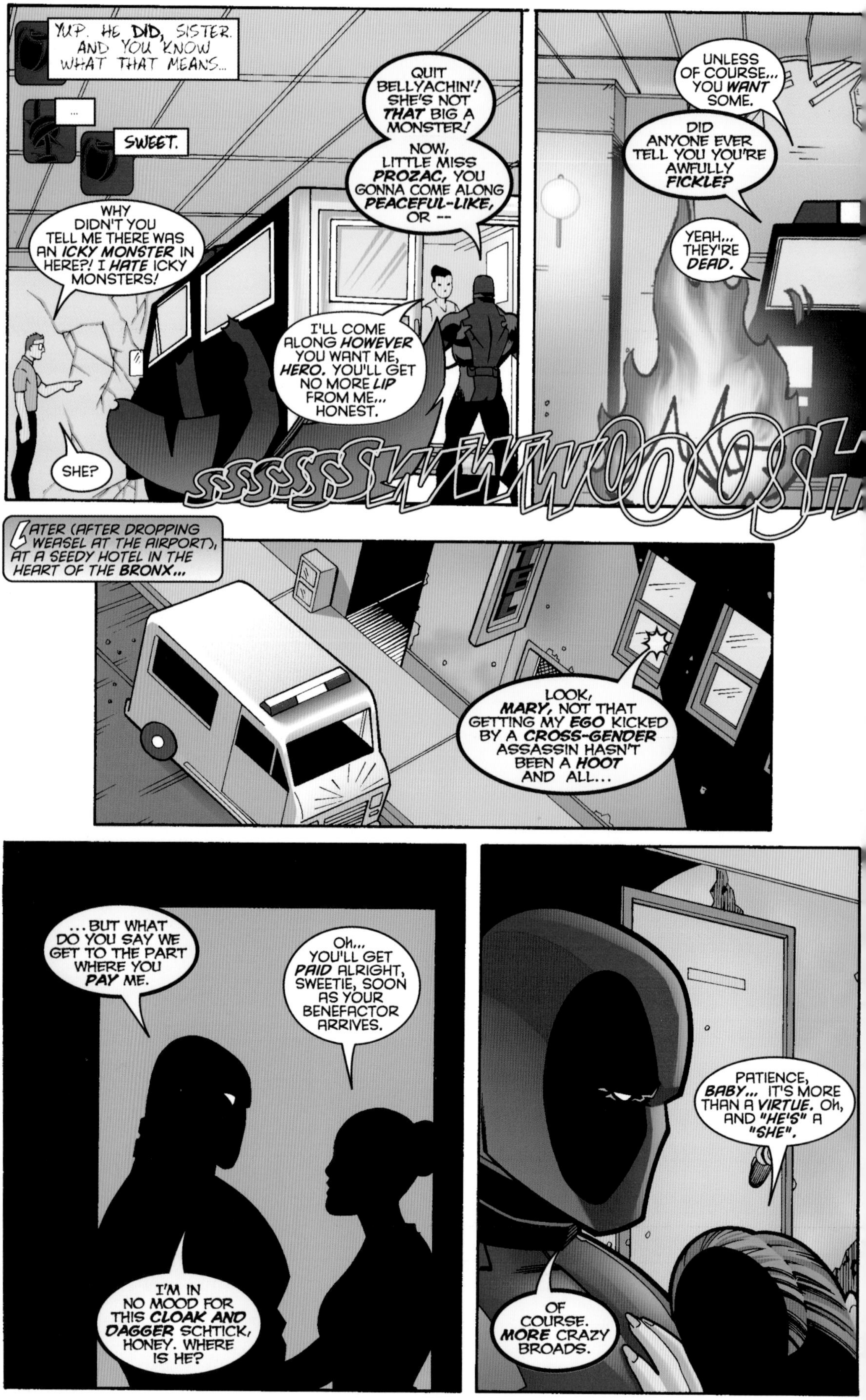
YUP. HE DID, SISTER. AND YOU KNOW WHAT THAT MEANS...
...
SWEET.
WHY DIDN'T YOU TELL ME THERE WAS AN ICKY MONSTER IN HERE?! I HATE ICKY MONSTERS!
SHE?
QUIT BELLYACHIN'! SHE'S NOT THAT BIG A MONSTER!
NOW, LITTLE MISS PROZAC, YOU GONNA COME ALONG PEACEFUL-LIKE, OR --
I'LL COME ALONG HOWEVER YOU WANT ME, HERO. YOU'LL GET NO MORE LIP FROM ME... HONEST.
UNLESS OF COURSE... YOU WANT SOME.
DID ANYONE EVER TELL YOU YOU'RE AWFULLY FICKLE?
YEAH... THEY'RE DEAD.
SSSSSSWWWWOOOOSH
LATER (AFTER DROPPING WEASEL AT THE AIRPORT), AT A SEEDY HOTEL IN THE HEART OF THE BRONX...
LOOK, MARY, NOT THAT GETTING MY EGO KICKED BY A CROSS-GENDER ASSASSIN HASN'T BEEN A HOOT AND ALL...
...BUT WHAT DO YOU SAY WE GET TO THE PART WHERE YOU PAY ME.
Oh... YOU'LL GET PAID ALRIGHT, SWEETIE, SOON AS YOUR BENEFACTOR ARRIVES.
I'M IN NO MOOD FOR THIS CLOAK AND DAGGER SCHTICK, HONEY. WHERE IS HE?
PATIENCE, BABY... IT'S MORE THAN A VIRTUE. Oh, AND "HE'S" A "SHE".
OF COURSE. MORE CRAZY BROADS.

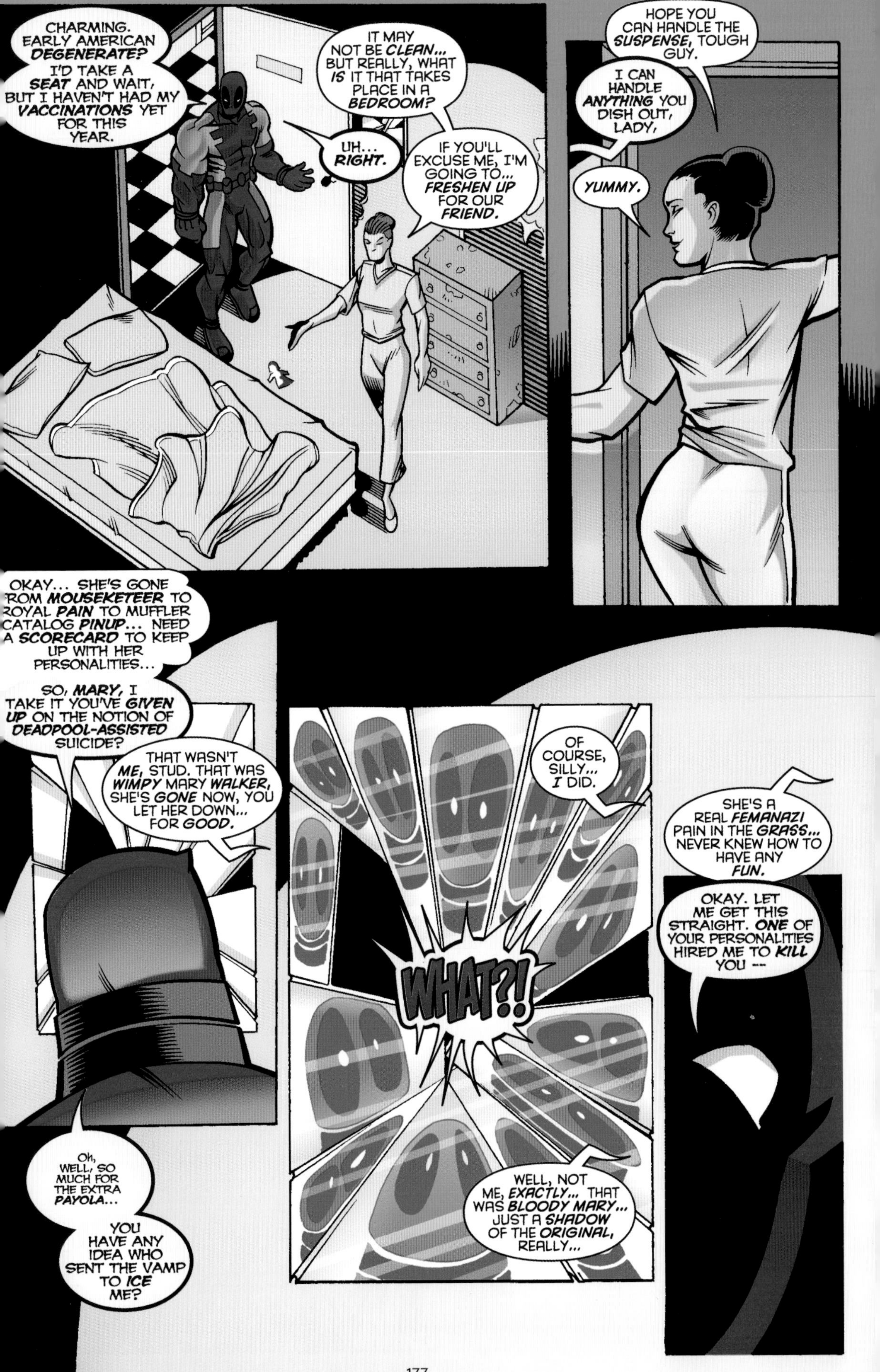

CHARMING. EARLY AMERICAN DEGENERATE?
I'D TAKE A SEAT AND WAIT, BUT I HAVEN'T HAD MY VACCINATIONS YET FOR THIS YEAR.
IT MAY NOT BE CLEAN... BUT REALLY, WHAT IS IT THAT TAKES PLACE IN A BEDROOM?
UH... RIGHT.
IF YOU'LL EXCUSE ME, I'M GOING TO... FRESHEN UP FOR OUR FRIEND.
HOPE YOU CAN HANDLE THE SUSPENSE, TOUGH GUY.
I CAN HANDLE ANYTHING YOU DISH OUT, LADY,
YUMMY.
OKAY... SHE'S GONE ROM MOUSEKETEER TO ROYAL PAIN TO MUFFLER CATALOG PINUP... NEED A SCORECARD TO KEEP UP WITH HER PERSONALITIES...
SO, MARY, I TAKE IT YOU'VE GIVEN UP ON THE NOTION OF DEADPOOL-ASSISTED SUICIDE?
THAT WASN'T ME, STUD. THAT WAS WIMPY MARY WALKER, SHE'S GONE NOW, YOU LET HER DOWN... FOR GOOD.
Oh, WELL, SO MUCH FOR THE EXTRA PAYOLA...
YOU HAVE ANY IDEA WHO SENT THE VAMP TO ICE ME?
OF COURSE, SILLY... I DID.
WHAT?!
WELL, NOT ME, EXACTLY... THAT WAS BLOODY MARY... JUST A SHADOW OF THE ORIGINAL, REALLY...
SHE'S A REAL FEMANAZI PAIN IN THE GRASS... NEVER KNEW HOW TO HAVE ANY FUN.
OKAY. LET ME GET THIS STRAIGHT. ONE OF YOUR PERSONALITIES HIRED ME TO KILL YOU --

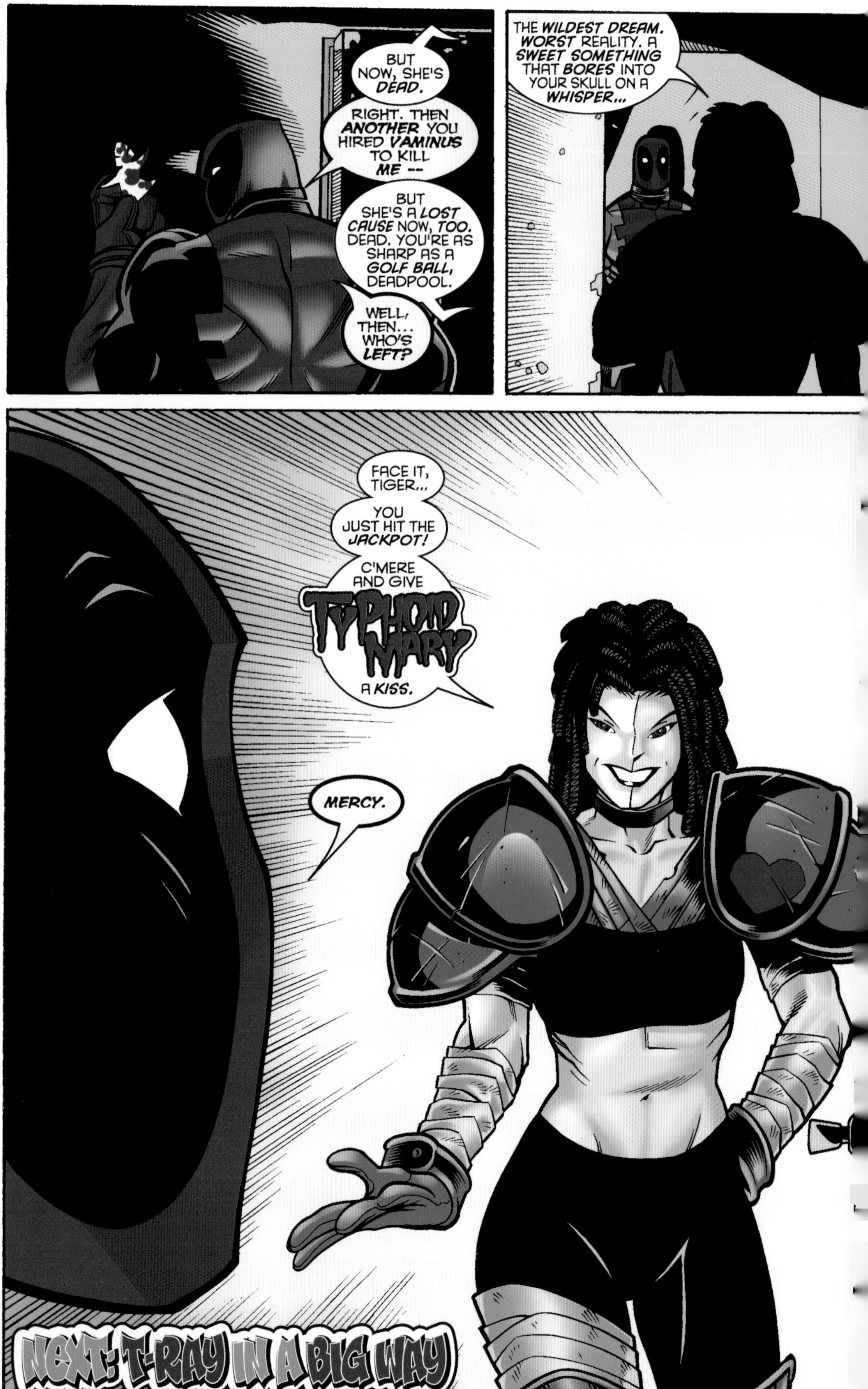
BUT NOW, SHE'S *DEAD.*
RIGHT. THEN *ANOTHER* YOU HIRED *VAMINUS* TO KILL *ME* --
BUT SHE'S A *LOST CAUSE* NOW, *TOO.* DEAD. YOU'RE AS SHARP AS A *GOLF BALL,* DEADPOOL.
WELL, THEN... WHO'S *LEFT?*
THE *WILDEST DREAM. WORST* REALITY. A *SWEET SOMETHING* THAT *BORES* INTO YOUR SKULL ON A *WHISPER...*
FACE IT, TIGER...
YOU JUST HIT THE *JACKPOT!*
C'MERE AND GIVE TYPHOID MARY A *KISS.*
MERCY.
NEXT: T-RAY IN A BIG WAY

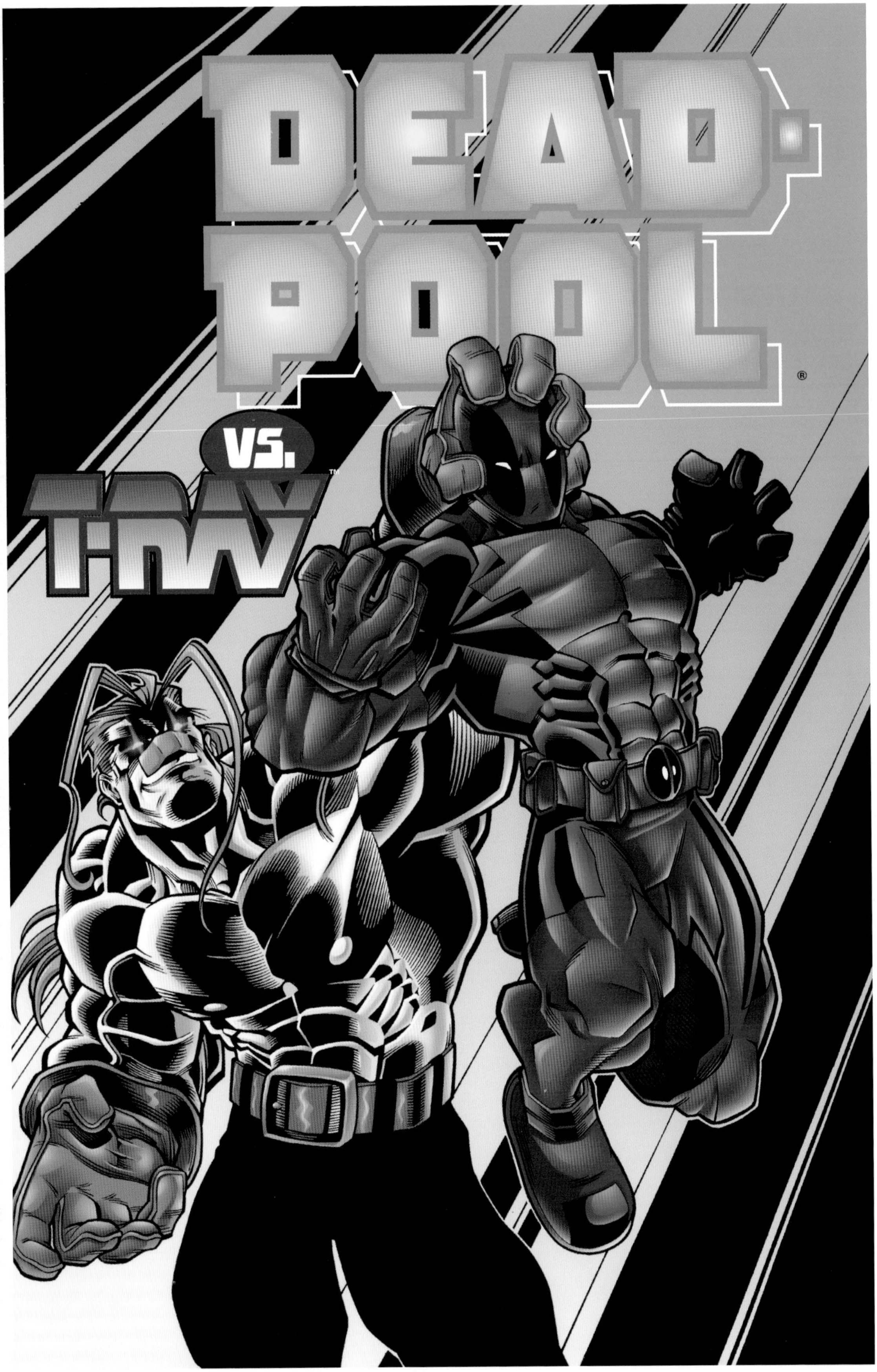
DEAD-POOL®
VS.
T-RAY™

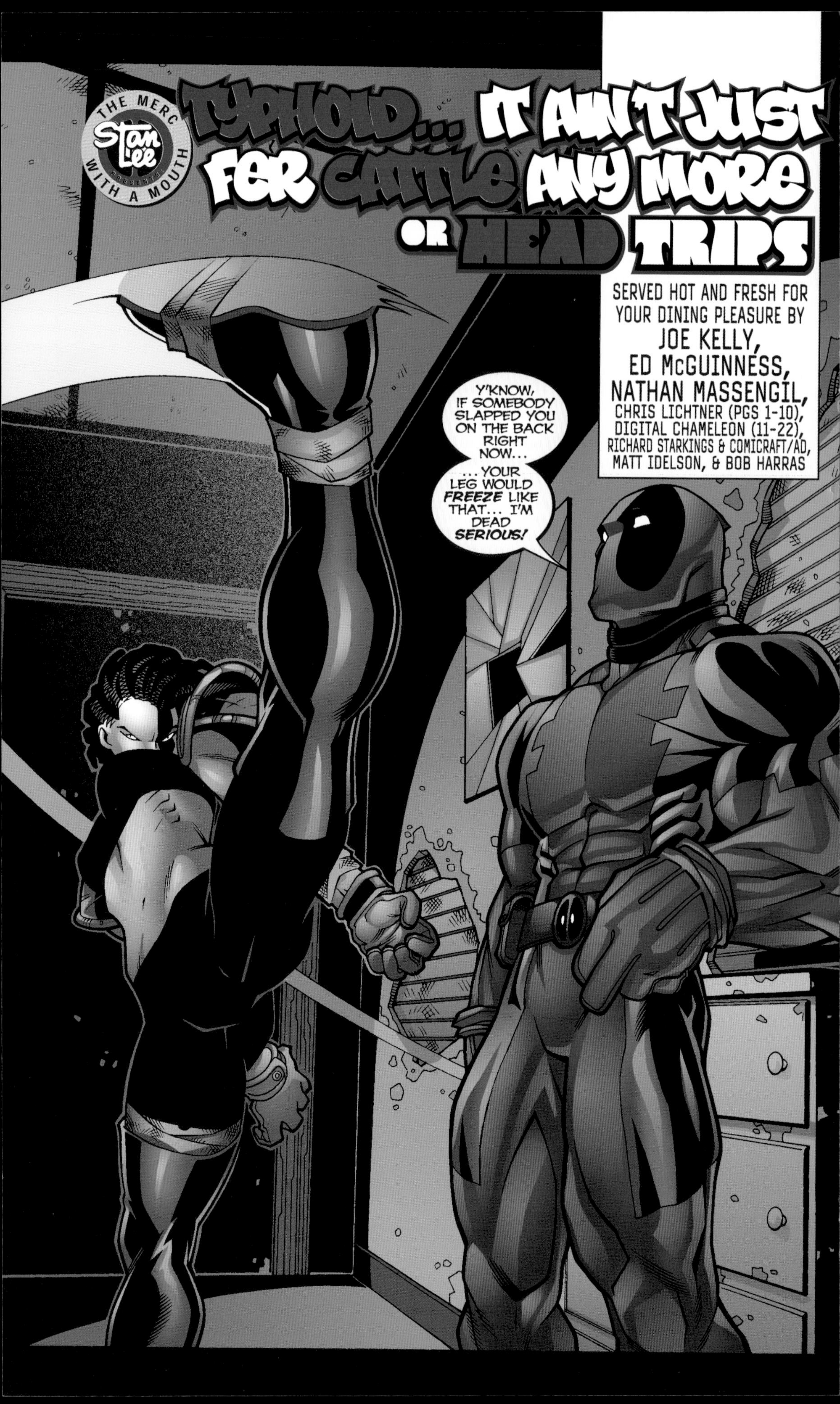
THE MERC WITH A MOUTH
Stan Lee PRESENTS:
TYPHOID... IT AIN'T JUST FOR CATTLE ANY MORE OR HEAD TRIPS
SERVED HOT AND FRESH FOR YOUR DINING PLEASURE BY
JOE KELLY,
ED McGUINNESS,
NATHAN MASSENGIL,
CHRIS LICHTNER (PGS 1-10),
DIGITAL CHAMELEON (11-22),
RICHARD STARKINGS & COMICRAFT/AD,
MATT IDELSON, & BOB HARRAS
Y'KNOW, IF SOMEBODY SLAPPED YOU ON THE BACK RIGHT NOW...
...YOUR LEG WOULD FREEZE LIKE THAT... I'M DEAD SERIOUS!

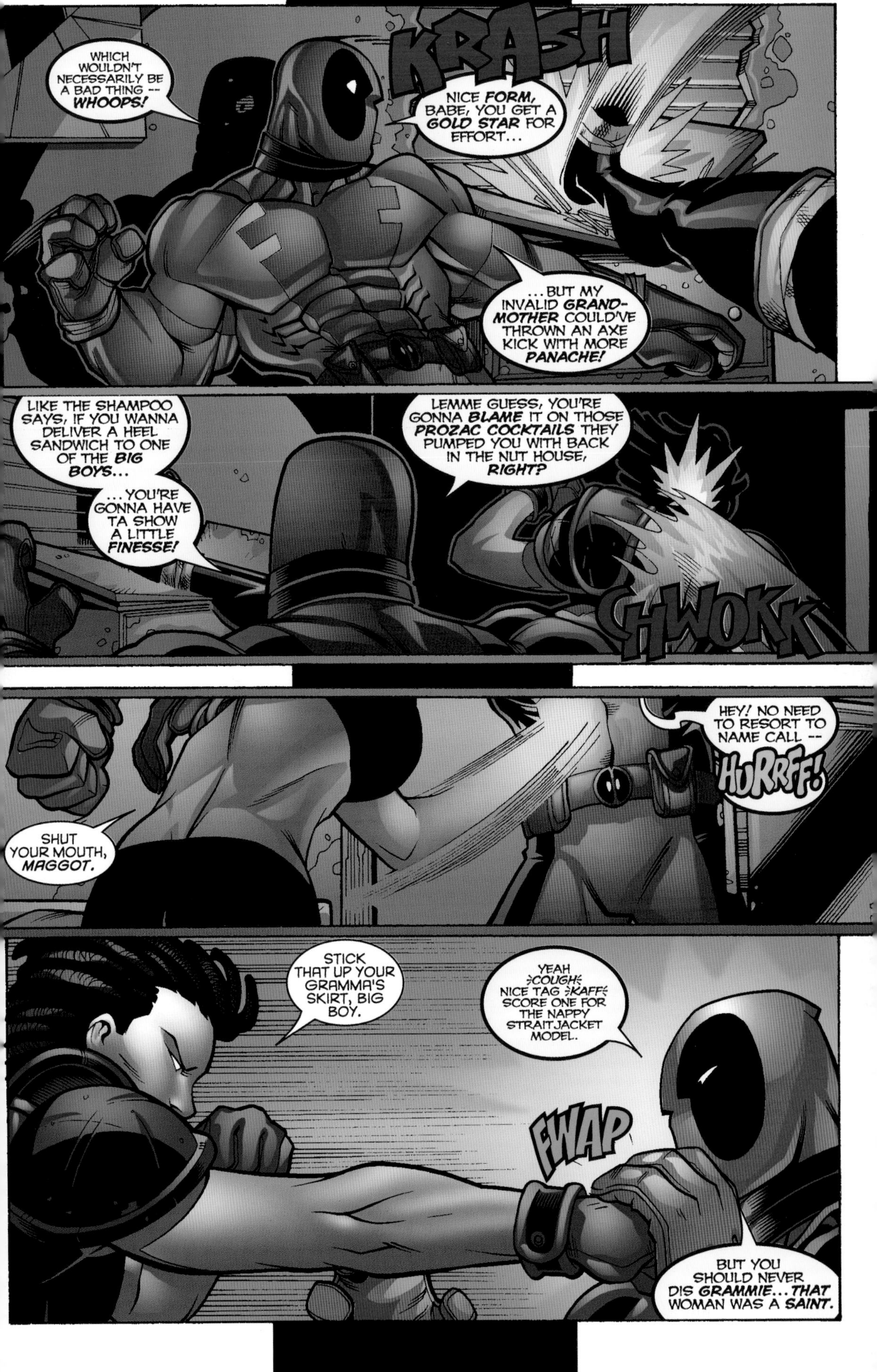
WHICH WOULDN'T NECESSARILY BE A BAD THING -- WHOOPS!
KRASH
NICE FORM, BABE, YOU GET A GOLD STAR FOR EFFORT...
...BUT MY INVALID GRAND-MOTHER COULD'VE THROWN AN AXE KICK WITH MORE PANACHE!
LIKE THE SHAMPOO SAYS, IF YOU WANNA DELIVER A HEEL SANDWICH TO ONE OF THE BIG BOYS...
...YOU'RE GONNA HAVE TA SHOW A LITTLE FINESSE!
LEMME GUESS, YOU'RE GONNA BLAME IT ON THOSE PROZAC COCKTAILS THEY PUMPED YOU WITH BACK IN THE NUT HOUSE, RIGHT?
CHWOKK
HEY! NO NEED TO RESORT TO NAME CALL --
HURRFF!
SHUT YOUR MOUTH, MAGGOT.
STICK THAT UP YOUR GRAMMA'S SKIRT, BIG BOY.
YEAH *COUGH* NICE TAG *KAFF* SCORE ONE FOR THE NAPPY STRAITJACKET MODEL.
FWAP
BUT YOU SHOULD NEVER DIS GRAMMIE...THAT WOMAN WAS A SAINT.

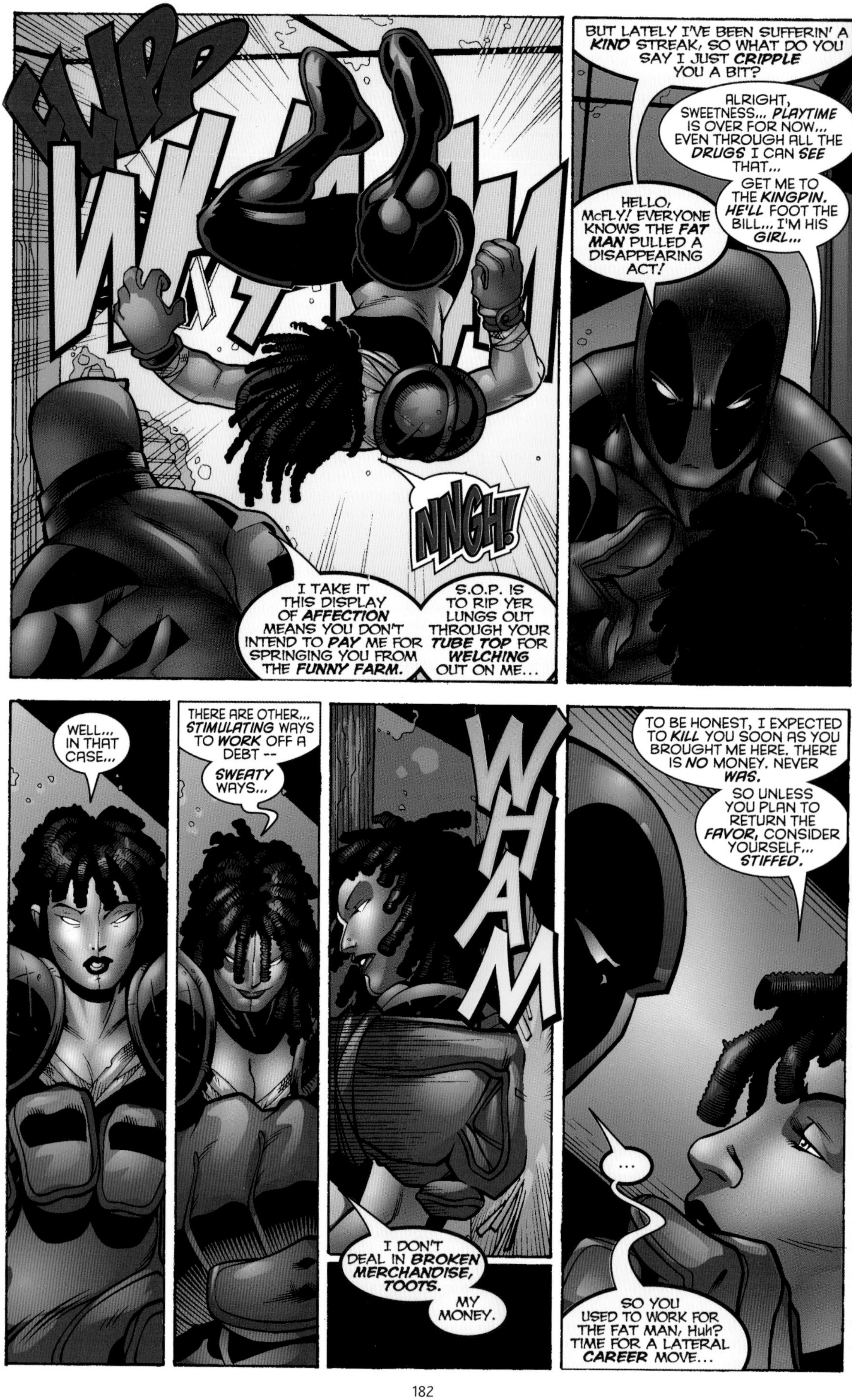
CLIPP
WHAM
NNGH!
I TAKE IT THIS DISPLAY OF AFFECTION MEANS YOU DON'T INTEND TO PAY ME FOR SPRINGING YOU FROM THE FUNNY FARM.
S.O.P. IS TO RIP YER LUNGS OUT THROUGH YOUR TUBE TOP FOR WELCHING OUT ON ME...
BUT LATELY I'VE BEEN SUFFERIN' A KIND STREAK, SO WHAT DO YOU SAY I JUST CRIPPLE YOU A BIT?
ALRIGHT, SWEETNESS... PLAYTIME IS OVER FOR NOW... EVEN THROUGH ALL THE DRUGS I CAN SEE THAT...
GET ME TO THE KINGPIN. HE'LL FOOT THE BILL... I'M HIS GIRL...
HELLO, McFLY! EVERYONE KNOWS THE FAT MAN PULLED A DISAPPEARING ACT!
WELL... IN THAT CASE...
THERE ARE OTHER... STIMULATING WAYS TO WORK OFF A DEBT --
SWEATY WAYS...
WHAM
I DON'T DEAL IN BROKEN MERCHANDISE, TOOTS.
MY MONEY.
TO BE HONEST, I EXPECTED TO KILL YOU SOON AS YOU BROUGHT ME HERE. THERE IS NO MONEY. NEVER WAS.
SO UNLESS YOU PLAN TO RETURN THE FAVOR, CONSIDER YOURSELF... STIFFED.
...
SO YOU USED TO WORK FOR THE FAT MAN, Huh? TIME FOR A LATERAL CAREER MOVE...

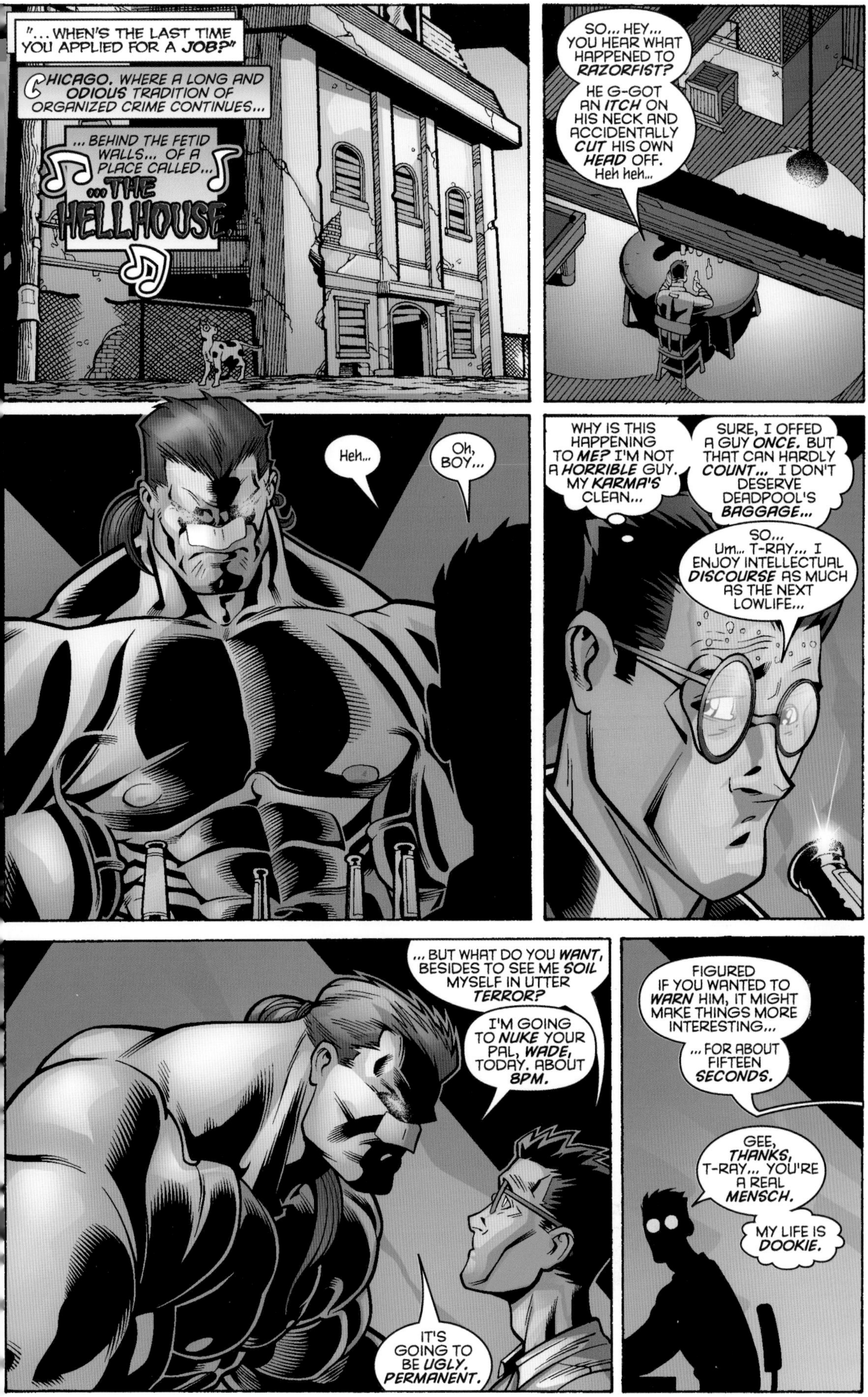
"...WHEN'S THE LAST TIME YOU APPLIED FOR A JOB?"
CHICAGO. WHERE A LONG AND ODIOUS TRADITION OF ORGANIZED CRIME CONTINUES...
...BEHIND THE FETID WALLS... OF A PLACE CALLED...
...THE HELLHOUSE.
SO... HEY... YOU HEAR WHAT HAPPENED TO RAZORFIST?
HE G-GOT AN ITCH ON HIS NECK AND ACCIDENTALLY CUT HIS OWN HEAD OFF. Heh heh...
Heh...
Oh, BOY...
WHY IS THIS HAPPENING TO ME? I'M NOT A HORRIBLE GUY. MY KARMA'S CLEAN...
SURE, I OFFED A GUY ONCE. BUT THAT CAN HARDLY COUNT... I DON'T DESERVE DEADPOOL'S BAGGAGE...
SO... Um... T-RAY... I ENJOY INTELLECTUAL DISCOURSE AS MUCH AS THE NEXT LOWLIFE...
...BUT WHAT DO YOU WANT, BESIDES TO SEE ME SOIL MYSELF IN UTTER TERROR?
I'M GOING TO NUKE YOUR PAL, WADE, TODAY. ABOUT 8PM.
IT'S GOING TO BE UGLY. PERMANENT.
FIGURED IF YOU WANTED TO WARN HIM, IT MIGHT MAKE THINGS MORE INTERESTING...
...FOR ABOUT FIFTEEN SECONDS.
GEE, THANKS, T-RAY... YOU'RE A REAL MENSCH.
MY LIFE IS DOOKIE.

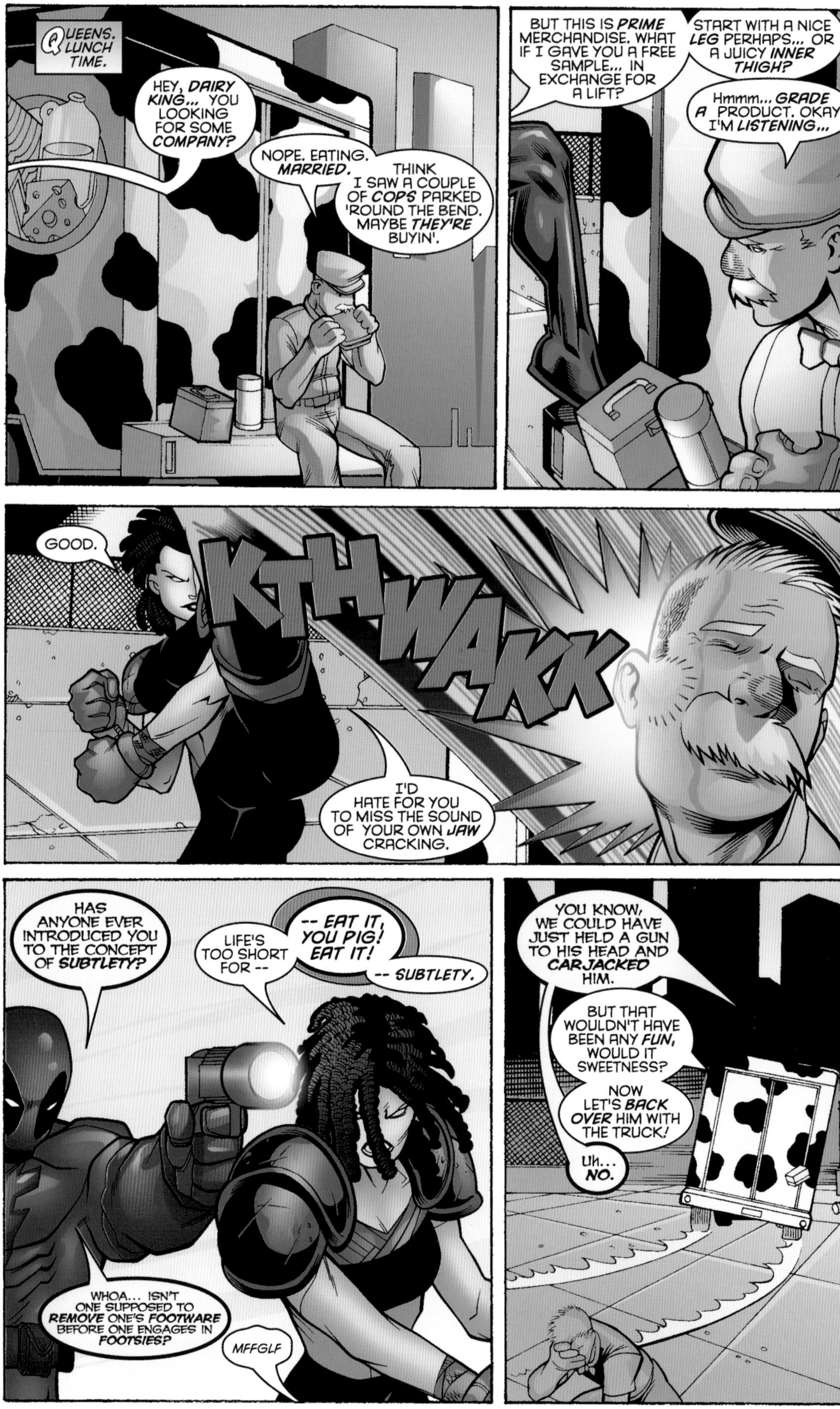
QUEENS. LUNCH TIME.
HEY, DAIRY KING... YOU LOOKING FOR SOME COMPANY?
NOPE. EATING. MARRIED.
THINK I SAW A COUPLE OF COPS PARKED 'ROUND THE BEND. MAYBE THEY'RE BUYIN'.
BUT THIS IS PRIME MERCHANDISE. WHAT IF I GAVE YOU A FREE SAMPLE... IN EXCHANGE FOR A LIFT?
START WITH A NICE LEG PERHAPS... OR A JUICY INNER THIGH?
Hmmm... GRADE A PRODUCT. OKAY, I'M LISTENING...
GOOD.
KTHWAKK
I'D HATE FOR YOU TO MISS THE SOUND OF YOUR OWN JAW CRACKING.
HAS ANYONE EVER INTRODUCED YOU TO THE CONCEPT OF SUBTLETY?
LIFE'S TOO SHORT FOR --
-- EAT IT, YOU PIG! EAT IT!
-- SUBTLETY.
WHOA... ISN'T ONE SUPPOSED TO REMOVE ONE'S FOOTWARE BEFORE ONE ENGAGES IN FOOTSIES?
MFFGLF
YOU KNOW, WE COULD HAVE JUST HELD A GUN TO HIS HEAD AND CARJACKED HIM.
BUT THAT WOULDN'T HAVE BEEN ANY FUN, WOULD IT SWEETNESS?
NOW LET'S BACK OVER HIM WITH THE TRUCK!
Uh... NO.

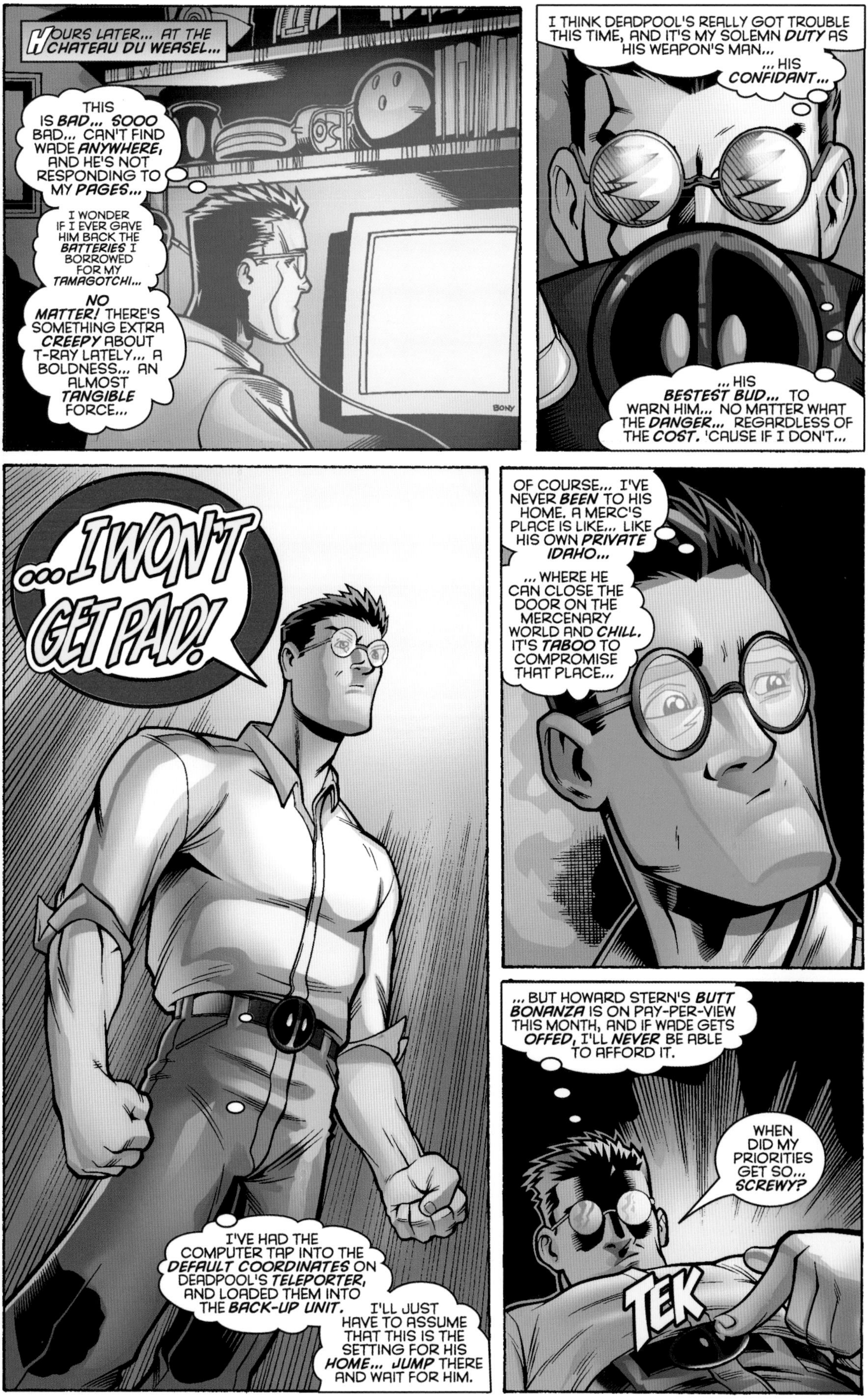
HOURS LATER... AT THE CHATEAU DU WEASEL...
THIS IS BAD... SOOO BAD... CAN'T FIND WADE ANYWHERE, AND HE'S NOT RESPONDING TO MY PAGES...
I WONDER IF I EVER GAVE HIM BACK THE BATTERIES I BORROWED FOR MY TAMAGOTCHI...
NO MATTER! THERE'S SOMETHING EXTRA CREEPY ABOUT T-RAY LATELY... A BOLDNESS... AN ALMOST TANGIBLE FORCE...
BONY
I THINK DEADPOOL'S REALLY GOT TROUBLE THIS TIME, AND IT'S MY SOLEMN DUTY AS HIS WEAPON'S MAN...
...HIS CONFIDANT...
...HIS BESTEST BUD... TO WARN HIM... NO MATTER WHAT THE DANGER... REGARDLESS OF THE COST. 'CAUSE IF I DON'T...
...I WON'T GET PAID!
I'VE HAD THE COMPUTER TAP INTO THE DEFAULT COORDINATES ON DEADPOOL'S TELEPORTER, AND LOADED THEM INTO THE BACK-UP UNIT.
I'LL JUST HAVE TO ASSUME THAT THIS IS THE SETTING FOR HIS HOME... JUMP THERE AND WAIT FOR HIM.
OF COURSE... I'VE NEVER BEEN TO HIS HOME. A MERC'S PLACE IS LIKE... LIKE HIS OWN PRIVATE IDAHO...
...WHERE HE CAN CLOSE THE DOOR ON THE MERCENARY WORLD AND CHILL. IT'S TABOO TO COMPROMISE THAT PLACE...
...BUT HOWARD STERN'S BUTT BONANZA IS ON PAY-PER-VIEW THIS MONTH, AND IF WADE GETS OFFED, I'LL NEVER BE ABLE TO AFFORD IT.
WHEN DID MY PRIORITIES GET SO... SCREWY?
TEK

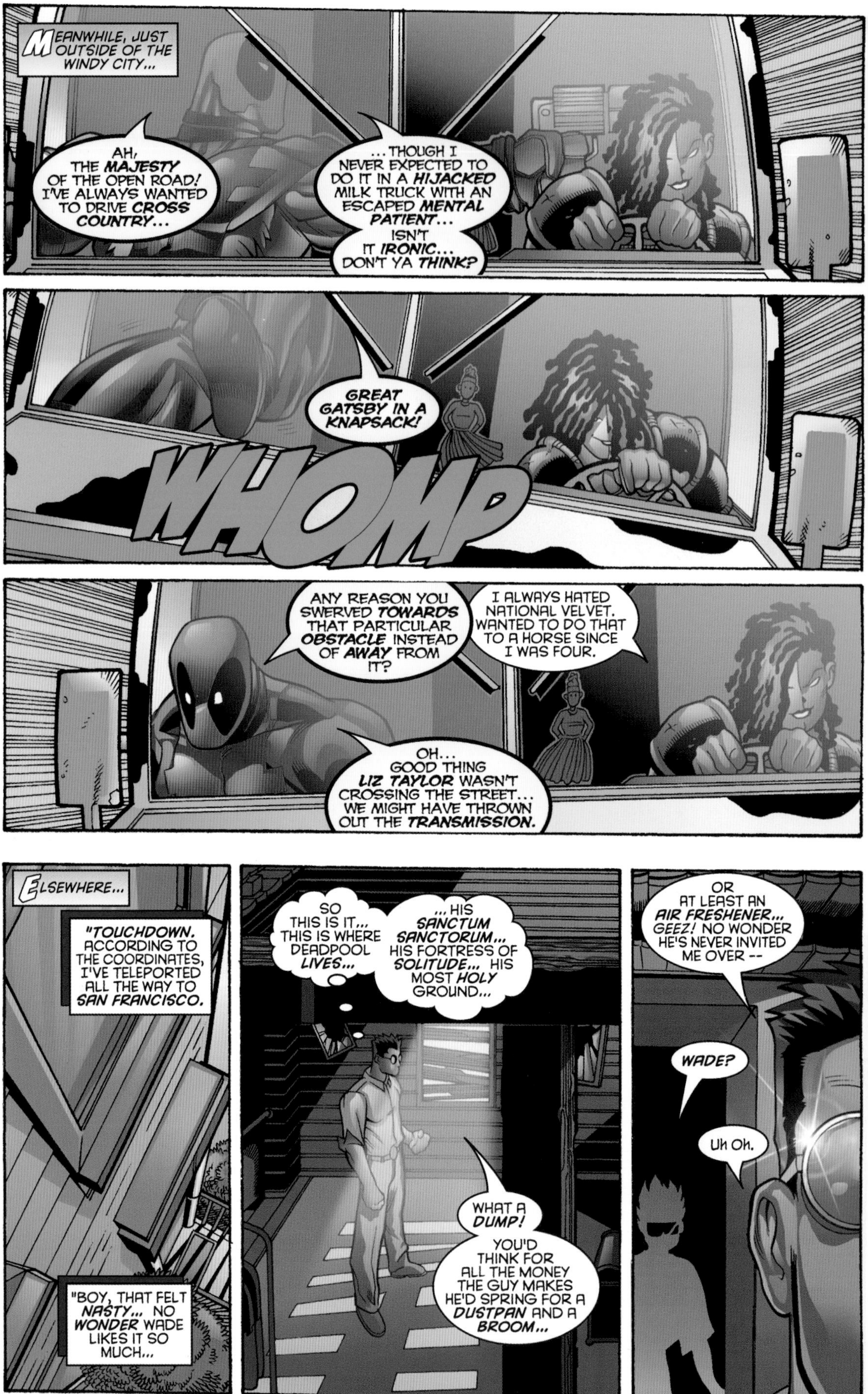
MEANWHILE, JUST OUTSIDE OF THE WINDY CITY...
AH, THE MAJESTY OF THE OPEN ROAD! I'VE ALWAYS WANTED TO DRIVE CROSS COUNTRY...
...THOUGH I NEVER EXPECTED TO DO IT IN A HIJACKED MILK TRUCK WITH AN ESCAPED MENTAL PATIENT...
ISN'T IT IRONIC... DON'T YA THINK?
GREAT GATSBY IN A KNAPSACK!
WHOMP
ANY REASON YOU SWERVED TOWARDS THAT PARTICULAR OBSTACLE INSTEAD OF AWAY FROM IT?
I ALWAYS HATED NATIONAL VELVET. WANTED TO DO THAT TO A HORSE SINCE I WAS FOUR.
OH... GOOD THING LIZ TAYLOR WASN'T CROSSING THE STREET... WE MIGHT HAVE THROWN OUT THE TRANSMISSION.
ELSEWHERE...
"TOUCHDOWN. ACCORDING TO THE COORDINATES, I'VE TELEPORTED ALL THE WAY TO SAN FRANCISCO.
"BOY, THAT FELT NASTY... NO WONDER WADE LIKES IT SO MUCH...
SO THIS IS IT... THIS IS WHERE DEADPOOL LIVES...
...HIS SANCTUM SANCTORUM... HIS FORTRESS OF SOLITUDE... HIS MOST HOLY GROUND...
WHAT A DUMP!
YOU'D THINK FOR ALL THE MONEY THE GUY MAKES HE'D SPRING FOR A DUSTPAN AND A BROOM...
OR AT LEAST AN AIR FRESHENER... GEEZ! NO WONDER HE'S NEVER INVITED ME OVER --
WADE?
Uh Oh.

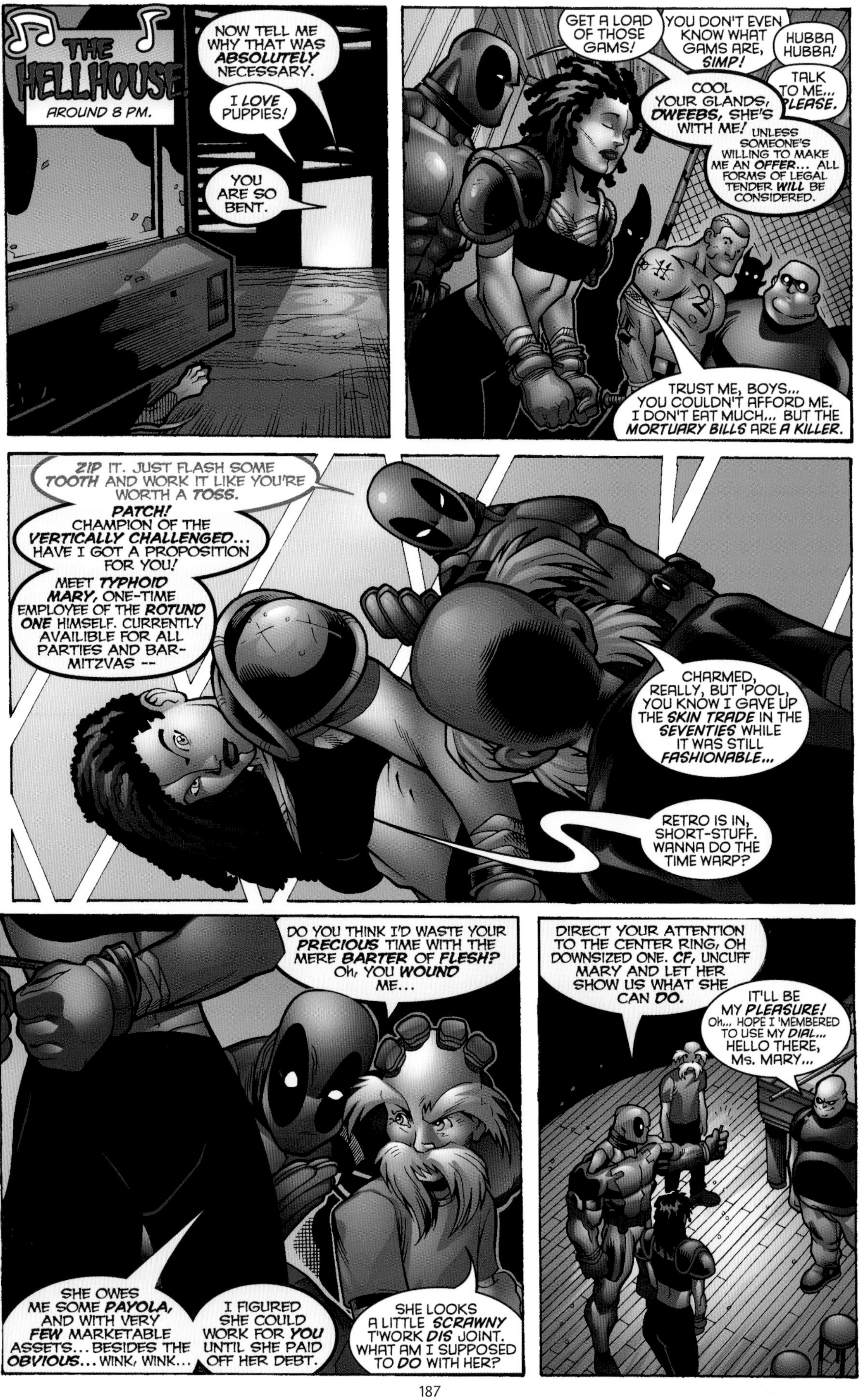

THE HELLHOUSE
AROUND 8 PM.
NOW TELL ME WHY THAT WAS ABSOLUTELY NECESSARY.
I LOVE PUPPIES!
YOU ARE SO BENT.
GET A LOAD OF THOSE GAMS!
YOU DON'T EVEN KNOW WHAT GAMS ARE, SIMP!
HUBBA HUBBA!
TALK TO ME... PLEASE.
COOL YOUR GLANDS, DWEEBS, SHE'S WITH ME! UNLESS SOMEONE'S WILLING TO MAKE ME AN OFFER... ALL FORMS OF LEGAL TENDER WILL BE CONSIDERED.
TRUST ME, BOYS... YOU COULDN'T AFFORD ME. I DON'T EAT MUCH... BUT THE MORTUARY BILLS ARE A KILLER.
ZIP IT. JUST FLASH SOME TOOTH AND WORK IT LIKE YOU'RE WORTH A TOSS.
PATCH! CHAMPION OF THE VERTICALLY CHALLENGED... HAVE I GOT A PROPOSITION FOR YOU!
MEET TYPHOID MARY, ONE-TIME EMPLOYEE OF THE ROTUND ONE HIMSELF. CURRENTLY AVAILIBLE FOR ALL PARTIES AND BAR-MITZVAS --
CHARMED, REALLY, BUT 'POOL, YOU KNOW I GAVE UP THE SKIN TRADE IN THE SEVENTIES WHILE IT WAS STILL FASHIONABLE...
RETRO IS IN, SHORT-STUFF. WANNA DO THE TIME WARP?
DO YOU THINK I'D WASTE YOUR PRECIOUS TIME WITH THE MERE BARTER OF FLESH? Oh, YOU WOUND ME...
SHE OWES ME SOME PAYOLA, AND WITH VERY FEW MARKETABLE ASSETS... BESIDES THE OBVIOUS... WINK, WINK...
I FIGURED SHE COULD WORK FOR YOU UNTIL SHE PAID OFF HER DEBT.
SHE LOOKS A LITTLE SCRAWNY T'WORK DIS JOINT. WHAT AM I SUPPOSED TO DO WITH HER?
DIRECT YOUR ATTENTION TO THE CENTER RING, OH DOWNSIZED ONE. CF, UNCUFF MARY AND LET HER SHOW US WHAT SHE CAN DO.
IT'LL BE MY PLEASURE! Oh... HOPE I 'MEMBERED TO USE MY DIAL... HELLO THERE, Ms. MARY...

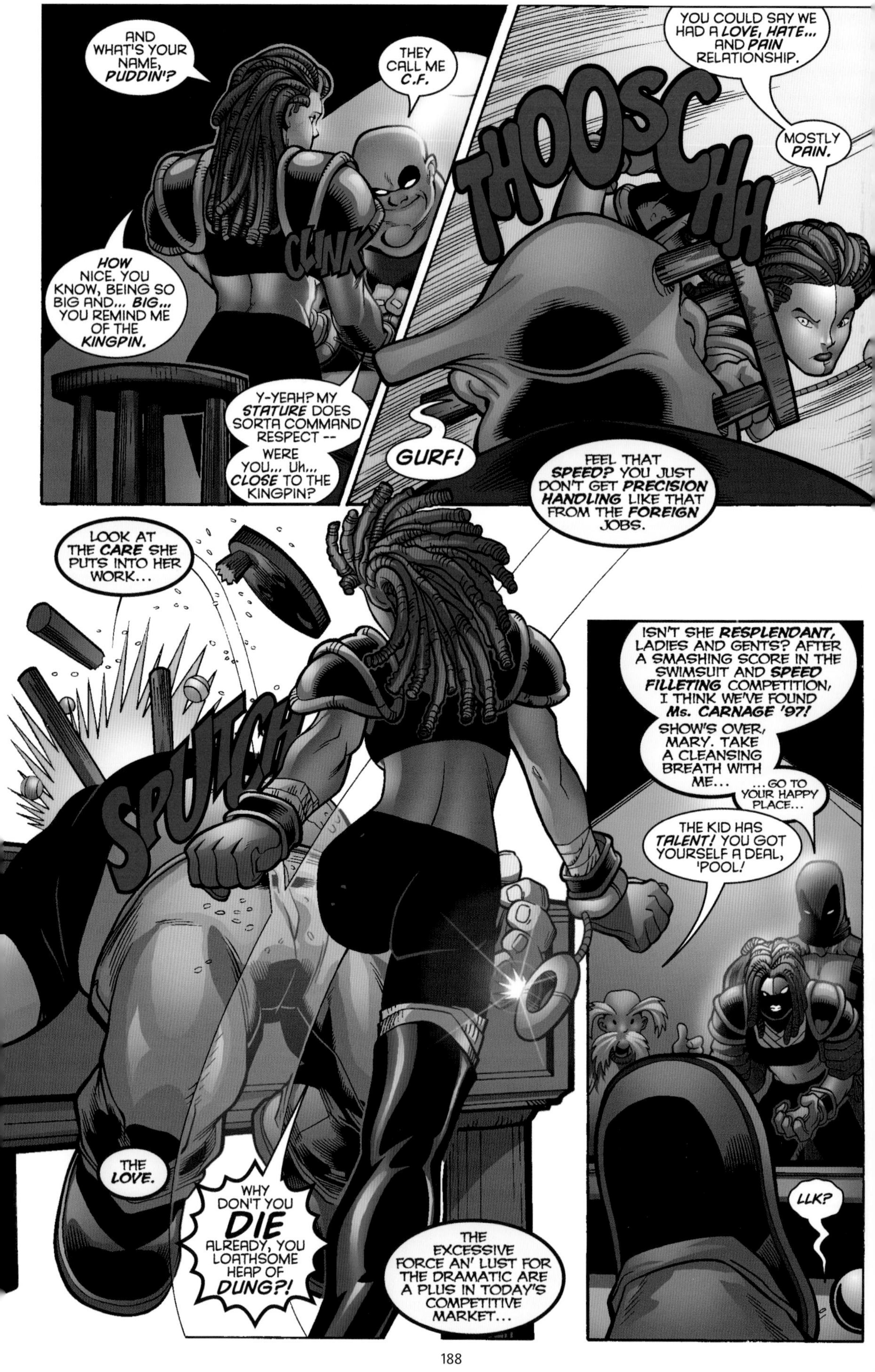
AND WHAT'S YOUR NAME, PUDDIN'?
THEY CALL ME C.F.
CLINK
HOW NICE. YOU KNOW, BEING SO BIG AND... BIG... YOU REMIND ME OF THE KINGPIN.
Y-YEAH? MY STATURE DOES SORTA COMMAND RESPECT --
WERE YOU... Uh... CLOSE TO THE KINGPIN?
YOU COULD SAY WE HAD A LOVE, HATE... AND PAIN RELATIONSHIP.
THOOSCHH
MOSTLY PAIN.
GURF!
FEEL THAT SPEED? YOU JUST DON'T GET PRECISION HANDLING LIKE THAT FROM THE FOREIGN JOBS.
LOOK AT THE CARE SHE PUTS INTO HER WORK...
SPUTCH
ISN'T SHE RESPLENDANT, LADIES AND GENTS? AFTER A SMASHING SCORE IN THE SWIMSUIT AND SPEED FILLETING COMPETITION, I THINK WE'VE FOUND Ms. CARNAGE '97!
SHOW'S OVER, MARY. TAKE A CLEANSING BREATH WITH ME...
...GO TO YOUR HAPPY PLACE...
THE KID HAS TALENT! YOU GOT YOURSELF A DEAL, 'POOL!
THE LOVE.
WHY DON'T YOU DIE ALREADY, YOU LOATHSOME HEAP OF DUNG?!
THE EXCESSIVE FORCE AN' LUST FOR THE DRAMATIC ARE A PLUS IN TODAY'S COMPETITIVE MARKET...
LLK?

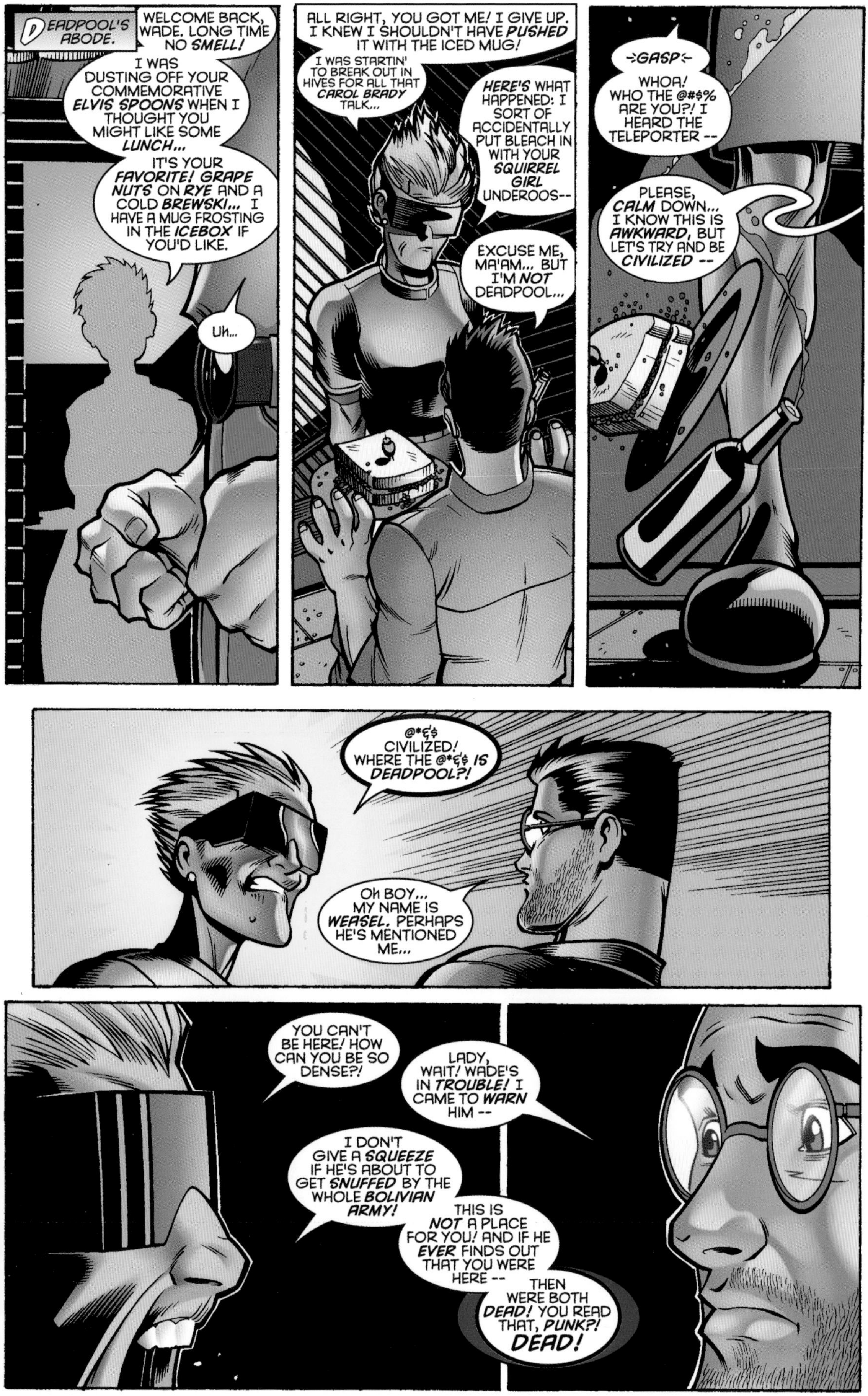
DEADPOOL'S ABODE.
WELCOME BACK, WADE. LONG TIME NO SMELL!
I WAS DUSTING OFF YOUR COMMEMORATIVE ELVIS SPOONS WHEN I THOUGHT YOU MIGHT LIKE SOME LUNCH...
IT'S YOUR FAVORITE! GRAPE NUTS ON RYE AND A COLD BREWSKI... I HAVE A MUG FROSTING IN THE ICEBOX IF YOU'D LIKE.
Uh...
ALL RIGHT, YOU GOT ME! I GIVE UP. I KNEW I SHOULDN'T HAVE PUSHED IT WITH THE ICED MUG!
I WAS STARTIN' TO BREAK OUT IN HIVES FOR ALL THAT CAROL BRADY TALK...
HERE'S WHAT HAPPENED: I SORT OF ACCIDENTALLY PUT BLEACH IN WITH YOUR SQUIRREL GIRL UNDEROOS--
EXCUSE ME, MA'AM... BUT I'M NOT DEADPOOL...
-GASP-
WHOA! WHO THE @#$% ARE YOU?! I HEARD THE TELEPORTER --
PLEASE, CALM DOWN... I KNOW THIS IS AWKWARD, BUT LET'S TRY AND BE CIVILIZED --
@*&$ CIVILIZED! WHERE THE @*&$ IS DEADPOOL?!
Oh BOY... MY NAME IS WEASEL. PERHAPS HE'S MENTIONED ME...
YOU CAN'T BE HERE! HOW CAN YOU BE SO DENSE?!
LADY, WAIT! WADE'S IN TROUBLE! I CAME TO WARN HIM --
I DON'T GIVE A SQUEEZE IF HE'S ABOUT TO GET SNUFFED BY THE WHOLE BOLIVIAN ARMY!
THIS IS NOT A PLACE FOR YOU! AND IF HE EVER FINDS OUT THAT YOU WERE HERE --
THEN WERE BOTH DEAD! YOU READ THAT, PUNK?! DEAD!

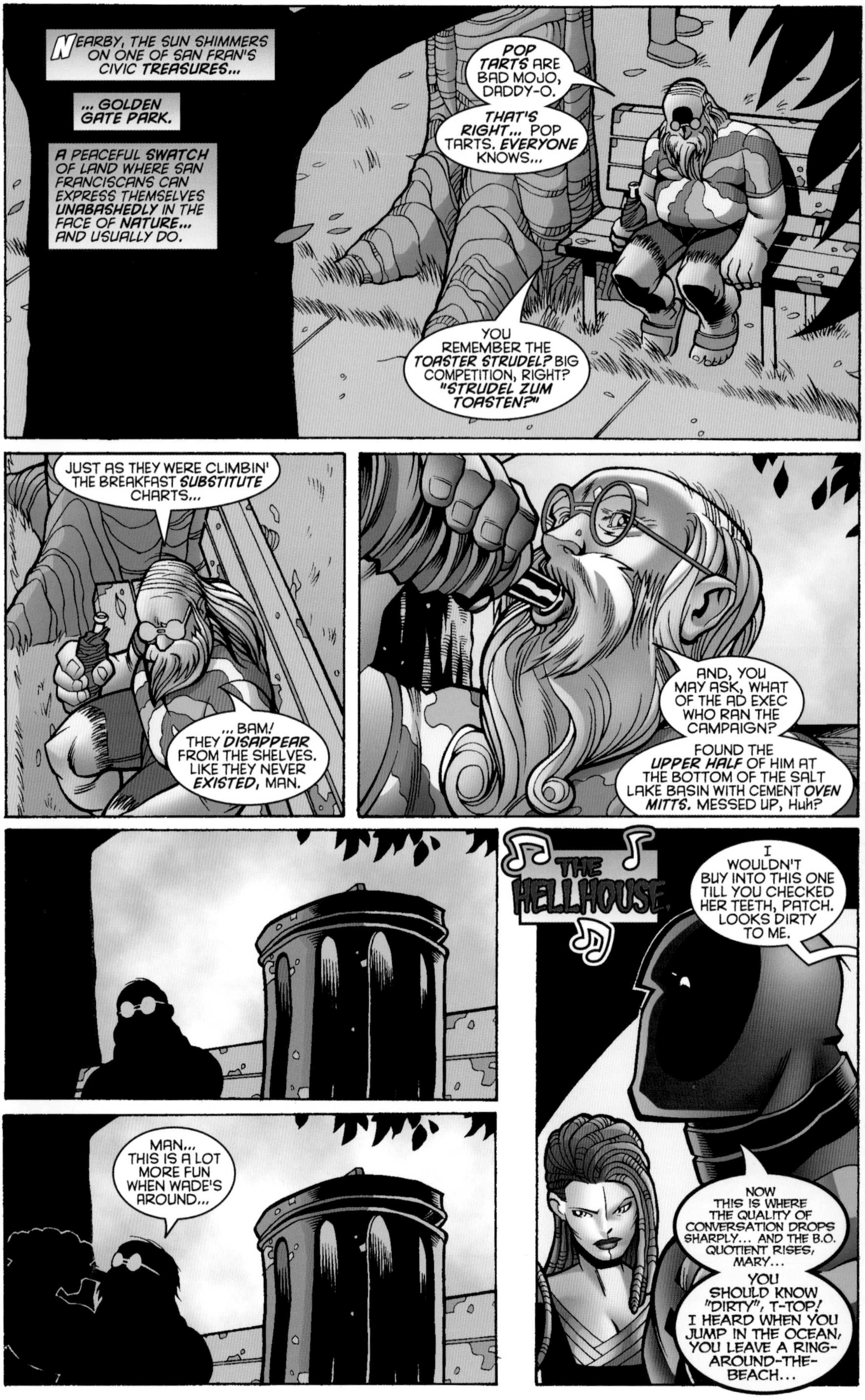
NEARBY, THE SUN SHIMMERS ON ONE OF SAN FRAN'S CIVIC TREASURES...
... GOLDEN GATE PARK.
A PEACEFUL SWATCH OF LAND WHERE SAN FRANCISCANS CAN EXPRESS THEMSELVES UNABASHEDLY IN THE FACE OF NATURE... AND USUALLY DO.
POP TARTS ARE BAD MOJO, DADDY-O.
THAT'S RIGHT... POP TARTS. EVERYONE KNOWS...
YOU REMEMBER THE TOASTER STRUDEL? BIG COMPETITION, RIGHT? "STRUDEL ZUM TOASTEN?"
JUST AS THEY WERE CLIMBIN' THE BREAKFAST SUBSTITUTE CHARTS...
... BAM! THEY DISAPPEAR FROM THE SHELVES. LIKE THEY NEVER EXISTED, MAN.
AND, YOU MAY ASK, WHAT OF THE AD EXEC WHO RAN THE CAMPAIGN?
FOUND THE UPPER HALF OF HIM AT THE BOTTOM OF THE SALT LAKE BASIN WITH CEMENT OVEN MITTS. MESSED UP, Huh?
MAN... THIS IS A LOT MORE FUN WHEN WADE'S AROUND...
THE HELLHOUSE
I WOULDN'T BUY INTO THIS ONE TILL YOU CHECKED HER TEETH, PATCH. LOOKS DIRTY TO ME.
NOW THIS IS WHERE THE QUALITY OF CONVERSATION DROPS SHARPLY... AND THE B.O. QUOTIENT RISES, MARY...
YOU SHOULD KNOW "DIRTY", T-TOP! I HEARD WHEN YOU JUMP IN THE OCEAN, YOU LEAVE A RING-AROUND-THE-BEACH...

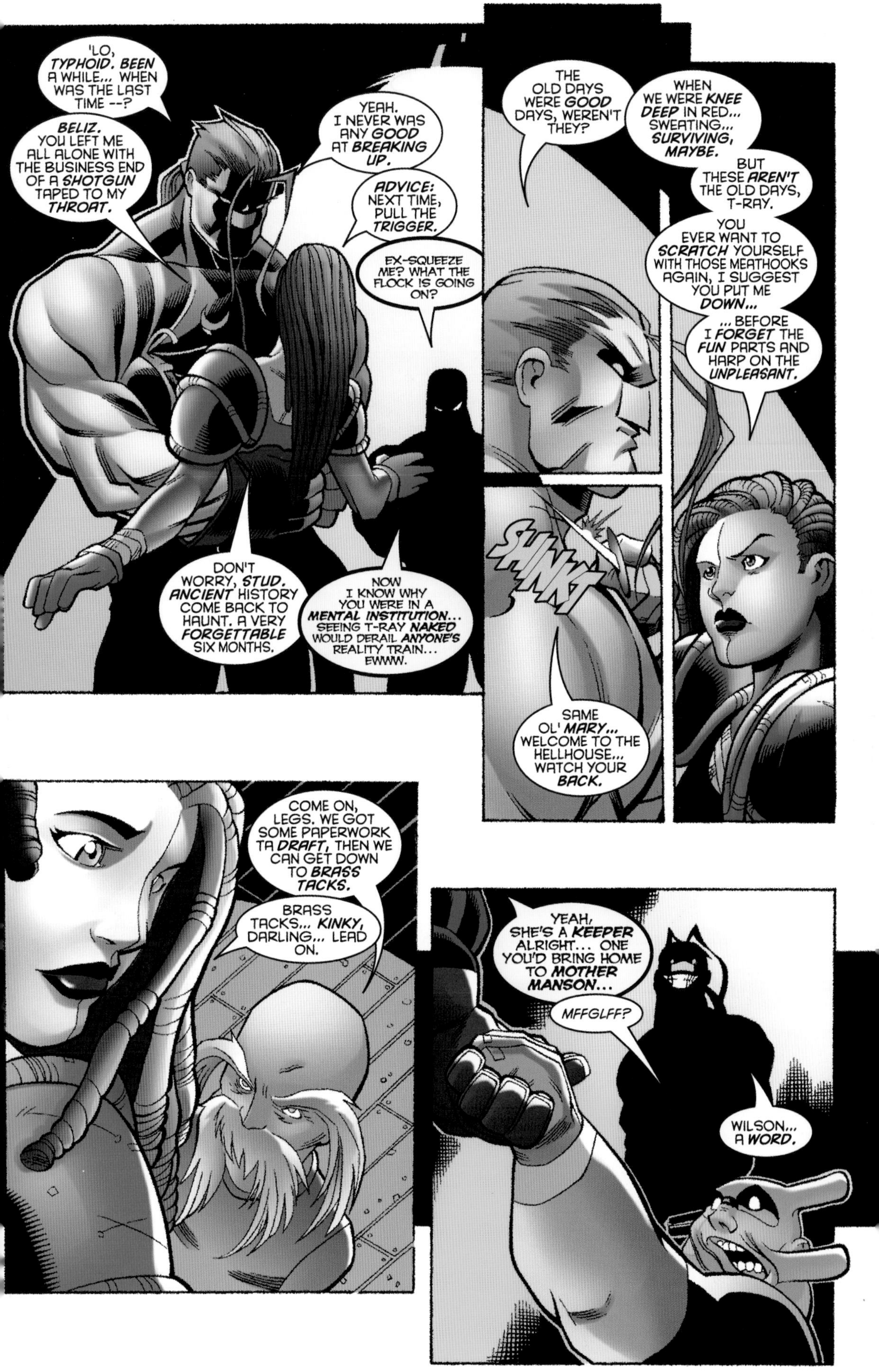
'LO, TYPHOID. BEEN A WHILE... WHEN WAS THE LAST TIME --?
BELIZ. YOU LEFT ME ALL ALONE WITH THE BUSINESS END OF A SHOTGUN TAPED TO MY THROAT.
YEAH. I NEVER WAS ANY GOOD AT BREAKING UP.
ADVICE: NEXT TIME, PULL THE TRIGGER.
EX-SQUEEZE ME? WHAT THE FLOCK IS GOING ON?
DON'T WORRY, STUD. ANCIENT HISTORY COME BACK TO HAUNT. A VERY FORGETTABLE SIX MONTHS.
NOW I KNOW WHY YOU WERE IN A MENTAL INSTITUTION... SEEING T-RAY NAKED WOULD DERAIL ANYONE'S REALITY TRAIN... EWWW.
THE OLD DAYS WERE GOOD DAYS, WEREN'T THEY?
WHEN WE WERE KNEE DEEP IN RED... SWEATING... SURVIVING, MAYBE.
BUT THESE AREN'T THE OLD DAYS, T-RAY.
YOU EVER WANT TO SCRATCH YOURSELF WITH THOSE MEATHOOKS AGAIN, I SUGGEST YOU PUT ME DOWN...
... BEFORE I FORGET THE FUN PARTS AND HARP ON THE UNPLEASANT.
SHINKT
SAME OL' MARY... WELCOME TO THE HELLHOUSE... WATCH YOUR BACK.
COME ON, LEGS. WE GOT SOME PAPERWORK TA DRAFT, THEN WE CAN GET DOWN TO BRASS TACKS.
BRASS TACKS... KINKY, DARLING... LEAD ON.
YEAH, SHE'S A KEEPER ALRIGHT... ONE YOU'D BRING HOME TO MOTHER MANSON...
MFFGLFF?
WILSON... A WORD.

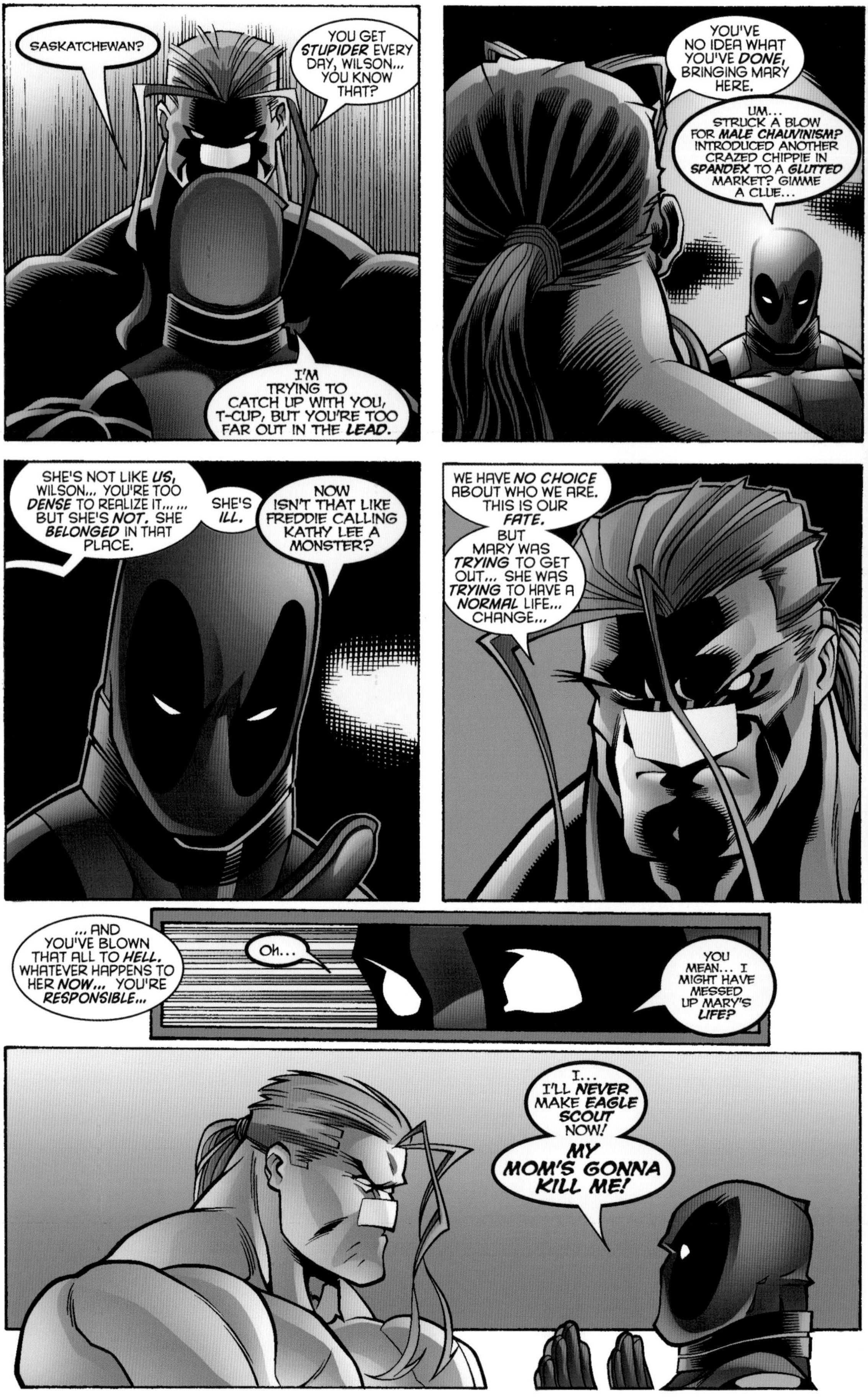
SASKATCHEWAN?
YOU GET STUPIDER EVERY DAY, WILSON... YOU KNOW THAT?
I'M TRYING TO CATCH UP WITH YOU, T-CUP, BUT YOU'RE TOO FAR OUT IN THE LEAD.
YOU'VE NO IDEA WHAT YOU'VE DONE, BRINGING MARY HERE.
UM... STRUCK A BLOW FOR MALE CHAUVINISM? INTRODUCED ANOTHER CRAZED CHIPPIE IN SPANDEX TO A GLUTTED MARKET? GIMME A CLUE...
SHE'S NOT LIKE US, WILSON... YOU'RE TOO DENSE TO REALIZE IT... ... BUT SHE'S NOT. SHE BELONGED IN THAT PLACE.
SHE'S ILL.
NOW ISN'T THAT LIKE FREDDIE CALLING KATHY LEE A MONSTER?
WE HAVE NO CHOICE ABOUT WHO WE ARE. THIS IS OUR FATE.
BUT MARY WAS TRYING TO GET OUT... SHE WAS TRYING TO HAVE A NORMAL LIFE... CHANGE...
... AND YOU'VE BLOWN THAT ALL TO HELL. WHATEVER HAPPENS TO HER NOW... YOU'RE RESPONSIBLE...
Oh...
YOU MEAN... I MIGHT HAVE MESSED UP MARY'S LIFE?
I... I'LL NEVER MAKE EAGLE SCOUT NOW!
MY MOM'S GONNA KILL ME!

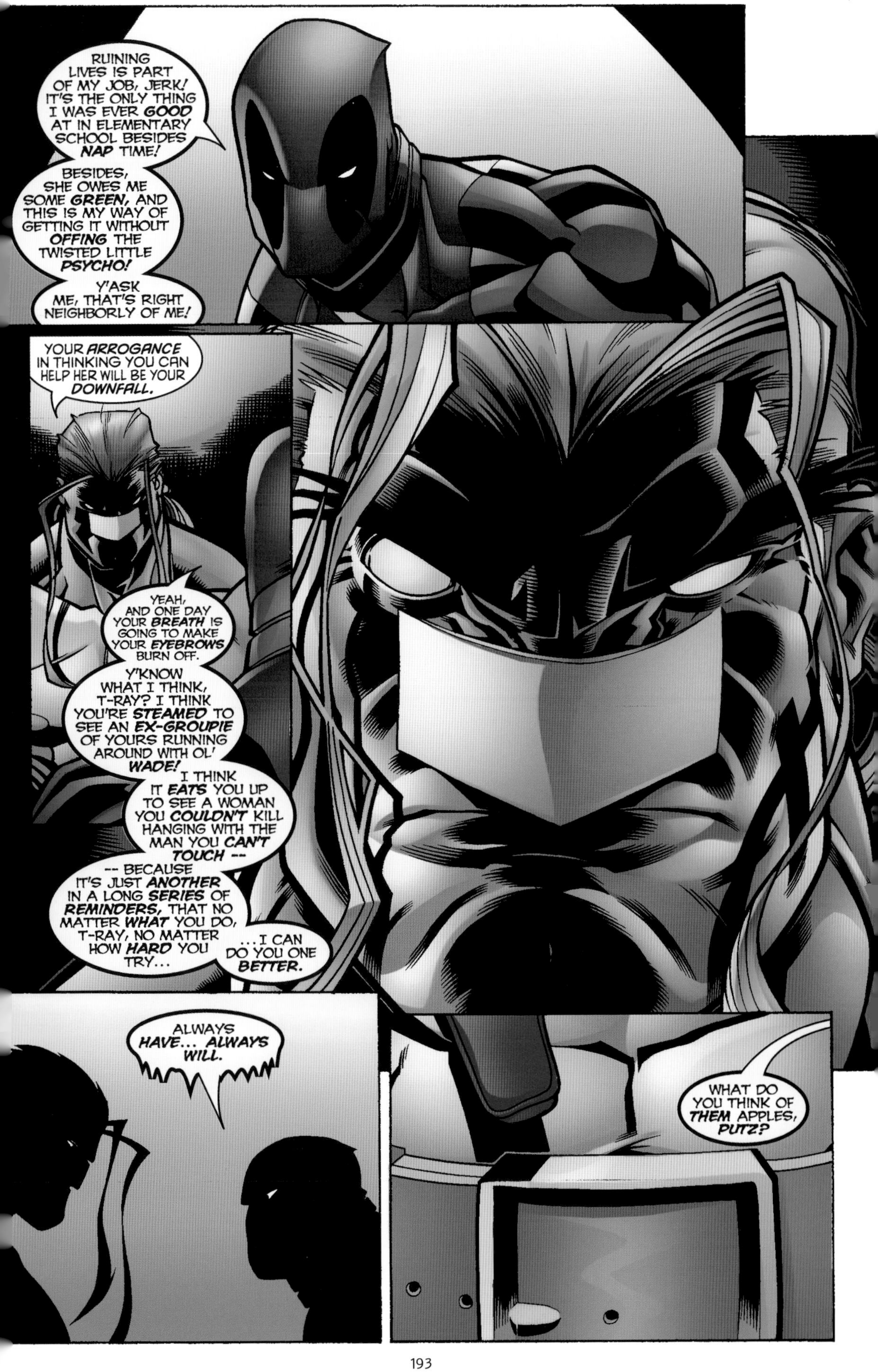
RUINING LIVES IS PART OF MY JOB, JERK! IT'S THE ONLY THING I WAS EVER GOOD AT IN ELEMENTARY SCHOOL BESIDES NAP TIME!
BESIDES, SHE OWES ME SOME GREEN, AND THIS IS MY WAY OF GETTING IT WITHOUT OFFING THE TWISTED LITTLE PSYCHO!
Y'ASK ME, THAT'S RIGHT NEIGHBORLY OF ME!
YOUR ARROGANCE IN THINKING YOU CAN HELP HER WILL BE YOUR DOWNFALL.
YEAH, AND ONE DAY YOUR BREATH IS GOING TO MAKE YOUR EYEBROWS BURN OFF.
Y'KNOW WHAT I THINK, T-RAY? I THINK YOU'RE STEAMED TO SEE AN EX-GROUPIE OF YOURS RUNNING AROUND WITH OL' WADE!
I THINK IT EATS YOU UP TO SEE A WOMAN YOU COULDN'T KILL HANGING WITH THE MAN YOU CAN'T TOUCH --
-- BECAUSE IT'S JUST ANOTHER IN A LONG SERIES OF REMINDERS, THAT NO MATTER WHAT YOU DO, T-RAY, NO MATTER HOW HARD YOU TRY...
...I CAN DO YOU ONE BETTER.
ALWAYS HAVE... ALWAYS WILL.
WHAT DO YOU THINK OF THEM APPLES, PUTZ?

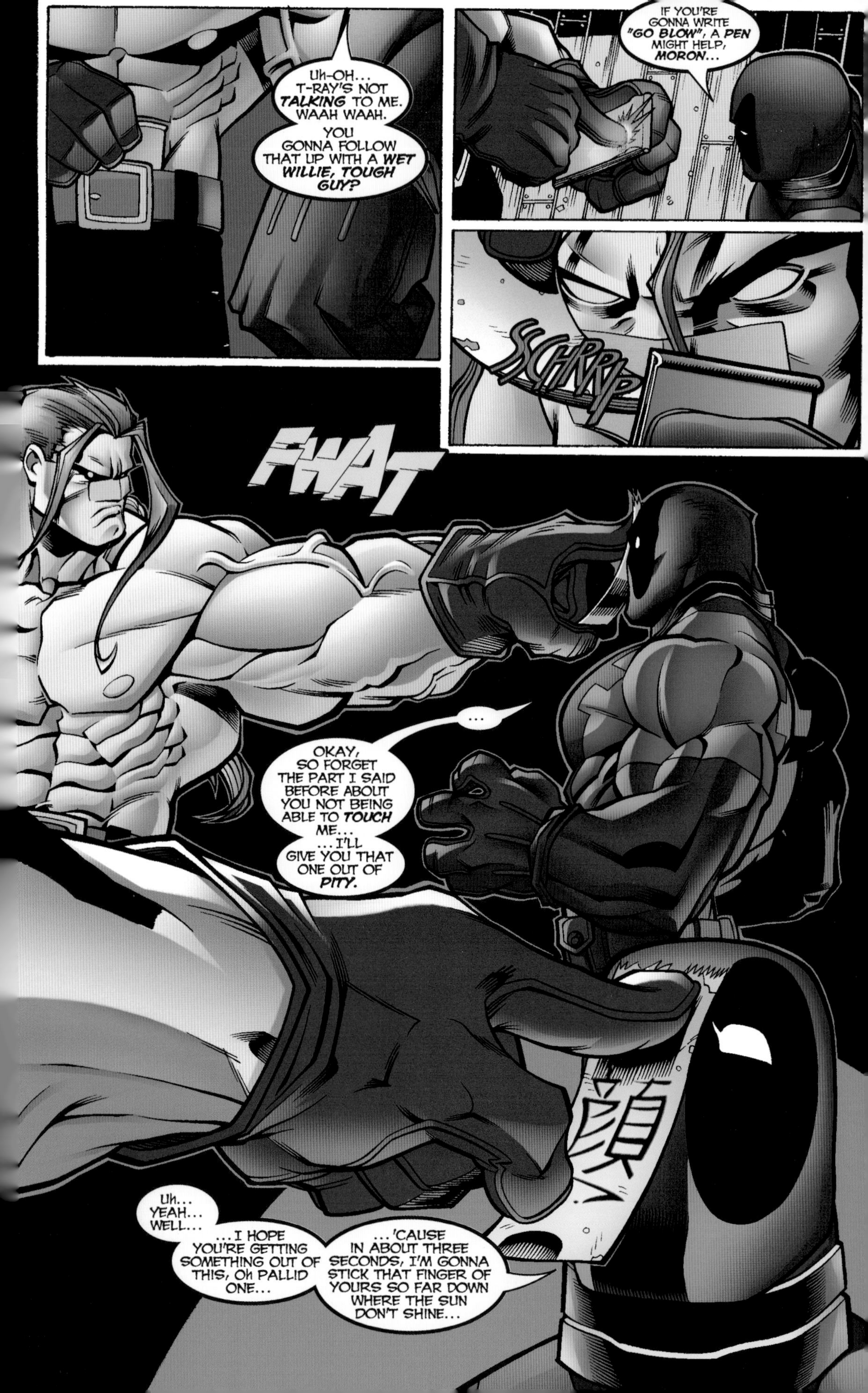
Uh-OH... T-RAY'S NOT TALKING TO ME. WAAH WAAH.
YOU GONNA FOLLOW THAT UP WITH A WET WILLIE, TOUGH GUY?
IF YOU'RE GONNA WRITE "GO BLOW", A PEN MIGHT HELP, MORON...
SCHRRIP
FWAT
...
OKAY, SO FORGET THE PART I SAID BEFORE ABOUT YOU NOT BEING ABLE TO TOUCH ME...
...I'LL GIVE YOU THAT ONE OUT OF PITY.
Uh... YEAH... WELL...
...I HOPE YOU'RE GETTING SOMETHING OUT OF THIS, Oh PALLID ONE...
...'CAUSE IN ABOUT THREE SECONDS, I'M GONNA STICK THAT FINGER OF YOURS SO FAR DOWN WHERE THE SUN DON'T SHINE...

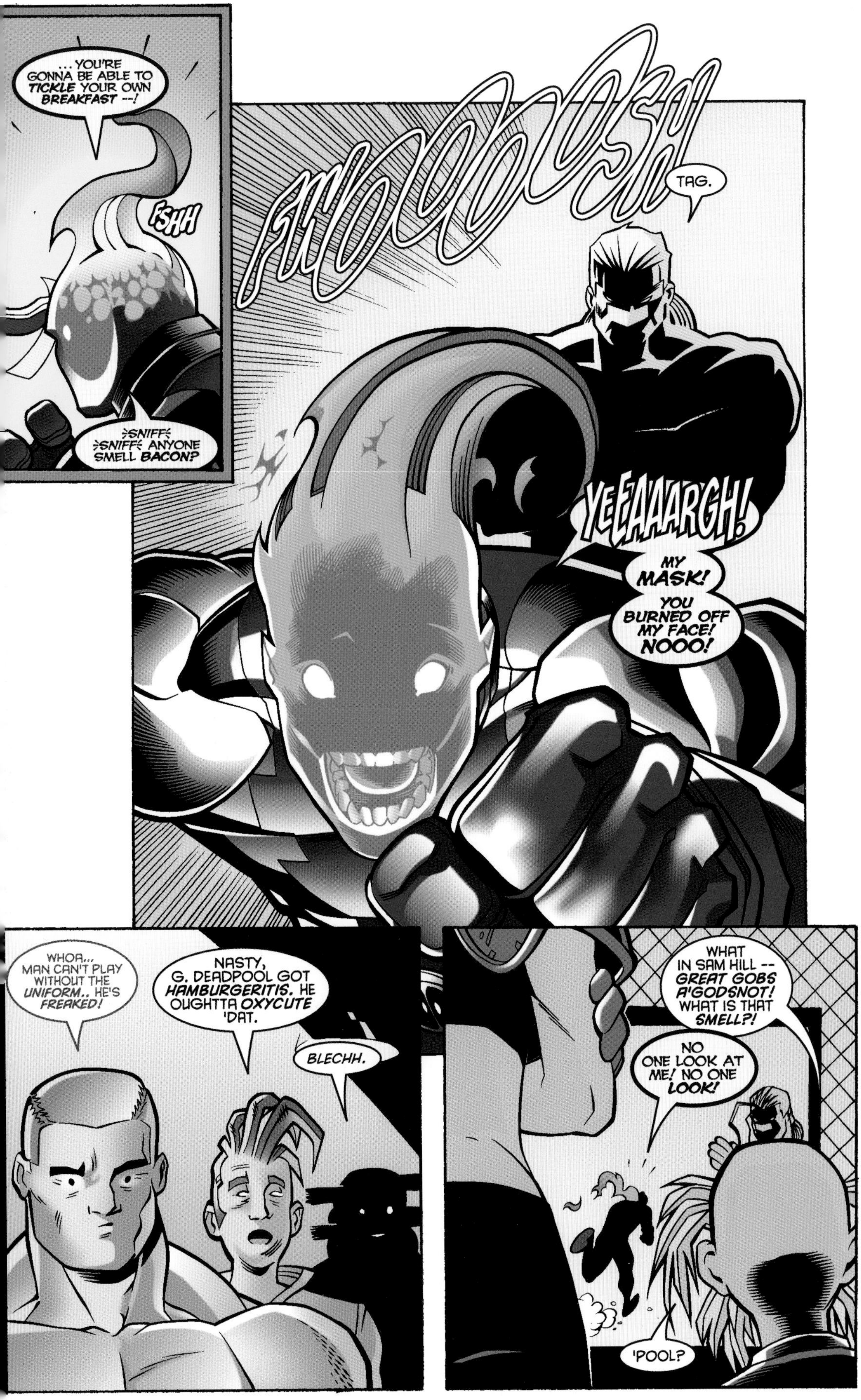
...YOU'RE GONNA BE ABLE TO TICKLE YOUR OWN BREAKFAST --!
FSHH
SNIFF SNIFF ANYONE SMELL BACON?
TAG.
YEEAAARGH!
MY MASK! YOU BURNED OFF MY FACE! NOOO!
WHOA... MAN CAN'T PLAY WITHOUT THE UNIFORM.. HE'S FREAKED!
NASTY, G. DEADPOOL GOT HAMBURGERITIS. HE OUGHTTA OXYCUTE 'DAT.
BLECHH.
WHAT IN SAM HILL -- GREAT GOBS A'GODSNOT! WHAT IS THAT SMELL?!
NO ONE LOOK AT ME! NO ONE LOOK!
'POOL?

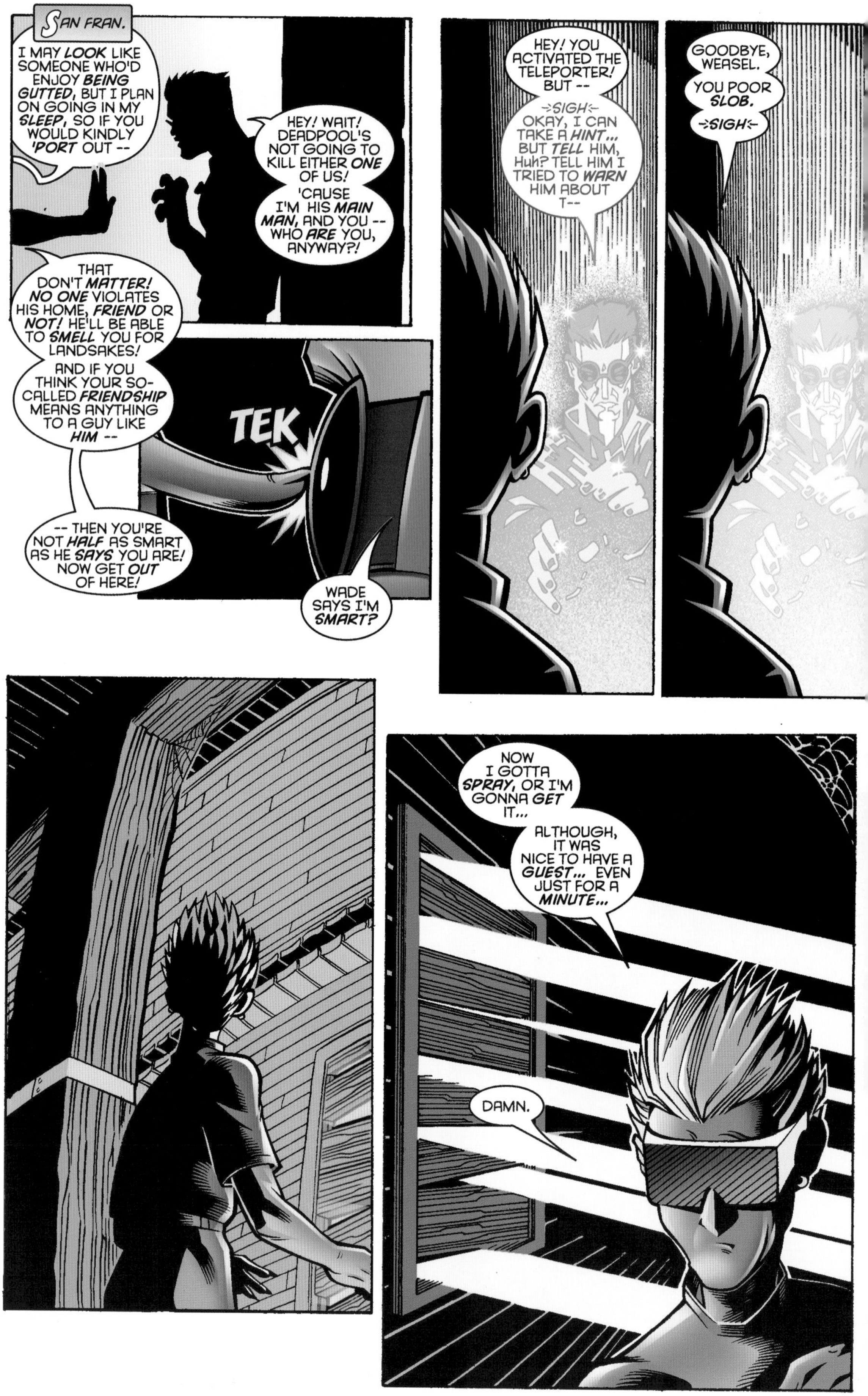
SAN FRAN.
I MAY LOOK LIKE SOMEONE WHO'D ENJOY BEING GUTTED, BUT I PLAN ON GOING IN MY SLEEP, SO IF YOU WOULD KINDLY 'PORT OUT --
HEY! WAIT! DEADPOOL'S NOT GOING TO KILL EITHER ONE OF US!
'CAUSE I'M HIS MAIN MAN, AND YOU -- WHO ARE YOU, ANYWAY?!
THAT DON'T MATTER! NO ONE VIOLATES HIS HOME, FRIEND OR NOT! HE'LL BE ABLE TO SMELL YOU FOR LANDSAKES!
AND IF YOU THINK YOUR SO-CALLED FRIENDSHIP MEANS ANYTHING TO A GUY LIKE HIM --
TEK
-- THEN YOU'RE NOT HALF AS SMART AS HE SAYS YOU ARE! NOW GET OUT OF HERE!
WADE SAYS I'M SMART?
HEY! YOU ACTIVATED THE TELEPORTER! BUT --
SIGH
OKAY, I CAN TAKE A HINT... BUT TELL HIM, Huh? TELL HIM I TRIED TO WARN HIM ABOUT T--
GOODBYE, WEASEL.
YOU POOR SLOB.
SIGH
NOW I GOTTA SPRAY, OR I'M GONNA GET IT...
ALTHOUGH, IT WAS NICE TO HAVE A GUEST... EVEN JUST FOR A MINUTE...
DAMN.

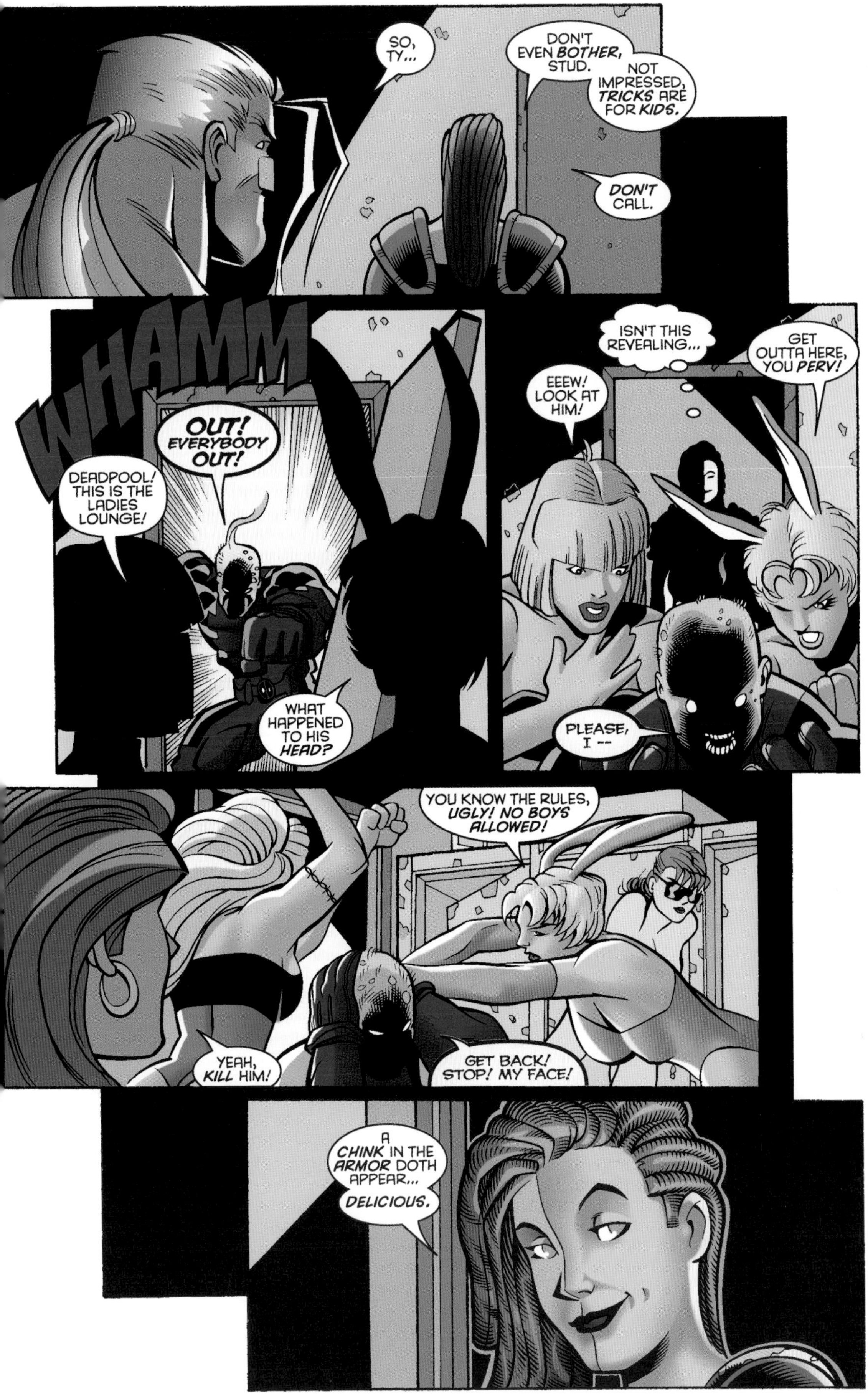
SO, TY...
DON'T EVEN BOTHER, STUD.
NOT IMPRESSED, TRICKS ARE FOR KIDS.
DON'T CALL.
WHAMM
OUT! EVERYBODY OUT!
DEADPOOL! THIS IS THE LADIES LOUNGE!
WHAT HAPPENED TO HIS HEAD?
ISN'T THIS REVEALING...
GET OUTTA HERE, YOU PERV!
EEEW! LOOK AT HIM!
PLEASE, I --
YOU KNOW THE RULES, UGLY! NO BOYS ALLOWED!
YEAH, KILL HIM!
GET BACK! STOP! MY FACE!
A CHINK IN THE ARMOR DOTH APPEAR... DELICIOUS.

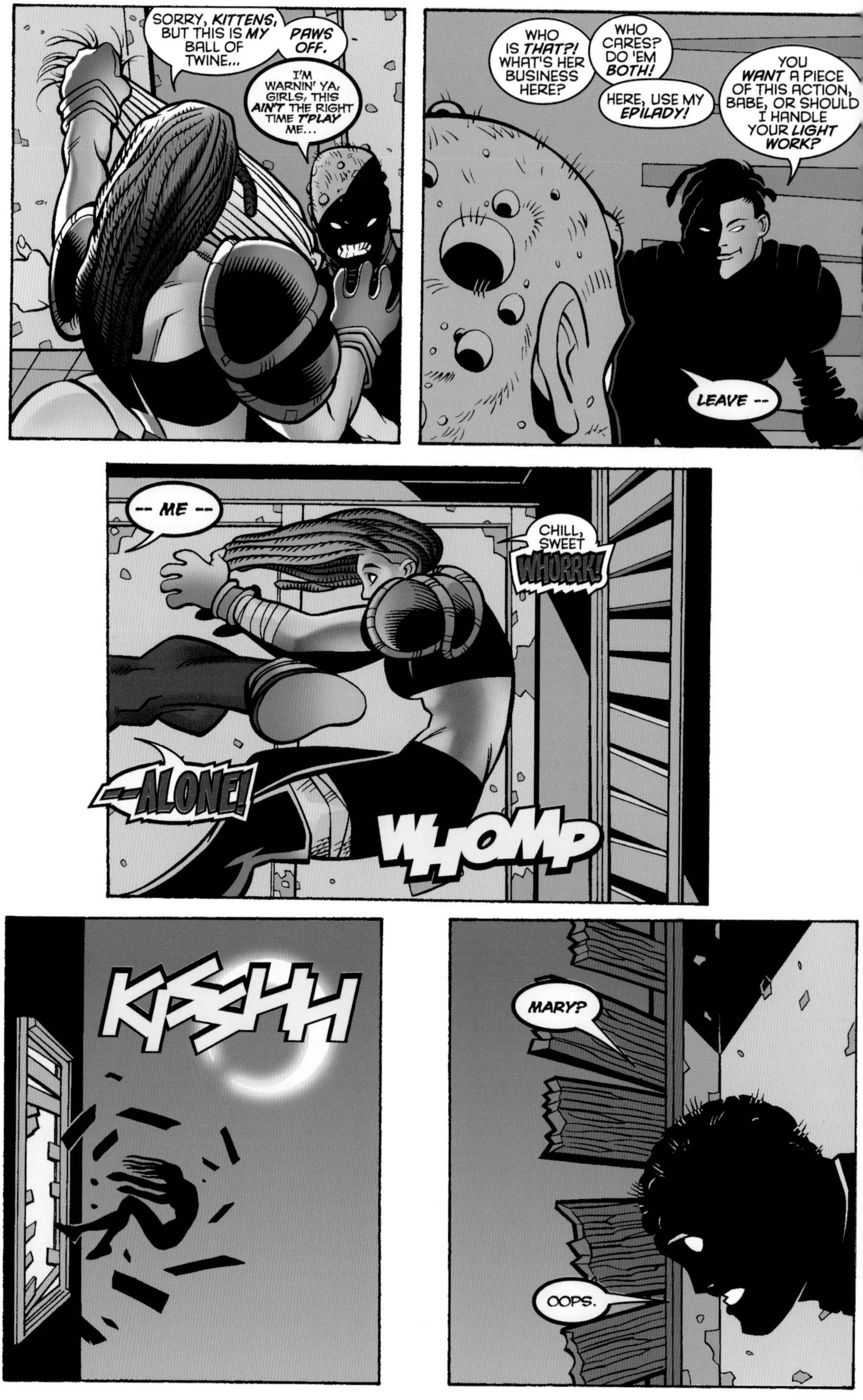

SORRY, KITTENS, BUT THIS IS MY BALL OF TWINE...
PAWS OFF.
I'M WARNIN' YA, GIRLS, THIS AIN'T THE RIGHT TIME T'PLAY ME...
WHO IS THAT?! WHAT'S HER BUSINESS HERE?
WHO CARES? DO 'EM BOTH!
HERE, USE MY EPILADY!
YOU WANT A PIECE OF THIS ACTION, BABE, OR SHOULD I HANDLE YOUR LIGHT WORK?
LEAVE --
-- ME --
CHILL, SWEET
WHORRK!
--ALONE!
WHOMP
KRSHH
MARY?
OOPS.

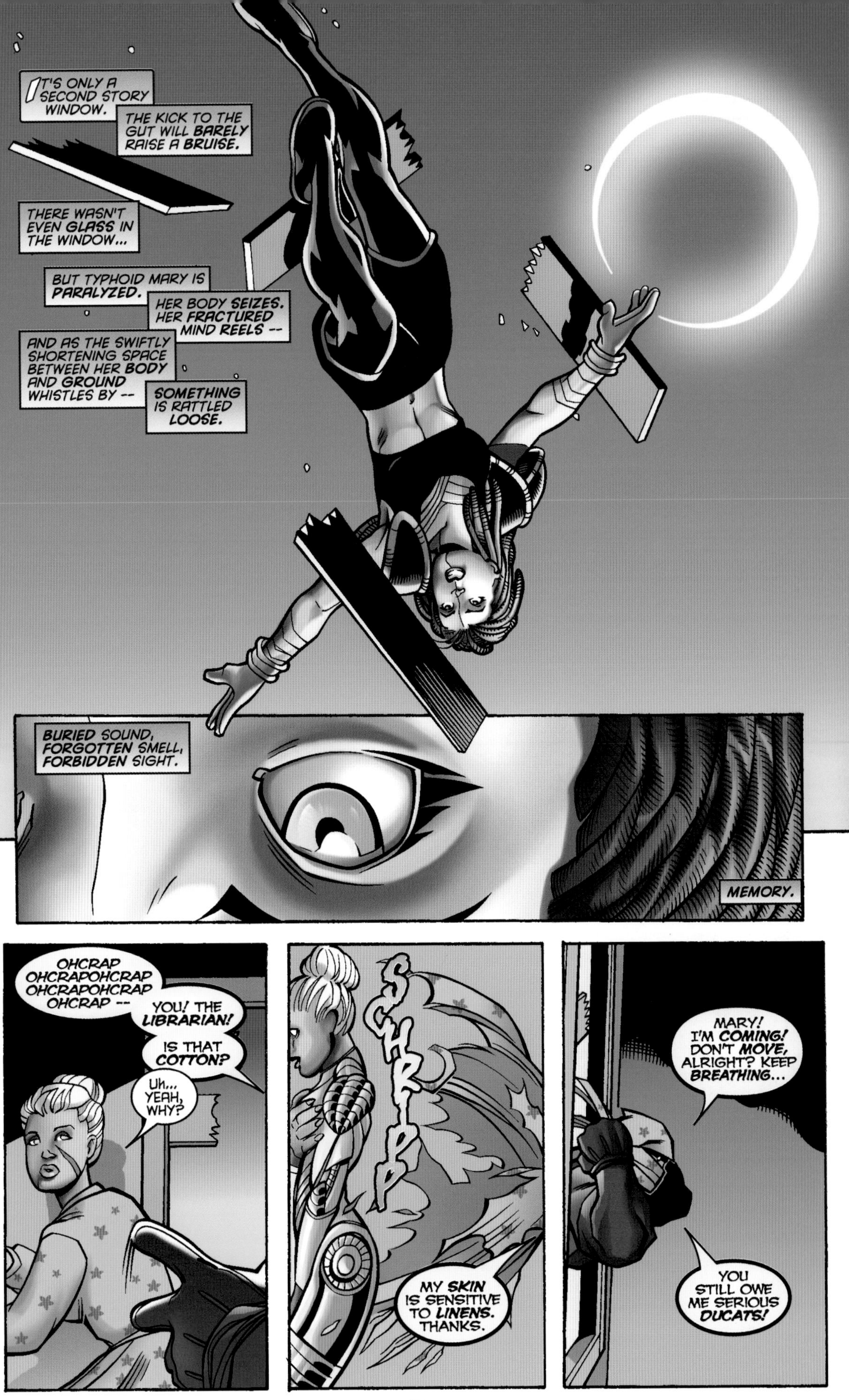
IT'S ONLY A SECOND STORY WINDOW.
THE KICK TO THE GUT WILL BARELY RAISE A BRUISE.
THERE WASN'T EVEN GLASS IN THE WINDOW...
BUT TYPHOID MARY IS PARALYZED.
HER BODY SEIZES. HER FRACTURED MIND REELS --
AND AS THE SWIFTLY SHORTENING SPACE BETWEEN HER BODY AND GROUND WHISTLES BY --
SOMETHING IS RATTLED LOOSE.
BURIED SOUND, FORGOTTEN SMELL, FORBIDDEN SIGHT.
MEMORY.
OHCRAP OHCRAPOHCRAP OHCRAPOHCRAP OHCRAP --
YOU! THE LIBRARIAN!
IS THAT COTTON?
Uh... YEAH, WHY?
SCHRIP
MY SKIN IS SENSITIVE TO LINENS. THANKS.
MARY! I'M COMING! DON'T MOVE, ALRIGHT? KEEP BREATHING...
YOU STILL OWE ME SERIOUS DUCATS!

FRIKKIN-FRAKKIN RASSUM-FRASSUM DING-DANG HORNGNOBBIT!

IF I TOLD YOU *ONCE*, T-RAY, I TOLD YA *FIFTEEN* TIMES, NO *SCRAPPIN'* IN THE HELLHOUSE!

YOU PUSHED IT *TOO* FAR THIS TIME! YOU'RE *OUTTA* HERE! ONE *MONTH* PROBATION! *NO JOBS!*

I'M SORRY, PATCH...

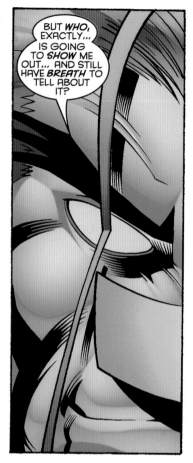

BUT *WHO*, EXACTLY... IS GOING TO *SHOW* ME OUT... AND STILL HAVE *BREATH* TO TELL ABOUT IT?

WHY YOU BELIGERENT, BACKWATER *PUNK*... YOU *CHALLENGIN'* ME IN MY OWN PLACE, BOY?

FINE.

THERE'S *TEN LARGE* FER THE FIRST *MOOK* T'BOUNCE THIS *TRASH* T'THE *CURB!*

AN EXTRA *THREE* IF YOU CAN DO IT WIT'OUT SCRATCHIN' UP THE NEW *FLOOR.*

WHICH ONE OF YOU *NASTY BOYS'RE* LOOKIN' FOR A *BONUS* THIS MONTH?

WELL?

WELL?

OUTSIDE...

IT WAS AN *ACCIDENT,* KID, HONEST... 'CAUSE *TRUST* ME, IF I'D *MEANT* TO KNOCK YOU OUT A WINDOW, YOU *WOULDN'T* BE GETTING UP.

AW GEEZ... LOOK AT YOU THERE, WITH YOUR *COOL SHOULDER PADS* ALL *LOPSIDED...*

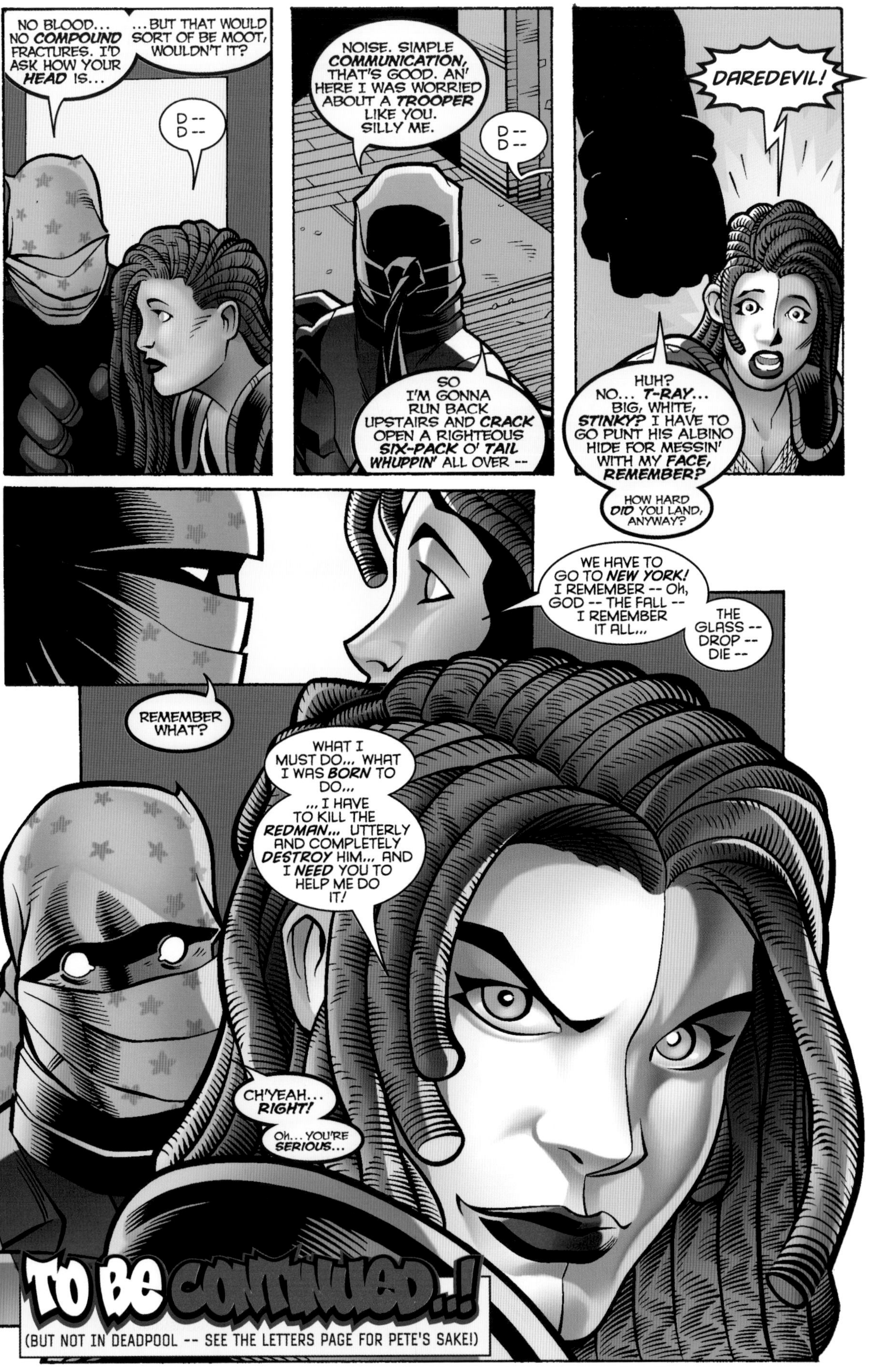
NO BLOOD... NO COMPOUND FRACTURES. I'D ASK HOW YOUR HEAD IS...
...BUT THAT WOULD SORT OF BE MOOT, WOULDN'T IT?
D -- D --
NOISE. SIMPLE COMMUNICATION, THAT'S GOOD. AN' HERE I WAS WORRIED ABOUT A TROOPER LIKE YOU. SILLY ME.
D -- D --
SO I'M GONNA RUN BACK UPSTAIRS AND CRACK OPEN A RIGHTEOUS SIX-PACK O' TAIL WHUPPIN' ALL OVER --
DAREDEVIL!
HUH? NO... T-RAY... BIG, WHITE, STINKY? I HAVE TO GO PUNT HIS ALBINO HIDE FOR MESSIN' WITH MY FACE, REMEMBER?
HOW HARD DID YOU LAND, ANYWAY?
WE HAVE TO GO TO NEW YORK! I REMEMBER -- Oh, GOD -- THE FALL -- I REMEMBER IT ALL...
THE GLASS -- DROP -- DIE --
REMEMBER WHAT?
WHAT I MUST DO... WHAT I WAS BORN TO DO...
... I HAVE TO KILL THE REDMAN... UTTERLY AND COMPLETELY DESTROY HIM... AND I NEED YOU TO HELP ME DO IT!
CH'YEAH... RIGHT!
Oh... YOU'RE SERIOUS...
TO BE CONTINUED..!
(BUT NOT IN DEADPOOL -- SEE THE LETTERS PAGE FOR PETE'S SAKE!)

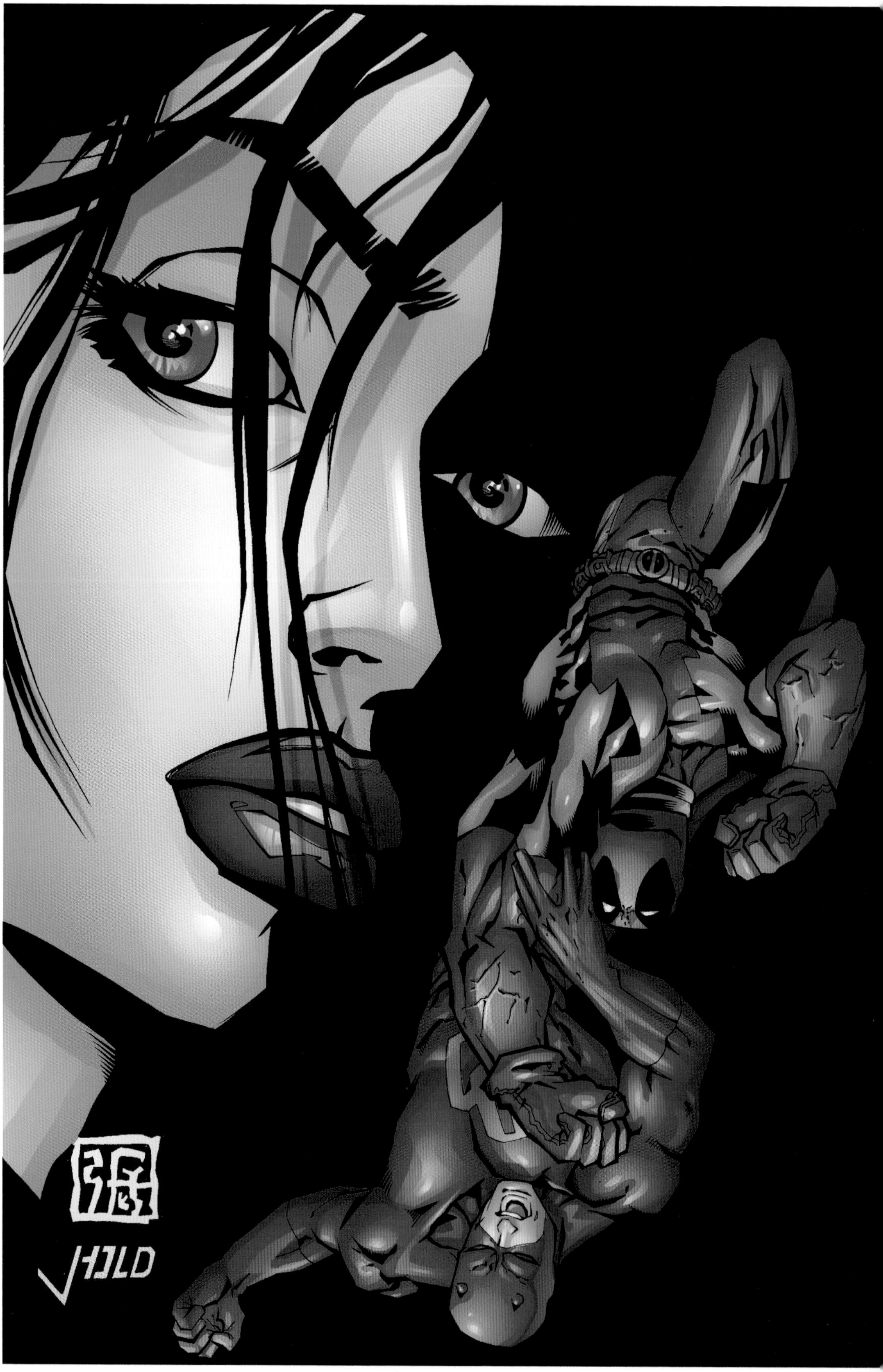

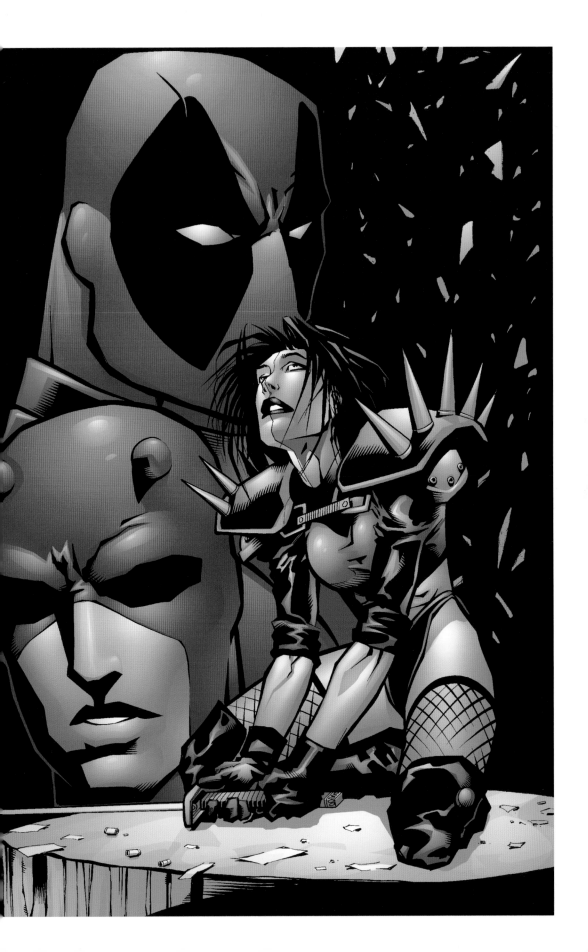

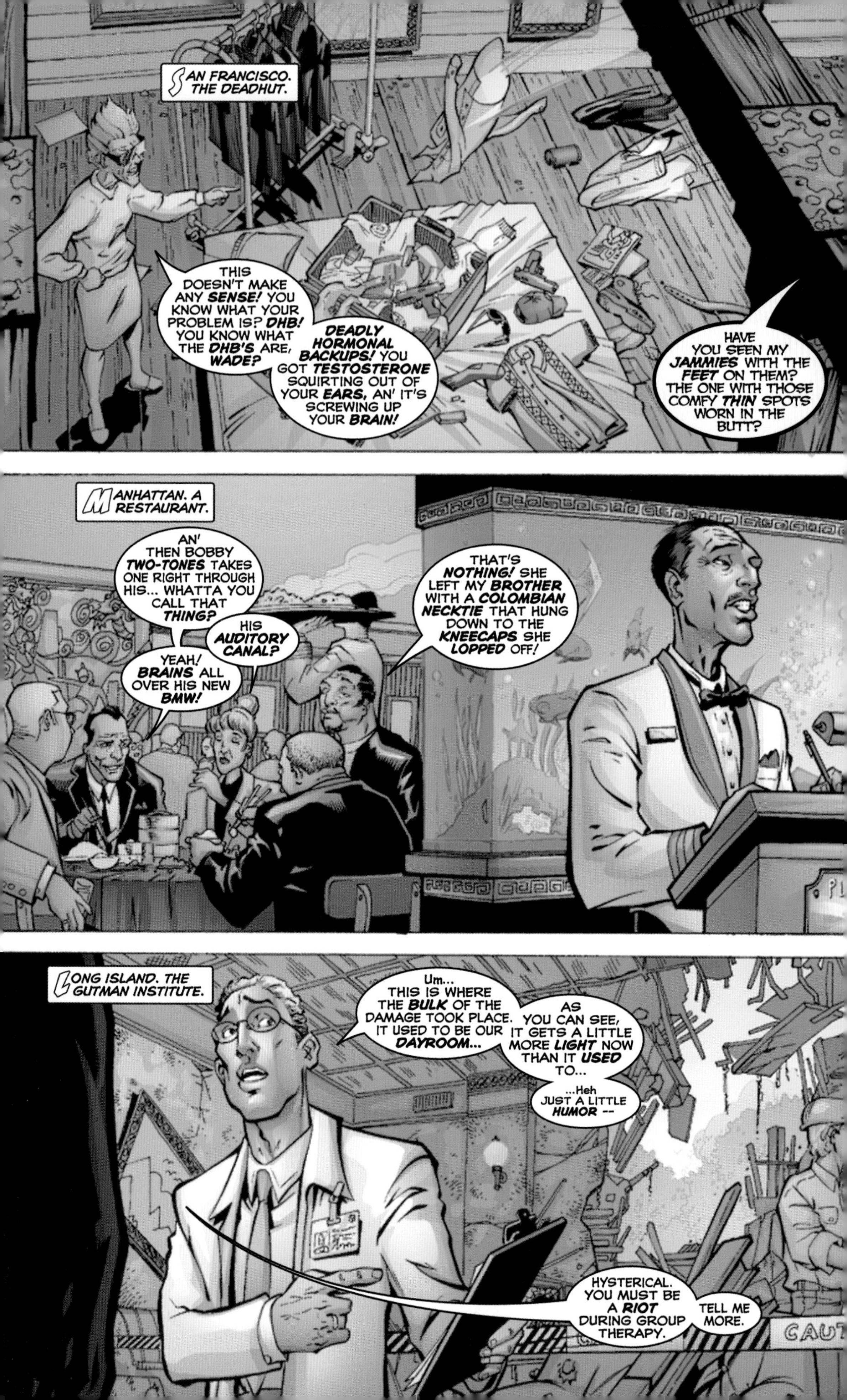
SAN FRANCISCO. THE DEADHUT.
THIS DOESN'T MAKE ANY SENSE! YOU KNOW WHAT YOUR PROBLEM IS? DHB! YOU KNOW WHAT THE DHB'S ARE, WADE?
DEADLY HORMONAL BACKUPS! YOU GOT TESTOSTERONE SQUIRTING OUT OF YOUR EARS, AN' IT'S SCREWING UP YOUR BRAIN!
HAVE YOU SEEN MY JAMMIES WITH THE FEET ON THEM? THE ONE WITH THOSE COMFY THIN SPOTS WORN IN THE BUTT?
MANHATTAN. A RESTAURANT.
AN' THEN BOBBY TWO-TONES TAKES ONE RIGHT THROUGH HIS... WHATTA YOU CALL THAT THING?
HIS AUDITORY CANAL?
YEAH! BRAINS ALL OVER HIS NEW BMW!
THAT'S NOTHING! SHE LEFT MY BROTHER WITH A COLOMBIAN NECKTIE THAT HUNG DOWN TO THE KNEECAPS SHE LOPPED OFF!
LONG ISLAND. THE GUTMAN INSTITUTE.
Um... THIS IS WHERE THE BULK OF THE DAMAGE TOOK PLACE. IT USED TO BE OUR DAYROOM...
AS YOU CAN SEE, IT GETS A LITTLE MORE LIGHT NOW THAN IT USED TO...
...Heh JUST A LITTLE HUMOR --
HYSTERICAL. YOU MUST BE A RIOT DURING GROUP THERAPY.
TELL ME MORE.

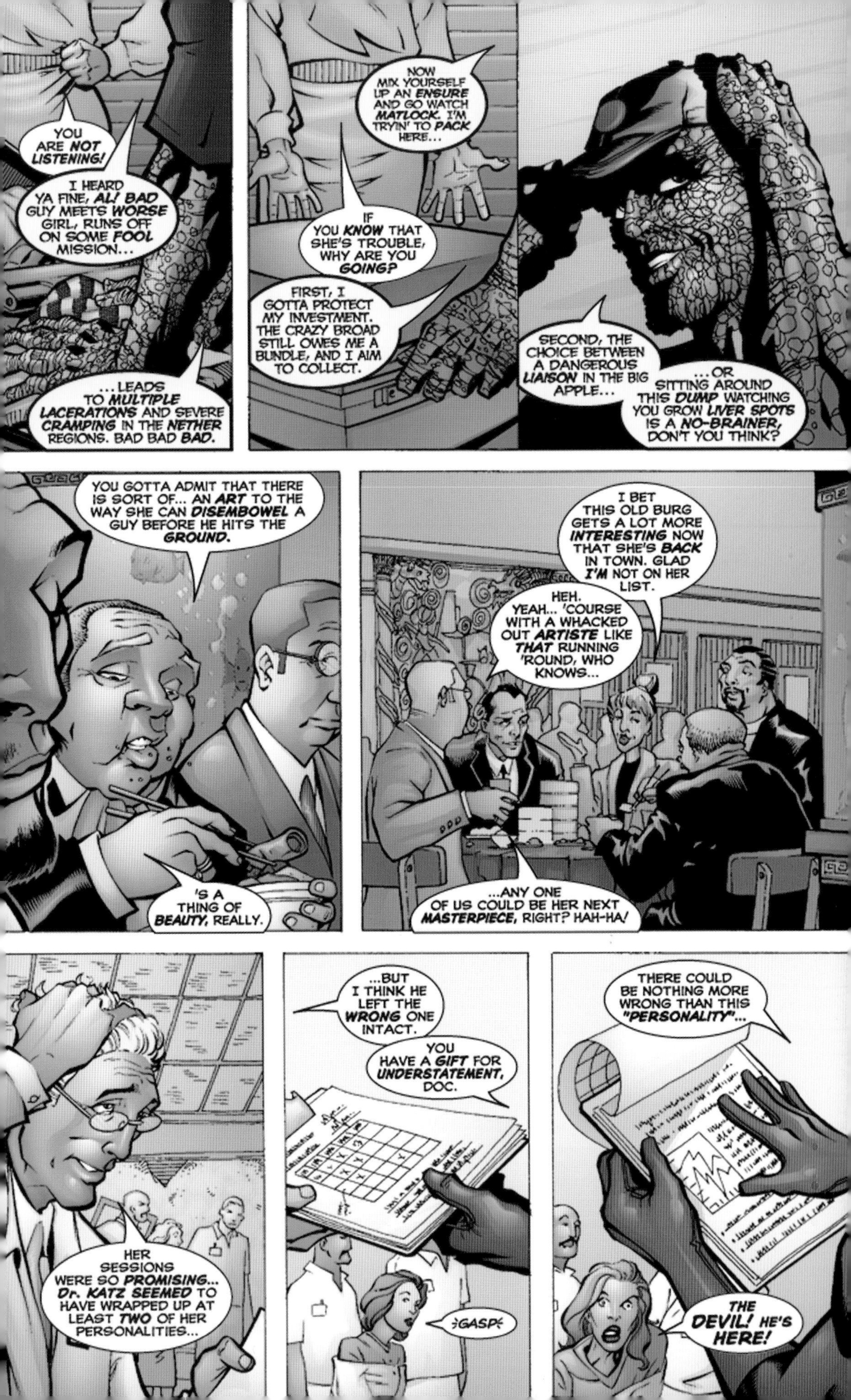
YOU ARE NOT LISTENING!
I HEARD YA FINE, AL! BAD GUY MEETS WORSE GIRL, RUNS OFF ON SOME FOOL MISSION...
...LEADS TO MULTIPLE LACERATIONS AND SEVERE CRAMPING IN THE NETHER REGIONS. BAD BAD BAD.
NOW MIX YOURSELF UP AN ENSURE AND GO WATCH MATLOCK. I'M TRYIN' TO PACK HERE...
IF YOU KNOW THAT SHE'S TROUBLE, WHY ARE YOU GOING?
FIRST, I GOTTA PROTECT MY INVESTMENT. THE CRAZY BROAD STILL OWES ME A BUNDLE, AND I AIM TO COLLECT.
SECOND, THE CHOICE BETWEEN A DANGEROUS LIAISON IN THE BIG APPLE...
...OR SITTING AROUND THIS DUMP WATCHING YOU GROW LIVER SPOTS IS A NO-BRAINER, DON'T YOU THINK?
YOU GOTTA ADMIT THAT THERE IS SORT OF... AN ART TO THE WAY SHE CAN DISEMBOWEL A GUY BEFORE HE HITS THE GROUND.
'S A THING OF BEAUTY, REALLY.
I BET THIS OLD BURG GETS A LOT MORE INTERESTING NOW THAT SHE'S BACK IN TOWN. GLAD I'M NOT ON HER LIST.
HEH. YEAH... 'COURSE WITH A WHACKED OUT ARTISTE LIKE THAT RUNNING 'ROUND, WHO KNOWS...
...ANY ONE OF US COULD BE HER NEXT MASTERPIECE, RIGHT? HAH-HA!
HER SESSIONS WERE SO PROMISING... Dr. KATZ SEEMED TO HAVE WRAPPED UP AT LEAST TWO OF HER PERSONALITIES...
...BUT I THINK HE LEFT THE WRONG ONE INTACT.
YOU HAVE A GIFT FOR UNDERSTATEMENT, DOC.
GASP
THERE COULD BE NOTHING MORE WRONG THAN THIS "PERSONALITY"...
THE DEVIL! HE'S HERE!

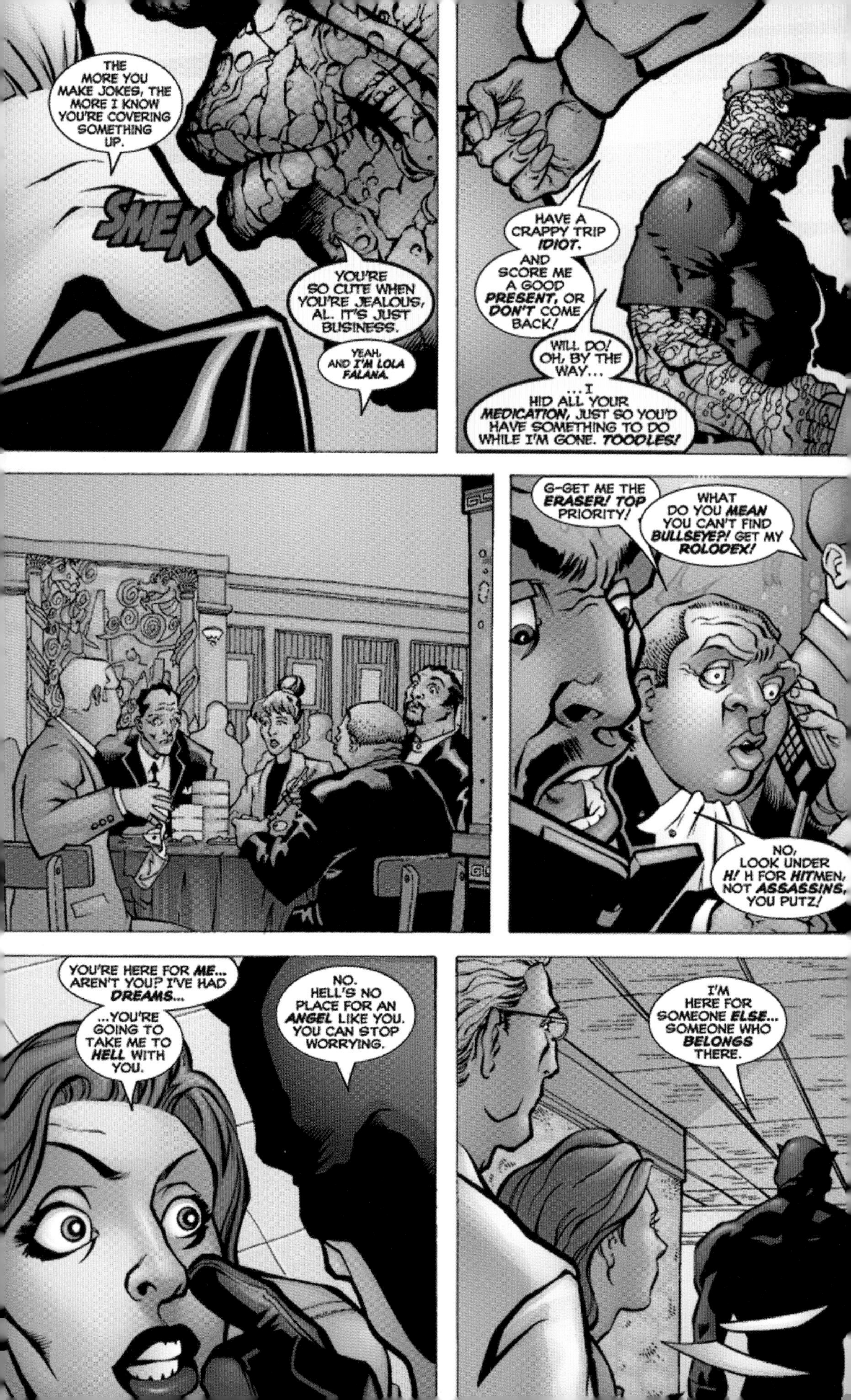
THE MORE YOU MAKE JOKES, THE MORE I KNOW YOU'RE COVERING SOMETHING UP.
SMEK
YOU'RE SO CUTE WHEN YOU'RE JEALOUS, AL. IT'S JUST BUSINESS.
YEAH, AND I'M LOLA FALANA.
HAVE A CRAPPY TRIP IDIOT.
AND SCORE ME A GOOD PRESENT, OR DON'T COME BACK!
WILL DO! OH, BY THE WAY...
...I HID ALL YOUR MEDICATION, JUST SO YOU'D HAVE SOMETHING TO DO WHILE I'M GONE. TOODLES!
G-GET ME THE ERASER! TOP PRIORITY!
WHAT DO YOU MEAN YOU CAN'T FIND BULLSEYE?! GET MY ROLODEX!
NO, LOOK UNDER H! H FOR HITMEN, NOT ASSASSINS, YOU PUTZ!
YOU'RE HERE FOR ME... AREN'T YOU? I'VE HAD DREAMS...
...YOU'RE GOING TO TAKE ME TO HELL WITH YOU.
NO. HELL'S NO PLACE FOR AN ANGEL LIKE YOU. YOU CAN STOP WORRYING.
I'M HERE FOR SOMEONE ELSE... SOMEONE WHO BELONGS THERE.

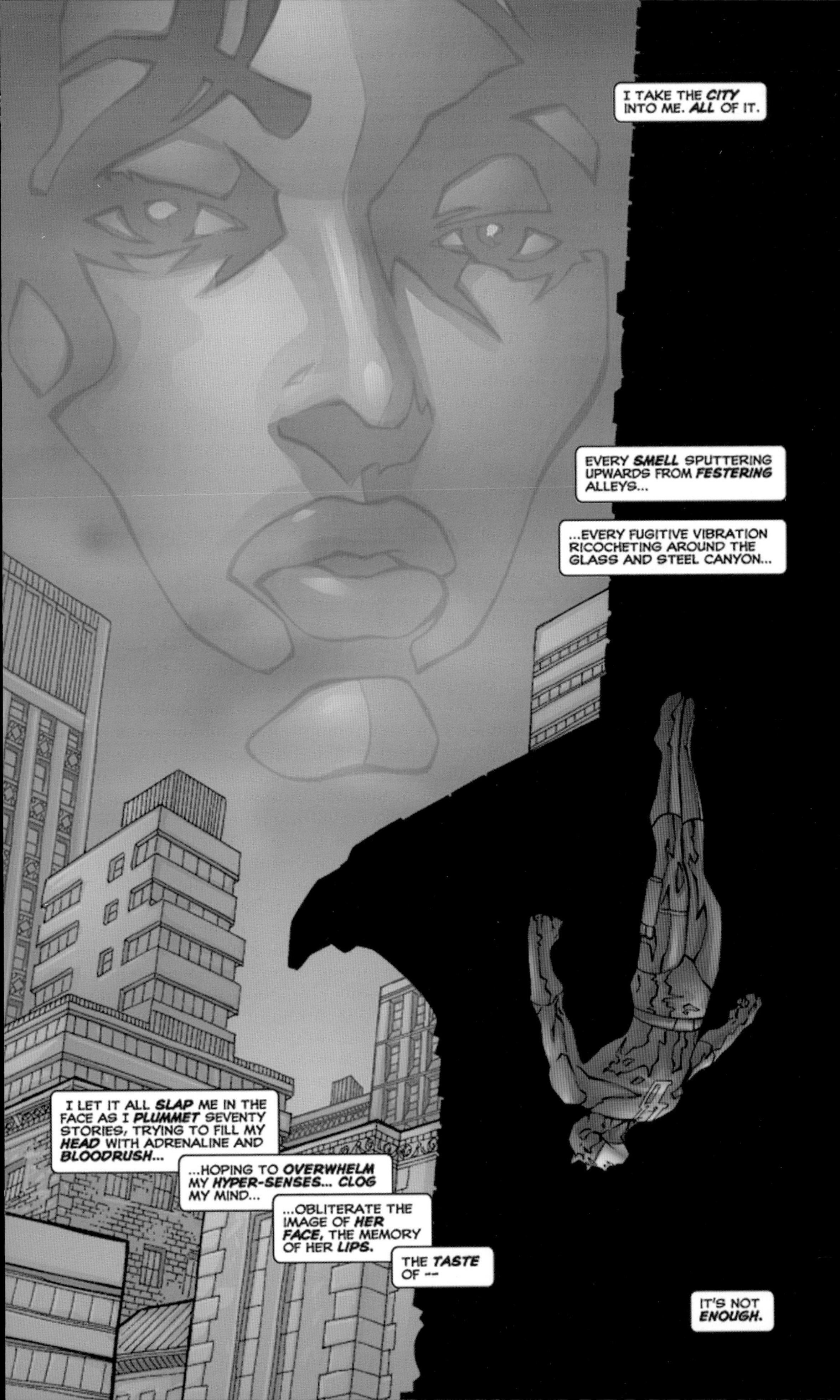

I TAKE THE *CITY* INTO ME. *ALL* OF IT.
EVERY *SMELL* SPUTTERING UPWARDS FROM *FESTERING* ALLEYS...
...EVERY FUGITIVE VIBRATION RICOCHETING AROUND THE GLASS AND STEEL CANYON...
I LET IT ALL *SLAP* ME IN THE FACE AS I *PLUMMET* SEVENTY STORIES, TRYING TO FILL MY *HEAD* WITH ADRENALINE AND *BLOODRUSH*...
...HOPING TO *OVERWHELM* MY *HYPER-SENSES... CLOG* MY MIND...
...OBLITERATE THE IMAGE OF *HER FACE*, THE MEMORY OF HER *LIPS*.
THE *TASTE* OF --
IT'S NOT *ENOUGH*.

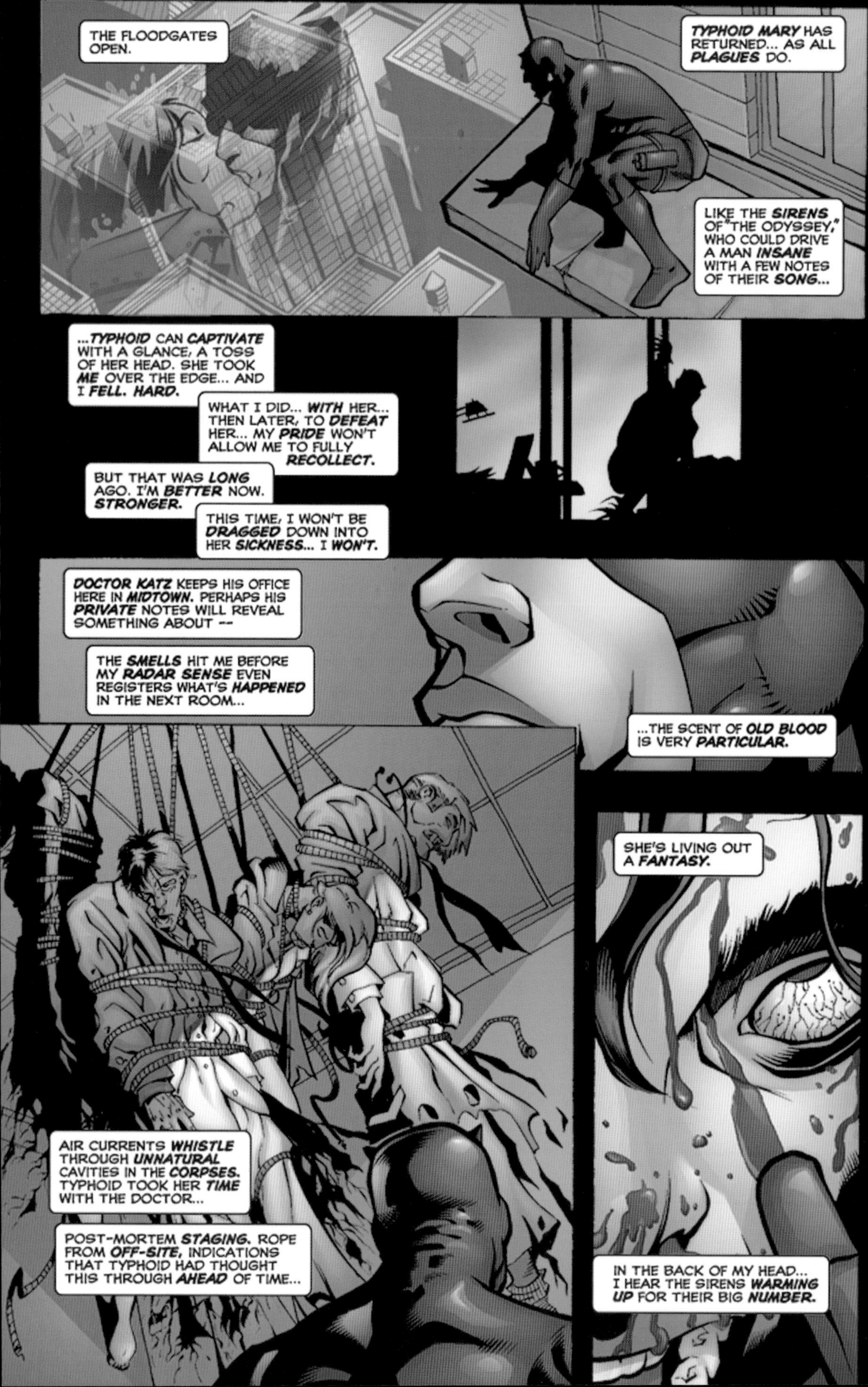
THE FLOODGATES OPEN.
TYPHOID MARY HAS RETURNED... AS ALL PLAGUES DO.
LIKE THE SIRENS OF "THE ODYSSEY," WHO COULD DRIVE A MAN INSANE WITH A FEW NOTES OF THEIR SONG...
...TYPHOID CAN CAPTIVATE WITH A GLANCE, A TOSS OF HER HEAD. SHE TOOK ME OVER THE EDGE... AND I FELL. HARD.
WHAT I DID... WITH HER... THEN LATER, TO DEFEAT HER... MY PRIDE WON'T ALLOW ME TO FULLY RECOLLECT.
BUT THAT WAS LONG AGO. I'M BETTER NOW. STRONGER.
THIS TIME, I WON'T BE DRAGGED DOWN INTO HER SICKNESS... I WON'T.
DOCTOR KATZ KEEPS HIS OFFICE HERE IN MIDTOWN. PERHAPS HIS PRIVATE NOTES WILL REVEAL SOMETHING ABOUT --
THE SMELLS HIT ME BEFORE MY RADAR SENSE EVEN REGISTERS WHAT'S HAPPENED IN THE NEXT ROOM...
...THE SCENT OF OLD BLOOD IS VERY PARTICULAR.
AIR CURRENTS WHISTLE THROUGH UNNATURAL CAVITIES IN THE CORPSES. TYPHOID TOOK HER TIME WITH THE DOCTOR...
POST-MORTEM STAGING. ROPE FROM OFF-SITE, INDICATIONS THAT TYPHOID HAD THOUGHT THIS THROUGH AHEAD OF TIME...
SHE'S LIVING OUT A FANTASY.
IN THE BACK OF MY HEAD... I HEAR THE SIRENS WARMING UP FOR THEIR BIG NUMBER.

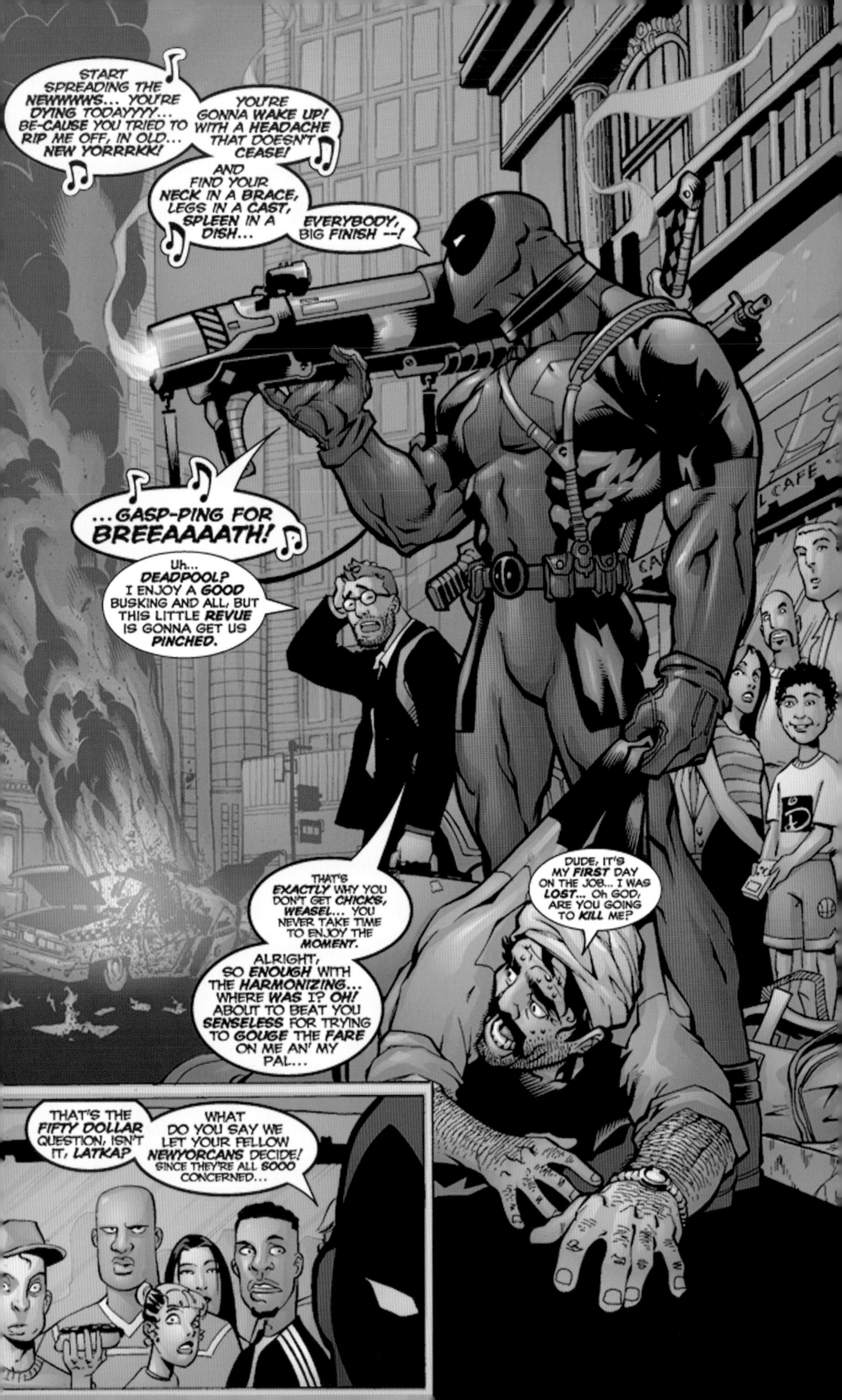
START SPREADING THE NEWWWWS... YOU'RE DYING TODAYYYY... BE-CAUSE YOU TRIED TO RIP ME OFF, IN OLD... NEW YORRRKK!
YOU'RE GONNA WAKE UP! WITH A HEADACHE THAT DOESN'T CEASE!
AND FIND YOUR NECK IN A BRACE, LEGS IN A CAST, SPLEEN IN A DISH...
EVERYBODY, BIG FINISH --!
...GASP-PING FOR BREEAAAATH!
Uh... DEADPOOL? I ENJOY A GOOD BUSKING AND ALL, BUT THIS LITTLE REVUE IS GONNA GET US PINCHED.
THAT'S EXACTLY WHY YOU DON'T GET CHICKS, WEASEL... YOU NEVER TAKE TIME TO ENJOY THE MOMENT.
ALRIGHT, SO ENOUGH WITH THE HARMONIZING... WHERE WAS I? OH! ABOUT TO BEAT YOU SENSELESS FOR TRYING TO GOUGE THE FARE ON ME AN' MY PAL...
DUDE, IT'S MY FIRST DAY ON THE JOB... I WAS LOST... Oh GOD, ARE YOU GOING TO KILL ME?
THAT'S THE FIFTY DOLLAR QUESTION, ISN'T IT, LATKA?
WHAT DO YOU SAY WE LET YOUR FELLOW NEWYORCANS DECIDE! SINCE THEY'RE ALL SOOO CONCERNED...

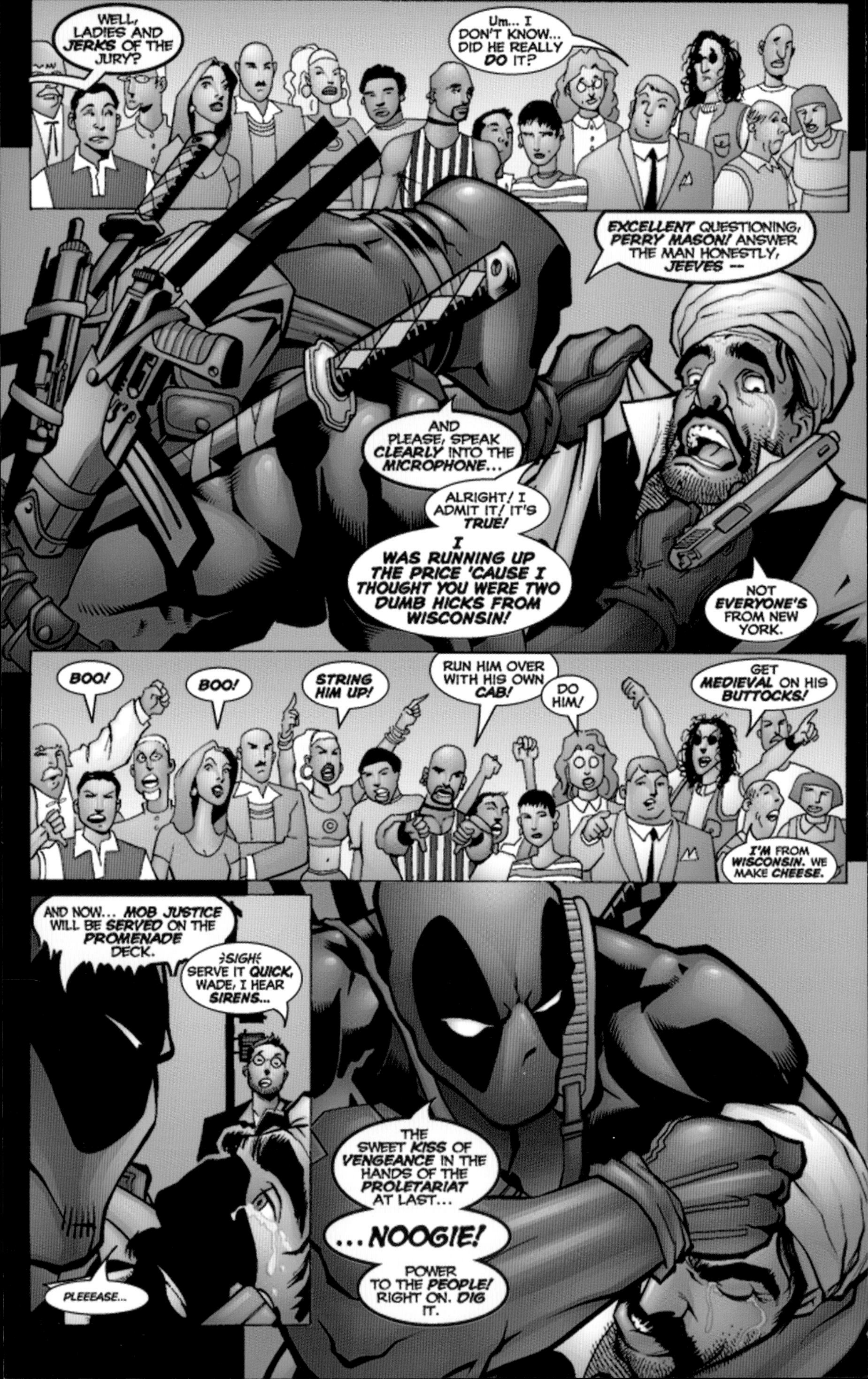

WELL, LADIES AND JERKS OF THE JURY?
Um... I DON'T KNOW... DID HE REALLY DO IT?
EXCELLENT QUESTIONING, PERRY MASON! ANSWER THE MAN HONESTLY, JEEVES --
AND PLEASE, SPEAK CLEARLY INTO THE MICROPHONE...
ALRIGHT! I ADMIT IT! IT'S TRUE!
I WAS RUNNING UP THE PRICE 'CAUSE I THOUGHT YOU WERE TWO DUMB HICKS FROM WISCONSIN!
NOT EVERYONE'S FROM NEW YORK.
BOO!
BOO!
STRING HIM UP!
RUN HIM OVER WITH HIS OWN CAB!
DO HIM!
GET MEDIEVAL ON HIS BUTTOCKS!
I'M FROM WISCONSIN. WE MAKE CHEESE.
AND NOW... MOB JUSTICE WILL BE SERVED ON THE PROMENADE DECK.
SIGH SERVE IT QUICK, WADE, I HEAR SIRENS...
THE SWEET KISS OF VENGEANCE IN THE HANDS OF THE PROLETARIAT AT LAST...
...NOOGIE!
POWER TO THE PEOPLE! RIGHT ON. DIG IT.
PLEEEASE...

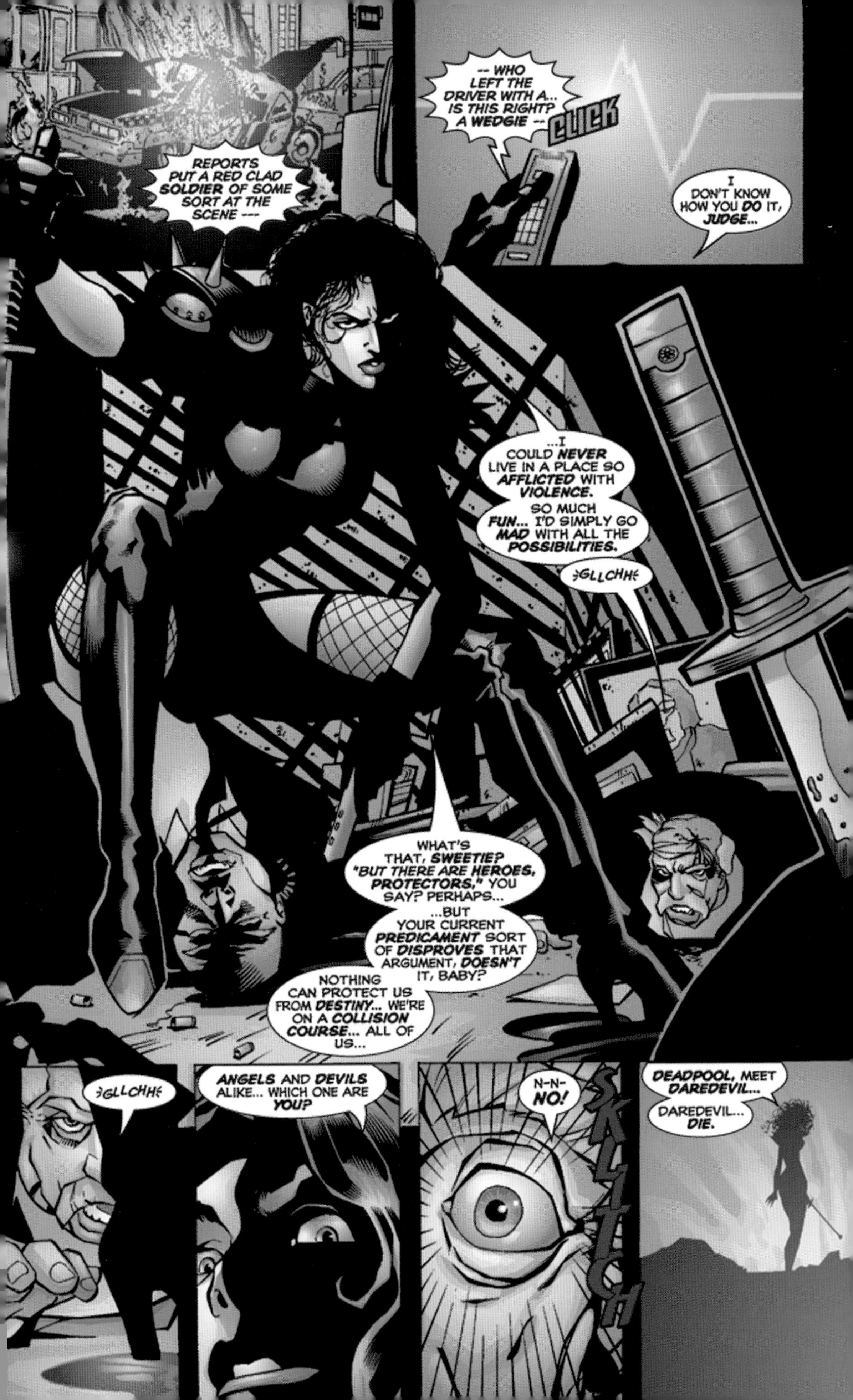
REPORTS PUT A RED CLAD SOLDIER OF SOME SORT AT THE SCENE ---
-- WHO LEFT THE DRIVER WITH A... IS THIS RIGHT? A WEDGIE --
CLICK
I DON'T KNOW HOW YOU DO IT, JUDGE...
...I COULD NEVER LIVE IN A PLACE SO AFFLICTED WITH VIOLENCE.
SO MUCH FUN... I'D SIMPLY GO MAD WITH ALL THE POSSIBILITIES.
GLLCHH
WHAT'S THAT, SWEETIE? "BUT THERE ARE HEROES, PROTECTORS," YOU SAY? PERHAPS...
...BUT YOUR CURRENT PREDICAMENT SORT OF DISPROVES THAT ARGUMENT, DOESN'T IT, BABY?
NOTHING CAN PROTECT US FROM DESTINY... WE'RE ON A COLLISION COURSE... ALL OF US...
GLLCHH
ANGELS AND DEVILS ALIKE... WHICH ONE ARE YOU?
N-N-NO!
SKLITCH
DEADPOOL, MEET DAREDEVIL...
DAREDEVIL... DIE.

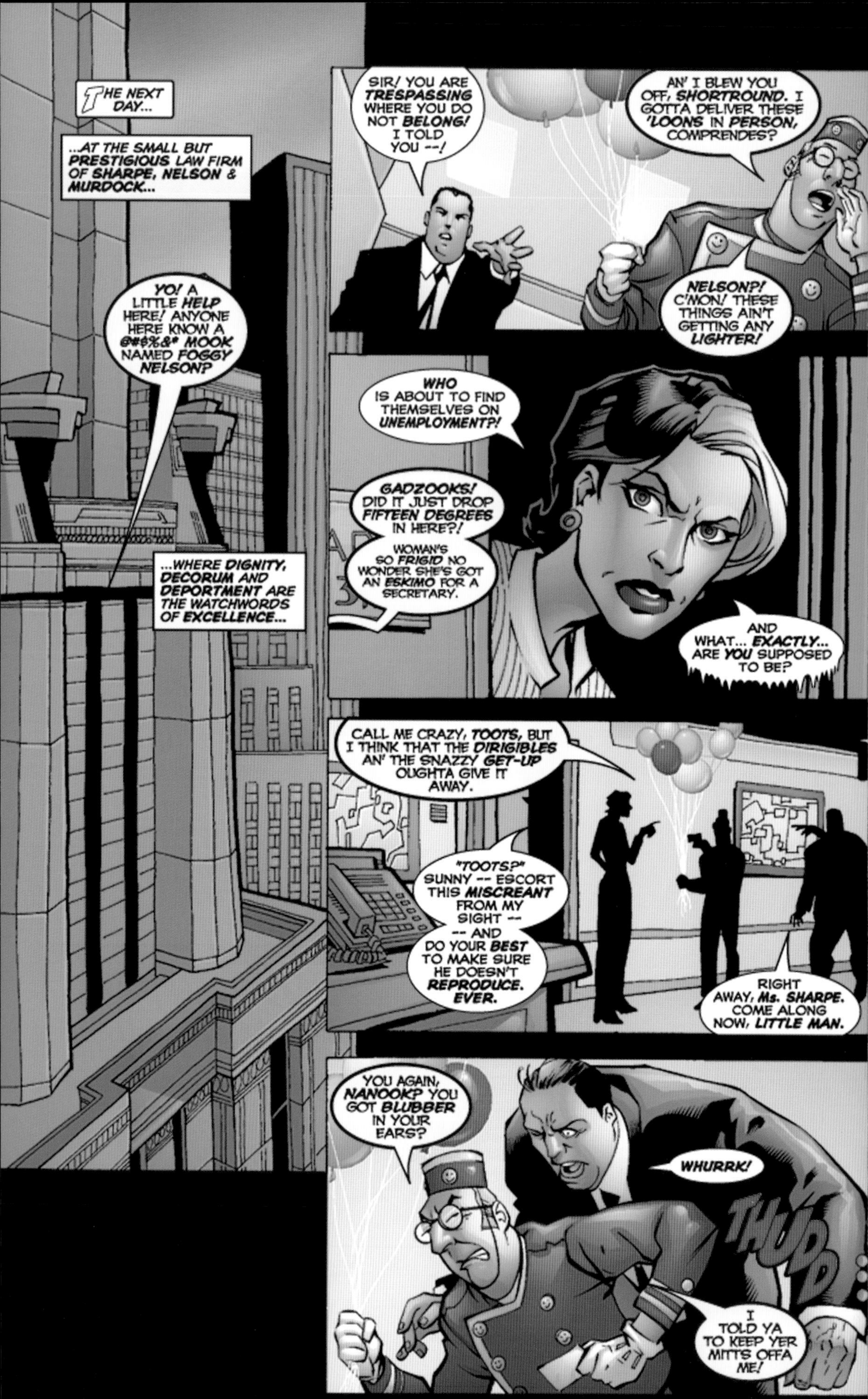
THE NEXT DAY...
...AT THE SMALL BUT PRESTIGIOUS LAW FIRM OF SHARPE, NELSON & MURDOCK...
YO! A LITTLE HELP HERE! ANYONE HERE KNOW A @#$%&* MOOK NAMED FOGGY NELSON?
...WHERE DIGNITY, DECORUM AND DEPORTMENT ARE THE WATCHWORDS OF EXCELLENCE...
SIR! YOU ARE TRESPASSING WHERE YOU DO NOT BELONG! I TOLD YOU --!
AN' I BLEW YOU OFF, SHORTROUND. I GOTTA DELIVER THESE 'LOONS IN PERSON, COMPRENDES?
NELSON?! C'MON! THESE THINGS AIN'T GETTING ANY LIGHTER!
WHO IS ABOUT TO FIND THEMSELVES ON UNEMPLOYMENT?!
GADZOOKS! DID IT JUST DROP FIFTEEN DEGREES IN HERE?!
WOMAN'S SO FRIGID NO WONDER SHE'S GOT AN ESKIMO FOR A SECRETARY.
AND WHAT... EXACTLY... ARE YOU SUPPOSED TO BE?
CALL ME CRAZY, TOOTS, BUT I THINK THAT THE DIRIGIBLES AN' THE SNAZZY GET-UP OUGHTA GIVE IT AWAY.
"TOOTS?" SUNNY -- ESCORT THIS MISCREANT FROM MY SIGHT --
-- AND DO YOUR BEST TO MAKE SURE HE DOESN'T REPRODUCE. EVER.
RIGHT AWAY, Ms. SHARPE. COME ALONG NOW, LITTLE MAN.
YOU AGAIN, NANOOK? YOU GOT BLUBBER IN YOUR EARS?
WHURRK!
THUDD
I TOLD YA TO KEEP YER MITTS OFFA ME!

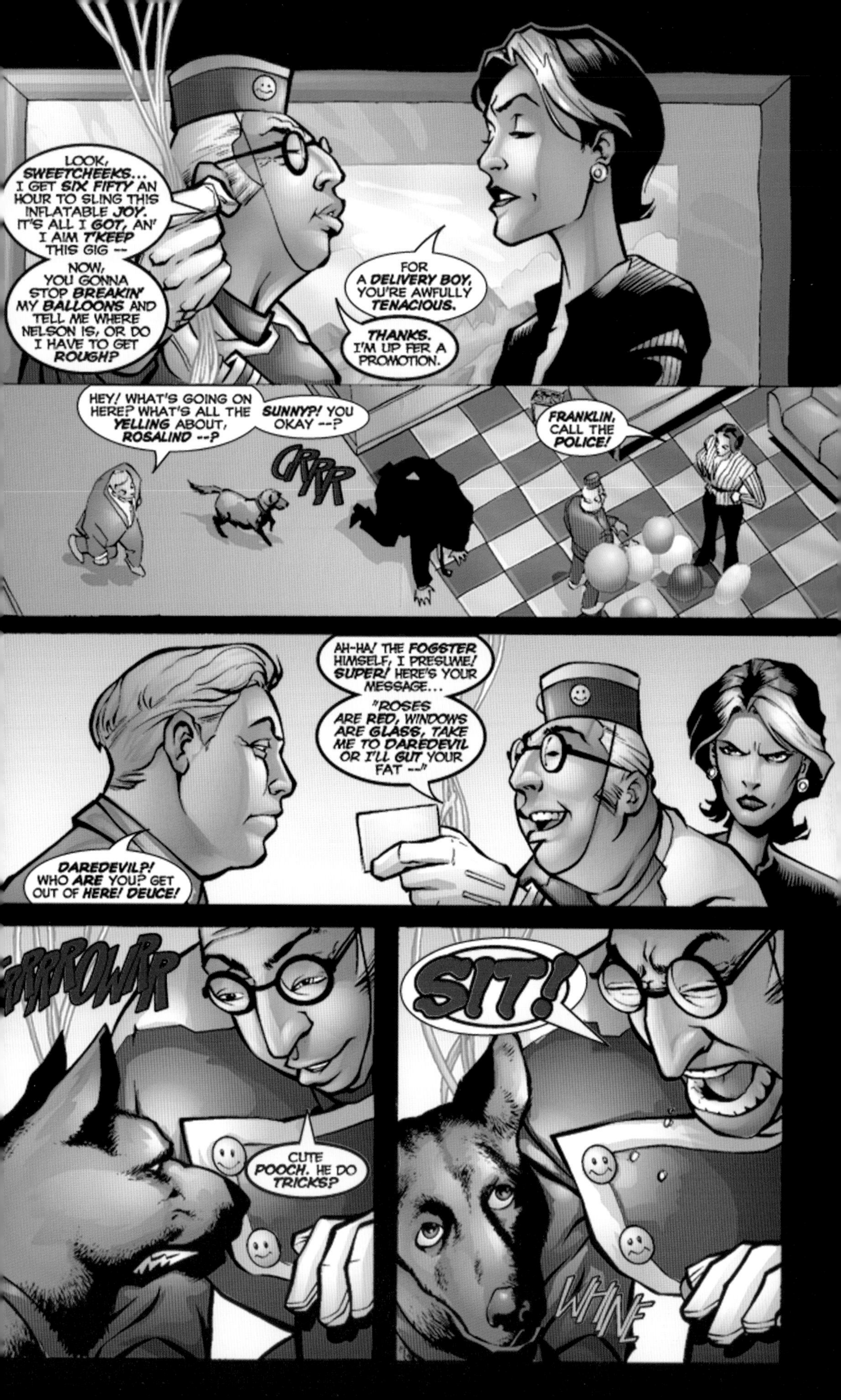
LOOK, SWEETCHEEKS... I GET SIX FIFTY AN HOUR TO SLING THIS INFLATABLE JOY. IT'S ALL I GOT, AN' I AIM T'KEEP THIS GIG --
NOW, YOU GONNA STOP BREAKIN' MY BALLOONS AND TELL ME WHERE NELSON IS, OR DO I HAVE TO GET ROUGH?
FOR A DELIVERY BOY, YOU'RE AWFULLY TENACIOUS.
THANKS. I'M UP FER A PROMOTION.
HEY! WHAT'S GOING ON HERE? WHAT'S ALL THE YELLING ABOUT, ROSALIND --?
SUNNY?! YOU OKAY --?
CRRR
FRANKLIN, CALL THE POLICE!
AH-HA! THE FOGSTER HIMSELF, I PRESUME! SUPER! HERE'S YOUR MESSAGE...
"ROSES ARE RED, WINDOWS ARE GLASS, TAKE ME TO DAREDEVIL OR I'LL GUT YOUR FAT --"
DAREDEVIL?! WHO ARE YOU? GET OUT OF HERE! DEUCE!
RRRROWRR
CUTE POOCH. HE DO TRICKS?
SIT!
WHINE

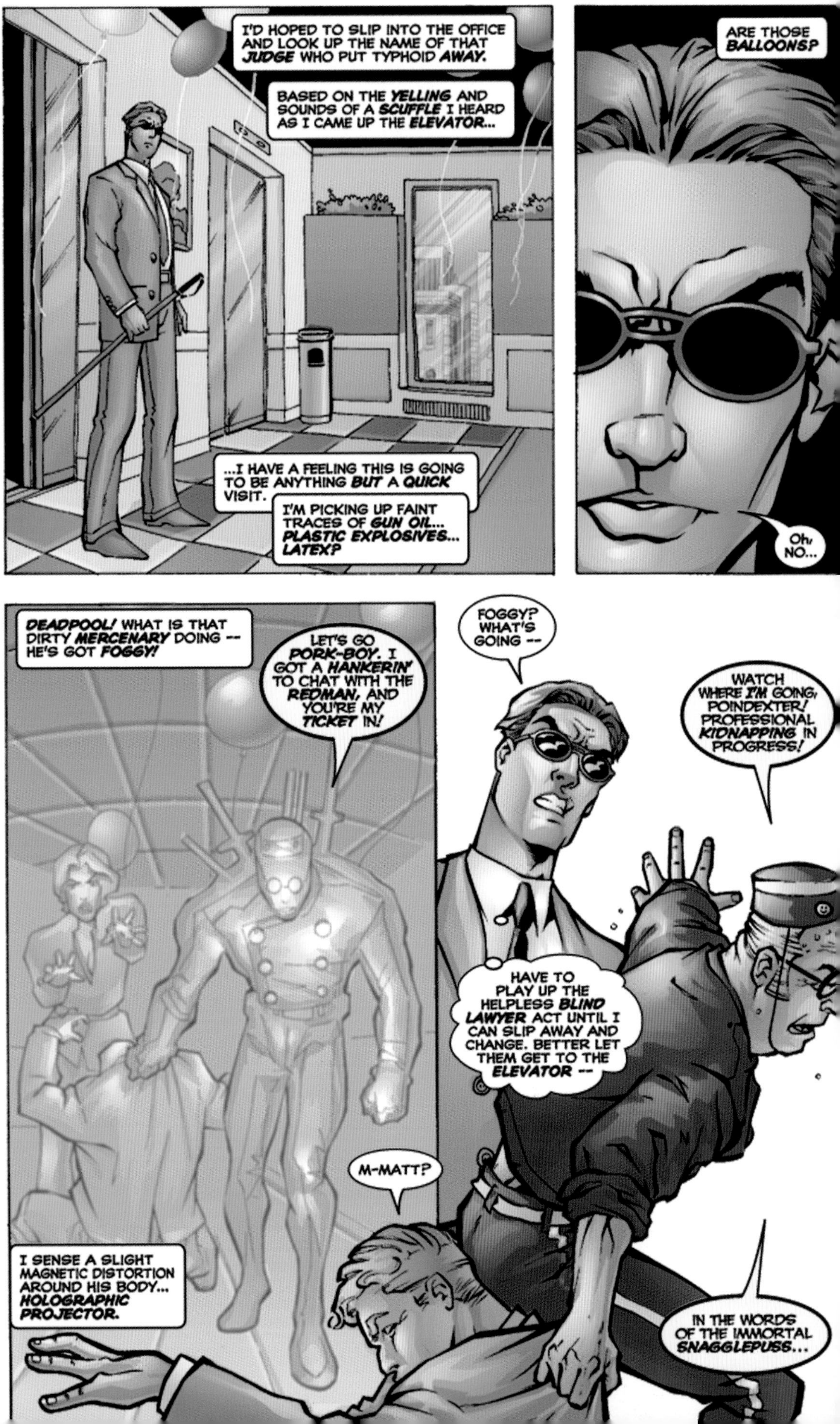

I'D HOPED TO SLIP INTO THE OFFICE AND LOOK UP THE NAME OF THAT JUDGE WHO PUT TYPHOID AWAY.
BASED ON THE YELLING AND SOUNDS OF A SCUFFLE I HEARD AS I CAME UP THE ELEVATOR...
...I HAVE A FEELING THIS IS GOING TO BE ANYTHING BUT A QUICK VISIT.
I'M PICKING UP FAINT TRACES OF GUN OIL... PLASTIC EXPLOSIVES... LATEX?
ARE THOSE BALLOONS?
Oh, NO...
DEADPOOL! WHAT IS THAT DIRTY MERCENARY DOING -- HE'S GOT FOGGY!
LET'S GO PORK-BOY. I GOT A HANKERIN' TO CHAT WITH THE REDMAN, AND YOU'RE MY TICKET IN!
FOGGY? WHAT'S GOING --
WATCH WHERE I'M GOING, POINDEXTER! PROFESSIONAL KIDNAPPING IN PROGRESS!
HAVE TO PLAY UP THE HELPLESS BLIND LAWYER ACT UNTIL I CAN SLIP AWAY AND CHANGE. BETTER LET THEM GET TO THE ELEVATOR --
M-MATT?
I SENSE A SLIGHT MAGNETIC DISTORTION AROUND HIS BODY... HOLOGRAPHIC PROJECTOR.
IN THE WORDS OF THE IMMORTAL SNAGGLEPUSS...

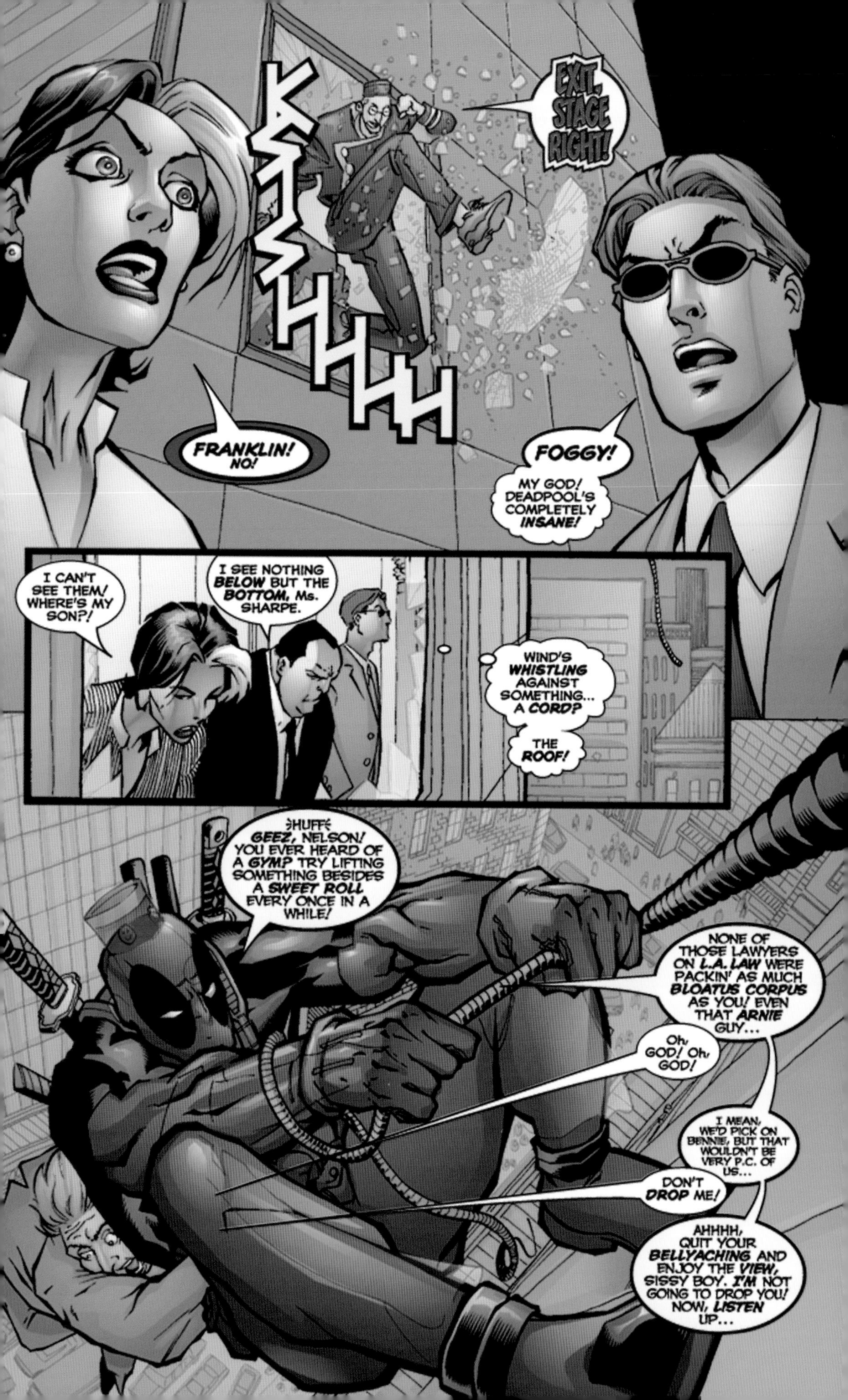
KRSSHHHH
EXIT, STAGE RIGHT!
FRANKLIN! NO!
FOGGY!
MY GOD! DEADPOOL'S COMPLETELY INSANE!
I CAN'T SEE THEM! WHERE'S MY SON?!
I SEE NOTHING BELOW BUT THE BOTTOM, Ms. SHARPE.
WIND'S WHISTLING AGAINST SOMETHING... A CORD?
THE ROOF!
HUFF GEEZ, NELSON! YOU EVER HEARD OF A GYM? TRY LIFTING SOMETHING BESIDES A SWEET ROLL EVERY ONCE IN A WHILE!
NONE OF THOSE LAWYERS ON L.A. LAW WERE PACKIN' AS MUCH BLOATUS CORPUS AS YOU! EVEN THAT ARNIE GUY...
Oh, GOD! Oh, GOD!
I MEAN, WE'D PICK ON BENNIE, BUT THAT WOULDN'T BE VERY P.C. OF US...
DON'T DROP ME!
AHHHH, QUIT YOUR BELLYACHING AND ENJOY THE VIEW, SISSY BOY. I'M NOT GOING TO DROP YOU! NOW, LISTEN UP...

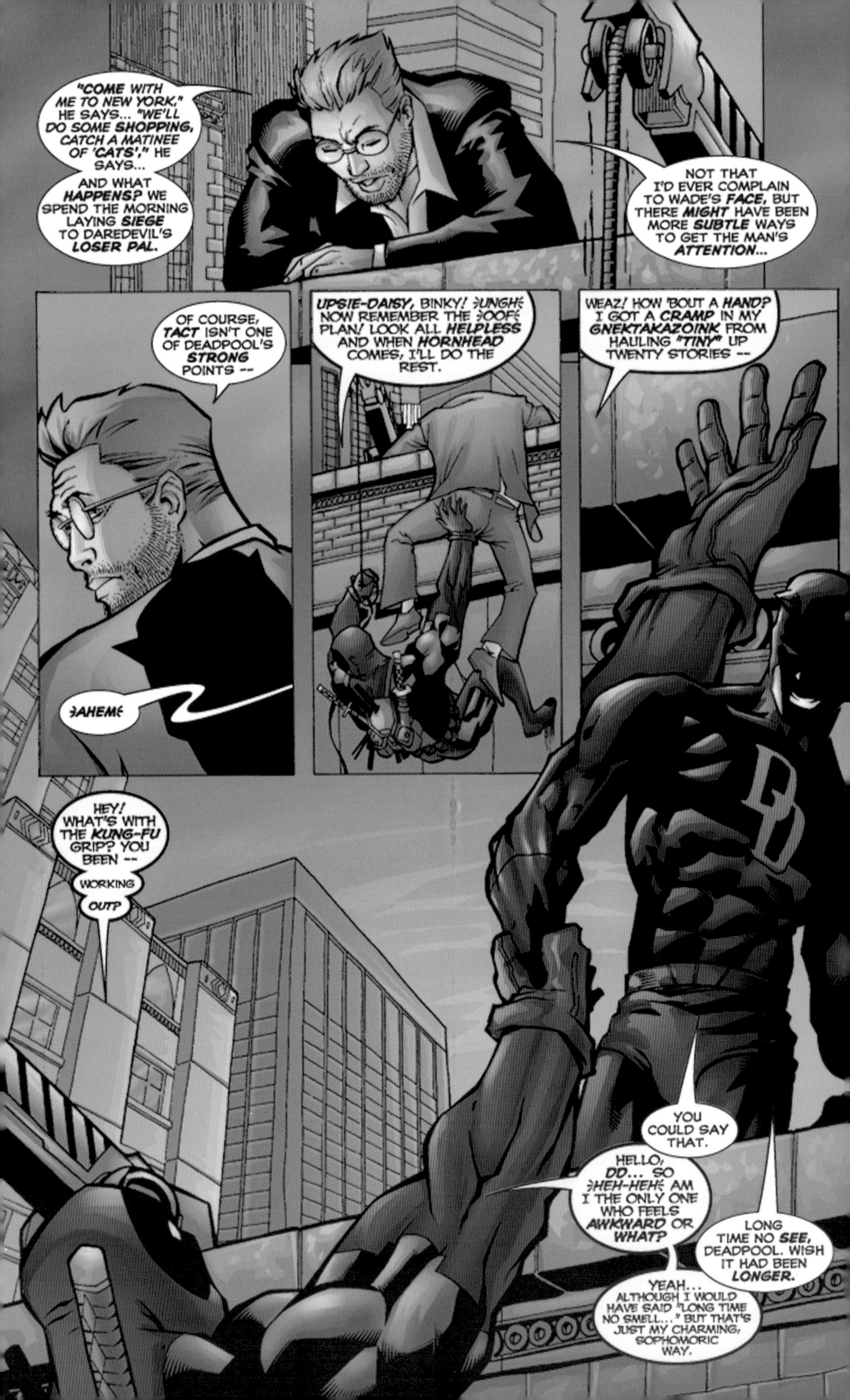
"COME WITH ME TO NEW YORK," HE SAYS... "WE'LL DO SOME SHOPPING, CATCH A MATINEE OF 'CATS'," HE SAYS...
AND WHAT HAPPENS? WE SPEND THE MORNING LAYING SIEGE TO DAREDEVIL'S LOSER PAL.
NOT THAT I'D EVER COMPLAIN TO WADE'S FACE, BUT THERE MIGHT HAVE BEEN MORE SUBTLE WAYS TO GET THE MAN'S ATTENTION...
OF COURSE, TACT ISN'T ONE OF DEADPOOL'S STRONG POINTS --
AHEM
UPSIE-DAISY, BINKY! UNGH NOW REMEMBER THE OOF PLAN! LOOK ALL HELPLESS AND WHEN HORNHEAD COMES, I'LL DO THE REST.
WEAZ! HOW 'BOUT A HAND? I GOT A CRAMP IN MY GNEKTAKAZOINK FROM HAULING "TINY" UP TWENTY STORIES --
HEY! WHAT'S WITH THE KUNG-FU GRIP? YOU BEEN --
WORKING
OUT?
YOU COULD SAY THAT.
HELLO, DD... SO HEH-HEH AM I THE ONLY ONE WHO FEELS AWKWARD OR WHAT?
LONG TIME NO SEE, DEADPOOL. WISH IT HAD BEEN LONGER.
YEAH... ALTHOUGH I WOULD HAVE SAID "LONG TIME NO SMELL..." BUT THAT'S JUST MY CHARMING, SOPHOMORIC WAY.

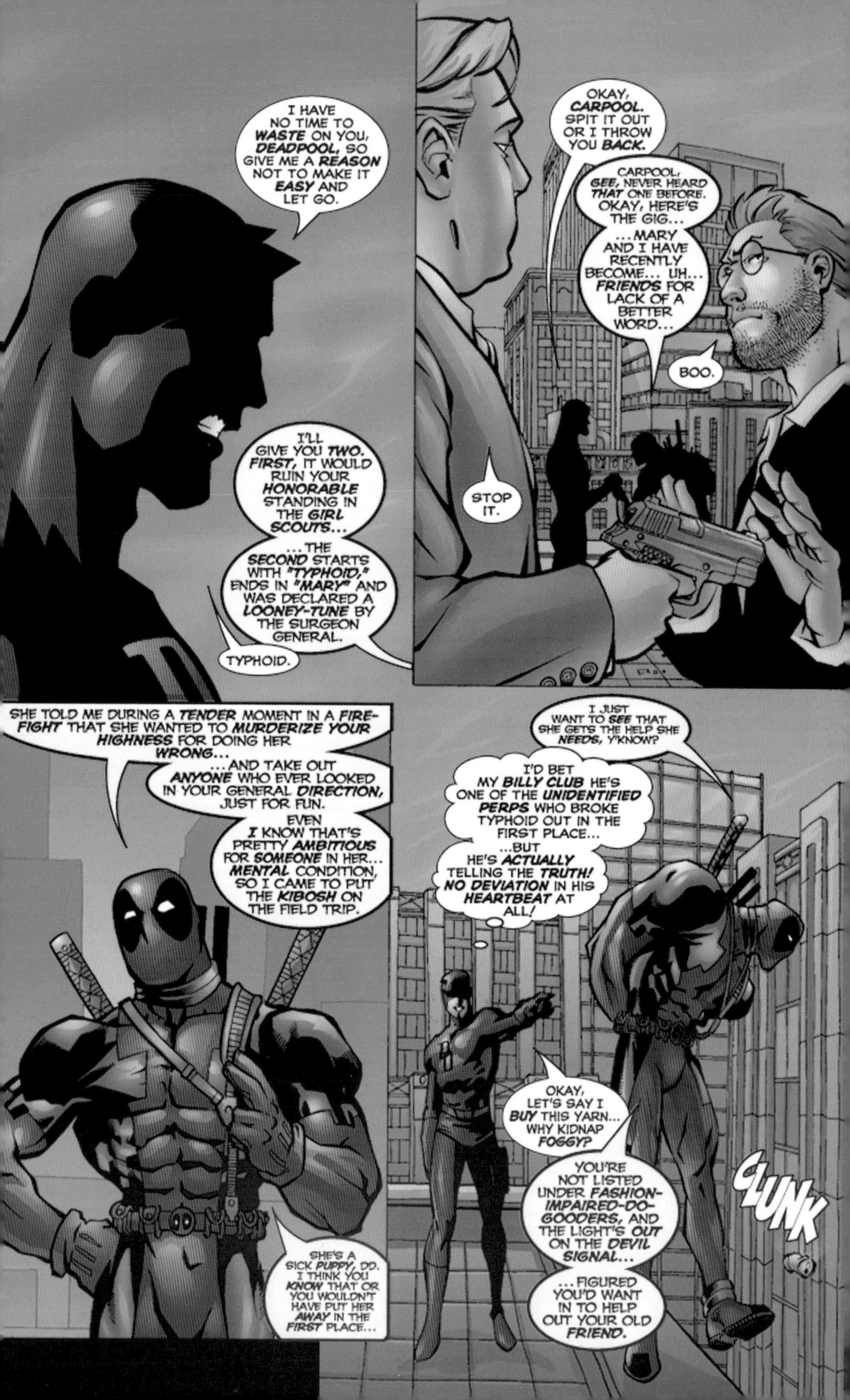
I HAVE NO TIME TO WASTE ON YOU, DEADPOOL, SO GIVE ME A REASON NOT TO MAKE IT EASY AND LET GO.
I'LL GIVE YOU TWO. FIRST, IT WOULD RUIN YOUR HONORABLE STANDING IN THE GIRL SCOUTS...
...THE SECOND STARTS WITH "TYPHOID," ENDS IN "MARY" AND WAS DECLARED A LOONEY-TUNE BY THE SURGEON GENERAL.
TYPHOID.
OKAY, CARPOOL. SPIT IT OUT OR I THROW YOU BACK.
CARPOOL, GEE, NEVER HEARD THAT ONE BEFORE. OKAY, HERE'S THE GIG...
...MARY AND I HAVE RECENTLY BECOME... UH... FRIENDS FOR LACK OF A BETTER WORD...
BOO.
STOP IT.
SHE TOLD ME DURING A TENDER MOMENT IN A FIRE-FIGHT THAT SHE WANTED TO MURDERIZE YOUR HIGHNESS FOR DOING HER WRONG...
...AND TAKE OUT ANYONE WHO EVER LOOKED IN YOUR GENERAL DIRECTION, JUST FOR FUN.
EVEN I KNOW THAT'S PRETTY AMBITIOUS FOR SOMEONE IN HER... MENTAL CONDITION, SO I CAME TO PUT THE KIBOSH ON THE FIELD TRIP.
SHE'S A SICK PUPPY, DD. I THINK YOU KNOW THAT OR YOU WOULDN'T HAVE PUT HER AWAY IN THE FIRST PLACE...
I JUST WANT TO SEE THAT SHE GETS THE HELP SHE NEEDS, Y'KNOW?
I'D BET MY BILLY CLUB HE'S ONE OF THE UNIDENTIFIED PERPS WHO BROKE TYPHOID OUT IN THE FIRST PLACE...
...BUT HE'S ACTUALLY TELLING THE TRUTH! NO DEVIATION IN HIS HEARTBEAT AT ALL!
OKAY, LET'S SAY I BUY THIS YARN... WHY KIDNAP FOGGY?
YOU'RE NOT LISTED UNDER FASHION-IMPAIRED-DO-GOODERS, AND THE LIGHT'S OUT ON THE DEVIL SIGNAL...
...FIGURED YOU'D WANT IN TO HELP OUT YOUR OLD FRIEND.
CLUNK

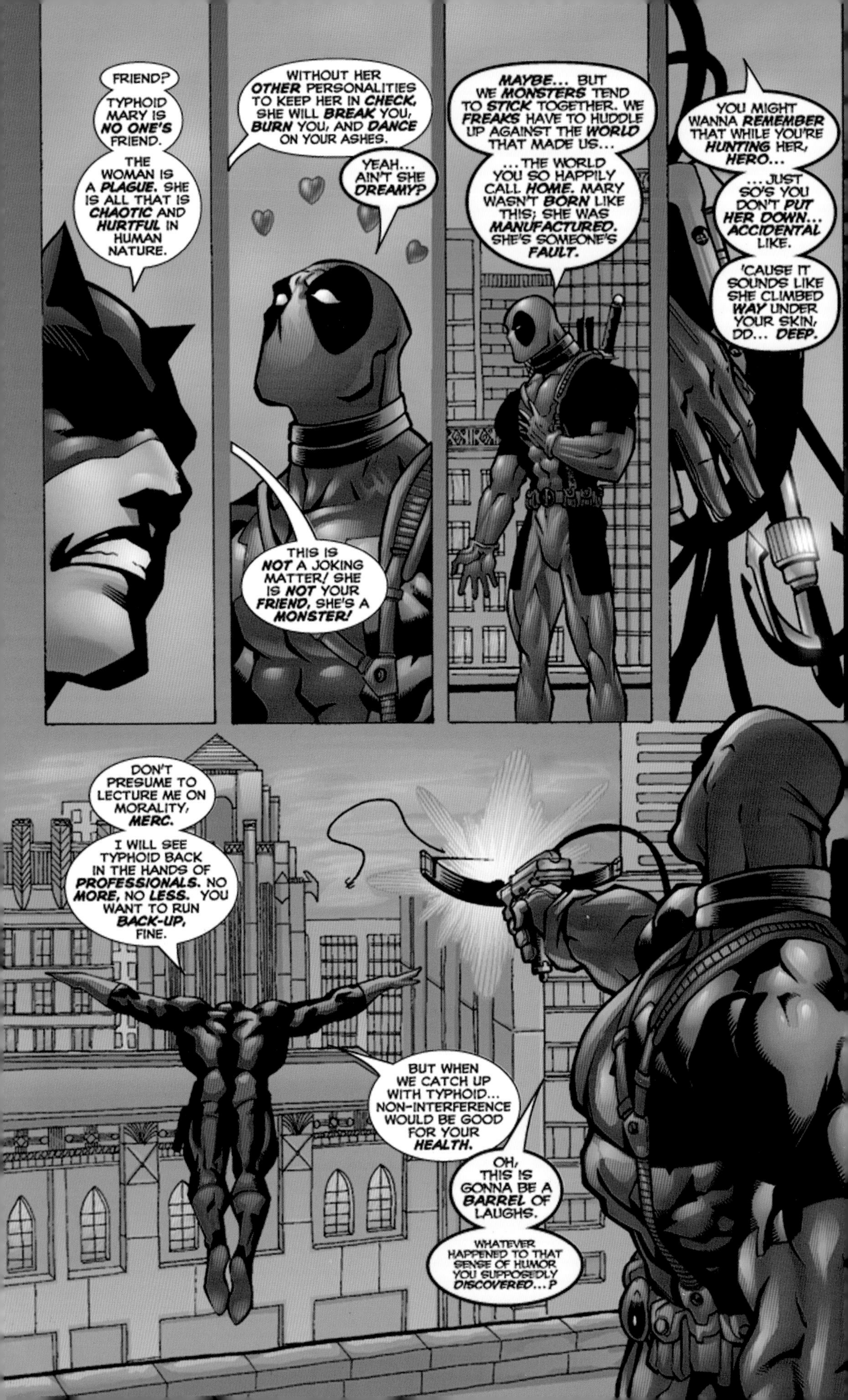

FRIEND?
TYPHOID MARY IS NO ONE'S FRIEND.
THE WOMAN IS A PLAGUE. SHE IS ALL THAT IS CHAOTIC AND HURTFUL IN HUMAN NATURE.
WITHOUT HER OTHER PERSONALITIES TO KEEP HER IN CHECK, SHE WILL BREAK YOU, BURN YOU, AND DANCE ON YOUR ASHES.
YEAH... AIN'T SHE DREAMY?
THIS IS NOT A JOKING MATTER! SHE IS NOT YOUR FRIEND, SHE'S A MONSTER!
MAYBE... BUT WE MONSTERS TEND TO STICK TOGETHER. WE FREAKS HAVE TO HUDDLE UP AGAINST THE WORLD THAT MADE US...
...THE WORLD YOU SO HAPPILY CALL HOME. MARY WASN'T BORN LIKE THIS; SHE WAS MANUFACTURED. SHE'S SOMEONE'S FAULT.
YOU MIGHT WANNA REMEMBER THAT WHILE YOU'RE HUNTING HER, HERO...
...JUST SO'S YOU DON'T PUT HER DOWN... ACCIDENTAL LIKE.
'CAUSE IT SOUNDS LIKE SHE CLIMBED WAY UNDER YOUR SKIN, DD... DEEP.
DON'T PRESUME TO LECTURE ME ON MORALITY, MERC.
I WILL SEE TYPHOID BACK IN THE HANDS OF PROFESSIONALS. NO MORE, NO LESS. YOU WANT TO RUN BACK-UP, FINE.
BUT WHEN WE CATCH UP WITH TYPHOID... NON-INTERFERENCE WOULD BE GOOD FOR YOUR HEALTH.
OH, THIS IS GONNA BE A BARREL OF LAUGHS.
WHATEVER HAPPENED TO THAT SENSE OF HUMOR YOU SUPPOSEDLY DISCOVERED...?

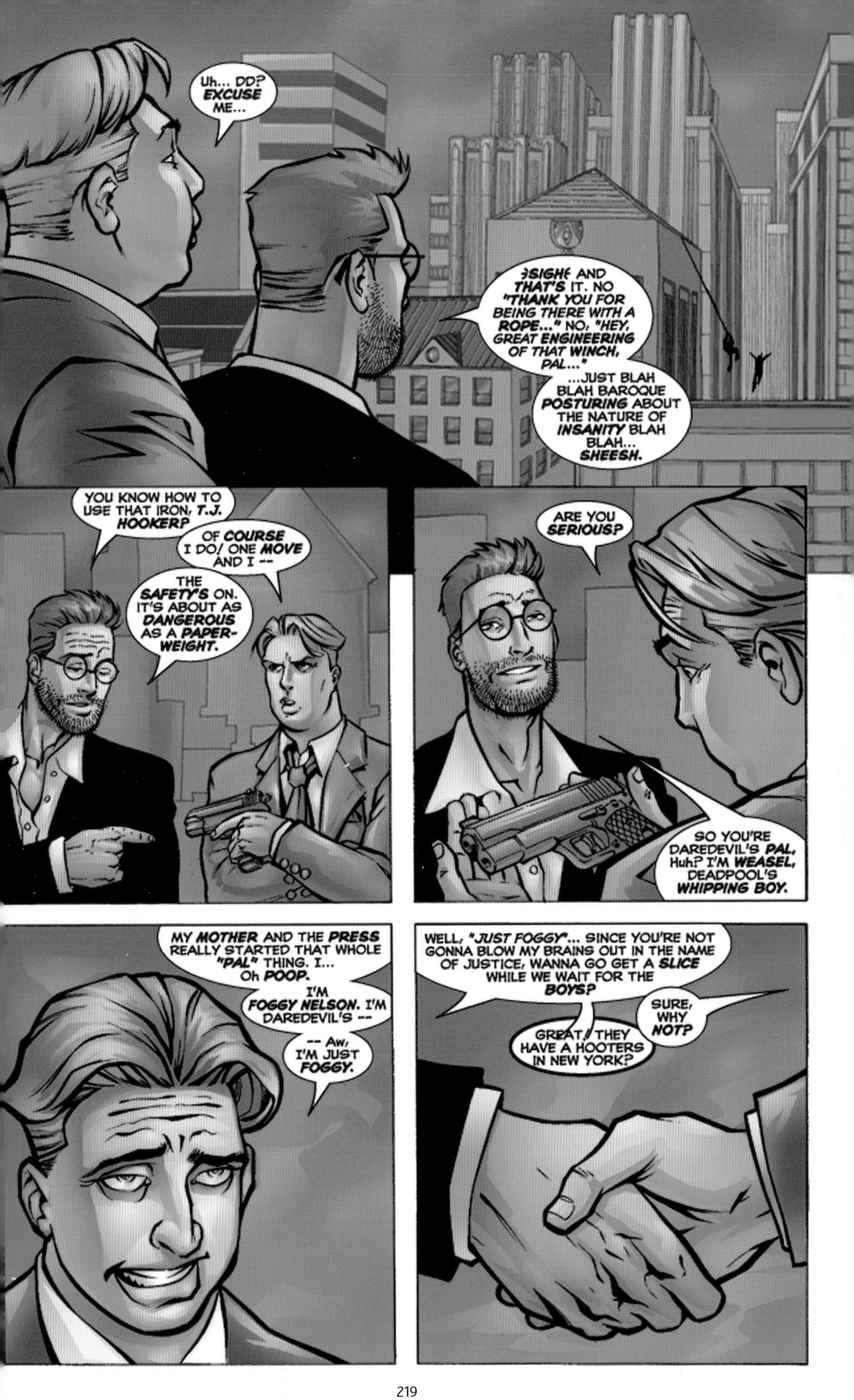
Uh... DD? EXCUSE ME...
?SIGH? AND THAT'S IT. NO "THANK YOU FOR BEING THERE WITH A ROPE..." NO, "HEY, GREAT ENGINEERING OF THAT WINCH, PAL..."
...JUST BLAH BLAH BAROQUE POSTURING ABOUT THE NATURE OF INSANITY BLAH BLAH... SHEESH.
YOU KNOW HOW TO USE THAT IRON, T.J. HOOKER?
OF COURSE I DO! ONE MOVE AND I --
THE SAFETY'S ON. IT'S ABOUT AS DANGEROUS AS A PAPER-WEIGHT.
ARE YOU SERIOUS?
SO YOU'RE DAREDEVIL'S PAL, Huh? I'M WEASEL, DEADPOOL'S WHIPPING BOY.
MY MOTHER AND THE PRESS REALLY STARTED THAT WHOLE "PAL" THING. I... Oh POOP.
I'M FOGGY NELSON. I'M DAREDEVIL'S --
-- Aw, I'M JUST FOGGY.
WELL, "JUST FOGGY"... SINCE YOU'RE NOT GONNA BLOW MY BRAINS OUT IN THE NAME OF JUSTICE, WANNA GO GET A SLICE WHILE WE WAIT FOR THE BOYS?
SURE, WHY NOT?
GREAT! THEY HAVE A HOOTERS IN NEW YORK?

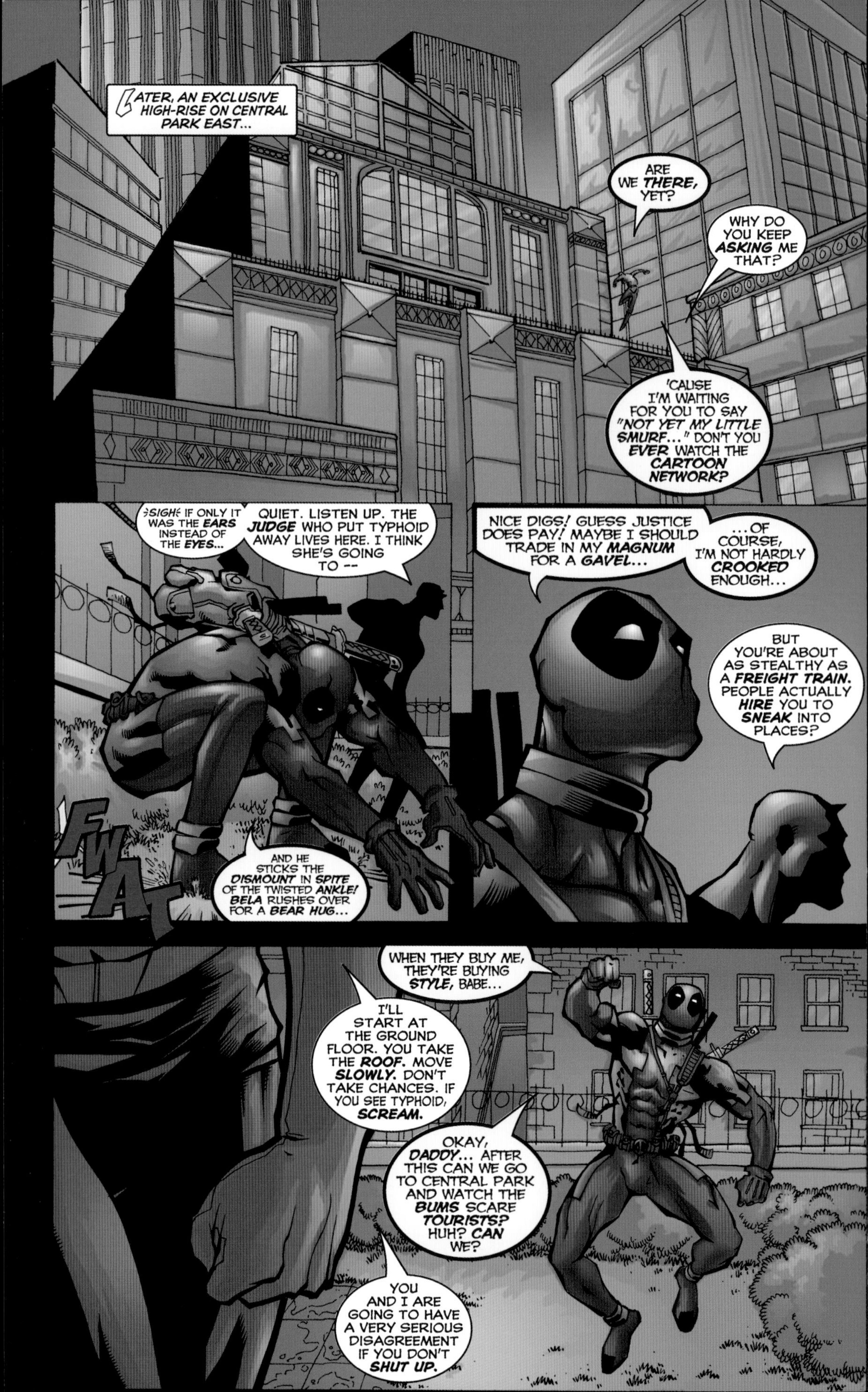
LATER, AN EXCLUSIVE HIGH-RISE ON CENTRAL PARK EAST...
ARE WE THERE, YET?
WHY DO YOU KEEP ASKING ME THAT?
'CAUSE I'M WAITING FOR YOU TO SAY "NOT YET MY LITTLE SMURF..." DON'T YOU EVER WATCH THE CARTOON NETWORK?
SIGH IF ONLY IT WAS THE EARS INSTEAD OF THE EYES...
QUIET. LISTEN UP. THE JUDGE WHO PUT TYPHOID AWAY LIVES HERE. I THINK SHE'S GOING TO --
FWAT
AND HE STICKS THE DISMOUNT IN SPITE OF THE TWISTED ANKLE! BELA RUSHES OVER FOR A BEAR HUG...
NICE DIGS! GUESS JUSTICE DOES PAY! MAYBE I SHOULD TRADE IN MY MAGNUM FOR A GAVEL...
...OF COURSE, I'M NOT HARDLY CROOKED ENOUGH...
BUT YOU'RE ABOUT AS STEALTHY AS A FREIGHT TRAIN. PEOPLE ACTUALLY HIRE YOU TO SNEAK INTO PLACES?
WHEN THEY BUY ME, THEY'RE BUYING STYLE, BABE...
I'LL START AT THE GROUND FLOOR. YOU TAKE THE ROOF. MOVE SLOWLY. DON'T TAKE CHANCES. IF YOU SEE TYPHOID, SCREAM.
OKAY, DADDY... AFTER THIS CAN WE GO TO CENTRAL PARK AND WATCH THE BUMS SCARE TOURISTS? HUH? CAN WE?
YOU AND I ARE GOING TO HAVE A VERY SERIOUS DISAGREEMENT IF YOU DON'T SHUT UP.

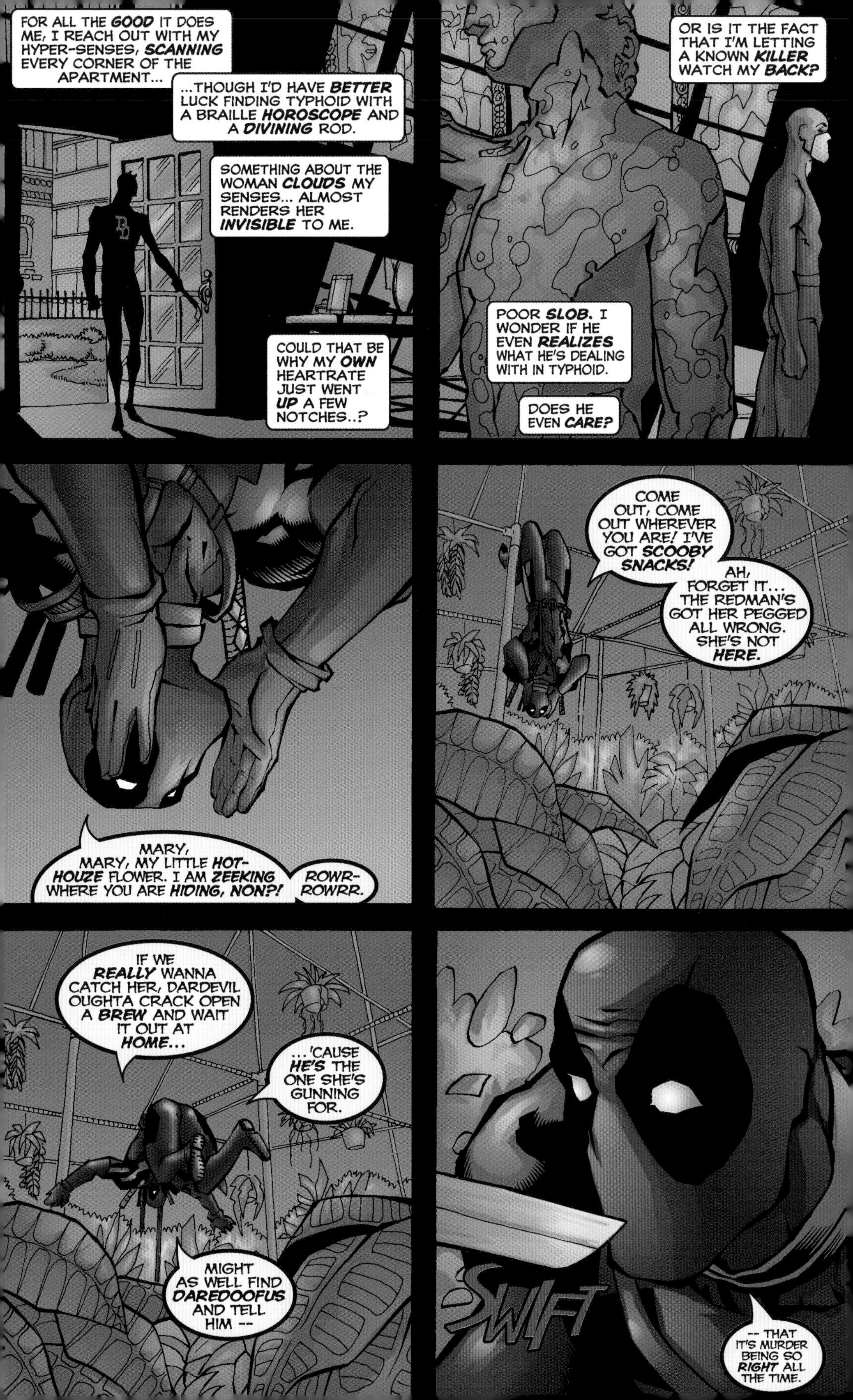
FOR ALL THE GOOD IT DOES ME, I REACH OUT WITH MY HYPER-SENSES, SCANNING EVERY CORNER OF THE APARTMENT...
...THOUGH I'D HAVE BETTER LUCK FINDING TYPHOID WITH A BRAILLE HOROSCOPE AND A DIVINING ROD.
SOMETHING ABOUT THE WOMAN CLOUDS MY SENSES... ALMOST RENDERS HER INVISIBLE TO ME.
COULD THAT BE WHY MY OWN HEARTRATE JUST WENT UP A FEW NOTCHES..?
OR IS IT THE FACT THAT I'M LETTING A KNOWN KILLER WATCH MY BACK?
POOR SLOB. I WONDER IF HE EVEN REALIZES WHAT HE'S DEALING WITH IN TYPHOID.
DOES HE EVEN CARE?
MARY, MARY, MY LITTLE HOT-HOUZE FLOWER. I AM ZEEKING WHERE YOU ARE HIDING, NON?!
ROWR-ROWRR.
COME OUT, COME OUT WHEREVER YOU ARE! I'VE GOT SCOOBY SNACKS!
AH, FORGET IT... THE REDMAN'S GOT HER PEGGED ALL WRONG. SHE'S NOT HERE.
IF WE REALLY WANNA CATCH HER, DARDEVIL OUGHTA CRACK OPEN A BREW AND WAIT IT OUT AT HOME...
...'CAUSE HE'S THE ONE SHE'S GUNNING FOR.
MIGHT AS WELL FIND DAREDOOFUS AND TELL HIM --
SWIFT
-- THAT IT'S MURDER BEING SO RIGHT ALL THE TIME.

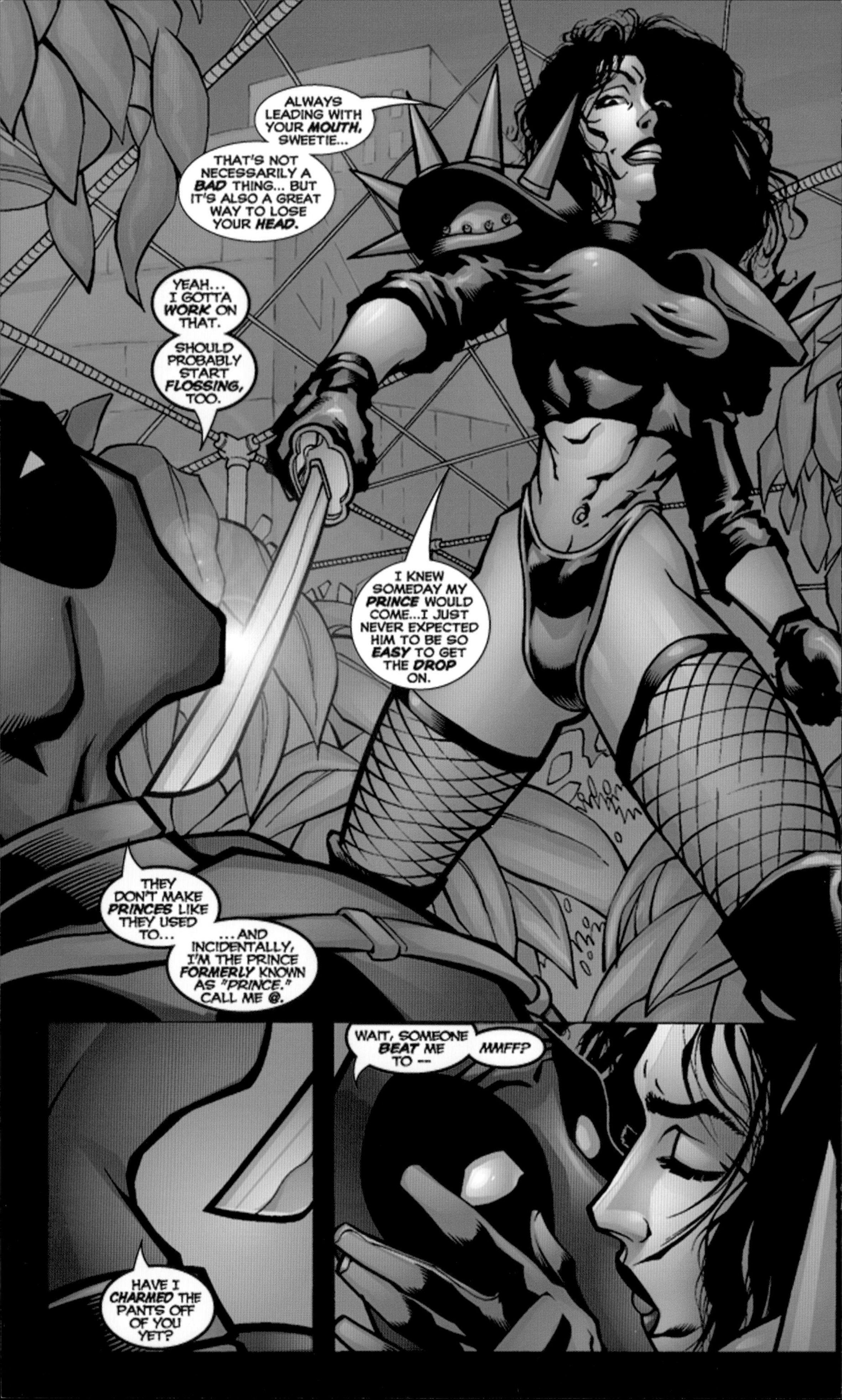
ALWAYS LEADING WITH YOUR MOUTH, SWEETIE...
THAT'S NOT NECESSARILY A BAD THING... BUT IT'S ALSO A GREAT WAY TO LOSE YOUR HEAD.
YEAH... I GOTTA WORK ON THAT.
SHOULD PROBABLY START FLOSSING, TOO.
I KNEW SOMEDAY MY PRINCE WOULD COME...I JUST NEVER EXPECTED HIM TO BE SO EASY TO GET THE DROP ON.
THEY DON'T MAKE PRINCES LIKE THEY USED TO...
...AND INCIDENTALLY, I'M THE PRINCE FORMERLY KNOWN AS "PRINCE." CALL ME @.
WAIT, SOMEONE BEAT ME TO --
MMFF?
HAVE I CHARMED THE PANTS OFF OF YOU YET?

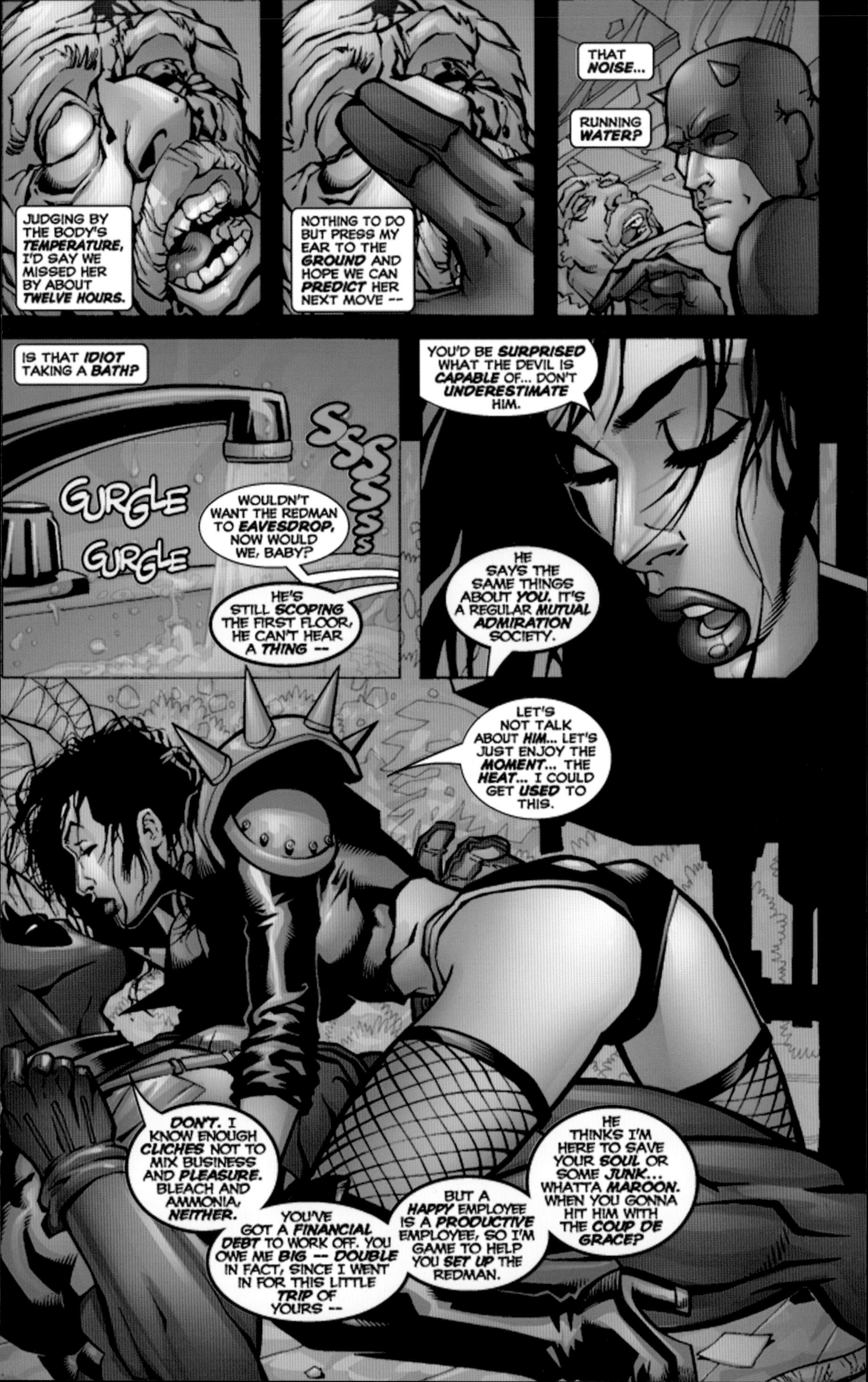

JUDGING BY THE BODY'S TEMPERATURE, I'D SAY WE MISSED HER BY ABOUT TWELVE HOURS.
NOTHING TO DO BUT PRESS MY EAR TO THE GROUND AND HOPE WE CAN PREDICT HER NEXT MOVE --
THAT NOISE...
RUNNING WATER?
IS THAT IDIOT TAKING A BATH?
SSSSSSS
GURGLE
GURGLE
WOULDN'T WANT THE REDMAN TO EAVESDROP, NOW WOULD WE, BABY?
HE'S STILL SCOPING THE FIRST FLOOR, HE CAN'T HEAR A THING --
YOU'D BE SURPRISED WHAT THE DEVIL IS CAPABLE OF... DON'T UNDERESTIMATE HIM.
HE SAYS THE SAME THINGS ABOUT YOU. IT'S A REGULAR MUTUAL ADMIRATION SOCIETY.
LET'S NOT TALK ABOUT HIM... LET'S JUST ENJOY THE MOMENT... THE HEAT... I COULD GET USED TO THIS.
DON'T. I KNOW ENOUGH CLICHES NOT TO MIX BUSINESS AND PLEASURE. BLEACH AND AMMONIA, NEITHER.
YOU'VE GOT A FINANCIAL DEBT TO WORK OFF. YOU OWE ME BIG -- DOUBLE IN FACT, SINCE I WENT IN FOR THIS LITTLE TRIP OF YOURS --
BUT A HAPPY EMPLOYEE IS A PRODUCTIVE EMPLOYEE, SO I'M GAME TO HELP YOU SET UP THE REDMAN.
HE THINKS I'M HERE TO SAVE YOUR SOUL OR SOME JUNK... WHATTA MAROON. WHEN YOU GONNA HIT HIM WITH THE COUP DE GRACE?

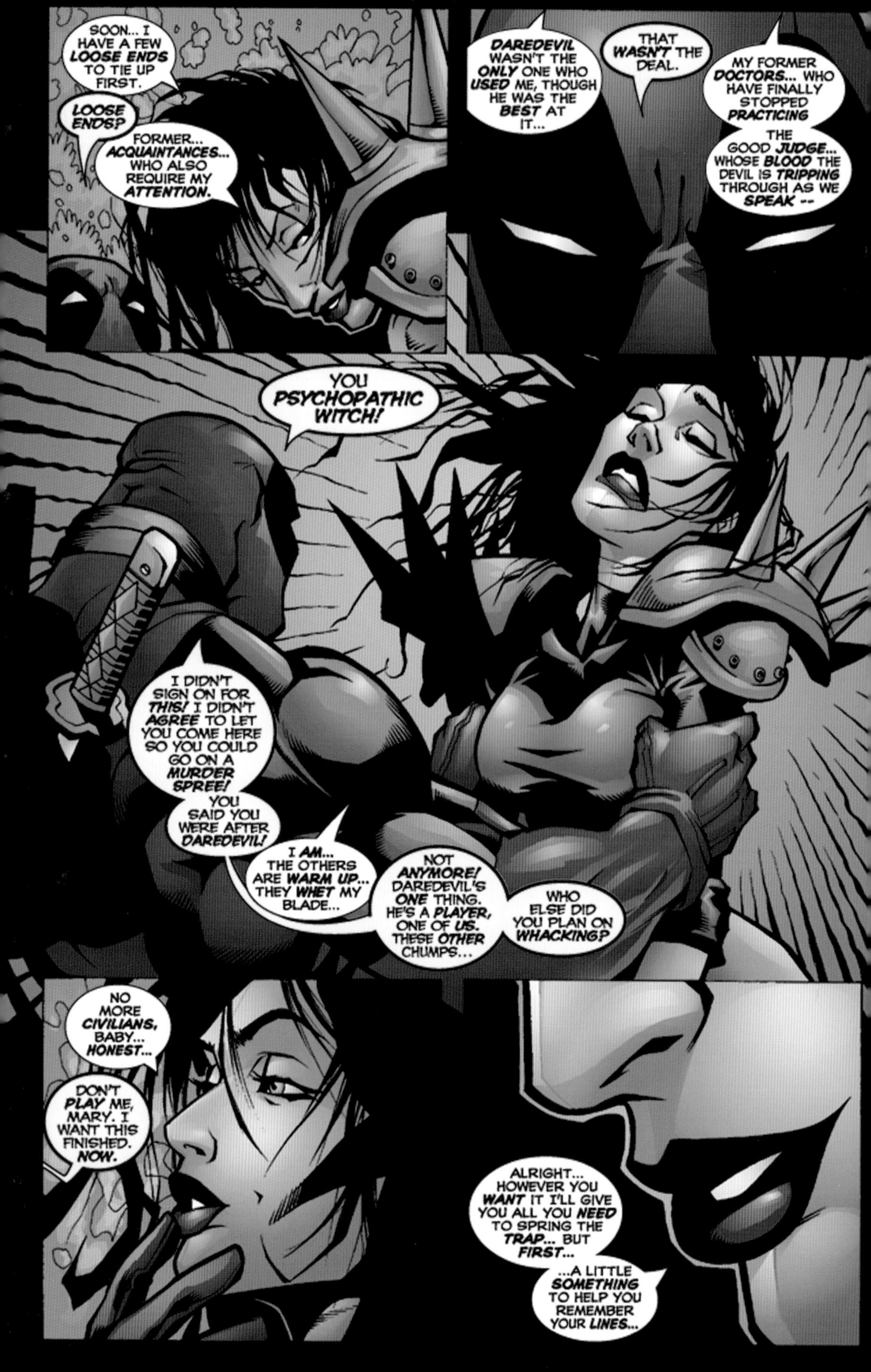

SOON... I HAVE A FEW LOOSE ENDS TO TIE UP FIRST.
LOOSE ENDS?
FORMER... ACQUAINTANCES... WHO ALSO REQUIRE MY ATTENTION.
DAREDEVIL WASN'T THE ONLY ONE WHO USED ME, THOUGH HE WAS THE BEST AT IT...
THAT WASN'T THE DEAL.
MY FORMER DOCTORS... WHO HAVE FINALLY STOPPED PRACTICING
THE GOOD JUDGE... WHOSE BLOOD THE DEVIL IS TRIPPING THROUGH AS WE SPEAK --
YOU PSYCHOPATHIC WITCH!
I DIDN'T SIGN ON FOR THIS! I DIDN'T AGREE TO LET YOU COME HERE SO YOU COULD GO ON A MURDER SPREE!
YOU SAID YOU WERE AFTER DAREDEVIL!
I AM... THE OTHERS ARE WARM UP... THEY WHET MY BLADE...
NOT ANYMORE! DAREDEVIL'S ONE THING. HE'S A PLAYER, ONE OF US. THESE OTHER CHUMPS...
WHO ELSE DID YOU PLAN ON WHACKING?
NO MORE CIVILIANS, BABY... HONEST...
DON'T PLAY ME, MARY. I WANT THIS FINISHED. NOW.
ALRIGHT... HOWEVER YOU WANT IT I'LL GIVE YOU ALL YOU NEED TO SPRING THE TRAP... BUT FIRST...
...A LITTLE SOMETHING TO HELP YOU REMEMBER YOUR LINES...

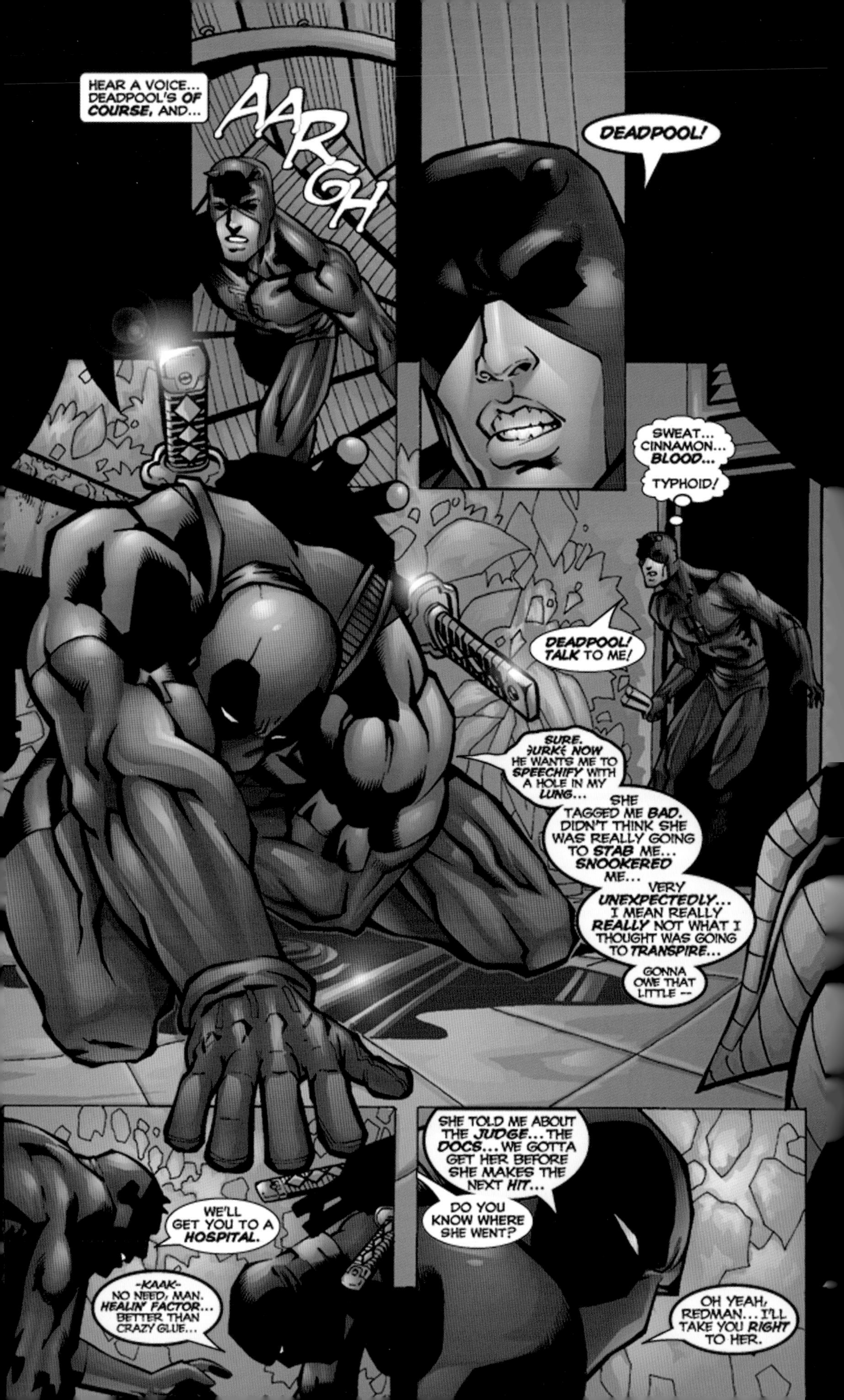

HEAR A VOICE... DEADPOOL'S OF COURSE, AND...
AARGH
DEADPOOL!
SWEAT... CINNAMON... BLOOD...
TYPHOID!
DEADPOOL! TALK TO ME!
SURE. ‹URK› NOW HE WANTS ME TO SPEECHIFY WITH A HOLE IN MY LUNG...
SHE TAGGED ME BAD. DIDN'T THINK SHE WAS REALLY GOING TO STAB ME... SNOOKERED ME... VERY UNEXPECTEDLY... I MEAN REALLY REALLY NOT WHAT I THOUGHT WAS GOING TO TRANSPIRE...
GONNA OWE THAT LITTLE --
WE'LL GET YOU TO A HOSPITAL.
-KAAK- NO NEED, MAN. HEALIN' FACTOR... BETTER THAN CRAZY GLUE...
SHE TOLD ME ABOUT THE JUDGE... THE DOCS... WE GOTTA GET HER BEFORE SHE MAKES THE NEXT HIT...
DO YOU KNOW WHERE SHE WENT?
OH YEAH, REDMAN... I'LL TAKE YOU RIGHT TO HER.

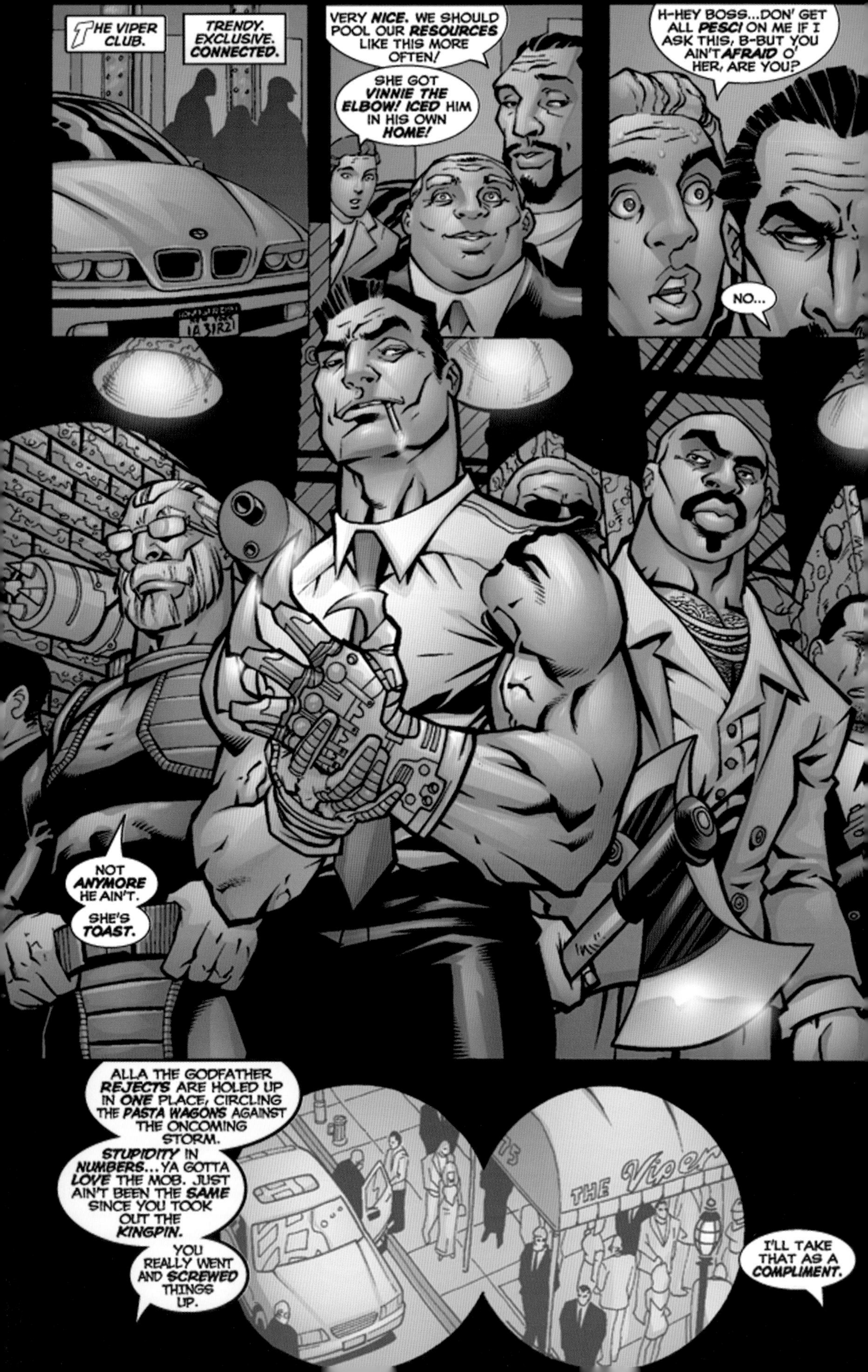
THE VIPER CLUB.
TRENDY. EXCLUSIVE. CONNECTED.
VERY NICE. WE SHOULD POOL OUR RESOURCES LIKE THIS MORE OFTEN!
SHE GOT VINNIE THE ELBOW! ICED HIM IN HIS OWN HOME!
H-HEY BOSS...DON' GET ALL PESCI ON ME IF I ASK THIS, B-BUT YOU AIN'T AFRAID O' HER, ARE YOU?
NO...
NOT ANYMORE HE AIN'T.
SHE'S TOAST.
ALLA THE GODFATHER REJECTS ARE HOLED UP IN ONE PLACE, CIRCLING THE PASTA WAGONS AGAINST THE ONCOMING STORM.
STUPIDITY IN NUMBERS...YA GOTTA LOVE THE MOB. JUST AIN'T BEEN THE SAME SINCE YOU TOOK OUT THE KINGPIN.
YOU REALLY WENT AND SCREWED THINGS UP.
THE Viper
I'LL TAKE THAT AS A COMPLIMENT.

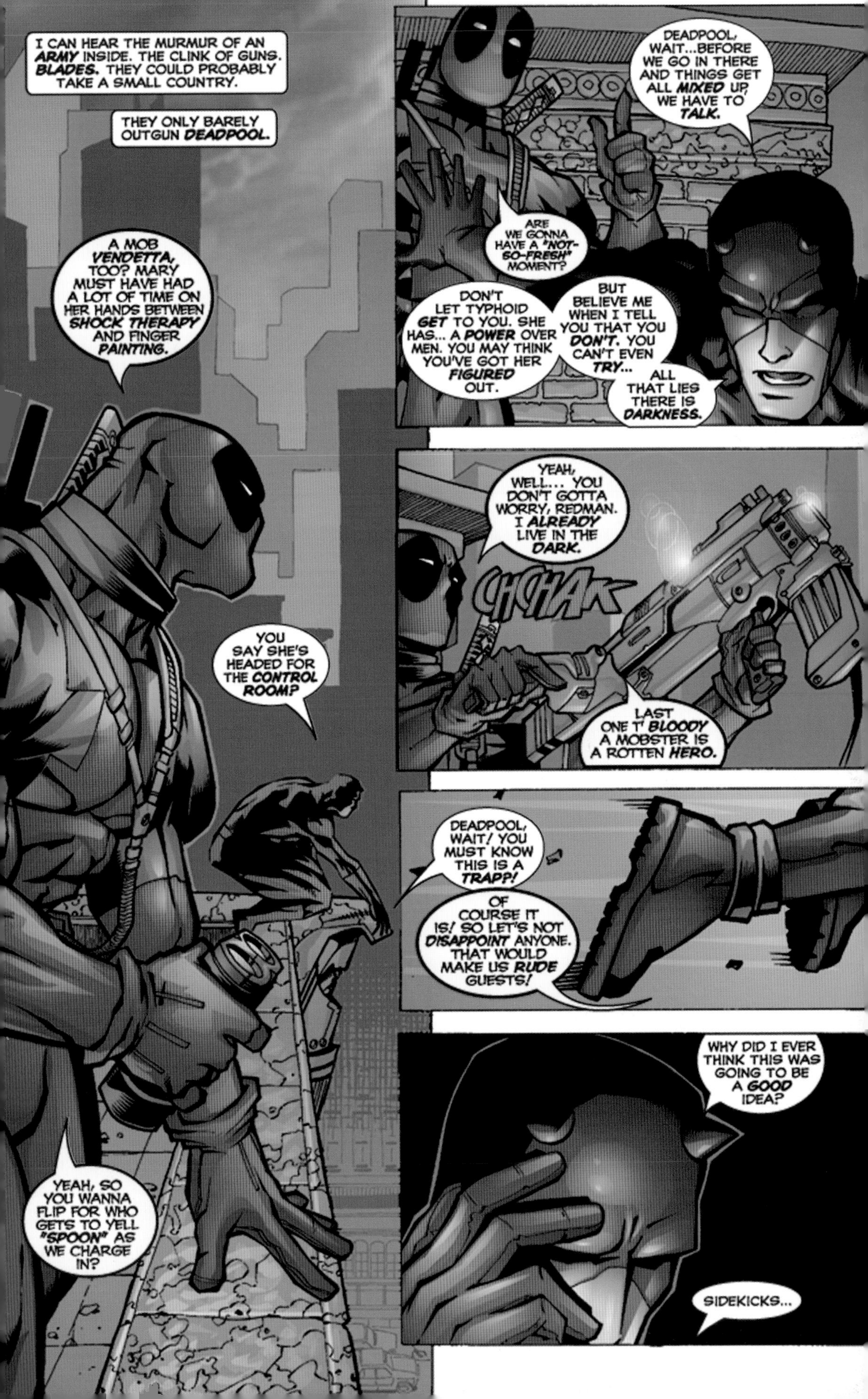

I CAN HEAR THE MURMUR OF AN ARMY INSIDE. THE CLINK OF GUNS. BLADES. THEY COULD PROBABLY TAKE A SMALL COUNTRY.
THEY ONLY BARELY OUTGUN DEADPOOL.
A MOB VENDETTA, TOO? MARY MUST HAVE HAD A LOT OF TIME ON HER HANDS BETWEEN SHOCK THERAPY AND FINGER PAINTING.
YOU SAY SHE'S HEADED FOR THE CONTROL ROOM?
YEAH, SO YOU WANNA FLIP FOR WHO GETS TO YELL "SPOON" AS WE CHARGE IN?
DEADPOOL, WAIT...BEFORE WE GO IN THERE AND THINGS GET ALL MIXED UP, WE HAVE TO TALK.
ARE WE GONNA HAVE A "NOT-SO-FRESH" MOMENT?
DON'T LET TYPHOID GET TO YOU. SHE HAS... A POWER OVER MEN. YOU MAY THINK YOU'VE GOT HER FIGURED OUT.
BUT BELIEVE ME WHEN I TELL YOU THAT YOU DON'T. YOU CAN'T EVEN TRY...
ALL THAT LIES THERE IS DARKNESS.
YEAH, WELL... YOU DON'T GOTTA WORRY, REDMAN. I ALREADY LIVE IN THE DARK.
CHCHAK
LAST ONE T' BLOODY A MOBSTER IS A ROTTEN HERO.
DEADPOOL, WAIT! YOU MUST KNOW THIS IS A TRAPP!
OF COURSE IT IS! SO LET'S NOT DISAPPOINT ANYONE. THAT WOULD MAKE US RUDE GUESTS!
WHY DID I EVER THINK THIS WAS GOING TO BE A GOOD IDEA?
SIDEKICKS...

Panel 1:

DOWNTOWN, AT A LITTLE JOINT IN THE VILLAGE...

MA___'S WORLD FAMOUS PIZZA

‹MMGLFF› S'EXCELLENT! YOU GOTTA TRY THE ‹SMAK› SHRIMP AND *FETA CHEESE* ONE! MMM -- IT'S TO *DIE*, WEASEL!

Oh, I DON'T KNOW, I'M SORT OF *STUFFED*...UNLESS YOU'RE, uh... PICKING UP THE *TAB*..?

SURE! WHAT GOOD'S BEING A LAWYER IF YOU CAN'T SPLURGE AFTER A *NEAR-DEATH* EXPERIENCE?

Panel 2:

EXCELLENT! HERE YOU GO, *POOCHIE*, DADDY'S PICKIN' UP THE TAB! SO *WELL TRAINED*... SEEIN' EYE DOG TOO, HUH?

SLURP

Panel 3:

SO, AS *DD'S* PAL, WHAT DO YOU DO, *EXACTLY?* MUST BE PRETTY *HOT* STUFF.

WELL, NOT --

ONE TIME, I SAVED POOL'S BACON BY *PLUGGING* A GUY RIGHT THROUGH THE *BRAINPAN!* BANG! COOL, RIGHT?

Panel 4:

Oh *HEAVENS*... NO, I DON'T DO ANYTHING LIKE THAT!

COME ON, *FOGGSTER*, YOU CAN TELL *ME*... HE MAKE YOU CLEAN HIS *WEAPONS?* *HACK* INTO CIA COMPUTERS?

Uh, NO... *TECHNOLOGY* AND I AREN'T VERY *COMPATIBLE*...

Panel 5:

HE EVER HAVE YOU OPEN ANY *TICKING PACKAGES?* USE YOU FOR *TARGET* PRACTICE? DRIVE HIM AT 3AM TO *GUNS'R'US?*

ACTUALLY, I DON'T HAVE A *LICENSE*, AND HE DOESN'T *MAKE* ME DO ANYTHING.

WE JUS', Y'KNOW... *HANG OUT*. PALS.

Panel 6:

DO YOU THINK... DAREDEVIL COULD USE *ANOTHER* PAL? I WON'T GET IN THE WAY, I *PROMISE*...

YOU DON'T LIKE BEING *DEADPOOL'S* PAL?

IT'S *GREAT*. THE BEST. YOU WANNA *TRADE?* YOU'LL HAVE *FUN*...‹SNIFF› I PROMISE...

228

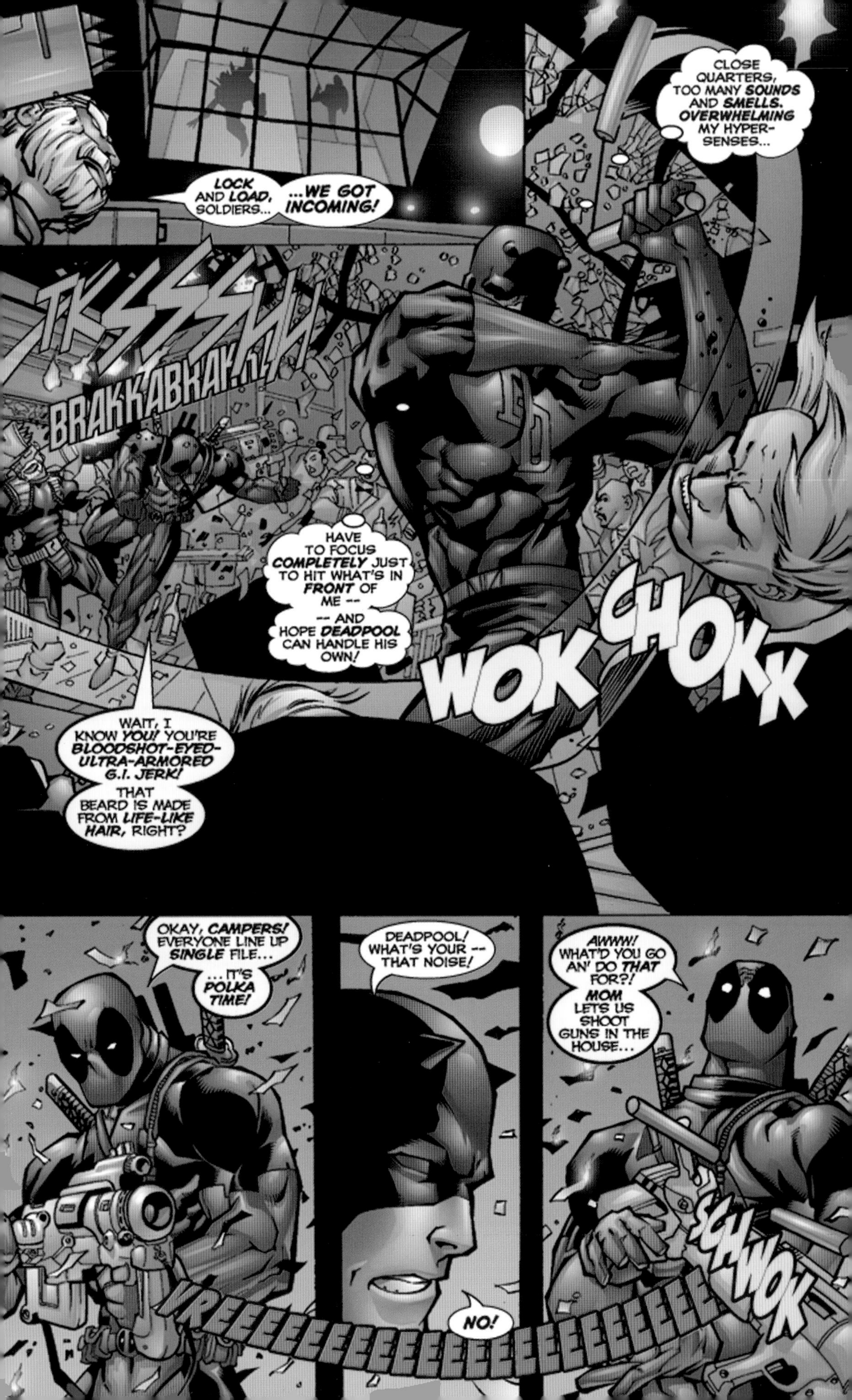
LOCK AND LOAD, SOLDIERS...
...WE GOT INCOMING!
CLOSE QUARTERS, TOO MANY SOUNDS AND SMELLS. OVERWHELMING MY HYPER-SENSES...
TKSSSHH
BRAKKABRAK
HAVE TO FOCUS COMPLETELY JUST TO HIT WHAT'S IN FRONT OF ME --
-- AND HOPE DEADPOOL CAN HANDLE HIS OWN!
WOK
CHOKK
WAIT, I KNOW YOU! YOU'RE BLOODSHOT-EYED-ULTRA-ARMORED G.I. JERK!
THAT BEARD IS MADE FROM LIFE-LIKE HAIR, RIGHT?
OKAY, CAMPERS! EVERYONE LINE UP SINGLE FILE...
...IT'S POLKA TIME!
DEADPOOL! WHAT'S YOUR -- THAT NOISE!
NO!
AWWW! WHAT'D YOU GO AN' DO THAT FOR?!
MOM LETS US SHOOT GUNS IN THE HOUSE...
SCHWOK

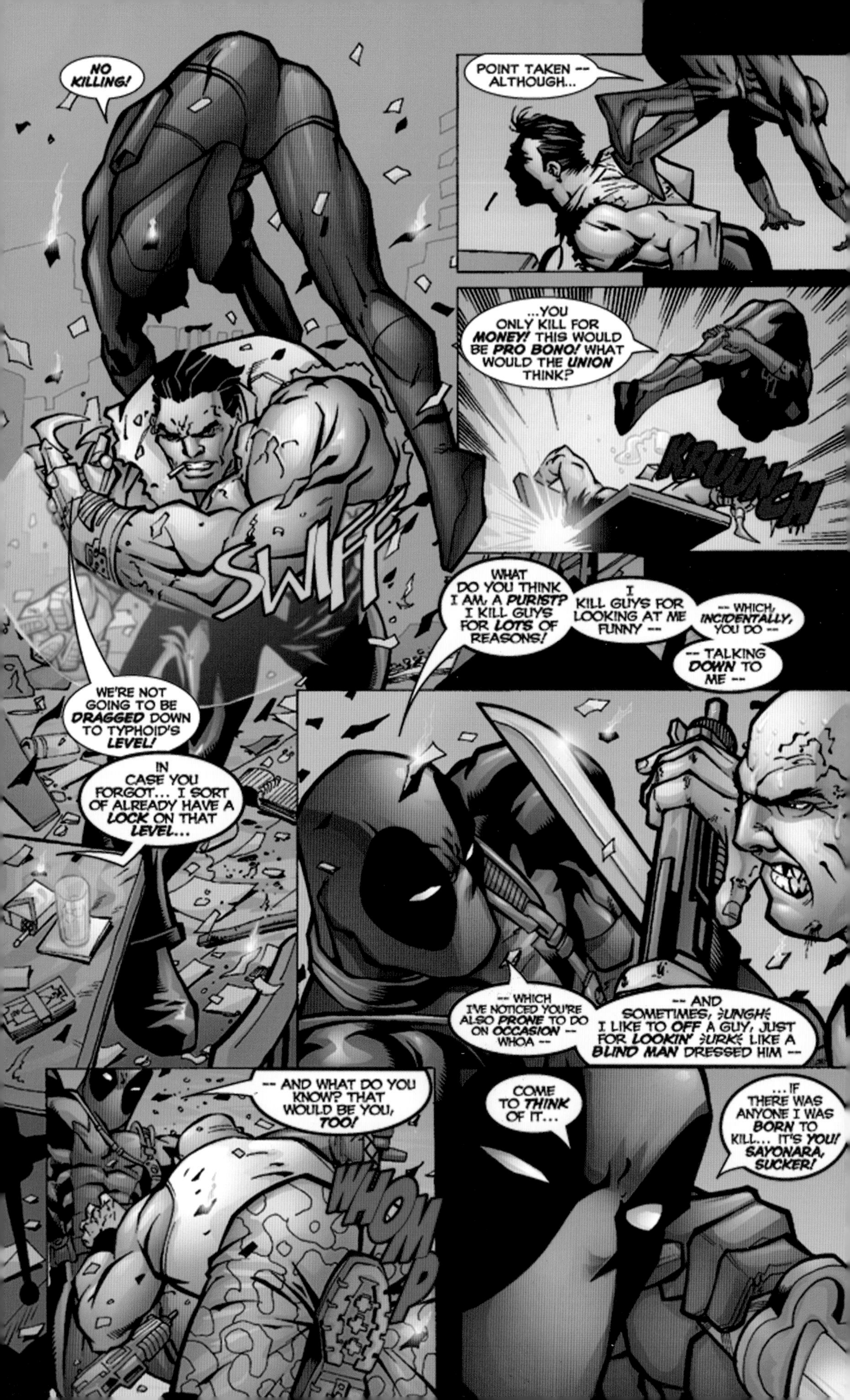
NO KILLING!
POINT TAKEN -- ALTHOUGH...
...YOU ONLY KILL FOR MONEY! THIS WOULD BE PRO BONO! WHAT WOULD THE UNION THINK?
KRUUNCH
SWIFF
WHAT DO YOU THINK I AM, A PURIST? I KILL GUYS FOR LOTS OF REASONS!
I KILL GUYS FOR LOOKING AT ME FUNNY --
-- WHICH, INCIDENTALLY, YOU DO --
-- TALKING DOWN TO ME --
WE'RE NOT GOING TO BE DRAGGED DOWN TO TYPHOID'S LEVEL!
IN CASE YOU FORGOT... I SORT OF ALREADY HAVE A LOCK ON THAT LEVEL...
-- WHICH I'VE NOTICED YOU'RE ALSO PRONE TO DO ON OCCASION -- WHOA --
-- AND SOMETIMES, UNGH I LIKE TO OFF A GUY, JUST FOR LOOKIN' URK LIKE A BLIND MAN DRESSED HIM --
-- AND WHAT DO YOU KNOW? THAT WOULD BE YOU, TOO!
COME TO THINK OF IT...
...IF THERE WAS ANYONE I WAS BORN TO KILL... IT'S YOU! SAYONARA, SUCKER!

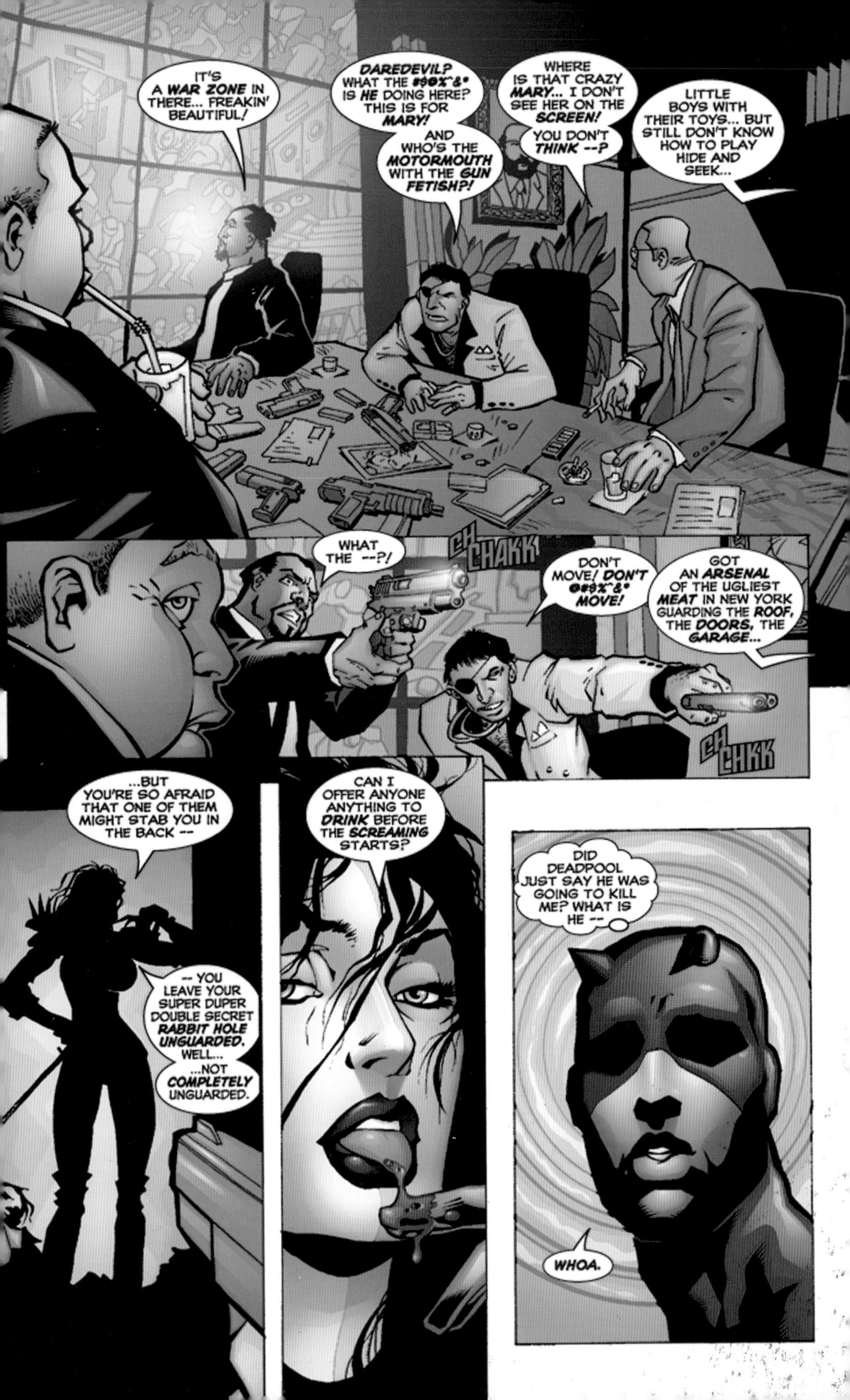

IT'S A WAR ZONE IN THERE... FREAKIN' BEAUTIFUL!
DAREDEVIL? WHAT THE #$@%^&* IS HE DOING HERE? THIS IS FOR MARY!
AND WHO'S THE MOTORMOUTH WITH THE GUN FETISH?!
WHERE IS THAT CRAZY MARY... I DON'T SEE HER ON THE SCREEN!
YOU DON'T THINK --?
LITTLE BOYS WITH THEIR TOYS... BUT STILL DON'T KNOW HOW TO PLAY HIDE AND SEEK...
WHAT THE --?!
CH CHAKK
DON'T MOVE! DON'T @#$%^&* MOVE!
GOT AN ARSENAL OF THE UGLIEST MEAT IN NEW YORK GUARDING THE ROOF, THE DOORS, THE GARAGE...
CH CHKK
...BUT YOU'RE SO AFRAID THAT ONE OF THEM MIGHT STAB YOU IN THE BACK --
-- YOU LEAVE YOUR SUPER DUPER DOUBLE SECRET RABBIT HOLE UNGUARDED. WELL...
...NOT COMPLETELY UNGUARDED.
CAN I OFFER ANYONE ANYTHING TO DRINK BEFORE THE SCREAMING STARTS?
DID DEADPOOL JUST SAY HE WAS GOING TO KILL ME? WHAT IS HE --
WHOA.

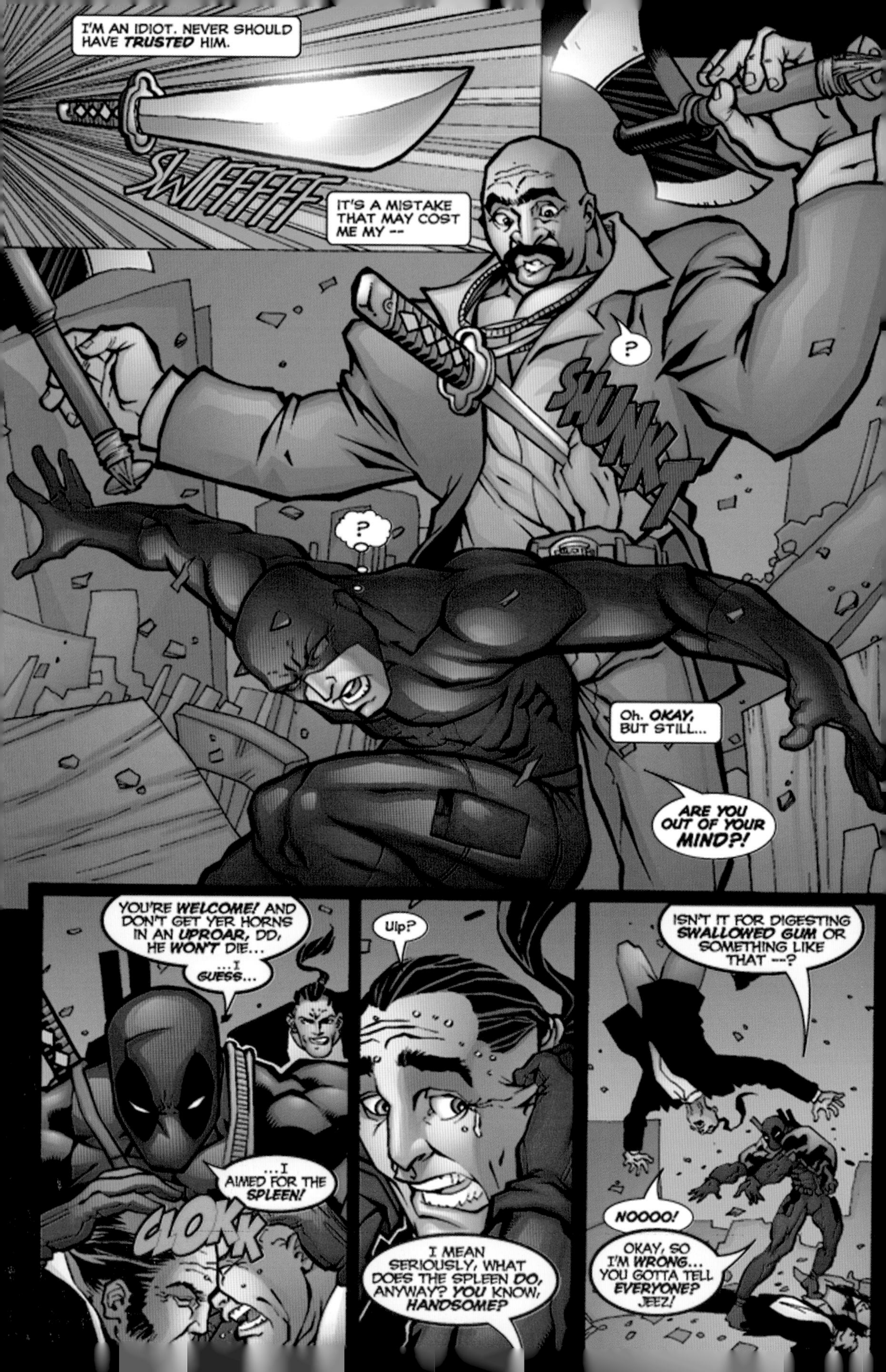

I'M AN IDIOT. NEVER SHOULD HAVE TRUSTED HIM.
SWFFFFF
IT'S A MISTAKE THAT MAY COST ME MY --
?
SHUNKT
?
Oh. OKAY, BUT STILL...
ARE YOU OUT OF YOUR MIND?!
YOU'RE WELCOME! AND DON'T GET YER HORNS IN AN UPROAR, DD, HE WON'T DIE...
...I GUESS...
...I AIMED FOR THE SPLEEN!
CLOKK
Ulp?
I MEAN SERIOUSLY, WHAT DOES THE SPLEEN DO, ANYWAY? YOU KNOW, HANDSOME?
ISN'T IT FOR DIGESTING SWALLOWED GUM OR SOMETHING LIKE THAT --?
NOOOO!
OKAY, SO I'M WRONG... YOU GOTTA TELL EVERYONE? JEEZ!

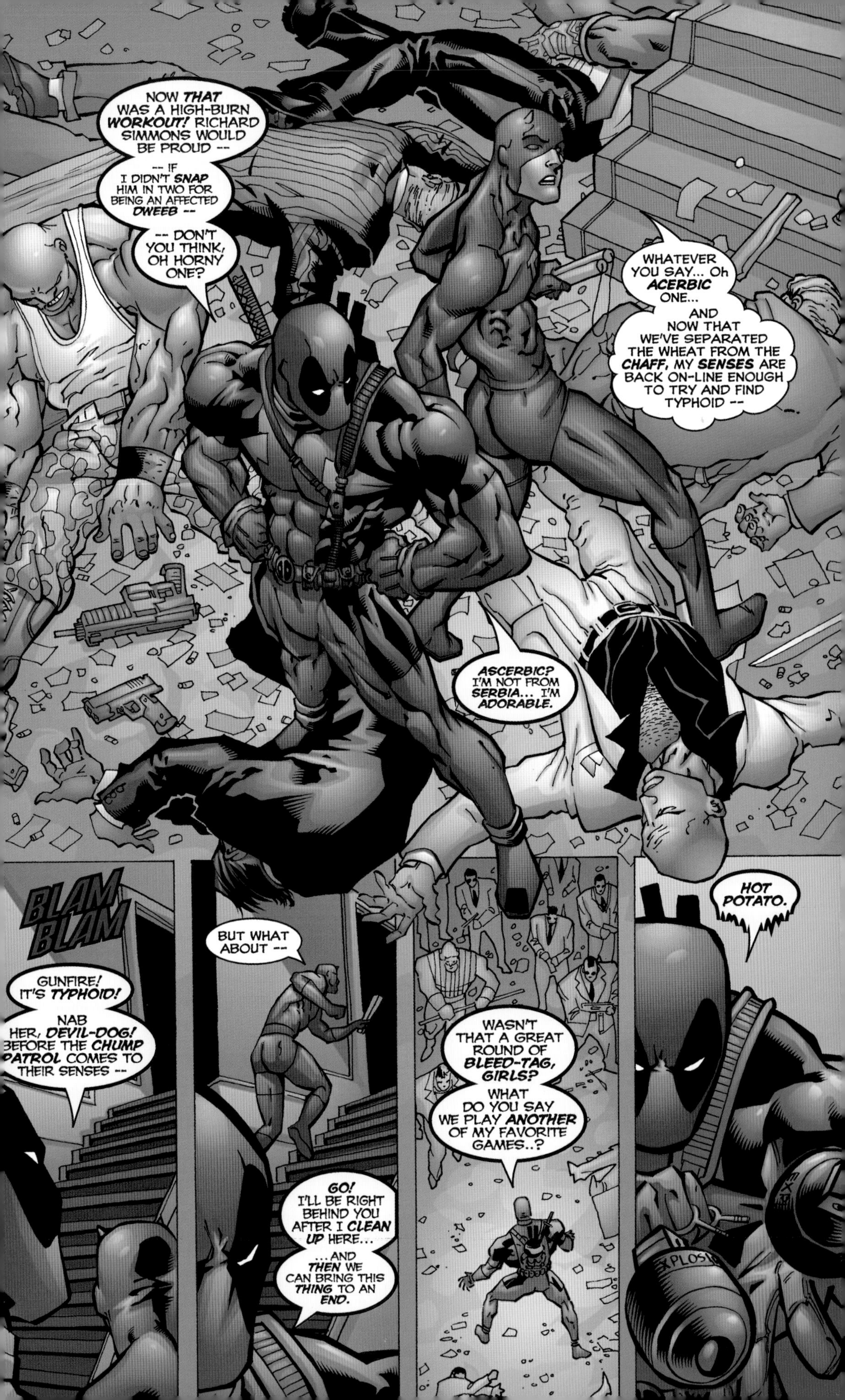
NOW THAT WAS A HIGH-BURN WORKOUT! RICHARD SIMMONS WOULD BE PROUD --
-- IF I DIDN'T SNAP HIM IN TWO FOR BEING AN AFFECTED DWEEB --
-- DON'T YOU THINK, OH HORNY ONE?
WHATEVER YOU SAY... Oh ACERBIC ONE...
AND NOW THAT WE'VE SEPARATED THE WHEAT FROM THE CHAFF, MY SENSES ARE BACK ON-LINE ENOUGH TO TRY AND FIND TYPHOID --
ASCERBIC? I'M NOT FROM SERBIA... I'M ADORABLE.
BLAM BLAM
GUNFIRE! IT'S TYPHOID!
NAB HER, DEVIL-DOG! BEFORE THE CHUMP PATROL COMES TO THEIR SENSES --
BUT WHAT ABOUT --
GO! I'LL BE RIGHT BEHIND YOU AFTER I CLEAN UP HERE...
...AND THEN WE CAN BRING THIS THING TO AN END.
WASN'T THAT A GREAT ROUND OF BLEED-TAG, GIRLS?
WHAT DO YOU SAY WE PLAY ANOTHER OF MY FAVORITE GAMES..?
HOT POTATO.

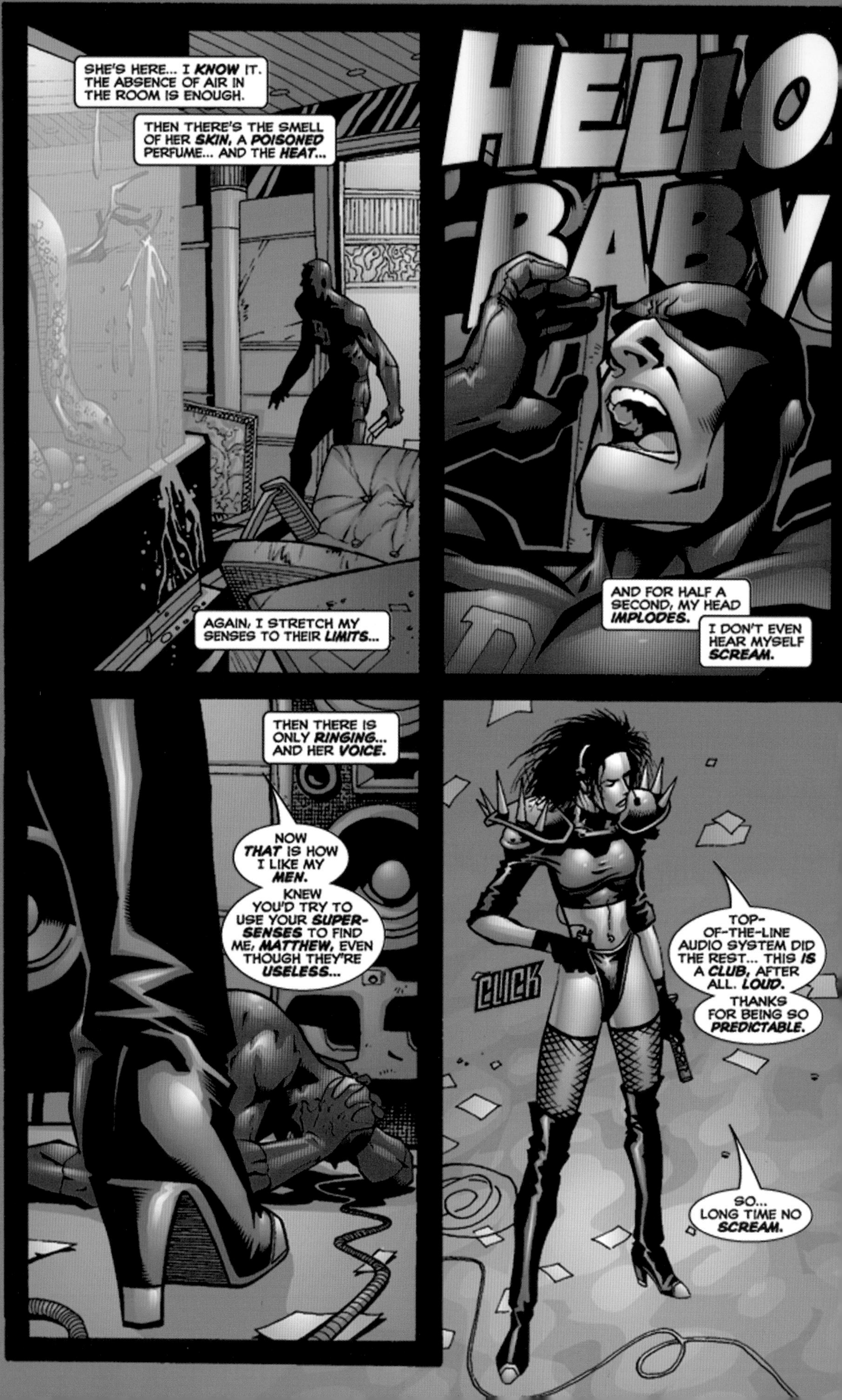
SHE'S HERE... I KNOW IT. THE ABSENCE OF AIR IN THE ROOM IS ENOUGH.
THEN THERE'S THE SMELL OF HER SKIN, A POISONED PERFUME... AND THE HEAT...
AGAIN, I STRETCH MY SENSES TO THEIR LIMITS...
HELLO BABY.
AND FOR HALF A SECOND, MY HEAD IMPLODES.
I DON'T EVEN HEAR MYSELF SCREAM.
THEN THERE IS ONLY RINGING... AND HER VOICE.
NOW THAT IS HOW I LIKE MY MEN.
KNEW YOU'D TRY TO USE YOUR SUPER-SENSES TO FIND ME, MATTHEW, EVEN THOUGH THEY'RE USELESS...
CLICK
TOP-OF-THE-LINE AUDIO SYSTEM DID THE REST... THIS IS A CLUB, AFTER ALL. LOUD.
THANKS FOR BEING SO PREDICTABLE.
SO... LONG TIME NO SCREAM.

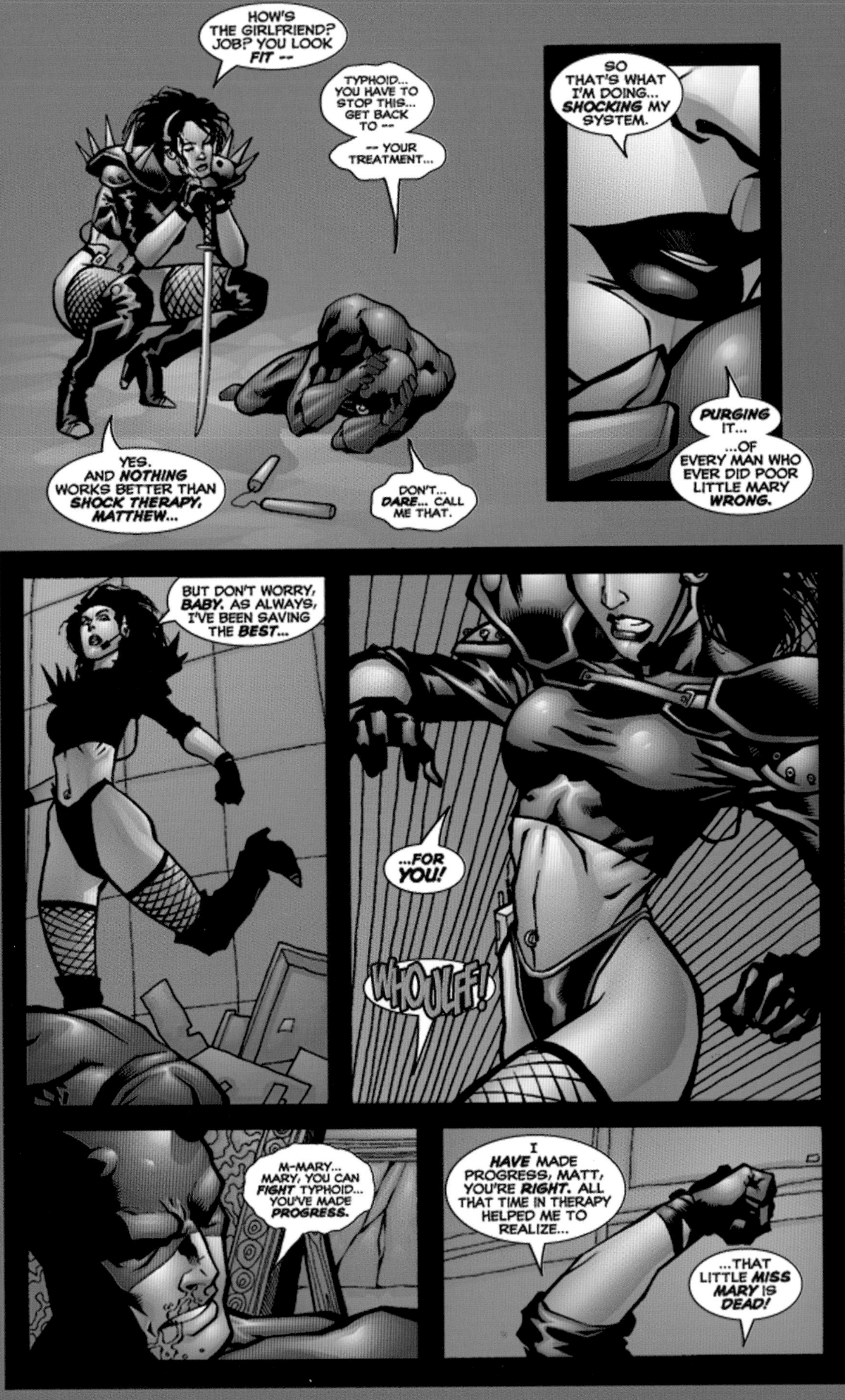

HOW'S THE GIRLFRIEND? JOB? YOU LOOK FIT --
TYPHOID... YOU HAVE TO STOP THIS... GET BACK TO --
-- YOUR TREATMENT...
YES. AND NOTHING WORKS BETTER THAN SHOCK THERAPY, MATTHEW...
DON'T... DARE... CALL ME THAT.
SO THAT'S WHAT I'M DOING... SHOCKING MY SYSTEM.
PURGING IT...
...OF EVERY MAN WHO EVER DID POOR LITTLE MARY WRONG.
BUT DON'T WORRY, BABY. AS ALWAYS, I'VE BEEN SAVING THE BEST...
...FOR YOU!
WHOOLFF!
M-MARY... MARY, YOU CAN FIGHT TYPHOID... YOU'VE MADE PROGRESS.
I HAVE MADE PROGRESS, MATT, YOU'RE RIGHT. ALL THAT TIME IN THERAPY HELPED ME TO REALIZE...
...THAT LITTLE MISS MARY IS DEAD!

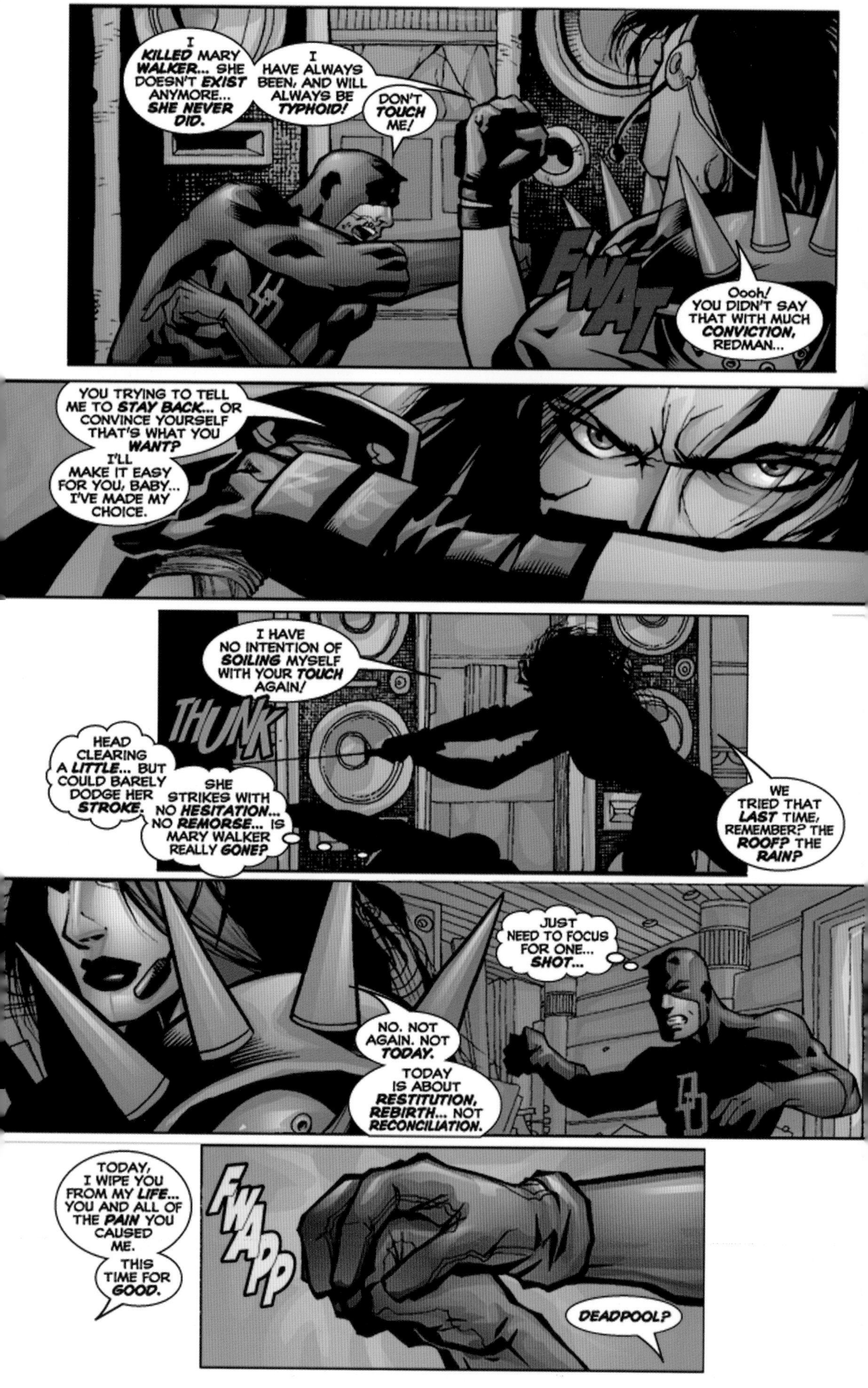

I KILLED MARY WALKER... SHE DOESN'T EXIST ANYMORE... SHE NEVER DID.
I HAVE ALWAYS BEEN, AND WILL ALWAYS BE TYPHOID!
DON'T TOUCH ME!
FWAT
Oooh! YOU DIDN'T SAY THAT WITH MUCH CONVICTION, REDMAN...
YOU TRYING TO TELL ME TO STAY BACK... OR CONVINCE YOURSELF THAT'S WHAT YOU WANT?
I'LL MAKE IT EASY FOR YOU, BABY... I'VE MADE MY CHOICE.
I HAVE NO INTENTION OF SOILING MYSELF WITH YOUR TOUCH AGAIN!
THUNK
HEAD CLEARING A LITTLE... BUT COULD BARELY DODGE HER STROKE.
SHE STRIKES WITH NO HESITATION... NO REMORSE... IS MARY WALKER REALLY GONE?
WE TRIED THAT LAST TIME, REMEMBER? THE ROOF? THE RAIN?
JUST NEED TO FOCUS FOR ONE... SHOT...
NO. NOT AGAIN. NOT TODAY.
TODAY IS ABOUT RESTITUTION, REBIRTH... NOT RECONCILIATION.
TODAY, I WIPE YOU FROM MY LIFE... YOU AND ALL OF THE PAIN YOU CAUSED ME.
THIS TIME FOR GOOD.
FWAPP
DEADPOOL?

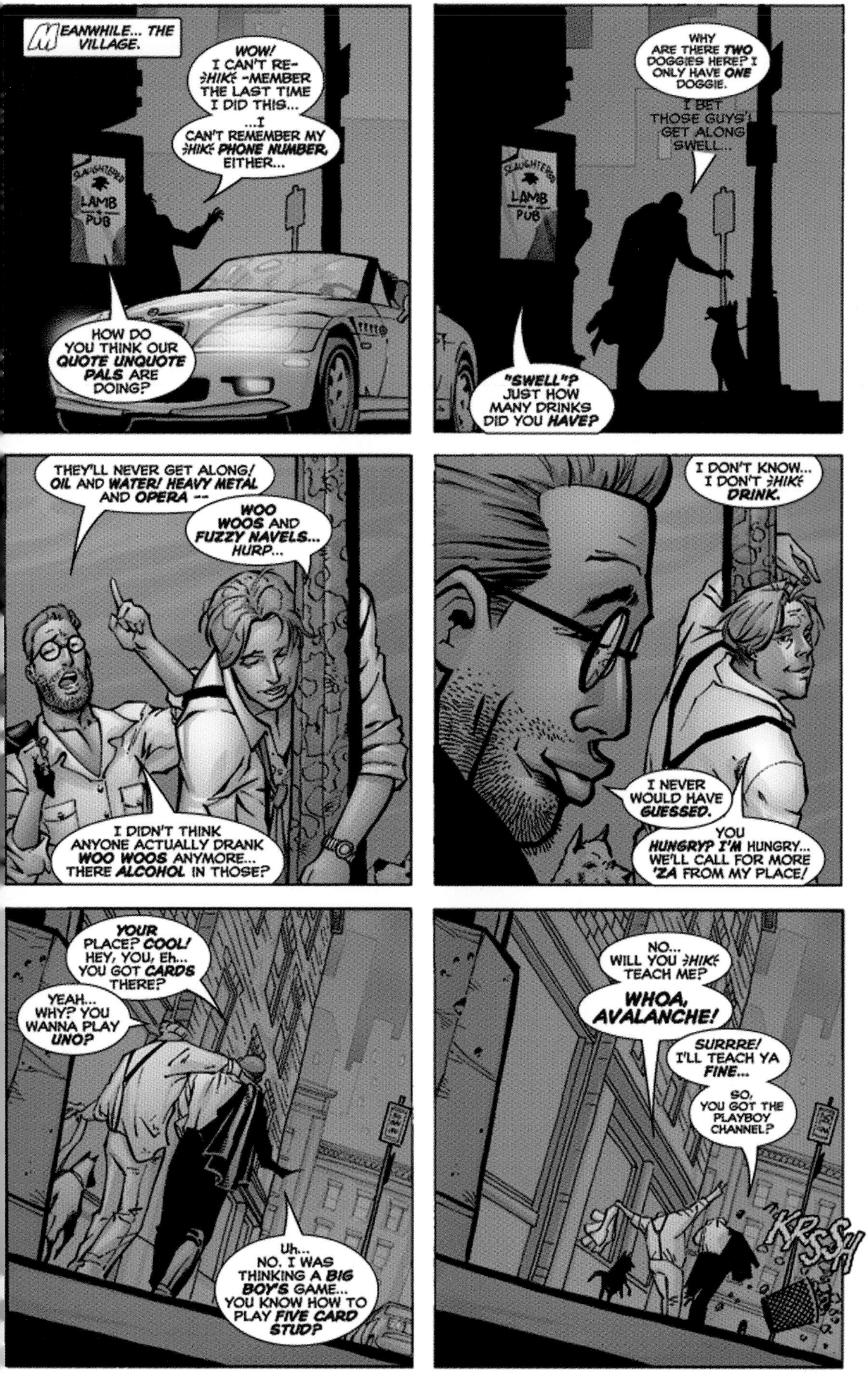
MEANWHILE... THE VILLAGE.
WOW! I CAN'T RE- HIK -MEMBER THE LAST TIME I DID THIS...
...I CAN'T REMEMBER MY HIK PHONE NUMBER, EITHER...
SLAUGHTERED LAMB PUB
HOW DO YOU THINK OUR QUOTE UNQUOTE PALS ARE DOING?
WHY ARE THERE TWO DOGGIES HERE? I ONLY HAVE ONE DOGGIE.
I BET THOSE GUYS'LL GET ALONG SWELL...
"SWELL"? JUST HOW MANY DRINKS DID YOU HAVE?
THEY'LL NEVER GET ALONG! OIL AND WATER! HEAVY METAL AND OPERA --
WOO WOOS AND FUZZY NAVELS... HURP...
I DIDN'T THINK ANYONE ACTUALLY DRANK WOO WOOS ANYMORE... THERE ALCOHOL IN THOSE?
I DON'T KNOW... I DON'T HIK DRINK.
I NEVER WOULD HAVE GUESSED.
YOU HUNGRY? I'M HUNGRY... WE'LL CALL FOR MORE 'ZA FROM MY PLACE!
YOUR PLACE? COOL! HEY, YOU, Eh... YOU GOT CARDS THERE?
YEAH... WHY? YOU WANNA PLAY UNO?
Uh... NO. I WAS THINKING A BIG BOY'S GAME... YOU KNOW HOW TO PLAY FIVE CARD STUD?
NO... WILL YOU HIK TEACH ME?
WHOA, AVALANCHE!
SURRRE! I'LL TEACH YA FINE...
SO, YOU GOT THE PLAYBOY CHANNEL?
KRSSH

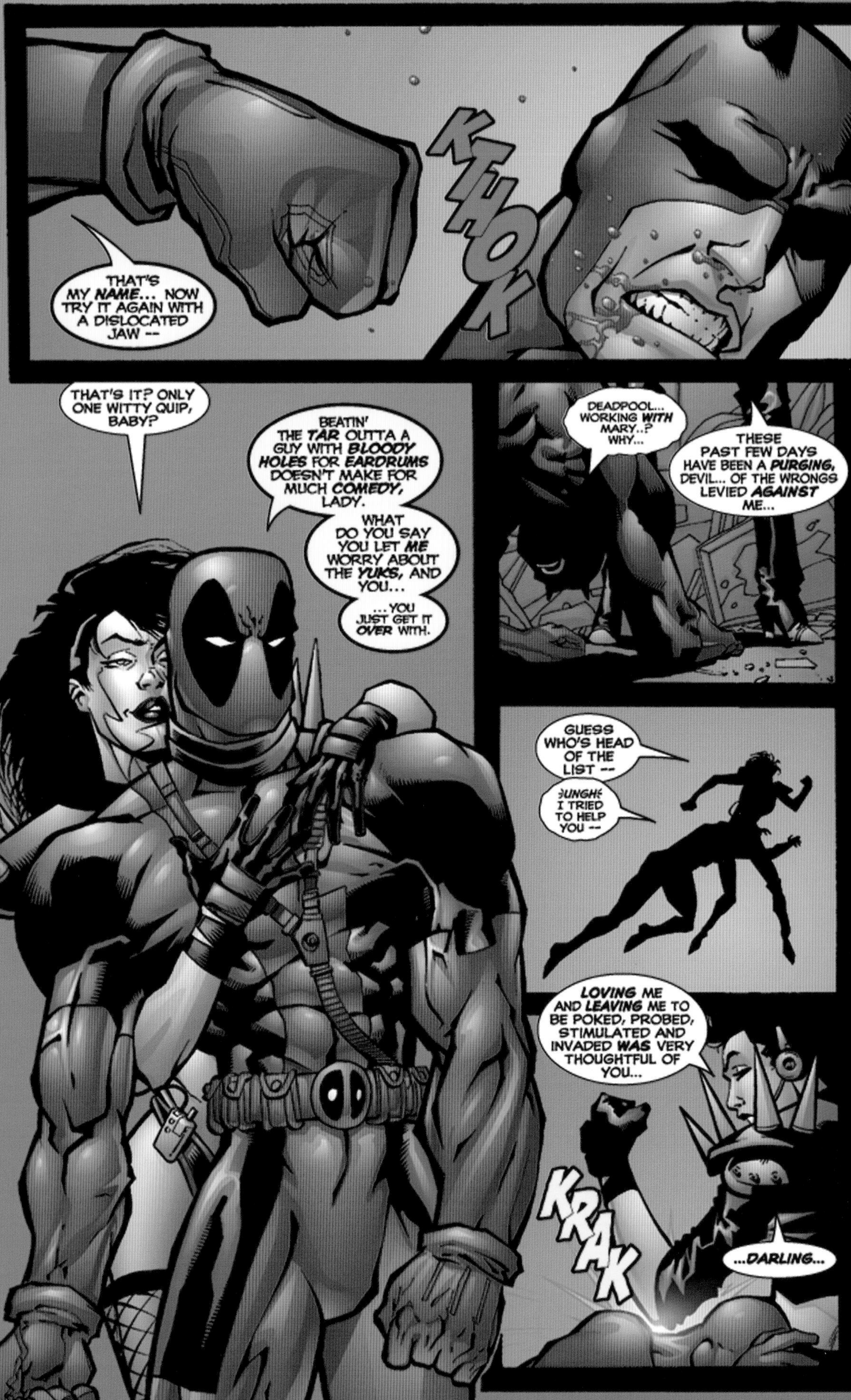

THAT'S MY NAME... NOW TRY IT AGAIN WITH A DISLOCATED JAW --
KTHOK
THAT'S IT? ONLY ONE WITTY QUIP, BABY?
BEATIN' THE TAR OUTTA A GUY WITH BLOODY HOLES FOR EARDRUMS DOESN'T MAKE FOR MUCH COMEDY, LADY.
WHAT DO YOU SAY YOU LET ME WORRY ABOUT THE YUKS, AND YOU...
...YOU JUST GET IT OVER WITH.
DEADPOOL... WORKING WITH MARY..? WHY...
THESE PAST FEW DAYS HAVE BEEN A PURGING, DEVIL... OF THE WRONGS LEVIED AGAINST ME...
GUESS WHO'S HEAD OF THE LIST --
UNGH! I TRIED TO HELP YOU --
LOVING ME AND LEAVING ME TO BE POKED, PROBED, STIMULATED AND INVADED WAS VERY THOUGHTFUL OF YOU...
KRAK
...DARLING...

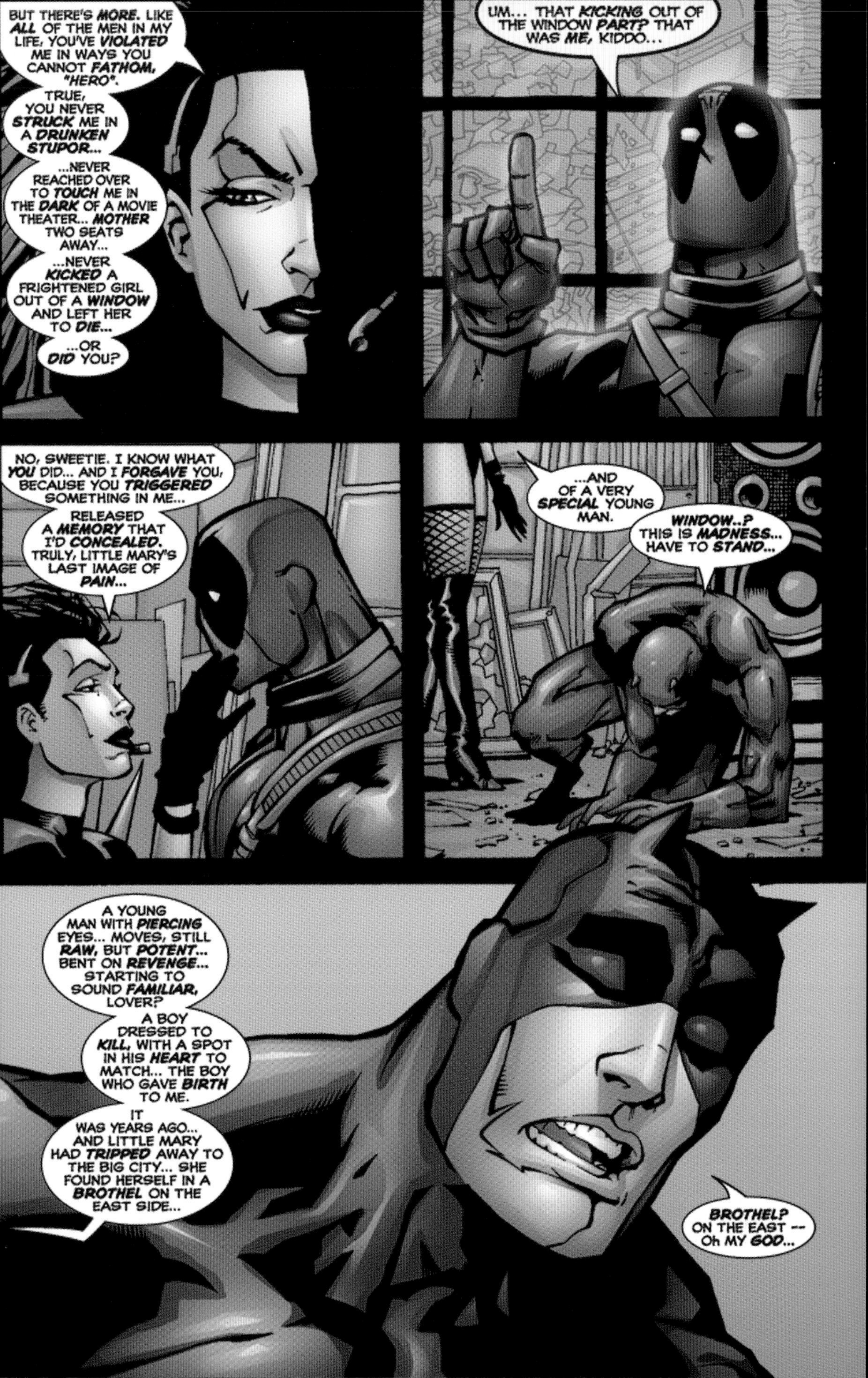
BUT THERE'S MORE. LIKE ALL OF THE MEN IN MY LIFE, YOU'VE VIOLATED ME IN WAYS YOU CANNOT FATHOM, "HERO".
TRUE, YOU NEVER STRUCK ME IN A DRUNKEN STUPOR...
...NEVER REACHED OVER TO TOUCH ME IN THE DARK OF A MOVIE THEATER... MOTHER TWO SEATS AWAY...
...NEVER KICKED A FRIGHTENED GIRL OUT OF A WINDOW AND LEFT HER TO DIE...
...OR DID YOU?
UM... THAT KICKING OUT OF THE WINDOW PART? THAT WAS ME, KIDDO...
NO, SWEETIE. I KNOW WHAT YOU DID... AND I FORGAVE YOU, BECAUSE YOU TRIGGERED SOMETHING IN ME...
RELEASED A MEMORY THAT I'D CONCEALED. TRULY, LITTLE MARY'S LAST IMAGE OF PAIN...
...AND OF A VERY SPECIAL YOUNG MAN.
WINDOW..? THIS IS MADNESS... HAVE TO STAND...
A YOUNG MAN WITH PIERCING EYES... MOVES, STILL RAW, BUT POTENT... BENT ON REVENGE... STARTING TO SOUND FAMILIAR, LOVER?
A BOY DRESSED TO KILL, WITH A SPOT IN HIS HEART TO MATCH... THE BOY WHO GAVE BIRTH TO ME.
IT WAS YEARS AGO... AND LITTLE MARY HAD TRIPPED AWAY TO THE BIG CITY... SHE FOUND HERSELF IN A BROTHEL ON THE EAST SIDE...
BROTHEL? ON THE EAST -- Oh MY GOD...

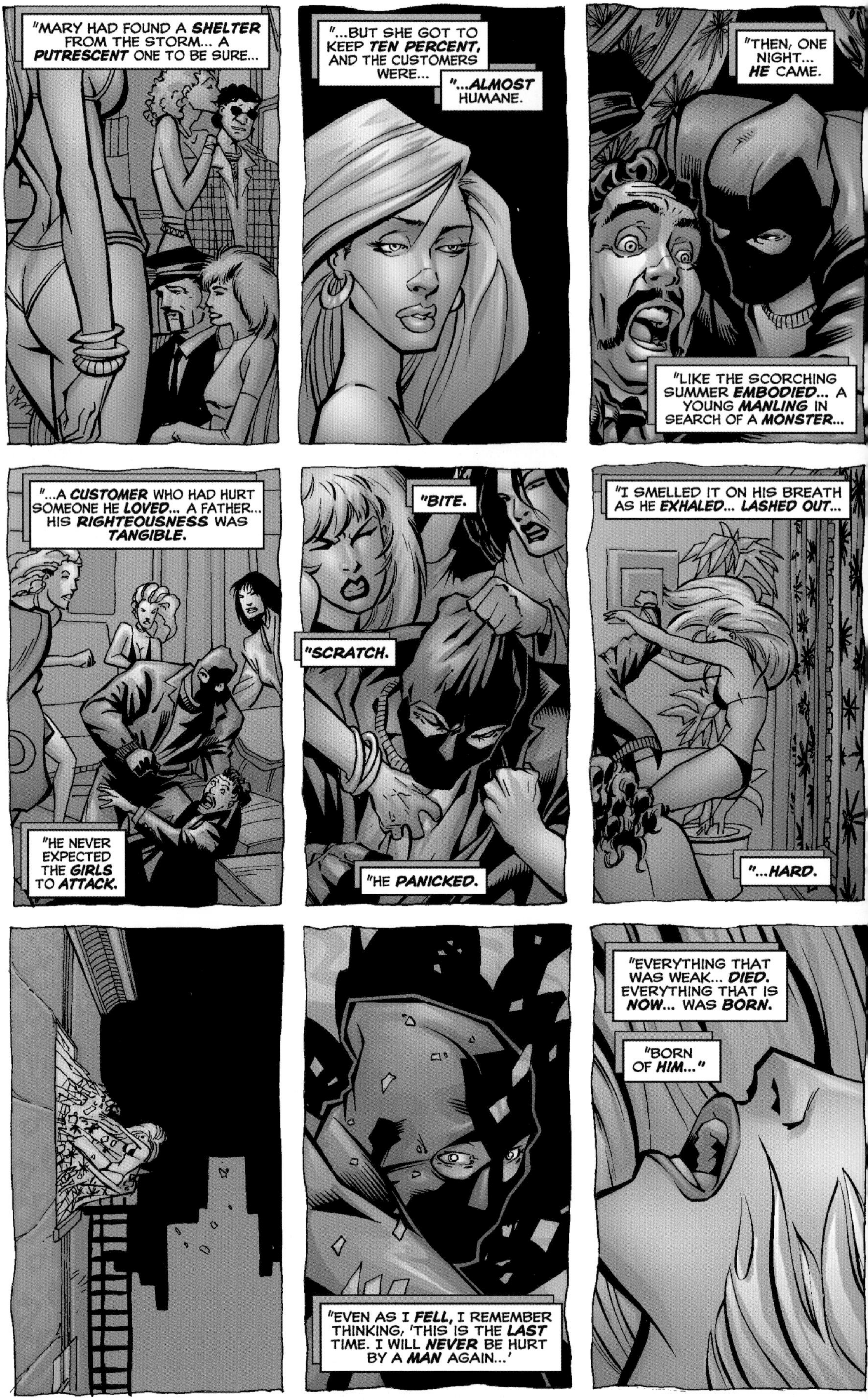
"MARY HAD FOUND A SHELTER FROM THE STORM... A PUTRESCENT ONE TO BE SURE...
"...BUT SHE GOT TO KEEP TEN PERCENT, AND THE CUSTOMERS WERE...
"...ALMOST HUMANE.
"THEN, ONE NIGHT... HE CAME.
"LIKE THE SCORCHING SUMMER EMBODIED... A YOUNG MANLING IN SEARCH OF A MONSTER...
"...A CUSTOMER WHO HAD HURT SOMEONE HE LOVED... A FATHER... HIS RIGHTEOUSNESS WAS TANGIBLE.
"HE NEVER EXPECTED THE GIRLS TO ATTACK.
"BITE.
"SCRATCH.
"HE PANICKED.
"I SMELLED IT ON HIS BREATH AS HE EXHALED... LASHED OUT...
"...HARD.
"EVEN AS I FELL, I REMEMBER THINKING, 'THIS IS THE LAST TIME. I WILL NEVER BE HURT BY A MAN AGAIN...'
"EVERYTHING THAT WAS WEAK... DIED. EVERYTHING THAT IS NOW... WAS BORN.
"BORN OF HIM..."

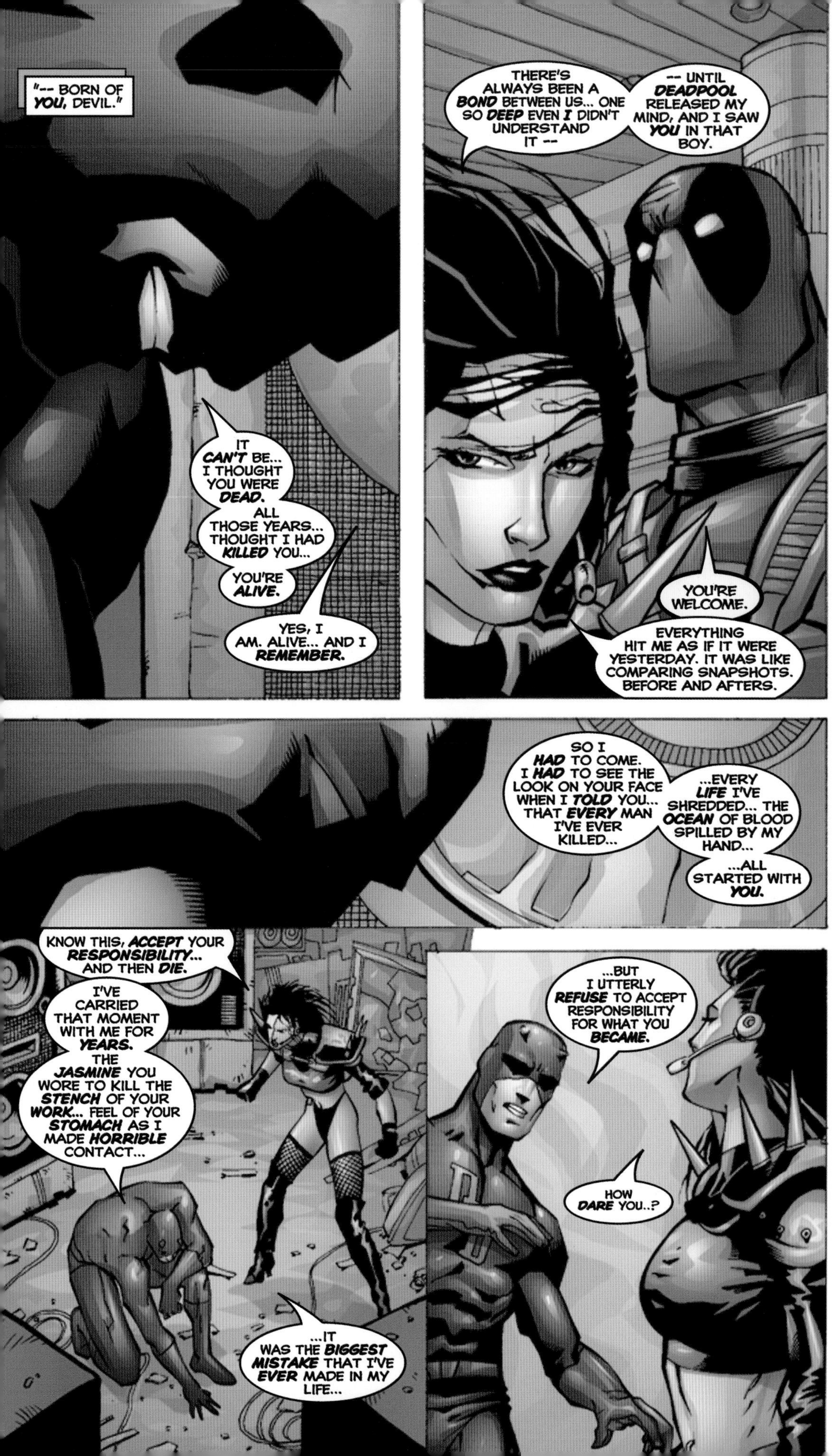
"-- BORN OF YOU, DEVIL."
IT CAN'T BE... I THOUGHT YOU WERE DEAD.
ALL THOSE YEARS... THOUGHT I HAD KILLED YOU...
YOU'RE ALIVE.
YES, I AM. ALIVE... AND I REMEMBER.
THERE'S ALWAYS BEEN A BOND BETWEEN US... ONE SO DEEP EVEN I DIDN'T UNDERSTAND IT --
-- UNTIL DEADPOOL RELEASED MY MIND, AND I SAW YOU IN THAT BOY.
YOU'RE WELCOME.
EVERYTHING HIT ME AS IF IT WERE YESTERDAY. IT WAS LIKE COMPARING SNAPSHOTS. BEFORE AND AFTERS.
SO I HAD TO COME. I HAD TO SEE THE LOOK ON YOUR FACE WHEN I TOLD YOU... THAT EVERY MAN I'VE EVER KILLED...
...EVERY LIFE I'VE SHREDDED... THE OCEAN OF BLOOD SPILLED BY MY HAND...
...ALL STARTED WITH YOU.
KNOW THIS, ACCEPT YOUR RESPONSIBILITY... AND THEN DIE.
I'VE CARRIED THAT MOMENT WITH ME FOR YEARS. THE JASMINE YOU WORE TO KILL THE STENCH OF YOUR WORK... FEEL OF YOUR STOMACH AS I MADE HORRIBLE CONTACT...
...IT WAS THE BIGGEST MISTAKE THAT I'VE EVER MADE IN MY LIFE...
...BUT I UTTERLY REFUSE TO ACCEPT RESPONSIBILITY FOR WHAT YOU BECAME.
HOW DARE YOU..?

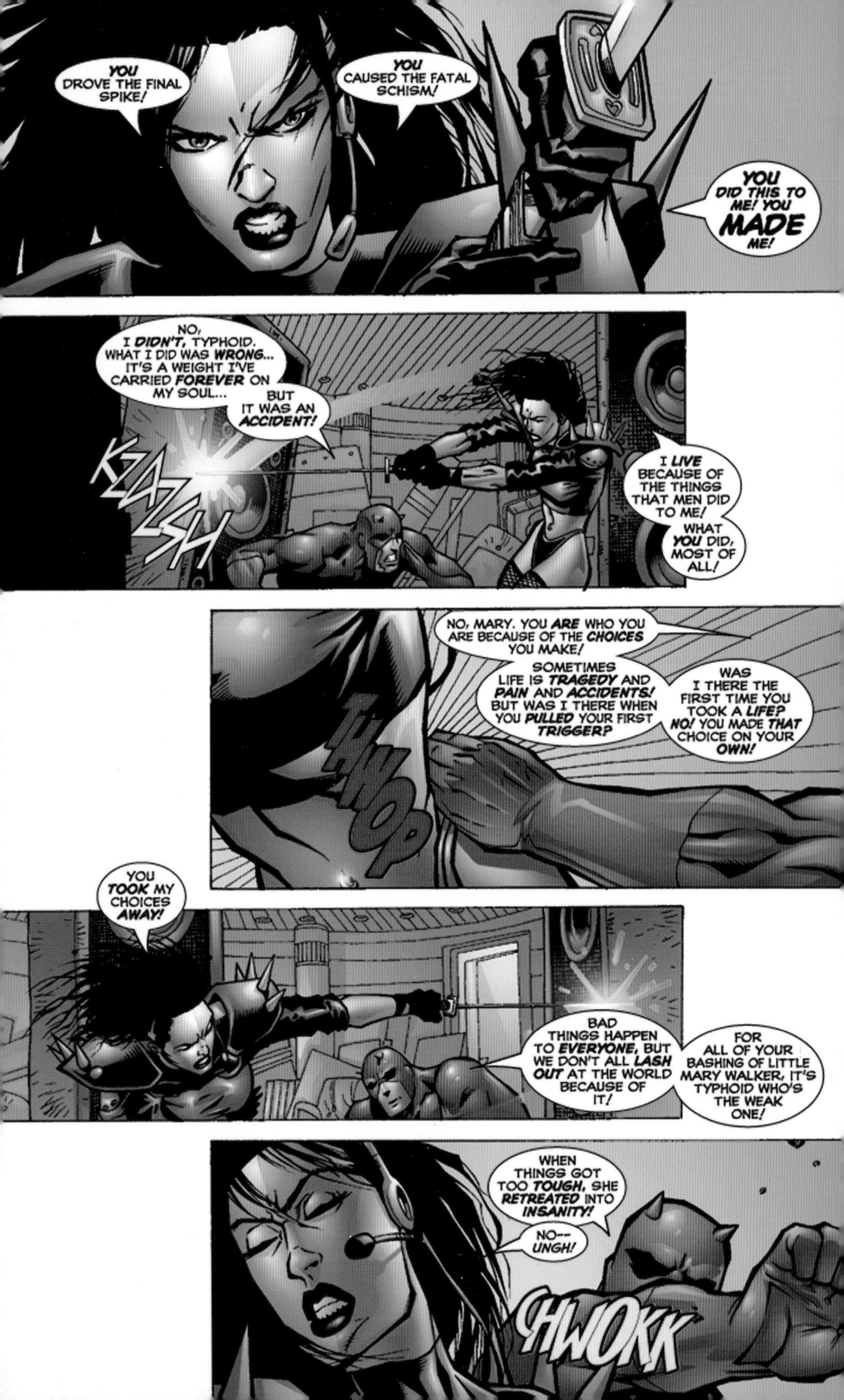
YOU DROVE THE FINAL SPIKE!
YOU CAUSED THE FATAL SCHISM!
YOU DID THIS TO ME! YOU MADE ME!
NO, I DIDN'T, TYPHOID. WHAT I DID WAS WRONG... IT'S A WEIGHT I'VE CARRIED FOREVER ON MY SOUL...
BUT IT WAS AN ACCIDENT!
KZZAZSH
I LIVE BECAUSE OF THE THINGS THAT MEN DID TO ME!
WHAT YOU DID, MOST OF ALL!
NO, MARY. YOU ARE WHO YOU ARE BECAUSE OF THE CHOICES YOU MAKE!
SOMETIMES LIFE IS TRAGEDY AND PAIN AND ACCIDENTS! BUT WAS I THERE WHEN YOU PULLED YOUR FIRST TRIGGER?
WAS I THERE THE FIRST TIME YOU TOOK A LIFE? NO! YOU MADE THAT CHOICE ON YOUR OWN!
THWOP
YOU TOOK MY CHOICES AWAY!
BAD THINGS HAPPEN TO EVERYONE, BUT WE DON'T ALL LASH OUT AT THE WORLD BECAUSE OF IT!
FOR ALL OF YOUR BASHING OF LITTLE MARY WALKER, IT'S TYPHOID WHO'S THE WEAK ONE!
WHEN THINGS GOT TOO TOUGH, SHE RETREATED INTO INSANITY!
NO-- UNGH!
CHWOKK

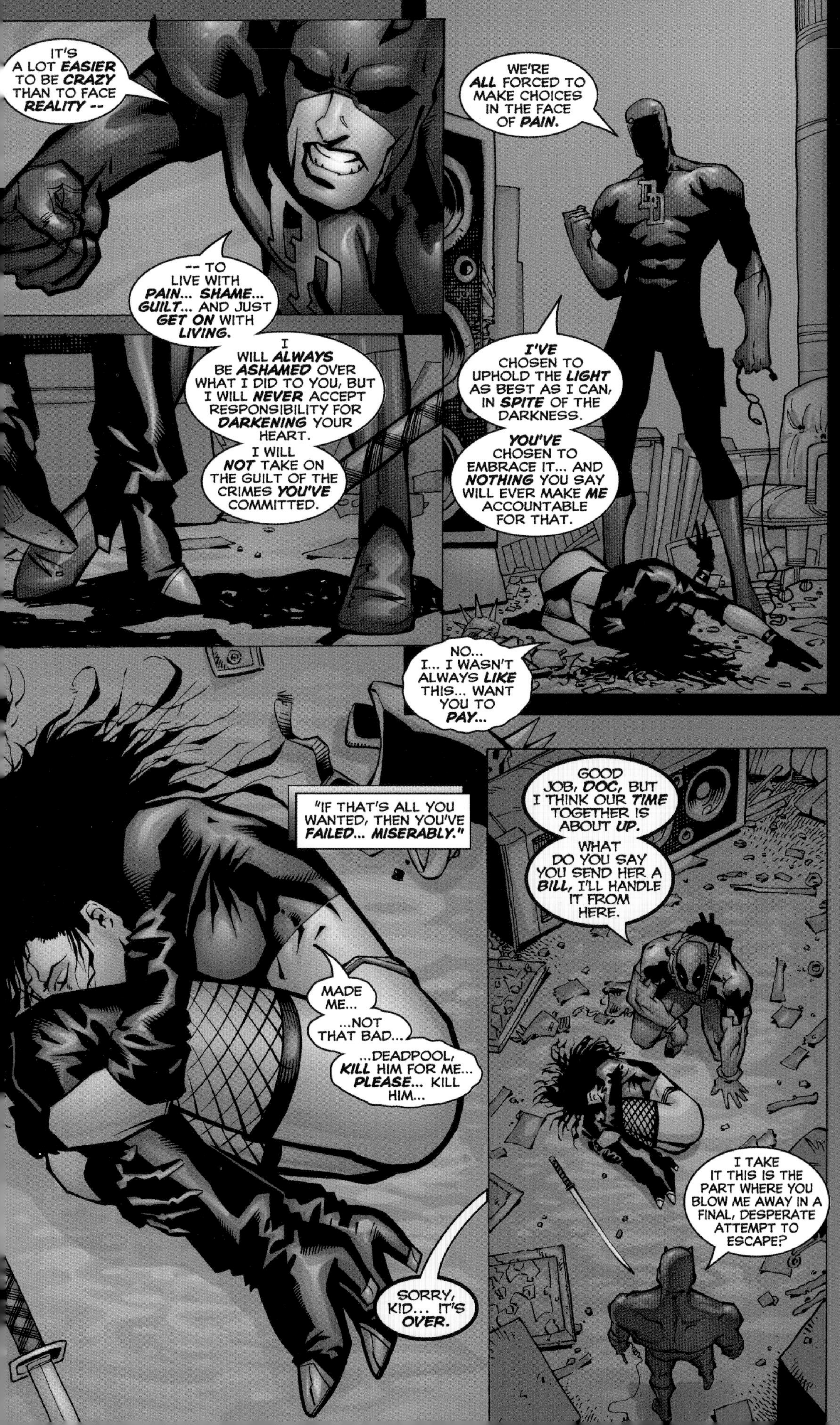
IT'S A LOT EASIER TO BE CRAZY THAN TO FACE REALITY --
-- TO LIVE WITH PAIN... SHAME... GUILT... AND JUST GET ON WITH LIVING.
WE'RE ALL FORCED TO MAKE CHOICES IN THE FACE OF PAIN.
I WILL ALWAYS BE ASHAMED OVER WHAT I DID TO YOU, BUT I WILL NEVER ACCEPT RESPONSIBILITY FOR DARKENING YOUR HEART.
I WILL NOT TAKE ON THE GUILT OF THE CRIMES YOU'VE COMMITTED.
I'VE CHOSEN TO UPHOLD THE LIGHT AS BEST AS I CAN, IN SPITE OF THE DARKNESS.
YOU'VE CHOSEN TO EMBRACE IT... AND NOTHING YOU SAY WILL EVER MAKE ME ACCOUNTABLE FOR THAT.
NO... I... I WASN'T ALWAYS LIKE THIS... WANT YOU TO PAY...
"IF THAT'S ALL YOU WANTED, THEN YOU'VE FAILED... MISERABLY."
MADE ME...
...NOT THAT BAD...
...DEADPOOL, KILL HIM FOR ME... PLEASE... KILL HIM...
SORRY, KID... IT'S OVER.
GOOD JOB, DOC, BUT I THINK OUR TIME TOGETHER IS ABOUT UP.
WHAT DO YOU SAY YOU SEND HER A BILL, I'LL HANDLE IT FROM HERE.
I TAKE IT THIS IS THE PART WHERE YOU BLOW ME AWAY IN A FINAL, DESPERATE ATTEMPT TO ESCAPE?

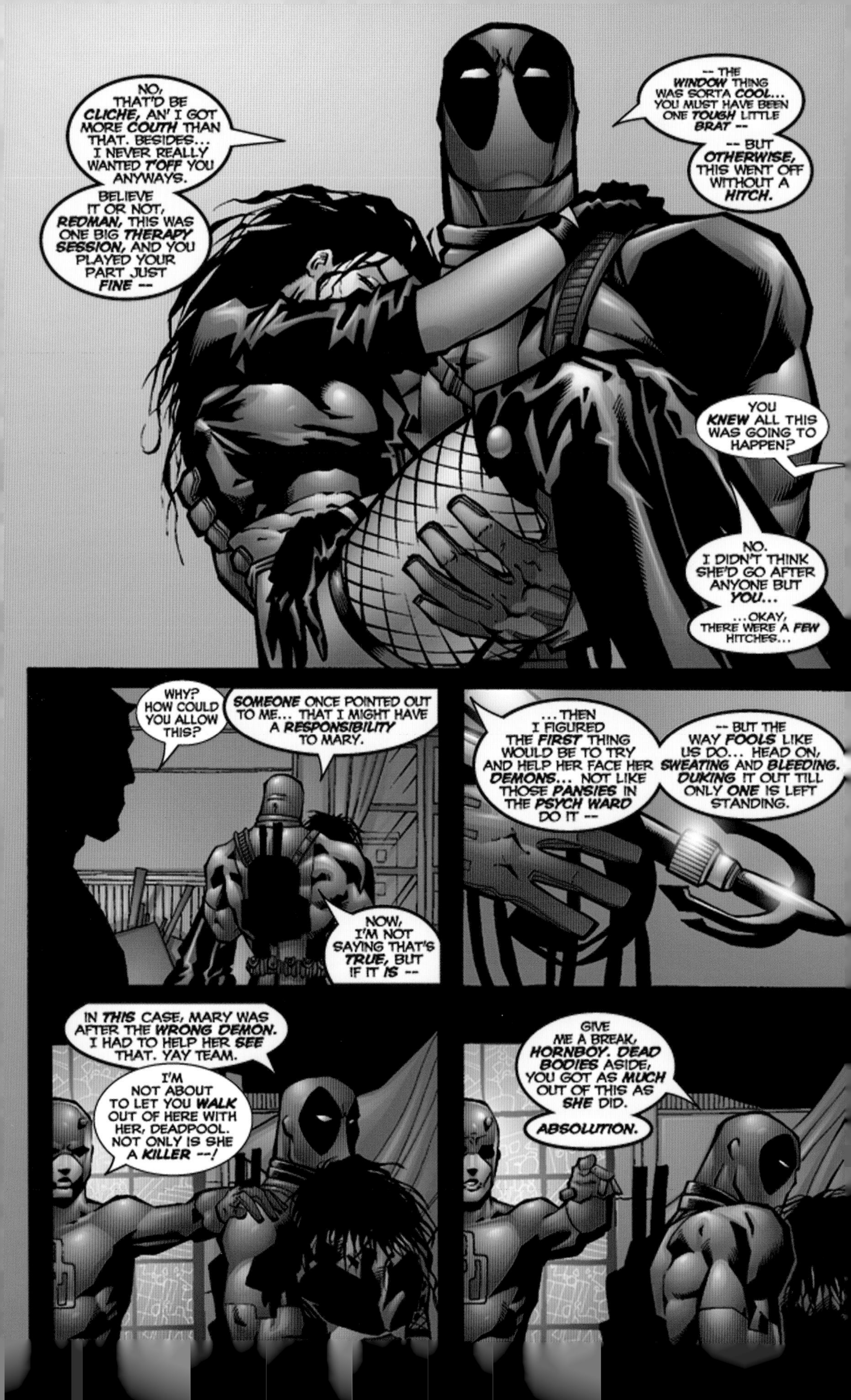
NO, THAT'D BE CLICHE, AN' I GOT MORE COUTH THAN THAT. BESIDES... I NEVER REALLY WANTED T'OFF YOU ANYWAYS.
BELIEVE IT OR NOT, REDMAN, THIS WAS ONE BIG THERAPY SESSION, AND YOU PLAYED YOUR PART JUST FINE --
-- THE WINDOW THING WAS SORTA COOL... YOU MUST HAVE BEEN ONE TOUGH LITTLE BRAT --
-- BUT OTHERWISE, THIS WENT OFF WITHOUT A HITCH.
YOU KNEW ALL THIS WAS GOING TO HAPPEN?
NO. I DIDN'T THINK SHE'D GO AFTER ANYONE BUT YOU...
...OKAY, THERE WERE A FEW HITCHES...
WHY? HOW COULD YOU ALLOW THIS?
SOMEONE ONCE POINTED OUT TO ME... THAT I MIGHT HAVE A RESPONSIBILITY TO MARY.
NOW, I'M NOT SAYING THAT'S TRUE, BUT IF IT IS --
...THEN I FIGURED THE FIRST THING WOULD BE TO TRY AND HELP HER FACE HER DEMONS... NOT LIKE THOSE PANSIES IN THE PSYCH WARD DO IT --
-- BUT THE WAY FOOLS LIKE US DO... HEAD ON, SWEATING AND BLEEDING. DUKING IT OUT TILL ONLY ONE IS LEFT STANDING.
IN THIS CASE, MARY WAS AFTER THE WRONG DEMON. I HAD TO HELP HER SEE THAT. YAY TEAM.
I'M NOT ABOUT TO LET YOU WALK OUT OF HERE WITH HER, DEADPOOL. NOT ONLY IS SHE A KILLER --!
GIVE ME A BREAK, HORNBOY. DEAD BODIES ASIDE, YOU GOT AS MUCH OUT OF THIS AS SHE DID.
ABSOLUTION.

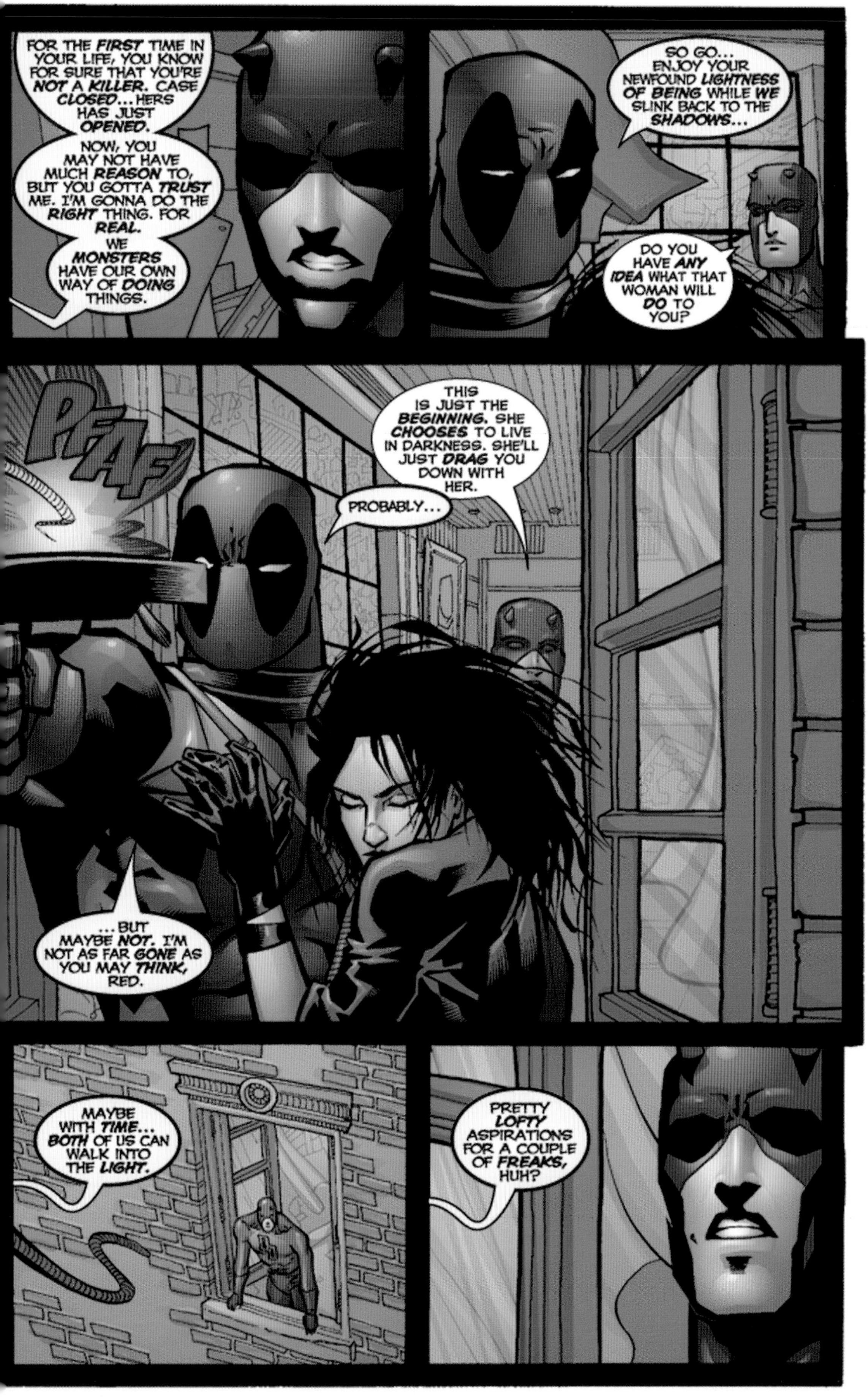
FOR THE FIRST TIME IN YOUR LIFE, YOU KNOW FOR SURE THAT YOU'RE NOT A KILLER. CASE CLOSED... HERS HAS JUST OPENED.
NOW, YOU MAY NOT HAVE MUCH REASON TO, BUT YOU GOTTA TRUST ME. I'M GONNA DO THE RIGHT THING. FOR REAL.
WE MONSTERS HAVE OUR OWN WAY OF DOING THINGS.
SO GO... ENJOY YOUR NEWFOUND LIGHTNESS OF BEING WHILE WE SLINK BACK TO THE SHADOWS...
DO YOU HAVE ANY IDEA WHAT THAT WOMAN WILL DO TO YOU?
PFAF
THIS IS JUST THE BEGINNING. SHE CHOOSES TO LIVE IN DARKNESS. SHE'LL JUST DRAG YOU DOWN WITH HER.
PROBABLY...
... BUT MAYBE NOT. I'M NOT AS FAR GONE AS YOU MAY THINK, RED.
MAYBE WITH TIME... BOTH OF US CAN WALK INTO THE LIGHT.
PRETTY LOFTY ASPIRATIONS FOR A COUPLE OF FREAKS, HUH?

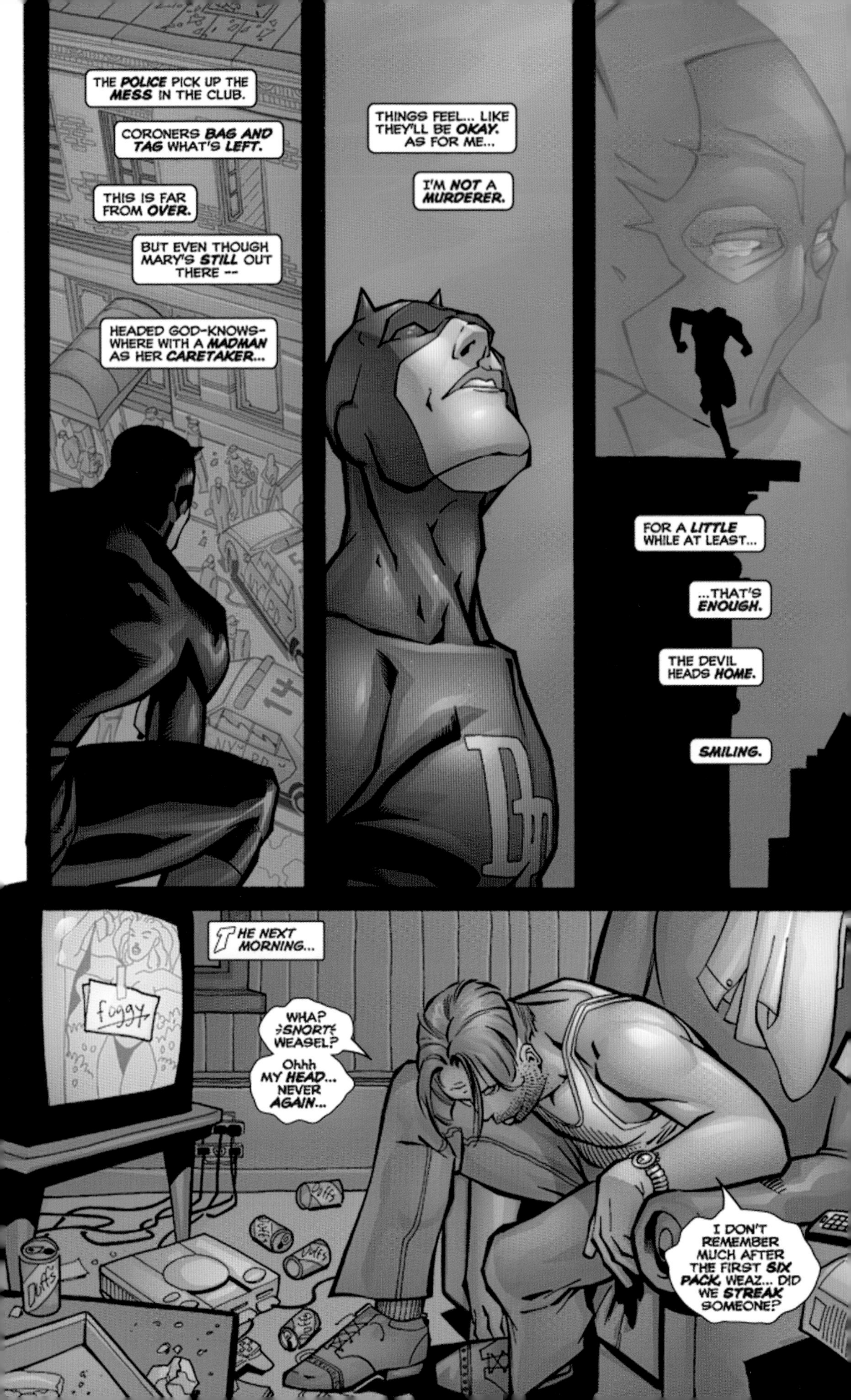
THE POLICE PICK UP THE MESS IN THE CLUB.
CORONERS BAG AND TAG WHAT'S LEFT.
THIS IS FAR FROM OVER.
BUT EVEN THOUGH MARY'S STILL OUT THERE --
HEADED GOD-KNOWS-WHERE WITH A MADMAN AS HER CARETAKER...
THINGS FEEL... LIKE THEY'LL BE OKAY. AS FOR ME...
I'M NOT A MURDERER.
FOR A LITTLE WHILE AT LEAST...
...THAT'S ENOUGH.
THE DEVIL HEADS HOME.
SMILING.
THE NEXT MORNING...
foggy
WHA? SNORT WEASEL?
Ohhh MY HEAD... NEVER AGAIN...
I DON'T REMEMBER MUCH AFTER THE FIRST SIX PACK, WEAZ... DID WE STREAK SOMEONE?

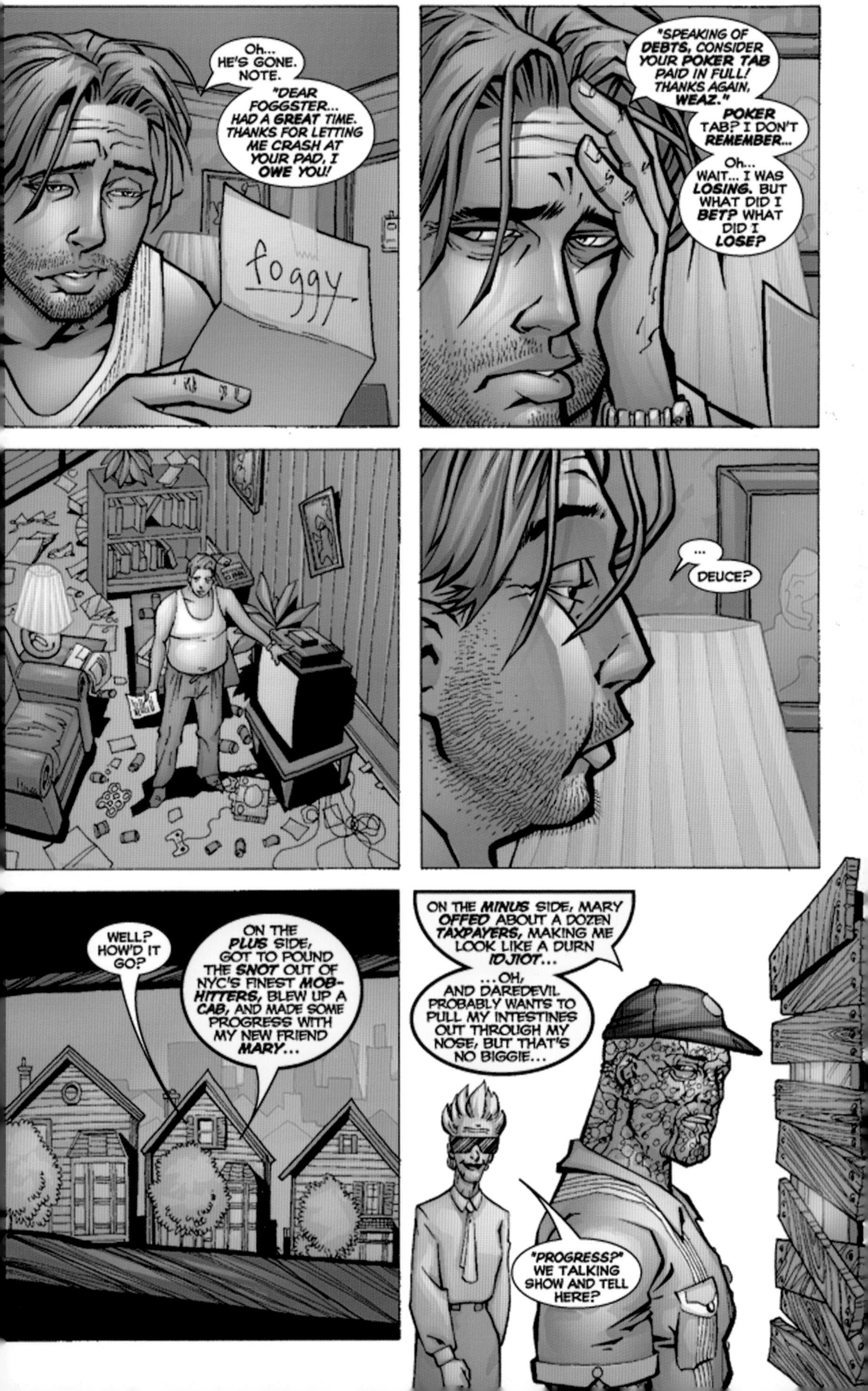
Oh... HE'S GONE. NOTE.
"DEAR FOGGSTER... HAD A GREAT TIME. THANKS FOR LETTING ME CRASH AT YOUR PAD, I OWE YOU!
foggy
"SPEAKING OF DEBTS, CONSIDER YOUR POKER TAB PAID IN FULL! THANKS AGAIN, WEAZ."
POKER TAB? I DON'T REMEMBER...
Oh... WAIT... I WAS LOSING. BUT WHAT DID I BET? WHAT DID I LOSE?
... DEUCE?
WELL? HOW'D IT GO?
ON THE PLUS SIDE, GOT TO POUND THE SNOT OUT OF NYC'S FINEST MOB-HITTERS, BLEW UP A CAB, AND MADE SOME PROGRESS WITH MY NEW FRIEND MARY...
ON THE MINUS SIDE, MARY OFFED ABOUT A DOZEN TAXPAYERS, MAKING ME LOOK LIKE A DURN IDJIOT...
...OH, AND DAREDEVIL PROBABLY WANTS TO PULL MY INTESTINES OUT THROUGH MY NOSE, BUT THAT'S NO BIGGIE...
"PROGRESS?" WE TALKING SHOW AND TELL HERE?

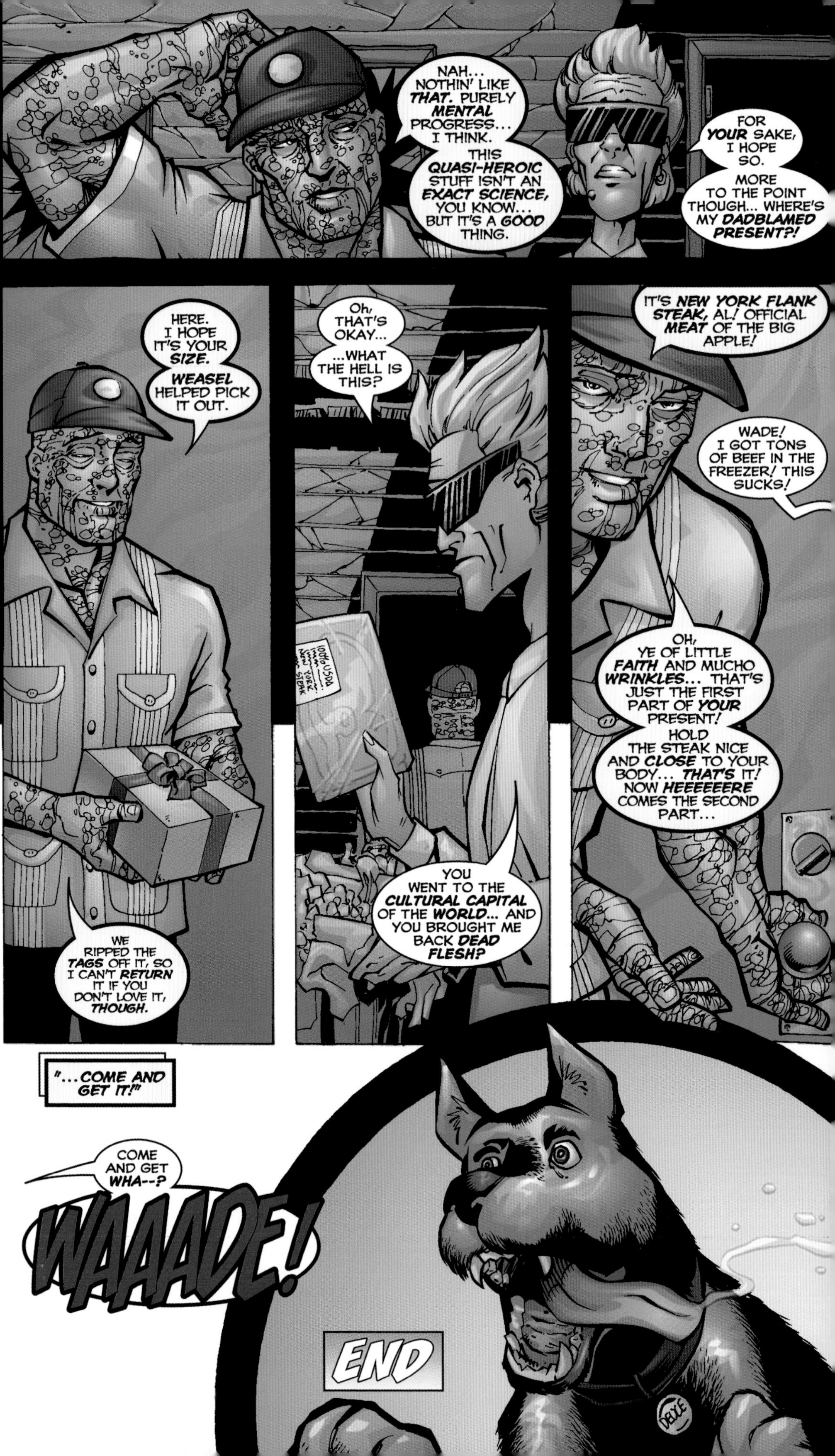
NAH... NOTHIN' LIKE THAT. PURELY MENTAL PROGRESS... I THINK.
THIS QUASI-HEROIC STUFF ISN'T AN EXACT SCIENCE, YOU KNOW... BUT IT'S A GOOD THING.
FOR YOUR SAKE, I HOPE SO.
MORE TO THE POINT THOUGH... WHERE'S MY DADBLAMED PRESENT?!
HERE. I HOPE IT'S YOUR SIZE.
WEASEL HELPED PICK IT OUT.
WE RIPPED THE TAGS OFF IT, SO I CAN'T RETURN IT IF YOU DON'T LOVE IT, THOUGH.
Oh, THAT'S OKAY...
...WHAT THE HELL IS THIS?
YOU WENT TO THE CULTURAL CAPITAL OF THE WORLD... AND YOU BROUGHT ME BACK DEAD FLESH?
IT'S NEW YORK FLANK STEAK, AL! OFFICIAL MEAT OF THE BIG APPLE!
WADE! I GOT TONS OF BEEF IN THE FREEZER! THIS SUCKS!
OH, YE OF LITTLE FAITH AND MUCHO WRINKLES... THAT'S JUST THE FIRST PART OF YOUR PRESENT!
HOLD THE STEAK NICE AND CLOSE TO YOUR BODY... THAT'S IT! NOW HEEEEEERE COMES THE SECOND PART...
"...COME AND GET IT!"
COME AND GET WHA--?
WAAADE!
END

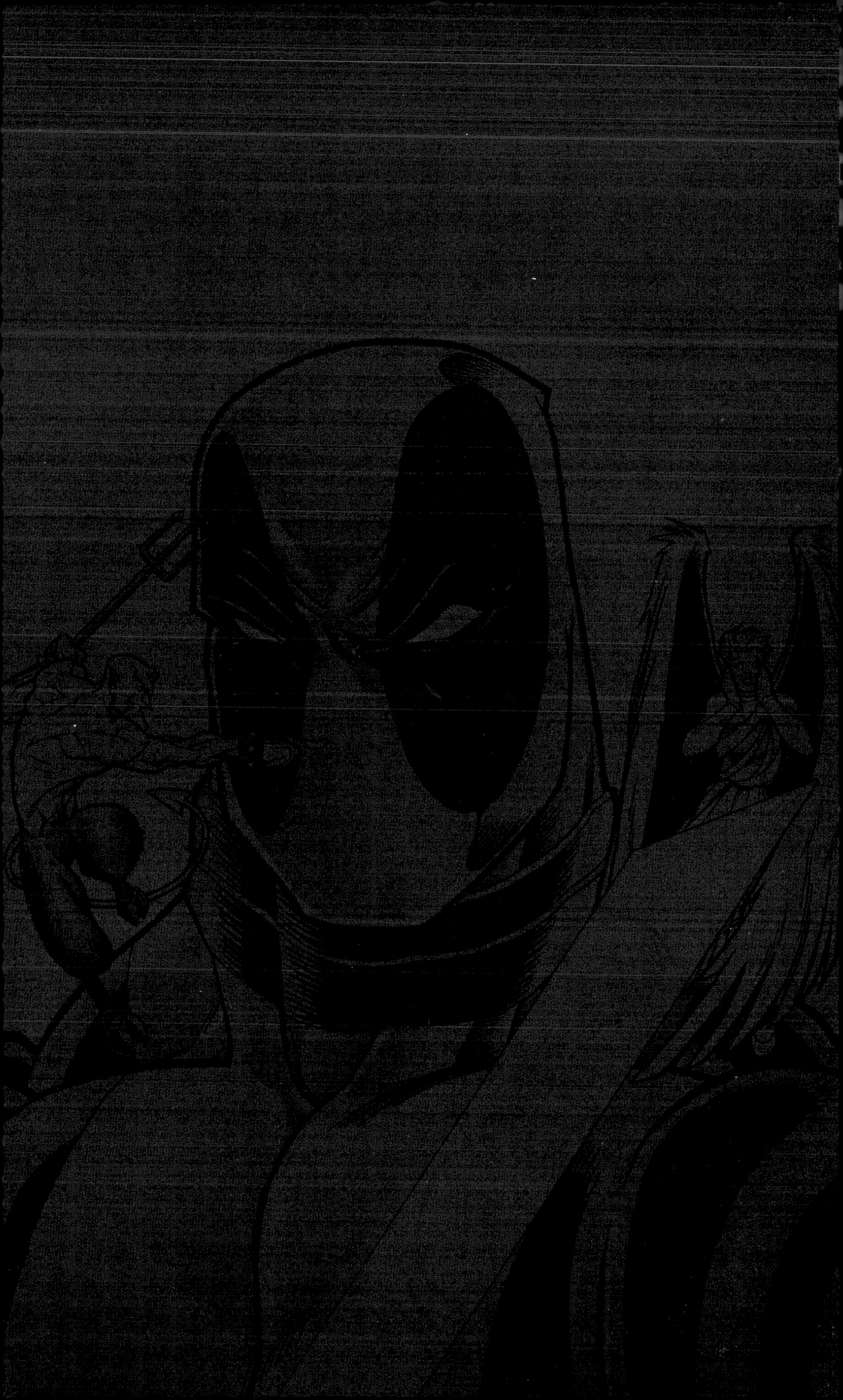

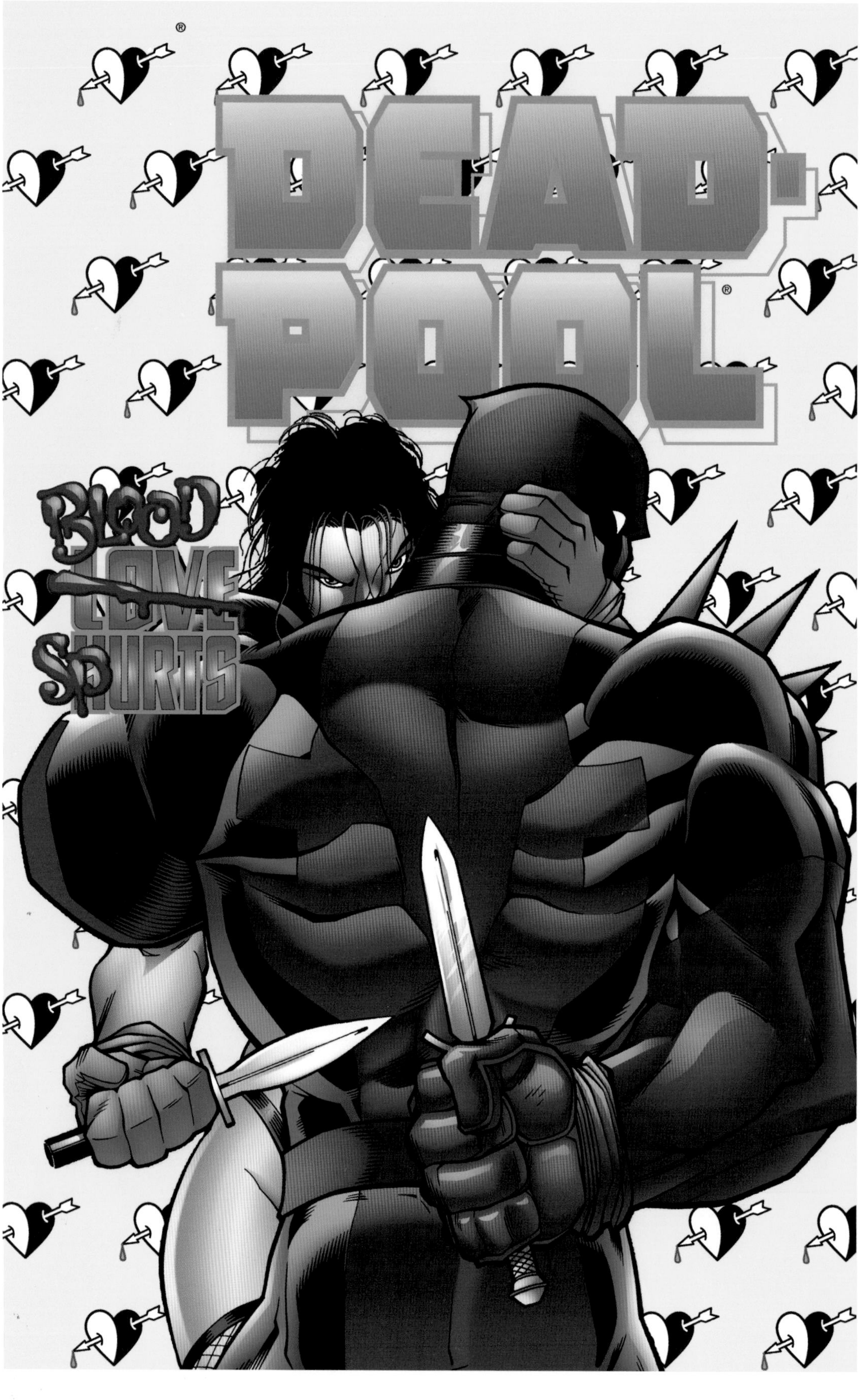
DEADPOOL
BLOOD LOVE SPURTS HURTS

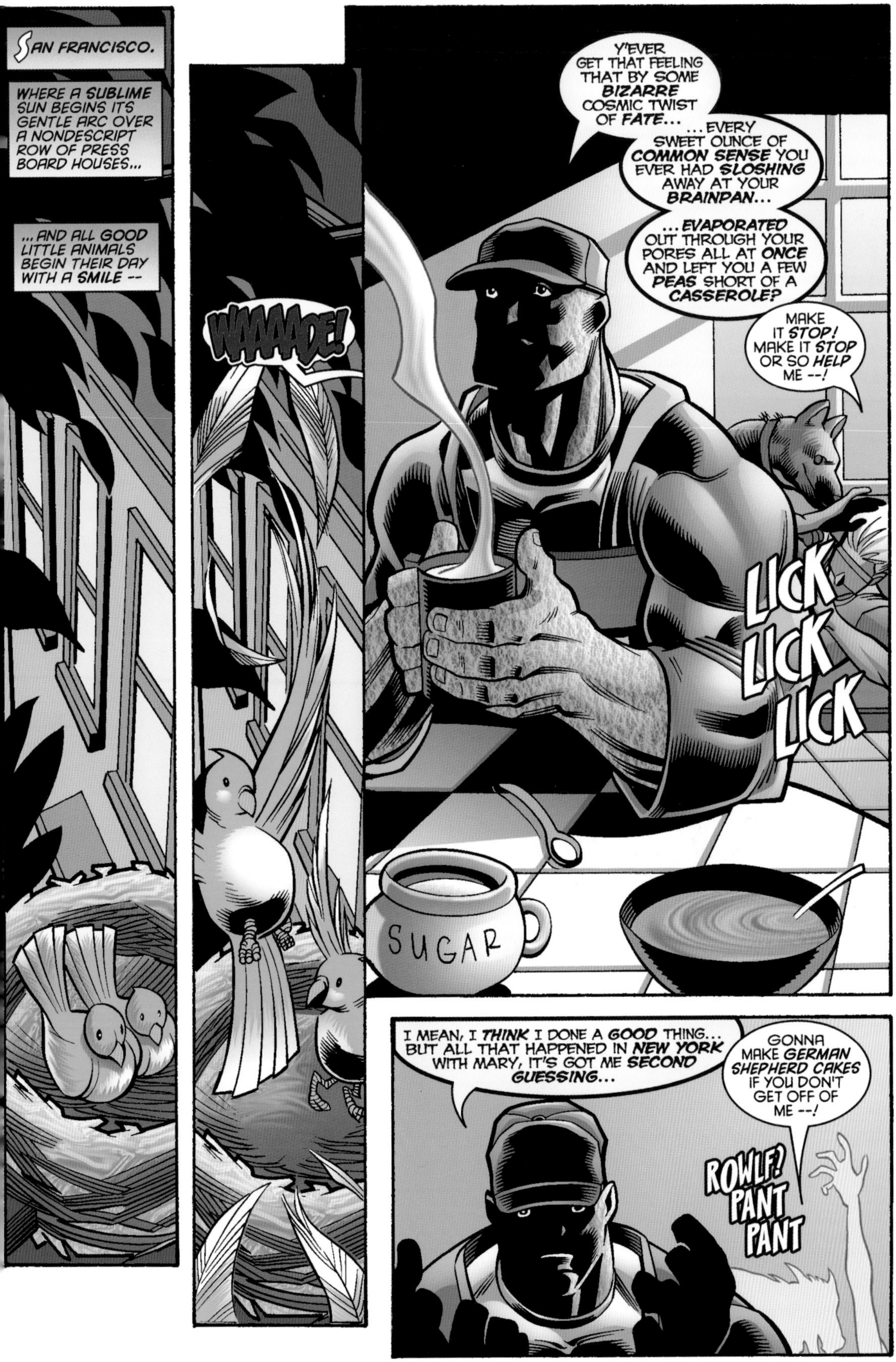
SAN FRANCISCO.
WHERE A SUBLIME SUN BEGINS ITS GENTLE ARC OVER A NONDESCRIPT ROW OF PRESS BOARD HOUSES...
...AND ALL GOOD LITTLE ANIMALS BEGIN THEIR DAY WITH A SMILE --
WAAAADE!
Y'EVER GET THAT FEELING THAT BY SOME BIZARRE COSMIC TWIST OF FATE...
...EVERY SWEET OUNCE OF COMMON SENSE YOU EVER HAD SLOSHING AWAY AT YOUR BRAINPAN...
...EVAPORATED OUT THROUGH YOUR PORES ALL AT ONCE AND LEFT YOU A FEW PEAS SHORT OF A CASSEROLE?
MAKE IT STOP! MAKE IT STOP OR SO HELP ME --!
LICK LICK LICK
SUGAR
I MEAN, I THINK I DONE A GOOD THING... BUT ALL THAT HAPPENED IN NEW YORK WITH MARY, IT'S GOT ME SECOND GUESSING...
GONNA MAKE GERMAN SHEPHERD CAKES IF YOU DON'T GET OFF OF ME --!
ROWLF? PANT PANT

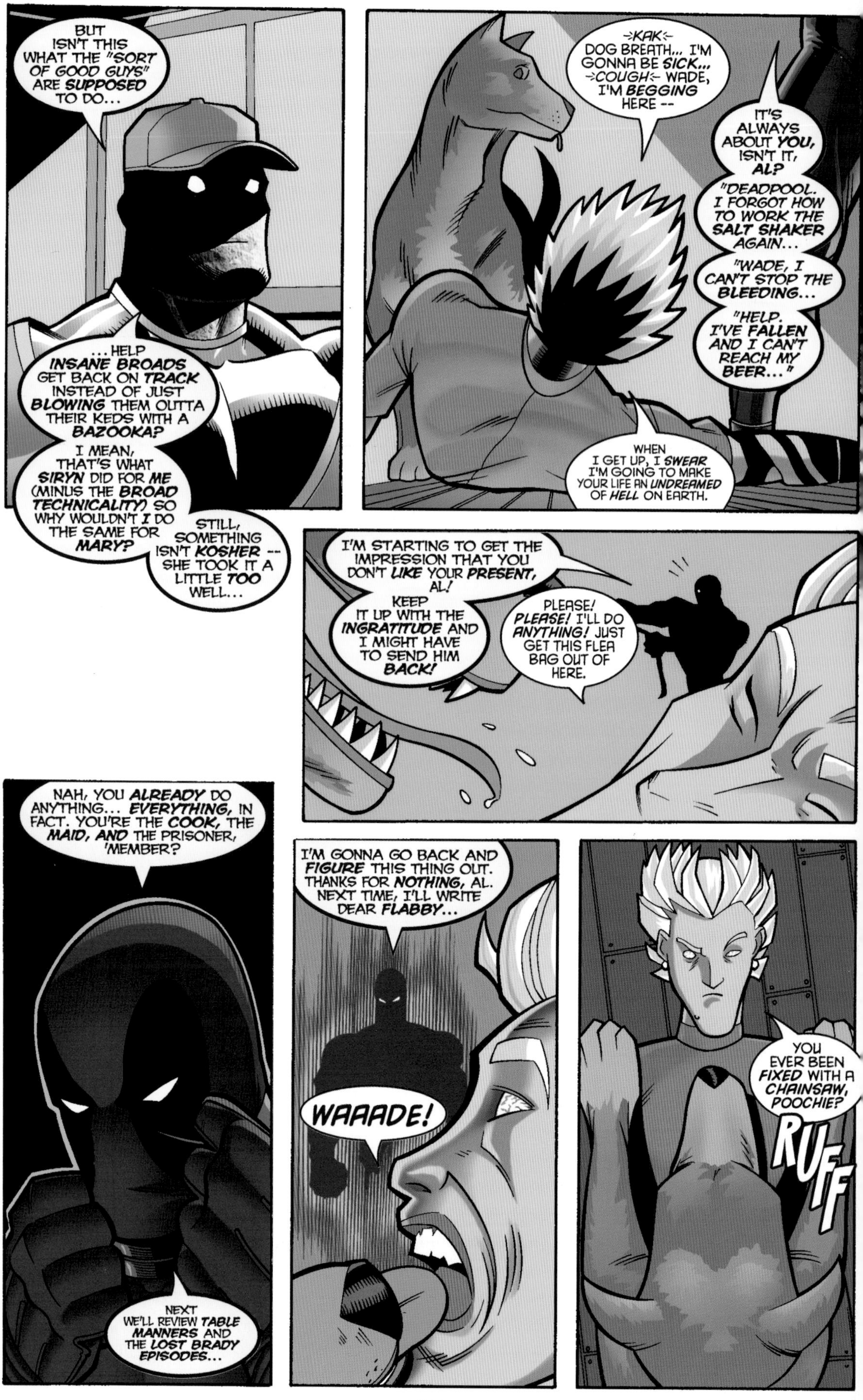
BUT ISN'T THIS WHAT THE "SORT OF GOOD GUYS" ARE SUPPOSED TO DO...
...HELP INSANE BROADS GET BACK ON TRACK INSTEAD OF JUST BLOWING THEM OUTTA THEIR KEDS WITH A BAZOOKA?
I MEAN, THAT'S WHAT SIRYN DID FOR ME (MINUS THE BROAD TECHNICALITY) SO WHY WOULDN'T I DO THE SAME FOR MARY?
STILL, SOMETHING ISN'T KOSHER -- SHE TOOK IT A LITTLE TOO WELL...
-KAK- DOG BREATH... I'M GONNA BE SICK... -COUGH- WADE, I'M BEGGING HERE --
IT'S ALWAYS ABOUT YOU, ISN'T IT, AL?
"DEADPOOL. I FORGOT HOW TO WORK THE SALT SHAKER AGAIN...
"WADE, I CAN'T STOP THE BLEEDING...
"HELP. I'VE FALLEN AND I CAN'T REACH MY BEER..."
WHEN I GET UP, I SWEAR I'M GOING TO MAKE YOUR LIFE AN UNDREAMED OF HELL ON EARTH.
I'M STARTING TO GET THE IMPRESSION THAT YOU DON'T LIKE YOUR PRESENT, AL!
KEEP IT UP WITH THE INGRATITUDE AND I MIGHT HAVE TO SEND HIM BACK!
PLEASE! PLEASE! I'LL DO ANYTHING! JUST GET THIS FLEA BAG OUT OF HERE.
NAH, YOU ALREADY DO ANYTHING... EVERYTHING, IN FACT. YOU'RE THE COOK, THE MAID, AND THE PRISONER, 'MEMBER?
NEXT WE'LL REVIEW TABLE MANNERS AND THE LOST BRADY EPISODES...
I'M GONNA GO BACK AND FIGURE THIS THING OUT. THANKS FOR NOTHING, AL. NEXT TIME, I'LL WRITE DEAR FLABBY...
WAAADE!
YOU EVER BEEN FIXED WITH A CHAINSAW, POOCHIE?
RUFF

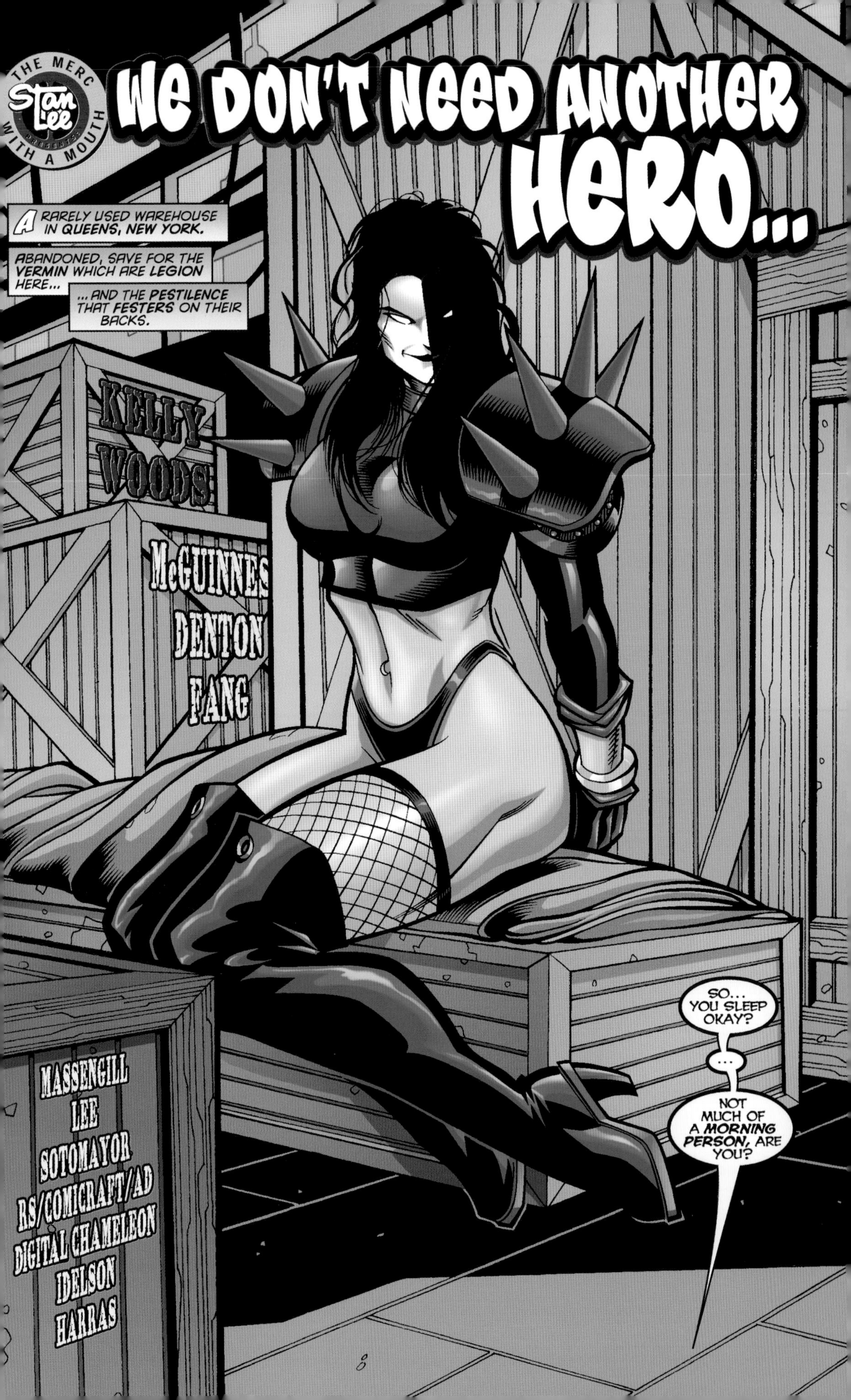
THE MERC WITH A MOUTH
Stan Lee PRESENTS
WE DON'T NEED ANOTHER HERO...
A RARELY USED WAREHOUSE IN QUEENS, NEW YORK.
ABANDONED, SAVE FOR THE VERMIN WHICH ARE LEGION HERE...
...AND THE PESTILENCE THAT FESTERS ON THEIR BACKS.
KELLY WOODS
McGUINNES DENTON FANG
MASSENGILL
LEE
SOTOMAYOR
RS/COMICRAFT/AD
DIGITAL CHAMELEON
IDELSON
HARRAS
SO... YOU SLEEP OKAY?
...
NOT MUCH OF A MORNING PERSON, ARE YOU?

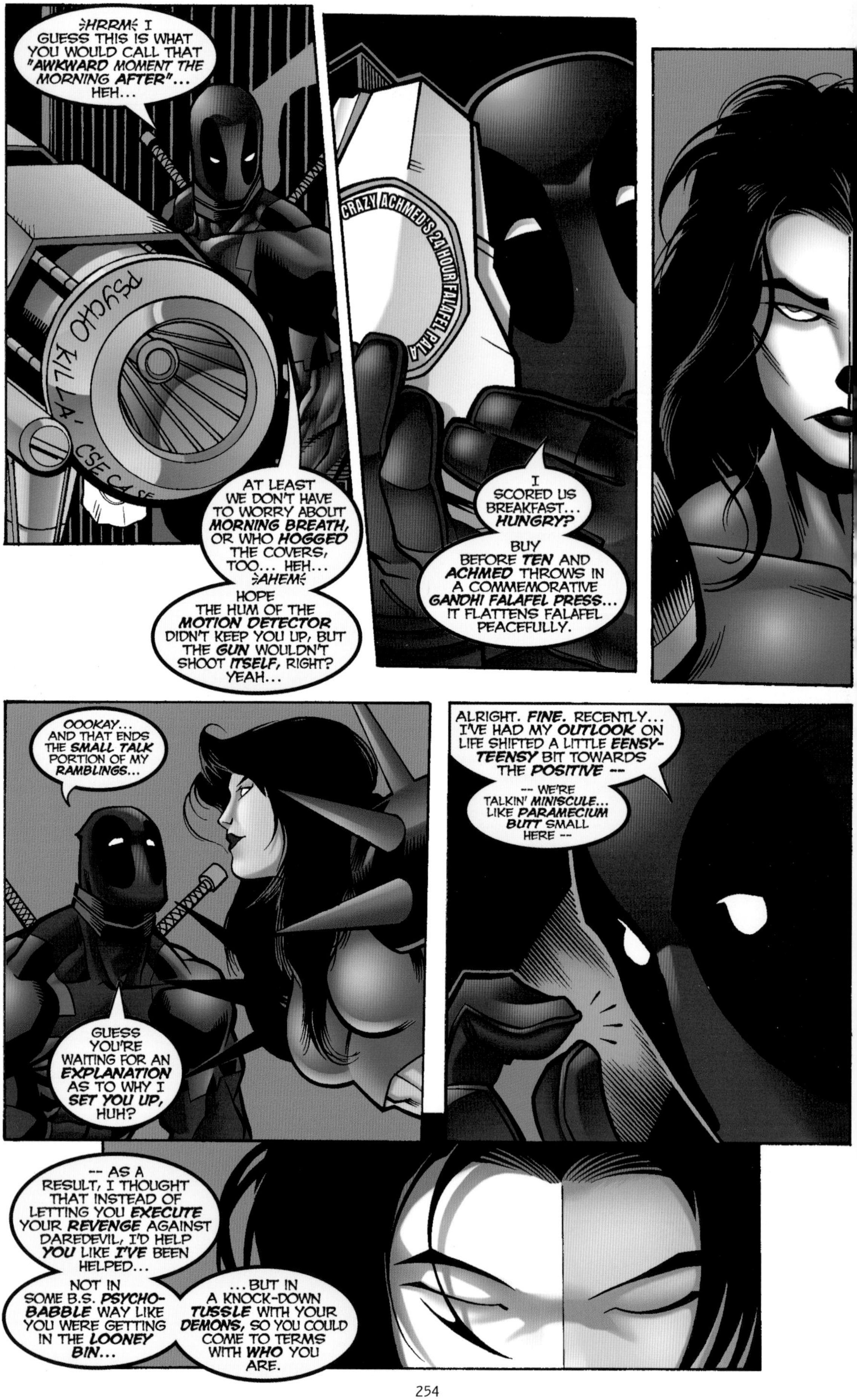

HRRM I GUESS THIS IS WHAT YOU WOULD CALL THAT "AWKWARD MOMENT THE MORNING AFTER"... HEH...
PSYCHO KILLA' CSE CASE
AT LEAST WE DON'T HAVE TO WORRY ABOUT MORNING BREATH, OR WHO HOGGED THE COVERS, TOO... HEH... AHEM
HOPE THE HUM OF THE MOTION DETECTOR DIDN'T KEEP YOU UP, BUT THE GUN WOULDN'T SHOOT ITSELF, RIGHT? YEAH...
CRAZY ACHMED'S 24 HOUR FALAFEL PALA
I SCORED US BREAKFAST... HUNGRY?
BUY BEFORE TEN AND ACHMED THROWS IN A COMMEMORATIVE GANDHI FALAFEL PRESS... IT FLATTENS FALAFEL PEACEFULLY.
OOOKAY... AND THAT ENDS THE SMALL TALK PORTION OF MY RAMBLINGS...
GUESS YOU'RE WAITING FOR AN EXPLANATION AS TO WHY I SET YOU UP, HUH?
ALRIGHT. FINE. RECENTLY... I'VE HAD MY OUTLOOK ON LIFE SHIFTED A LITTLE EENSY-TEENSY BIT TOWARDS THE POSITIVE --
-- WE'RE TALKIN' MINISCULE... LIKE PARAMECIUM BUTT SMALL HERE --
-- AS A RESULT, I THOUGHT THAT INSTEAD OF LETTING YOU EXECUTE YOUR REVENGE AGAINST DAREDEVIL, I'D HELP YOU LIKE I'VE BEEN HELPED...
NOT IN SOME B.S. PSYCHO-BABBLE WAY LIKE YOU WERE GETTING IN THE LOONEY BIN...
...BUT IN A KNOCK-DOWN TUSSLE WITH YOUR DEMONS, SO YOU COULD COME TO TERMS WITH WHO YOU ARE.

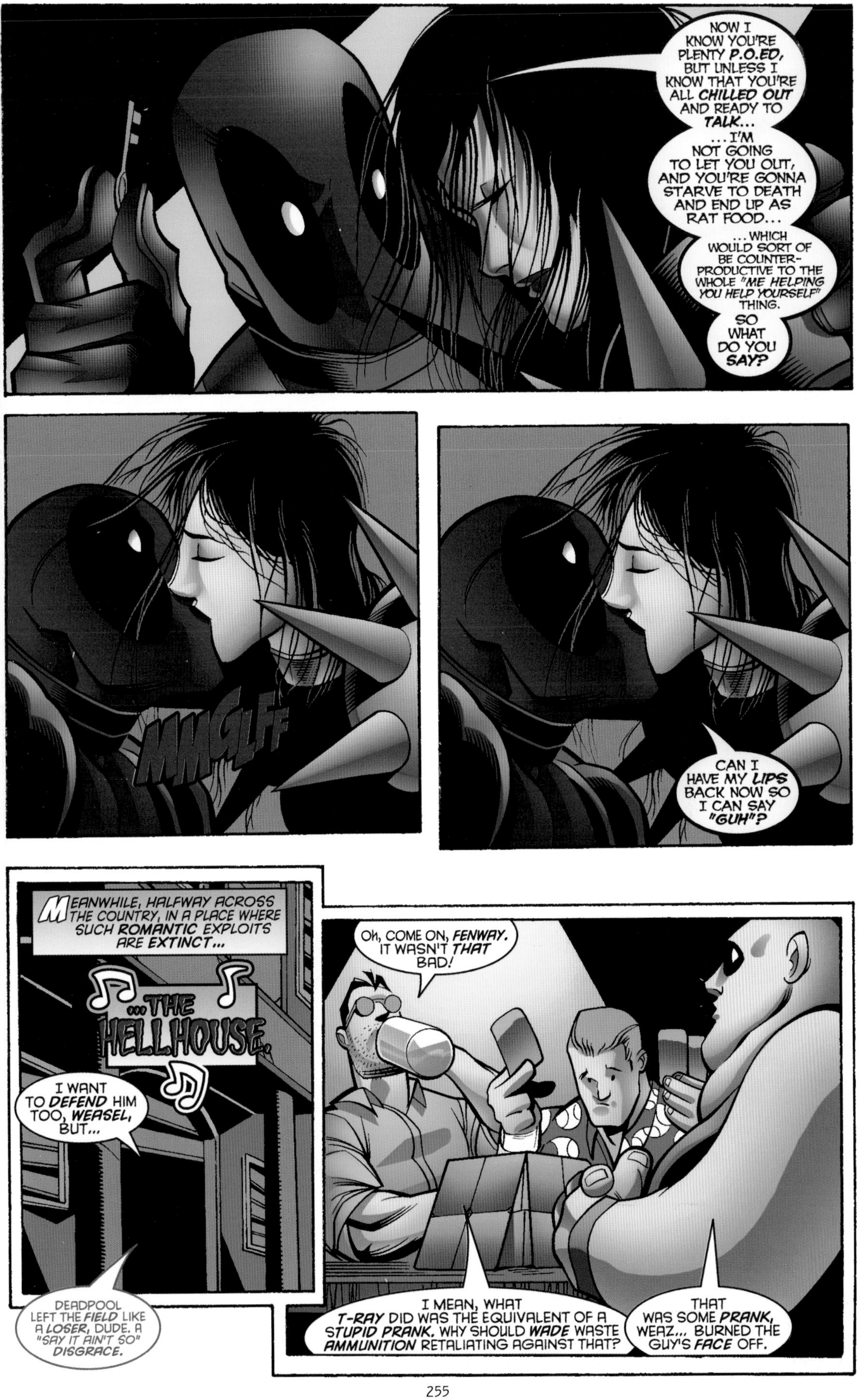
NOW I KNOW YOU'RE PLENTY P.O.ED, BUT UNLESS I KNOW THAT YOU'RE ALL CHILLED OUT AND READY TO TALK...
...I'M NOT GOING TO LET YOU OUT, AND YOU'RE GONNA STARVE TO DEATH AND END UP AS RAT FOOD...
...WHICH WOULD SORT OF BE COUNTER-PRODUCTIVE TO THE WHOLE "ME HELPING YOU HELP YOURSELF" THING.
SO WHAT DO YOU SAY?
MMGLFF
CAN I HAVE MY LIPS BACK NOW SO I CAN SAY "GUH"?
MEANWHILE, HALFWAY ACROSS THE COUNTRY, IN A PLACE WHERE SUCH ROMANTIC EXPLOITS ARE EXTINCT...
...THE HELLHOUSE.
I WANT TO DEFEND HIM TOO, WEASEL, BUT...
DEADPOOL LEFT THE FIELD LIKE A LOSER, DUDE. A "SAY IT AIN'T SO" DISGRACE.
Oh, COME ON, FENWAY. IT WASN'T THAT BAD!
I MEAN, WHAT T-RAY DID WAS THE EQUIVALENT OF A STUPID PRANK. WHY SHOULD WADE WASTE AMMUNITION RETALIATING AGAINST THAT?
THAT WAS SOME PRANK, WEAZ... BURNED THE GUY'S FACE OFF.

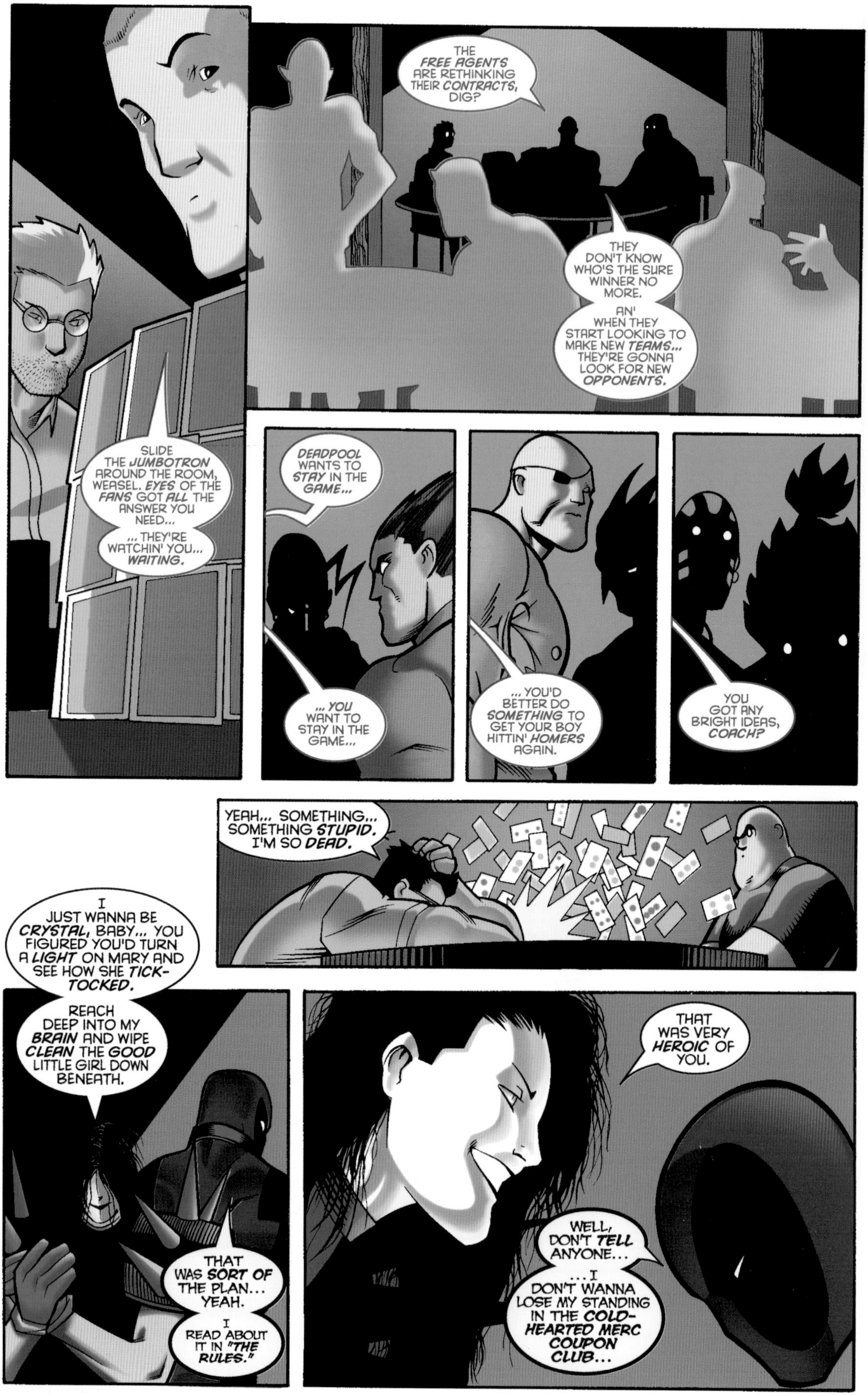
THE FREE AGENTS ARE RETHINKING THEIR CONTRACTS, DIG?
THEY DON'T KNOW WHO'S THE SURE WINNER NO MORE.
AN' WHEN THEY START LOOKING TO MAKE NEW TEAMS... THEY'RE GONNA LOOK FOR NEW OPPONENTS.
SLIDE THE JUMBOTRON AROUND THE ROOM, WEASEL. EYES OF THE FANS GOT ALL THE ANSWER YOU NEED...
... THEY'RE WATCHIN' YOU... WAITING.
DEADPOOL WANTS TO STAY IN THE GAME...
... YOU WANT TO STAY IN THE GAME...
... YOU'D BETTER DO SOMETHING TO GET YOUR BOY HITTIN' HOMERS AGAIN.
YOU GOT ANY BRIGHT IDEAS, COACH?
YEAH... SOMETHING... SOMETHING STUPID. I'M SO DEAD.
I JUST WANNA BE CRYSTAL, BABY... YOU FIGURED YOU'D TURN A LIGHT ON MARY AND SEE HOW SHE TICK-TOCKED.
REACH DEEP INTO MY BRAIN AND WIPE CLEAN THE GOOD LITTLE GIRL DOWN BENEATH.
THAT WAS SORT OF THE PLAN... YEAH.
I READ ABOUT IT IN "THE RULES."
THAT WAS VERY HEROIC OF YOU.
WELL, DON'T TELL ANYONE...
... I DON'T WANNA LOSE MY STANDING IN THE COLD-HEARTED MERC COUPON CLUB...

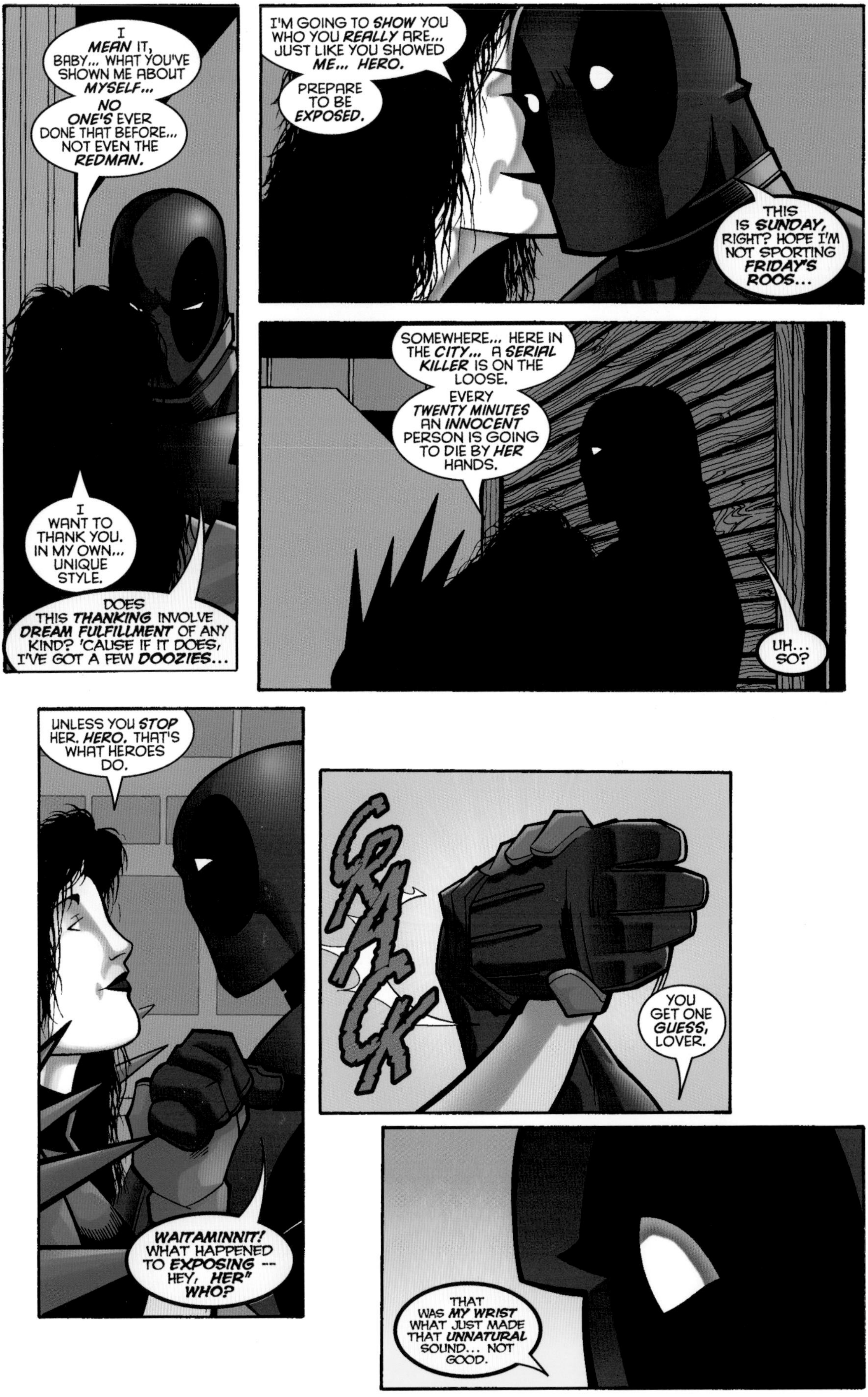
I MEAN IT, BABY... WHAT YOU'VE SHOWN ME ABOUT MYSELF...
NO ONE'S EVER DONE THAT BEFORE... NOT EVEN THE REDMAN.
I WANT TO THANK YOU. IN MY OWN... UNIQUE STYLE.
DOES THIS THANKING INVOLVE DREAM FULFILLMENT OF ANY KIND? 'CAUSE IF IT DOES, I'VE GOT A FEW DOOZIES...
I'M GOING TO SHOW YOU WHO YOU REALLY ARE... JUST LIKE YOU SHOWED ME... HERO.
PREPARE TO BE EXPOSED.
THIS IS SUNDAY, RIGHT? HOPE I'M NOT SPORTING FRIDAY'S ROOS...
SOMEWHERE... HERE IN THE CITY... A SERIAL KILLER IS ON THE LOOSE.
EVERY TWENTY MINUTES AN INNOCENT PERSON IS GOING TO DIE BY HER HANDS.
UH... SO?
UNLESS YOU STOP HER. HERO. THAT'S WHAT HEROES DO.
WAITAMINNIT! WHAT HAPPENED TO EXPOSING -- HEY, HER" WHO?
CRACK
YOU GET ONE GUESS, LOVER.
THAT WAS MY WRIST WHAT JUST MADE THAT UNNATURAL SOUND... NOT GOOD.

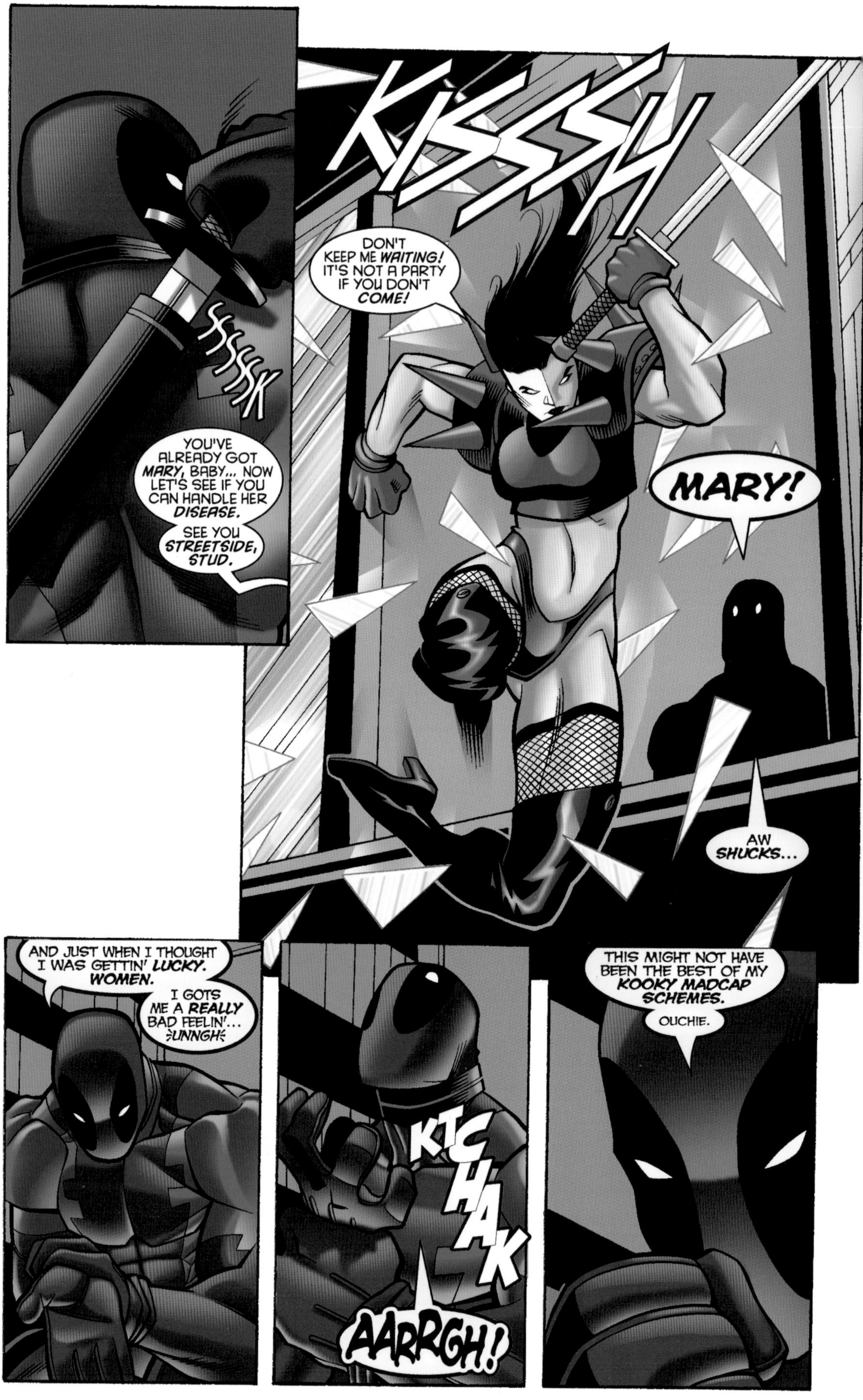
KISSSH
DON'T KEEP ME WAITING! IT'S NOT A PARTY IF YOU DON'T COME!
SSSSK
YOU'VE ALREADY GOT MARY, BABY... NOW LET'S SEE IF YOU CAN HANDLE HER DISEASE.
SEE YOU STREETSIDE, STUD.
MARY!
AW SHUCKS...
AND JUST WHEN I THOUGHT I WAS GETTIN' LUCKY. WOMEN.
I GOTS ME A REALLY BAD FEELIN'... UNNGH
KTCHAK
AARRGH!
THIS MIGHT NOT HAVE BEEN THE BEST OF MY KOOKY MADCAP SCHEMES.
OUCHIE.

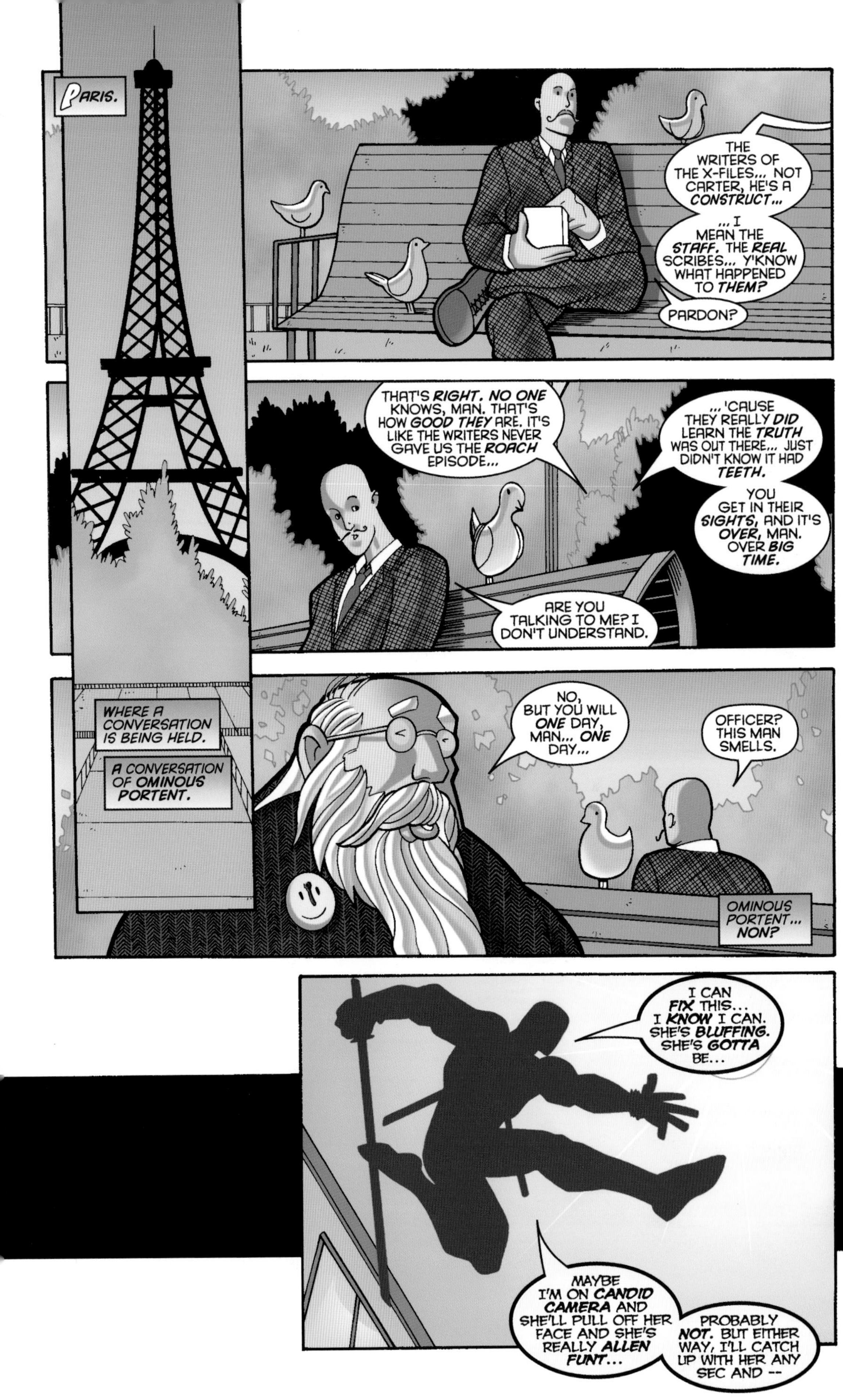
PARIS.
THE WRITERS OF THE X-FILES... NOT CARTER, HE'S A CONSTRUCT...
...I MEAN THE STAFF. THE REAL SCRIBES... Y'KNOW WHAT HAPPENED TO THEM?
PARDON?
THAT'S RIGHT. NO ONE KNOWS, MAN. THAT'S HOW GOOD THEY ARE. IT'S LIKE THE WRITERS NEVER GAVE US THE ROACH EPISODE...
...'CAUSE THEY REALLY DID LEARN THE TRUTH WAS OUT THERE... JUST DIDN'T KNOW IT HAD TEETH.
YOU GET IN THEIR SIGHTS, AND IT'S OVER, MAN. OVER BIG TIME.
ARE YOU TALKING TO ME? I DON'T UNDERSTAND.
WHERE A CONVERSATION IS BEING HELD.
A CONVERSATION OF OMINOUS PORTENT.
NO, BUT YOU WILL ONE DAY, MAN... ONE DAY...
OFFICER? THIS MAN SMELLS.
OMINOUS PORTENT... NON?
I CAN FIX THIS... I KNOW I CAN. SHE'S BLUFFING. SHE'S GOTTA BE...
MAYBE I'M ON CANDID CAMERA AND SHE'LL PULL OFF HER FACE AND SHE'S REALLY ALLEN FUNT...
PROBABLY NOT. BUT EITHER WAY, I'LL CATCH UP WITH HER ANY SEC AND --

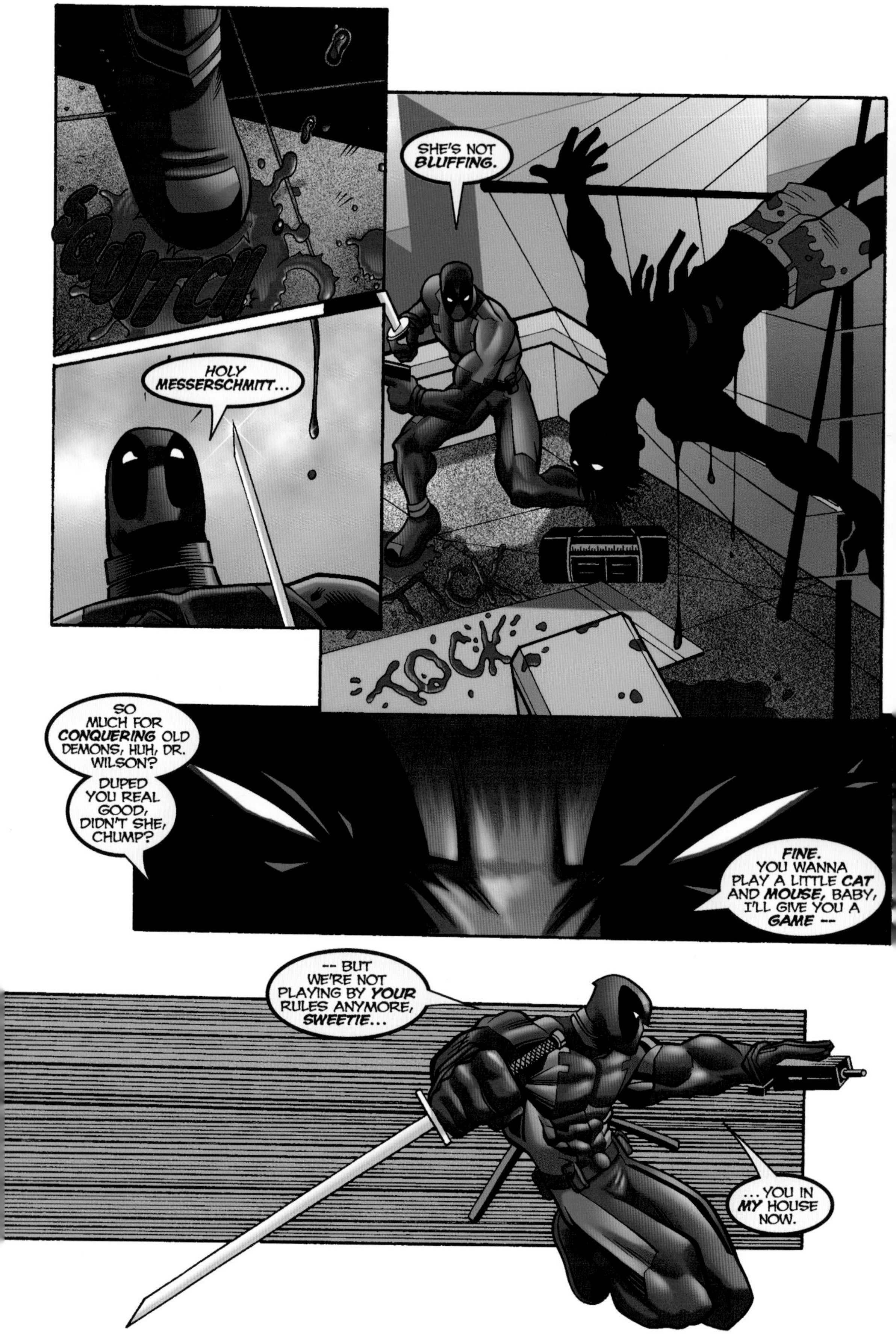
SQUITCH
HOLY MESSERSCHMITT...
SHE'S NOT BLUFFING.
TOCK
TOCK
SO MUCH FOR CONQUERING OLD DEMONS, HUH, DR. WILSON?
DUPED YOU REAL GOOD, DIDN'T SHE, CHUMP?
FINE. YOU WANNA PLAY A LITTLE CAT AND MOUSE, BABY, I'LL GIVE YOU A GAME --
-- BUT WE'RE NOT PLAYING BY YOUR RULES ANYMORE, SWEETIE...
...YOU IN MY HOUSE NOW.

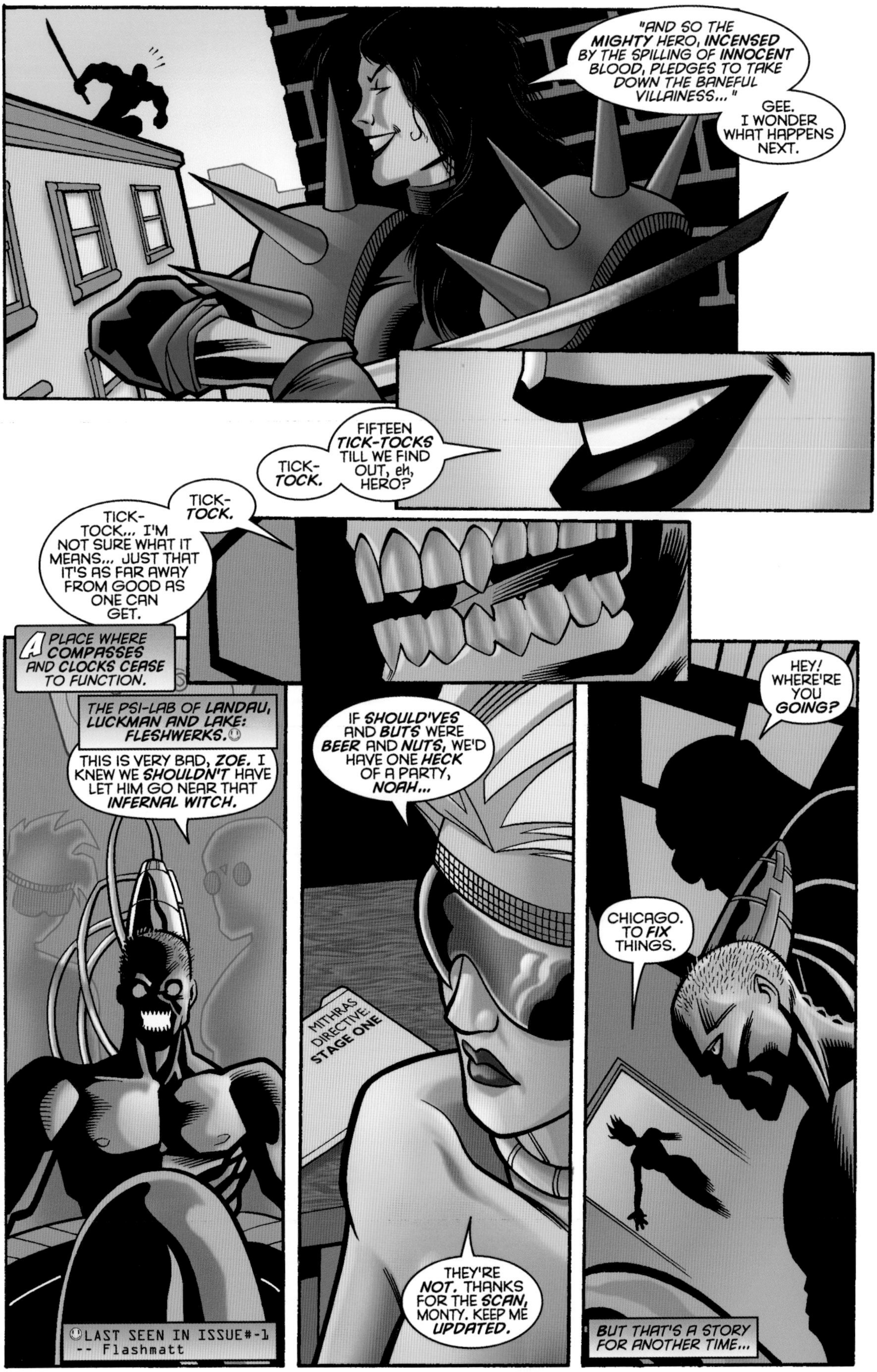
"AND SO THE MIGHTY HERO, INCENSED BY THE SPILLING OF INNOCENT BLOOD, PLEDGES TO TAKE DOWN THE BANEFUL VILLAINESS..."
GEE. I WONDER WHAT HAPPENS NEXT.
FIFTEEN TICK-TOCKS TILL WE FIND OUT, eh, HERO?
TICK-TOCK.
TICK-TOCK.
TICK-TOCK... I'M NOT SURE WHAT IT MEANS... JUST THAT IT'S AS FAR AWAY FROM GOOD AS ONE CAN GET.
A PLACE WHERE COMPASSES AND CLOCKS CEASE TO FUNCTION.
THE PSI-LAB OF LANDAU, LUCKMAN AND LAKE: FLESHWERKS.
THIS IS VERY BAD, ZOE. I KNEW WE SHOULDN'T HAVE LET HIM GO NEAR THAT INFERNAL WITCH.
LAST SEEN IN ISSUE#-1 -- Flashmatt
IF SHOULD'VES AND BUTS WERE BEER AND NUTS, WE'D HAVE ONE HECK OF A PARTY, NOAH...
MITHRAS DIRECTIVE: STAGE ONE
THEY'RE NOT. THANKS FOR THE SCAN, MONTY. KEEP ME UPDATED.
HEY! WHERE'RE YOU GOING?
CHICAGO. TO FIX THINGS.
BUT THAT'S A STORY FOR ANOTHER TIME...

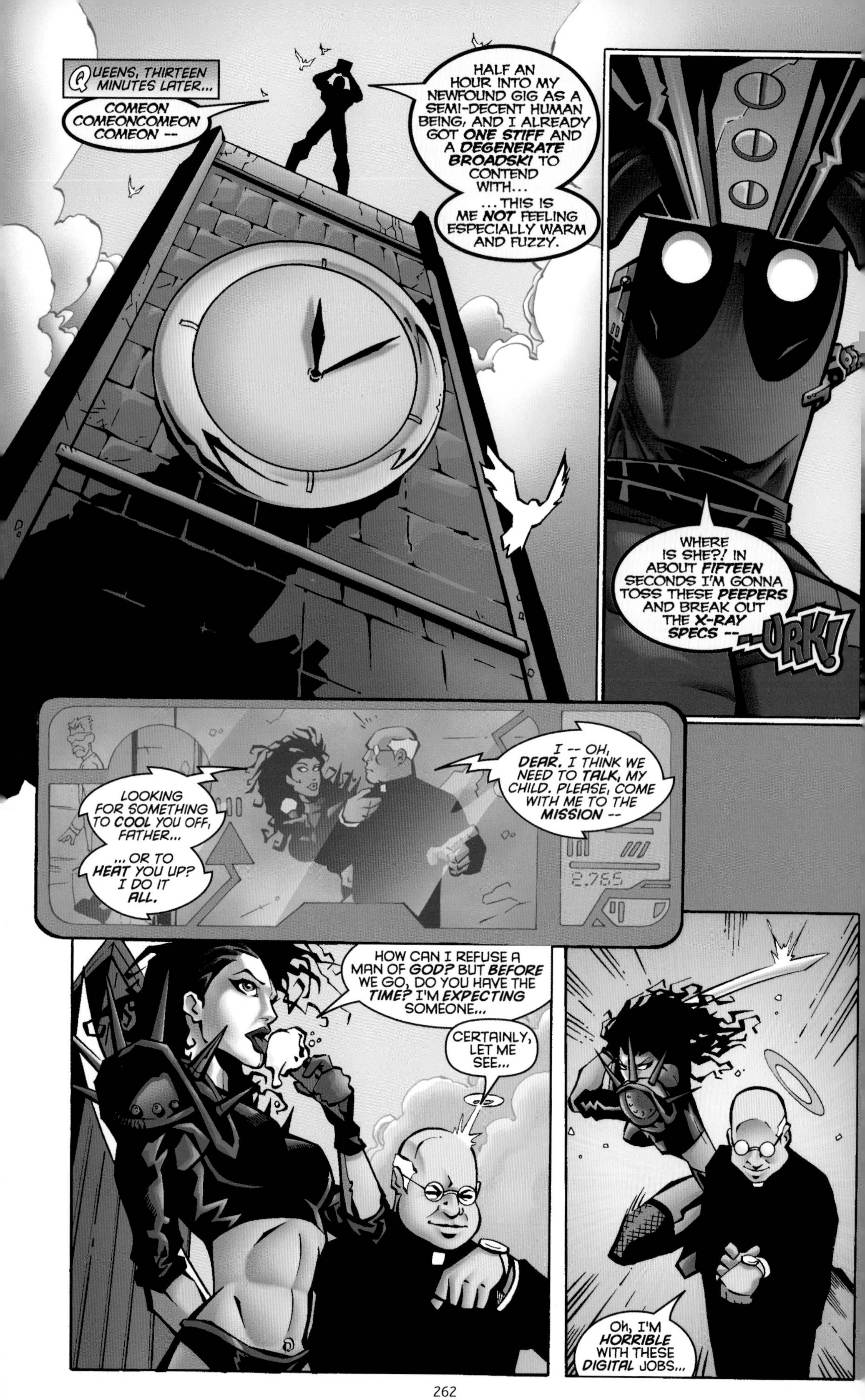
QUEENS, THIRTEEN MINUTES LATER...
COMEON COMEONCOMEON COMEON --
HALF AN HOUR INTO MY NEWFOUND GIG AS A SEMI-DECENT HUMAN BEING, AND I ALREADY GOT ONE STIFF AND A DEGENERATE BROADSKI TO CONTEND WITH...
...THIS IS ME NOT FEELING ESPECIALLY WARM AND FUZZY.
WHERE IS SHE?! IN ABOUT FIFTEEN SECONDS I'M GONNA TOSS THESE PEEPERS AND BREAK OUT THE X-RAY SPECS --
--URK!
LOOKING FOR SOMETHING TO COOL YOU OFF, FATHER...
...OR TO HEAT YOU UP? I DO IT ALL.
I -- OH, DEAR. I THINK WE NEED TO TALK, MY CHILD. PLEASE, COME WITH ME TO THE MISSION --
2.765
HOW CAN I REFUSE A MAN OF GOD? BUT BEFORE WE GO, DO YOU HAVE THE TIME? I'M EXPECTING SOMEONE...
CERTAINLY, LET ME SEE...
Oh, I'M HORRIBLE WITH THESE DIGITAL JOBS...

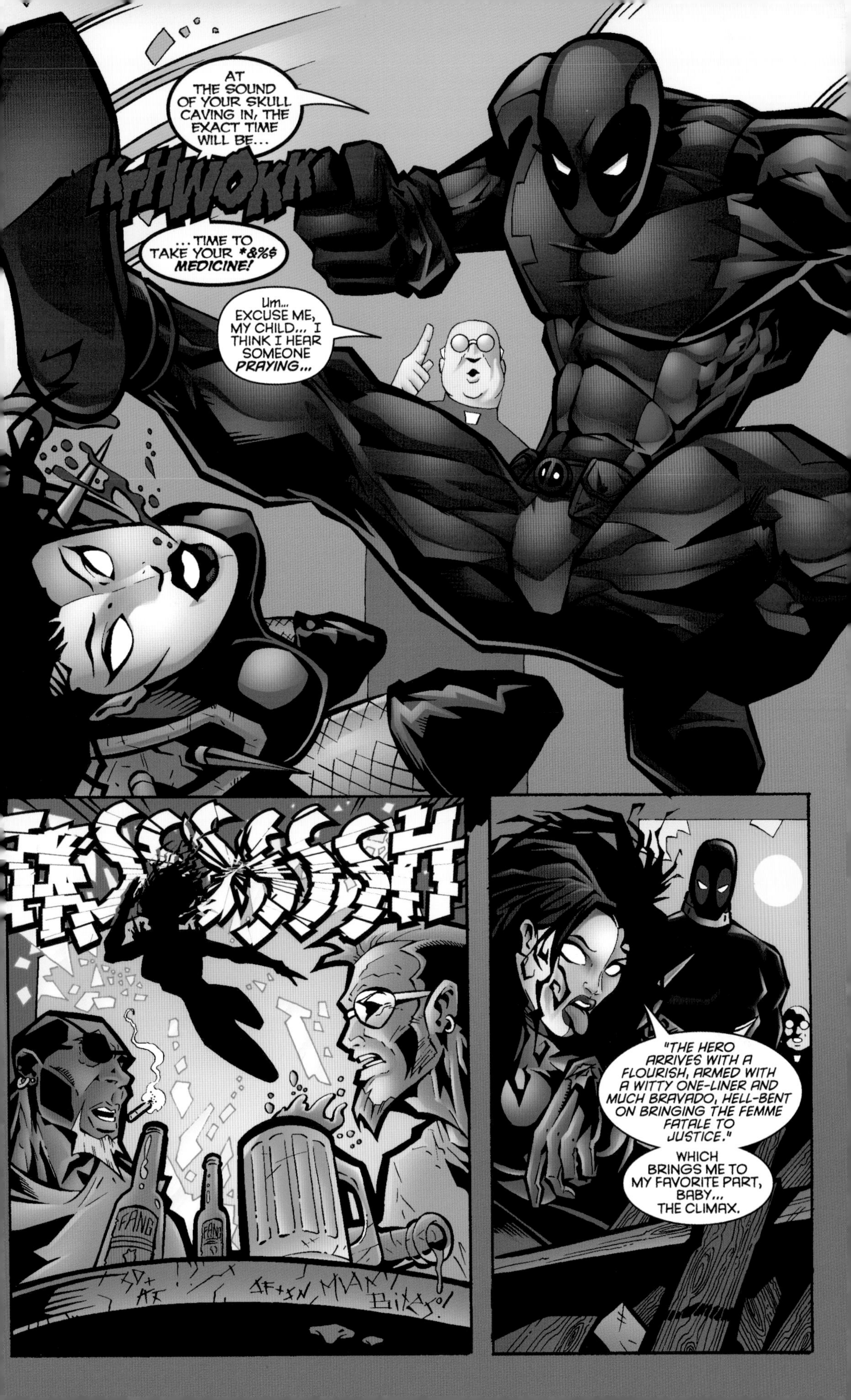

AT THE SOUND OF YOUR SKULL CAVING IN, THE EXACT TIME WILL BE...
KRHWOKK
...TIME TO TAKE YOUR *&%$ MEDICINE!
Um... EXCUSE ME, MY CHILD... I THINK I HEAR SOMEONE PRAYING...
KRSSSSSH
"THE HERO ARRIVES WITH A FLOURISH, ARMED WITH A WITTY ONE-LINER AND MUCH BRAVADO, HELL-BENT ON BRINGING THE FEMME FATALE TO JUSTICE."
WHICH BRINGS ME TO MY FAVORITE PART, BABY... THE CLIMAX.

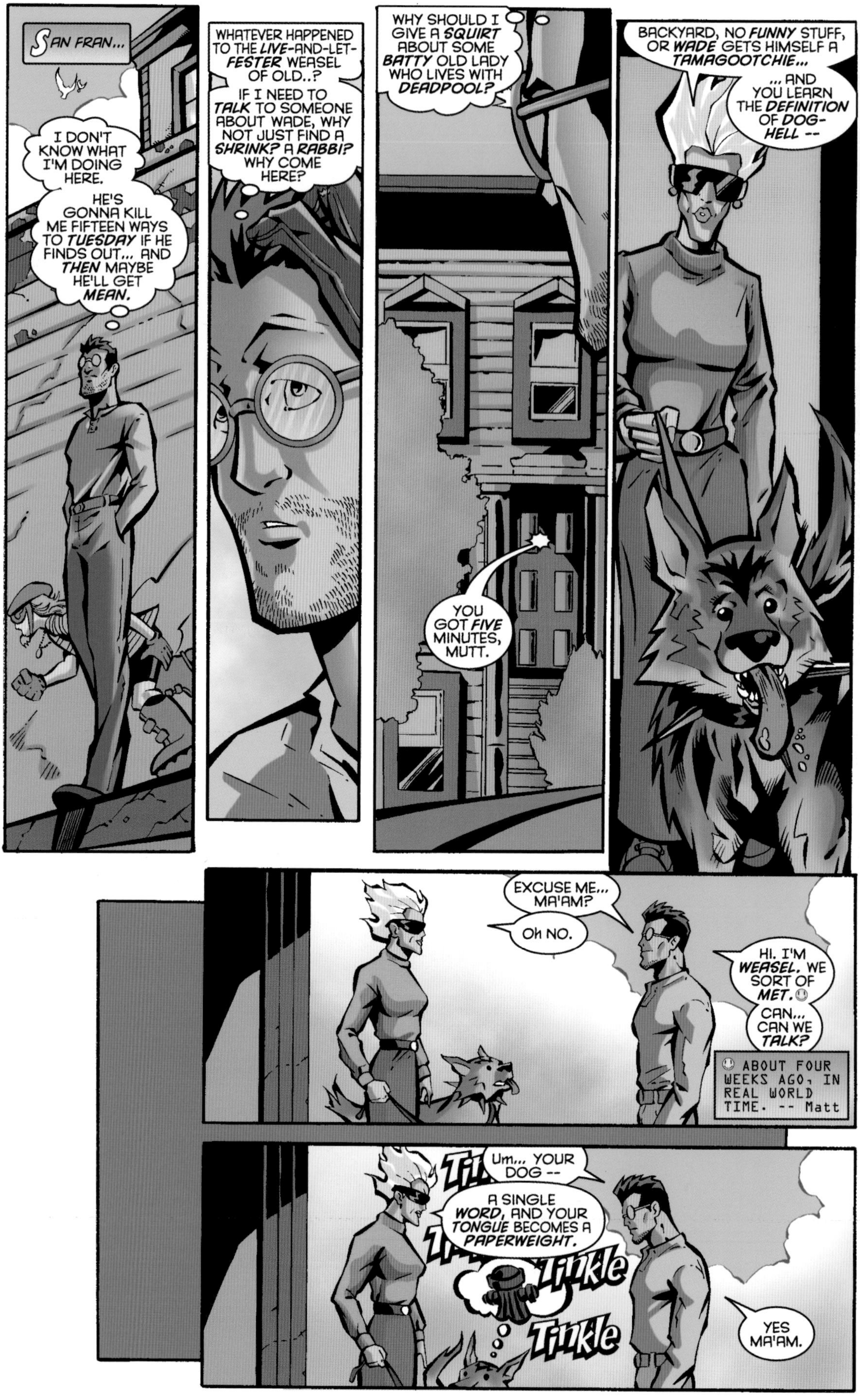
SAN FRAN...
I DON'T KNOW WHAT I'M DOING HERE.
HE'S GONNA KILL ME FIFTEEN WAYS TO TUESDAY IF HE FINDS OUT... AND THEN MAYBE HE'LL GET MEAN.
WHATEVER HAPPENED TO THE LIVE-AND-LET-FESTER WEASEL OF OLD..?
IF I NEED TO TALK TO SOMEONE ABOUT WADE, WHY NOT JUST FIND A SHRINK? A RABBI? WHY COME HERE?
WHY SHOULD I GIVE A SQUIRT ABOUT SOME BATTY OLD LADY WHO LIVES WITH DEADPOOL?
YOU GOT FIVE MINUTES, MUTT.
BACKYARD, NO FUNNY STUFF, OR WADE GETS HIMSELF A TAMAGOOTCHIE...
... AND YOU LEARN THE DEFINITION OF DOG-HELL --
EXCUSE ME... MA'AM?
Oh NO.
HI. I'M WEASEL. WE SORT OF MET. ☺
CAN... CAN WE TALK?
☺ ABOUT FOUR WEEKS AGO, IN REAL WORLD TIME. -- Matt
Um... YOUR DOG --
A SINGLE WORD, AND YOUR TONGUE BECOMES A PAPERWEIGHT.
Tinkle
Tinkle
YES MA'AM.

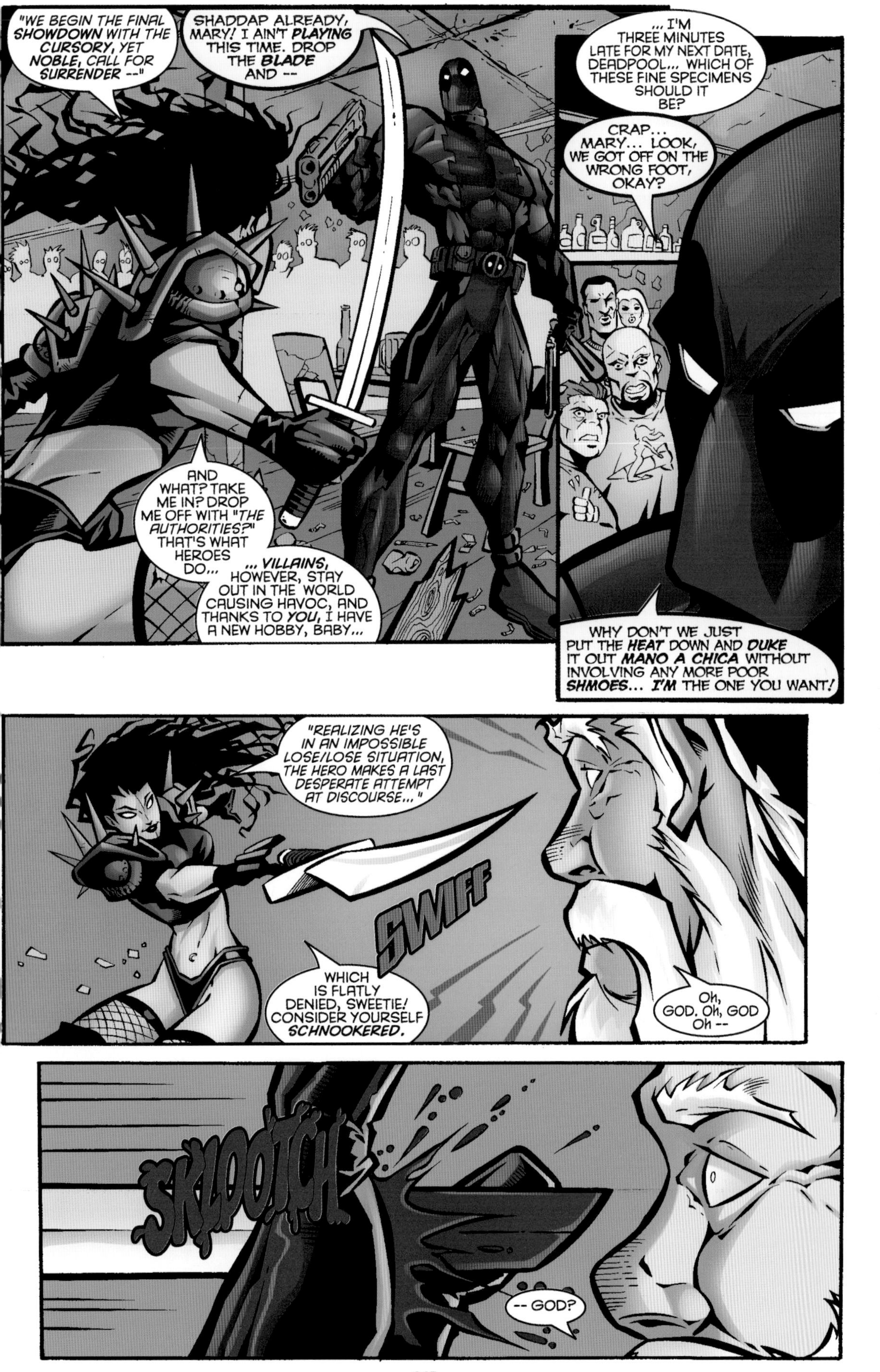
"WE BEGIN THE FINAL SHOWDOWN WITH THE CURSORY, YET NOBLE, CALL FOR SURRENDER --"
SHADDAP ALREADY, MARY! I AIN'T PLAYING THIS TIME. DROP THE BLADE AND --
AND WHAT? TAKE ME IN? DROP ME OFF WITH "THE AUTHORITIES?" THAT'S WHAT HEROES DO...
... VILLAINS, HOWEVER, STAY OUT IN THE WORLD CAUSING HAVOC, AND THANKS TO YOU, I HAVE A NEW HOBBY, BABY...
... I'M THREE MINUTES LATE FOR MY NEXT DATE, DEADPOOL... WHICH OF THESE FINE SPECIMENS SHOULD IT BE?
CRAP... MARY... LOOK, WE GOT OFF ON THE WRONG FOOT, OKAY?
WHY DON'T WE JUST PUT THE HEAT DOWN AND DUKE IT OUT MANO A CHICA WITHOUT INVOLVING ANY MORE POOR SHMOES... I'M THE ONE YOU WANT!
"REALIZING HE'S IN AN IMPOSSIBLE LOSE/LOSE SITUATION, THE HERO MAKES A LAST DESPERATE ATTEMPT AT DISCOURSE..."
SWIFF
WHICH IS FLATLY DENIED, SWEETIE! CONSIDER YOURSELF SCHNOOKERED.
Oh, GOD. Oh, GOD Oh --
SKLOOTCH
-- GOD?

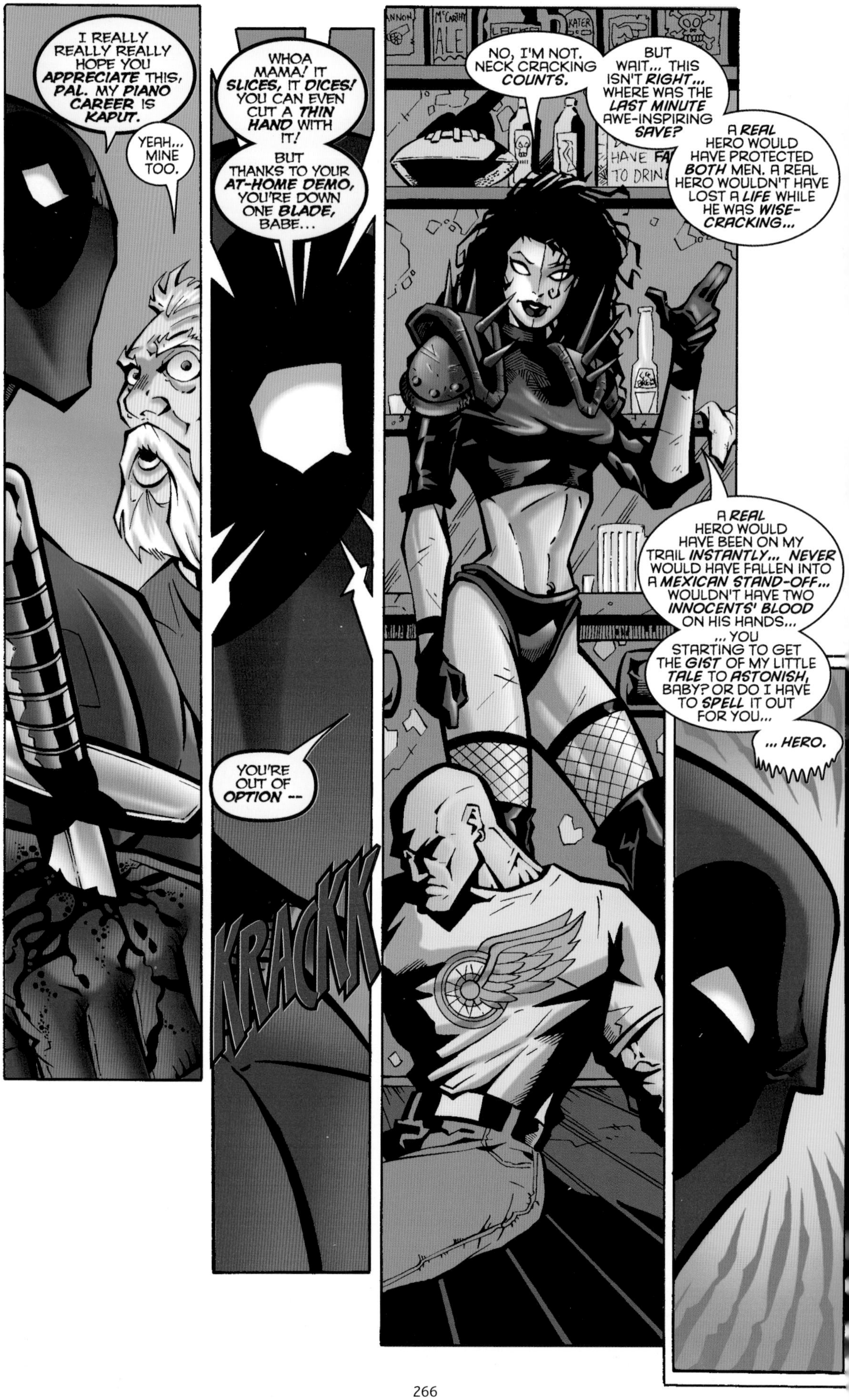
I REALLY REALLY REALLY HOPE YOU APPRECIATE THIS, PAL. MY PIANO CAREER IS KAPUT.
YEAH... MINE TOO.
WHOA MAMA! IT SLICES, IT DICES! YOU CAN EVEN CUT A THIN HAND WITH IT!
BUT THANKS TO YOUR AT-HOME DEMO, YOU'RE DOWN ONE BLADE, BABE...
YOU'RE OUT OF OPTION --
KRACKK
NO, I'M NOT. NECK CRACKING COUNTS.
BUT WAIT... THIS ISN'T RIGHT... WHERE WAS THE LAST MINUTE AWE-INSPIRING SAVE?
A REAL HERO WOULD HAVE PROTECTED BOTH MEN. A REAL HERO WOULDN'T HAVE LOST A LIFE WHILE HE WAS WISE-CRACKING...
A REAL HERO WOULD HAVE BEEN ON MY TRAIL INSTANTLY... NEVER WOULD HAVE FALLEN INTO A MEXICAN STAND-OFF... WOULDN'T HAVE TWO INNOCENTS' BLOOD ON HIS HANDS...
... YOU STARTING TO GET THE GIST OF MY LITTLE TALE TO ASTONISH, BABY? OR DO I HAVE TO SPELL IT OUT FOR YOU...
... HERO.

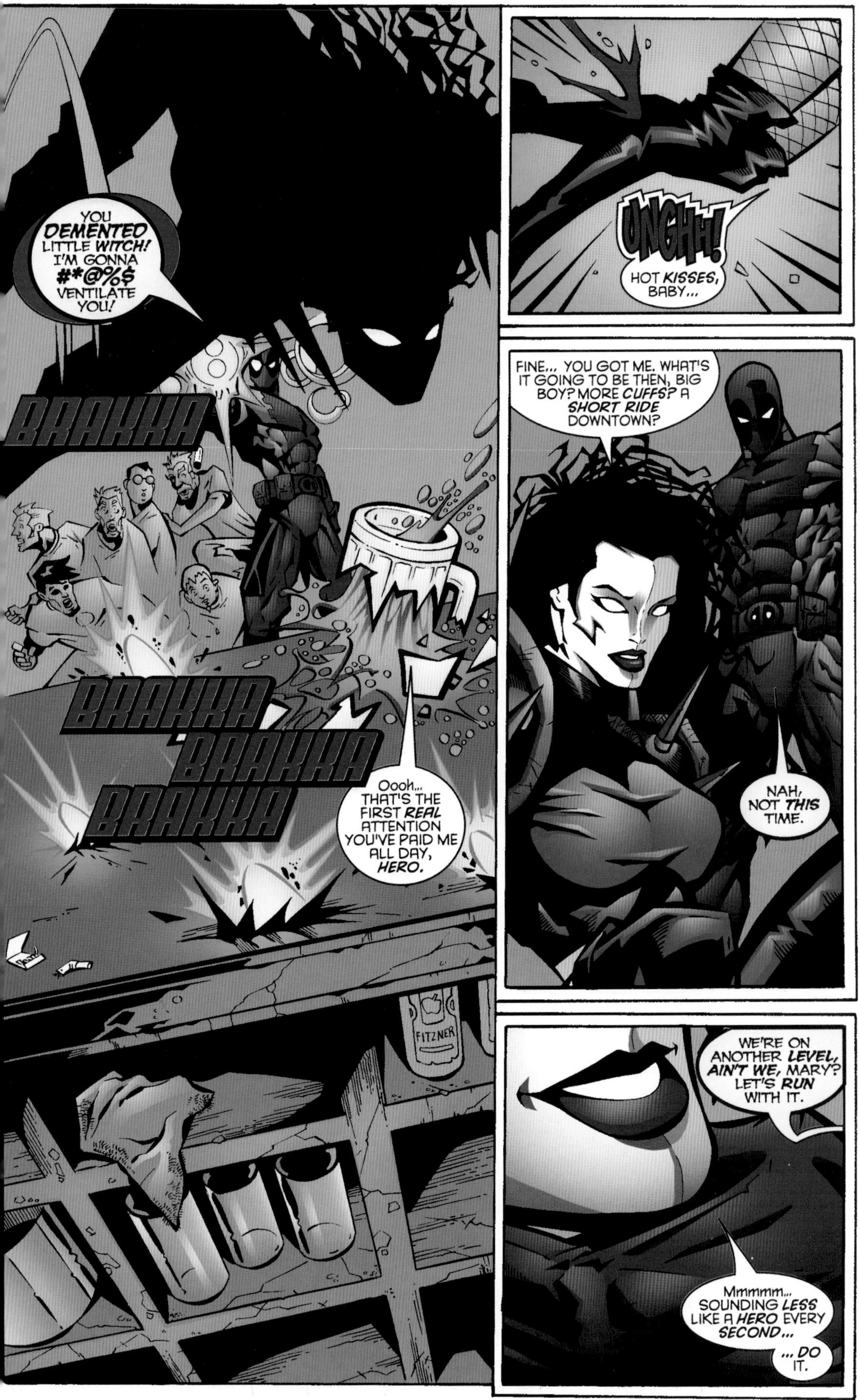
YOU DEMENTED LITTLE WITCH! I'M GONNA #*@%$ VENTILATE YOU!
BRAKKA
BRAKKA
BRAKKA
BRAKKA
Oooh... THAT'S THE FIRST REAL ATTENTION YOU'VE PAID ME ALL DAY, HERO.
FITZNER
UNGHH!
HOT KISSES, BABY...
FINE... YOU GOT ME. WHAT'S IT GOING TO BE THEN, BIG BOY? MORE CUFFS? A SHORT RIDE DOWNTOWN?
NAH, NOT THIS TIME.
WE'RE ON ANOTHER LEVEL, AIN'T WE, MARY? LET'S RUN WITH IT.
Mmmmm... SOUNDING LESS LIKE A HERO EVERY SECOND...
...DO IT.

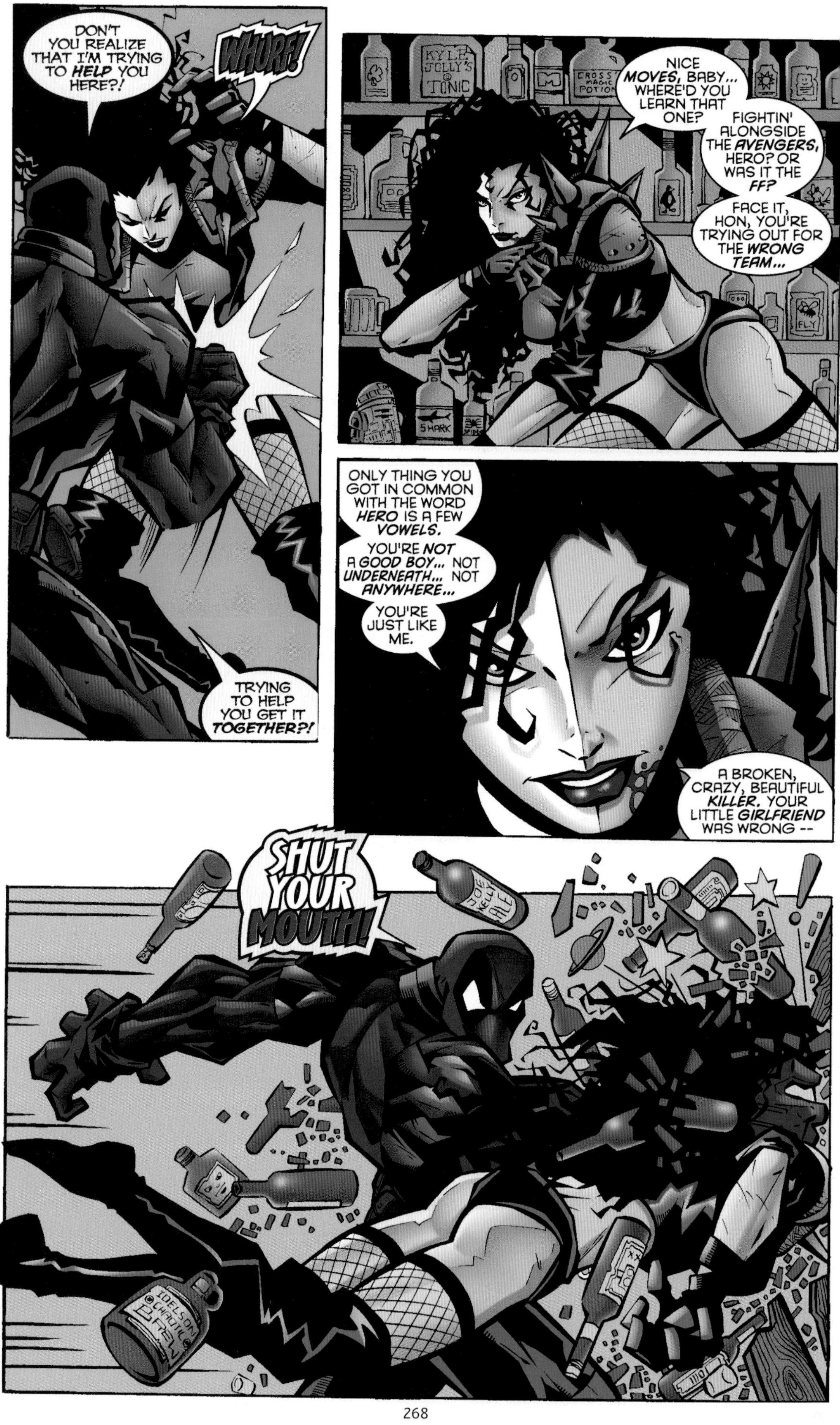
DON'T YOU REALIZE THAT I'M TRYING TO HELP YOU HERE?!
WHURF!
TRYING TO HELP YOU GET IT TOGETHER?!
NICE MOVES, BABY... WHERE'D YOU LEARN THAT ONE?
FIGHTIN' ALONGSIDE THE AVENGERS, HERO? OR WAS IT THE FF?
FACE IT, HON, YOU'RE TRYING OUT FOR THE WRONG TEAM...
ONLY THING YOU GOT IN COMMON WITH THE WORD HERO IS A FEW VOWELS.
YOU'RE NOT A GOOD BOY... NOT UNDERNEATH... NOT ANYWHERE...
YOU'RE JUST LIKE ME.
A BROKEN, CRAZY, BEAUTIFUL KILLER. YOUR LITTLE GIRLFRIEND WAS WRONG --
SHUT YOUR MOUTH!

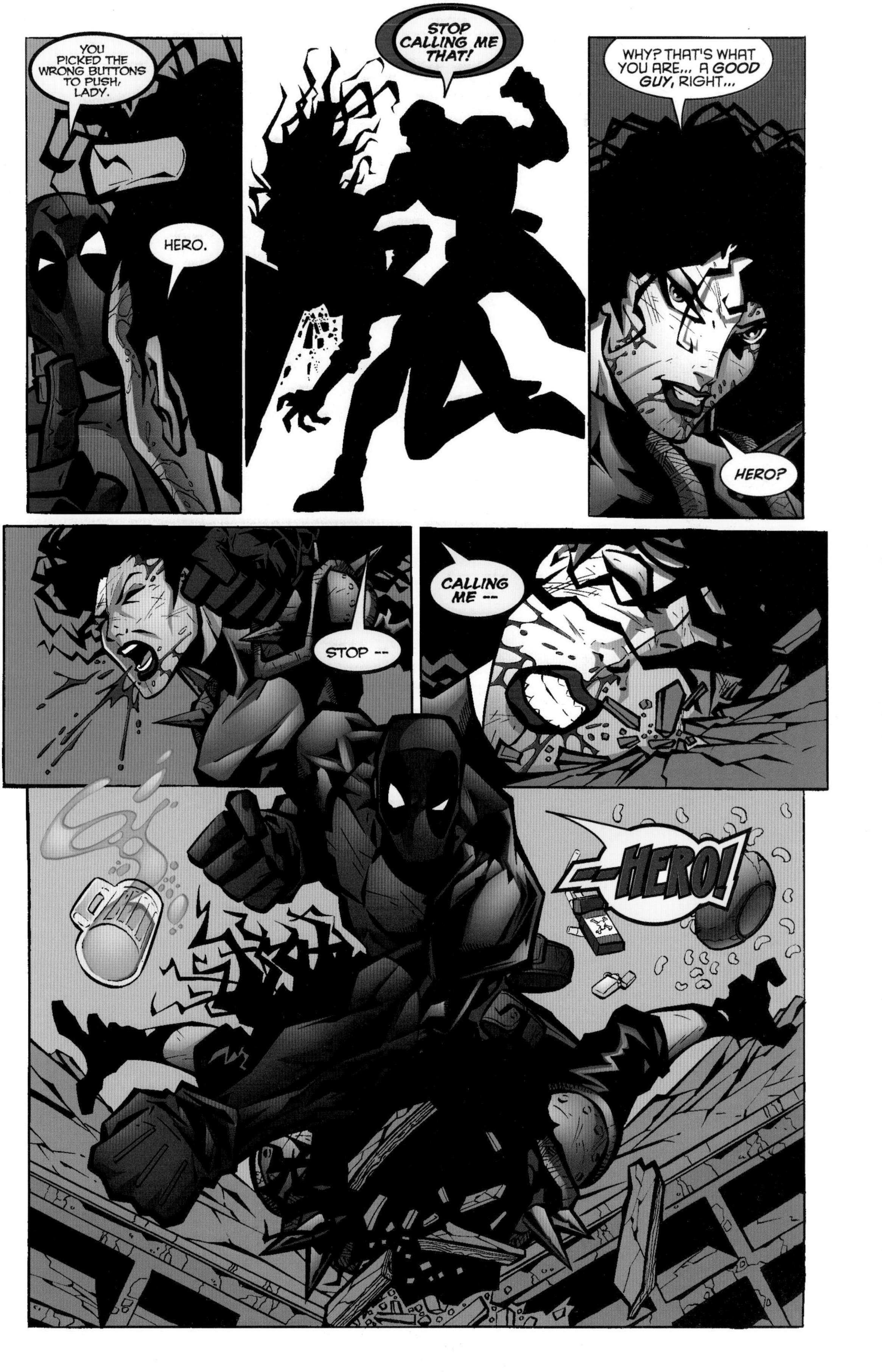
YOU PICKED THE WRONG BUTTONS TO PUSH, LADY.
HERO.
STOP CALLING ME THAT!
WHY? THAT'S WHAT YOU ARE... A GOOD GUY, RIGHT...
HERO?
STOP --
CALLING ME --
--HERO!

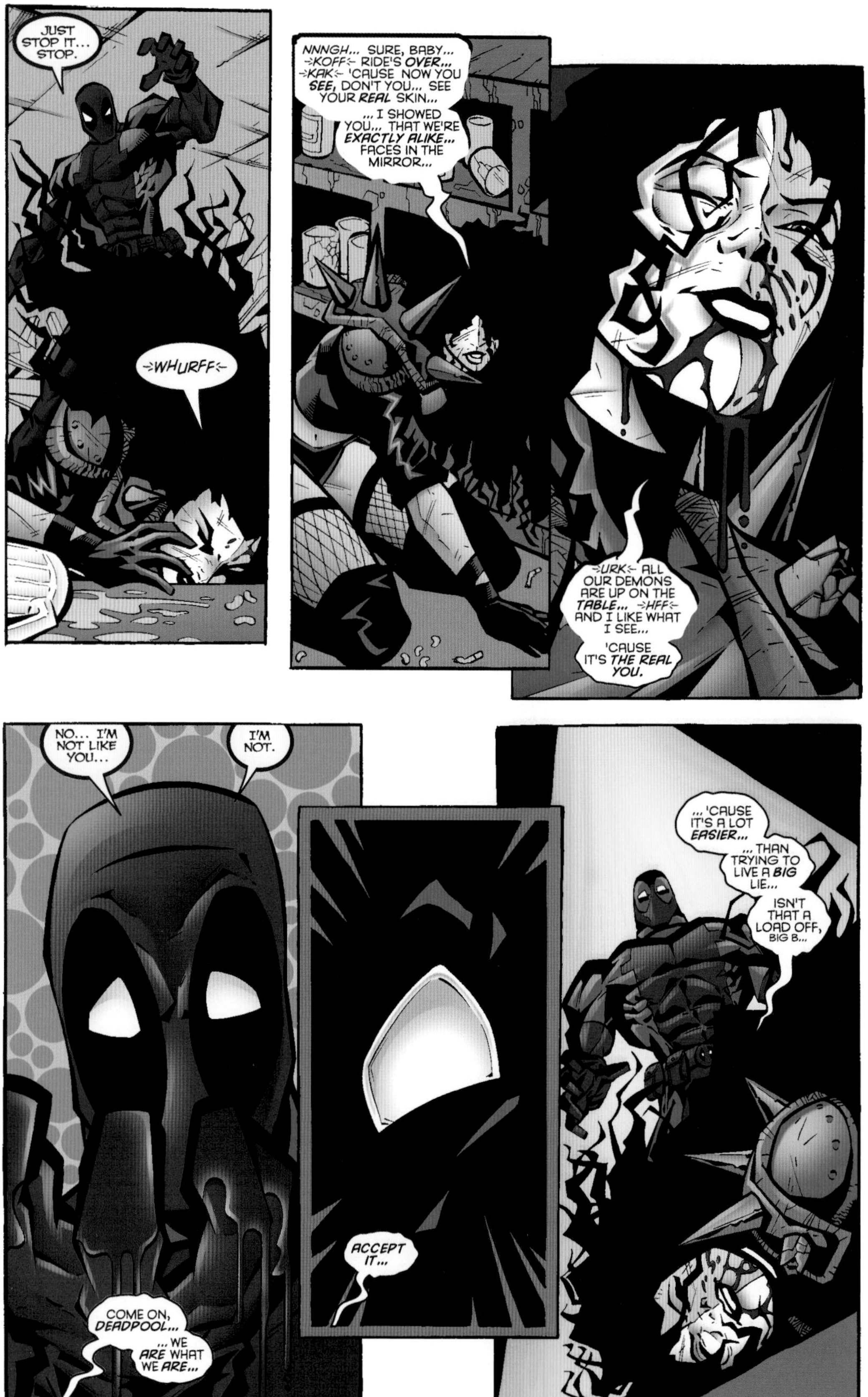
JUST STOP IT... STOP.
WHURFF
NNNGH... SURE, BABY... KOFF RIDE'S OVER... KAK 'CAUSE NOW YOU SEE, DON'T YOU... SEE YOUR REAL SKIN...
... I SHOWED YOU... THAT WE'RE EXACTLY ALIKE... FACES IN THE MIRROR...
URK ALL OUR DEMONS ARE UP ON THE TABLE... HFF AND I LIKE WHAT I SEE...
'CAUSE IT'S THE REAL YOU.
NO... I'M NOT LIKE YOU...
I'M NOT.
COME ON, DEADPOOL...
... WE ARE WHAT WE ARE...
ACCEPT IT...
... 'CAUSE IT'S A LOT EASIER...
... THAN TRYING TO LIVE A BIG LIE...
ISN'T THAT A LOAD OFF, BIG B...

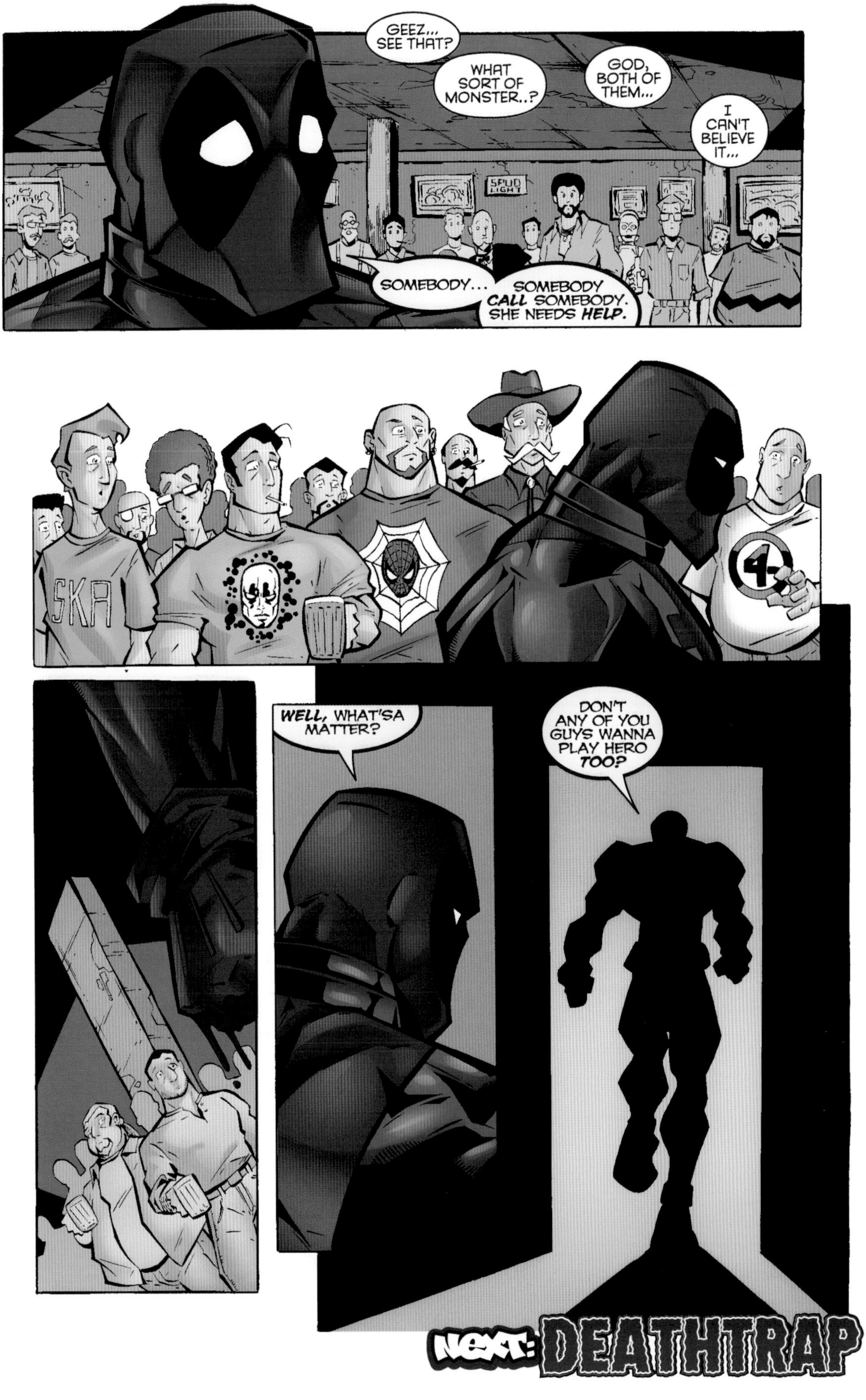
GEEZ... SEE THAT?
WHAT SORT OF MONSTER..?
GOD, BOTH OF THEM...
I CAN'T BELIEVE IT...
SPUD LIGHT
SOMEBODY...
SOMEBODY CALL SOMEBODY. SHE NEEDS HELP.
SKA
WELL, WHAT'SA MATTER?
DON'T ANY OF YOU GUYS WANNA PLAY HERO TOO?
NEXT: DEATHTRAP

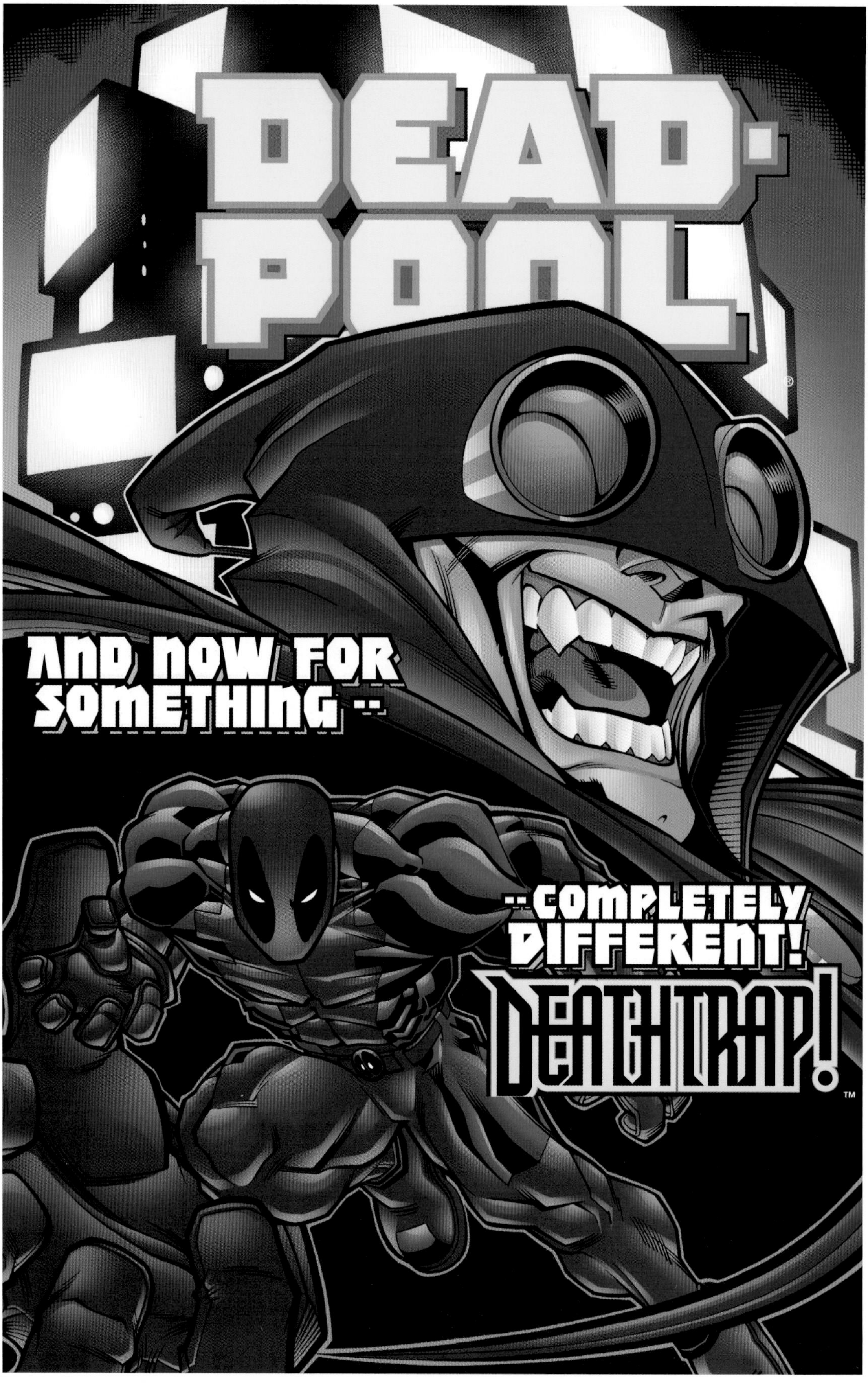
DEAD-POOL®
AND NOW FOR SOMETHING --
--COMPLETELY DIFFERENT!
DEATHTRAP!™

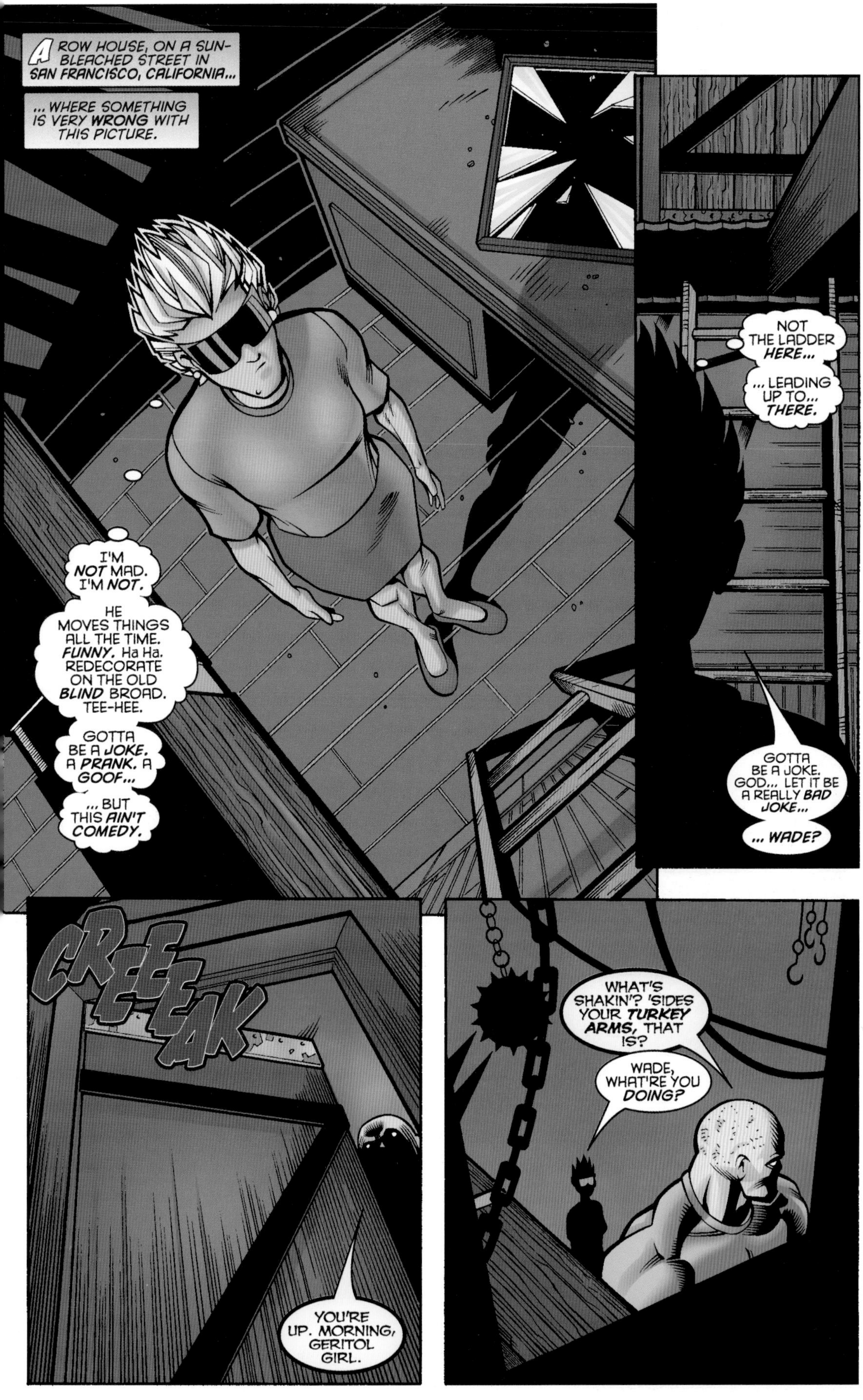
A ROW HOUSE, ON A SUN-BLEACHED STREET IN SAN FRANCISCO, CALIFORNIA...
... WHERE SOMETHING IS VERY WRONG WITH THIS PICTURE.
I'M NOT MAD. I'M NOT.
HE MOVES THINGS ALL THE TIME. FUNNY. Ha Ha. REDECORATE ON THE OLD BLIND BROAD. TEE-HEE.
GOTTA BE A JOKE. A PRANK. A GOOF...
... BUT THIS AIN'T COMEDY.
NOT THE LADDER HERE...
... LEADING UP TO... THERE.
GOTTA BE A JOKE. GOD... LET IT BE A REALLY BAD JOKE...
... WADE?
CREEEAK
YOU'RE UP. MORNING, GERITOL GIRL.
WHAT'S SHAKIN'? 'SIDES YOUR TURKEY ARMS, THAT IS?
WADE, WHAT'RE YOU DOING?

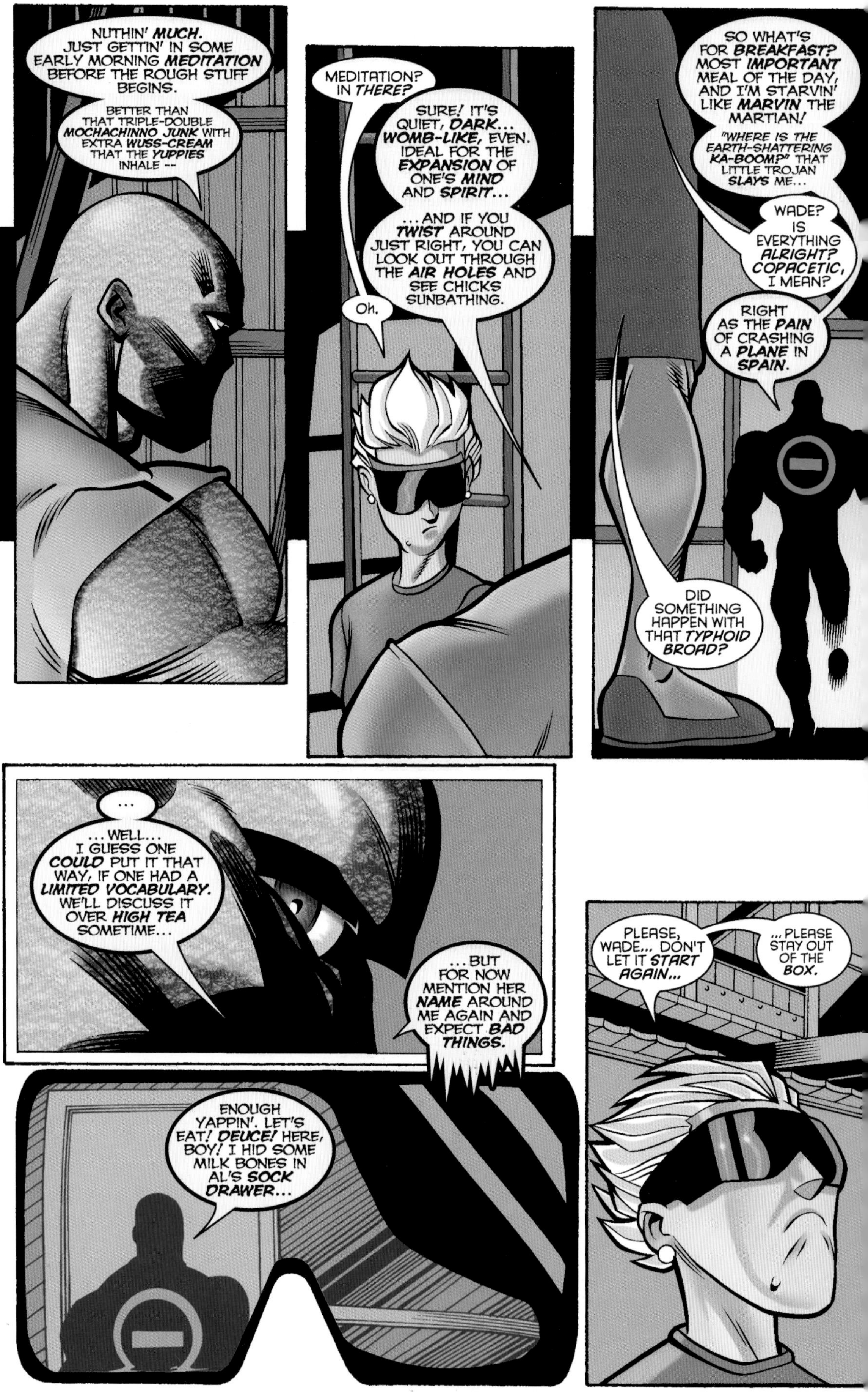

NUTHIN' MUCH. JUST GETTIN' IN SOME EARLY MORNING MEDITATION BEFORE THE ROUGH STUFF BEGINS.
BETTER THAN THAT TRIPLE-DOUBLE MOCHACHINNO JUNK WITH EXTRA WUSS-CREAM THAT THE YUPPIES INHALE --
MEDITATION? IN THERE?
SURE! IT'S QUIET, DARK... WOMB-LIKE, EVEN. IDEAL FOR THE EXPANSION OF ONE'S MIND AND SPIRIT...
...AND IF YOU TWIST AROUND JUST RIGHT, YOU CAN LOOK OUT THROUGH THE AIR HOLES AND SEE CHICKS SUNBATHING.
Oh.
SO WHAT'S FOR BREAKFAST? MOST IMPORTANT MEAL OF THE DAY, AND I'M STARVIN' LIKE MARVIN THE MARTIAN!
"WHERE IS THE EARTH-SHATTERING KA-BOOM?" THAT LITTLE TROJAN SLAYS ME...
WADE? IS EVERYTHING ALRIGHT? COPACETIC, I MEAN?
RIGHT AS THE PAIN OF CRASHING A PLANE IN SPAIN.
DID SOMETHING HAPPEN WITH THAT TYPHOID BROAD?
...
...WELL... I GUESS ONE COULD PUT IT THAT WAY, IF ONE HAD A LIMITED VOCABULARY. WE'LL DISCUSS IT OVER HIGH TEA SOMETIME...
...BUT FOR NOW MENTION HER NAME AROUND ME AGAIN AND EXPECT BAD THINGS.
ENOUGH YAPPIN'. LET'S EAT! DEUCE! HERE, BOY! I HID SOME MILK BONES IN AL'S SOCK DRAWER...
PLEASE, WADE... DON'T LET IT START AGAIN...
...PLEASE STAY OUT OF THE BOX.

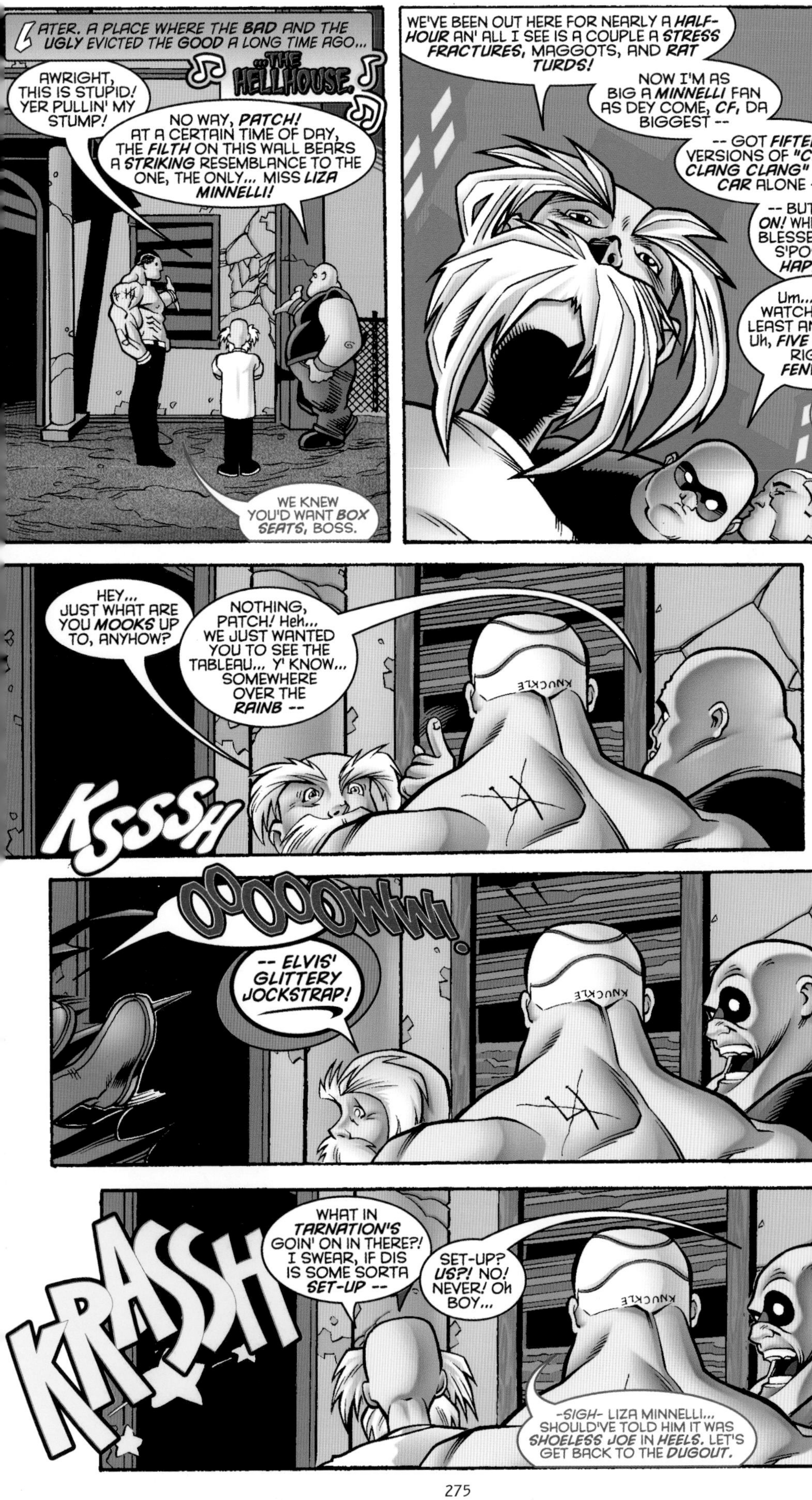
LATER. A PLACE WHERE THE BAD AND THE UGLY EVICTED THE GOOD A LONG TIME AGO...
...THE HELLHOUSE.
AWRIGHT, THIS IS STUPID! YER PULLIN' MY STUMP!
NO WAY, PATCH! AT A CERTAIN TIME OF DAY, THE FILTH ON THIS WALL BEARS A STRIKING RESEMBLANCE TO THE ONE, THE ONLY... MISS LIZA MINNELLI!
WE KNEW YOU'D WANT BOX SEATS, BOSS.
WE'VE BEEN OUT HERE FOR NEARLY A HALF-HOUR AN' ALL I SEE IS A COUPLE A STRESS FRACTURES, MAGGOTS, AND RAT TURDS!
NOW I'M AS BIG A MINNELLI FAN AS DEY COME, CF, DA BIGGEST --
-- GOT FIFTEEN VERSIONS OF "CLANG CLANG CLANG" IN MY CAR ALONE --
-- BUT COME ON! WHEN'S THIS BLESSED EVENT S'POSED T' HAPPEN?
Um... LET'S WATCH FOR AT LEAST ANOTHER... Uh, FIVE MINUTES. RIGHT, FENWAY?
THE UMP NEEDS AT LEAST TEN --
HEY... JUST WHAT ARE YOU MOOKS UP TO, ANYHOW?
NOTHING, PATCH! Heh... WE JUST WANTED YOU TO SEE THE TABLEAU... Y' KNOW... SOMEWHERE OVER THE RAINB --
KNUCKLE
KSSSH
OOOOOWW!
-- ELVIS' GLITTERY JOCKSTRAP!
KNUCKLE
KRASSH
WHAT IN TARNATION'S GOIN' ON IN THERE?! I SWEAR, IF DIS IS SOME SORTA SET-UP --
SET-UP? US?! NO! NEVER! Oh BOY...
KNUCKLE
-SIGH- LIZA MINNELLI... SHOULD'VE TOLD HIM IT WAS SHOELESS JOE IN HEELS. LET'S GET BACK TO THE DUGOUT.

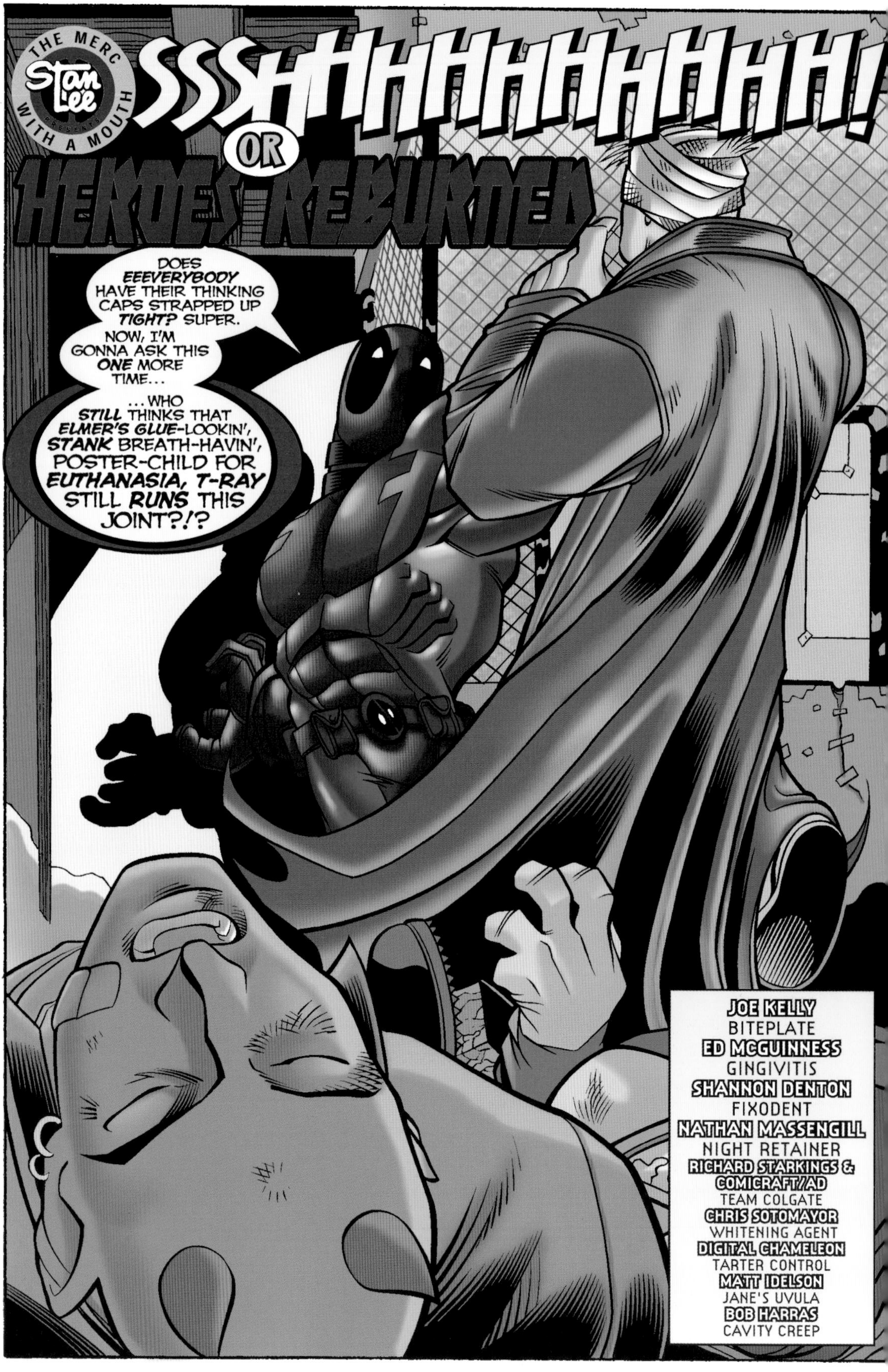
THE MERC WITH A MOUTH
Stan Lee PRESENTS
SSSHHHHHHHHHHHH!
OR
HEROES REBURNED
DOES EEEVERYBODY HAVE THEIR THINKING CAPS STRAPPED UP TIGHT? SUPER. NOW, I'M GONNA ASK THIS ONE MORE TIME...
...WHO STILL THINKS THAT ELMER'S GLUE-LOOKIN', STANK BREATH-HAVIN', POSTER-CHILD FOR EUTHANASIA, T-RAY STILL RUNS THIS JOINT?!?
JOE KELLY
BITEPLATE
ED MCGUINNESS
GINGIVITIS
SHANNON DENTON
FIXODENT
NATHAN MASSENGILL
NIGHT RETAINER
RICHARD STARKINGS & COMICRAFT/AD
TEAM COLGATE
CHRIS SOTOMAYOR
WHITENING AGENT
DIGITAL CHAMELEON
TARTER CONTROL
MATT IDELSON
JANE'S UVULA
BOB HARRAS
CAVITY CREEP

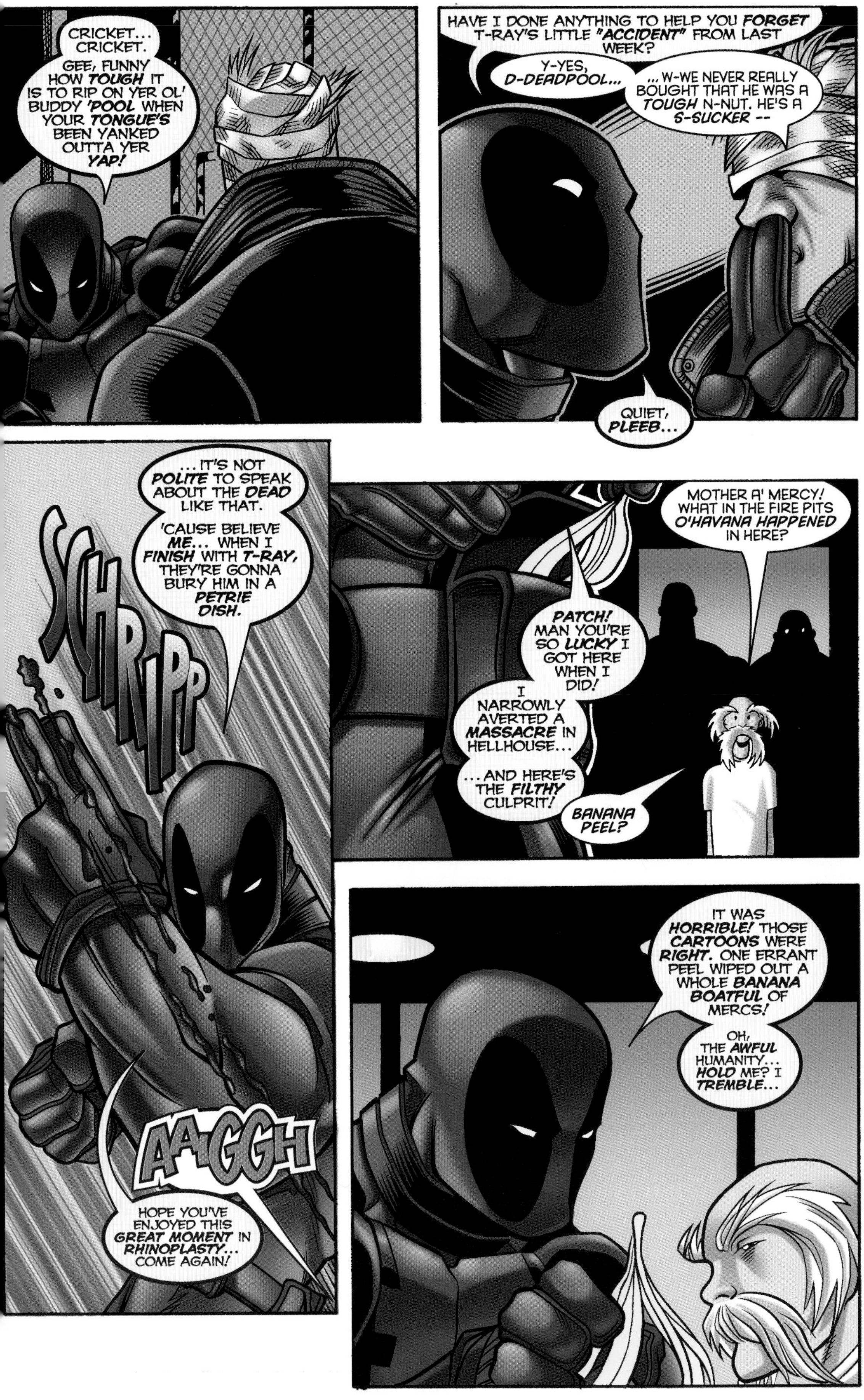
CRICKET... CRICKET.
GEE, FUNNY HOW TOUGH IT IS TO RIP ON YER OL' BUDDY 'POOL WHEN YOUR TONGUE'S BEEN YANKED OUTTA YER YAP!
HAVE I DONE ANYTHING TO HELP YOU FORGET T-RAY'S LITTLE "ACCIDENT" FROM LAST WEEK?
Y-YES, D-DEADPOOL...
... W-WE NEVER REALLY BOUGHT THAT HE WAS A TOUGH N-NUT. HE'S A S-SUCKER --
QUIET, PLEEB...
... IT'S NOT POLITE TO SPEAK ABOUT THE DEAD LIKE THAT.
'CAUSE BELIEVE ME... WHEN I FINISH WITH T-RAY, THEY'RE GONNA BURY HIM IN A PETRIE DISH.
SCHRIPP
AAGGH
HOPE YOU'VE ENJOYED THIS GREAT MOMENT IN RHINOPLASTY... COME AGAIN!
MOTHER A' MERCY! WHAT IN THE FIRE PITS O'HAVANA HAPPENED IN HERE?
PATCH! MAN YOU'RE SO LUCKY I GOT HERE WHEN I DID!
I NARROWLY AVERTED A MASSACRE IN HELLHOUSE...
...AND HERE'S THE FILTHY CULPRIT!
BANANA PEEL?
IT WAS HORRIBLE! THOSE CARTOONS WERE RIGHT. ONE ERRANT PEEL WIPED OUT A WHOLE BANANA BOATFUL OF MERCS!
OH, THE AWFUL HUMANITY... HOLD ME? I TREMBLE...

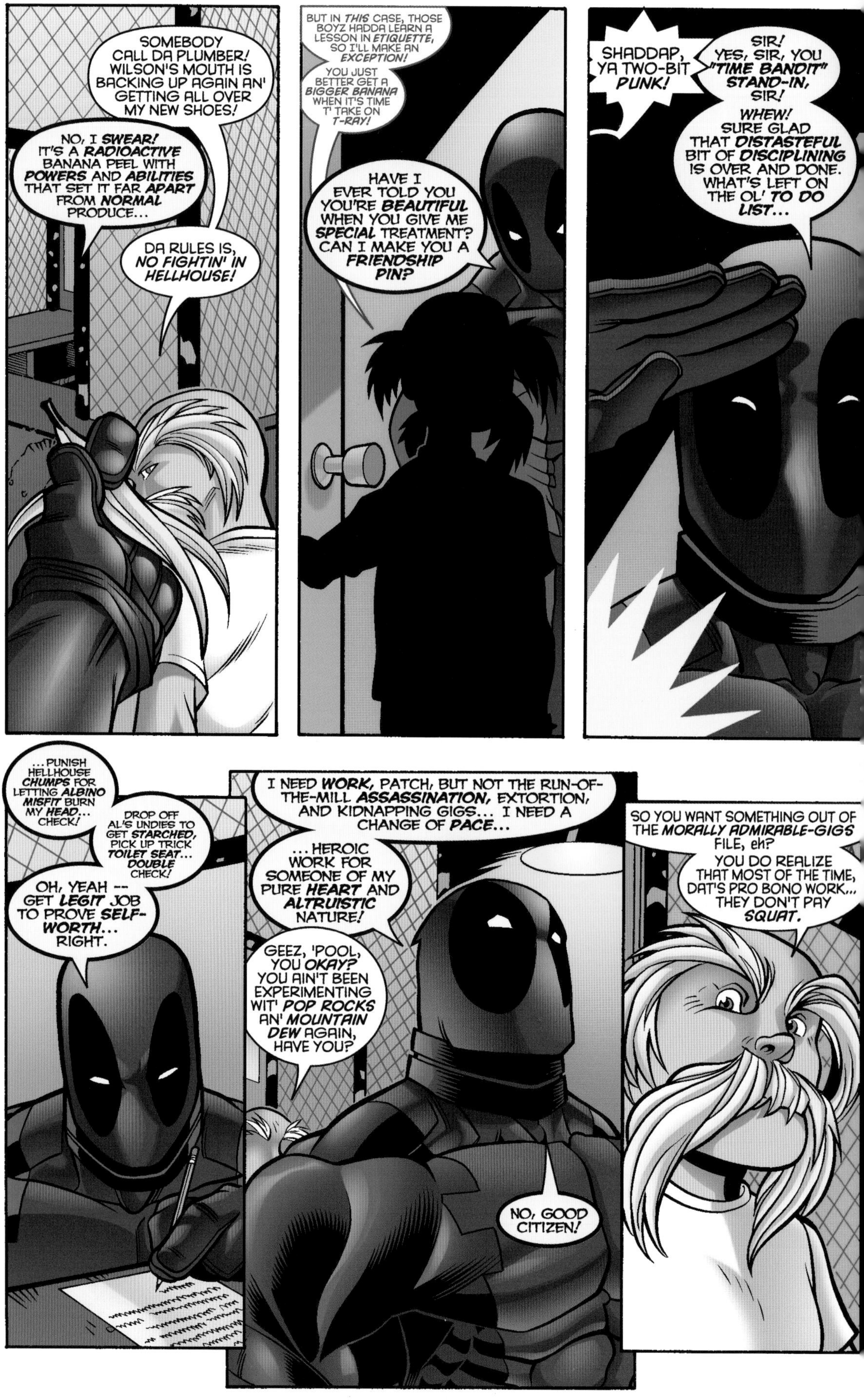
SOMEBODY CALL DA PLUMBER! WILSON'S MOUTH IS BACKING UP AGAIN AN' GETTING ALL OVER MY NEW SHOES!
NO, I SWEAR! IT'S A RADIOACTIVE BANANA PEEL WITH POWERS AND ABILITIES THAT SET IT FAR APART FROM NORMAL PRODUCE...
DA RULES IS, NO FIGHTIN' IN HELLHOUSE!
BUT IN THIS CASE, THOSE BOYZ HADDA LEARN A LESSON IN ETIQUETTE, SO I'LL MAKE AN EXCEPTION!
YOU JUST BETTER GET A BIGGER BANANA WHEN IT'S TIME T' TAKE ON T-RAY!
HAVE I EVER TOLD YOU YOU'RE BEAUTIFUL WHEN YOU GIVE ME SPECIAL TREATMENT? CAN I MAKE YOU A FRIENDSHIP PIN?
SHADDAP, YA TWO-BIT PUNK!
SIR! YES, SIR, YOU "TIME BANDIT" STAND-IN, SIR!
WHEW! SURE GLAD THAT DISTASTEFUL BIT OF DISCIPLINING IS OVER AND DONE. WHAT'S LEFT ON THE OL' TO DO LIST...
...PUNISH HELLHOUSE CHUMPS FOR LETTING ALBINO MISFIT BURN MY HEAD... CHECK!
DROP OFF AL'S UNDIES TO GET STARCHED, PICK UP TRICK TOILET SEAT... DOUBLE CHECK!
OH, YEAH -- GET LEGIT JOB TO PROVE SELF-WORTH... RIGHT.
I NEED WORK, PATCH, BUT NOT THE RUN-OF-THE-MILL ASSASSINATION, EXTORTION, AND KIDNAPPING GIGS... I NEED A CHANGE OF PACE...
...HEROIC WORK FOR SOMEONE OF MY PURE HEART AND ALTRUISTIC NATURE!
GEEZ, 'POOL, YOU OKAY? YOU AIN'T BEEN EXPERIMENTING WIT' POP ROCKS AN' MOUNTAIN DEW AGAIN, HAVE YOU?
NO, GOOD CITIZEN!
SO YOU WANT SOMETHING OUT OF THE MORALLY ADMIRABLE-GIGS FILE, eh?
YOU DO REALIZE THAT MOST OF THE TIME, DAT'S PRO BONO WORK... THEY DON'T PAY SQUAT.

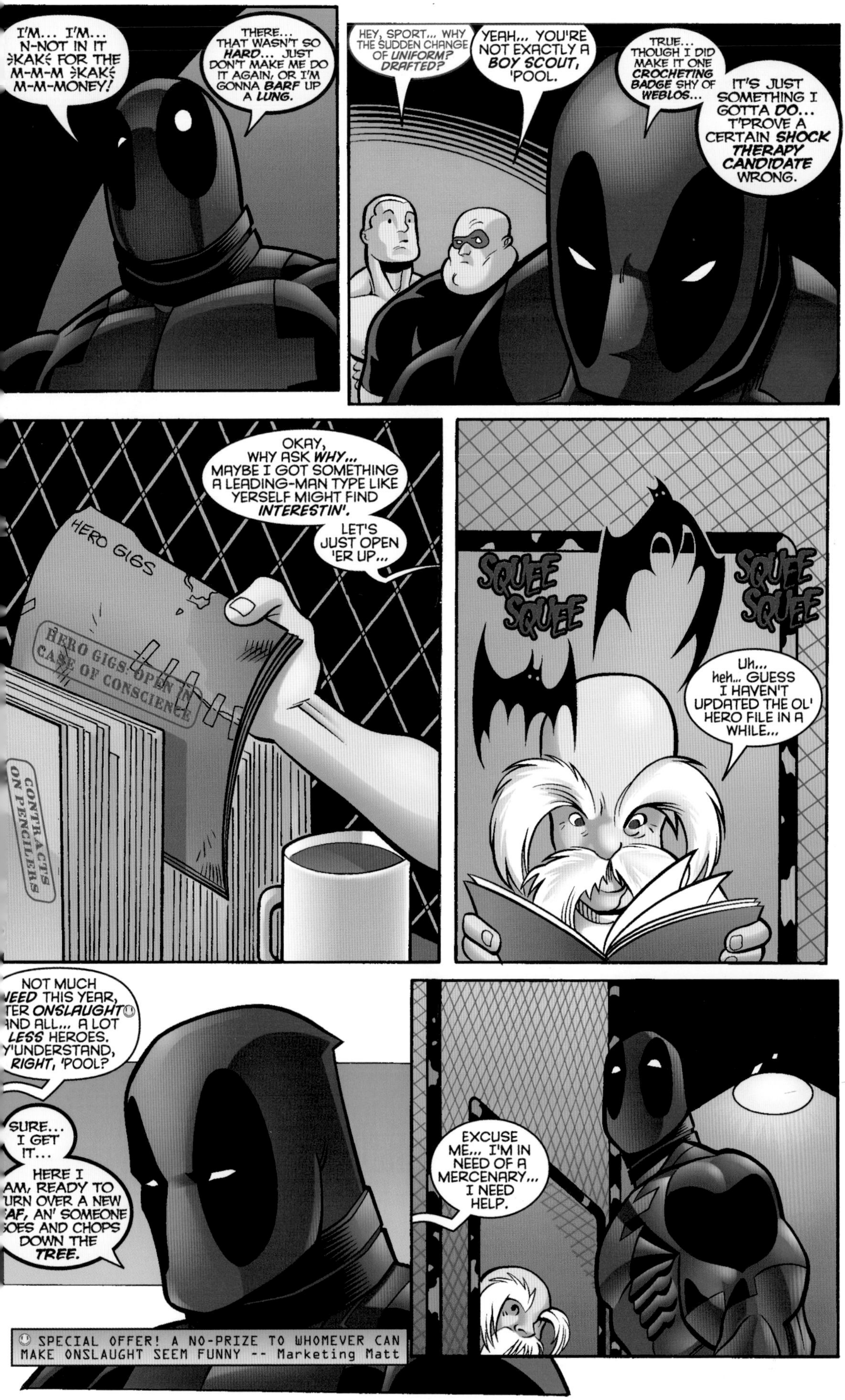
I'M... I'M... N-NOT IN IT ✶KAK✶ FOR THE M-M-M ✶KAK✶ M-M-MONEY!
THERE... THAT WASN'T SO HARD... JUST DON'T MAKE ME DO IT AGAIN, OR I'M GONNA BARF UP A LUNG.
HEY, SPORT... WHY THE SUDDEN CHANGE OF UNIFORM? DRAFTED?
YEAH... YOU'RE NOT EXACTLY A BOY SCOUT, 'POOL.
TRUE... THOUGH I DID MAKE IT ONE CROCHETING BADGE SHY OF WEBLOS...
IT'S JUST SOMETHING I GOTTA DO... T'PROVE A CERTAIN SHOCK THERAPY CANDIDATE WRONG.
OKAY, WHY ASK WHY... MAYBE I GOT SOMETHING A LEADING-MAN TYPE LIKE YERSELF MIGHT FIND INTERESTIN'.
LET'S JUST OPEN 'ER UP...
HERO GIGS
HERO GIGS: OPEN IN CASE OF CONSCIENCE
CONTRACTS ON PENCILERS
SQUEE SQUEE
SQUEE SQUEE
Uh... heh... GUESS I HAVEN'T UPDATED THE OL' HERO FILE IN A WHILE...
NOT MUCH NEED THIS YEAR, AFTER ONSLAUGHT AND ALL... A LOT LESS HEROES. Y'UNDERSTAND, RIGHT, 'POOL?
SURE... I GET IT...
HERE I AM, READY TO TURN OVER A NEW LEAF, AN' SOMEONE GOES AND CHOPS DOWN THE TREE.
EXCUSE ME... I'M IN NEED OF A MERCENARY... I NEED HELP.
SPECIAL OFFER! A NO-PRIZE TO WHOMEVER CAN MAKE ONSLAUGHT SEEM FUNNY -- Marketing Matt

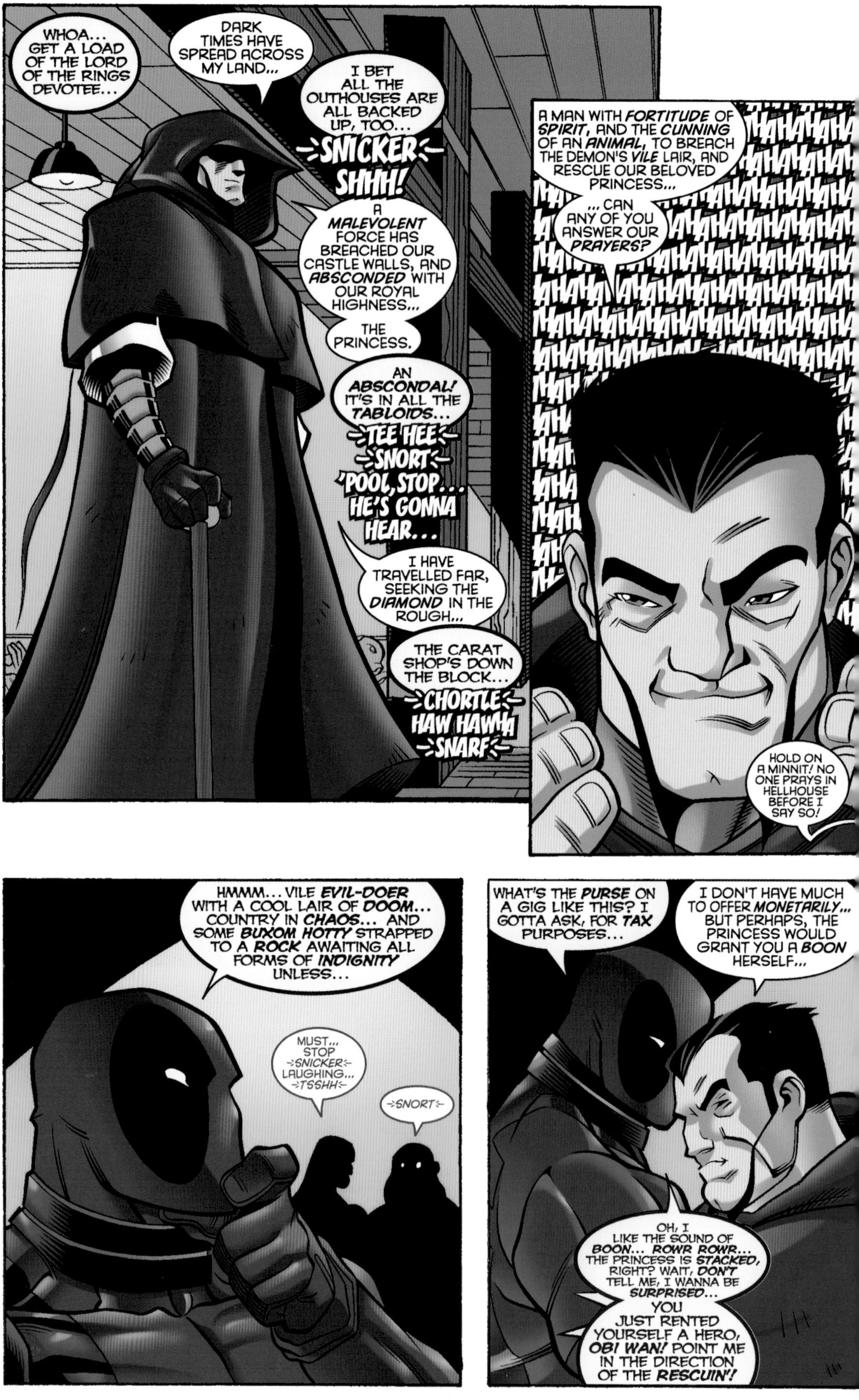
WHOA... GET A LOAD OF THE LORD OF THE RINGS DEVOTEE...
DARK TIMES HAVE SPREAD ACROSS MY LAND...
I BET ALL THE OUTHOUSES ARE ALL BACKED UP, TOO...
SNICKER
SHHH!
A MALEVOLENT FORCE HAS BREACHED OUR CASTLE WALLS, AND ABSCONDED WITH OUR ROYAL HIGHNESS...
THE PRINCESS.
AN ABSCONDAL! IT'S IN ALL THE TABLOIDS...
TEE HEE
SNORT
'POOL, STOP... HE'S GONNA HEAR...
I HAVE TRAVELLED FAR, SEEKING THE DIAMOND IN THE ROUGH...
THE CARAT SHOP'S DOWN THE BLOCK...
CHORTLE
HAW HAWHA
SNARF
A MAN WITH FORTITUDE OF SPIRIT, AND THE CUNNING OF AN ANIMAL, TO BREACH THE DEMON'S VILE LAIR, AND RESCUE OUR BELOVED PRINCESS...
... CAN ANY OF YOU ANSWER OUR PRAYERS?
HAHAHAHAHA
HOLD ON A MINNIT! NO ONE PRAYS IN HELLHOUSE BEFORE I SAY SO!
HMMM... VILE EVIL-DOER WITH A COOL LAIR OF DOOM... COUNTRY IN CHAOS... AND SOME BUXOM HOTTY STRAPPED TO A ROCK AWAITING ALL FORMS OF INDIGNITY UNLESS...
MUST... STOP SNICKER LAUGHING... TSSHH
SNORT
WHAT'S THE PURSE ON A GIG LIKE THIS? I GOTTA ASK, FOR TAX PURPOSES...
I DON'T HAVE MUCH TO OFFER MONETARILY... BUT PERHAPS, THE PRINCESS WOULD GRANT YOU A BOON HERSELF...
OH, I LIKE THE SOUND OF BOON... ROWR ROWR... THE PRINCESS IS STACKED, RIGHT? WAIT, DON'T TELL ME, I WANNA BE SURPRISED...
YOU JUST RENTED YOURSELF A HERO, OBI WAN! POINT ME IN THE DIRECTION OF THE RESCUIN'!

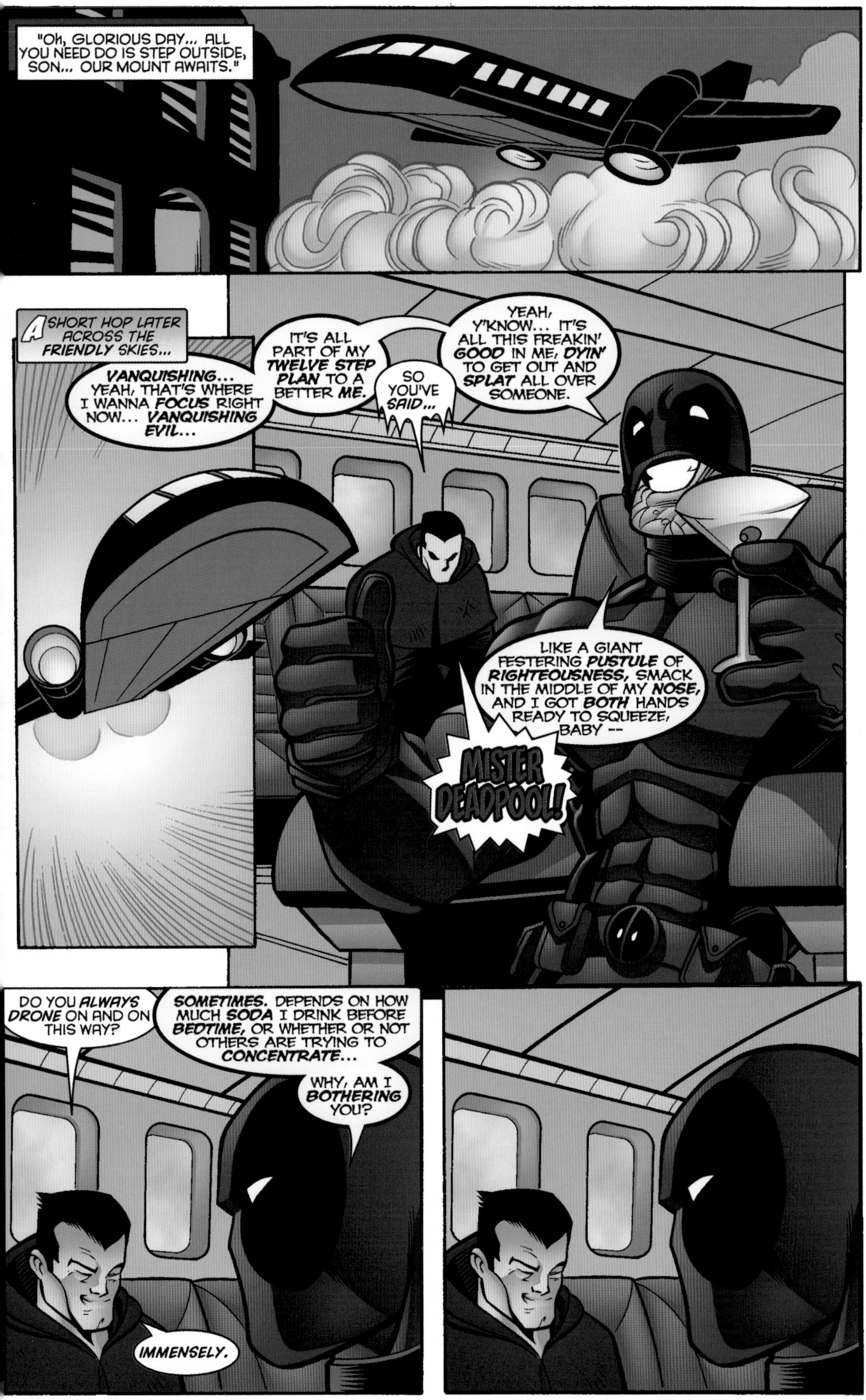

"OH, GLORIOUS DAY... ALL YOU NEED DO IS STEP OUTSIDE, SON... OUR MOUNT AWAITS."
A SHORT HOP LATER ACROSS THE FRIENDLY SKIES...
VANQUISHING... YEAH, THAT'S WHERE I WANNA FOCUS RIGHT NOW... VANQUISHING EVIL...
IT'S ALL PART OF MY TWELVE STEP PLAN TO A BETTER ME.
SO YOU'VE SAID...
YEAH, Y'KNOW... IT'S ALL THIS FREAKIN' GOOD IN ME, DYIN' TO GET OUT AND SPLAT ALL OVER SOMEONE.
LIKE A GIANT FESTERING PUSTULE OF RIGHTEOUSNESS, SMACK IN THE MIDDLE OF MY NOSE, AND I GOT BOTH HANDS READY TO SQUEEZE, BABY --
MISTER DEADPOOL!
DO YOU ALWAYS DRONE ON AND ON THIS WAY?
SOMETIMES. DEPENDS ON HOW MUCH SODA I DRINK BEFORE BEDTIME, OR WHETHER OR NOT OTHERS ARE TRYING TO CONCENTRATE...
WHY, AM I BOTHERING YOU?
IMMENSELY.

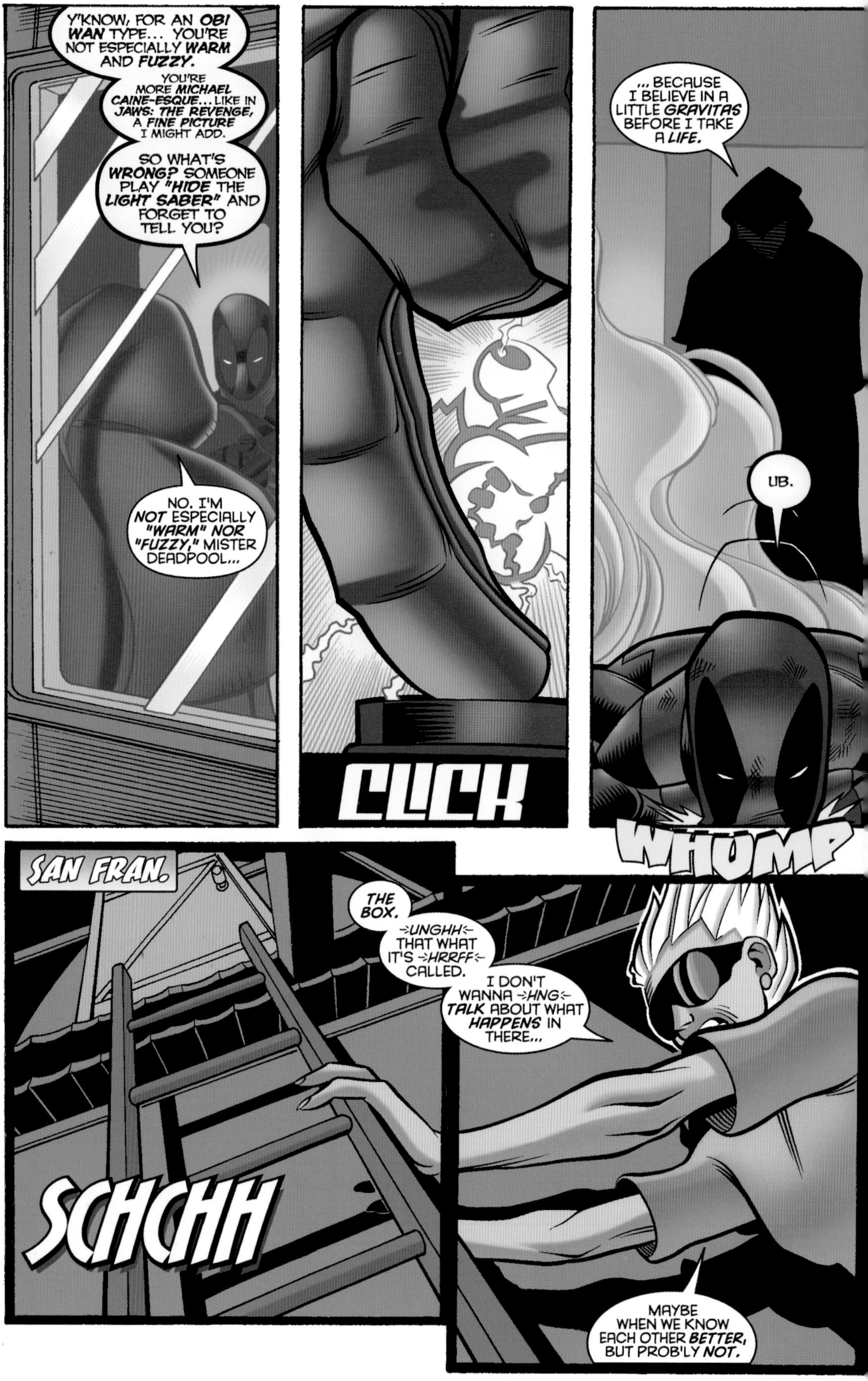

Y'KNOW, FOR AN OBI WAN TYPE... YOU'RE NOT ESPECIALLY WARM AND FUZZY.
YOU'RE MORE MICHAEL CAINE-ESQUE... LIKE IN JAWS: THE REVENGE, A FINE PICTURE I MIGHT ADD.
SO WHAT'S WRONG? SOMEONE PLAY "HIDE THE LIGHT SABER" AND FORGET TO TELL YOU?
NO. I'M NOT ESPECIALLY "WARM" NOR "FUZZY," MISTER DEADPOOL...
CLICK
...BECAUSE I BELIEVE IN A LITTLE GRAVITAS BEFORE I TAKE A LIFE.
UB.
WHUMP
SAN FRAN.
SCHHH
THE BOX.
UNGHH THAT WHAT IT'S HRRFF CALLED.
I DON'T WANNA HNG TALK ABOUT WHAT HAPPENS IN THERE...
MAYBE WHEN WE KNOW EACH OTHER BETTER, BUT PROB'LY NOT.

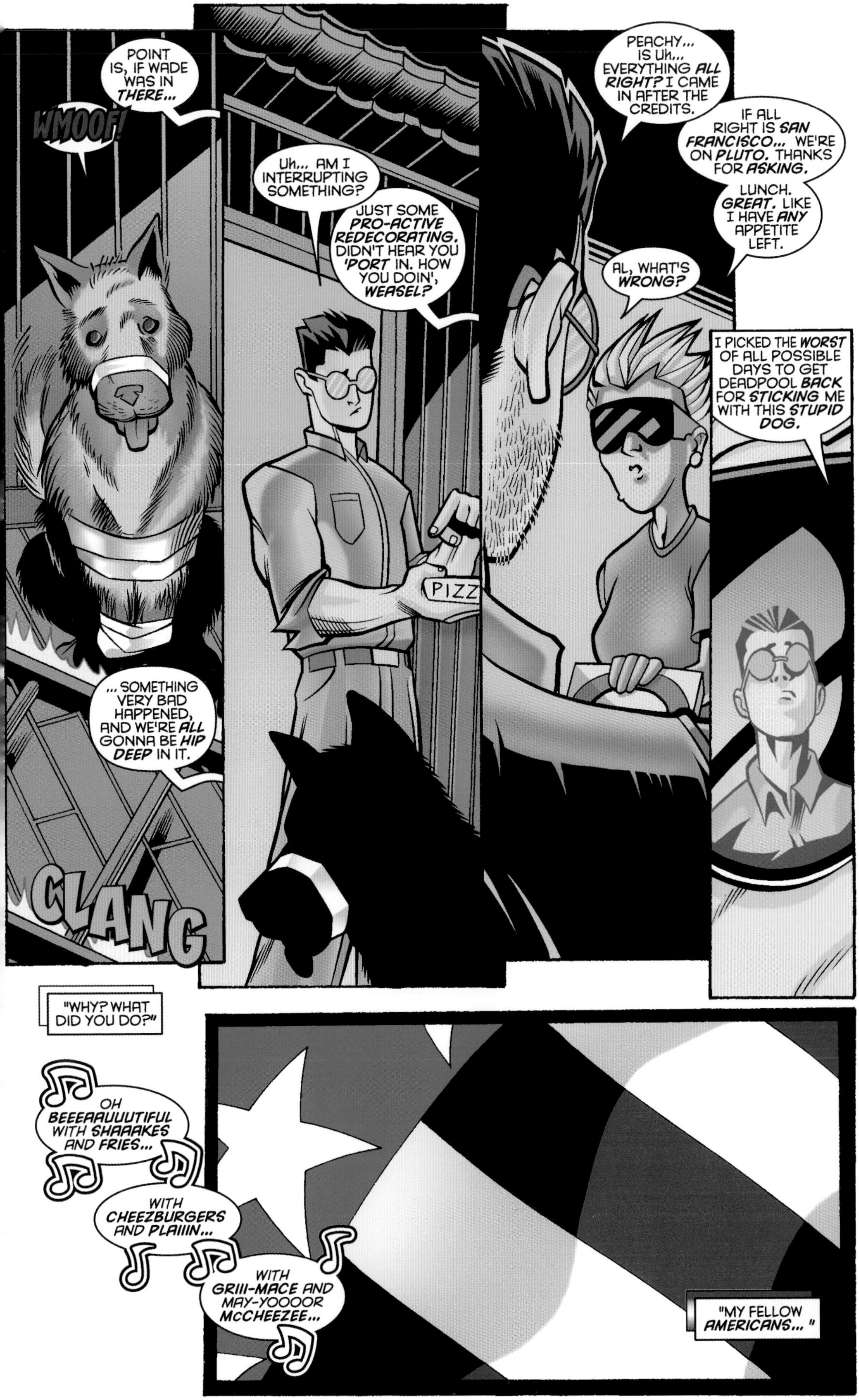
POINT IS, IF WADE WAS IN THERE...
WMOOF!
...SOMETHING VERY BAD HAPPENED, AND WE'RE ALL GONNA BE HIP DEEP IN IT.
CLANG
Uh... AM I INTERRUPTING SOMETHING?
JUST SOME PRO-ACTIVE REDECORATING. DIDN'T HEAR YOU 'PORT IN. HOW YOU DOIN', WEASEL?
PIZZ
PEACHY... IS Uh... EVERYTHING ALL RIGHT? I CAME IN AFTER THE CREDITS.
IF ALL RIGHT IS SAN FRANCISCO... WE'RE ON PLUTO. THANKS FOR ASKING.
LUNCH. GREAT. LIKE I HAVE ANY APPETITE LEFT.
AL, WHAT'S WRONG?
I PICKED THE WORST OF ALL POSSIBLE DAYS TO GET DEADPOOL BACK FOR STICKING ME WITH THIS STUPID DOG.
"WHY? WHAT DID YOU DO?"
OH BEEEAAUUUTIFUL WITH SHAAAKES AND FRIES...
WITH CHEEZBURGERS AND PLAIIIN...
WITH GRIII-MACE AND MAY-YOOOOR McCHEEZEE...
"MY FELLOW AMERICANS..."

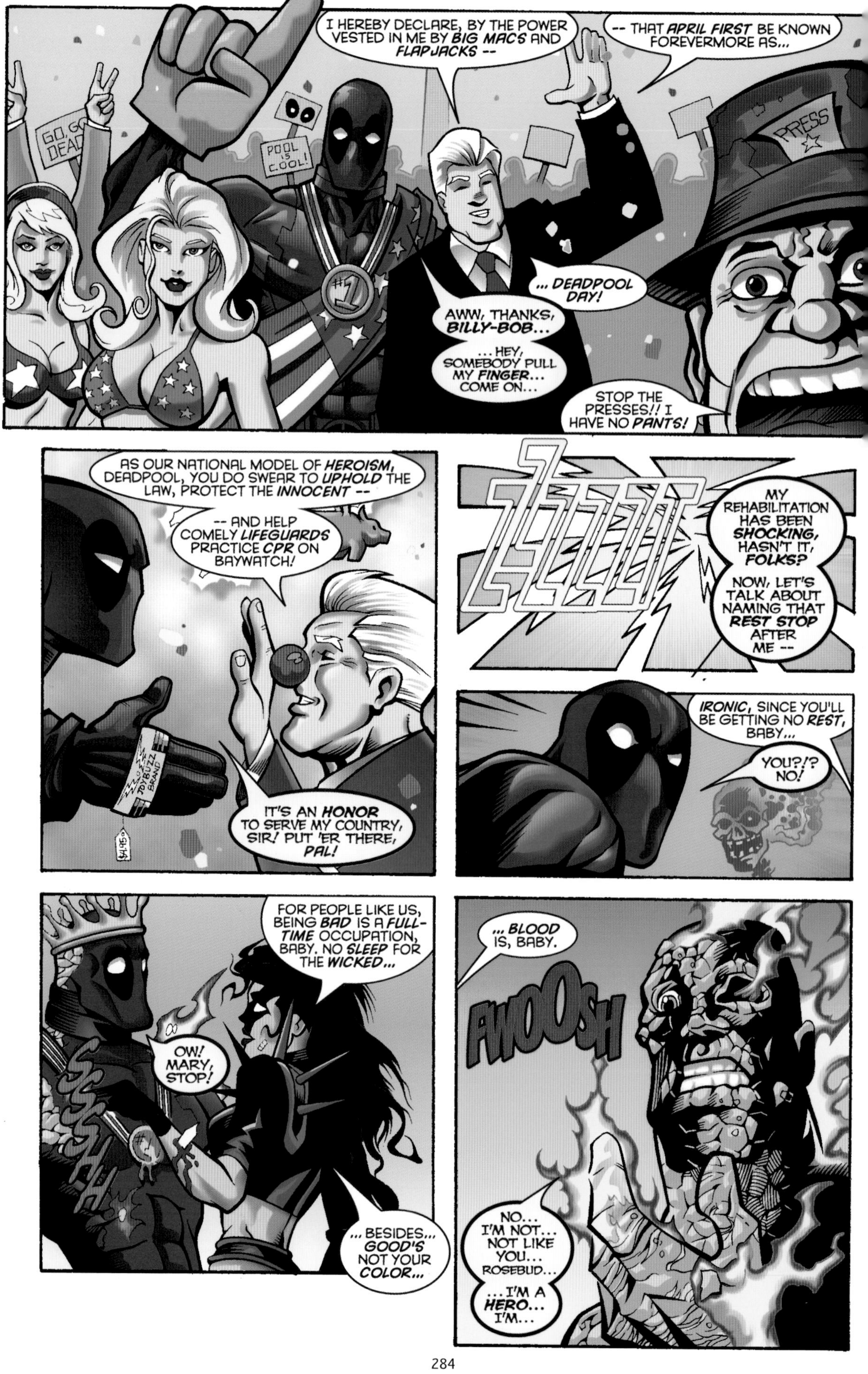
I HEREBY DECLARE, BY THE POWER VESTED IN ME BY BIG MACS AND FLAPJACKS --
-- THAT APRIL FIRST BE KNOWN FOREVERMORE AS...
GO, GO DEAD
POOL IS COOL!
PRESS
... DEADPOOL DAY!
AWW, THANKS, BILLY-BOB...
... HEY, SOMEBODY PULL MY FINGER... COME ON...
STOP THE PRESSES!! I HAVE NO PANTS!
AS OUR NATIONAL MODEL OF HEROISM, DEADPOOL, YOU DO SWEAR TO UPHOLD THE LAW, PROTECT THE INNOCENT --
-- AND HELP COMELY LIFEGUARDS PRACTICE CPR ON BAYWATCH!
JOYBUZZ BRAND
$1.95
IT'S AN HONOR TO SERVE MY COUNTRY, SIR! PUT 'ER THERE, PAL!
MY REHABILITATION HAS BEEN SHOCKING, HASN'T IT, FOLKS?
NOW, LET'S TALK ABOUT NAMING THAT REST STOP AFTER ME --
IRONIC, SINCE YOU'LL BE GETTING NO REST, BABY...
YOU?!? NO!
FOR PEOPLE LIKE US, BEING BAD IS A FULL-TIME OCCUPATION, BABY. NO SLEEP FOR THE WICKED...
OW! MARY, STOP!
... BESIDES... GOOD'S NOT YOUR COLOR...
... BLOOD IS, BABY.
FWOOSH
NO... I'M NOT... NOT LIKE YOU... ROSEBUD...
... I'M A HERO... I'M...

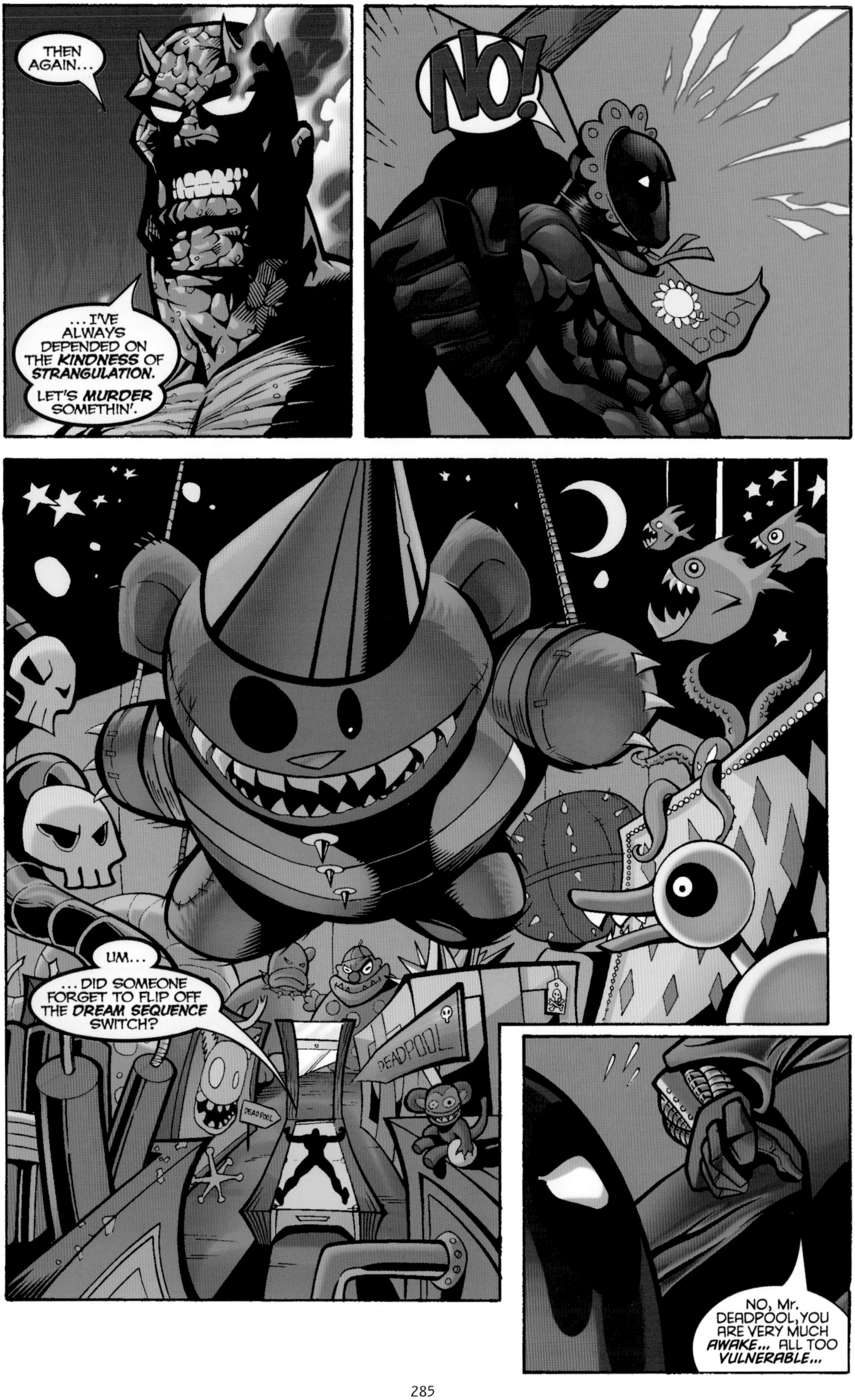

THEN AGAIN...
...I'VE ALWAYS DEPENDED ON THE KINDNESS OF STRANGULATION.
LET'S MURDER SOMETHIN'.
NO!
baby
UM...
...DID SOMEONE FORGET TO FLIP OFF THE DREAM SEQUENCE SWITCH?
DEADPOOL
DEADPOOL
NO, Mr. DEADPOOL, YOU ARE VERY MUCH AWAKE... ALL TOO VULNERABLE...

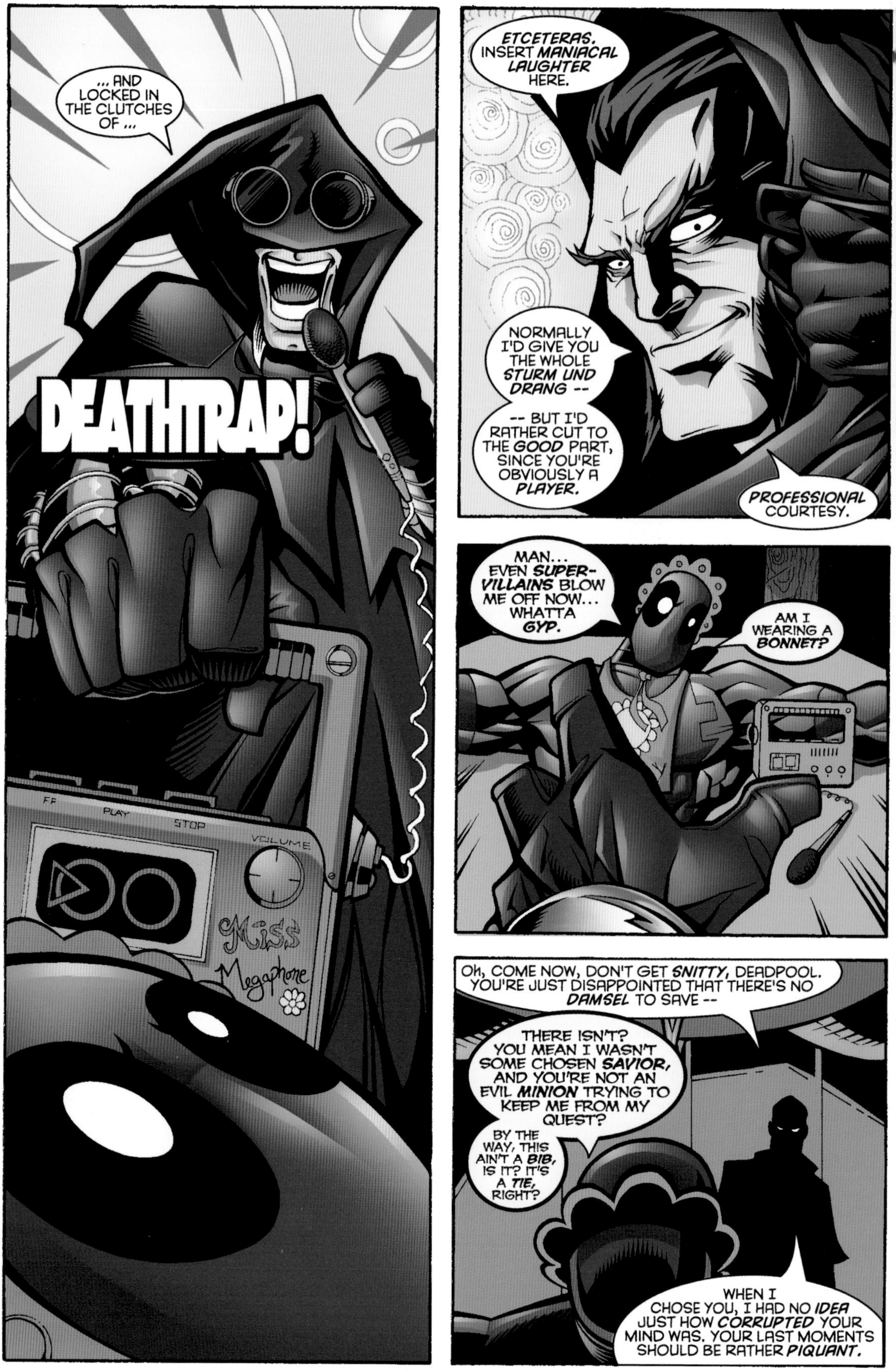
... AND LOCKED IN THE CLUTCHES OF ...
DEATHTRAP!
FF
PLAY
STOP
VOLUME
Miss Megaphone
ETCETERAS. INSERT MANIACAL LAUGHTER HERE.
NORMALLY I'D GIVE YOU THE WHOLE STURM UND DRANG --
-- BUT I'D RATHER CUT TO THE GOOD PART, SINCE YOU'RE OBVIOUSLY A PLAYER.
PROFESSIONAL COURTESY.
MAN... EVEN SUPER-VILLAINS BLOW ME OFF NOW... WHATTA GYP.
AM I WEARING A BONNET?
Oh, COME NOW, DON'T GET SNITTY, DEADPOOL. YOU'RE JUST DISAPPOINTED THAT THERE'S NO DAMSEL TO SAVE --
THERE ISN'T? YOU MEAN I WASN'T SOME CHOSEN SAVIOR, AND YOU'RE NOT AN EVIL MINION TRYING TO KEEP ME FROM MY QUEST?
BY THE WAY, THIS AIN'T A BIB, IS IT? IT'S A TIE, RIGHT?
WHEN I CHOSE YOU, I HAD NO IDEA JUST HOW CORRUPTED YOUR MIND WAS. YOUR LAST MOMENTS SHOULD BE RATHER PIQUANT.

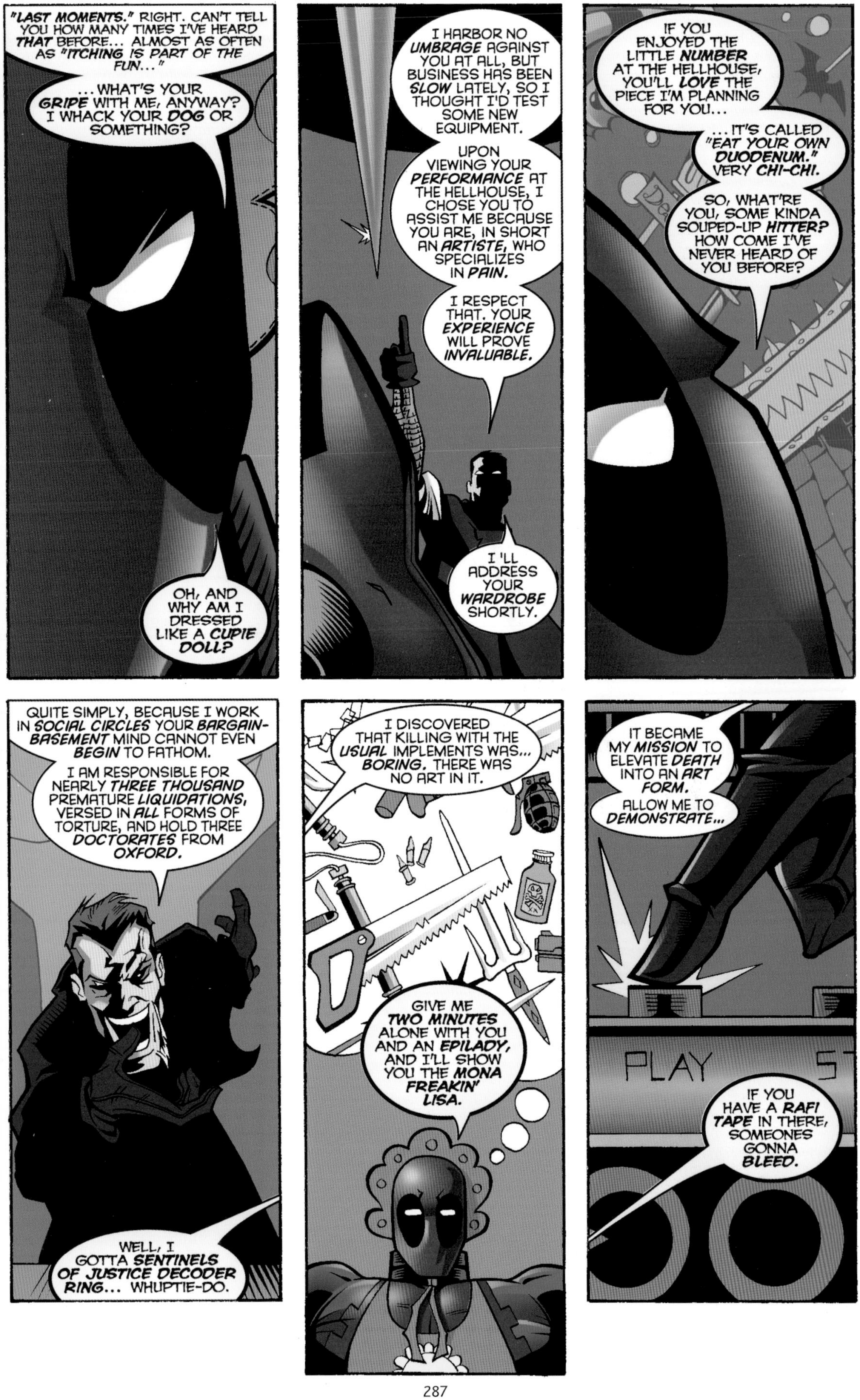
"LAST MOMENTS." RIGHT. CAN'T TELL YOU HOW MANY TIMES I'VE HEARD THAT BEFORE... ALMOST AS OFTEN AS "ITCHING IS PART OF THE FUN..."
...WHAT'S YOUR GRIPE WITH ME, ANYWAY? I WHACK YOUR DOG OR SOMETHING?
OH, AND WHY AM I DRESSED LIKE A CUPIE DOLL?
I HARBOR NO UMBRAGE AGAINST YOU AT ALL, BUT BUSINESS HAS BEEN SLOW LATELY, SO I THOUGHT I'D TEST SOME NEW EQUIPMENT.
UPON VIEWING YOUR PERFORMANCE AT THE HELLHOUSE, I CHOSE YOU TO ASSIST ME BECAUSE YOU ARE, IN SHORT AN ARTISTE, WHO SPECIALIZES IN PAIN.
I RESPECT THAT. YOUR EXPERIENCE WILL PROVE INVALUABLE.
I'LL ADDRESS YOUR WARDROBE SHORTLY.
IF YOU ENJOYED THE LITTLE NUMBER AT THE HELLHOUSE, YOU'LL LOVE THE PIECE I'M PLANNING FOR YOU...
...IT'S CALLED "EAT YOUR OWN DUODENUM." VERY CHI-CHI.
SO, WHAT'RE YOU, SOME KINDA SOUPED-UP HITTER? HOW COME I'VE NEVER HEARD OF YOU BEFORE?
QUITE SIMPLY, BECAUSE I WORK IN SOCIAL CIRCLES YOUR BARGAIN-BASEMENT MIND CANNOT EVEN BEGIN TO FATHOM.
I AM RESPONSIBLE FOR NEARLY THREE THOUSAND PREMATURE LIQUIDATIONS, VERSED IN ALL FORMS OF TORTURE, AND HOLD THREE DOCTORATES FROM OXFORD.
WELL, I GOTTA SENTINELS OF JUSTICE DECODER RING... WHUPTIE-DO.
I DISCOVERED THAT KILLING WITH THE USUAL IMPLEMENTS WAS... BORING. THERE WAS NO ART IN IT.
GIVE ME TWO MINUTES ALONE WITH YOU AND AN EPILADY, AND I'LL SHOW YOU THE MONA FREAKIN' LISA.
IT BECAME MY MISSION TO ELEVATE DEATH INTO AN ART FORM.
ALLOW ME TO DEMONSTRATE...
PLAY
IF YOU HAVE A RAFI TAPE IN THERE, SOMEONES GONNA BLEED.

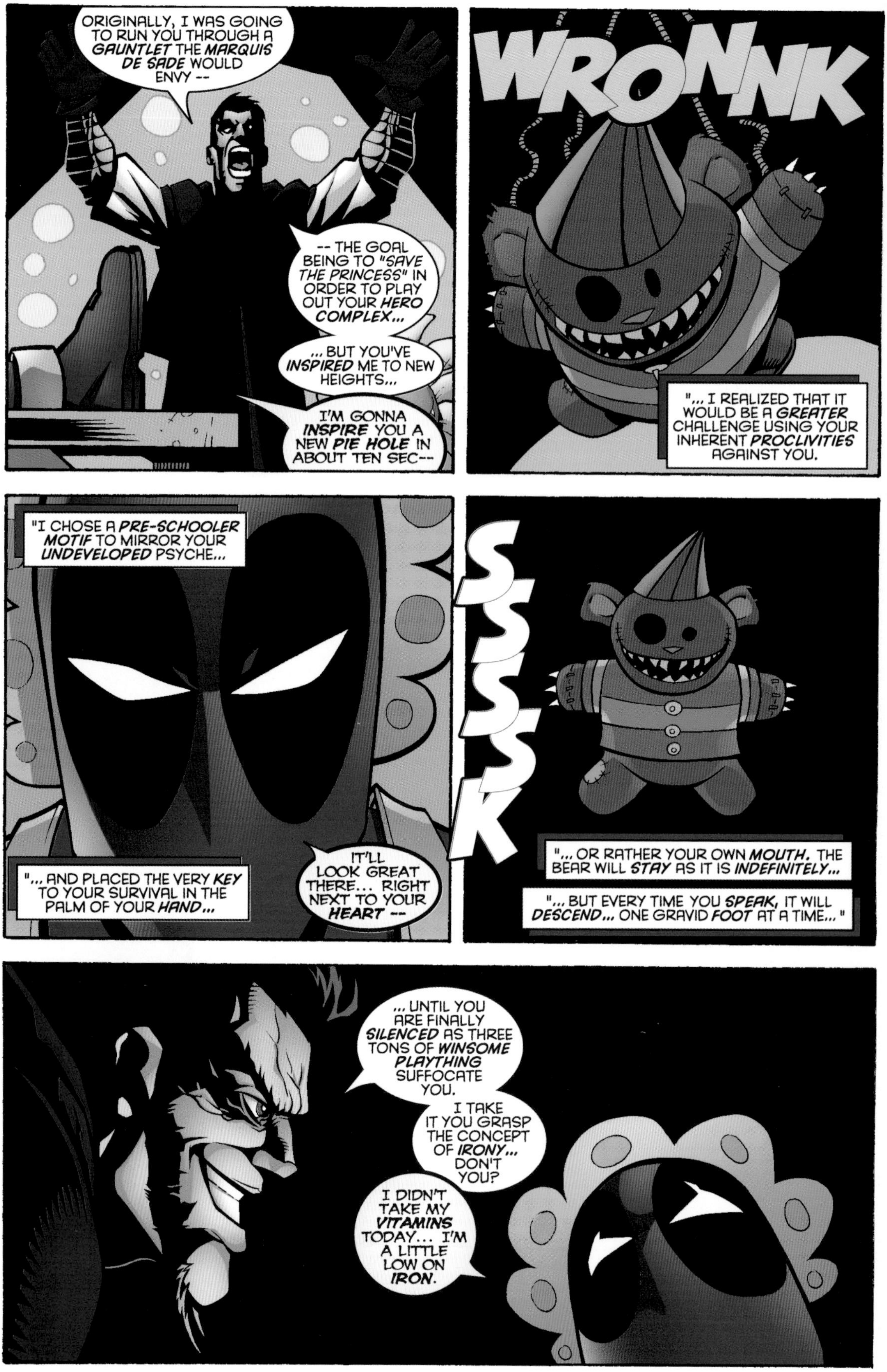
ORIGINALLY, I WAS GOING TO RUN YOU THROUGH A GAUNTLET THE MARQUIS DE SADE WOULD ENVY --
-- THE GOAL BEING TO "SAVE THE PRINCESS" IN ORDER TO PLAY OUT YOUR HERO COMPLEX...
... BUT YOU'VE INSPIRED ME TO NEW HEIGHTS...
I'M GONNA INSPIRE YOU A NEW PIE HOLE IN ABOUT TEN SEC--
WRONNK
"... I REALIZED THAT IT WOULD BE A GREATER CHALLENGE USING YOUR INHERENT PROCLIVITIES AGAINST YOU.
"I CHOSE A PRE-SCHOOLER MOTIF TO MIRROR YOUR UNDEVELOPED PSYCHE...
"... AND PLACED THE VERY KEY TO YOUR SURVIVAL IN THE PALM OF YOUR HAND...
IT'LL LOOK GREAT THERE... RIGHT NEXT TO YOUR HEART --
SSSSK
"... OR RATHER YOUR OWN MOUTH. THE BEAR WILL STAY AS IT IS INDEFINITELY...
"... BUT EVERY TIME YOU SPEAK, IT WILL DESCEND... ONE GRAVID FOOT AT A TIME..."
... UNTIL YOU ARE FINALLY SILENCED AS THREE TONS OF WINSOME PLAYTHING SUFFOCATE YOU.
I TAKE IT YOU GRASP THE CONCEPT OF IRONY... DON'T YOU?
I DIDN'T TAKE MY VITAMINS TODAY... I'M A LITTLE LOW ON IRON.

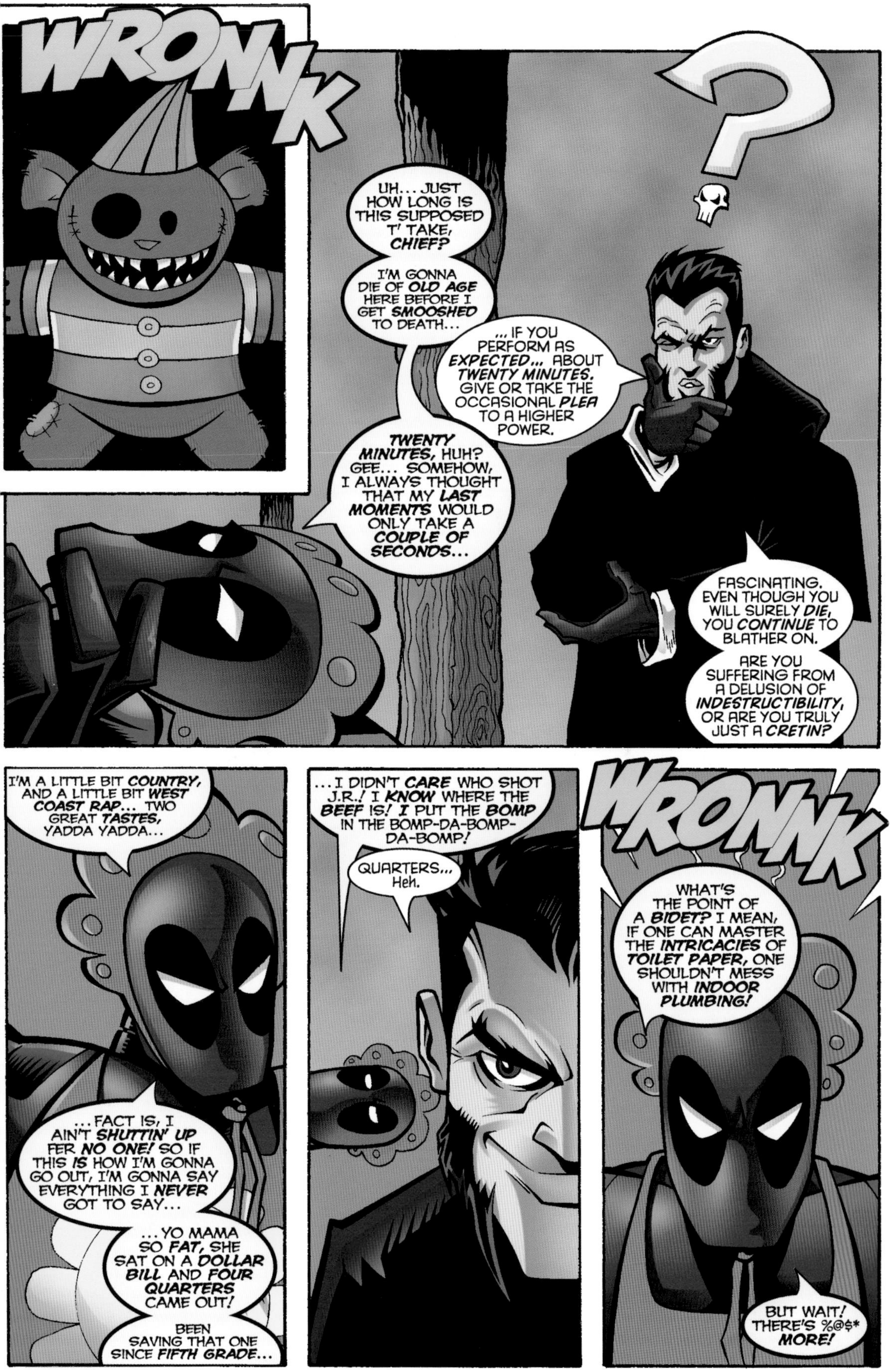
WRONNK
UH... JUST HOW LONG IS THIS SUPPOSED T' TAKE, CHIEF?
I'M GONNA DIE OF OLD AGE HERE BEFORE I GET SMOOSHED TO DEATH...
...IF YOU PERFORM AS EXPECTED... ABOUT TWENTY MINUTES. GIVE OR TAKE THE OCCASIONAL PLEA TO A HIGHER POWER.
TWENTY MINUTES, HUH? GEE... SOMEHOW, I ALWAYS THOUGHT THAT MY LAST MOMENTS WOULD ONLY TAKE A COUPLE OF SECONDS...
FASCINATING. EVEN THOUGH YOU WILL SURELY DIE, YOU CONTINUE TO BLATHER ON.
ARE YOU SUFFERING FROM A DELUSION OF INDESTRUCTIBILITY, OR ARE YOU TRULY JUST A CRETIN?
I'M A LITTLE BIT COUNTRY, AND A LITTLE BIT WEST COAST RAP... TWO GREAT TASTES, YADDA YADDA...
...FACT IS, I AIN'T SHUTTIN' UP FER NO ONE! SO IF THIS IS HOW I'M GONNA GO OUT, I'M GONNA SAY EVERYTHING I NEVER GOT TO SAY...
...YO MAMA SO FAT, SHE SAT ON A DOLLAR BILL AND FOUR QUARTERS CAME OUT!
BEEN SAVING THAT ONE SINCE FIFTH GRADE...
...I DIDN'T CARE WHO SHOT J.R.! I KNOW WHERE THE BEEF IS! I PUT THE BOMP IN THE BOMP-DA-BOMP-DA-BOMP!
QUARTERS... Heh.
WRONNK
WHAT'S THE POINT OF A BIDET? I MEAN, IF ONE CAN MASTER THE INTRICACIES OF TOILET PAPER, ONE SHOULDN'T MESS WITH INDOOR PLUMBING!
BUT WAIT! THERE'S %@$* MORE!

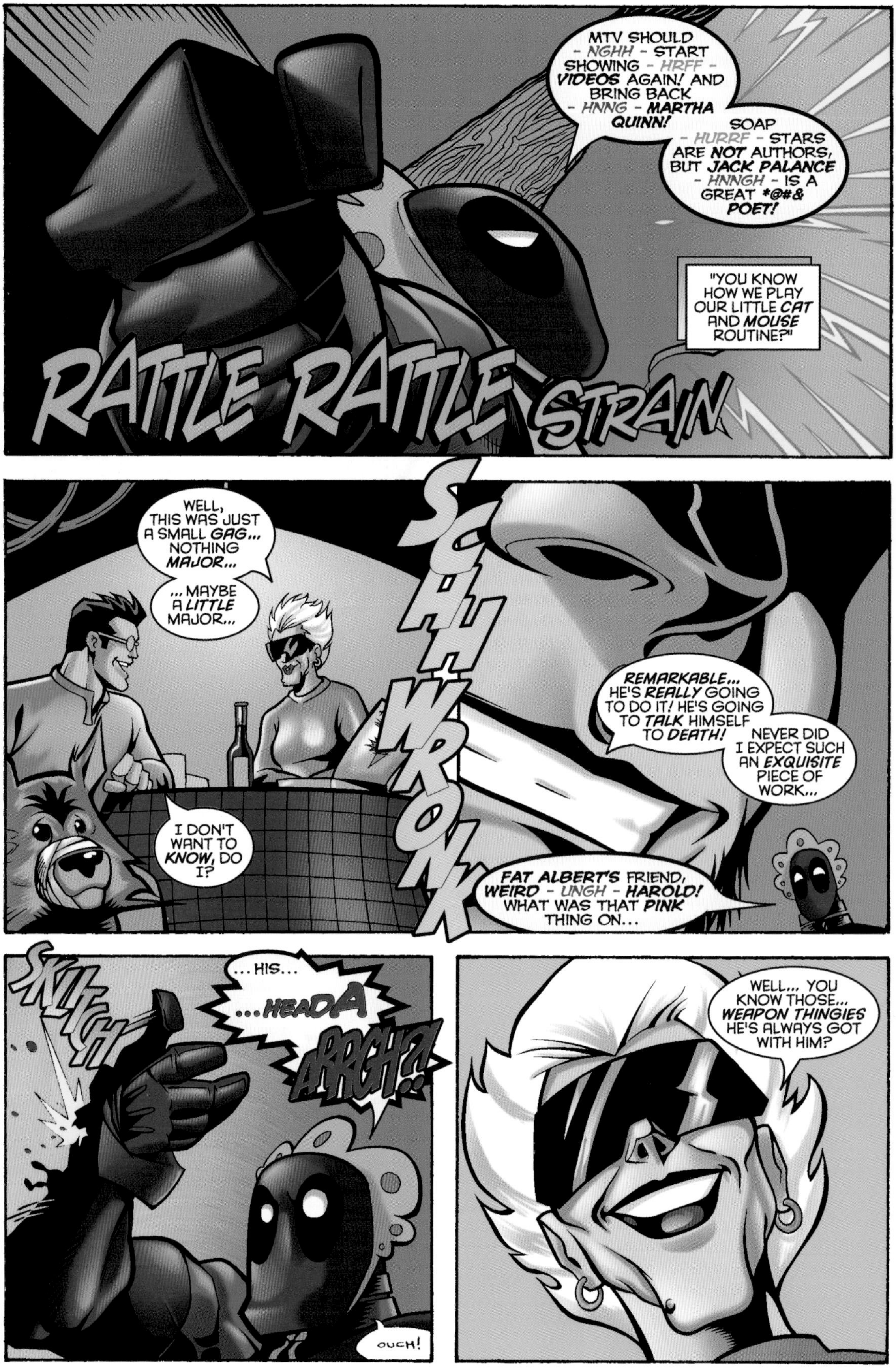
MTV SHOULD - NGHH - START SHOWING - HRFF - VIDEOS AGAIN! AND BRING BACK - HNNG - MARTHA QUINN!
SOAP - HURRF - STARS ARE NOT AUTHORS, BUT JACK PALANCE - HNNGH - IS A GREAT *@#& POET!
"YOU KNOW HOW WE PLAY OUR LITTLE CAT AND MOUSE ROUTINE?"
RATTLE RATTLE STRAIN
WELL, THIS WAS JUST A SMALL GAG... NOTHING MAJOR...
... MAYBE A LITTLE MAJOR...
SCHHWRONK
REMARKABLE... HE'S REALLY GOING TO DO IT! HE'S GOING TO TALK HIMSELF TO DEATH!
NEVER DID I EXPECT SUCH AN EXQUISITE PIECE OF WORK...
I DON'T WANT TO KNOW, DO I?
FAT ALBERT'S FRIEND, WEIRD - UNGH - HAROLD! WHAT WAS THAT PINK THING ON...
SKLITCH
... HIS...
...HEADA
ARRGH?!
OUCH!
WELL... YOU KNOW THOSE... WEAPON THINGIES HE'S ALWAYS GOT WITH HIM?

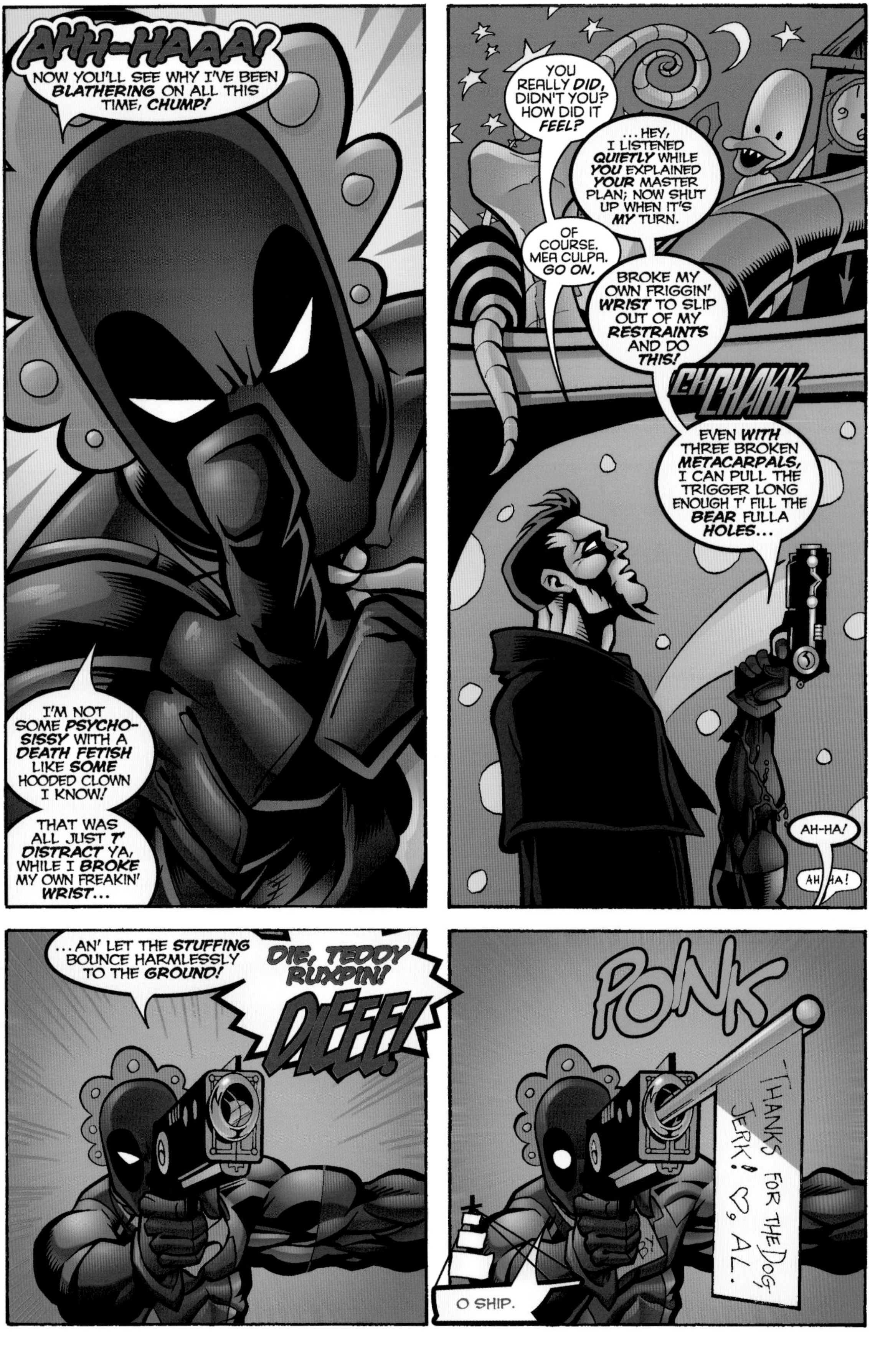
AHH-HAAA!
NOW YOU'LL SEE WHY I'VE BEEN BLATHERING ON ALL THIS TIME, CHUMP!
I'M NOT SOME PSYCHO-SISSY WITH A DEATH FETISH LIKE SOME HOODED CLOWN I KNOW!
THAT WAS ALL JUST T' DISTRACT YA, WHILE I BROKE MY OWN FREAKIN' WRIST...
YOU REALLY DID, DIDN'T YOU? HOW DID IT FEEL?
...HEY, I LISTENED QUIETLY WHILE YOU EXPLAINED YOUR MASTER PLAN; NOW SHUT UP WHEN IT'S MY TURN.
OF COURSE. MEA CULPA. GO ON.
BROKE MY OWN FRIGGIN' WRIST TO SLIP OUT OF MY RESTRAINTS AND DO THIS!
CHCHAKK
EVEN WITH THREE BROKEN METACARPALS, I CAN PULL THE TRIGGER LONG ENOUGH T' FILL THE BEAR FULLA HOLES...
AH-HA!
AH-HA!
...AN' LET THE STUFFING BOUNCE HARMLESSLY TO THE GROUND!
DIE, TEDDY RUXPIN!
DIEEE!
PONK
THANKS FOR THE DOG, JERK! ♡, AL.
O SHIP.

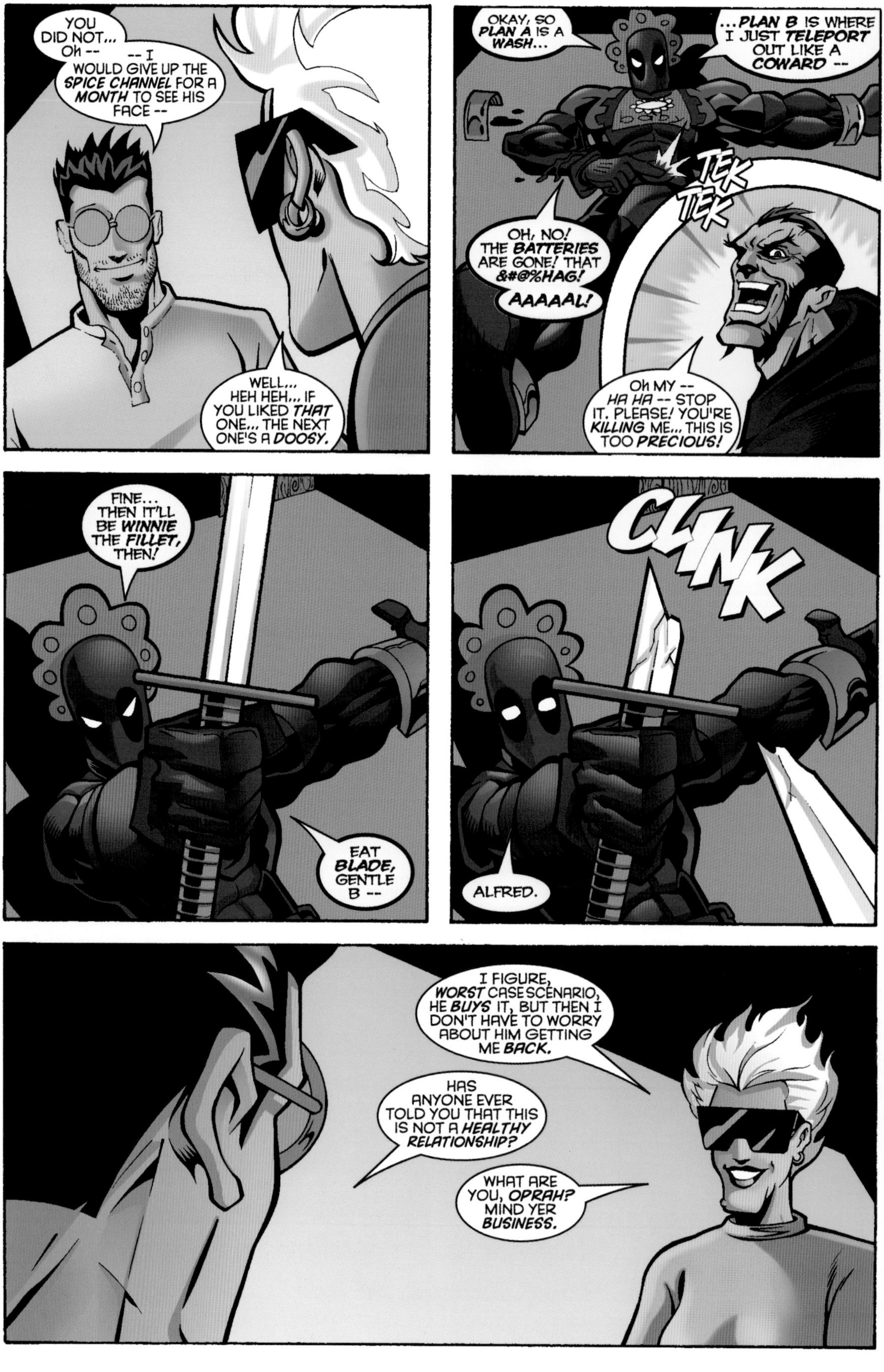

YOU DID NOT... Oh -- -- I WOULD GIVE UP THE SPICE CHANNEL FOR A MONTH TO SEE HIS FACE --
WELL... HEH HEH... IF YOU LIKED THAT ONE... THE NEXT ONE'S A DOOSY.
OKAY, SO PLAN A IS A WASH...
...PLAN B IS WHERE I JUST TELEPORT OUT LIKE A COWARD --
TEK TEK
OH, NO! THE BATTERIES ARE GONE! THAT &#@%HAG!
AAAAAL!
Oh MY -- HA HA -- STOP IT. PLEASE! YOU'RE KILLING ME... THIS IS TOO PRECIOUS!
FINE... THEN IT'LL BE WINNIE THE FILLET, THEN!
EAT BLADE, GENTLE B --
CLINK
ALFRED.
I FIGURE, WORST CASE SCENARIO, HE BUYS IT, BUT THEN I DON'T HAVE TO WORRY ABOUT HIM GETTING ME BACK.
HAS ANYONE EVER TOLD YOU THAT THIS IS NOT A HEALTHY RELATIONSHIP?
WHAT ARE YOU, OPRAH? MIND YER BUSINESS.

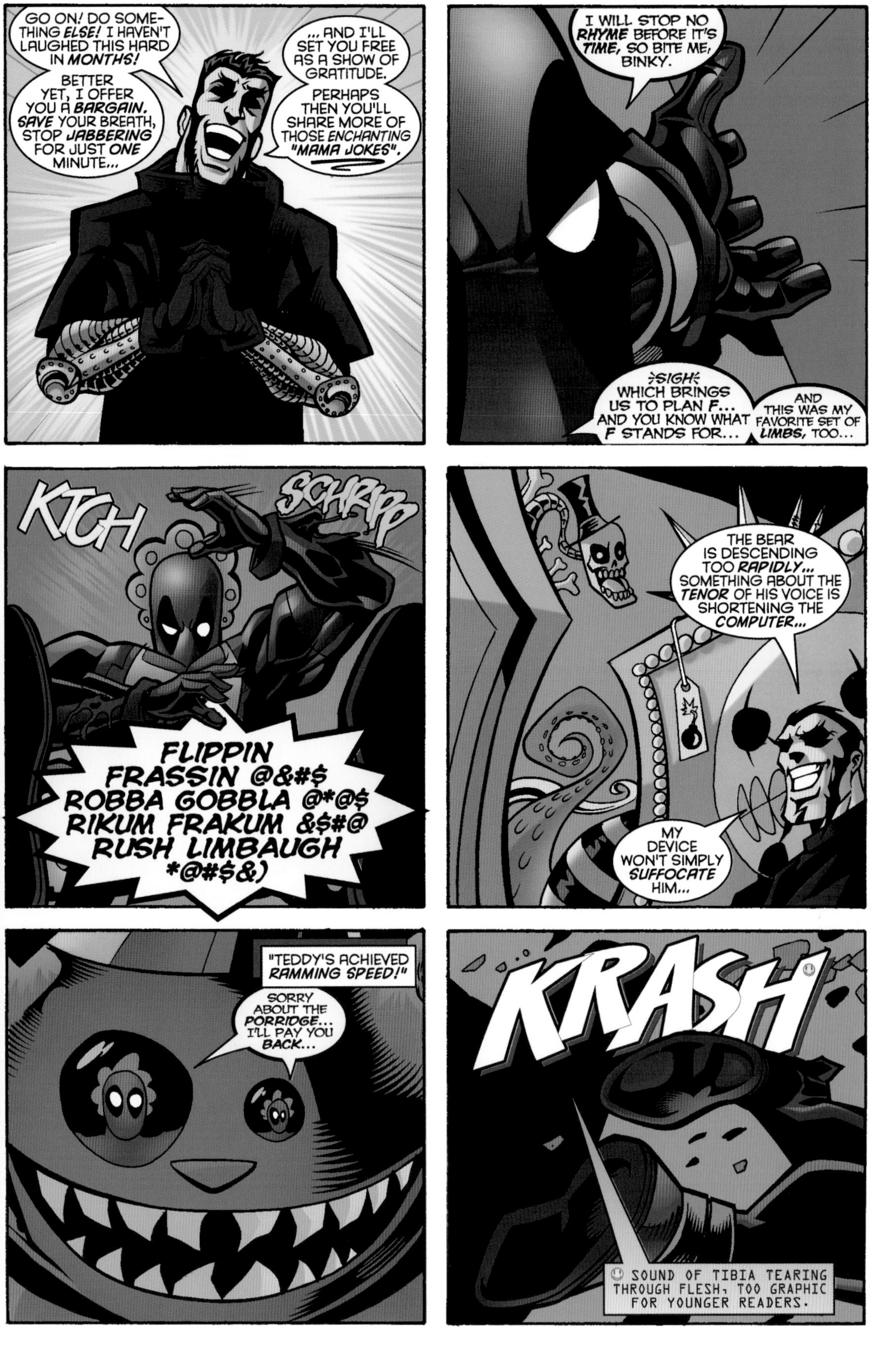

GO ON! DO SOMETHING ELSE! I HAVEN'T LAUGHED THIS HARD IN MONTHS!
BETTER YET, I OFFER YOU A BARGAIN. SAVE YOUR BREATH, STOP JABBERING FOR JUST ONE MINUTE...
...AND I'LL SET YOU FREE AS A SHOW OF GRATITUDE.
PERHAPS THEN YOU'LL SHARE MORE OF THOSE ENCHANTING "MAMA JOKES".
I WILL STOP NO RHYME BEFORE IT'S TIME, SO BITE ME, BINKY.
SIGH WHICH BRINGS US TO PLAN F... AND YOU KNOW WHAT F STANDS FOR...
AND THIS WAS MY FAVORITE SET OF LIMBS, TOO...
KTCH
SCHRIPP
FLIPPIN FRASSIN @&#$ ROBBA GOBBLA @*@$ RIKUM FRAKUM &$#@ RUSH LIMBAUGH *@#$&)
THE BEAR IS DESCENDING TOO RAPIDLY... SOMETHING ABOUT THE TENOR OF HIS VOICE IS SHORTENING THE COMPUTER...
MY DEVICE WON'T SIMPLY SUFFOCATE HIM...
"TEDDY'S ACHIEVED RAMMING SPEED!"
SORRY ABOUT THE PORRIDGE... I'LL PAY YOU BACK...
KRASH
SOUND OF TIBIA TEARING THROUGH FLESH, TOO GRAPHIC FOR YOUNGER READERS.

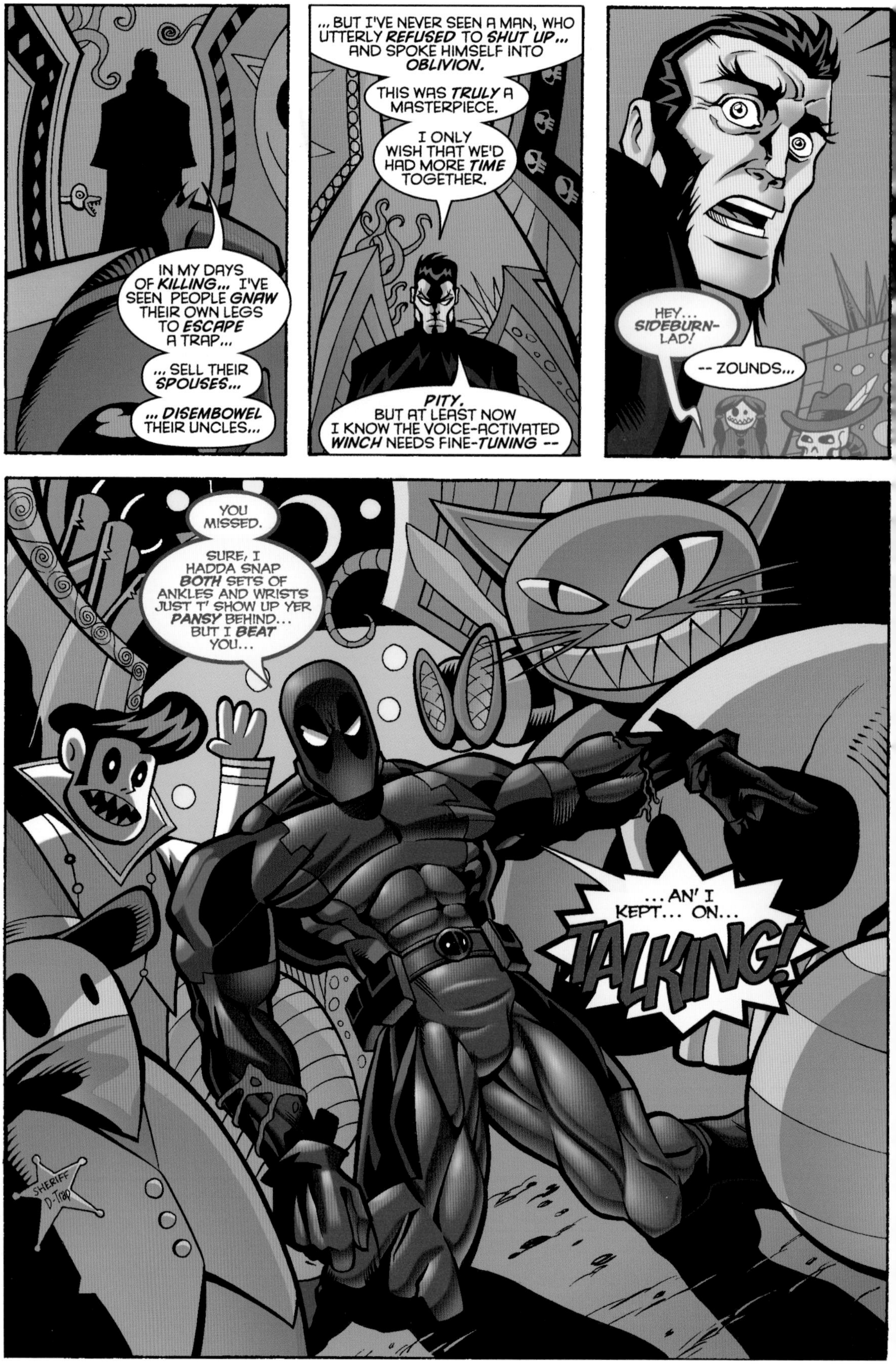
IN MY DAYS OF KILLING... I'VE SEEN PEOPLE GNAW THEIR OWN LEGS TO ESCAPE A TRAP...
... SELL THEIR SPOUSES...
... DISEMBOWEL THEIR UNCLES...
... BUT I'VE NEVER SEEN A MAN, WHO UTTERLY REFUSED TO SHUT UP... AND SPOKE HIMSELF INTO OBLIVION.
THIS WAS TRULY A MASTERPIECE.
I ONLY WISH THAT WE'D HAD MORE TIME TOGETHER.
PITY. BUT AT LEAST NOW I KNOW THE VOICE-ACTIVATED WINCH NEEDS FINE-TUNING --
HEY... SIDEBURN-LAD!
-- ZOUNDS...
YOU MISSED.
SURE, I HADDA SNAP BOTH SETS OF ANKLES AND WRISTS JUST T' SHOW UP YER PANSY BEHIND... BUT I BEAT YOU...
... AN' I KEPT... ON... TALKING!
SHERIFF D-Trap

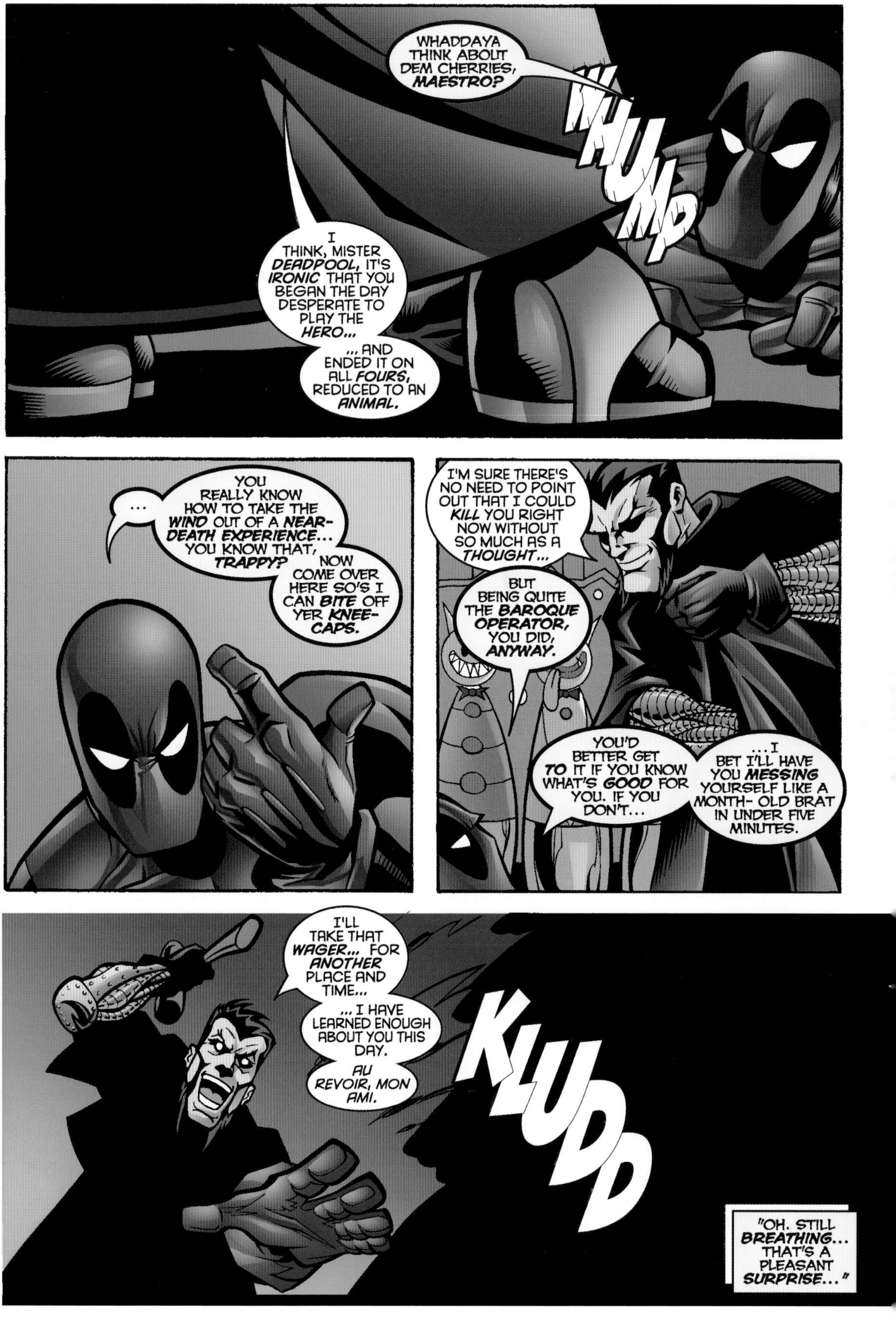
WHADDAYA THINK ABOUT DEM CHERRIES, MAESTRO?
WHUMP
I THINK, MISTER DEADPOOL, IT'S IRONIC THAT YOU BEGAN THE DAY DESPERATE TO PLAY THE HERO...
... AND ENDED IT ON ALL FOURS, REDUCED TO AN ANIMAL.
...
YOU REALLY KNOW HOW TO TAKE THE WIND OUT OF A NEAR-DEATH EXPERIENCE... YOU KNOW THAT, TRAPPY?
NOW COME OVER HERE SO'S I CAN BITE OFF YER KNEE-CAPS.
I'M SURE THERE'S NO NEED TO POINT OUT THAT I COULD KILL YOU RIGHT NOW WITHOUT SO MUCH AS A THOUGHT...
BUT BEING QUITE THE BAROQUE OPERATOR, YOU DID, ANYWAY.
YOU'D BETTER GET TO IT IF YOU KNOW WHAT'S GOOD FOR YOU. IF YOU DON'T...
... I BET I'LL HAVE YOU MESSING YOURSELF LIKE A MONTH- OLD BRAT IN UNDER FIVE MINUTES.
I'LL TAKE THAT WAGER... FOR ANOTHER PLACE AND TIME...
... I HAVE LEARNED ENOUGH ABOUT YOU THIS DAY.
AU REVOIR, MON AMI.
KLUDD
"OH. STILL BREATHING... THAT'S A PLEASANT SURPRISE..."

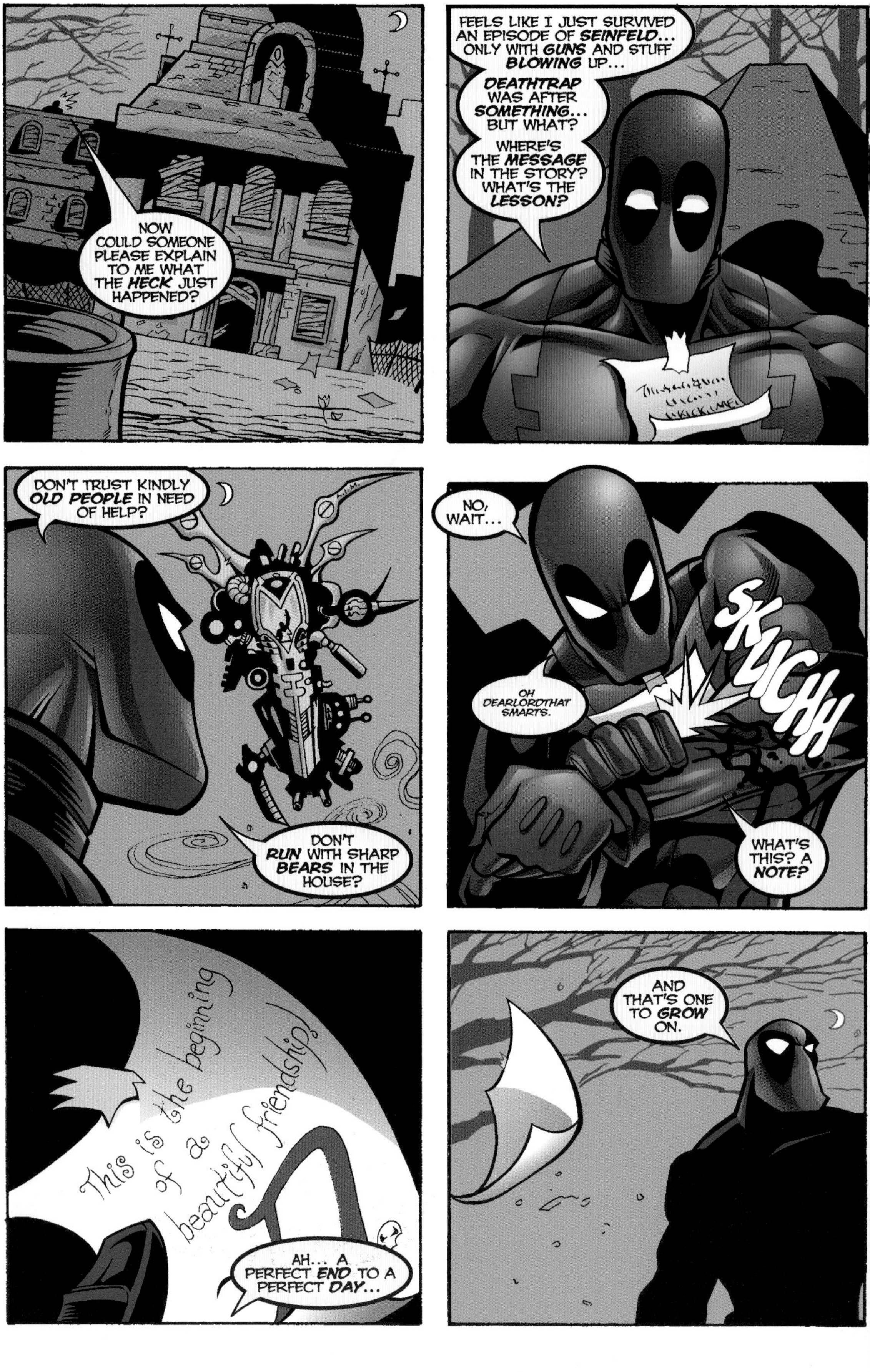
NOW COULD SOMEONE PLEASE EXPLAIN TO ME WHAT THE HECK JUST HAPPENED?
FEELS LIKE I JUST SURVIVED AN EPISODE OF SEINFELD... ONLY WITH GUNS AND STUFF BLOWING UP...
DEATHTRAP WAS AFTER SOMETHING... BUT WHAT?
WHERE'S THE MESSAGE IN THE STORY? WHAT'S THE LESSON?
DON'T TRUST KINDLY OLD PEOPLE IN NEED OF HELP?
DON'T RUN WITH SHARP BEARS IN THE HOUSE?
NO, WAIT...
SKLUCHH
OH DEARLORDTHAT SMARTS.
WHAT'S THIS? A NOTE?
This is the beginning of a beautiful friendship!
AH... A PERFECT END TO A PERFECT DAY...
AND THAT'S ONE TO GROW ON.

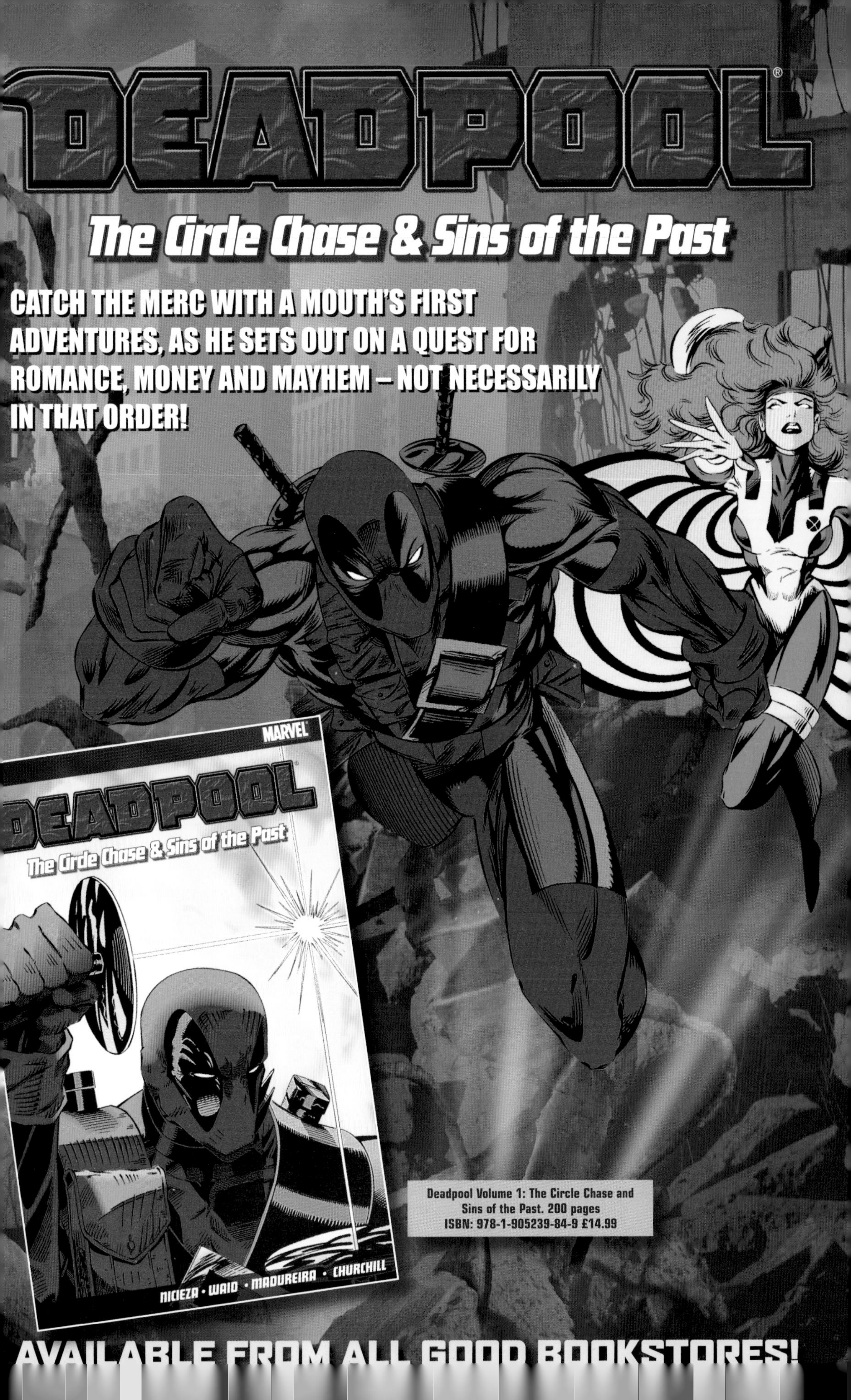
DEADPOOL®
The Circle Chase & Sins of the Past
CATCH THE MERC WITH A MOUTH'S FIRST ADVENTURES, AS HE SETS OUT ON A QUEST FOR ROMANCE, MONEY AND MAYHEM – NOT NECESSARILY IN THAT ORDER!
MARVEL
DEADPOOL
The Circle Chase & Sins of the Past
NICIEZA • WAID • MADUREIRA • CHURCHILL
Deadpool Volume 1: The Circle Chase and Sins of the Past. 200 pages
ISBN: 978-1-905239-84-9 £14.99
AVAILABLE FROM ALL GOOD BOOKSTORES!

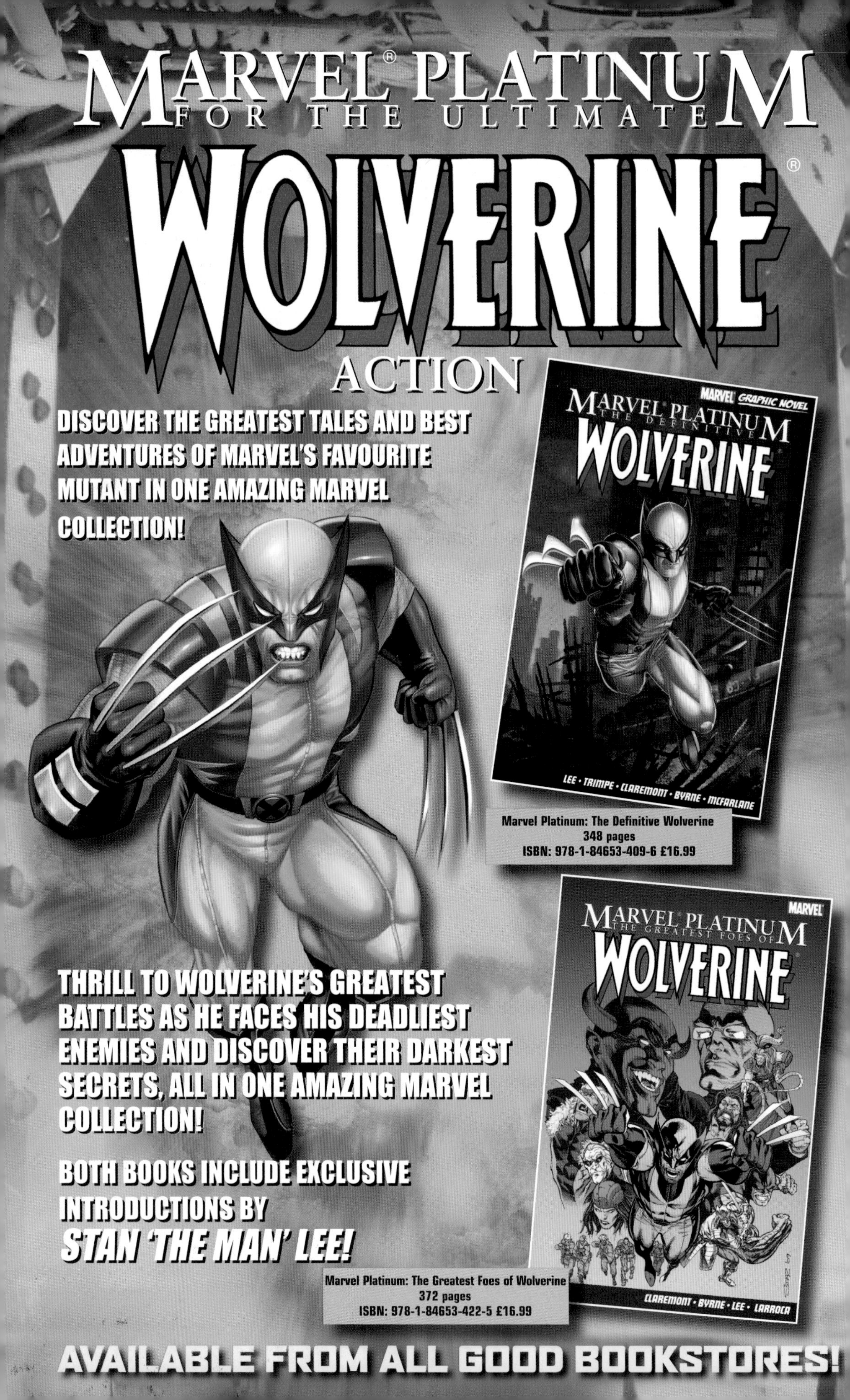

MARVEL® PLATINUM
FOR THE ULTIMATE
WOLVERINE®
ACTION
DISCOVER THE GREATEST TALES AND BEST ADVENTURES OF MARVEL'S FAVOURITE MUTANT IN ONE AMAZING MARVEL COLLECTION!
MARVEL GRAPHIC NOVEL
MARVEL PLATINUM
THE DEFINITIVE
WOLVERINE
LEE • TRIMPE • CLAREMONT • BYRNE • MCFARLANE
Marvel Platinum: The Definitive Wolverine
348 pages
ISBN: 978-1-84653-409-6 £16.99
MARVEL
MARVEL PLATINUM
THE GREATEST FOES OF
WOLVERINE
CLAREMONT • BYRNE • LEE • LARROCA
THRILL TO WOLVERINE'S GREATEST BATTLES AS HE FACES HIS DEADLIEST ENEMIES AND DISCOVER THEIR DARKEST SECRETS, ALL IN ONE AMAZING MARVEL COLLECTION!
BOTH BOOKS INCLUDE EXCLUSIVE INTRODUCTIONS BY
STAN 'THE MAN' LEE!
Marvel Platinum: The Greatest Foes of Wolverine
372 pages
ISBN: 978-1-84653-422-5 £16.99
AVAILABLE FROM ALL GOOD BOOKSTORES!

CHAPTER 2

Exhilaration shot through Buffy as she rushed down the corridor toward a red, glowing EXIT sign. The sign itself—an indication that this place had originally been used by humans—made the whole scene almost surreal, and she felt giddy with her freedom.

Freedom.

But she wasn't free yet. Her captors had kept a hood over her head when they brought her here years before, so she had no idea what surrounded the building she was in. Things were bad. That was all she had learned from August, but it was enough to set her nerves on edge.

Thoughts of August made her flinch and swallow hard. Nausea roiled in her gut and bile rose up in the back of her throat. The girl had forced her hand, and even then Buffy had done everything she could to avoid killing her, but August was dead. When she thought of that, and the things she'd had to do to herself to feign her own death, her feet began to slow beneath her.

Buffy could not afford to slow down.

She took a deep breath, picked up her pace again, and silently cursed the vampires for not having any wood around. A chair leg, anything at all, would have made it possible for her to dust them without feeling so much like it had been a massacre.

In her mind, she saw a quick flash of herself slamming the huge steel door closed on Maddox's neck, severing his head. The spray of dust that had resulted was welcome, but despite her years of hatred for her jailer, there was no triumph in it.

Not that she had any sympathy, either. What unnerved her was that the deaths she had dealt out to the guards had been so intimate. She did not want to get that close to the undead. Not ever. They were abominations, unclean things; a truth she had come to realize more and more during her captivity. Her calling was to eliminate them, but it was a filthy job.

The sick feeling in her stomach abated somewhat, but a faint, sour taste remained in her mouth. She shook her head once to clear her mind, then shoved through the door at the end of the hall. It swung too wide, and would have clanged off the wall if she had not caught it quickly enough.

A momentary pause to be certain no one was near,

and then she started up a set of stairs in front of her. A long oak railing was bolted to the wall. Buffy stopped halfway up and lashed out with a snap kick that cracked the railing in two. The halves dangled down, tearing at their moorings. Another kick, aimed at one of the sagging halves, and a fifteen-inch length of splintered oak clattered to the stairs. The Slayer snatched it and continued upward.

It was too thick by far. Her grip did not come close to reaching all the way around it. But it would do. It would most certainly do.

There was a door at the top of the stairs. As she raced toward it, the door began to open. A vampire poked his head into the stairwell with a predator's curiosity, his nostrils flaring as he scented the air. The black tattoo splayed across his features, bat wings extending down his cheeks into a thin beard, made the blazing orange fire of his eyes stand out in ghostly fashion, there in the darkened stairwell.

Those ghostfire eyes widened as he spotted her. "Oh, sh—"

Buffy pivoted and popped a kick at the door. It clanged into his head and the vampire stumbled back into the corridor. She hauled the door open and pursued him.

Though she sensed some alarm in him, the vampire faced her without hesitation. "She's out!" he yelled into the empty corridor. "The Slayer's out!"

"Tattletale," Buffy rasped.

Expressionless, she backhanded him. He tried to

block the blow, but she was too fast for him. Faster than ever before. It had been a long time since she had fought anything but shadows, and it was going to take some getting used to, but she was at almost her most powerful now.

The makeshift oak stake flashed down and punched an enormous hole in his chest. The vampire dusted.

From around a corner off to her left came the sound of running feet. Her eyes flickered closed for a moment: three, no four of them. Though the stake felt good in her hand, and though she wanted to eliminate all of her captors, her priorities began to assert themselves.

Primary among them was simply to get out, to escape, to see the sky again. To breathe fresh air.

Buffy took off down the corridor, away from her pursuers. The structure she was in appeared to have once housed offices, for there were doors and glass windows looking inward all along the hall. Each office was dark and lifeless inside. The hallway itself had no external windows, however. At least not here.

Up ahead, the hall turned right. Buffy rounded the corner just as she heard shouts behind her. The vampires had seen her. That was all right, though. She could practically smell the outdoors now. Nothing was going to stand in her way.

Even as that thought skittered across her brain, she looked up. At the end of the hall in front of her, the structure opened up into a wide lobby area. The door was all glass. The walls on either side of the door were glass. All of it was painted black.

A pair of vampires stood blocking the door, arms crossed. They did not flinch as she approached, did not even attempt the arrogant, menacing grin that their kind had mastered long ago. But Buffy remembered all too well how this breed of vampires worked, these servants of Camazotz. The demon-god who was their master had trained them to be silent and fearless. Yet she had seen fear in the tattooed eyes of the ones she had killed in her cell, and knew that it was there in them.

"You can get away from the door, or you can *be* the door," she told them grimly.

In unison, they unfolded their arms and prepared to fight her. Behind her, Buffy heard more shouts as her pursuers caught sight of her again. Ahead, the door sentries stood firm, eyes crackling with energy.

Buffy rushed headlong at them without breaking stride. She was three feet away when they lunged for her. The Slayer froze in place, both of the sentries' reach fell short. Buffy leaped up, spun into a roundhouse kick that caught one of the sentries in the jaw and sent him reeling back toward the blacked out glass door.

In the instant before the glass shattered, she punched the splintered oak railing through the heart of the other. As he dusted, his partner crashed through the glass door. The darkness fell away, and the daylight poured in.

The sun.

A grin slipped across Buffy's features as she watched the other sentry scramble to his feet among shards of black glass and try to get inside. He began to smoke, and then to burn, and just before he would have reached the shade, he exploded into a cloud of cinder and ash.

The Slayer stepped calmly out into the sunshine, sneakers crunching shattered glass. Then she turned, bathed in the light, and eyed the bat-faced vampires who had been rushing at her from within. They all stopped short ten feet from the door, avoiding the perilous splash of sun that spread across the floor.

Once upon a time, Buffy would have teased them, said something funny. She didn't feel funny anymore. With a flourish, she made an obscene gesture, turned, and walked away.

But she felt their burning eyes upon her back.

The building she had been in was a three-story office with no name or insignia on the front, and no sign. Only a street number, One Five Seven.

It was a beautiful Southern California day, the kind of glorious day she had always taken for granted growing up. This was, after all, what California was all about. Today, however, she reveled in it. Birds sang. A sparrow glided across the street in front of her. The breeze carried sweet smells to her, like springtime, though she was not sure of the season.

Free.

Though Buffy knew she had to act immediately, to figure out the lay of the land, to find her friends and discover what horror had driven August so wild, she was overwhelmed for several moments simply with being outside again. She had to shield her eyes or look down at the ground for the first few minutes, so unaccustomed was she to the brilliance of the daylight.

A relief surged through her unlike anything she had ever felt. Along with it came a feeling of power, as though some long dead battery within her was being recharged.

The block she was on was lined with faceless buildings similar to the one she had escaped from. Boring corporate shells. As she strode toward an intersection ahead, though, she frowned. Something was not right. Even out here, something was intensely not right.

Disconnected as she had been for so long, it took her a moment to put it together. An ominous feeling descended upon her. Then she knew. It was not the presence of something dreadful, but an absence. The absence of life, of bustle, even of traffic. The birds were the only activity in sight.

Greatly troubled, she began to run again. At the intersection, she glanced both ways along a street dotted with trendy storefront boutiques and sandwich shops. Though she had not been there since shortly after moving to Sunnydale, Buffy recognized the town. She was in El Suerte, maybe fifteen minutes from home.

Hope rose again within her, punctuated by the appearance, far down the street, of several cars crossing at another intersection. Then, off to her left, an engine caught her attention. She turned to see an SUV cruising along among the shops. It halted abruptly in front of a sandwich shop and the driver, a middle-aged man in a well-tailored suit, popped out and took a look around. He spotted her, frowned, then hurried into the shop.

Moments later he emerged again, carrying several plastic bags she presumed were filled with sandwiches and drinks. Buffy's only thought was of home, of getting back to Sunnydale. Quickly, she trotted across the street to catch the man before he could drive away.

"Hey!" she called.

Eyes wide, he stared at her in alarm. Buffy slowed, wondering if he was some sort of paranoid.

"Why aren't you working?" he demanded, gaze darting up and down the street as though afraid he might be seen speaking to someone slacking off.

"Umm, day off?" Buffy shrugged. "Do you know where I can catch a bus to Sunnydale?"

He laughed, but it was a tiny sound, almost as though he were coughing instead. "What are you, some kind of nut? Who in their right mind would ever *want* to go there?"

Again he glanced around. "You better get off the street, sweetheart."

Then he ducked into the SUV and locked the doors even before starting the engine, as though afraid she might try to carjack him. A moment later, he pulled away. Buffy called after him, but he didn't even look into the rearview mirror.

Angry now, she turned toward the sandwich shop, determined to get answers. When she glanced at the door, however, she saw a dark-haired man with a thick mustache turning a key in the lock. He pulled back from the door when their eyes met, as if he did not want to be seen. Then he closed the blinds that hung by the door, and she could not see him or the inside of the shop anymore.

"What the hell's wrong with you people?" Buffy shouted.

But a deep dread had filled her, a horrible feeling that she knew exactly what was wrong with them. It was impossible, of course. A whole town could not be terrorized like this. But they were.

A sudden squeal from a siren startled her. Buffy turned to see a police car cruising slowly toward her. It rolled up beside her. Two cops jumped out with the engine still running and began to walk toward her. They began to reach for their weapons.

"Excuse me, Miss Summers, but we're going to have to ask you to come with us."

Miss Summers. They knew who she was. They were looking for her. Her suspicion of moments earlier had become a reality. The people terrified to be on the streets, the police looking for her. She had not been the only captive in El Suerte. The vampires held the entire town prisoner.

The two police officers drew their weapons and aimed at her.

"Miss Summers."

"I don't think so," Buffy replied. "It isn't as though they're going to let you kill me."

One of the cops, a tall, dark-complexioned guy with sad eyes, looked extremely uncomfortable. His partner was a heavyset man with pasty skin and thick glasses.

Pastyface smiled. "I can shoot both kneecaps, maybe your shoulders. You'll recover, but it'll hurt like hell. One way or another, you're coming with us."

Buffy sighed. "I don't think so. Thanks for the ride, though."

Pastyface looked confused. With a single, fluid motion, Buffy spiraled in the air toward him and kicked the gun from his hand, shattering his fingers in the process. He let out a scream even as the tall man fired. Buffy was still in motion, however, and the bullet whistled past her cheek, close enough that she could feel the air pressure change by her skin.

Then the tall man stared down at his hand, stunned that his gun had somehow disappeared. Buffy showed it to him, then tossed it over her shoulder. As he watched it sail through the air, she punched him hard enough to spin him around. He tumbled like a felled redwood on top of his partner.

Alarm bells continued to go off in her head, but they had nothing to do with the cops. They were practically forgotten already. All she could think of was the reaction of the sandwich man in the SUV when she had mentioned Sunnydale.

Who in their right mind would ever want to go there?

He lived in El Suerte, a prisoner of the vampires who ran the town, and he thought the idea of anyone going to Sunnydale was crazy.

Tendrils of ice spread throughout her body, wrapping around her spine and curling up in her gut. Grim-faced, she went to the police car and slid into the driver's seat. As she put it in gear she caught sight of her reflection in the rearview mirror.

A shock ran through her.

For just a moment, she saw herself at nineteen. Then the illusion faded and she saw the way she truly looked, the hard line of her jaw, the ragged cut of her long, blond hair, the crinkles at the corners of her eyes and mouth, the furious glare of her eyes. It was startling, after so long, to see her own reflection. She saw that it was not only the world they had changed, but her as well.

Buffy hated them all the more for it.

In her mind, she saw again the image of herself at nineteen. That was how it was supposed to be. None of this was meant to happen. For a short while, she had almost forgotten that. Yet again the voice of her younger self rose up within her, took control.

I've got to get back. I've got to fix this.

The words meant so many things. Whatever was happening in the here and now, she had to do something about it, true. But that was the older Buffy's priority. Within her body was also a girl out of time, a college girl who only ever wanted to be normal. A young woman who had been told by a ghost that she would make a mistake that would have catastrophic results. She could not help but think that she lived amongst those results even now.

I have to go back, she thought again. *Figure out what I did wrong, find a way back, and stop it.* It never occurred to her to wonder if such a thing were possible. After all, the being called The Prophet had somehow cast the spirit of her younger self forward to inhabit her future body. If that was possible, there had to be a way to reverse the process.

For the moment, though, she had to figure out just how far the vampires' influence had spread, and stop them. It was what she did, who she was. The Slayer. Before The Prophet had touched her, had sent her forward in time, Buffy had been determined to dedicate herself wholly to being the Slayer, and also to having a life of her own. One hundred percent Slayer, one hundred percent Buffy. An impossible task, but she had done impossible things before. Yet that struggle had frustrated those close to her, and might have indirectly led to her current situation. If she had not made such a mess of things, she would never have been in a position to rely upon The Prophet, would never have ended up here.

A grim smile cut through her melancholy now. For in this future she did not have to worry about trying to live two lives to their fullest, about filling two roles. The things that had made up the life of Buffy Summers seemed to have been torn away, leaving only this monstrous landscape where vampires ruled. No one needed Buffy anymore. She didn't need to live two lives . . . only one.

She was just the Slayer now. There was a freedom in that, and it felt good.

Knuckles white where she gripped the steering wheel, she accelerated and raced out of El Suerte, headed for Sunnydale. Soon enough, they would know she had taken the car. Her only hope was that they would not realize where she was headed.

Though she tried not to, Buffy wondered what had become of her mother and her friends, her old gang. Not only now, but *then*. Willow, Oz, Xander, and Anya. Not to mention Giles, and even Angel. What had happened to them that day, after The Prophet had cast her out of her body?

In the past . . .

It was difficult to breathe. Willow glanced around the dorm room she shared with Buffy, and shuddered. It was a pretty big room, but she felt claustrophobic in it for the first time. Oz sat beside her, and she reached out to squeeze his hand for reassurance. Xander and Anya were there as well. Quite a crowd for her little summoning, in the darkened room, with the shades pulled down.

But even in the darkness, the thing that shimmered in the middle of the room, beside Buffy, was darker still. It made her think of black holes, the way it swirled, oily and black, there in the air, a rip in the fabric of the world.

Willow had summoned Lucy Hanover, the ghost of a long-dead Slayer, who now aided lost souls in the afterworld. The ghost had heard dire predictions from this thing, called The Prophet, and had agreed to try to bring it forth to communicate those prophecies more precisely.

But now that it was here, Willow only wanted to send the thing back. Just being in its presence made her skin crawl like nothing she had ever felt before. And now it seemed to float nearer to Buffy; or, perhaps more accurately, it seemed to consume the space between them, to slither across reality as it reached for her.

No! Willow thought. *Buffy, don't let it near!* But somehow she had lost the strength to cry out.

The specter of Lucy Hanover lingered, hovering near the window, watching the proceedings as Buffy spoke to The Prophet. The entity's words stunned them all.

"The future cannot be prevented now. Already the clockwork grinds on," it said, voice like whispered profanity. *"But I can show you my vision, share with you the sight, so you may see what is coming and perhaps better prepare for it."*

Buffy flinched away from it and glanced over at Willow. Silently, she urged the Slayer to say no. Anxiously, Willow bit her lip. The ghost of Lucy Hanover reached out phantom hands toward Buffy as though she wanted to help. But she was already dead. This was all the help she could offer.

Buffy sat up straighter and stared at The Prophet, the flowing black presence in the room. "Show me."

Willow shook her head slowly, warning, but Buffy did not see. Still, somehow, she felt unable to speak.

"I must only touch you, and you may see."

"Do it," Buffy instructed The Prophet.

The Prophet's slick, shimmering form slithered toward her. The tear in the fabric of the world extended toward her, fingers like tendrils reached for her.

Finally, Willow felt something give way within her, as though the grip of some hideous force had finally loosened.

"Buffy," she said cautiously. "Maybe this isn't such a good—"

But it was too late. The Prophet touched Buffy. And Buffy screamed.

The Slayer's eyes went wide and she stared as though she were seeing a vision of unspeakable horror. Her mouth remained open but the ragged, high-pitched scream died on her lips. Her chest began to heave, and Buffy started to hyperventilate.

"Buffy!" Willow cried.

She ran to her best friend and grabbed hold just as Buffy began to fall limp. Angry, and fearful for her, Willow glanced around the room. Oz was beside her, Xander and Anya behind him, looking on worriedly.

Otherwise the room was empty.

"Where . . . where'd they go?" Willow asked softly.

The others glanced around as well, apparently equally mystified.

"That's just like a disembodied clairvoyant," Xander muttered. "Offer up the ominous future, then skip town before the questions start rolling in."

"I'm going to open the shade now. I've had enough darkness for today," Anya said in clipped tones.

When the shades were up, and the sunlight streamed in, Willow felt a little better. Buffy was still breathing, though her eyes were closed and she was pale. Her skin felt too cold.

But she was alive. And she was the Slayer.

"What do you think's up?" Oz asked.

Willow swallowed hard. "Well, I'm sorta hoping I'm wrong. And it bothers me to think about how often I feel that way. But I'm guessing whatever future that thing showed Buffy, it was too much for her to handle. Kinda think she's in shock."

"Whoa. Red light," Xander said. "She's the Slayer. How could just seeing something put her into a state of shock?"

"I'm thinkin' it depends what she saw," Oz noted.

Anya threw her hands up in exasperation. "See! Why does this stuff always happen?" She rounded on Xander, a small pout on her lips. "Why do we live *here*? In all the world, *this* is where you want to live? Can't we go far away from the impending apocalypse?"

"You could," Willow said sadly, still gazing at her

best friend's pale features. "But that wouldn't keep it from coming."

For another few moments, Willow cradled Buffy gently in her arms. Then, with a suddenness that gave her a start, the Slayer opened her eyes. Her skin was still cold and white, but her eyes were as fierce and determined as always.

Fierce and determined . . . and yet there was something else there as well.

"Buffy!" Willow cried.

"See!" Xander said. "She's okay."

Buffy sat up and shook Willow's hands off her. She stretched like a cat, as if testing her body to see if she was harmed in some way. Flexing her fingers, she stared at her hands as though they were some newly invented marvel. Then she stood up carefully, a bit off-balance. She nearly collapsed, and Willow thought of a foal just testing its legs for the first time.

"You are okay, right?" Xander asked doubtfully.

The Slayer glanced around the dorm room. A sly grin stole across her features for one moment, and then was gone. She went to the closet, reached inside and grabbed a black leather jacket, though it was too warm outside for the coat.

"Buffy?" Willow asked. "Come on. I know you want to protect us, but we're part of this. It's our future, too. What did you see?"

As she slipped the jacket on, Buffy turned to regard them all. There was no emotion on her face now.

Her eyes flickered with some sort of light, as though from within.

"Everything will be fine," she said, a peculiar slurring to her voice.

"You're not all right," Willow told her. "Come on. Just give yourself an hour's rest. Then we'll figure out what to do about Giles. You've got to talk to us, Buffy. Let us help."

But Buffy shook her head. "There is nothing you can do."

"So you're going to go after Giles alone, after all this?" Xander demanded.

He sounded ticked off, and Willow didn't blame him.

"Do not concern yourself," Buffy said bluntly.

With that, the Slayer turned and left the room, not even bothering to close the door behind her.

"Great," Xander sighed. "Now she's back to that again. Omnipotent Slayer-girl. Taking it all on herself."

"I don't know," Willow said slowly, staring at the half-open door.

Oz sidled up beside her. "What don't you know?" he asked, brow furrowed.

"I don't think this is about that," she said. "This is something else. Something new and family-size creepy. Or, okay, could be just Willow-paranoia. But I'm thinking The Prophet touching Buffy? Possibly more to it than just a Viewmaster of Doom."

"There was a sinister vibe around that thing," Anya agreed. "But what do you think it did, exactly?"

Willow stared at the door. "Remember the part where I said 'I don't know?' "

"Well, we'll keep an eye on her. See what's what," Xander suggested.

Willow nodded, deeply troubled, and afraid for Buffy. She didn't know if the future was going to be as The Prophet had predicted, but she had a sinking feeling it was going to be ugly, one way or another.

As she drove along nearly deserted roads, Buffy was chilled by the changes she saw around her. A few cars passed by, and some stores were open, but many others were boarded up. The skating rink just off I-17 had been partially destroyed by fire, and the parking lot was cracked and overgrown. There were no rollerbladers, no joggers, no bicyclists. Other than those few cars, the only people she saw were a pair of homeless men raiding a Dumpster behind a Chinese restaurant that was apparently still in operation, and they scrambled back through a broken fence behind the place when she drove by.

Buffy decided it was perhaps best to enter the town quietly, perhaps even invisibly. They'd be looking for the car, after all. Buffy ditched the El Suerte police car in the overgrown lot that had once been the Sunnydale Twin Drive-In.

It rolled across the cracked pavement, four-foot weeds whisking against the grille of the car. Buffy killed the engine, took a long breath, and laid her forehead upon the steering wheel for a moment. A slight motion, and she flinched at the sudden pain in her broken nose. Along with her other wounds, it had begun to heal quickly. That was part of being the Slayer. But it was still very sore.

Resolute, she popped open the door and climbed out, then hesitated. Inside the police car was a shotgun locked in a brace between seats. It would be a simple thing to snap the brace and take it with her. Buffy glanced into the car and looked at the gleaming barrel of the gun. Then she shook her head. What she wanted was a crossbow. Maybe even a sword. But after all this time she suspected that the weapons caches at Giles's apartment and her mother's house, not to mention her dorm room back at U.C. Sunnydale, would have been cleaned out. Even if they were still there, the Kakchiquels, Camazotz's vampire followers, would likely be keeping an eye on those places in case she should return.

Without those weapons, without even a knife, she would have to fashion some crude, makeshift stakes, and hope that was enough.

Buffy left the car where it was and began to walk back toward the road. After a moment she paused and glanced back at the concrete structure on the far side of the lot that had once served as both projection booth and concession stand. Once upon a time, like any abandoned structure in Sunnydale, it had been a prime nesting place for vampires and other creatures of darkness.

Best to make sure, she thought.

In a light jog, she crossed the lot without any attempt to hide herself. If anyone were inside the bunker-like edifice, they would already have seen her. The metal door was rusted and hung off its hinges. The sky above was blue as a robin's egg, the wind whispered through the overgrown brush in the lot, the sunlight painted the world around her in bright hues. But the beauty of the day ended at that rusty door. The gaping maw of the place almost seemed to swallow the sunlight. Within was impenetrable darkness.

Nothing moved inside.

Buffy kicked the door loose and it crashed down onto concrete inside. She paused for a moment, then slipped into the dark. It took a moment for her eyes to adjust. Blinking, she ventured farther into the now gray, dusty interior of the building.

Nothing. Something scuffled in the walls, but that was all. It was little more than a tomb for several generations of mice. There were counters of shattered glass where concession snacks had once been offered. Empty now.

Head cocked to one side, Buffy listened, searching for some sound that did not represent rodents. Convinced she was alone, she turned to leave and then thought better of it. Upstairs in the projection booth she was likely to find furniture of some kind. And it was easier to turn smashed furniture into stakes than to forge them out of downed tree limbs, particularly when she had nothing to whittle with.

Sure enough, at the top of the stairs, in the box of a

room where the projectionist had once done his work, she found a small table and several wooden chairs, the legs of which would be satisfactory for her purposes. Buffy crossed to the table, pulled out the nearest chair, and froze with astonishment as she gazed at what lay upon it.

A crossbow.

More accurately, *her* crossbow, the one Giles had given her when they first began to train together. Beside it, a folded bone-white card with two words printed neatly on the front: FOR BUFFY.

Doubt flooded her and she glanced around anxiously, suddenly sure she must have been mistaken. Someone had to be here—otherwise how could she explain the weapon's presence?

Yet her senses confirmed it. She was alone.

Tentatively, she reached out to pick up the crossbow, studying it intently to be sure there was no tripwire or other trap involved. There was not. Only the crossbow, and on the chair opposite that one, a small quiver containing bolts for it.

Profoundly unnerved, a thousand questions in her head, Buffy shattered one of the chairs, snapped the legs and back into half a dozen usable stakes, and carried them under one arm with the quiver. In the other hand she held the crossbow. On alert, skin prickling as she searched around her for any sign of another presence, she hurried down the stairs and out into the sun.

With the blue sky above, she felt a little better, but

not much. This was a mystery that disturbed her deeply. Someone had known or at least suspected that she would find her way to this spot, or had been here upon her arrival and left these things for her to find.

And all across the lot, the shadows cast by nearby trees and the remnants of the drive-in screens had grown longer. The afternoon was waning, and night was only a few hours away.

Buffy hurried to the police car again. She opened the trunk, and was relieved to find a canvas bag that had belonged to one of the police officers inside. There were cotton sweatpants and a sweatshirt in there, as well as a large pair of sneakers. She dumped the clothes out, dropped the weapons into the bag, then noticed a small box of roadside flares and took those as well. She slung the bag over her shoulder and headed, not for the road, but for the chain link fence at the far side of the lot.

It felt to her as though there were eyes upon her, now. The crossbow was almost warm in her grip. Buffy vaulted the fence and set off through a stretch of woods that would lead up to a power plant, from which she could work her way eventually into Hammersmith Park, and then into the backyards of residential Sunnydale.

Stay off the street, she told herself.

CHAPTER 3

If the silence in El Suerte had been surreal, the ravaged streets of Sunnydale were all *too* real. As Buffy made her way through back alleys and across fire escapes, hugging the shadows to keep out of plain sight, a constant current of alarm and abhorrence ran through her body. Her town had become an abomination.

The parks were ravaged, statues destroyed. Every few blocks she passed a row of buildings or houses that had been burned out completely, leaving a charred shell behind. It was unnerving, seeing some shops and markets apparently thriving, while so many other businesses had been ransacked, shattered windows in the front a sure sign of what she would find inside.

Three times she had entered such a store, and each time the result was the same. Christabel's Consignments, The Flower Cart, and Quarryhouse Pizza. Each store had been torn apart, ripped and shattered, but it had obviously happened long ago and a thick layer of dust, umblemished by the footprint of a single intruder, lay upon everything. In the back of each of those businesses, Buffy discovered the remains of the owners, so decayed that there was no way to tell how they died. She could only assume the vampires had killed them.

And yet the others, the stores that were still running, were equally disturbing to see, for Buffy knew that their proprietors must be cooperating with the vampires, serving both the humans who still lived in Sunnydale and the monsters who ruled it.

With each block she drove, Buffy's mood became even more grim. Questions about her mother's fate, and that of her friends, kept forcing their way into her mind, but Buffy pushed them away. Before she could help anyone, she had to know exactly what the situation was, what she was dealing with. Someone had been there, at the Twin Drive-In. They knew she was on her way here. No way could she risk going by her house just yet.

In a way, despite her horror at the devastation that had occurred in some places in town, it disturbed her even more deeply when she saw that other businesses and homes seemed remarkably well-preserved. Downtown was deserted, and yet many of the businesses actually still had lights on. Curious, Buffy broke in through the back door of the Espresso Pump. The machines hummed quietly, the coolers still working, red lights winking on coffee machines, ready for business.

Buffy made her way through the darkened store to the front door and looked at the posted hours of business. There were three words printed there: OPEN ALL NIGHT. Simple enough, but they created more questions. The Espresso Pump was still in operation, as were most of the bars she had seen, as well as video stores, a couple of small markets, and the Sun Cinema. But were they run by vampires or humans? *Were* there many humans left?

As she had made her way around town, she had seen several police cars cruising slowly down deserted streets. *Probably looking for me,* she'd thought. But she had also seen a few other vehicles, including two gray vans with no rear windows and blacked-out windshields.

Just inside the Espresso Pump, Buffy stepped back a bit from the door when she saw another of those gray vans cruise by slowly. It seemed too quiet, almost as though it were rolling along without an engine. Ridiculous, of course. She had not heard anything because of the hum of the many machines inside the café. But eerie nevertheless.

A car pulled up in front of the Sun Cinema across the street. Buffy was only slightly surprised to see a haggard-looking middle-aged couple climb out together. They walked around to the trunk, from which they retrieved a trio of large film canisters. Revulsion rippled through her as she realized what was going on. These people were collaborators. Whatever was in the canisters, they were films that had been brought in to be screened for the vampires that now populated Sunnydale.

Maybe they had no choice, Buffy thought. But she knew that they all had a choice, the people who still lived in this town. Some of them might not be cooperating with the vampires, but rather were paralyzed by their fear, too terrified to fight. The people remaining in Sunnydale could have banded together and killed their masters, or simply run off while the sun was up. Some probably *had* fled. But Buffy knew that she would have to be careful. Whether collaborators or simply ruled by their fear, she could not afford to trust anyone who was still here.

The whole town belonged to the monsters now, one enormous lair for the vampires she had come to know as Kakchiquels, the servants of Camazotz. With this as the epicenter, they were building a kingdom, an empire even. Their control extended at least to El Suerte, probably farther.

Buffy needed answers.

As soon as the human couple had disappeared inside the theater, Buffy went back out into the alley behind the Espresso Pump again. With the canvas bag of weapons slung across her back, she moved lithely through the hidden places of Sunnydale, always alert for watchful eyes. Even the humans here could not be trusted, that much was now certain.

The going was slow due to the need for stealth, but within twenty minutes she found herself on a block of warehouses, factories and office buildings that ran parallel to the street where the Bronze sat. There were other bars there as well, and it stood to reason she might be able to catch a human out during the daylight.

Answers. The need to hear it from the lips of a living, breathing human being was strong in here. Her instinct, and her own memories of the place, had suggested this would be a good neighborhood to start. If that didn't work, she might try at the college, or simply break into a home that looked as though it were still occupied.

It had occurred to her that the initial skirmishes she'd had with the Kakchiquels all those years ago had been in Docktown, but it would take too long for her to get over there. She had a couple of hours, probably less, before dark. If possible, she wanted to be out of Sunnydale by then. Otherwise she would need a safe place to use as her base, and had no idea where to begin.

Buffy slid between an enormous trash bin and the brick wall of a warehouse. Fifteen feet above the ground was an iron ladder that led to the roof. Without hesitation, she splayed her hands against the brick on one side and the metal bin on the other and crawled up between the two. Muscles rippled like cables in her arms.

With a push off the wall, she landed atop the trash bin, balanced on the metal lip of the thing. Buffy sprang from her perch and both hands locked around the bottom rung of the ladder. Feet against the building, she pulled herself up and then was scrambling hand over hand to the roof.

Crouched low, she sprinted across the rooftop to the opposite corner, where she could see the street that ran in front of the Bronze, as well as the alley beside the building she was on. Disappointment deflated her. The street below was empty of movement of any kind. A stray beer bottle, pushed by the wind, rolled across pavement with a tinkle of glass. Otherwise, all was silence.

For ten minutes or more, Buffy sat there at the edge of the roof. From that height, she could see almost as far as Docktown to the east, the blazing sun on top of the cinema downtown off to the north, and to the south, the tops of houses in residential neighborhoods.

It was as though the entire town had been killed, drained by a vampire. Yet it seethed with menace, as if at any moment its eyes would open, burning orange, and it would rise with fangs gnashing, thirsting for blood.

Anxious, Buffy bounced on the balls of her feet and glanced time and again at the deepening hues of blue on the horizon and the long afternoon shadows on the street.

"I've gotta get out of here," she whispered.

Almost as if on cue, the sound of a distant engine came to her. Buffy crouched down even farther and glanced furtively up and down the street. A moment later, she saw the same gray van—or another exactly like it—cruising toward her.

CITY COLLEGE

With a small squeak of brakes, it stopped in front of the Bronze. There was a moment's pause and then the horn blared twice and the passenger door opened.

The figure that emerged from the van made Buffy shiver, though the sun shone warmly on her. She could not see if it was male or female, but it was clothed in a silver radiation suit that covered it from head to toe. Only the black goggles across its eyes broke up the endless silver. Not an inch of skin was visible.

Vampire, she thought, and instantly knew it was true. Daylight reflected off the folds in its silver suit, but the monster was safe within that protective garb.

The driver of the van beeped again and the front door of the Bronze slammed open. A tall human man with black hair came out of the club, hands in the air.

"All right, all right! Keep your shirt on!" he snapped.

The vampire walked around to the back of the van and opened the door. From what Buffy could tell from that angle, there was nothing inside the van. Then the man turned back toward the Bronze and shouted inside.

"Move it! Come on, kiddies. Everyone has to take a turn."

Almost immediately, six more people came out of the club, all in their late teens, early twenties. Three male, three female. One of the girls began to sob and hesitate, unwilling to climb into the van with the others. The dark-haired man went to her, held her face in his hands and whispered something that made her stiffen, wide-eyed. After that she went meekly to the back of the van and climbed in.

The vampire returned to the front of the van, climbed in, and then the vehicle rolled away.

For a moment, the dark-haired man stared after it. Then he went to the door of the Bronze and locked it up before walking to a brand-new convertible Mercedes parked along the road amongst several other cars.

He got in and started the engine. Then he took a moment to tilt his head back and regard himself in the mirror, fussing with his hair.

Which was when Buffy recognized him.

"Oh my God," she whispered. *"Parker."*

The last time she had seen him he had been a freshman in college. He had seduced her, used her, and then pretended he had done nothing wrong. Now he was five years older, and Parker Abrams was not only collaborating with the vampires, he seemed to be enjoying himself.

"Son of a bitch," Buffy muttered angrily.

She withdrew from the edge of the building eight or ten feet, paused, then ran full tilt. With a grunt of effort and anger, she sprang out across the narrow alleyway below. The gap was broader than she had judged and she extended her body forward, turned her leap into a dive. Buffy made it across with room to spare, hit the roof of the Bronze and tucked into a roll.

Without a pause, she flowed back to her feet and ran across the building to stare down at Parker's car. The Mercedes slid into reverse, but moved only two feet as he attempted to pull out from between two other vehicles.

He was right below her.

Buffy leaped out into open air, her hair whipping behind her as she fell straight down, canvas bag dragging behind her like an unopened parachute. Though it lasted only a heartbeat or two, the fall seemed extremely slow to her. Parker had turned the steering wheel and put the car in drive again, and even as she fell he began to pull forward slowly, at pains to be sure he cleared the bumper of the car in front of him.

Her boots slammed the hood of the Mercedes with a loud crumpling noise. The impact made her teeth clack together and drove her to her knees.

Parker screamed in surprise and fear and for just a moment, forgot he was driving. The bumper of the Mercedes rapped lightly against the car in front of it.

He didn't even notice. He only stared at her. "What—" he muttered. "Who the—" Parker's eyes went wide, and she knew then that he had recognized her.

"Oh Jesus. *You.*"

Buffy rose from the dented hood and gripped the top of the convertible's windshield. Parker gripped the wheel, cut it as far to the left as he could, and pressed the accelerator. He clipped the other car's bumper again, but Buffy flipped herself over the windshield and into the passenger's seat.

"No!" Parker yelled.

Beside him now, Buffy shot her right hand out and latched on to his throat, squeezing.

"Stop the car."

Parker slammed on the brakes. "Buffy, please," he rasped hoarsely, eyes roving desperately, searching the streets.

It turned her stomach to think that he might be hoping the vampires might still be there, might protect him from her.

"You remember me. You know who I am. Let me ask you, do you know *what* I am?"

Choking, he managed a wheezing "yes." His eyes were on her, and Buffy stared back at him until Parker looked away. She released his throat and he began to massage it, almost whimpering. When she reached around to pull her canvas bag into her lap, he flinched.

"I'm going to ask questions. You're going to drive. If I think you're lying, I'll snap your neck. Any doubt in your mind that I mean what I say?" she demanded.

He hesitated. Then he smiled, as if relieved. His eyes still had the sparkle that had charmed her once upon a time. "Buffy," he said amiably. "You don't have to threaten me."

Nostrils flaring, she turned to glare at him. "You took advantage of me once, Parker. But that was a long time ago. Do I look like that girl to you now?"

Cowed, he gave her the once-over, then shook his head.

"I'll break you," she promised. "Just drive."

"Where to?"

Her thoughts skittered off in several directions at once. There was no way to know how far Camazotz's influence had spread. But she was certain that there was no way a city the size of Los Angeles could have been overrun. If it had, they wouldn't still be based here in Sunnydale.

"South," she said.

Parker drove.

A car passed going the other direction. She watched to be sure Parker made no attempt to signal the driver, likely another collaborator on his way to open up some business that would serve the vampires. The shadows had grown longer. The sky on the western horizon had begun to darken.

Nightfall was imminent.

"Faster," Buffy instructed.

"Your wish is my command."

"Guess you're pretty good at that response," Buffy snarled. "How long have they been in control here?"

"In Sunnydale? Going on four years, I guess. It started small at first, a few people here and there disappeared. Then the cops and the professors up at the college started acting weird. The new mayor, too. Night classes. Evening press conferences. At some point, there were enough of them to just take the town. They did it all in one night, after that. The winter solstice, y'know? Longest night of the year."

The wind seemed almost chilly as it whipped around the convertible.

"How many are there?"

Parker shrugged. "No idea."

"My friends. My mother. What happened to them?"

"I never met your mother. And I haven't seen Willow or that other guy since before that night."

Buffy winced, hurt by his ignorance. She wanted so badly to know what had become of her friends. But Parker could not help her.

"How far does their influence extend?"

"I heard they've turned the governor. But that's just the beginning of the king's plans for the state. Same as he did here, he's gonna turn officials and people in power, then build up enough of an army to take the whole state at once. Right now it's just around here. Sunnydale's like ground zero, with maybe thirty square miles in his control. He's smart about it, though. Keeps other towns functioning, even has people in some of them thinking nothing's changed, not even knowing the vampires have taken over. Morons. The leeches keep reproducing, though. It's only a matter of time."

His words chilled and infuriated her.

"Those people, the ones you gave to the vampires, who were they?"

Parker swallowed loud enough for her to hear it. He twitched a little. "They're . . . like me. We play along, we live pretty good. But we all have to take turns going to the lair. They . . . use us. Drink, whatever else they want. One night only. Then they throw us back until it's our turn again."

Bile rose in the back of Buffy's throat and her stomach convulsed. She nearly threw up right there in the car. Her nose crinkled with her distaste. Then she remembered something else he'd said.

"King."

"What's that?"

"Camazotz has them all calling him 'the king' now? It wasn't enough being the god of bats?"

Parker actually chuckled and shook his head. "You really have been away, haven't you, Buffy?"

Buffy frowned. "What the hell's that supposed to mean?"

But he did not answer. The evening had darkened the eastern sky to a bruised purple, though to the west it was still a baby blue. Minutes left before true night.

Ahead was the intersection with Royal Street, which ran alongside the north end of Hammersmith Park, a quarter of a mile from her mother's house. The light was yellow.

Parker began to slow down.

"Don't stop."

But he only smiled. Alarmed, Buffy turned to see a gray van speeding up behind them.

"Go!" she snapped at him.

Up ahead, a second van barreled down Royal Street. Its brakes squealed as it came to a shuddering halt, blocking the way in front of them. The van behind them slewed sideways, preventing them from retreating.

Furious, Buffy shot an elbow into Parker's side, then punched him in the side of the head. The car was hemmed in front and back. Resigned to a fight, wary of the encroaching dark, she grabbed her bag and leaped up to stand on the seat. Her hands went into the bag and withdrew the crossbow, nocking a bolt into place. She shot a glance at Parker and saw that he was groggy, but conscious. He reached for the steering wheel and the gearshift.

With a grunt, Buffy kicked him in the head and he slumped over the wheel. The car horn began to blare incessantly.

Ahead of her, four vampires in silver suits climbed out of the van. Three others emerged from the vehicle behind her.

Seven. She'd faced worse odds.

The sky seemed to grow darker in the space between one blink and another. It seemed to Buffy that eyes stared ominously down at her from the windows of every building around her. She thought of her mother's house, so close and yet impossibly far, and tried not to think of what she might find if she dared go there.

On the corner was a coffee and doughnut place she and her mother had been to a hundred times. Its familiar presence seemed almost to mock the way she knew the world *should* be. The nineteen-year-old soul that shared a double existence with its older counterpart inside her retreated even farther within.

"Come on!" she cried, outraged, prepared to tear down this ugly new world and rebuild the old, even if she had to do it alone.

The four vampires in front of the Mercedes started toward her. Buffy laughed darkly and shot a crossbow bolt at the one in front. It exploded into a burst of dust inside its silver suit, and the suit crumpled to the ground, empty. Buffy had nocked another bolt into the crossbow in an instant.

Then the vampires began to remove their goggles and hoods. It was dark enough now, and it was as though they wanted her to see them, to realize that they did not fear her. She might kill them, they seemed to be saying, but she was in enemy territory, surrounded now, and with more on the way.

Buffy fired again, but this time the vampire that was her target moved swiftly, dodging the bolt.

She nocked another one, prepared to fire as one by one they removed their hoods. With a harsh intake of breath, she recognized two of the vampires in front of her. One was a female with green-dyed punk hair, face covered in garish, red and white greasepaint. The other was an ugly male who seemed always to accompany her. Though Buffy did not know their real names, during their skirmishes—years ago—she had come to think of them as Clownface and Bulldog.

They knew, she thought. *Knew where I was, all along.* It could not be coincidence that of all the vampires in Sunnydale, these two were the ones who had caught up with her.

Out of the corner of her eye, Buffy caught motion behind her. Alert, ready to defend herself, she spun to see that the other three had also begun to approach her. They had already removed their hoods and goggles.

She knew them all.

Blond, bubbly Harmony had been in her high school class. The dead girl waved almost shyly, a sweet, stupid grin on her face. But Harmony did not worry her. It was the other two that made Buffy curse out loud.

Spike and Drusilla.

Willow sat in her dormitory room amidst a circle of white candles, their flames casting a sickly yellow glow upon the walls, flickering shadows of things that had no form. It was dark outside, but clouds blotted out the stars.

Something prevented her from summoning Lucy Hanover. For more than an hour she had tried. Now she bit her lip and fought the despair that threatened to overwhelm her.

"Lucy, please," Willow whispered into the seething shadows. "I need help. You're the only one who might have answers. Please."

With her heart and soul she reached out into the dark, into the spiritual ether she had mentally touched several times before. Something cold touched Willow's back, and she flinched in fear and shock.

"Lucy?"

As one, the candles blew out, smoke wafting up from each of them, glittering in the dark. The tendrils seemed to reach out to one another, to twine into a web of smoke, to spin and weave together into a hideous shadow face, a snarling, horned thing whose eyes seemed like endless black pits.

"Noooooo . . ." it groaned with pain and anger.

Though the windows were closed, a sudden wind rushed through the room and the smoke dissipated. Willow shivered as the temperature dropped precipitously. She blinked, searching for some sign of that malevolent presence.

Lucy was there, hovering half a foot above the ground. Her spectral form seemed even more faint than ever, a ghost of a ghost. Willow whispered her name and the spirit smiled weakly.

"I am here, friend Willow," Lucy said, her otherworldly voice quavering.

"What was that?"

"The creature was a soul-eater. My will proved too strong for it, but it has been thwarting my attempts to reach you. It attacked me here on the Ghost Roads, in the moment just before The Prophet showed the Slayer the future. I fear that it may not have been coincidence."

Willow slumped over, one hand over her mouth, and squeezed her eyes shut. Only for a moment, though. Then she stood, determined, and faced the ghost.

"You've gotta help me figure out what's going on," she said. "Ever since that night, Buffy's been all wigged. At first I thought maybe she was just pushing us away, that she was gonna go all Lone Ranger, take Camazotz down herself and get Giles back."

Something rolled over in Willow's stomach and she shuddered.

"She hasn't even tried, Lucy. I live here. I see her. She goes to half her classes, and she's looking over her shoulder all the time, paranoid, like any second, hello, ambush! But she's the Slayer. She gets ambushed all the time. Comes with the territory. And not usually during the day. It just isn't like her."

Willow paused, a chill creeping through her. When she looked up, she saw the phantom of the dead Slayer gazing dolefully down upon her, swaying slightly in the dim room.

"Lucy?"

"Where are your friends? Do they agree?"

"Definitely. It's been two days and Buffy hasn't done anything about Giles, so we're going to do it ourselves. Oz is tracking down the ship, and Xander and Anya are getting some weapons from Giles's apartment. We're going in tonight to save him, with or without her."

"Of course I will aid as best I can," Lucy agreed. *"But what of Buffy? Your words have given rise to a terrible suspicion. I think it best we find her and put that suspicion to the test before even attempting the rescue you have planned."*

Willow hesitated. A whispered voice in the back of her mind told her that it was already too late for Giles. But she would not listen. She was determined to find him and bring him back alive. The last thing she wanted to do was to wait another day.

"We're going in after Giles in the morning," she said. "I don't know what to do about—"

A key rattled in the lock. The door opened, and Buffy walked in. Willow's breath caught in her throat as she saw her friend stiffen, a dark look spreading across the Slayer's face.

"Buffy," Willow whispered.

"No," Lucy Hanover said, her voice like a breeze rustling through the trees. *"That is not Buffy Summers."*

Willow shot a glance at the ghost, then back at the doorway. She shook her head, not understanding. Buffy shot the gossamer spirit of the former Slayer a hard look, then smiled grimly.

It was the smile that convinced Willow.

"Oh my God."

Buffy crossed to her bed, bent down and reached beneath it, and retrieved a duffel bag. Willow could only stare at her, frozen with shock and grief.

"It is The Prophet," Lucy said. *"Whatever she is, the creature has taken Buffy's physical form."*

The Slayer began to open drawers and throw clothes into the bag. "It was foolish of me to think I would be able to stay here. Though it would have been more convenient, it is simpler to start over."

Willow could only stare as she zipped the bag, but as soon as The Prophet began to move toward the door, she moved to block the way. Fear and disbelief were supplanted within her by a kind of anger unlike anything she had ever known. She shook her head, jaw clenched tightly.

"You're not leaving," Willow said. "Not until you bring Buffy back."

A brittle, severe expression settled upon Buffy's face, and Willow wondered how she could not have noticed the change in her best friend. This thing in front of her was not Buffy.

"Move, witch."

Willow glanced once at Lucy, hoping that the ghost would have some way to remove The Prophet. But the specter only floated, a soul-haze and nothing more. She could not help. Willow swallowed hard and begin to inscribe arcane symbols upon the air with her fingers. Her lips moved silently as she mouthed a spell that would lock them all in the room.

With a guttural laugh, The Prophet backhanded Willow, who staggered backward and slammed into her desk before crumbling to the floor.

Dazed, she dragged herself to her feet.

But the door hung open, and The Prophet was gone. Buffy was gone.

And if Willow did not catch up with her, she might never know what had truly become of her best friend.

The car horn kept blaring. Parker, unconscious, was slumped over the wheel and Buffy could not spare even a moment to slide him off.

Spike and Drusilla.

"Well, well, Dru, look what we've got here," Spike called happily, preening like a rooster as he took a few steps toward the car. His hair was longer now, almost shaggy, giving him a more feral aspect. "That little Summers girl, isn't it? I thought she was a house pet now. Soft little kitten."

Drusilla's mad eyes widened and she made tiny

scratching motions in the air, then licked her lips. "Ooh, I love kittens. We know just what to do with kitties, don't we, Spike?"

There was bloodlust in Spike's eyes. "Oh, we certainly do, pet. We certainly do."

Harmony stared at Drusilla. "You don't hurt kittens. Tell me you don't hurt kittens."

Dru seemed shocked. "Only when I'm hungry. I'm not a monster."

It took Buffy only a heartbeat to calculate the odds. These three behind her, three more in front. Parker's Mercedes was hemmed in on both sides. Six of them. She'd killed six at once before. More than that, in fact.

But not *these* six.

Harmony and the stranger wouldn't be a problem. But Buffy knew from experience that Clownface and Bulldog were tough enough. Spike and Drusilla, though, that was the final nail.

I'm not ready. Not now. The world had changed and she had to find her place in it. At the same time, she knew that another world awaited her in the past, a place . . . a home . . . where she was desperately needed. She had to return there.

What had she told Faith, so long ago? The first rule of slaying: *Don't die.*

Once the decision was made within her, Buffy acted in an instant. She ratcheted around, fired a crossbow bolt at Spike. He snatched it out of the air, and then glared at her as though his feelings were hurt.

Buffy dove across the unconscious Parker, who slid off the horn. She popped open the door, then used her prodigious strength to shove him out onto the pavement. Her bag dropped onto the seat beside her with the crossbow, and she reached into it for one of the stakes she had made.

The vampires saw that she intended to flee, and rushed at the car.

"Dammit, Buffy! I never took you for a coward," Spike snapped at her. "I'm disappointed."

Buffy slammed the Mercedes into reverse and floored the gas. Spike and Drusilla had learned to be fast. It was part of the reason they had stayed alive as long as they had. They split up, each diving out of the way of the car in opposite directions.

Harmony stood frozen behind the car, her mouth open as though she were somehow offended. The Mercedes slammed into her, drove her back with all the horsepower the engine had. The car crashed broadside into the van with Harmony in the middle. There was a sickening crunch and she screamed, a shriek so wild and agonized that it seemed to be tearing her throat apart.

Buffy spun the wheel to the right in order to avoid running over Parker, dropped it into drive, and floored it again. Spike and Drusilla had gotten up and were rushing at her from either side, but the tires spun under the Mercedes, laying a black rubber patch on the pavement, and the car lurched forward, away from them.

Behind her, Harmony tumbled to the ground, the

top and bottom of her body only connected by torn flesh and a crushed spine. Her upper torso twitched as though she were having a seizure, but her legs lay still.

In the rearview, Buffy caught a glimpse of Spike and Drusilla running to their van.

The Mercedes raced around to one side of the van in front, but the other three vampires were there already, coming for her. Buffy lifted up the crossbow in her right hand, targeted the one she did not recognize, and fired even as he leaped toward the car. The bolt found its mark and the monster dusted, orange-blazing eyes the last to disintegrate.

Buffy tossed the empty crossbow into the backseat as Clownface jumped onto the hood of the Mercedes at the last possible moment. Then Bulldog leaped onto the trunk and tossed himself into the backseat. The Slayer swore loudly.

Her right hand gripped the stake that lay beside her. With all her strength, she stomped on the brake.

Clownface sailed off the hood and rolled onto the pavement, even as Bulldog was thrown into the front seat. The pug-faced vampire slammed his head against the dashboard, but struggled to right himself.

Buffy punched the stake through his heart and he imploded, scattering dust all over the upholstery.

She accelerated again. Just as Clownface was getting up, Buffy ran her down. The car rocked as she drove right over the vampire, and then she was away, leaving them behind. Spike and Drusilla gave chase in the van, but they had no hope of catching up to her. Not in the Mercedes.

Clownface wasn't dead. Buffy knew that. But three out of six wasn't bad for a girl who was only trying to get away. *Maybe I should have stayed,* she thought. But she pushed the idea away. *Priorities.*

A few miles and a left turn out of view, and she had lost Spike and Drusilla. As she drove through the darkness, streetlights flashing across her face, Buffy kept an eye out for other gray vans, or any vehicle that might try to get in her way.

She had gotten away, but she wasn't free. Not until she had traveled beyond the area Camazotz controlled. And Buffy had a feeling that was not going to be easy.

CITY COLLEGE
LEARNING RESOURCE SERVICE

CHAPTER 4

The houses on Redwood Lane reminded Buffy painfully of the neighborhood where she had lived during high school. Perfectly groomed lawns, a smattering of trees—though none of them redwoods—and a minivan or SUV in every driveway. She had abandoned the Mercedes three blocks away, and as she skulked along from house to house, it unnerved her how silent they were. No loud voices, no radios. The few lights inside barely showed through the curtains and shades drawn across every window.

Six miles from the center of town, and still no one dared breathe loud enough to attract the vampires' attention.

Halfway down the block, Buffy paused in front of an imposing Spanish-style house, and put her back against the stucco just beside a side window. From within, she could just barely hear a television set. In the driveway sat a Volvo sedan, maybe three or four years old.

She hesitated only for a moment. Then she slipped around the back of the house and across the patio to the rear door. A heavy wooden door, not a glass slider. That was good. Less noise.

Buffy kicked the door open and the three locks on it splintered the frame with a tearing of wood. It crashed open, the sound echoing out into the night. She only hoped that, locked up tight in their homes, no one would hear it.

"Oh God, no!" someone cried within the house.

Buffy rushed through the kitchen and into the living room where a haggard looking couple in their late forties cowered in a corner by the television set.

"How . . . we didn't invite you in!" the man shouted, panicked.

They thought she was a vampire.

"No," Buffy said, both hands up as she approached them. "Just sit tight, right there, and I won't hurt you. I swear I won't. Cooperate, and maybe I can even get you out of here."

They stared at her as though she were mad.

"Where's the phone?"

"What do you mean out of here? You're not trying to leave, are you?" the woman said, horrified.

"You *want* to stay?" Buffy asked. "Where's the phone?"

"On the wall in the kitchen," the man said. "You passed right by it. But please don't talk to anyone like this on our phone. They'll hear you. They'll think we're involved."

Buffy had already started back toward the kitchen, but paused at his words. She turned to stare at him again.

"What do you mean 'they'll hear'?"

"They listen," the woman replied.

With a sigh, Buffy shook her head. "Of course they do. Can't have anybody spilling the blood-soaked beans, now, can we? Still, they can't listen to every phone twenty-four hours a day. They've got you scared 'cause you never know when they're listening.

"Look, it doesn't matter anyway. We'll be gone by the time anyone can get here." She regarded them closely. "I'm Buffy. What are your names?"

The couple exchanged a tired, frightened glance. The woman stood up first, followed by her husband, but they kept their distance.

"I'm Nadine Ross. This is my husband Andrew."

"Nice to meet you. Sorry about the door. Come into the kitchen." Buffy led the way, and the Rosses followed. "Have a seat," she said, gesturing toward the breakfast table. They slid chairs out and stood gazing at her anxiously as she picked up the phone.

There was a strange clicking sound before the dial tone.

Buffy stared at it for a second. Of all the phone numbers she knew by heart, most of them would be useless now. Her mother's. The numbers of all her friends in Sunnydale. But there were two others, one that she had used only a few times, and another she had never even dialed, yet she knew both of them by heart.

The first was a Los Angeles number. Angel's number. Holding her breath, Buffy dialed, but the number was out of service. She closed her eyes and held the phone against her forehead.

Where are you, Angel?

"Please," the woman whispered behind her.

Ignoring her, Buffy dialed information for Los Angeles. She asked for the number for Angel Investigations, but the operator said there was no listing under that name. Wesley Wyndam-Pryce? Again, no listing. Cordelia Chase?

Unlisted.

As disappointed as she was, this last bit of information fanned a tiny spark of hope in Buffy's chest. It might be unlisted, but Cordelia had a phone number. Somewhere in this insane world, someone she knew still lived.

Buffy thumbed a button on the phone to disconnect, then waited for a new dial tone. There was only one other number she might call for help. It was a long sequence. Time might have caused part of it to change. Given that she had only memorized it, but never used it, she feared that she might have gotten it wrong.

Her chest rose and fell more quickly as she punched in the numbers. She felt the eyes of the people whose home she had invaded, and she shifted uncomfortably under their fearful, accusing gaze.

Somewhere on the other side of the Atlantic, a phone began to ring. Buffy let out a shuddering breath of relief as the tinny sound reached her ears. There was a click as the call was answered.

"Yes?"

The voice was British. Buffy had never heard such a welcome sound.

"This is Buffy Summers."

A pause, a harsh intake of breath. "That isn't funny. Who is this?"

"Who the hell is this?" she snapped, angry and frustrated. "Put Quentin Travers on the phone!"

Another pause. "Dear God, it really is you, isn't it? My name is Alan Fontaine, Miss Summers. Quentin Travers is dead. Where are you?"

"Behind enemy lines and headed south," she said. "Can you help?"

"Hold on."

She heard a muffled sound and assumed he had put a hand over the phone. Dull voices could be heard, and a moment later, Fontaine came back on the line.

"Do you know Donatello's? An Italian restaurant just off your one-oh-nine freeway?"

Buffy thought about it, found a vague recollection of the place. "I think so."

"That's the border. We can have an extraction team waiting for you there. One hour."

One hour, Buffy thought. A smile spread across

her face. One hour, and then she could begin to make sense of this insane world, this horrid future.

"If I'm not there it means I'm dead," she replied. "Oh, and this line is bugged. There could be a Welcome Wagon there waiting for me and for your team."

"One hour," Fontaine repeated. "And Buffy?"

"Yes?"

"I'm glad you're alive."

He hung up, and before she could do the same, Buffy heard a series of rapid clicks on the other end. Though she knew there was no way the vampires could monitor all calls at all times, a dreadful certainty filled her that they had listened to at least part of *this* call.

One hour.

She hung up the phone and turned to the Rosses. They flinched, and would not meet her gaze.

"Keys to the Volvo. Now."

Andrew Ross shook a bit as he stood to face her, face growing red. "Just a goddamn second. Maybe you scare me. Hell, you kicked in a door with three deadbolts in it. But I'm not just going to hand you my keys."

"Are you kidding?" Buffy asked, amazed. "I'm not going to leave you two here. You're coming with me."

"They'll kill us," Nadine hissed, scandalized.

Andrew crossed his arms defiantly. "We're not going anywhere."

Buffy gaped at them. After a moment, she shook her head in astonishment. "All right, look, I'm not going to make you come. The last thing I need is to wrestle with people I'm trying to help. And maybe you're right, maybe you're safer here until the nest is destroyed. But I need your car, and I'm taking it.

"Now, keys."

"They'll . . . they'll think we helped you," Andrew stammered.

With a sigh, Buffy strode across the room and decked him. She pulled the punch, but it would leave a hell of a bruise. Andrew moaned as he sat up on the linoleum. Nadine just stared at them both.

"*Now* they won't think you helped by choice. I don't have time to be nice. Give me the keys."

Nadine hurried across the kitchen and picked up her purse, rifled through it and dug out a key ring. She tossed them, jangling, to Buffy.

"I'll be back," Buffy told them.

The couple only stared at her, Nadine with her purse clutched defensively in front of her and Andrew on his butt on the floor, one hand over the rapidly rising welt on his face.

"What's wrong with you people? I want to help."

"No one can help," Nadine whispered.

"This is helping?" Andrew snapped. "You can go to hell."

"This *is* hell," Buffy told them grimly. "And I've already stayed too long. I'm outta here."

She went out the front door and loped across the lawn to the Volvo. As she drove, Buffy tried not to think about the Rosses and the fear that kept them from even trying to run away. Her destination, Donatello's, was about nine miles away. If the vampires were listening, they knew where she was headed. The only advantages she had at the moment were that they did not know what she was driving, and that she knew the roads. There were half a dozen ways to get where she was going.

The hard part was going to be guessing correctly which one of them would get her there alive.

After high school graduation, Xander Harris had retreated to the basement of his parents' house and a series of dead-end jobs, not because he could do nothing else, but because he was burdened with a depressing ambivalence. He just had no idea what he wanted to do next. All he did know was that he did not want to sit in another classroom as long as he lived. And, while hanging out in the cramped, damp space he called an apartment while his parents battled it out upstairs was not his ideal living arrangement, it had a certain charm in the area of personal finance.

Still, he knew there was more for him to do in life. It was only that he could not figure out what that might be. Thinking about it made his head ache, but once he started, it was impossible to turn the flow of thoughts off. *Ironic,* he thought, given that his girlfriend was curled up naked under the sheets, half asleep with her head on his chest and one leg thrown over his torso.

"Mmm," Anya purred.

Xander sighed. Between his general dissatisfaction with the way his life was headed and the fact that despite her vow to rescue Giles, Buffy hadn't done a damn thing to get him away from the demon Camazotz, he could barely concentrate on Anya. Buffy was acting so weird, that they were all going to go after Giles tonight, to rescue him themselves. He and Anya had even done a little old-fashioned trespassing at the ex-Watcher's house to gather up the weapons they'd need.

It's not fair, he thought sullenly.

His eyes fluttered closed. Anya snuggled up closer and Xander felt himself at last begin to relax. Though he knew Willow and Oz were due in the next hour or so, sleep seemed to be his only escape from the confusion and worry that plagued him.

Bamm! Bamm! Bamm!

His eyes snapped open and he stared at the ceiling for a minute, wondering if he had dreamed the knocking. Anya had not stirred at all. Then it came again, a hard rapping at the door that led out into the backyard, the door people used if they wanted to visit him. Willow was early.

Anya shifted, moaned a bit, and one eye slitted open. "Make them go away or I'll put a pox on them."

Xander smiled down at her uncertainly. "You're not a demon anymore, sweetie, remember?"

She sighed. "There are times . . ."

But Anya did not finish the thought. Xander climbed out of bed and pulled on sweatpants and a tee shirt as he went to open the door. As soon as it was open a crack, Willow pushed her way in. She had an enormous red welt on the side of her face, and a crazed look in her eyes.

"Xander, we have to find Buffy. She's not Buffy. I think she's going to try to leave town and we have to stop her."

Oz followed her at a more leisurely pace. Xander stared at Willow for a second, then glanced at Oz.

"Hey," Xander said.

"Hey."

"What's all this about not-Buffy?"

Oz nodded. "Possessed, apparently. Body thief, I'm guessing."

Anya sat up in bed, covers clutched at her throat, and glared daggers at all of them. "You are early."

Willow shot her a hard look, then rolled her eyes and looked at Xander again. "Come on. Saddle up. We're not gonna let this happen. If Buffy—or whoever hijacked her—gives us the slip, we may never get our friend back."

"Okay, okay, we just need to get dressed. But what about Giles? I mean, not that I was looking forward to sashaying into the lair of the ancient bat-god with a passel of vampires running around the place, but someone's gotta get him out."

Oz raised an eyebrow. "Sashaying?"

Willow rounded on Xander then, but there was no anger in her eyes, just fear and a lingering sadness. "Confession? Always kinda hoped I'd leak our plan to Buffy and she'd feel all guilty and go do the rescuing herself. Apparently no longer in the cards. I don't even want to think about Giles right now, Xander. I can't, because then I'll remember how I'm thinking, hey, he's probably dead, and I can't handle that grief. It would paralyze me, you understand?"

It was as though, with Buffy and Giles out of action, Willow had just stepped right up to the plate. She was in charge, all of a sudden, and Xander was surprised with how all right with that he was.

"Poor Giles," Anya said. "It's Buffy's fault, you know. If she hadn't been all high and mighty—"

"*If* Giles is still alive, we have to pray he lasts until morning," Willow went on. "Whatever this thing is that's taken Buffy over, Lucy Hanover is following it. Following . . . her. Right now, that's our priority. We're going to find a way to expel this thing out of Buffy. You and Oz may have to hold her long enough for me to do the spell, but—"

Xander held up a hand. *"Un momento,"* he interrupted. "Some evil spirit is holding the reins on Buffy's Slayer-powered figure, and we're supposed to hold on to her."

Willow shot him a withering glare.

"Just checking," Xander added quietly. "Wouldn't miss it, personally."

On her way south, Buffy passed through Citrus Beach, a tiny, trendy little hamlet with a single block of bistros and shops frequented only by the wealthy and their parasites.

In that respect, it had not changed.

As she drove along the strip in Citrus Beach, Buffy slowed the Volvo and peered out the window. The sidewalks were swarming with nightlife, packs of drunken Kakchiquels, their trademark black tattoos gleaming as headlights splashed across them. They sat in outdoor patio dining areas at the bistros, served by human waiters, many of whom had wide, terrified eyes, though others only looked numb, shell-shocked. The vampires roamed the streets in packs like Mardi Gras revelers, crying catcalls at passing cars.

It wasn't just vampires, either. For each clutch of undead, there were humans as well. Men and women who fawned over the Kakchiquels or gazed at them like obedient lap dogs. Buffy spotted a man on a leash, his head shaved bald, clothed only in ragged blue jeans and garish, obscene tattoos that had been etched into his skin, presumably by his masters.

Amongst the throng she spotted several demons as well.

I should stop, she thought. *These people . . .*

The thought dissipated. *First rule of Slaying.* Buffy gripped the wheel tighter, her knuckles whitening, but she kept driving, even accelerated. Several of the Kakchiquels hooted at her as she passed, beastly vampire faces on display for the world to see. Buffy flashed back to the others of their tribe she had known, the grim, silent, deadly killers. These were nothing like the others, and she wondered why.

Questions. Too many questions in her head.

A pair of blond, female vampires clad in tight, red

leather pants and matching tops began to move into the street ahead of her. There was menace in their gaze and their stride, and Buffy had to speed up and swerve around them. She checked the rearview mirror and saw one of the twins make a gesture, but they did not pursue her.

Even so, Buffy did not slow down.

Now, more than ever, she wanted to put Sunnydale and Citrus Beach and the Kakchiquels behind her. The lights of the town flashed across her face, but soon she traveled into darkness again. The road wound south, away from Citrus Beach.

I'll come back, she thought, a silent vow to everyone still alive behind her.

It wasn't long before she came in sight of Freeway 109, but Buffy did not dare go that way. More than likely, the Kakchiquels would be waiting to ambush her there. Instead, she said a tiny prayer she would not get lost, and took a left onto a secondary road she thought would eventually take her, in a roundabout way, within a quarter mile of her destination.

For several minutes, she drove in silence, not even the radio for company. The smattering of neighborhoods and gas stations gave way to trees on both sides of the road. A gentle rise curved around and through the thick woods, and Buffy became alarmed. She did not recall a forest on this road and she could not afford to become lost.

Keep going, she told herself. *South. Just get out of here. A few more miles.*

The Volvo crested the hill. The road curved again as it began its descent on the other side. There were a few homes in amongst the trees, but these had lights on inside. She was not out of their territory yet, but those lights gave her hope.

The headlights washed over the trees, then the road straightened out. In the darkness far ahead, three cars were parked at odd angles, blocking the way completely.

"Dammit," Buffy whispered, there in the glow of the dash.

Instinctively, she reached out to shut off the headlights, but stopped herself. It was too late. They would have been watching for her, would have seen her coming long before she had noticed them. Her mind whirled. The Kakchiquels must have set roadblocks up along every route south. They were a couple of miles from the restaurant where she was supposed to meet the extraction team.

Her foot came off the brake. Almost before she knew what she was doing, Buffy floored the accelerator. Her seat belt was cinched tight, her hands gripped the wheel, and she aimed the nose of the Volvo right at the point where two of the cars ahead met grille to grille.

Don't die! an alarmed voice cried in her mind.

Working on it, she silently replied.

Vampires popped up from behind the cars. Doors opened and others stepped out. From the forest around the roadblock, others appeared, moving slowly down toward the road. Buffy's fingers flexed on the wheel. The headlights seemed to grow brighter, silhouetting each one of them, and the engine roared as she built up speed.

Buffy grinned.

She was doing better than sixty when the Volvo crashed into the roadblock. Buffy was thrust forward, the seat belt grabbed hold, bruised her, broke a rib, then the airbag erupted into her face and pushed her back against the seat. There was a screeching of metal like nothing she had ever heard, a shattering of glass as the Volvo rammed through the two cars, battering them aside, crushing at least one vampire.

The Volvo's bumper was caved in, scarred, twisted metal thrust down, punctured the tire. It blew, and the car slewed to one side, then flipped. Buffy struck her head against the driver's side window hard enough to break it as the Volvo rolled toward the tree line, and for a moment, she was unconscious.

When her eyes fluttered open she heard shouts of pain and fury. Her ribs hurt, and it felt as though someone had hammered a nail into each of her temples. She squeezed her eyes shut, then reached up to wipe the blood from her face. It was a surprise to find that the car had come to rest right side up. The airbag pressed her against the seat, but she reached out, clutched a large shard of glass, and punctured it.

As she looked out through the shattered glass, the vampires began to cluster around the ruined vehicles they had used for their roadblock. It was steel and fiberglass carnage. The headlights of the one car that was mostly intact shone in oily sparkles off the gasoline that seeped from the other two ravaged cars. The Kakchiquels seemed stunned for a moment, as though they had no idea how to proceed.

Then, among them, Buffy saw a pale, raven-haired creature rise up, gossamer gown fluttering around her.

Drusilla.

Perhaps thirty yards separated them. The others were dazed, but in a moment, they would come for her, surround the car, drag her out. She counted at least a dozen. If she didn't move quickly, by numbers alone they might have her.

Her chest hurt with every breath, but Buffy built a wall between herself and that pain. There was no time for it. With the shouts of the vampires in her ears and the ghostly image of Drusilla rising from the wreckage burned into her mind, Buffy released her seat belt and lunged for the canvas bag that lay on the floor. Her fingers closed around the strap and she tried to pop open the door.

It was jammed shut from the crash.

She swung the bag out the broken window, then climbed out, tiny shards of glass pinpricking the backs of her legs. The wound she had gotten in her side while fighting August earlier that day—it seemed like forever to her now—tore open again.

"Smell her, puppies!" Drusilla cried in her singsong voice, hoarse with desire. "Like cinnamon and nutmeg. A fox hunt, now! A taste of her boldness to the first to make her scream, but save the eyes for me!"

Buffy shuddered, but would not look away from Drusilla's crazed, wide-eyed gaze. They thought she was going to run away.

No more running.

Instead, Buffy strode purposefully across the pavement toward them. The vampires had begun to lope toward her, but they paused in confusion when she did not flee. Even Drusilla cocked her head sideways, where it lolled as though broken.

"What's this?" the lunatic inquired in a childlike voice.

"This?" Buffy rammed a hand into the canvas bag and pulled out a road flare. "This is for Kendra."

She ignited the flare, then threw it skittering across the pavement into the pool of gasoline that spread across the road beneath the cars and around the feet of the vampires. There was a heartbeat when nothing happened, and all eyes turned to the blazing flare.

Buffy sprinted toward the tree line.

With a sound like an enormous flag flapping in the wind, the gas ignited into a sheet of flame. Vampires screamed as the fire engulfed them. Then the first of the gas tanks exploded, and the force of it thumped through Buffy's chest like the thunder of fireworks on the Fourth of July multiplied a thousandfold. She was thrown off her feet into the undergrowth at the edge of the woods, where she kept her head down.

The other two cars exploded in quick succession

and blazing chunks of their frames struck the pavement all around. Buffy felt the heat even through her clothes, and her arms felt as though she had been sunburned. She bled from dozens of tiny wounds, and ached as though she'd been worked over good.

But she was alive.

Buffy stood up, glanced down in surprise to find the canvas bag still clutched in her hand, then surveyed the conflagration in front of her. Most of the vampires had been incinerated already. On the other side of the inferno she could see four or five of them running up the road in the other direction.

Sudden motion, much closer, caught her eye. In the midst of the blaze, burning wreckage all around, Drusilla twirled in a mad ballet of fire, her arms flung out like a little girl, her head back. The vampire's hair had been scorched from her head and her entire body was in flames, yet she danced and giggled in a high, wild, disturbingly beautiful voice.

Then she burst into a swirling tornado of burning embers, ash and charred bone fragments . . . and then she was only dust, spinning still, blown about and then drifting across the night sky like confetti.

"For Kendra," the Slayer whispered.

Buffy turned and ran up into the trees, still headed south.

CITY COLLEGE

CHAPTER 5

The inside of Oz's van smelled like pine trees. When his band, Dingoes Ate My Baby, had a gig, he usually ended up carrying either the rest of the band or a lot of their equipment back and forth. Not one but three cardboard air fresheners hung from the dashboard to combat the smell of sweaty musicians and beer.

Willow liked the pine scent. It comforted her, the way anything about Oz did. He was not a big guy, not a particularly strong guy, but he was resolute as stone. She had no doubt at all that he would always be there to watch her back.

As Oz drove toward the Sunnydale bus station, Willow glanced at him from time to time. In the soft glow from the dash, his face was expressionless as always, but his eyes were alive, intense and filled with a fierce tenacity. Simply having him there with her made Willow think it was all possible. They could save Buffy.

They had to.

Anya and Xander had been silent in the backseat, but now Xander shifted forward.

"Where do you think she's headed?" he asked.

Willow shook her head. "I don't know. If we knew who she is . . . what she is . . . but we don't. And we've run out of time for research."

"Does it matter where she's going?" Anya asked. "It's almost ten o'clock. There can't be many more buses leaving tonight. The L.A. express, the airport shuttle, and probably one to Las Vegas. There's always one to Las Vegas. For the gambling and carousing."

Slowly, Willow turned to regard her quizzically.

Anya shrugged. "I've left town in a hurry once or twice."

"But you came back," Xander said softly, and slipped an arm around her.

As the lampposts above the bus station parking lot came into view ahead, Oz leaned forward and killed the headlights. He braked, and pulled to the curb before turning the engine off.

"How are we doing this?" he asked.

Willow took a calming breath, a bit unnerved by her sudden, unwanted promotion to leader-girl. Buffy was supposed to be the boss, Giles the strategist. *But they're not here,* she told herself. *It's on you, now.*

Self-conscious, she reached up to gingerly touch

the bruise on the side of her face where this not-Buffy had struck her. It hurt far more than had the older, fading bruise where her best friend had accidentally hit her days before. Willow wondered why that was, but thought she knew. This new one ached deeply, all the way down to her heart.

Another breath, as she forced the coming moments into a semblance of logic in her mind. Lucy Hanover had appeared to them while they were doing research and told them that the thing that had hijacked Buffy's body had come to rest at the bus station, where she now sat waiting for her bus to arrive.

"We have to assume that Buffy . . . that she didn't take off in the few minutes Lucy's ghost was with us. If she's still there, inside the station, I'm going to try the spell from the parking lot, out of sight of the windows. Anya's going to help. It may be that she'll sense me trying to drive her out. That's where you guys come in," Willow said, glancing from Oz to Xander and back. "If she runs, you have to stop her. Keep her down long enough for me to finish the spell."

Xander cleared his throat. "But you said 'cause you don't know what this thing is, you're not even sure it's going to work. What happens if it doesn't?"

Anya smiled at him. "Well, you two will be brutally thrashed, of course. This thing has all of Buffy's gifts as the Slayer. On the bright side, though, Willow and I will think you both incredibly brave."

Xander did not smile in return. "I'll try to remember that during the thrashing."

For a moment, the four friends seemed to take a collective breath. Then, as one, they slipped out of the van as quietly as they were able and started off toward the bus station. The parking lot was far too well lit for them to simply walk across it without drawing attention to themselves. A chain link fence ran the entire perimeter.

Xander was in the lead, and he paused and gestured toward the fence. "We'll have to go around," he whispered. "Anybody notice, no buses? That's a good thing, I think."

The bus station was bordered on this side by a corporate office complex. The drive that led up to the darkened buildings had lights as well, but they were far enough away that the four of them were able to slip along the outside of the chain link fence in relative darkness. They went all the way around to the back of the station, then climbed the fence and dropped down in the parking lot. The rear of the station was plain brick, unbroken by windows, with only a rear exit door Willow thought was likely for maintenance use.

Out in the open like that, the lights of the lot spotlighting them, she felt exposed and vulnerable. With a bag of items she had collected from her own stash and Giles's apartment, she sprinted across the lot toward that rear wall. The others followed quickly. As they reached the station, the ghost of Lucy Hanover appeared suddenly among them. In the glaring overhead lights, the phantom of the dead Slayer shimmered, barely there, as though her form had been woven with spiderwebs.

"She's still here?" Willow asked.

"Indeed," Lucy confirmed. *"She awaits within, anxious and angry. I believe that she can feel me watching."*

Willow stood before the ghost, aware that the others would not come closer. Though they rarely mentioned it, not even Xander, they were always deeply disturbed by Lucy's presence.

"Whatever happens now, we wouldn't even have gotten a chance to save her without your help," Willow said. "Thanks."

"I wish I could do more," the specter whispered in her eerie voice.

"Stand by. You might get your chance. If we can drive her out, it's going to be up to you to make sure she doesn't try to invade anyone else."

Lucy nodded wordlessly and simply hovered there, the solidity of her form wavering as though the breeze disrupted it. Willow turned to her friends, smiled encouragingly, then set her bag down gently. As she reached in and withdrew the contents of the bag, she glanced up at Oz and Xander.

"Go around to either side. Just be ready. But don't pass by the windows. Don't give her a chance to see you."

They complied without another word. Willow was tempted to kiss Oz once before he went, for luck, but he was gone too quickly for her to act on the impulse, and she dared not call him back. Instead, with Anya and the ghost watching over her, she laid out the contents of the bag carefully. A small ampule of white rose oil had made it intact, despite the jostling the bag had taken. Willow daubed a bit of it on her forehead, throat and wrists, then gestured for Anya to do the same.

Quickly as she could manage, she took a small cone of black construction paper and set a piece of incense within it, then repeated the process four times. Willow drew a power circle around herself, and a star at its center, then placed the incense at each of the points of the star. With a deep breath, she sat cross-legged at the center of the circle and glanced up at Anya.

"Go ahead and light them," she said.

Anya complied quickly, using long wooden matches to set fire to the paper the incense was in. The tiny blazes flared up quickly, the paper burning, and the incense in each began to smoke.

"Wormwood," Lucy Hanover observed.

"Artemisia," Willow corrected, using a more modern name for the herb in the incense.

"What you attempt is dangerous, friend Willow," Lucy cautioned. *"If you do not know the name of the spirit you are trying to draw forth, you may succeed only in drawing it into yourself rather than simply expelling it from your friend."*

Willow paused.

"You didn't tell us that," Anya said, suddenly alarmed. "We should have used a different spell."

"Yeah, with all that extra time we had for research," Willow replied dryly.

"But . . . what if that happens? If this thing comes out of Buffy and into you, nobody else is witchy enough to get it out of you."

Willow was touched by the girl's concern, particularly in light of Anya's tenure as a demon. But she had no satisfactory answer.

"If it possesses me, Buffy will go rescue Giles and he'll figure it out."

"Not if he's dead," Anya muttered.

Willow shushed her, closed her eyes to calm herself, inhaled the fumes rising from the artemisia burning all around her. "Infernal power, you who carry disturbance into the universe, you who have intruded upon the flesh of the living, I call you forth."

As instructed, Anya scattered powdered lodestone around the circle.

"Be you *exurgent mortui,* shade, or demon, leave your somber habitation within living flesh and render yourself back unto the spirit world," Willow continued.

Anya lay a branch of hazelwood upon the pavement, pointing from the magick circle toward the brick wall of the station. The smoke rising from the burning incense seemed to pause in the air, and then to flow as one in a line along the path pointed by the hazel branch.

"Render yourself back unto the spirit world," Willow repeated.

As though it were her will alone and not the power of the spell, she could feel the magick prodding Buffy's body. In her mind's eye, she could picture the inside of the bus station as though she were truly seeing it herself.

The incense smoke is invisible now, but inhabited by the spell Willow had cast, and it works against Buffy's flesh, into her mouth and nostrils and eardrums, circling like tentacles around the thing that has possessed the Slayer's body.

Buffy tenses. Her eyes snap open.

Outside, under the glare of the lampposts, Willow stiffened at the center of the magick circle. "Uh-oh," she mumbled.

"Uh-oh?" Anya demanded, alarmed. "What's uh-oh?"

Both of them glanced over to where Lucy Hanover had been observing them, but the ghost was suddenly gone. Willow had known she would be, for in that last moment she had felt Lucy trying to help her push the invasive entity out of Buffy's body.

But they had failed. The thing had sensed her, and pushed back.

"Come on!" Willow snapped.

Anya was right behind her as they ran around the side of the bus station just in time to see Buffy—or whatever wore her body—slam the door open hard enough that the glass in it shattered. Xander was there, only a few feet away, and he leaped at her. Guilt surged up within Willow, for Xander had been badly injured only days before.

Still, they had no choice.

"We have to help him," Willow said.

But it was too late. Buffy hit him once, twice, then spun and kicked him hard enough that Xander sailed off the concrete walk and into the parking lot. Oz came running around the front of the station then, but there was nothing he could do. Nothing anyone could have done. Willow had known from the beginning that if her spell failed, they were lost.

"We're not going to just let you take her body and leave!" Willow shouted angrily, tears beginning to well up in her eyes.

The thing that was Buffy froze, turned and looked at her, almost kindly. "I have no choice," it said. "And neither do you. Try to restrain me, and I shall kill you all."

The half-dozen other people who had been inside the bus station stood just inside the panoramic plate glass window now, watching the action unfold. Willow looked from Buffy's face to the people inside. She could cast a glamour on them later to make them forget. For now, she couldn't think about what they might see.

"If I can't stop you, I can hurt you," Willow said, wiping at her eyes. She prayed now that pain might drive the thing out.

With a single gesture, her moderate magickal ability amped up by the adrenaline rushing through her, Willow caused all of the broken glass to levitate off the ground. A flick of her wrist sent the hundreds of pieces scything through the air at Buffy, who dodged what she could, and screamed as the others sliced into her.

The beast that lived in her now glared at Willow

with red-rimmed, furious eyes. "If you had walked away, you would have lived."

"That wouldn't have been living," Willow said, fighting back the fear that rose up in her then. She felt the presence of her friends around her. "Take her down now, or we've lost her forever."

Together, the four of them rushed at Buffy.

With a loud pop, all the power in the bus station and the parking lot went out. The lot was cast into darkness, the building's interior dark as pitch. Shouts of alarm came from the travelers inside. Willow and the others all faltered, keeping their distance in a rough circle around Buffy in a bizarre standoff.

"Will," Xander began, "did you—"

"Not me," she said quickly.

"Somebody cut the power off," Anya added.

Oz moved toward Willow, still keeping his eyes on Buffy, just as they all were. "Or blew the transformer out on the street," he suggested.

Inside the bus station, people began to scream. They all glanced over to see blood spattering the plate glass. Motion drew Willow's attention off to the left, and then all around.

A band of vampires swarmed across the parking lot toward them. Others slipped slowly out of the bus station, hands covered with the blood of the dead travelers.

"No!" Buffy snapped, exasperated. "What have you done?" she sneered at Willow. "He has found me."

"Indeed," came a slithering voice from within the darkened station. "I have."

With the dry whisper of ravaged wings that beat uselessly at the air, a creature Willow knew must be the bat-god Camazotz stepped out into the lot. He pointed at Buffy with a long, tapered claw.

"She's mine. Kill the others."

Buffy crouched in the darkened interior of an abandoned gas station and peered across the street at Donatello's Italian Restaurant. The place was all white stucco, glass, and brass, the sort of place where local high school kids might have their prom if their class was small enough. It disturbed her to find that the restaurant was open for business.

She had broken into the gas station almost twenty minutes earlier and found cobwebs gathering in the darkest corners. The cooler at the front was still packed with soda, and the racks under the cashier's counter still loaded with candy bars.

There were no looters in Kakchiquel territory.

Yet the place was dark, not even the hum of electricity to indicate that it might come alive again. Buffy suspected it might be used to refuel now and again, when the vampires needed it. But like so many other businesses in the region they had laid claim to, its owners had either been murdered or had fled. This close to the edge of things, Buffy suspected the latter.

And it was close, indeed. Donatello's was perhaps two hundred yards up the road, and the taint of the undead had not yet fallen upon it. *Creepy and strange,* she thought. Parker had said the vampires' expansion had been methodical, but this brought it home to her more than anything else.

As Buffy watched, late dinner customers emerged from within the restaurant. Even across the distance, a seemingly unbridgeable gulf between them, she could hear the echo of their laughter like a cold blade knifing into her gut.

Though she had somehow managed to combine the two personas within her, the two spirits, the two Buffys . . . there was no denying that there were indeed two. To the older Slayer, who had spent so long as a prisoner, that glimpse of normalcy was the first hint of happiness she had seen in more than five years. To the younger Buffy, it was a painful reminder of all she had lost by being thrust into this dark, malevolent future.

It drew her with a magnetic allure. Her heart ached to be across the invisible barrier that marked the border of Kakchiquel territory. The temptation to simply run for it was enormous. But she had told the Watcher on the phone that she would wait for the extraction team he promised to send, and she knew it was sensible to do just that. Particularly given the half-dozen cars parked on either side of the road between the abandoned gas station and Donatello's.

Though she could not really see into the interior of those ominously silent vehicles, cigarette embers burned inside three of them, and there were at least a dozen vampires that stood sentry around the cars, watching for her. Even a conservative bit of mathematics gave them more than twenty against her one, and she suspected that if she tried to cut around the intersection by diverting behind buildings and into a neighborhood, they would have scouts on the lookout for her there.

It didn't matter. They had heard the phone conversation. They knew she was coming here. Knew that the opposition was coming to bring her out.

At some point.

Another hour passed and Buffy's patience crumbled. Carefully, she slipped out of the darkness of the gas station and ran in a crouch to the silent gas pumps. It had brought her only a dozen yards closer to her goal, but that was something. In a minute or two, she was going to take the crossbow and makeshift stakes out of the canvas bag in her hand and walk right down the middle of the street toward the restaurant.

When the momentum that was tugging at her, the yearning to be free, could not be put off for one more second, she stepped out from behind the pumps and began to sprint.

They were slow. She had counted to nine in her head before the shouting began, before the car doors opened and more vampires leaped out. She had been too conservative. There were enough that she could not count them with a simple glance, and she was going to have to fight them hand to hand. All of them.

Should have waited for the extraction team, Buffy thought.

But it was too late, and she cursed herself for her impatience. She had been through too much to have it end now over a stupid mistake, her own impatience and arrogance.

Not the first time they've gotten me into trouble, she thought, as her younger self recalled her conflict with Willow and Giles only days before, and yet also many years before. Days, years, were one and the same. *No, not the first time. But maybe the last.*

On the other side of the street, the driver's door of the last of the cars opened and Spike stepped out. A lit cigarette dangled from his mouth. His face was misshapen, the countenance of the vampire within him, and in contrast to the furious rage of the others who scurried around preparing to fight her, he walked calmly away from the car, his jacket flapping behind him.

The others had swords, axes, some even had guns in spite of the vampires' usual distaste for such things. Spike was empty-handed. Dead, face as pale as his bleached-white hair, he seemed to drift along the street toward her like the scythe of the Reaper himself, gliding toward her.

Spike raised a hand and the rest of them froze, waiting for his command. He took a long drag from the cigarette and then flicked the ash away.

"You killed her." Spike did not even look at her as he spoke.

A bitter taste in her mouth, Buffy felt a hate rise up in her as powerful as any she had ever known. She remained silent, glaring at him until at last Spike turned to meet her gaze.

"She was dancing when she died," Buffy told him. A smile flickered at the corners of her mouth. "I thought you'd like to know."

Spike took another long drag, then glanced at a clutch of vampires to his right. "Kill her."

"But we're not supposed to . . ." one of the creatures replied hesitantly. "I mean—"

"Oh, bloody hell. Right, then, catch her, and bring her to me."

They moved as one, running and loping and scuttling toward her, a pack of wolves and vermin. Buffy stood her ground, lifted the crossbow, and dusted the foremost from twenty-five yards away. She nocked and aimed and released twice more, killing both her targets, before they were too close for the crossbow.

It clattered to the pavement as they swarmed her, and she pulled the stake she had brought from the rear waistband of her jeans. This was it. Five years of shadow-boxing and private *kata*, of exercise and anger.

Buffy began to move. They came at her and she flowed in a dance of death, kicking and thrusting and spinning, using their numbers against them, drawing them close to keep the others away, slaughtering them in a cloud of their own ashen remains. Gunfire erupted and a bullet grazed her shoulder. Warm blood spilled down her back, but it did not slow her. A sword point punctured her side, just below the rib cage, but she was fluid, in motion, and its owner was dead before he could harm her any further.

Then Buffy had the sword. The stake was forgotten. The sword flashed and vampires died and she choked on their floating, snowflake flesh, the nuclear fallout of slain undead. It stung her eyes and forced her to hold her breath.

Another gunshot.

A bullet through her back.

A club across the back of her head.

Buffy staggered. Fell to her knees, the sword wavering in her hands.

Spike stood over her, an ax in his hands. "So much for the not killing you thing, eh?" he asked sweetly. Cigarette firmly clenched in his lips, its tip flaring bright, he snarled at her. "Your turn now, Buffy. Let's see if you dance."

The others all stood back, but none of them dared to challenge his action. Dazed from loss of blood, Buffy was still able to make a rough guess that she had killed over a dozen of them. That was good. That was something.

But it was not going to keep her from breaking the first rule of Slaying. Spike raised the battleax, and Buffy knew she was about to die. The blade gleamed in the moonlight and somewhere nearby, probably from the parking lot at the restaurant, she heard the echo of several people, normal humans, shouting in alarm at the grotesque, macabre tableau being played out in the street.

But they were on the other side of the border. There was nothing they could do.

The blade fell toward her. The other vampires seemed to pull back even one step farther. There seemed to be more of them now, as though others had arrived, reinforcements.

Buffy tried to lift the sword.

Spike grinned.

Then his eyes went wide and his lips dropped open and the cigarette fell end over burning end from his mouth. His body jittered a little bit and he dropped the ax and stumbled toward her. Buffy aimed the blade of the sword at him and it sliced right through his abdomen, impaling him.

"Kill them!" the vampires screamed.

That woke Buffy up. *Kill who?*

She shoved the moaning Spike away from her and struggled to stand. The Kakchiquels closest to her attacked. Though she was wounded, slowed, still she spun and decapitated the nearest one, who exploded into dust. With an elbow, she drove a second back. The third grabbed her from behind, began to choke her, then he too began to jitter madly.

This time she felt the surge of electricity pass from the vampire and into her. The shock made every muscle in her body contract and ache, made her eyes go wide and her teeth feel like she had just bitten through aluminum foil. The vampire went down at her feet, and Buffy looked up to see a grim-faced man standing before her with a taser gun. A long crescent-shaped scar striped the left side of his face, cutting into the bristly stubble on his chin. His black hair was too long, hanging as a curtain that nearly hid his eyes.

It had been this man who had saved her.

"Thank you," Buffy rasped as she shook off the electrocution.

He shocked the fallen vampire again, blue electricity arcing from the weapon into the Kakchiquel on the ground. As he did, this grave, scarred warrior shook the hair back from his face and regarded her with an urgency in his sad eyes.

"We need to go," he said.

Buffy froze, staring at him, not breathing. Joy and grief clashed within her as she recognized the man.

"Xander," she whispered. "Oh my God. Xander."

"We need to go," he replied sternly, not even a flicker of a smile.

Though she bled now from so many wounds, she stood tall, held the sword up and ready, and nodded at him. "Let's go, then."

The vampires were all around them, but they were being driven back by other men and women with taser guns and crossbows. Their numbers were deteriorating even as Buffy followed Xander . . . this sad, brooding man she had once known . . . in a run for the invisible border. In the parking lot of the restaurant, she now saw a pair of black sedans and a military troop carrier that had not been there before.

Engines roared, headlights flashed, and more cars came racing down from the north, from vampire territory. They slewed sideways and bat-tattooed Kakchi-quels with orange, jack-o'-lantern eyes burning, piled out with weapons in hand.

"Go, go, get the Slayer to safety!" snapped a commanding female voice behind her.

Buffy turned, saw the extraction team still fighting, but now withdrawing. The command had come from a woman with long red hair tied in a ponytail. The lithe woman raised her hands, gestured madly in the air, and cried out something in Latin that Buffy did not understand. Three vampires within several feet of her turned to glass and another member of the team shattered them all.

Her voice still echoed in Buffy's mind.

"Willow," she whispered to herself.

"Come on!" Xander snapped, grasping at her arm.

She shook him free, staring at the back of the extraction team commander. The woman turned, then, and Buffy saw her face. Willow Rosenberg at twenty-four, determined, very much in charge. When she saw Buffy looking at her, she grinned.

Buffy grinned back.

But then the newly arrived cadre of Kakchiquels rushed into the fray, and Willow's attention was back on the fight. One of them was Clownface, white greasepaint ghostly in the dark. Buffy went to go back, to help out, but Xander grabbed her with more strength than she would ever have imagined.

"No. We're not here to win. We're here to get you out."

For a long, last moment, Buffy watched. Willow set a pair of vampires on fire simply by touching them. Then she screamed out a name Buffy knew.

"Oz!"

From the midst of the melee came a sudden howl that made the hairs on the back of Buffy's neck stand up. Amidst the vampires, one of the members of the team changed in an instant. In the confusion, Buffy had not noticed him. Now there was no mistaking that it was him.

The werewolf raged, its black snout glistening, its ears twitching, teeth gnashing at the air as it charged at the approaching group. Clownface was in the lead and the werewolf rose up on its hind legs, grabbed the vampire, and tore her head off.

Oz? Buffy thought, horrified by how savage he was. The beast within him had been set loose at Willow's order, though the moon was not full.

He began to attack others, using powerful jaws and claws to tear into them, but then Willow shouted for them all to fall back. The extraction team complied instantly. Xander hauled on Buffy's arm, and then she was running toward the restaurant parking lot, mind spinning, almost blacking out. It was all too much for her.

Then they were at one of the sedans. Xander shoved her into the backseat, then jumped in front and started it up. Through the tinted windows Buffy watched the vampires give chase, but only for a few seconds. The team loaded into the military transport and the other sedan, and the vampires stopped as though they had also been ordered to fall back.

The passenger door opened and Willow dropped into the seat beside Xander.

"Spike," Buffy said. "Did you get him?"

"He disappeared," Willow replied. "He'll always save his own ass first." Then she glanced at Xander. "Move out."

He complied instantly, tearing out of the restaurant parking lot with the other sedan and the troop transport close behind. As they went, Buffy craned her neck to look out the rear window. The vampires who had survived were also retreating. They had climbed into their cars, both those that had been on sentry and the late arrivals, and begun to return the way they had come, as though the carnage had never happened, as though the people in the parking lot had not witnessed something horrible.

One car had not moved. It seemed aimed at them, headlights on high beam. They were several hundred yards away now, but Buffy could make out the form of a man standing in front of the car, his body silhouetted by the harsh lights, backlit so that he seemed more like a dark hole in the air than a man, like a thing of darkness painted over the face of the world.

Whoever he was, he stood calmly and watched them drive away.

Buffy shivered, there in the car, with these people who had once been her friends but whom she now barely knew. As they rounded a corner and the dark figure slipped out of sight behind them, she thought of the feeling she had had in the projection house at the drive-in. She thought of the crossbow that had been left there, just for her.

The two spirits that coexisted within her exulted simultaneously. Buffy was free. Yet somehow she felt her fear even more keenly than before, and a terrible dread was born within her.

CHAPTER 6

Willow felt frozen in place, there in the darkened parking lot of the Sunnydale bus station. She did not know if Camazotz's vampire followers had cut the power, or if the outage was simple coincidence, but she knew that in the end it would not really matter. The vampires scrambled across the lot from both sides, fifteen, maybe twenty. They were silent as wraiths. The night air crackled with menace.

The half that were nearest to Buffy formed a sort of semicircle around her, even as their master, the bat-god Camazotz, sprang toward her on cloven feet. Whatever had possessed Buffy, it was clear that the thing was running from Camazotz. Now that he had found her, the demon thing planned to destroy her himself. Buffy would die so that Camazotz could destroy the entity inhabiting her body.

Camazotz moved in to attack her. Buffy blocked his lunge, then shot a hard kick at his midsection that drove the bat-god backward.

"I came a long way to take the Slayer's body," the thing inside Buffy snapped. "Now you'll see why."

The vampires around her moved in, but Camazotz snarled at them and they moved back. The other cluster of vampires rushed at Willow, Oz, Xander, and Anya, who stood their ground, though they had no weapons at all. Xander and Oz had already been battered around by the Slayer. Even if they were fresh for the fight, and these were normal vampires— which, given their tattooed features and blazing orange eyes, and the way their bodies seemed to spark with energy, they most certainly weren't—even then the odds would have been against them.

With a single, muttered word and a wave of her hands, Willow drew upon the heat in the air around her, and a wall of fire suddenly blazed up from the pavement, a barrier of raging flame that gave the predators pause. They seemed, just then, like some species of ancient animal, these creatures who stared across the wall of flames, their flickering fire-eyes purely evil within the pitch black of the bat tattoos on their faces.

"Way to go, Willow!" Xander cried happily. "Torch 'em all!"

But she knew she did not have the mastery of magick to be able to do that. She had risked setting herself and her friends on fire with the spell she had just cast. Willow shot a quick glance at Buffy. She was in motion, kicking, punching, parrying blows, but Camazotz had already slashed her and she bled from several wounds.

No choice. They had no choice at all. Willow turned to her friends. "Run!" she barked.

"What about Buffy?" Oz asked, where he stood just beside her.

"We'll come back for her."

With that, Willow turned and ran toward the street side of the parking lot, toward the fence on the other side of which the van was still parked. Oz was right behind her, but Xander and Anya hung back a little, slowed down as Xander was by the beating Buffy had given him.

Willow glanced at Oz. "Get to the van. Start it up. Break out the weapons."

He sprinted even faster, and she dropped back to help Anya with Xander. Behind them the fire barrier had diminished and the vampires surged across, still unnervingly silent. Willow wished they would scream or make threats. Quiet as they were, the Kakchiquels made her mouth go dry and her skin prickle with cold fear.

"Willow, they're catching up!" Anya snapped, both petulant and afraid. "Some more fire would be nice!"

But Willow said nothing. It was hard for her to concentrate right now, and she needed focus to do magick. Without the van, without weapons, they would die. Simple as that. Her magick could protect them briefly, but that would not be enough. And even if she could keep them safe until sunrise, what about Buffy?

"Willow!" Anya shouted.

"Just run!" Willow replied curtly.

They were rushing along, Xander's arms over their shoulders, helping him to stay up and keep moving.

"Just go!" Xander said. "I'll catch up!"

Willow glanced at him, saw everything in his eyes in that one moment, his fear and courage, and his determination. But she knew Anya would not leave him behind, and neither would she.

Which was when Xander stopped. He simply planted his feet and pulled himself away from them. Before Willow or Anya could say anything, he had turned to face the Kakchiquels, who were closing in now. One of them, perhaps the hungriest, was far ahead of the others.

Xander crouched in a fighting stance. "Come on, then, you son of a—"

The vampire leaped on him, drove Xander down hard on the pavement. His head struck the ground with a loud *thunk* that seemed to echo in the silence. Anya screamed his name.

But Willow could not speak, could not scream. She saw them coming, smiling grimly now. Saw the one on top of Xander as it gripped his hair and dropped its fangs toward his throat. No words came up from within her, but something did, a dark anger she could barely control.

Her hands twitched, then lashed at the air as though it were the object of her rage. The vampire on top of Xander burst into flame, shrieking in agony at its immolation. Xander's clothes began to burn and he too cried out in pain as the heat seared his hands and face.

Anya kicked the vampire down onto the ground and began to beat at Xander's burning clothes. In an instant the flames were out.

"Not so quiet now," Willow said to the blazing Kakchiquel.

It glared at her, black tattoo blistering, and then it disintegrated in a puff of embers. The others who ran toward them faltered when they saw this, and Willow turned to face them, hands raised, ready for a fight. She wasn't exactly sure how she had managed to pinpoint that spell, knew she had nearly killed Xander, and was far from sure she could manage it again.

But they didn't know that.

"Come on, then!" she snapped.

Which was when the roar of an engine surged through the dark behind them. Headlights washed across them and Oz's van barreled into the parking lot.

Anya hustled Xander to the rear doors, opened them, and then helped him in. The Kakchiquels stood there, staring nervously at Willow, but then they began to inch closer.

"Willow," Oz's voice called from behind her. "Down!"

She dropped to a crouch on the pavement. Two of the vampires were struck in the chest with crossbow bolts. One dusted, but the other was not hit through the heart and grunted in pain instead, clutching at the wooden bolt in his chest.

Willow turned and ran for the van. Oz leaned out the driver's side window with a crossbow and fired again. Anya was in the other window, fitting a bolt into another.

"Go!" Willow said. "Can we just go, please?"

Oz pulled back into the van, put it in drive, and swung around just as Willow ran up toward the back. The rear door was open and she dove inside, then pulled it shut behind her.

Xander sat, face contorted with pain, leaning against the wall of the van.

"Hold on," she told him.

"Buffy," he muttered through gritted teeth. "We can't just leave her."

"We're not," Willow promised. Then she called to Oz up front. "Run them down. Get to Buffy."

"On it," Oz replied as he floored the accelerator.

The van rocked as he slammed into several of the Kakchiquels. Willow moved up between the front seats in time to see them smashed down under the van's wheels. They attacked the sides, and at least one of them managed to get on top and hold on.

The van raced toward the bus station and plowed through several of the Kakchiquels who had gathered as spectators around Camazotz's fight with Buffy.

They were not dead, but some at least were broken and out of the fight.

Oz said her name and Willow's heart broke. Her boyfriend felt things very deeply, but his expression and tone almost never revealed those feelings. Now, though, with just the two syllables of her name, he communicated all too much. Horror, grief, the desire to protect her from the scene that was playing out before them.

Willow sagged against the seats, her heart breaking.

As though they were actors on a stage, pinpointed by the headlights of the van, Camazotz held Buffy two feet off the ground, her feet kicking uselessly beneath her. One of her shoes had come off.

While Willow watched, tears beginning to slide down her face, Camazotz pulled Buffy toward him. A long, forked tongue snaked out of the bat-god's mouth and slipped down inside her throat. It was obscene, an intimate intrusion, a violent attack as vicious as if it had been a blade. The demon's tongue thrust between Buffy's lips and she choked and gagged. Her eyes rolled up in her head.

Willow and the others saw it all, a grotesque tableau before them. The van shook as more vampires attacked it. The passenger window cracked. The rear doors were dented.

Her heart was broken, but an even greater horror threatened to break Willow's spirit. For she understood with perfect clarity that they were too late. There was nothing left for them to do.

The passenger window shattered. Anya screamed as vampires reached in. Oz shot a crossbow bolt at one of them.

Willow did not even look. Her eyes were still locked on Buffy and Camazotz.

Suddenly, the bat-god's tongue began to slither back, inch after inch pulling out of Buffy's throat. The dead, scorched wings on Camazotz's back fluttered obscenely, like the wagging of a dog's tail. The orange fire that sparked in its eyes and those of its servants now seemed to blaze up all over the thing's body, as though electricity were passing all through him.

Buffy went rigid in Camazotz's grasp, as suddenly a dark, writhing, oily thing began to slip from her open lips, dragged out of her by the bat-god's probing tongue. It was an ephemeral thing, a dark ghost of boiling tar, a twitching, roiling cloud of blackness.

Willow had seen it before. *The Prophet.*

Somehow, Camazotz was tearing the entity right out of Buffy.

A pair of arms surged through the passenger window, grabbed Anya by the shoulder and by the hair, and began to pull her out. Her shoulder was slashed with broken glass and she cried out.

Suddenly Xander thrust a hand up from the back of the van and slapped a crucifix down on the vampire's arm. It smoked and burned and the van was filled with the smell of rotten meat cooking. The vampire withdrew, but there were others waiting.

Buffy hung limply in Camazotz's grasp as his tongue dragged the black thing from within her.

"We can't win this," Anya snapped. "We've got to go!"

"Not without *her*," Willow insisted. "Oz, run them both down. Camazotz *and* Buffy!"

"But Willow—" Xander began.

"She'll survive it. She has to. But it's the only way to buy us a few seconds to drag her in here."

"What if she *doesn't* survive it?" Oz asked calmly.

Willow didn't answer.

In the backseat of the sedan, Buffy shifted painfully on the seat, her blood sticky on the leather upholstery. Willow, beautiful and confident, watched her with great curiosity from the front seat.

Xander drove and said nothing, never even turned his head.

"You ran me over?" Buffy asked, stunned. A great deal of the story Willow was telling—of the night five years ago when they had tried to save her from Camazotz—stunned her. "I don't remember any of that."

Willow offered a brief smile. "You weren't yourself, Buffy. First you were possessed by Zotziloha, and then you were unconscious."

"Zotzil-who?" Buffy asked.

The sedan knifed through the darkness. But it was a darkness lit with streetlights and businesses and homes, a place where real people lived out from under the control of the vampires. Through the windshield, Buffy saw a large, ornate church ahead, its stained-glass windows gleaming in the night. It heartened her to know that there were still people who had faith in something.

"Zotziloha was Camazotz's wife. You knew her as The Prophet. She was a noncorporeal goddess entity, a demon yes, but not as evil as her mate. She fled him, but knew he would eventually catch up to her. Which was why she possessed you."

"Then he drove her out?" Buffy asked.

"That's one way to put it."

And then they captured me, and kept me locked up all this time, Buffy thought. But the other Buffy inside her had more questions, and other priorities. Throughout the trek she had made to get away from the vampires, the two personas' priorities had been the same, and it had been simple for them to coexist. Now, though, they were split again.

"I remember coming around while they were bringing me to my cell," Buffy said, her voice a low rasp. "But nothing before that."

Even as she said it, the younger Buffy within her knew that it was no longer as simple as returning to her own time. Given what Willow had told her, she knew that her spirit—the spirit of Buffy at nineteen—would eventually be drawn back to the time and the body it was supposed to inhabit. But she did not know *when.* Any day, any hour, any minute, she could not know when. This Zotziloha entity had been driven out of her that night five years earlier, and her spirit returned. But now, in this dark future, she could not simply wait for that to happen. Unless she could find a way for her displaced spirit to return to her correct time earlier, *before* The Prophet, Zotziloha, possessed her body, then this future could not be avoided.

"God, my head hurts," Buffy whispered. Then she looked at Willow. There was a hesitation between them, an awkwardness that five years apart had created. But Willow was still her friend, and Buffy knew that she had all the help she needed, the greatest ally she could ask for. "You and I have a lot of things to talk about, Will."

"Yeah," Willow agreed. "And soon. You have a lot of catching up to do, a lot for me to tell you. A lot of it bad. But at the moment . . ." she turned around to look out the windshield again. "Here we are."

The sky had been lightening as they drove, and now the eastern horizon was bright and blue. The sedan pulled into an unmarked street. A line of trees had been planted along the road. They drove along until they came to a building that looked like a hospital or office complex, the other vehicles close behind. The troop transport went past them, into a large lot beside the building, but the two sedans parked right up in front among some other cars.

"This is home base," Willow said.

Buffy stared at the front of the building. "Big operation."

The three of them climbed out of the car. Without a

word or a glance, Xander started for the building, but Buffy and Willow hung back, walking slowly side by side. After a moment, both women paused. Buffy and Willow turned to gaze at each other. The Slayer was overcome with emotion, a release of despair that she had fought against for so long. Willow bit her lip, a tiny smile twitching at her lips, and then the women embraced. Best friends, too long apart, they had built up walls around their hope that they would be together again. Buffy still felt some distance between them, knew that it would take time for them to be comfortable with each other again.

But this was a start.

After a moment, they stepped back from each other. Buffy began to walk toward the building, but paused again and glanced curiously at this woman Willow had become.

"I know we have a million things to talk about—you have no idea—but you know what's nagging at me? If all Camazotz wanted was his wife back, then why did he capture me afterward? Why bother with me at all? He could have just killed me and gone home. All this conqueror stuff, I mean, what does that have to do with chasing his wife?"

Willow's eyes went wide as Buffy spoke. When only silence hung between them, Willow lifted a hand to her mouth as though afraid of the words that might come out. After a moment, she shook her head.

"God, Buffy, I'm sorry. I . . . it never occurred to me that you didn't know."

Icy tendrils of dread clutched at Buffy's heart. "Didn't know what?"

"Nobody's seen Camazotz for years. If he's still alive, he's probably as much a prisoner as you were."

Buffy frowned. "I don't understand."

The van rocked back and forth as the Kakchiquels tried to tip it over. Anya held up a crucifix in front of her broken window. Willow stared through the windshield and saw Camazotz retract his tongue. The black, viscous thing that had been pulled from inside Buffy's throat undulated at the end of the bat-god's tongue. Buffy was limp in his clutches but the thing was out of her body, at least.

Camazotz sucked the twitching black thing into his mouth and swallowed it whole. The bat-god's withered wings fluttered mightily and he threw his disgusting head back and laughed, needle teeth flashing in the starlight.

"Run him down," Willow said, stomach roiling in disgust. "Go!"

Oz put the van in drive and was about to floor it when there came a soft tap at the driver's-side window.

They all glanced that way at once, surprised by the subtle noise amidst the violent cacophony around them.

Giles stood beside the van, just outside Oz's window. He no longer wore his glasses, and his eyes blazed brightly with orange flame. He bore no tattoo on his face, but when he smiled at them, Willow saw the pale outline of fangs.

Something crumbled inside her then. "No," she whispered, shaking her head in despair. "No, no, no!"

"Giles," Anya said. "He's a . . ."

"You can't win," Giles called amiably, loud enough to be heard through the window. "You can only die. Don't worry, though. Buffy will live. I wouldn't dream of killing *her*."

With that he turned away from the van and strode toward Camazotz. Through Anya's shattered window they heard Giles shout at the bat-god.

"Careful with her! Don't forget, if you kill her, another will rise in her place. The only way to defeat the Slayer is to cage her. If we can't send her to Hell, bringing Hell to her here on Earth is the next best thing."

Camazotz hesitated, but after a moment he dropped Buffy on the ground. Giles motioned to several of the others, who picked her up, and then they all retreated into the night, beyond the reach of the van's headlights, carrying Buffy with them.

In a moment, the van idled in the parking lot, and they were alone save for the dead travelers inside the bus station.

They had been left alive, but Willow knew it was not because the monster who had once been their friend had spared them. It was because they were an afterthought. With the Slayer a prisoner, they didn't matter to him. Not at all.

"Oh, man. Giles," Oz said, voice hushed.

"What do we do now?" Xander asked. "We are *so* screwed."

Willow began to cry, there in the back of the van, great heaving sobs that seemed to be torn right out of her. She didn't think she would ever be able to stop.

Buffy stared at Willow, eyes wide. She had never felt so cold. Of all she had seen and heard in this horrid future, this was the hardest blow of all. She bit her lip, tears slipping down her cheeks, and shook her head slowly.

"No, Willow. Oh, no," she whispered. "Not Giles."

For Willow, that night was five years in the past. And yet the pain of it still haunted her eyes. She pulled Buffy to her again, held her for a long moment. Suddenly Buffy pulled away.

"Giles," the Slayer said, wiping at her eyes. "Giles is a vampire."

Willow paused, then glanced away. "Not just a vampire," she said. "The most brilliant, most evil, most dangerously organized vampire who has ever lived. He's their leader.

"Their king."

To Be Continued . . .

ABOUT THE AUTHOR

CHRISTOPHER GOLDEN is the award-winning, *L.A. Times* best-selling author of such novels as *Straight on 'Til Morning, Strangewood, Prowlers,* and the *Body of Evidence* series of teen thrillers.

Golden has also written a great many books and comic books related to the TV series *Buffy the Vampire Slayer* and *Angel.* His other comic book work includes stories featuring such characters as Batman, Wolverine, Spider-Man, The Crow, and Hellboy, among many others.

As a pop culture journalist, he was the editor of the Bram Stoker Award–winning book of criticism, *CUT!: Horror Writers on Horror Film,* and co-author of both *Buffy the Vampire Slayer: The Monster Book* and *The Stephen King Universe.*

Golden was born and raised in Massachusetts, where he still lives with his family. He graduated from Tufts University. He is currently at work on the third book in the *Prowlers* series, *Predator and Prey,* and a new novel for Signet called *The Ferryman.* There are more than four million copies of his books in print. Please visit him at his website, www.christophergolden.com.

Everyone's got his demons....

ANGEL™

If it takes an eternity, he will make amends.

◆

Original stories based
on the TV show
Created by Joss Whedon
& David Greenwalt

Available from Pocket Pulse
Published by Pocket Books

™ and © 2000 Twentieth Century Fox Film Corporation. All Rights Reserved.

2311-01

**At a time when most kids
are trying to figure out who they are,
they're trying to figure out WHAT they are.**

ROSWELL HIGH™

*Where school is an entirely
different experience...*

**Read the books that started it all
and watch ROSWELL™ this fall on the WB**

Published by Pocket Books

TM & © 1999 by Pocket Books. All Rights Reserved